AMERICA

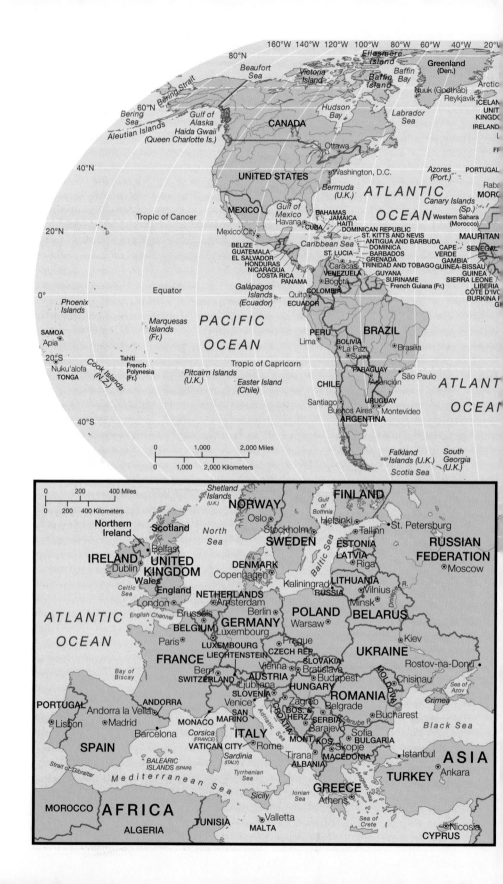

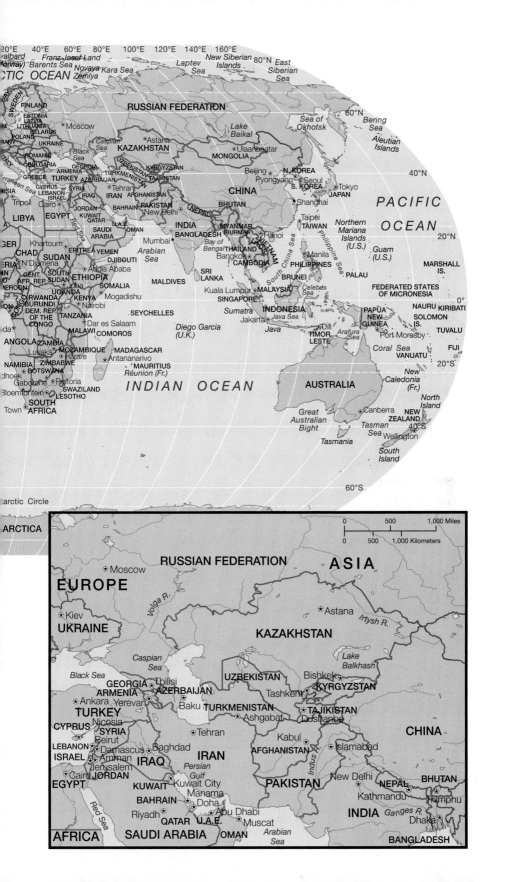

brief tenth edition
VOLUME 2

AMERICA

A Narrative History

David Emory Shi

George Brown Tindall

W. W. NORTON & COMPANY, INC.
New York • London

W. W. Norton & Company has been independent since its founding in 1923, when William Warder Norton and Mary D. Herter Norton first published lectures delivered at the People's Institute, the adult education division of New York City's Cooper Union. The firm soon expanded its program beyond the Institute, publishing books by celebrated academics from America and abroad. By midcentury, the two major pillars of Norton's publishing program—trade books and college texts—were firmly established. In the 1950s, the Norton family transferred control of the company to its employees, and today—with a staff of four hundred and a comparable number of trade, college, and professional titles published each year—W. W. Norton & Company stands as the largest and oldest publishing house owned wholly by its employees.

Editor: Jon Durbin
Associate Editors: Justin Cahill and Scott Sugarman
Project Editors: Melissa Atkin and Linda Feldman
Editorial Assistant: Travis Carr
Managing Editor, College: Marian Johnson
Managing Editor, College Digital Media: Kim Yi
Production Manager: Ashley Horna
Media Editor: Laura Wilk
Media Project Editor: Penelope Lin
Media Editorial Assistant: Chris Hillyer
Marketing Manager, History: Sarah England
Design Director: Hope Goodell-Miller
Photo Editor: Stephanie Romeo
Permissions Manager: Megan Jackson
Composition: Jouve North America
Manufacturing: Quad Graphics Taunton

Permission to use copyrighted material is included on page A151.

The Library of Congress has cataloged the full edition as follows:

Shi, David E. Tindall, George Brown.
  America: a narrative history / David Emory Shi, George Brown Tindall.
Tenth edition. New York: W. W. Norton & Company, 2016.
  Includes index.
LCCN 2015036484
  ISBN 9780393265934 (hardcover)
LCSH: United States—History—Textbooks.
LCC E178.1 .T55 2017 DDC 973—dc23 LC record available at http://lccn.loc.gov/2015036484

This edition: **9780393265989 (pbk.)**

W. W. Norton & Company, Inc., 500 Fifth Avenue, New York, NY 10110-0017
wwnorton.com
W. W. Norton & Company Ltd., 15 Carlisle Street, London W1D 3BS

2 3 4 5 6 7 8 9 0

FOR
MY WIFE,
ANGELA HALFACRE SHI

DAVID E. SHI is a professor of history and the president emeritus of Furman University. He is the author of several books on American cultural history, including the award-winning *The Simple Life: Plain Living and High Thinking in American Culture* and *Facing Facts: Realism in American Thought and Culture, 1850–1920*.

GEORGE B. TINDALL, recently of the University of North Carolina, Chapel Hill, was an award-winning historian of the South with a number of major books to his credit, including *The Emergence of the New South, 1913–1945* and *The Disruption of the Solid South*.

CONTENTS

16 The Era of Reconstruction, 1865–1877 578

PART FIVE GROWING PAINS 615

17 Business and Labor in the Industrial Era, 1860–1900 618

PART SEVEN THE AMERICAN AGE 997

MAPS

PREFACE

This Tenth Edition of *America: A Narrative History* seeks to improve upon a textbook grounded in a compelling narrative history of the American experience. From the start of our collaboration in 1984, George Tindall and I strove to write an engaging book focused on political and economic developments but animated by colorful characters, informed by balanced analysis and social texture, and guided by the unfolding of key events. Those classic principles, combined with a handy format and low price, have helped make *America: A Narrative History* one of the most popular and well-respected American history textbooks. This brief edition, which I have crafted by streamlining the narrative by nearly 20 percent, remains the most coherent and lively of its kind.

This Tenth Brief Edition of *America* features a number of important changes designed to make the text more teachable and classroom-friendly. Chief among them are major structural changes, including the joining of several chapters to reduce the overall number from thirty-four to thirty-two as well as the resequencing of several chapters to make the narrative flow more smoothly for students. Major organizational changes include:

- New Chapter 6, *Strengthening the New Nation*, combines *Shaping a Federal Union* and *The Federalist Era* from previous editions to better integrate the events after the Revolution.
- New Chapter 19, *Political Stalemate and Rural Revolt, 1865–1900* combines *The Emergence of Urban America* and *Gilded Age Politics and Agrarian Revolt* from previous editions to connect the clash of urban and rural cultures.

In terms of content changes, the overarching theme of the new edition is the importance of the culture of everyday life in understanding American history. While an introductory textbook must necessarily focus on major political, constitutional, diplomatic, economic, and social changes, it is also important to understand how ordinary people managed everyday concerns: housing, jobs, food, recreation, religion, and entertainment.

I have looked to broaden the political narrative by incorporating more social and cultural history into the text, primarily using the refreshed and expanded coverage of the culture of everyday life as the main vehicle for doing so. Key new discussions include:

- Chapter 1, *The Collision of Cultures*, features new material about Native American religious beliefs and practices as well as aspects of everyday life.
- Chapter 2, *England's Colonies*, provides additional insights into the status of indentured servants and slavery in the colonies.
- Chapter 3, *Colonial Ways of Life,* includes a new portrait of Antonio, an enslaved African brutalized by his Dutch owner in Maryland in the mid-seventeenth century. There is also new material about colonial houses, taverns, diets, and the competition among American colonists for British luxury goods in the 1760s and 1770s.
- Chapter 4, *From Colonies to States,* has more material on the nonimportation efforts (boycotts of British goods imported into America) led by ordinary Americans. It also includes new material about the conversion of farmers into soldiers after the shooting at Lexington and Concord.
- Chapter 5, *The American Revolution, 1776–1783*, includes more material about slaves who took advantage of the war to escape or join the British forces, and about the ways in which women, Native Americans, and slaves became engaged in the war effort.
- Chapter 6, *Strengthening the New Nation,* includes more about Shays's Rebellion and other expressions of agrarian discontent across the nation that occurred after the Revolution, and more on how women, Native Americans, and slaves figured into the thinking of the Founding Fathers during the Constitutional Convention in 1787.
- Chapter 7, *The Early Republic, 1800–1815*, has new material on the way in which the War of 1812 affected slavery/blacks.
- Chapter 8, *The Emergence of a Market Economy, 1815–1850*, includes new discussions of the emergence of the cotton culture in the South, the nature of farming, canals, boats, and steamship travel, and the plight of the Irish fleeing the famine at home and heading to America.
- Chapter 9, *Nationalism and Sectionalism, 1815–1828*, more fully fleshes out the role of labor advocates and unions in helping to forge what would become the Jacksonian movement.
- Chapter 10, *The Jacksonian Era, 1828–1840*, describes the effects of the Panic of 1837 and the ensuing depression on the working poor.

- Chapter 11, *The South, Slavery, and King Cotton, 1800–1860*, has substantial new material related to slavery, cotton, and everyday life within African American society. There is also a new discussion of a New Orleans slave uprising led by Charles Deslondes in 1811, the largest slave revolt in American history.
- Chapter 12, *Religion, Romanticism, and Reform, 1800–1860*, includes enriched treatment of the revivalism of the Second Great Awakening, a rewritten discussion of Mormonism, and a new section on Sylvester Graham and his health reform movement (Grahamism).
- Chapter 13, *Western Expansion, 1830-1848*, is enlivened by textured portraits of John Fremont and Sam Houston and a much fuller profile of James K. Polk.
- Chapter 15, *The War of the Union, 1861–1865*, includes new material about the social history of the Civil War, including more material on the everyday life of common soldiers, rioting in opposition to the military draft, and backwoods violence rarely included in discussions of the war, such as the summary of the execution of thirteen Unionists in Madison County, North Carolina.
- Chapter 16, *The Era of Reconstruction, 1865–1877*, has more material about former slaves—from their perspective. It also includes new examples of the ways in which the Freedmen's Bureau helped negotiate labor contracts between white planters and freedmen.
- Chapter 17, *Business and Labor in the Industrial Era, 1860–1900*, discusses the emergence of a new middle class during the Gilded Age, and includes substantially revised material on women's and labor history.
- Chapter 18, *The New South and the New West, 1865–1900*, includes a rewritten section on the emergence of new racial segregation in the South, and also new material about the everyday realities of Western expansion.
- Chapter 21, *The Progressive Era, 1890–1920*, includes new sections on the attitudes of Theodore Roosevelt and Woodrow Wilson concerning race.
- Chapter 22, *America and the Great War, 1914–1920*, now discusses the war's social effects in the United States, with special attention to women, blacks, and Mexican Americans. There is also new material about the grim nature of trench warfare.
- Chapter 23, *A Clash of Cultures, 1920–1929*, includes new material on the consumer culture, women's history, and revised material on the Harlem Renaissance with a new profile of Zora Neale Hurston. There are also fresh treatments of the impact of the radio, automobiles, cinema, and airplanes.

- Chapter 26, *The Second World War, 1933–1945*, includes new material about the social effects of the war at home, including the wartime experience of Mexican Americans.
- Chapter 27, *The Cold War and the Fair Deal, 1945–1952*, includes new coverage of George Kennan's role in inspiring the containment doctrine, women industrial workers, and also the efforts of Latinos to gain equal rights in the aftermath of World War II.
- Chapter 28, *Cold War America, 1950-1959*, features enhanced treatments of the emerging civil rights movement.
- Chapter 29, *A New Frontier and a Great Society, 1960–1968*, includes a new portrait of Fannie Lou Hamer, a black Mississippi activist, in the section on the early civil rights movements.
- Chapter 30, *Rebellion and Reaction, 1960s and 1970s*, includes new material on the women's movement, Mexican Americans, and Native Americans.
- Chapter 32, *Twenty-First-Century America, 1993–Present*, features developments in the twenty-first century—the presidency of Barack Obama , the killing of al-Qaida leader Osama bin Laden, the emergence of the Tea Party and the Occupy Wall Street movements—as well as the stagnant economy in the aftermath of the Great Recession.

In addition, I have incorporated throughout this edition fresh insights from important new scholarly works dealing with many significant topics. Whether you consider yourself a political, social, cultural, or economic historian, you'll find new material to consider and share with your students.

As part of making the new editions even more teachable and classroom friendly, the new Tenth Brief Edition of *America: A Narrative History* also makes history an immersive experience through its innovative pedagogy and digital resources. Norton InQuizitive for History—Norton's groundbreaking, formative, and adaptive new learning program—enables both students and instructors to assess learning progress at the individual and classroom level. The Norton Coursepack provides an array of support materials—free to instructors—who adopt the text for integration into their local learning-management system. The Norton Coursepack includes valuable assessment and skill-building activities like new primary source exercises, guided reading exercises, review quizzes, and interactive map resources. In addition, we've created new Office Hours videos that help students understand the Focus Questions and make history relevant for them (see pages xxv–xxvii for information about student and instructor resources).

Media Resources for Instructors and Students

America's new student resources are designed to make them better readers, guiding them through the narrative while at the same time developing their critical thinking and history skills.

The comprehensive ancillary package features a groundbreaking new formative and adaptive system, as well as innovative interactive resources, including maps and primary sources, to help students master the Focus Questions in each chapter and continue to strengthen the skills they need to do the work of historians. Norton is unique in partnering exclusively with subject-matter experts who teach the course to author these resources. As a result, instructors have all of the course materials they need to successfully manage their U.S. history survey course, whether they are teaching face-to-face, online, or in a hybrid setting.

Instructor Resources

learning management system coursepacks: strong assessment and lecture tools

- **New! Office Hour Videos:** These segments feature David Shi speaking for 90 seconds on the Focus Questions of each chapter. There are over 100 of these new video segments.
- **New! Primary Source Exercises:** These activities feature several primary sources with multiple-choice and short essay questions to encourage close reading and analysis.
- **Guided Reading Exercises:** These exercises are designed by P. Scott Corbett (Ventura College) to help students learn how to read a textbook and, more important, comprehend what they are reading. The reading exercises instill a three-step Note-Summarize-Assess pedagogy. Exercises are based on actual passages from the textbook, and sample feedback is provided to model responses.
- **Interactive iMaps:** These interactive tools challenge students to better understand the nature of change over time by allowing them to explore the different layers of the maps from the book. Follow-up map worksheets help build geography skills by allowing students to test their knowledge by labeling.
- **Review Quizzes:** Multiple-choice, true/false, and chronological-sequence questions allow students to test their knowledge of the chapter content

and identify where they need to focus their attention to better understand difficult concepts.

- **Primary Sources:** Over 400 primary source documents and images are available on the Student Site that accompanies *America: A Narrative History*, Tenth Edition. Instructors and students can use these resources for assignments and further research on each chapter.
- **Norton American History Digital Archive:** The Digital Archive offers roughly 2,000 images and audio and video files spanning American history. The comprehensive collection provides endless opportunities to enhance lecture presentations, build new assignments, and expand your students' comprehension through visual history and artifacts. From government documents, to personal artifacts, this collection enhances students' understanding of history.

INSTRUCTOR'S MANUAL

The Instructor's Manual for *America: A Narrative History*, Tenth Brief Edition, is designed to help instructors prepare lectures and exams. The Instructor's Manual contains detailed chapter outlines, lecture ideas, in-class activities, discussion questions, as well as chapter concept maps.

TEST BANK

The Test Bank contains over 2,000 multiple-choice, true/false, and essay questions. This edition of the Test Bank has been completely revised for content and accuracy. All test questions are now aligned with Bloom's Taxonomy for greater ease of assessment.

LECTURE POWERPOINT SLIDES

These ready-made presentations provide comprehensive outlines of each chapter, as well as discussion prompts to encourage student comprehension and engagement.

STUDENT RESOURCES

NEW! NORTON INQUIZITIVE FOR HISTORY

This groundbreaking formative, adaptive learning tool improves student understanding of the Focus Questions in each chapter. Students receive personalized quiz questions on the topics with which they need the most help. Questions range from vocabulary and concepts to interactive maps and primary sources that challenge students to begin developing the skills necessary to do the work of a historian. Engaging game-like elements motivate students as they learn. As a result, students come to class better prepared to participate in discussions and activities.

NEW! STUDENT SITE

wwnorton.com/college/history/America10

Free and open to all students, Norton Student Site includes additional resources and tools to ensure they come to class prepared and ready to actively participate.

- **Office Hour Videos:** These segments feature David Shi speaking for 90 seconds on the Focus Questions of each chapter. There are over 100 of these new video segments.
- **iMaps:** Interactive maps challenge students to explore change over time by navigating the different layers of the maps from the book. Practice worksheets help students build their geography skills by labeling the locations.
- **Online Reader:** The online reader offers a diverse collection of primary source readings for use in assignments and activities.

PRIMARY SOURCE READERS TO ACCOMPANY *AMERICA: A NARRATIVE HISTORY*

- **New** sixth edition of *For the Record: A Documentary History of America*, by David E. Shi and Holly A. Mayer (Duquesne University), is the perfect companion reader for *America: A Narrative History*. *For the Record* now has 250 primary-source readings from diaries, journals, newspaper articles, speeches, government documents, and novels, including a number of readings that highlight the substantially updated theme of African American history in this new edition of *America*. If you haven't scanned *For the Record* in a while, now would be a good time to take a look.
- **New Norton Mix: American History** enables instructors to build their own custom reader from a database of nearly 300 primary- and secondary-source selections. The custom readings can be packaged as a standalone reader or integrated with chapters from *America* into a custom textbook.

ACKNOWLEDGMENTS

This Tenth Brief Edition of *America: A Narrative History* has been a team effort. Several professors who have become specialists in teaching the introductory survey course helped create the test bank, interactive media, and primary source exercises:

Erik Anderson, San Antonio College
Melissa Weinbrenner, Northeast Texas College
Mark Goldman, Tallahassee Community College
Brian McKnight, University of Virginia at Wise
Laura Farkas, Ivy Tech College–West Lafayette
Jon Lee, San Antonio College

The quality and range of reviews on this project were truly exceptional. The book and its accompanying media components were greatly influenced by the thoughts and ideas of numerous instructors.

Milan Andrejevich, Ivy Tech College–South Bend
Evan Bennett, Florida Atlantic University
Laura Bergstrom, Ivy Tech College–Sellersburg
Keith Berry, Hillsborough Community College
Albert Broussard, Texas A&M, College Station
Blanche Brick, Blinn College
Cory Burger, Ivy Tech College–Terre Haute
Brian Cervantez, Tarrant County College–Northwest Campus

Michael L. Collins, Midwestern State University
Lee Cowan, Tarrant County College
Thomas A. DeBlack, Arkansas Tech University
Scott Derr, Ivy Tech College–Bloomington
S. Matthew DeSpain, Rose State College
Michael Downs, Tarrant County College–Northeast Campus
Shannon Duffy, Southwest Texas State University
Karen Dunn-Haley, University of California, Davis
Stephen D. Engle, Florida Atlantic University
Laura Farkas, Ivy Tech College–West Lafayette
David Haney, Austin Community College
Andrew Hollinger, Tarrant County College–Southeast Campus
Frances Jacobson, Tidewater Community College
Robert MacDonald, Ivy Tech College–Lafayette
Richard McCaslin, University of North Texas–Denton
Suzanne McFadden, Austin Community College
Joel McMahon, Kennesaw State University
Greg Miller, Hillsborough Community College
Catherine Parzynski, Montgomery County Community College
R. Lynn Rainard, Tidewater Community College
Hazel Ramos, Glendale Community College
Nicole Ribianszky, Georgia Gwinnett College
Allen Smith, Ivy Tech College–Indianapolis
Bruce Solheim, Citrus College
Mark Stanley, University of North Texas–Denton
Melissa Weinbrenner, Northeast Texas College

As always, my colleagues at W. W. Norton shared with me their dedicated expertise and their poise amid tight deadlines, especially Jon Durbin, Justin Cahill, Melissa Atkin, Linda Feldman, Travis Carr, Ashley Horna, Laura Wilk, Chris Hillyer, Sarah England, Hope Goodell Miller, Stephanie Romeo, Marne Evans, John Gould, Heather Laskey, and Donna Ranieri.

In addition, Jim Stewart, a patient friend and consummate editor, helped winnow my wordiness.

Finally, I have dedicated this Tenth Brief Edition of *America* to Angela Halfacre Shi, my radiant wife who makes the present as fascinating as the past.

AMERICA

16 The Era of Reconstruction

1865–1877

A Visit from the Old Mistress **(1876)** This powerful painting by Winslow Homer depicts a plantation mistress visiting her former slaves in the postwar South. Although their living conditions are humble, these freedwomen stand firmly and eye-to-eye with the woman who had kept them in bondage.

I n the spring of 1865, the Civil War was finally over. The war to restore the Union ended up transforming American life. The United States was a "new nation," said an Illinois congressman, because it was now "wholly free." At a cost of some 730,000 lives and the destruction of the southern economy, the Union had won the terrible war, and almost 4 million enslaved Americans had won their freedom. This was the most dramatic social change in the history of the nation, but the end of slavery did not bring the end of racism.

The Confederacy had its world turned upside down. The abolition of slavery, the war-related disruptions to the southern economy, and the horrifying human losses had destroyed the plantation system and upended racial relations in the South, which now had to come to terms with a new era and a new order as the United States government set about "reconstructing" the region—and policing defiant ex-Confederates. Diarist Mary Chesnut expressed the frustration felt by the defeated southern white elite when she wished that "they were *all* dead—all Yankees!"

Freed slaves felt just the opposite. Yankees were their saviors. No longer would enslaved workers be sold and separated from their families or prevented from learning to read and write or attending church. "I felt like a bird out of a cage," said former slave Houston Holloway of Georgia, who had been sold to three different owners during his first twenty years. "Amen. Amen. Amen. I could hardly ask to feel any better than I did that day."

Few owners, however, willingly freed their slaves until forced to by the arrival of Union soldiers. A North Carolina planter pledged that he and other whites "will never get along with the free negroes" because they were an "inferior race." Similarly, a Mississippi planter predicted that "these niggers will all be slaves again in twelve months."

focus questions

1. What major challenges faced the federal government in reconstructing the South after the Civil War during the period from 1865 to 1877?

2. How and why did Reconstruction policies change over time?

3. In what ways did white and black southerners react to Reconstruction?

4. What were the political and economic factors that helped lead to the end of Reconstruction in 1877?

5. What was the significance of Reconstruction for the nation's future?

At war's end in the spring of 1865, Henry Adams left the Louisiana plantation where he had been enslaved "to see whether I am free by going without a pass." A group of whites confronted him on the road, asked his owner's name, and beat him when he declared that "I now belong to no one." Some newly freed slaves rushed to give themselves new names to symbolize their changed status. Others left plantations and farms for towns and cities, where, as one of them said, "freedom was free-er."

The ratification of the Thirteenth Amendment to the U.S. Constitution in December 1865 was intended to end all doubt about the status of former slaves by abolishing slavery everywhere. Now the nation faced the huge task of "reconstructing" and reuniting a war-ravaged South while transforming ex-slaves into free workers and equal citizens.

It would not be easy. Freedom did not bring independence or self-reliance for millions of former slaves. At the same time, many white southerners resented and resisted efforts to "reconstruct" their region. As a South Carolina planter told a federal official in the fall of 1865, "The war is not over."

During the Reconstruction era, from 1865 to 1877, political leaders wrestled with how best to bring the Confederate states back into the Union and how best to help former slaves make the transition from bondage to citizenship. Those turbulent years witnessed a complex debate about the role of the federal government in ensuring civil rights.

Some northerners wanted the former Confederate states returned to the Union with little or no changes in their social, political, and economic life. Others called for former Confederate political and military leaders to be imprisoned or executed and the South rebuilt in the image of the rest of the nation. The editors of the nation's most popular magazine, *Harper's Weekly*, expressed this vengeful attitude when they declared that "the forgive-and-forget policy . . . is mere political insanity and suicide."

Although the Reconstruction era lasted only twelve years, it was one of the most significant periods in U.S. history. The decisions made and the policies enacted are still shaping American life nearly 150 years later.

THE WAR'S AFTERMATH IN THE SOUTH

The postwar South presented a sharp contrast to the victorious North, where the economy had been strengthened by the war efforts. Between 1860 and 1870, northern wealth grew by 50 percent while southern wealth dropped 60 percent. Along the path that General William Tecumseh Sherman's Union army had blazed across Georgia and the Carolinas, one observer reported in 1866, the countryside "looked for many miles like a broad black streak of ruin and desolation." Burned-out Columbia, South Carolina, said another witness, was "a wilderness of ruins"; Charleston, the birthplace of secession, had become a place of "vacant houses, of widowed women, of rotting wharves, of deserted warehouses, of weed-wild gardens, of miles of grass-grown streets, of acres of pitiful and voiceless barrenness."

Throughout the South, property values had collapsed. In the year after the war ended, eighty-one plantations in Mississippi were sold for less than a tenth of what they had been worth in 1860. Confederate bonds and paper money were worthless; personal savings had vanished.

Union soldiers who fanned out across the defeated South to impose order were cursed and spat upon. A Virginia woman expressed a spirited defiance common among her circle of friends: "Every day, every hour, that I live increases my hatred and detestation, and loathing of that race. They [Yankees] disgrace our common humanity. As a people I consider them vastly inferior to the better classes of our slaves." Fervent southern nationalists, both men and

Richmond after the Civil War Before evacuating the capital of the Confederacy, Richmond, Virginia, Rebels set fire to warehouses and factories to prevent their falling into Union hands. Pictured here is one of Richmond's burnt districts in April 1865. Women in mourning attire walk among the shambles.

women, implanted in their children a similar hatred of Yankees and a defiance of northern rule.

Many of the largest southern cities—Richmond, Atlanta, Charleston—were in ruins; most railroads were damaged or destroyed. Cotton that had not been destroyed by invading Union armies was seized by federal troops. Emancipation had eliminated $4 billion invested in slaves and left the agricultural economy in confusion. In 1860, just before the war began, the South generated 30 percent of the nation's wealth; in 1870, only ten years later, it produced but 12 percent.

Many southerners were homeless and hungry, emotionally exhausted and physically disabled. Countless families had lost sons and husbands, and many surviving war veterans returned home with one or more limbs missing. In 1866, the state of Mississippi spent a fifth of its annual budget on artificial limbs for Confederate soldiers.

Rebuilding the former Confederacy would not be easy, and the issues related to reconstruction were often complicated and controversial. For example, the process of forming new state governments first required determining the official status of the states that had seceded. Were they now conquered territories? If so, then the Constitution assigned Congress authority to re-create their state governments. But what if, as Abraham Lincoln had argued, the Confederate states had never officially left the Union because the act of secession was itself illegal? In that circumstance, the president would be responsible for re-forming state governments.

Whichever branch of government—Congress or the presidency—directed the reconstruction of the South, it would have to address the most difficult issue: What would be the political, social, and economic status of the freed slaves? Were they citizens? If not, what was their status as Americans? What the freed slaves wanted most was to become self-reliant as soon as possible. That meant being able to control their labor, reunite with their family members, gain education for their children, enjoy full participation in political life, and create their own community organizations and social life. Many whites were just as determined to prevent that from happening.

DEBATES OVER POLITICAL RECONSTRUCTION

The reconstruction of former Confederate states actually began during the war and went through several phases, the first of which was Presidential Reconstruction. In 1862, with Union forces advancing into the South, President Lincoln had named army generals to serve as temporary military governors for conquered Confederate areas. By the end of 1863, he had formulated a plan to reestablish governments in states liberated from Confederate rule.

LINCOLN'S PLAN   In late 1863, President Lincoln issued a Proclamation of Amnesty and Reconstruction, under which any Confederate state could re-create a Union government once a number equal to 10 percent of those who had voted in 1860 swore allegiance to the Constitution and the Union. They also received a presidential pardon acquitting them of treason. Certain groups, however, were denied pardons: Confederate government officials; senior officers of the Confederate army and navy; judges, congressmen, and military officers of the United States who had left their posts to aid the rebellion; and those who had abused captured African American soldiers.

CONGRESSIONAL PLANS   Northern politicians, however, disagreed over who had the authority to restore Rebel states to the Union. Many Republicans, especially the so-called Radicals, argued that Congress, not the president, should supervise Reconstruction. A few conservative and most moderate Republicans supported Lincoln's program that immediately restored pro-Union southern governments.

The **Radical Republicans**, however, favored a drastic transformation of southern society based upon granting freed slaves full citizenship rights. Many Radical Republican leaders, motivated primarily by religious values and moral ideals, believed that all people, regardless of race, were equal in God's eyes. They wanted no compromise with the "sin" of racism.

The Radicals also hoped to replace the white, Democratic planter elite with a new generation of small farmers, along with wage-earning and middle-class Republicans, both black and white. "The middling classes who own the soil, and work it with their own hands," explained Radical leader Thaddeus Stevens, "are the main support of every free government."

THE WADE-DAVIS BILL   In 1864, with the war still raging, the Radical Republicans tried to take charge of Reconstruction by passing the Wade-Davis Bill, sponsored by Senator Benjamin Franklin Wade of Ohio and Representative Henry Winter Davis of Maryland. Unlike Lincoln's 10-percent plan, the Wade-Davis Bill required that a *majority* of white males swear their allegiance to the Union before a Confederate state could be readmitted.

But the Wade-Davis Bill never became law: Lincoln vetoed it as being too harsh. In retaliation, Republicans issued the Wade-Davis Manifesto, which accused Lincoln of exceeding his constitutional authority. Unfazed, Lincoln moved ahead with his efforts to restore the Confederate states to the Union. He also acted boldly to provide assistance to the freed slaves in the South.

THE FREEDMEN'S BUREAU In early 1865, Congress approved the Thirteenth Amendment to the Constitution, officially abolishing slavery in the United States. The amendment, and the war that enabled it, liberated almost 4 million slaves. Yet what did freedom mean for the former slaves, most of whom had no land, no home, no food, no jobs, and no education? Throughout the major northern cities, people had formed Freedmen's Aid Societies to raise funds and recruit volunteers to help the African Americans in the South. Many churches did the same. But the needs far exceeded such grassroots efforts.

It soon fell to the federal government to address the desperate plight of the former slaves. On March 3, 1865, Congress created the **Freedmen's Bureau** (within the War Department) to assist the "freedmen and their wives and children." It was the first federal experiment in providing assistance directly to people rather than to states.

In May 1865, General Oliver O. Howard, commissioner of the Freedmen's Bureau, declared that freed slaves "must be free to choose their own employers, and be paid for their labor." He sent agents to the South to negotiate labor contracts between blacks and white landowners, many of whom resisted. The Bureau provided former slaves with medical care and food and clothing, and also helped set up schools.

By 1870, the Bureau was supervising nearly 4,000 new schools serving almost 250,000 students, many of whose teachers were initially women volunteers from the North. The Freedmen's Bureau also helped former slaves reconnect with family members. Marriages that had been prohibited during slavery were now made legal.

FREED SLAVES AND LAND A few northerners argued that what ex-slaves needed most was their own land. A New Englander traveling in the postwar South noted that the "sole ambition of the freedman" was " . . . to become the owner of a little piece of land, there to erect a humble home, and to dwell in peace and security at his own free will and pleasure." In coastal South Carolina and in Mississippi, former slaves had been "given" land by Union armies that had taken control of Confederate areas during the war.

Even northern abolitionists balked at Radical proposals to confiscate white-owned land and distribute it to the freed slaves, however. Citizenship and legal rights were one thing, wholesale confiscation of property and land redistribution quite another. Nonetheless, the discussions fueled false rumors that freed slaves would get "forty acres and a mule," a slogan that swept across the South. Ulysses S. Grant, still general-in-chief of the U.S. Army, reported that the mistaken belief among the freed slaves that they would receive land was "seriously interfering" with their willingness to sign labor contracts agreeing to work as farmhands for pay.

In July 1865, hundreds of freed slaves gathered near an old church on St. Helena Island off the South Carolina coast. There, Virginia-born freeman Martin Delaney, the highest-ranking officer in the 104th U.S. Colored Troops, addressed them. Before the Civil War, he had been a prominent abolitionist in the North. Now, Major Delaney assured the gathering that slavery had been "absolutely abolished." But abolition, he stressed, was less the result of Abraham Lincoln's leadership than the outcome of former slaves and free blacks like him deciding to resist and undermine the Confederacy. Slavery was dead, and freedom was now in their hands. "Yes, yes, yes," his listeners shouted.

Delaney then noted that many white planters in the area claimed that the former slaves were lazy and "have not the intelligence to get on for yourselves without being guided and driven to the work by [white] overseers." Delaney dismissed such assumptions as lies intended to restore a system of forced labor for blacks. He told the freed slaves that their best hope was to become self-sustaining farmers: "Get a community and get all the lands you can—if you cannot get any singly." Then "grow as much vegetables etc., as you want for your families; on the other part of land, you cultivate rice and cotton." They must find ways to become economically self-reliant. Otherwise, he said, they would find themselves slaves again.

Several white planters attended Delaney's talk, and an army officer at the scene reported that they "listened with horror depicted in their faces" when Delaney urged the former slaves to become independent farmers. The planters predicted that such speeches would incite "open rebellion" among southern blacks.

DEATH OF A PRESIDENT The possibility of a lenient reconstruction of the Confederacy would die with Abraham Lincoln. The president offered his last view of Reconstruction in the final speech of his life. On April 11, 1865, he rejected calls by Radicals for a vengeful peace. He wanted "no persecution, no bloody work," no hangings of Confederate leaders, and no extreme efforts to restructure southern social and economic life. Three days later, on April 14, Lincoln and his wife Mary went to see a play at Ford's Theatre in Washington, D.C.

With his trusted bodyguard called away to Richmond, Lincoln was defenseless as John Wilkes Booth, a popular actor and a rabid Confederate, slipped into the unguarded presidential box and shot the president in the head. Lincoln, Booth claimed, was the cause of all the nation's "troubles," and God had directed him to kill the president. As the mortally wounded Lincoln slumped forward, Booth stabbed a military aide and jumped from the box to the stage, breaking his leg in the process. Booth limped out a stage door, mounted a waiting horse, and fled the city. Lincoln died nine hours later.

At the same time that Booth was shooting the president, other assassins were targeting Vice President Andrew Johnson and Secretary of State William H. Seward. Johnson escaped injury because his would-be assassin got cold feet and wound up tipsy in the barroom of the vice president's hotel. Seward and four others, including his son, suffered severe knife wounds when attacked at home.

The nation extracted a full measure of vengeance from the conspirators. After a desperate eleven-day manhunt, Booth was pursued into Virginia and killed in a burning barn. Three of his collaborators were convicted by a military court and hanged, as was Mary Surratt, who owned the Washington boardinghouse where the assassinations had been planned.

JOHNSON'S PLAN Lincoln's shocking death propelled into the White House Andrew Johnson of Tennessee, a pro-Union Democrat who had been added to the National Union ticket in 1864 solely to help Lincoln win reelection. Humorless and insecure, combative and obstinate, Johnson nursed fierce prejudices (he hated both the white southern elite and the idea of racial equality) and a weakness for liquor. At the inaugural ceremonies in early 1865, he had delivered his vice-presidential address in a state of slurring drunkenness.

Like Lincoln, Johnson was a self-made, self-taught man. Born in poverty in Raleigh, North Carolina, he never attended school. At age thirteen he relocated to Greeneville, in the mountains of east Tennessee, where he became a tailor and learned to read. Eventually, as the self-proclaimed friend of the "common man," he served as the mayor, a state legislator, governor, congressional representative, and U.S. senator.

Johnson's supporters were primarily small farmers and the working poor. He called himself a Jacksonian Democrat "in the strictest meaning of the term. I am for putting down the [Confederate] rebellion, because it is a war [of wealthy plantation owners] against democracy." Yet he also shared the racist attitudes of most southern whites. "Damn the negroes," he exclaimed to a friend during the war. "I am fighting those traitorous aristocrats, their masters." As a states' rights Democrat, he strongly opposed Republican economic policies designed to spur industrial development and insisted that the federal government should be as small and inactive as possible.

With Congress in recess, Johnson was temporarily in control of what he called the "restoration" of the Union. He needed to put his plan in place over the next seven months before the new Congress convened and the Republicans would take charge. In May 1865, he issued a new Proclamation of Amnesty that excluded not only those ex-Confederates whom Lincoln had barred from a presidential pardon but also anyone with property worth more than $20,000.

Johnson was determined to keep the wealthiest southerners from regaining political power. Surprisingly, however, he eventually pardoned most of the white "aristocrats" he claimed to despise. What brought about this change of heart? Johnson had decided that he could buy the political support of prominent southerners by pardoning them, improving his chances of reelection.

Johnson's Restoration Plan included the appointment of a Unionist as provisional governor in each southern state, a position with the authority to call a convention of men elected by "loyal" (that is, not Confederate) voters. His plan required that each state convention ratify the Thirteenth Amendment ending slavery before the state could be

Andrew Johnson A pro-Union Democrat from Tennessee.

readmitted to the Union. Johnson also encouraged the conventions to consider giving a few blacks voting rights, especially those with some education or with military service, so as to "disarm" the Republican "radicals who are wild upon" giving *all* African Americans the right to vote. Except for Mississippi, each state of the former Confederacy held a convention that met Johnson's requirements but ignored his suggestion about voting rights for blacks.

THE RADICALS REBEL Johnson's initial assault on the southern planter elite won him the support of the Radical Republicans, but not for long. Many Radicals who wanted "Reconstruction" to provide social and political equality for blacks were infuriated by Johnson's efforts to bring the South back into the Union as quickly as possible.

The leading Radical Republicans, such as Thaddeus Stevens of Pennsylvania and Charles Sumner of Massachusetts, wanted to deny former Confederates the right to vote to keep them from reelecting the old planter elite and to enable the Republican party to gain a foothold in the region. Stevens argued that the Civil War was intended to be a "*radical* revolution": the "whole fabric of southern society must be changed" to "revolutionize southern institutions, habits, and manners."

The iron-willed Stevens viewed the Confederate states as "conquered provinces" to be readmitted to the Union by the U.S. Congress, not the president.

President Johnson, however, balked at such an expansion of federal authority. He was committed to the states' rights to control their affairs. "White men alone must manage the South," Johnson told a visitor.

By the end of 1865, the Radical Republicans had gained a majority in Congress and were warring with Johnson over control of Reconstruction. On December 4, 1865, the president announced that the South had been restored to the Union. The final step in reconstruction, he added, would be for Congress to admit the newly elected southern representatives to their seats in the House and Senate.

Republicans, however, were not about to welcome back former Confederate leaders who had been elected to Congress. Georgia, for example, had elected Alexander Stephens, former vice president of the Confederacy. Across the South, four Confederate generals, eight colonels, six Confederate cabinet members, and fifty-eight Confederate legislators were elected. Outraged Republicans denied seats to all "Rebel" officials and appointed a congressional committee to develop a new plan to "reconstruct" the South.

JOHNSON VERSUS THE RADICALS President Johnson started a war with Congress over reconstruction when he vetoed a bill that renewed funding for the Freedmen's Bureau and allowed the federal agency to begin providing homesteads and schools to former slaves in the South as well as the border states. Thaddeus Stevens and other Radicals realized that Johnson and the Democrats were trying to redefine the Civil War as a conflict between states' rights and federal power, not a struggle over slavery.

In mid-March 1866, the Radical-led Congress passed the pathbreaking Civil Rights Act, which announced that "all persons born in the United States" (except Indians) were citizens entitled to "full and equal benefit of all laws."

The new legislation enraged Johnson. Congress, he bristled, had no authority to grant citizenship to lazy former slaves who did not deserve it, and he argued that the Civil Rights Act discriminated against the "white race." So he vetoed both bills.

Now it was the Republicans' turn to be infuriated. In April 1866, Congress overrode Johnson's vetoes. From that point on, Johnson, a stubborn, uncompromising loner, steadily lost both public and political support.

Soon thereafter, in the spring and summer of 1866, rampaging white mobs in the South murdered and wounded hundreds of African Americans during race riots in Memphis and New Orleans. A Memphis newspaper glorified the killings: "The negroes now know, to their sorrow, that it is best not to arouse the fury of the white man." Northerners were incensed. The massacres, Radical Republicans argued, resulted from Andrew Johnson's lenient policy toward white supremacists. "Witness Memphis, witness New Orleans," Massachusetts senator Charles Sumner cried. "Who can doubt that the President is the author of these tragedies?" The mob attacks helped motivate Congress to pass the Fourteenth Amendment, extending federal civil rights protections to blacks.

BLACK CODES The violence was partly triggered by African American protests over restrictive laws passed by the new all-white southern state legislatures in 1865 and 1866. These "**black codes**," a white southerner explained, were intended to make sure "the ex-slave was not a free man; he was a free Negro." A northerner visiting the South said the black codes were intended to enforce a widespread insistence that "the blacks at large belong to the whites at large."

The black codes differed from state to state, but their purpose was clear: to restore white supremacy. While black marriages were recognized, African Americans could not vote, serve on juries, testify against whites, or attend public schools. They could not own farmland in Mississippi or city property in South Carolina. In Alabama, they could not own guns. In Mississippi, every black male over the age of eighteen had to be apprenticed to a white, preferably a former slave owner. Virtually all black codes required that adult freed slaves sign annual labor contracts. Otherwise, they would be jailed as "vagrants." If they could not pay the vagrancy fine— and most could not—they were forced to work for whites as convict laborers.

The black codes disgusted Republicans. "We must see to it," Senator William Stewart of Nevada resolved, "that the man made free by the Constitution of the United States is a freeman indeed." And that is what they set out to do. A former slave who had served in the Union army shared the disbelief felt by most African Americans at the black codes: "If you call this Freedom, what do you call Slavery?"

"(?) Slavery Is Dead (?)" (1867)
Thomas Nast's cartoon argues that southern blacks were still being treated as slaves despite the passage of the Fourteenth Amendment. This detail illustrates a case in Raleigh, North Carolina: a black man was whipped for a crime despite federal orders specifically prohibiting such forms of punishment.

FOURTEENTH AMENDMENT To ensure the legality of the new federal Civil Rights Act, the Congressional Joint Committee on Reconstruction proposed in April 1866 a pathbreaking **Fourteenth Amendment** to the U.S. Constitution. It guaranteed citizenship to anyone born or naturalized in the United States, except Native Americans. It also prohibited any efforts to violate the civil rights of "citizens," black or white; to deprive any person "of life, liberty, or property, without due process of law"; or to "deny any person . . . the equal protection of the laws." With the Fourteenth Amendment, Congress gave the federal government responsibility for protecting (and enforcing) the civil rights of virtually all Americans. The amendment was approved by Congress on June 16, 1866. Not a single Democrat in the House or Senate voted for it. All states in the former Confederacy were required to ratify the amendment before they could be readmitted to the Union and to Congress.

Again, President Johnson fumed. "This is a country for white men," he insisted, "and, by God, as long as I am President, it shall be a government by white men." Johnson urged the southern states to refuse to ratify the amendment. He predicted that the Democrats would win the congressional elections in November and then nix the new amendment.

JOHNSON VERSUS RADICALS To win votes for Democratic candidates, Johnson went on a speaking tour of the Midwest during which he denounced Radical Republicans as traitors who should be hanged. Several of his speeches backfired, however. In Cleveland, Ohio, Johnson exchanged hot-tempered insults with a heckler. At another stop, while the president was speaking from the back of a railway car, the engineer mistakenly pulled the train out of the station, making the president appear quite the fool. Republicans charged that such unseemly incidents confirmed Johnson's image as a "ludicrous boor" and a "drunken imbecile."

In the end, the 1866 congressional elections were a devastating defeat for Johnson and the Democrats; in each house, Radical Republican candidates won more than a two-thirds majority, the margin required to override presidential vetoes. Congressional Republicans would now take over the process of reconstructing the former Confederacy.

CONGRESS TAKES CHARGE On March 2, 1867, the new Congress passed, over Johnson's vetoes, three crucial laws creating what came to be called **Congressional Reconstruction**: the Military Reconstruction Act, the Command of the Army Act, and the Tenure of Office Act.

The Military Reconstruction Act was the capstone of the Congressional Reconstruction plan. It abolished all new governments "in the rebel States" established under President Johnson's lenient reconstruction policies. In their place, Congress established military control over ten of the eleven former Confederate states. Tennessee was exempted because it had already ratified the Fourteenth Amendment. The other ten states were divided into five military districts, each commanded by a general who acted as governor.

The Military Reconstruction Act required each state to create a new constitution that guaranteed the right to vote for all adult males—black or white, rich or poor, landless or property owners. Women—black or white—did not yet have the vote and were not included in the discussions.

The Military Reconstruction Act also stipulated that the new state constitutions were to be drafted by conventions elected by male citizens "of whatever race, color, or previous condition." Each constitution had to guarantee African American males the right to vote. Once a constitution was ratified by a majority of voters and accepted by Congress, other criteria had to be met. The state legislature had to ratify the Fourteenth Amendment, and once the amendment became part of the Constitution, any given state would be entitled to representation in Congress. Several hundred African American delegates participated in the statewide constitutional conventions.

The Command of the Army Act required that the president issue all army orders through General in Chief Ulysses S. Grant. The Radical Republicans feared that President Johnson would appoint generals to head the military districts who would be too lenient. So they bypassed the president and entrusted Grant to enforce Congressional Reconstruction in the South.

The Tenure of Office Act required Senate permission for the president to remove any federal official whose appointment the Senate had confirmed. This act was intended to prevent Johnson from firing Secretary of War Edwin Stanton, the president's most outspoken critic in the cabinet.

Congressional Reconstruction embodied the most sweeping peacetime legislation in American history to that point. It sought to ensure that freed slaves could participate in the creation of new state governments in the former Confederacy. As Thaddeus Stevens explained, the Congressional Reconstruction plan was designed to create a "perfect republic" based on the principle of *equal rights* for all citizens. "This is the promise of America," he insisted. "No More. No Less."

IMPEACHING THE PRESIDENT The first two years of Congressional Reconstruction produced dramatic changes in the South, as new state legislatures rewrote their constitutions and ratified the Fourteenth Amendment. Radical Republicans now seemed fully in control of Reconstruction, but one person still stood in their way—Andrew Johnson. During 1867 and early 1868, more and more Radicals decided that the defiant Democratic president must be removed from office.

Johnson himself opened the door to impeachment (the formal process by which Congress charges the president with "high crimes and misdemeanors") when, in violation of the Tenure of Office Act, he fired Secretary of War Edwin Stanton, who had refused to resign from the cabinet despite his harsh criticism of the president's Reconstruction policy. Johnson, who considered the Tenure of Office Act an illegal restriction of presidential power, fired Stanton on August 12, 1867, and replaced him with Ulysses S. Grant.

The Radical Republicans now saw their chance. By removing Stanton without congressional approval, Johnson had violated the law. On February 24, 1868, the Republican-dominated House passed eleven articles of impeachment (that is, specific charges against the president), most of which dealt with Stanton's firing, and all of which were flimsy. In reality, the essential grievance against the president was that he had opposed the policies of the Radical Republicans.

The first Senate trial of a sitting president began on March 5, 1868 with Chief Justice Salmon P. Chase presiding. It was a dramatic spectacle before a packed gallery of journalists, foreign dignitaries, corporate executives, and political officials. As the trial began, Thaddeus Stevens, the Radical leader, warned the president: "Unfortunate, unhappy man, behold your doom!"

The five-week trial ended in stunning fashion, but not as the Radicals had hoped. The Senate voted 35 to 19 for conviction, only *one* vote short of the two-thirds needed for removal from office. Senator Edmund G. Ross, a young Radical from Kansas, cast the deciding vote in favor of acquittal, knowing that his vote would ruin his political career. "I almost literally looked down into my open grave," Ross explained afterward. "Friendships, position, fortune, everything that makes life desirable . . . were about to be swept away by the breath of my mouth." Ross was thereafter shunned by the Republicans. He lost his reelection campaign and died in near poverty.

The effort to remove Johnson was in the end a grave political mistake, for it weakened public support for Congressional Reconstruction. Nevertheless, the Radical cause did gain something: to avoid being convicted, Johnson had privately agreed to stop obstructing Congressional Reconstruction.

REPUBLICAN RULE IN THE SOUTH In June 1868, congressional Republicans announced that eight southern states were allowed again to send delegates to Congress. The remaining former Confederate states—Virginia, Mississippi, and Texas—were readmitted in 1870, with the added requirement that they ratify the **Fifteenth Amendment**, which gave voting rights to African American men. As black leader Frederick Douglass, himself a former slave, had declared in 1865, "slavery is not abolished until the black man has the ballot."

The Fifteenth Amendment prohibited states from denying any man the vote on grounds of "race, color, or previous condition of servitude." But Susan B. Anthony and Elizabeth Cady Stanton, seasoned leaders of the movement to secure an "honorable independence" and voting rights for women, demanded that the amendment be revised to include women. As Anthony stressed in a famous speech, the U.S. Constitution said: "we, the people; not we, the white male citizens; nor yet we, the male citizens; but we, the whole people, who formed the Union—women as well as men." Most men, however, remained unreconstructed when it came to voting rights for women. Radical Republicans tried to deflect the issue by declaring that it was the "Negro's hour." Women would have to wait—another fifty years, as it turned out.

Blacks under Reconstruction

When a federal official asked Garrison Frazier, a former slave in Georgia, if he and others wanted to live among whites, he said that they preferred "to live by ourselves, for there is a prejudice against us in the South that will take years to get over." In forging new lives, Frazier and many other former slaves set about creating their own social institutions.

FREED BUT NOT EQUAL White southerners used terror, intimidation, and violence to suppress black efforts to gain social and economic equality. In Texas, a white farmer told a former slave that his freedom would do him "damned little good . . . as I intend to shoot you"—and he did. In July 1866, a black woman in Clinch County, Georgia, was arrested and given sixty-five lashes for "using abusive language" during an encounter with a white woman. The Civil War had brought freedom to enslaved African Americans, but it did not bring them protection against exploitation or abuse.

Participation in the Union army or navy had provided many freedmen with training in leadership. Black military veterans would form the core of the first generation of African American political leaders in the postwar South. Military service gave many former slaves their first opportunities to learn to read and write, and army life alerted them to new opportunities for economic advancement, social respectability, and civic leadership. Fighting for the Union also instilled a fervent sense of nationalism. A Virginia freedman explained that the United States was "now *our* country—made emphatically so by the blood of our brethren."

BLACK CHURCHES AND SCHOOLS African American religious life in the South was transformed during and after the war. Many former slaves identified with the biblical Hebrews, who were led out of slavery into the "promised land." Emancipation demonstrated that God was on *their* side. Before the war, slaves who were allowed to attend white churches were forced to sit in the back. After the war, with the help of many northern Christian missionaries, both black and white, ex-slaves eagerly established their own African American churches.

The black churches were the first social institutions the former slaves could control and quickly became the crossroads for black community life. Black ministers emerged as social and political leaders as well as preachers. Many African Americans became Baptists or Methodists, in part because these were already the largest denominations in the South, and in part because they reached out to the working poor. In 1866 alone, the African Methodist Episcopal (AME) Church gained 50,000 members. By 1890, more than 1.3 million African Americans in the South had become Baptists, nearly three times as many as had joined any other denomination.

African American communities also rushed to establish schools. Education, said a freed slave in Mississippi, was "the next best thing to liberty." Most plantation owners had denied education to blacks in part because they feared that literate slaves would read abolitionist literature and organize uprisings. After the war, the white elite worried that formal education would encourage poor whites and poor blacks to leave the South in search of better social and economic opportunities.

White opposition made education all the more important to African Americans. South Carolina's Mary McLeod Bethune rejoiced in the opportunity: "The whole world opened to me when I learned to read." She earned a scholarship to college and went on to become the first black woman to found a school that became a four-year college: what is today known as Bethune-Cookman University, in Daytona Beach, Florida.

AFRICAN AMERICANS IN SOUTHERN POLITICS Groups encouraging freed slaves to embrace the Republican party were organized throughout the South. They were chiefly sponsored by the Union League, founded in Philadelphia in 1862. League recruiters enrolled African Americans and loyal whites, initiated them into the secrets and rituals of the order, and instructed them "in their rights and duties." The Union League was so

African American political figures of Reconstruction Blanche K. Bruce (left) and Hiram Revels (right) served in the U.S. Senate. Frederick Douglass (center) was a major figure in the abolitionist movement.

successful in recruiting African Americans that in 1867, it had eighty-eight chapters in South Carolina alone. The League claimed to have enrolled almost every adult black male in the state.

Of course, any African American participation in southern political life was a first. Some 600 blacks—most of them former slaves—served as state legislators under Congressional Reconstruction. In Louisiana, Pinckney Pinchback, a northern free black and former Union soldier, was elected lieutenant governor. Several other African Americans were elected lieutenant governor, state treasurer, or secretary of state. There were two black senators in Congress, Hiram Revels and Blanche K. Bruce, both Mississippi natives who had been educated in the North, as well as fourteen black members of the U.S. House of Representatives.

White southerners were appalled at the election of black politicians. Democrat extremists claimed that Radicals were trying to "organize a hell in the South" by putting "the Caucasian race" under the rule of "their own negroes." Southern whites complained that freed slaves were illiterate and had no civic experience or appreciation of political issues and processes. In this regard,

Freedmen voting in New Orleans The Fifteenth Amendment, ratified in 1870, guaranteed at the federal level the right of citizens to vote regardless of "race, color, or previous condition of servitude." But former slaves had been registering to vote—and voting in large numbers—in some state elections since 1867, as in this scene.

blacks were no different from millions of poor or immigrant white males who had been allowed to vote in many jurisdictions for years.

LAND, LABOR, AND DISAPPOINTMENT A few northerners argued that what the former slaves needed most was their own land, where they could gain economic self-sufficiency. Freed slaves felt the same way. Freedom, explained a black minister from Georgia, meant the freedom for blacks to "reap the fruit of our own labor, and take care of ourselves."

In several southern states, former slaves had been "given" land by Union armies after they had taken control of Confederate areas during the war. But transfers of white-owned property to former slaves were reversed during 1865 by President Andrew Johnson. In South Carolina, the Union general responsible for evicting former slaves urged them to "lay aside their bitter feelings, and become reconciled to their old masters." But the assembled freedmen shouted "No, never!" and "Can't do it!" They knew that ownership of land was the foundation of their freedom.

Tens of thousands of former slaves were forced to return their farms to the white owners. In addition, it was virtually impossible for former slaves to get loans to buy farmland because so few banks were willing to lend to blacks. Their sense of betrayal was profound. Reconstruction of the South would not include the redistribution of southern property.

What emerged was the labor system called **sharecropping**—where the landowner provided land, seed, and tools to a poor farmer in exchange for a *share* of the crop. Many freed blacks preferred sharecropping over working for wages, since it freed them from

Sharecroppers A family is shown outside their Virginia home in this 1899 photograph, taken by Frances Benjamin Johnston, one of the earliest American female photojournalists.

day-to-day supervision by white landowners. But over time, most sharecroppers, black and white, found themselves deep in debt to the landowner, with little choice but to remain tied to the same discouraging system of dependence that, over the years, felt much like slavery. As a former slave acknowledged, he and others had discovered that "freedom could make folks proud but it didn't make 'em rich."

TENSIONS AMONG SOUTHERN BLACKS African Americans in the postwar South were by no means a uniform community. They had their own differences and disputes, especially between the few who owned property and the many who did not.

Affluent northern blacks and the southern free black elite, most of whom were city dwellers and mulattos (people of mixed parentage), often opposed efforts to redistribute land to the freedmen, and many insisted that political equality did not mean social equality. In general, however, unity rather than dissension prevailed, and African Americans focused on common concerns, such as full equality under the law. "All we ask," said a black member of the state constitutional convention in Mississippi, "is justice, and to be treated like human beings."

With little or no training or political experience, many African Americans served in state governments with distinction. Nonetheless, the scornful label "black Reconstruction," used by critics then and since, distorts African

American political influence. Such criticism also overlooks the political clout of the large number of white Republicans, especially in the mountain areas of the Upper South, who favored the Radical plan for Reconstruction. Only South Carolina's Republican state convention had a black majority. Louisiana's was evenly divided racially, and in only two other state conventions were more than 20 percent of the members black: Florida and Virginia.

"CARPETBAGGERS" AND "SCALAWAGS"   Most of the offices in the new southern state governments went to white Republicans, who were dismissed as "carpetbaggers" or "scalawags." Carpetbaggers, critics argued, were scheming northerners who rushed South with all their belongings in cheap suitcases made of carpeting ("carpetbags") to grab political power.

Some northerners were indeed corrupt opportunists. However, most were Union military veterans drawn to the South by the desire to rebuild the region's devastated economy. New Yorker George Spencer, for example, arrived in Alabama with the Union army during the war and decided to pursue his "chances of making a fortune" in selling cotton and building railroads. He eventually was elected to the U.S. Senate. Many other so-called carpetbaggers were teachers, social workers, or ministers motivated by a genuine desire to help the free blacks and poor whites improve the quality of their lives.

The scalawags, or white southern Republicans, were especially hated by southern Democrats, who considered them traitors. A Nashville newspaper editor called them the "merest trash."

Most scalawags had been Unionists opposed to secession. They were especially prominent in mountain counties as far south as Georgia and Alabama and especially in the hills of eastern Tennessee. Among the scalawags were several distinguished figures, including former Confederate general James Longstreet, who decided after Appomattox that the Old South must change its ways. He became a successful cotton broker in New Orleans, joined the Republican party, and supported the Radical Reconstruction program. Other scalawags were former Whigs attracted by the Republican party's economic program of industrial and commercial expansion. What the diverse "scalawags" had in common was a willingness to work with Republicans to rebuild the southern economy.

SOUTHERN RESISTANCE AND WHITE "REDEMPTION"
Most southern whites viewed secession not as a mistake but as a noble "lost cause." They used all means possible—legal and illegal—to "redeem" their beloved South from northern control, Republican rule, and black assertive-

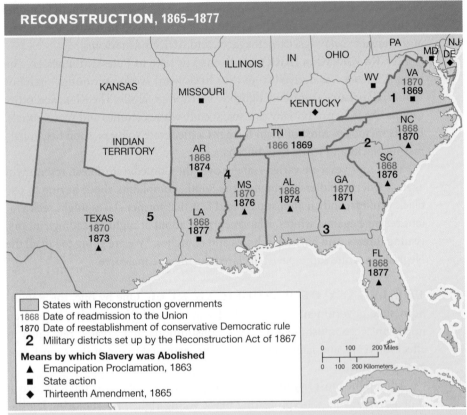

RECONSTRUCTION, 1865–1877

States with Reconstruction governments
1868 Date of readmission to the Union
1870 Date of reestablishment of conservative Democratic rule
2 Military districts set up by the Reconstruction Act of 1867

Means by which Slavery was Abolished
▲ Emancipation Proclamation, 1863
■ State action
◆ Thirteenth Amendment, 1865

- How did the Military Reconstruction Act reorganize governments in the South in the late 1860s and 1870s?
- What did the former Confederate states have to do to be readmitted to the Union?
- Why did "Conservative" white parties gradually regain control of the South from the Republicans in the 1870s?

ness. White southern ministers, for example, assured their congregations that God endorsed white supremacy.

The Civil War had brought freedom to enslaved African Americans, but it did not bring them protection against exploitation or abuse. The "black codes" created in 1865 and 1866 were the first of many continuing efforts to deny equality to African Americans. With each passing year, southern whites used terror, intimidation, and violence to prevent blacks from exercising their political rights, and resistance to Congressional Reconstruction and Radical Republican ("Radical") rule became more and more violent. Hundreds were killed and many more injured in systematic efforts to "keep blacks in their place." Several secret terrorist groups, including the Ku Klux Klan, the Knights of the White Camelia, and the White League, emerged to harass, intimidate, and even kill scalawags, carpetbaggers, and African Americans.

The **Ku Klux Klan (KKK)** was formed in 1866 in Pulaski, Tennessee. The name *Ku Klux* was derived from the Greek word *kuklos,* meaning "circle" or "band." *Klan* came from the English word *clan,* or family. The Klan, and other groups like it, began initially as a social club, with costumes and secret rituals. But its members, most of them former Confederate soldiers, soon began harrassing blacks and white Republicans.

Their motives were varied—anger over the Confederate defeat, resentment against federal soldiers occupying the South, complaints about having to pay black workers, and an almost paranoid fear that former slaves might seek violent revenge against whites. Klansmen rode about at night spreading rumors, issuing threats, and burning schools and churches. "We are going to kill all the Negroes," a white supremacist declared during one massacre.

THE LEGACY OF REPUBLICAN RULE One by one, the Republican state governments were gradually overturned. Yet they left behind an important accomplishment: the new constitutions they created remained in effect for years, and later constitutions incorporated many of their most progressive features.

Among the most significant innovations brought about by the Republican state governments were protecting black voting rights, restructuring legislatures to reflect shifting populations, and making more state offices elective to weaken the "good old boy" tradition of rewarding political supporters with state government jobs. In South Carolina, former Confederate leaders opposed the Republican state legislature not simply because of its black members but because poor whites were also enjoying political clout for the first time, thereby threatening the traditional power of wealthy white plantation owners and merchants.

Given the hostile circumstances under which Republican state governments operated in the South, their achievements were remarkable. They constructed an extensive railroad network and established public, though racially segregated, school systems funded by state governments and open to all children. Some 600,000 black pupils were enrolled in southern schools by 1877.

The Radicals also gave more attention to the poor and to orphanages, asylums, and institutions for the deaf and blind of both races. Public roads, bridges, and buildings were repaired or rebuilt. African Americans achieved rights and opportunities that would repeatedly be violated in coming decades but would never completely be taken away, at least in principle: equality before the law and the rights to own property, attend schools, learn to read and write, enter professions, and carry on business.

Yet several Republican state governments also engaged in corrupt practices. Bribes and kickbacks, whereby companies received government contracts in return for giving government officials cash or stock, were commonplace. In Louisiana, a twenty-six-year-old carpetbagger, Henry Clay Warmoth, a Union war veteran and an attorney, somehow turned an annual salary of $8,000 into a million-dollar fortune over four years as governor. (He was eventually impeached and removed from office.) "I don't pretend to be honest," he admitted. "I only pretend to be as honest as anybody in politics."

As was true in the North and the Midwest at the time, southern state governments awarded money to corporations, notably railroads, under conditions that invited shady dealings and outright corruption. In fact, some railroad officials received state funds but never built any railroads. Such corruption was not invented by the Radical Republican regimes, nor did it die with them. Governor Warmoth recognized as much: "Corruption is the fashion" in Louisiana, he explained.

THE GRANT ADMINISTRATION

Andrew Johnson's crippled presidency created an opportunity for Republicans to elect one of their own in 1868. Both parties wooed Ulysses S. Grant, the "Lion of Vicksburg" credited by most Americans with the Union victory in the Civil War. His falling-out with President Johnson, however, had pushed him toward the Republicans, who unanimously nominated him as their candidate.

THE ELECTION OF 1868 The Republican party platform endorsed Congressional Reconstruction. More important, however, were the public expectations driving the candidacy of Ulysses S. Grant, whose campaign slogan was "Let us have peace." Grant promised that, if elected, he would enforce the laws and promote prosperity for all.

The Democrats charged that the Radical Republicans were subjecting the South "to military despotism and Negro supremacy." They nominated Horatio Seymour, the wartime governor of New York and a passionate critic of Congressional Reconstruction. His running mate, Francis P. Blair Jr., a former Union general from Missouri who had served in Congress, appealed directly to white bigotry when he denounced Republicans for promoting equality for "a semi-barbarous race" of black men who sought to "subject the white women to their unbridled lust."

A Democrat later said that Blair's "stupid and indefensible" remarks cost Seymour a close election. Grant swept the electoral college, 214 to 80, but his popular majority was only 307,000 out of almost 6 million votes. More than 500,000 African American voters, mostly in the South, accounted for Grant's margin of victory. The efforts of Radical Republicans to ensure voting rights for southern blacks had paid off and would continue to do so throughout the nineteenth century. As Frederick Douglass, the revered black leader, explained, "the Republican party is the ship and all else is the sea" as far as black voters were concerned.

Grant, the youngest president ever (forty-six years old at the time of his inauguration), had proved himself a great military leader, but he was not a strong politician. He passively followed the lead of Congress and was often blind to the political forces and self-serving influence peddlers around him. Members of his own party would become his greatest disappointments and worst enemies. A failure as a storekeeper before the Civil War, Grant was awestruck by men of wealth who lavished gifts on him. He also showed poor judgment in his selection of cabinet members, often favoring friendship and loyalty over integrity and ability.

During Grant's two terms in office, his seven cabinet positions changed twenty-four times. Some of the men betrayed his trust and engaged in criminal behavior. His former comrade in arms, General William T. Sherman, said he felt sorry for Grant because so many supposedly "loyal" Republicans used the president for their own selfish gains. Carl Schurz, a Union war hero who became a Republican senator from Missouri, expressed frustration that Grant was misled by cunning advisers who "prostituted" his administration.

SCANDALS President Grant's administration was quickly mired in scandal. In the summer of 1869, two unprincipled financial schemers, Jay Gould and the colorful James Fisk Jr. (known as "Diamond Jim"), both infamous for bribing politicians and judges, plotted with Abel Corbin, the president's brother-in-law, to corner the gold market. They intended to create a public craze for gold by purchasing massive quantities of the precious metal to drive up its value. The only danger to the complicated scheme lay in the possibility that the federal Treasury would burst the bubble by selling large amounts of its gold supply, which would deflate the value of gold by putting more in circulation. When Grant was seen in public with Gould and Fisk, people assumed that he supported their scheme. As the false rumor spread in New York City's financial district that the president endorsed the run-up in gold, its value soared.

On September 24, 1869—soon to be remembered as "Black Friday"—the scheme to drive up the price of gold worked, at least at first. Starting at $150 an ounce, the bidding for gold started to rise, first to $160, then $165, leading more and more investors across the nation and around the world to join the stampede. Then, around noon, President Grant and his Treasury secretary realized what was happening and began selling huge amounts of government gold. Within fifteen minutes, the bubble created by Fisk and Gould burst, and the price of gold plummeted to $138. People who had bought gold in large amounts lost fortunes. Their agony, said a New Yorker, "made one feel as if the Battle of Gettysburg had been lost and the Rebels were marching down Broadway."

Soon, the turmoil spread to the entire stock market, claiming thousands of victims. As Fisk noted, "It was each man drag out his own corpse." For weeks after the gold bubble collapsed, financial markets were paralyzed and business confidence was shaken.

The plot to corner the gold market was only the first of several scandals that rocked the Grant administration. The secretary of war, it turned out, had accepted bribes from merchants who traded with Indians at army posts in the West. In St. Louis, whiskey distillers—dubbed the "whiskey ring" in the press—bribed federal agents in an effort to avoid taxes, bilking the government out of millions of dollars in revenue. Grant's personal secretary was enmeshed in the scheme.

Congressional committees investigated most of the scandals but uncovered no evidence that Grant himself was ever involved. His poor choice of associates, however, earned him widespread criticism. Democrats scolded Republicans for their "monstrous corruption and extravagance" and reinforced the public suspicion that elected officials were less servants of the people than they were self-serving bandits.

THE MONEY SUPPLY Complex financial issues—especially monetary policy—dominated Grant's presidency. Prior to the Civil War, the economy operated on a gold standard; state banks issued paper money that could be exchanged for an equal value of gold coins. So both gold coins and state bank notes circulated as currency. **Greenbacks** (so called because of the dye color used on the printed dollars) were issued during the Civil War to help pay for the war.

When a nation's supply of money grows faster than the economy itself, prices for goods and services increase (inflation). This happened when the greenbacks were issued. After the war, the U.S. Treasury assumed that the greenbacks would be recalled from circulation so that consumer prices would decline and the nation could return to a "hard-money" currency—gold, silver, and copper coins—which had always been viewed as more reliable in value than paper currency.

The most vocal supporters of a return to "hard money" were eastern creditors (mostly bankers and merchants) who did not want their debtors to pay them in paper currency. Critics of the gold standard tended to be farmers and other debtors. These so-called soft-money advocates opposed taking greenbacks out of circulation because shrinking the supply of money would bring lower prices (deflation) for their crops and livestock, thereby reducing their income and making it harder for them to pay their long-term debts. In 1868, congressional supporters of such a "soft-money" policy—mostly Democrats—forced the Treasury to stop withdrawing greenbacks from circulation.

President Grant sided with the "hard-money" camp. On March 18, 1869, he signed the Public Credit Act, which said that the investors who purchased government bonds to help finance the war effort must be paid back in gold. The Public Credit Act led to a decline in consumer prices that hurt debtors and helped creditors. It also ignited a ferocious political debate over the merits of "hard" and "soft" money that would last throughout the nineteenth century—and beyond.

FINANCIAL PANIC President Grant's effort to withdraw the greenbacks from circulation unintentionally helped cause a major economic collapse. During 1873, two dozen overextended railroads stopped paying their bills, forcing Jay Cooke and Company, the nation's leading business lender, to go bankrupt and close its headquarters on September 18, 1873. The shocking news created a snowball effect, as hard-pressed banks began shutting down. A Republican senator sent Grant an urgent telegram from New York City: "Results of today indicate imminent danger of general national bank panic."

The resulting **Panic of 1873** triggered a deep economic depression. Tens of thousands of businesses closed, millions of workers lost their jobs, and those with jobs saw their wages slashed. In the major cities, unemployed, homeless Americans formed long lines at charity soup kitchens.

The depression led the U.S. Treasury to reverse course and begin printing more greenbacks. For a time, the supporters of paper money celebrated, but in 1874, Grant, after a period of agonized reflection, overruled his cabinet and vetoed a bill to issue even more greenbacks. His decision pleased the financial community but also ignited a barrage of criticism. A prominent Republican, Edwards Pierrepont, telegraphed Grant that his veto represented "the bravest battle and biggest victory of your life." A Tennessee Republican congressman, however, called the veto of the currency bill "cold-blooded murder." In the end, Grant's decision only prolonged what was then the worst depression in the nation's history.

LIBERAL REPUBLICANS The sudden collapse of the economy in 1873 contributed to northerners' losing interest in Reconstruction and Republicans dividing into two factions: the Liberals (or Conscience Republicans) and the Capitalists (Stalwart Republicans). The Liberal Republicans, led by senators Charles Sumner and Carl Schurz, called for the "best elements" in both national parties to join together. Their goal was to oust the "tyrannical" Grant from the presidency, end federal Reconstruction efforts in the South, lower tariffs intended to line the pockets of big corporations, and promote "civil service reforms" to end the "partisan tyranny" of the "patronage system" whereby new presidents rewarded the "selfish greed" of political supporters with federal government jobs. The Liberal Republicans charged that Grant and his cronies were making decisions solely to benefit themselves, putting profits above principles.

In 1872, the breakaway Liberal Republicans, many of whom were newspaper editors suspicious of the "working classes," held their own national convention in Cincinnati, at which they accused the Grant administration of corruption, incompetence, and "despotism." They then committed political suicide by nominating an unlikely and ill-suited presidential candidate: Horace Greeley, editor of the *New York Tribune* and a longtime champion of a variety of causes: abolitionism, socialism, vegetarianism, and spiritualism. His image as an eccentric who repeatedly reversed his political positions was complemented by his record of hostility to the Democrats, whose support the Liberal Republicans needed if they were going to win the election.

The Democrats nevertheless gave their nomination to Greeley. Southern Democrats liked his criticism of federal reconstruction policies. His *New York Tribune*, for example, claimed that "ignorant, superstitious, semi-barbarian" former slaves were "extremely indolent, and will make no exertion beyond what is necessary to obtain food enough to satisfy their hunger." Moreover, Radical Republicans had given the vote to "ignorant" former slaves whose "Nigger Government" exercised "absolute political supremacy" in several states and was transferring the wealth from the "most intelligent" and "influential" southern whites to themselves.

Most northerners, however, were appalled at Greeley's candidacy. By nominating Greeley, said the *New York Times*, the Liberal Republicans and Democrats had killed any chance of electoral victory. Greeley carried only six southern states and none in the North. Grant won thirty-one states and car-

"Worse Than Slavery" This Thomas Nast cartoon condemns the Ku Klux Klan for promoting conditions "worse than slavery" for southern blacks after the Civil War.

ried the national election by 3,598,235 votes to 2,834,761. An exhausted Greeley confessed that he was "the worst beaten man who ever ran for high office." He died three weeks later. Grant was delighted that the "soreheads and thieves who had deserted the Republican party" were defeated, and he promised to be a better president by avoiding the "mistakes" he had made in his first term.

WHITE TERROR President Grant initially fought to enforce federal efforts to reconstruct the postwar South. But southern resistance to "Radical rule" increased and turned brutally violent. In Grayson County, Texas, a white man and two friends murdered three former slaves because they wanted to "thin the niggers out and drive them to their holes."

Klansmen focused their program of murder, violence, and intimidation on prominent Republicans, black and white—elected officials, teachers in black schools, state militias. They intentionally avoided clashes with federal troops. In Mississippi, they killed a black Republican leader in front of his family. Three white "scalawag" Republicans were murdered in Georgia in 1870. That same year, an armed mob of whites launched an attack at a Republican political rally in Alabama, killing four blacks and wounding fifty-four. An Alabama Republican pleaded with Grant to intervene. "Give us poor people some guarantee of our lives," G. T. F. Boulding wrote. "We are hunted and shot down as if we were wild beasts."

At the urging of President Grant, Republicans in Congress responded with three Enforcement Acts (1870–1871). The first of these measures imposed penalties on anyone who interfered with any citizen's right to vote. The second dispatched federal supervisors and marshals to monitor elections in southern districts where political terrorism flourished. The third, called the Ku Klux Klan Act, outlawed the main activities of the KKK—forming conspiracies, wearing disguises, resisting officers, and intimidating officials.

In general, however, the Enforcement Acts were not consistently enforced. As a result, the efforts of southern whites to use violence to thwart Reconstruction escalated. On Easter Sunday in 1873 in Colfax, Louisiana, a mob of white vigilantes, most of them ex-Confederate soldiers disappointed by local election results, used a cannon, rifles, and pistols to attack a group of black Republicans in the courthouse, slaughtering eighty-one and burning down the building. It was the bloodiest racial incident during the Reconstruction period.

SOUTHERN "REDEEMERS" The Ku Klux Klan's impact on southern politics varied from state to state. In the Upper South, it played only a modest role in helping Democrats win local elections. In the Lower South, however, Klan violence and intimidation had more serious effects. In overwhelmingly black Yazoo County, Mississippi, vengeful whites used terrorism to reverse the political balance of power. In the 1873 elections, for example, the Republicans cast 2,449 votes and the Democrats 638; two years later, the Democrats polled 4,049 votes, the Republicans 7.

Throughout the South, the activities of white supremacists disheartened black and white Republicans alike. "We are helpless and unable to organize," wrote a Mississippi scalawag. We "dare not attempt to canvass [campaign for candidates], or make public speeches." At the same time, northerners displayed a growing weariness with using federal troops to reconstruct the South. "The plain truth is," noted the *New York Herald*, "the North has got tired of the Negro."

President Grant, however, desperately wanted to use more federal force to preserve peace and asked Congress to pass new legislation that would "leave my duties perfectly clear." Congress responded with the Civil Rights Act of 1875, the most comprehensive guarantee of civil rights to that point. It said that people of all races must be granted equal access to hotels and restaurants, railroads and stagecoaches, theaters, and other places of public entertainment. Unfortunately for Grant, however, the new law provided little authority to enforce its provisions. Those who felt their rights were being violated had to file suit in court, and the penalties for violators were modest.

Public interest in protecting civil rights in the South continued to wane as other issues emerged to distract northerners. Western expansion, Indian wars, and economic issues surged to the forefront of voter concerns.

Republican political control in the South gradually loosened as all-white "Conservative" parties mobilized the anti-Reconstruction vote. White Democrats—the so-called **redeemers** who supposedly "saved" the South from Republican control and "black rule"—used the race issue to excite the white electorate and intimidate black voters. Where persuasion failed to work, Democrats used trickery. As one enthusiastic Democrat boasted, "The white and black Republicans may outvote us, but we can outcount them."

The Compromise of 1877 This illustration represents the compromise between Republicans and southern Democrats that elected Rutherford B. Hayes and ended Radical Reconstruction.

Republican political control ended in Virginia and Tennessee as early as 1869; in Georgia and North Carolina, it collapsed in 1870, although North Carolina had a Republican governor until 1876. Reconstruction lasted longest in the Lower South, where whites abandoned Klan robes for barefaced intimidation in paramilitary groups such as the Mississippi Rifle Club and the South Carolina Red Shirts. The last Radical Republican regimes collapsed, however, after the elections of 1876, and the return to power of the old white political elite in the South further undermined the country's commitment to Congressional Reconstruction.

THE CONTESTED ELECTION OF 1877 President Grant wanted to run for an unprecedented third term in 1876, but many Republicans had lost confidence in his leadership. In the summer of 1875, Grant acknowledged the inevitable, announced that he would retire, and admitted that he had entered the White House with "no political training" and had made "errors in judgment." James Gillespie Blaine of Maine, former Speaker of the House, was the likeliest Republican to succeed Grant, but his candidacy crumbled when it was revealed that he had promised political favors to railroad executives in exchange for shares of stock in the company.

The scandal led the Republican convention to pass over Blaine in favor of Ohio's favorite son, Rutherford B. Hayes. Elected governor of Ohio three times, most recently as a "hard money" gold advocate, Hayes also was a civil service reformer eager to reduce the number of federal jobs subject to political appointment. But his chief virtue was that he offended neither Radicals nor reformers. As a journalist put it, he was "obnoxious to no one."

The Democratic convention was uncharacteristically harmonious from the start. The nomination went to Samuel J. Tilden, a wealthy corporate lawyer and reform governor of New York.

The 1876 campaign avoided controversial issues. Both candidates favored relaxing federal military authority in the South. In the absence of strong ideological differences, Democrats highlighted the scandals embroiling the Republicans. In response, Republicans ignored the depression and repeatedly waved "the bloody shirt," linking the Democrats to secession, civil war, and the violence committed against Republicans in the South. As Robert G. Ingersoll, the most celebrated Republican public speaker of the time, insisted: "The man that assassinated Abraham Lincoln was a Democrat. . . . Soldiers, every scar you have on your heroic bodies was given you by a Democrat!"

Despite the lack of major issues, the 1876 election generated the most votes of any national election in U.S. history to that point. Early returns pointed to a victory for Tilden. Nationwide, he outpolled Hayes by almost 300,000 votes; by midnight following Election Day, Tilden had won 184 electoral votes, just one short of the total needed for victory. Overnight, however, Republican activists realized that the election hinged on 19 disputed electoral votes from Florida, Louisiana, and South Carolina.

The Democrats needed only one of the challenged votes to claim victory; the Republicans needed all nineteen. Republicans in those key states had engaged in election fraud, while Democrats had used physical intimidation to keep black voters at home. But all three states were governed by a Republican who appointed the election boards, each of which reported narrow victories for Hayes. The Democrats immediately challenged the results.

In all three states, rival election boards submitted conflicting vote counts. The nation watched and wondered as days, then weeks, passed with no solution. On January 29, 1877, Congress set up an electoral commission to settle the dispute. It met daily for weeks trying to verify the disputed vote counts.

Finally, on March 1, 1877, the commission voted 8 to 7 along party lines in favor of Hayes. The next day, the House of Representatives declared Hayes president by an electoral vote of 185 to 184. Tilden decided not to protest the decision. His campaign manager explained that they preferred "four years of Hayes's administration to four years of civil war."

Hayes's victory hinged on the defection of key southern Democrats, who, it turned out, had made a number of secret deals with the Republicans. On February 26, 1877, prominent Ohio Republicans and powerful southern Democrats struck a private bargain—the **Compromise of 1877**—at Wormley's Hotel in Washington, D.C. The Republicans promised that if Hayes were named president, he would remove the last federal troops from the South.

THE END OF RECONSTRUCTION In 1877, newly inaugurated President Hayes withdrew federal troops from Louisiana and South Carolina, whose Republican governments collapsed soon thereafter. Hayes insisted that it was not his fault: "The practical destruction of the Republican organization in the South was accomplished before my southern policy was announced."

Over the next thirty years, the protection of black civil rights in the South crumbled. As Henry Adams, a former Louisiana slave, observed in 1877, "The whole South—every state in the South—has got [back] into the hands of the very men that held us as slaves." New white state governments rewrote their constitutions, rid their administrations of "carpetbaggers, scalawags, and blacks," and cut spending. "The Yankees helped free us, so they say," a former North Carolina slave named Thomas Hall remembered, "but [in 1877] they let us be put back in slavery again."

RECONSTRUCTION'S SIGNIFICANCE

Congressional Reconstruction gave African Americans an opportunity to experience freedom—but not security or equality. As Thomas Hall noted in acknowledging the end of Reconstruction, African Americans were still dependent "on the southern white man for work, food, and clothing," and most southern whites remained hostile to the notion of civil rights and social equality. The collapse of Congressional Reconstruction in 1877 had tragic consequences, as the South aggressively renewed traditional patterns of discrimination against African Americans. Black activist W. E. B. DuBois called the effort to make slaves into citizens a "splendid failure."

Yet for all of the unfulfilled promises of Congressional Reconstruction, it left an enduring legacy—the Thirteenth, Fourteenth, and Fifteenth Amendments. If Reconstruction's experiment in interracial democracy did not provide true social equality or substantial economic opportunities for African Americans, it did create the essential constitutional foundation for future advances in the quest for equality and civil rights—and not just for African Americans, but for women and other minority groups. Until the pivotal Reconstruction era, the states were responsible for protecting citizens' rights. Thereafter, thanks to the Fourteenth and Fifteenth Amendments, blacks had gained equal rights (in theory), and the federal government had assumed responsibility for ensuring that states treated blacks equally. A hundred years later, the cause of civil rights would be embraced again by the federal government—this time permanently.

CHAPTER REVIEW

SUMMARY

- **Reconstruction Challenges**   With the defeat of the Confederacy and the passage of the Thirteenth Amendment, the federal government had to develop policies and procedures to address a number of vexing questions: What was the status of the defeated states and how would they be reintegrated into the nation's political life? What would be the political status of the former slaves and what would the federal government do to integrate them into the nation's social and economic fabric?

- **Reconstruction over Time**   Abraham Lincoln and his successor, southerner Andrew Johnson, wanted a lenient plan for Reconstruction. The *Freedmen's Bureau* helped to educate and aid freed slaves, negotiate labor contracts, and reunite families. Lincoln's assassination led many northerners to favor the *Radical Republicans*, who wanted to end the grasp of the old plantation elite on the South's society and economy. Whites resisted and established *black codes* to restrict the freedom of former slaves. *Congressional Reconstruction* responded by stipulating that to reenter the Union, former Confederate states had to ratify the *Fourteenth* and *Fifteenth Amendments* to the U.S. Constitution to protect the rights of African Americans. Congress also passed the Military Reconstruction Act, which used federal troops to enforce the voting and civil rights of African Americans.

- **Views of Reconstruction**   Many former slaves found comfort in their families and in the churches they established, but land ownership reverted to the old white elite, reducing newly freed blacks to *sharecropping*. African Americans enthusiastically participated in politics, with many serving as elected officials. Along with white southern Republicans (scalawags) and northern carpetbaggers, they worked to rebuild the southern economy. Many white southerners, however, supported the *Ku Klux Klan's* violent intimidation of the supporters of Reconstruction and pursued "redemption," or white Democratic control of southern state governments.

- **Political and Economic Developments and the End of Reconstruction**   Scandals during the Grant administration involved an attempt to corner the gold market, and the "whiskey ring's" plan to steal millions of dollars in tax revenue. In the face of these troubles and the economic downturn caused by both the *Panic of 1873* and disagreement over whether to continue the use of *greenbacks* or return to the gold standard, northern support for the status quo in government eroded and weakened Reconstruction. Southern white "*redeemers*" were elected in 1874, successfully reversing the political progress of Republicans and blacks. In the *Compromise of 1877*, Democrats agreed to the election of Republican Rutherford B. Hayes, who put an end to the Radical Republican administrations in the southern states.

- **The Significance of Reconstruction**   Southern state governments quickly renewed long-standing patterns of discrimination against African Americans, but the

Fourteenth and Fifteenth Amendments remained enshrined in the Constitution, creating the essential constitutional foundation for future advances in civil rights.

CHRONOLOGY

1865	Congress sets up the Freedmen's Bureau
April 14, 1865	Lincoln assassinated
1865	Johnson issues Proclamation of Amnesty
	All-white southern state legislatures pass various "black codes"
1866	Ku Klux Klan organized
	Congress passes the Civil Rights Act
1867	Congress passes the Military Reconstruction Act
1868	Fourteenth Amendment is ratified
	The U.S. House of Representatives impeaches President Andrew Johnson; the Senate fails to convict him
	Grant elected president
	Eight former Confederate states readmitted to the Union
1869	Reestablishment of white conservative rule ("redeemers") in some former Confederate states.
1870	Fifteenth Amendment ratified
	First Enforcement Acts passed in response to white terror in the South
1872	Grant wins reelection
1873	Panic of 1873 triggers depression
1877	Compromise of 1877 ends Reconstruction; Hayes becomes president

KEY TERMS

Radical Republicans p. 583

Freedmen's Bureau p. 584

Johnson's Restoration Plan p. 587

black codes p. 589

Fourteenth Amendment (1866) p. 589

Congressional Reconstruction p. 590

Fifteenth Amendment (1870) p. 592

sharecropping p. 597

Ku Klux Klan (KKK) p. 600

greenbacks p. 603

Panic of 1873 p. 604

redeemers p. 607

Compromise of 1877 p. 610

 INQUIZITIVE

Go to InQuizitive to see what you've learned—and learn what you've missed—with personalized feedback along the way.

part five

GROWING PAINS

The defeat of the Confederacy in 1865 restored the Union and, in the process, helped accelerate America's transformation into an agricultural empire and an industrial powerhouse. A stronger sense of nationalism began to replace the regional conflicts of the prewar era. During and after the Civil War, the Republican-led Congress pushed through legislation to promote industrial and commercial development and western expansion at the same time that it was "reconstructing" the former Confederate states. The United States forged a dynamic new industrial economy serving an increasingly national and international market for American goods. Yet, that progress, and the process of settling the rest of the continent, was tarnished by the relentless and ruthless relocation of Native Americans onto reservations and the exploitation of the continent's natural resources.

Fueled by innovations in mass production and mass marketing, and by advances in transportation and communications such as transcontinental railroads and transatlantic telegraph systems, huge corporations began to dominate the economy by the end of the nineteenth century. As the prominent social theorist William Graham Sumner remarked, the process of industrial development "controls us all because we are all in it. It creates the conditions of our own existence, sets the limits of our social activity, and regulates the bonds of our social relations."

Late-nineteenth-century American life drew much of its energy from the mushrooming industrial cities. "This is the age of cities," declared Midwestern writer Hamlin Garland. "We are now predominantly urban." But the transition from an economy made up of mostly small local and regional businesses to one dominated by large-scale national and international corporations affected rural life as well.

As early as 1869, novelist Harriet Beecher Stowe reported that the "simple, pastoral" America "is a thing forever gone. The hurry of railroads, and the rush and roar of business" had displaced the Jeffersonian ideal of America as a nation of small farms. She exaggerated, of course. Small farms and small towns survived the impact of the Industrial Revolution, but farm folk, as one New Englander stressed, must now "understand farming as a business; if they do not it will go hard with them." The friction between the new forces of the national marketplace and the traditional folkways of small-scale family farming generated social unrest and political revolts (what one writer called "a seismic shock, a cyclonic violence") during the last quarter of the nineteenth century.

The clash between tradition and modernity, sleepy farms and bustling cities, peaked during the 1890s, one of the most strife-ridden decades in American history. A deep economic depression, political activism by farmers, and violent conflicts between industrial workers and employers transformed the presidential campaign of 1896 into a clash between rival visions of America's future.

The Republican candidate, William McKinley, campaigned on modern urban and industrial values. By contrast, William Jennings Bryan, the nominee of both the Democratic and the Populist parties, was an eloquent defender of America's rural past. McKinley's victory proved to be a turning point in American political and social history. By 1900, the United States had emerged as one of the world's greatest industrial powers, and it would thereafter assume a new leadership role in world affairs—for good and for ill.

17

Business and Labor in the Industrial Era

1860–1900

Carnegie Steel Company Steelworkers operate the massive and dangerous Bessemer converters at Andrew Carnegie's huge steel mill in Pittsburgh, Pennsylvania.

T he Civil War devastated the economy of the South. In the North, however, the need to supply the massive Union armies with shoes, boots, uniforms, weapons, supplies, food, wagons, and railroads ushered in an era of unprecedented industrial development. The scope of the war favored large-scale business enterprises and hastened the maturation of a truly national economy. An Indiana congressman told business leaders in 1864 that the war effort had sparked the development of "resources and capabilities such as you never before dreamed you possessed."

During the war years, the number of manufacturing companies in the United States almost doubled, and between the end of the war and 1900, America experienced explosive growth. The nation's population tripled, agricultural production more than doubled, and manufacturing output grew *six* times over. In the thirty-five years after the Civil War, the United States achieved the highest rate of economic growth in the world, more than double that of its closest rival, Great Britain. By 1900, American industries and corporate farms dominated global markets in steel and oil, wheat and cotton.

Such phenomenal growth caused profound social changes, the most visible of which was the sudden prospering of large industrial cities such as Pittsburgh, Chicago, and Cleveland. Millions of young adults left farms and villages to work in factories, mines, and mills, and to revel in the energies of city life. In growing numbers, women left the "cult of domesticity" and entered the urban-industrial workplace as clerks, typists, secretaries, teachers, nurses, and seamstresses.

focus questions

1. What primary factors stimulated the unprecedented industrial and agricultural growth in the late nineteenth century?

2. Who were the leading entrepreneurs who pioneered the growth of Big Business? What were their goals and what strategies did they use to dominate their respective industries?

3. What role did the federal government play in the nation's economic development during this period?

4. In what ways did the social class structure and lives of women change in the late nineteenth century?

5. How effective were the efforts of workers to organize unions to promote their interests during this era?

While a few people made enormous fortunes, however, most laborers remained in unskilled, low-wage jobs. Big Business, a term commonly used to refer to the giant corporations that emerged after the Civil War, was as untamed and reckless as the cow towns and mining camps of the West. New technologies and business practices outpaced the ability of the outdated legal system to craft new laws and fashion rules of ethics to govern the rapidly changing economy. Business owners took advantage of this lawless environment to build fortunes, destroy reputations, exploit both workers and the environment, and gouge consumers. Yet out of the scramble for profits emerged an undreamed-of prosperity and a rising standard of living that became the envy of the world.

In the process of generating wealth, capitalism fosters inequality. People with different talents, opportunities, and resources receive unequal rewards from their labors and innovations. In a capitalist democracy like America, the tensions between equal political rights and unequal economic status produce inherent social instability. The overwhelming influence exercised by business tycoons led to tensions that spurred the formation of labor unions and farm associations. Increasingly, the tensions erupted into violent clashes that demanded government intervention and produced class conflict.

INDUSTRIAL AND AGRICULTURAL GROWTH

Several factors converged during the second half of the nineteenth century to accelerate the nation's industrial development. Perhaps the most important was the creation of new transportation systems—canals, steamboats, railroads—along with instantaneous communication networks (telegraph and, later, telephone), which combined to create a truly national marketplace for the sale and distribution of goods and services.

In addition, Americans enjoyed the benefits of vast and valuable natural resources—land, forests, minerals, oil, coal, water, and iron ore. At the same time, a rising tide of immigrants created an army of low-wage, high-energy workers while expanding the pool of consumers eager to buy new products. Between 1865 and 1900, more than 15 million newcomers arrived in the United States.

A new generation of business leaders drove the transition to an urban-industrial society. Investment banker Jay Cooke marveled at the new breed of cold-blooded capitalists who emerged during and after the Civil War, most of them northerners and all of them driven by the "same all-pervading, all-engrossing anxiety to grow rich."

The uncommon men who spearheaded the postwar economic boom elicited both praise and scorn. Admirers called them "captains of industry," while critics called them "robber barons" because they controlled the flow of money and commerce. Whatever the label, the post–Civil War business tycoons were shrewd men determined to create large enterprises never before imagined. They were proponents of free enterprise and self-reliance who were convinced that what was good for their businesses was good for the country as a whole. Hated, feared, envied, or admired, the titans of the industrial era were the catalysts for a new America of cities and factories, prosperity amid poverty, and growing social strife and political corruption.

Bigness was the driving goal of industrial capitalism. Mass, scale, and size were the watchwords of the day. Daring entrepreneurs took advantage of new money-making opportunities, new technologies, and political lobbying (including bribery) to build gigantic corporations (called *trusts*) that dominated industries such as oil refining, steel, sugar, and meatpacking.

The promoters of Big Business scrambled for wealth by ruthlessly improving efficiency and productivity, cutting costs, buying politicians, and suppressing competition. These predatory men—Cornelius Vanderbilt, John D. Rockefeller, Andrew Carnegie, and J. P. Morgan, among others—wanted to *dominate* their industries. When Vanderbilt, a commodore first of steamboats and then railroads, learned that some rivals had tried to steal one of his properties while he was away, he penned a brief message: "Gentlemen: You have undertaken to cheat me. I will not sue you, for law takes too long. I will ruin you." And he did.

Corporate Agriculture

At the same time that the manufacturing sector was experiencing rapid growth, the agricultural sector was also shifting to a large-scale industrial model of operation. Giant corporate-owned "bonanza" farms (growing mostly wheat and corn on thousands of acres) spread across the West. They were run like factories by professional, college-educated managers, who during harvest season would hire hundreds of migrant workers to bring in the crops, usually wheat or corn destined for eastern or foreign markets.

The farm sector stimulated the industrial sector—and vice versa. In the West, bonanza farms using the latest machinery and scientific techniques became internationally famous for their productivity. By 1870, the United States had become the world's leading agricultural producer. And, with the growth of the commercial cattle industry, the process of slaughtering, packing, and shipping cattle, hogs, and sheep began to stimulate major enterprises.

TECHNOLOGICAL INNOVATIONS

America has always nurtured a culture of invention and innovation. Abraham Lincoln had often praised the nation's peculiar talent for "discoveries and inventions," which was especially evident in the decades after the Civil War. Inventors, scientists, research laboratories, and business owners developed labor-saving machinery and mass-production techniques (such as the use of interchangeable parts) that spurred dramatic advances in efficiency, productivity, and the size of industrial enterprises.

Such innovations helped businesses turn out more products more cheaply while enabling more people to buy more of them. Technological advances created *economies of scale*, whereby larger business enterprises, including huge commercial farms, could afford expensive new machinery and large workforces that boosted their productivity.

After the Civil War, technological improvements spurred phenomenal increases in industrial productivity. The U.S. Patent Office, which had recorded only 276 inventions during the 1790s, registered almost 235,000 new patents in the 1890s. The list of innovations was lengthy: barbed wire; mechanical harvesters, reapers, and combines; refrigerated railcars; air brakes for trains; steam turbines; typewriters; sewing machines; vacuum cleaners; electric motors; and countless others.

BELL'S TELEPHONE Few, if any, inventions could rival the importance of the telephone. In 1875, twenty-eight-year-old Alexander Graham Bell began experimenting with the concept of a "speaking telegraph," or talking through wires. The following year, he developed a primitive "electric speaking telephone" that enabled him to send a famous message to his assistant in another room: "Mr. Watson, come here, I want to see you." Bell then patented his device and started a company, the American Telephone and Telegraph Company (AT&T), to begin manufacturing telephones. Five years later, he perfected the long-distance telephone lines that revolutionized communication. By 1895, there were more than 300,000 telephones in use. Bell's patent became the most valuable one ever issued.

TYPEWRITERS AND SEWING MACHINES Other inventions changed the nature of work. Typewriters, for example, transformed the operations of business offices. Because women showed greater dexterity in their fingers, business owners hired them to operate typewriters, in part because they could be paid much less than men. Clerical positions soon became the fastest-growing job category for women.

Office typists In new roles enabled by typewriters, women served as clerks or secretaries at many offices, such as the Remington Typewriter Company, pictured here.

Likewise, the introduction of sewing machines for the mass production of clothing and linens opened new doors to women—if not usually pleasant ones to walk through. So-called sweatshops emerged in the major cities, where large numbers of mostly young women, often immigrants, worked long hours in cramped, stifling conditions.

THOMAS EDISON No American inventor was more influential or prolific than Thomas Alva Edison. As a boy in Michigan, he could not sit still; he loved to "make things" and "do things." His mother home-schooled him and allowed him to explore the outdoors and perform chemical "experiments," except when he "mussed things up."

When Edison was twelve, he began working for the local railroad, selling newspapers, food, and candy to passengers. "Being poor," he explained, "I already knew that money is a valuable thing." One day he was late for the train and ran after it. A conductor reached down and lifted him into the train by his ears. Edison felt something snap in his head, and soon he was deaf. Despite losing his hearing, however, he said that his work as a trainboy "was the happiest time of my life."

Despite having no formal scientific education, the self-taught Edison developed an insatiable curiosity and mechanical genius. In January 1869, at the age of twenty-one, he announced that he would "hereafter devote his full time to bringing out his inventions." He moved to New York City to be closer to the center of America's financial district. He developed dozens of new machines, including a "stock market ticker" that would report the transactions on Wall Street in real time. Soon, job offers and "real money" flooded his way. Edison, however, had a different goal: he wanted to become a full-time inventor, an electrical engineer devoted to creating new products.

In 1876, he moved into his "science village" in Menlo Park, New Jersey, twenty-five miles southwest of New York City. There, Edison became a mass-production inventor, promising to produce "a minor invention every ten days and a big thing every six months or so."

In the nation's first industrial research laboratory, Edison and his assistants created the first phonograph in 1877 and long-lasting electric lightbulb in 1879. He also improved upon the telephone. By the ripe age of thirty, Edison was the nation's foremost inventor. Altogether, he created or perfected hundreds of new devices and processes, including the storage battery, Dictaphone, mimeograph copier, electric motor, and motion picture camera and projector.

Edison soon became world famous. A magazine saluted him as the "Wizard of Menlo Park" and called him one of the "wonders of the world." President Rutherford B. Hayes invited him to the White House, and Congress honored him.

GEORGE WESTINGHOUSE AND ELECTRIC POWER Until the 1880s, buildings and streets were lit mostly by kerosene or gas lamps. In 1882, the Edison Electric Illuminating Company, later renamed General Electric, supplied electrical current to eighty-five customers in New York City, launching the electric utility industry. Several companies that made lightbulbs merged into the Edison General Electric Company in 1888.

The use of direct electrical current, however, limited Edison's lighting system to a radius of about two miles. To cover greater distances required an alternating current, which could be transmitted at high voltage and then stepped down by transformers. George Westinghouse, inventor of the railway air brake, developed the first alternating-current electric system in 1886, and set up the Westinghouse Electric Company to manufacture the equipment.

Edison resisted the new method as too risky, but the Westinghouse system of transmitting electricity over long distances won the "battle of the currents," and the Edison companies had to switch over to AC (alternating current) from

DC (direct current). After the invention in 1887 of the alternating-current motor by a Croatian immigrant named Nikola Tesla, Westinghouse improved upon it, and the company began selling dynamos.

The invention of dynamos, or electric motors, dramatically increased the power, speed, and efficiency of machinery. Electricity enabled factories to be located wherever the owners wished; industry no longer had to cluster around waterfalls and coal deposits to have a ready supply of energy. Electricity also spurred urban growth by improving lighting, facilitating the development of trolley and subway systems, and stimulating the creation of elevators that enabled the construction of taller buildings.

THE RAILROAD REVOLUTION

More than any other industry, the railroads symbolized the impact of innovative technologies on industrial development. No other form of transportation played so large a role in the development of the interconnected national marketplace.

TRAINS AND TIME Railroads compressed time and distance. They moved masses of people and goods faster and farther than any other form of transportation. The railroad network prompted the creation of national and international time zones and spurred the use of wristwatches, for the trains were scheduled to run on time. Towns that had rail stations thrived; those that did not died. A town's connection to a railroad, observed Anthony Trollope, a celebrated British writer touring the United States, was "the first necessity of life, and gives the only hope of wealth."

Although the first great wave of railroad building occurred in the 1850s, the most spectacular growth took place during the quarter century after the Civil War. From about 35,000 miles of track in 1865, the national rail network grew to nearly 200,000 miles by 1897. Such a sprawling railroad system was expensive, and the long-term debt required to finance it would become a major cause of the financial panic of 1893 and the ensuing depression.

TRAINS AND THE INDUSTRIAL ERA Railroads were America's first truly *big business*, the first beneficiary of the great financial market known as Wall Street in New York City, the first industry to have operations in many locations, and the first to develop a large-scale management bureaucracy.

The railroad boom was the catalyst for America's transition to an urban-industrial economy. For a century, from the 1860s to the 1960s, most people entered or left a city through its railroad stations. Trains opened the West to economic development, enabled federal troops to suppress Indian resistance, ferried millions of European and Asian immigrants across the country, helped transform commercial agriculture into a major international industry, and transported raw materials to factories and finished goods to retailers.

Railroads were expensive enterprises, however. Locomotives, railcars (called "rolling stock"), and the construction of tracks, trestles, and bridges required enormous investments. Railroads became the first industry to contract with "investment banks" to raise capital by selling shares of stock to investors. They also stimulated other industries through their mammoth purchases of iron and steel, coal, timber, leather (for seats), and glass. In addition, railroad companies were the nation's largest employers. By the 1870s, the Pennsylvania Railroad alone had 55,000 employees, as many as the entire federal government.

THE DOWNSIDE OF THE RAILROAD BOOM Many developers, however, cared more about making money than building safe railroads. Companies often overlooked dangerous working conditions that caused thousands of laborers to be killed or injured. Too many unneeded railroads were built; by the 1880s, there were twice as many railroad companies as the economy could support.

Some railroads were poorly or even criminally managed and went bankrupt. Those that succeeded often broke the rules. Railroad lobbyists helped to corrupt state and federal legislators by "buying" the votes of politicians with cash or shares of stock in the new railroad companies. Admitted Charles Francis Adams Jr., head of the Union Pacific Railroad, "Our method of doing business is founded upon lying, cheating, and stealing—all bad things."

BUILDING THE TRANSCONTINENTALS

For decades, visionaries had dreamed of the United States being the first nation in the world to build a railroad spanning a continent. In the 1860s, the dream became reality as construction began on the first of four rail lines that would bridge the nation—and, as one promoter boasted, establish "our empire on the Pacific."

THE "WORK OF GIANTS" The transcontinental railroads were, in the words of General William T. Sherman, the "work of giants." Their construction required heroic feats by the surveyors, engineers, and laborers who laid the rails, built the bridges, and gouged out the tunnels through rugged mountains.

The first transcontinental railroads were much more expensive to build than were the shorter "trunk" lines in the East. Because the western routes passed through vast stretches of unpopulated plains and deserts, construction materials, as well as workers and their food and water, had to be hauled long distances. Locomotives, railcars, rails, ties, spikes, and much more were often shipped from the East Coast to San Francisco and then moved by train to the remote construction sites.

The construction process was like managing a moving army. Herds of cattle, horses, mules, and oxen had to be fed and tended. Huge mobile camps, called "Hell on Wheels," had to be built to house the crews. Construction camps included tents for dance halls, saloons, gambling, and prostitution. Night-life was raucous. A British reporter wrote, "Soldiers, herdsmen, teamsters, women, railroad men, are dancing, singing, or gambling. There are men here who would murder a fellow-creature for five dollars. Nay, there are men who have already done it. Not a day passes but a dead body is found somewhere in the vicinity with pockets rifled of their contents."

The Union Pacific meets the Central Pacific On May 10, 1869, the celebration of the first transcontinental railroad's completion took place in Promontory, Utah.

THE PACIFIC RAILWAY ACT (1862) Before the Civil War, construction of a transcontinental line had been delayed because northern and southern congressmen clashed over the choice of routes. Secession and the departure of southern congressmen for the Confederacy in 1861 finally permitted Republicans in Congress to pass the Pacific Railway Act in 1862. It authorized construction along a north-central route by two competing companies: the Union Pacific Railroad (UP) westward from Omaha, Nebraska, across the prairie, and the Central Pacific Railroad (CP) eastward from Sacramento, California, through the Sierra Nevada. Both companies began construction during the war, but most of the work was done after 1865.

Constructing a railroad across the continent entailed feats of daring, engineering, and construction, often punctuated by heartbreak and heroism. Laying rail around and through the mountains required extensive use of gunpowder, dynamite, and costly tunnels and bridges; harsh weather caused frequent work disruptions. Many workers were killed or injured in the process. At times, some 15,000 people, mostly men, worked for each of the companies as they literally raced against each other to complete their tasks. The company that laid the most track in the shortest time would be awarded more money by Congress.

The competition led both companies to cut corners. Collis Huntington, one of the CP owners, confessed that his goal was to build "the cheapest road that I could . . . so that it moves ahead fast." If bridges or trestles collapsed under the weight of freight trains, they could be fixed later. Mark Hopkins, one of Huntington's partners, agreed, noting that his goal was to build as "poor a road as we can."

RAILROAD WORKERS The UP crews were composed largely of young, unmarried former Civil War soldiers, both Union and Confederate, along with ex-slaves and Irish and German immigrants. The CP crews were mainly young Chinese workers lured to America by the California gold rush or by the railroad jobs. Most of these "coolie" laborers were single men eager to make money to take back to China, where they could then afford to marry and buy a parcel of land. Their temporary status and dreams of a good life made them more willing than American laborers to endure the low pay, dangerous working conditions, and intense racial prejudice.

The process of building the rail lines involved a series of sequential tasks. First came the surveyors, who selected and mapped the routes and measured the grade changes. Engineers then designed the bridges, trestles, tunnels, and snowsheds. Tree cutters and graders followed by preparing the rail beds. Wooden cross ties were then placed in the ground and leveled before thirty-foot-long iron rails weighing 560 pounds were laid atop them. Next came spikers, who used special hammers to wallop two-pound spikes attaching the rails to the ties. Finally, workers shoveled gravel between the ties to stabilize them against the weight of rolling trains. A journalist reported that "all this work is executed with great rapidity and mechanical regularity."

Yet for all of its precision and efficiency, the process of building the lines faced constant interruptions: terrible weather, late deliveries of key items, accidents, epidemics, or Indian attacks. Arthur Ferguson, a supervisor who kept a daily journal, frequently noted the hazards of constructing the first transcontinental in 1868:

> May 17—Two more men drowned in the river yesterday.
> June 4—At about sunrise, were attacked by Indians and succeeded in shooting one.
> June 21—Indians killed two men. Both had been horribly mutilated about the face by cuts made by a knife or a tomahawk.
> June 30—Four men were killed and scalped today about two miles above camp.

But it was not only Indians doing the killing. Workers often fought and killed each other. On June 7, Ferguson recorded that "two men were shot this evening in a drunken row—one was instantly killed, and the other is not expected to live."

THE RACE TO THE FINISH The drama of constructing the first transcontinental railroad seized the nation's imagination. Every major newspaper carried stories about the progress of the two competing companies. Finally, on May 10, 1869, former California governor Leland Stanford, one of the owners of the Central Pacific, drove a gold spike to complete the line at Promontory Summit in the Utah Territory north of the Great Salt Lake. The Union Pacific had built 1,086 miles of track compared with the Central Pacific's 689. The railroad builders had changed the landscape and widened the horizons of American ambition.

The golden spike used to connect the final rails symbolized the uniting of East and West, just as Robert E. Lee's surrender four years earlier had come to represent the reunion of North and South. Soon, the entire process would be repeated, as other companies constructed more lines across the continent.

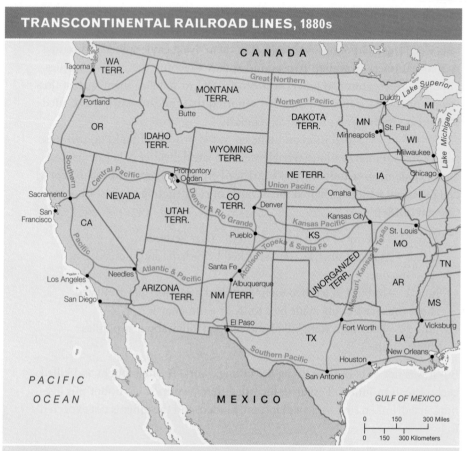

TRANSCONTINENTAL RAILROAD LINES, 1880s

- What was the route of the first transcontinental railroad, and why was it not in the South?
- Who built the railroads? How were they financed?

THE RISE OF BIG BUSINESS

The transcontinental railroads were the first of many investor-owned, publicly traded corporations during the industrial era. The emergence of "Big Business" was one of the most significant developments in American history. Corporations grew much larger and more powerful, transacting business across the nation and abroad. They were also much more influential politically as they worked to influence governors, legislators, Congress, and presidents.

Before the Civil War, most businesses had been small, local enterprises. After 1865, much of America suddenly got bigger—towns and cities, ships, locomotives, factories, machines, mines, and mills—and business organizations followed the same path. The rapid expansion in businesses, however, created problems. "The growing wealth and influence of our large corporations," warned the *New York Times*, "is one of the most alarming phenomena of our time. Our public companies already wield gigantic power, and they use it like unscrupulous giants."

THE GROWTH OF CORPORATIONS

As businesses grew, they took one of several different forms. Some were owned by an individual, usually their founder; others were partnerships involving several owners. Increasingly, however, large companies that served national and international markets were converted into "corporations"—legal entities that separate the *ownership* of an enterprise from the *management* of its operations.

Once a corporation is registered ("chartered" or "incorporated") with a state government, it can raise money to operate ("capital") by selling shares of stock—representing partial ownership of the company—to people not otherwise involved with it. Shareholders elect a board of directors who appoint and evaluate the corporation's executives ("management"). One of the most important benefits of a corporation is "limited legal liability": stockholders share in its profits but cannot be held liable for its debts if it fails.

FIGHTING COMPETITION

Competition is supposed to be the great virtue of capitalism, since it forces businesses to place a premium on efficiency and produce better products at the lowest cost. As many businesses became giant corporations, however, some business titans came to view competition as a burden rather than a blessing. Competition, many owners argued, created a chaotic and wasteful economic environment. Financier J. P. Morgan, for example, claimed that "bitter, destructive competition" always led to "destruction and ruin."

To eliminate cutthroat competition and thereby stabilize production, wages, and prices, rival companies selling similar products often formed "pools" whereby they secretly agreed to keep production and prices at specified levels. Such pools rarely lasted long, however, because they were unenforceable. One or more participants usually violated the agreement by cutting prices or increasing production—or both. The more effective strategy for the most aggressive companies was to get rid of weaker competitors by driving them out of business or buying them out.

Strategies like these, as well as the methods used to carry them out, led critics to call the corporate titans "robber barons." In the process of forming huge companies and eliminating competition, many business leaders cut corners, bribed politicians, double-crossed partners, exploited workers, hired strikebreakers, and broke laws. When asked how people might react to the shady methods he used to build his network of railroads, William Henry Vanderbilt famously replied: "The public be damned!"

THE BARONS OF BUSINESS

Most of the men (few women had such opportunities) who created big businesses in the late nineteenth century were driven by a compulsive desire to become rich and influential. Moreover, during and after the Civil War, becoming rich emerged as a national ideal sanctified by many religious leaders. "To secure wealth is an honorable ambition," stressed Russell Conwell, a prominent Baptist minister who crisscrossed the nation preaching a sermon called "Acres of Diamonds," in which he celebrated the benefits of hard work and its just rewards. "Money is power," he explained, and "every good man and woman ought to strive for power, to do good with it when obtained. I say, get rich! get rich!"

The industrial and financial giants personified the values that Conwell celebrated. They were men of grit and genius who found innovative—and at times unethical—ways to increase production, create efficiencies, and eliminate competition. The captains of commerce were also mercilessly adept at cutting costs and lowering prices.

Several of the post–Civil War business barons stood out for their extraordinary accomplishments: John D. Rockefeller and Andrew Carnegie for their innovations in organization, and J. Pierpont Morgan for his development of investment banking. In their different ways, each dealt a mortal blow to the small-scale economy of the early republic, fostering vast enterprises that forever altered the size and scope of business and industry.

JOHN D. ROCKEFELLER   Born in New York in 1839, John D. Rockefeller moved as a child to Cleveland, Ohio. Soon thereafter, his con-man father abandoned the family. Raised by his mother, a devout Baptist, Rockefeller developed a single-minded passion for systematic organization. As a young man in the 1860s, he decided to bring order and rationality to the new boom-and-bust oil industry. He was ambitious, disciplined, and obsessed with precision, efficiency, tidiness—and money.

The railroad and shipping connections around Cleveland made it a strategic location for serving the booming oil fields of nearby western Pennsylvania.

The first oil well in the United States began producing in 1859 in Titusville, Pennsylvania, and led to the Pennsylvania oil rush of the 1860s. Because oil could be refined into kerosene, which was widely used for lighting, heating, and cooking, the economic importance of the oil rush soon outstripped that of the California gold rush ten years earlier. Well before the end of the Civil War, oil refineries sprang up in Pittsburgh and Cleveland. Of the two cities, Cleveland had better rail service, so Rockefeller focused his energies there.

In 1870, Rockefeller teamed with his brother William and two other businessmen, Henry M. Flagler and Samuel Andrews (inventor of an inexpensive means of refining crude oil) to establish the **Standard Oil Company** of Ohio. Although the company quickly became the largest oil refiner in the nation, John Rockefeller wanted to eliminate his competitors and take control of the entire industry, in large part because he believed his competitors were inefficient and distracting.

John D. Rockefeller Co-founder of the Standard Oil Company.

During the 1870s, Rockefeller used various schemes to eliminate his competitors. Early on, he pursued a strategy that came to be called **horizontal integration**, in which a dominant corporation buys or forces out most of its competitors. Rockefeller viewed competition as a form of warfare. In a few cases, he hired former competitors as executives, but only "the big ones," he said, "those who have already proved they can do a *big business*. As for the others, unfortunately they will have to *die*."

By 1879, Standard Oil controlled more than 90 percent of the nation's oil refining business. Still, Rockefeller intended "to secure the entire refining business of the world." His goal was a **monopoly**, a business so large that it effectively controls an entire industry.

Rockefeller was an innovative genius with the fierce focus of a shark and the pinched priorities of a bookkeeper obsessed with the smallest details. He methodically reduced expenses, incorporated the latest technologies, and eliminated any hint of waste while paying "nobody a profit." Because he shipped so much oil by rail, he forced railroads to pay him secret "rebates" on the shipments, enabling him to pay less for shipping than his competitors paid.

Most important, instead of depending upon the products or services of other firms, known as middlemen, Standard Oil eventually owned everything it needed to produce, refine, and deliver oil—from wells to the finished product. The company had its own pipelines, built factories to make its own wagons and storage barrels, did its own hauling, owned its own storage tanks and tanker ships. In economic terms, this business strategy is called **vertical integration**. Rockefeller's Standard Oil Company was both horizontally and vertically integrated.

During the 1870s, Standard Oil bought so many of its competitors that it developed a virtual monopoly over the industry. Many state legislatures responded by outlawing the practice of one corporation owning stock in competing ones. In 1882, Rockefeller tried to get around such laws by organizing the Standard Oil Trust.

A **trust** gives a person or corporation (the "trustee") the legal power to manage another person's money or another company. Instead of owning other companies outright, the Standard Oil Trust controlled more than thirty companies by having their stockholders transfer their shares "in trust" to Rockefeller and eight other trustees. In return, the stockholders received "trust certificates," which paid them annual dividends from the trust's earnings. The Standard Oil Trust was Rockefeller's attempt to hide his virtual monopoly over the American oil industry.

Soon, however, the formation of huge corporate trusts, a practice widely copied by other industries, generated intense criticism. In 1890, Congress responded by passing the Sherman Anti-Trust Act with only one dissenting vote. It declared that corporate efforts to monopolize industries and thereby "restrain" competition were illegal. But the bill's language was so vague that it proved to be virtually toothless.

State laws against monopolies were initially more effective than the Sherman Act. In 1892, Ohio's Supreme Court ordered the Standard Oil Trust dissolved. A furious Rockefeller then developed another way to maintain control of his numerous companies: a **holding company**, which is a huge corporation that controls other companies by "holding" most or all of their stock certificates. A holding company produces nothing itself; it simply owns a majority of the stock in other companies.

Rockefeller was convinced that ending competition among companies was a good thing for the nation. Monopolies, he insisted, were the natural result of capitalism at work. "It is too late," he declared in 1899, "to argue about the advantages of [huge] industrial combinations. They are a necessity. The day of individualism is gone. Never to return." That year, Rockefeller brought his empire under the direction of the Standard Oil Company of New Jersey, a gigantic holding company.

ANDREW CARNEGIE Like Rockefeller, Andrew Carnegie, who created the largest steel company in the world, rose to wealth from boyhood poverty. Born in Scotland, the son of weavers, he migrated with his family in 1848 to western Pennsylvania. At age thirteen, he went to work in a textile mill. In 1853, he became personal secretary to Thomas Scott, then district superintendent of the Pennsylvania Railroad and later its president. When Scott moved up, the shrewd and charming Carnegie became superintendent in a region "teeming with treasure." During the Civil War, when Scott became assistant secretary of war in charge of transportation, Carnegie went with him to Washington, D.C., and helped develop a military telegraph system.

The ambitious Carnegie worked his way up—from telegraphy to railroading to bridge building, and then to steelmaking and investments. In the early 1870s, he decided "to concentrate on the manufacture of iron and steel and be master in that." A tiny man (barely five feet tall), Carnegie wanted to tower over the steel industry, just as John D. Rockefeller was doing with oil. Like Rockefeller, Carnegie accumulated vast wealth, and he often treated his workers ruthlessly.

Until the mid–nineteenth century, steel, which is stronger and more flexible than iron, could be made only from wrought iron—itself expensive since it had to be imported from Sweden—and could only be manufactured in small quantities. Bars of wrought iron were heated with charcoal over several days to add carbon and produce steel. It took three tons of coke, a high-burning fuel derived from coal, to produce one ton of steel. As a result, steel was too costly to make in large quantities.

Andrew Carnegie Established the Carnegie Steel Company and became the wealthiest man in the world.

That changed in the 1850s, when England's Sir Henry Bessemer invented the **Bessemer converter**, a process by which high-quality steel could be produced more quickly by blasting oxygen through the molten iron in a furnace. In the early 1870s, Carnegie decided to concentrate on steel, because Bessemer's process had made it so inexpensive to produce and the railroad industry required massive amounts of it.

As more steel was produced, its price dropped and its industrial uses soared. In 1860, the United States produced only 13,000 tons of steel. By 1880, production had reached 1.4 million tons annually. Between 1880 and 1900, Carnegie dominated the steel industry, acquiring competitors or driving them out of business by cutting prices and taking their customers. By 1900, the United States was producing more steel than Great Britain and Germany combined.

Carnegie was a resilient promoter, salesman, and organizer. He insisted upon up-to-date machinery and equipment, expanded production quickly and cheaply by purchasing struggling companies, and preached a philosophy of continuous innovation to reduce operating costs.

He also sought to expand his industry by vertical integration—gaining control of every phase of the steelmaking business. He owned coal mines in West Virginia, bought huge deposits of iron ore in Michigan and Wisconsin, and transported the ore in his own ships across the Great Lakes and then by rail to his steel mills in Pittsburgh.

The result was phenomenal. By 1900, the **Carnegie Steel Company**, with 20,000 employees, was the largest industrial company in the world. And Carnegie worked his people hard. His mills operated nonstop, with two 12-hour shifts every day and night.

Carnegie insisted that what he, Rockefeller, and other titans of industry were doing in forging dominant corporations was simply the wave of the future. Rockefeller agreed, saying that the formation of huge trusts was simply "the working out of a law of nature and a law of God."

J. PIERPONT MORGAN Unlike Rockefeller and Carnegie, J. Pierpont Morgan was born to wealth. His father was a partner in a large English bank. After attending school in Switzerland and college in Germany, Morgan was sent in 1857 to work in New York City for a new enterprise, **J. Pierpont Morgan and Company**. The firm, under various names, invested European money into American businesses. It grew into a financial power by helping competing corporations merge and by purchasing massive amounts of stock in American companies and selling them at a profit.

Morgan took over poorly run companies, appointed new executives, and supervised operations. Like Rockefeller and Carnegie, he believed in capitalism but hated the chaos of competition. In his view, high profits required order and stability, and stability required consolidating competitors into trusts that he would own and manipulate.

Morgan recognized early on the importance of railroads, and by the 1890s, he controlled a sixth of the nation's railway system. But his crowning triumph was the consolidation of the steel industry. After a rapid series of mergers, he bought out Andrew Carnegie's huge steel and iron holdings in 1901. Morgan added scores of related companies to form the United States Steel Corporation, the world's first billion-dollar corporation, employing 168,000 people. It was the climactic event in the efforts of the great financial capitalists to reduce competition and form ever-larger corporations capable of dominating their industries.

J. Pierpont Morgan Despite his privileged upbringing and financial success, he was self-conscious about his deformed nose, caused by chronic skin diseases.

THE "GOSPEL OF WEALTH"

However harsh the methods employed by the captains of industry, the men were convinced that they benefited the public by accelerating America's transformation into an industrial colossus. In their eyes, it was a law of societal evolution that those most talented at producing wealth should accumulate enormous personal fortunes.

Some of them, however, insisted that great wealth brought great responsibilities. In his essay "The Gospel of Wealth" (1889), Andrew Carnegie argued that "not evil, but good, has come to the [Anglo-Saxon] race from the accumulation of wealth by those who have the ability and energy that produces it." But he also felt the need to justify his wealth and denounced the "worship of money." He and John D. Rockefeller gave much of their money back to society.

By 1900, Rockefeller had become the world's leading philanthropist. "I have always regarded it as a religious duty," he said late in life, "to get all I could honorably and to give all I could." He donated more than $500 million during his lifetime, including tens of millions to Baptist causes and $35 million to found the University of Chicago. His philanthropic influence continues today through the Rockefeller Foundation.

As for Carnegie, after retiring from business at age sixty-five, he declared that the "man who dies rich dies disgraced" and devoted himself to dispensing his $400 million fortune. Calling himself a "distributor" of wealth (he disliked the term *philanthropy*), he gave huge sums to numerous universities; built 2,500 public libraries; and helped fund churches, hospitals, parks, and halls for meetings and concerts, including New York City's Carnegie Hall.

THE ALLIANCE OF BUSINESS AND POLITICS

The building of big businesses depended on more than just entrepreneurial energy. Most corporate leaders developed cozy relationships with local, state, and federal officials, a process of buying influence ("lobbying") that continues to this day. Big Business has legitimate political interests, but, because of its size and resources, it also at times exercises a corrupt influence on government. Nowhere was this conflicting role more evident than during the decades after the Civil War.

REPUBLICANS AND BIG BUSINESS During and after the Civil War, the Republican party and state and federal governments grew increasingly allied with Big Business. A key element of this alliance was tariff policy. Since 1789, the federal government had imposed **tariffs**—taxes on imported goods—to raise revenue and to benefit American manufacturers by penalizing their foreign competitors. In 1861, as the Civil War was starting, the Republican-dominated Congress enacted the Morrill Tariff, which doubled tax rates on hundreds of imported items as a means of raising money for the war and rewarding the businesses that supported the Republican party.

After the war, President Ulysses S. Grant, and later, Republican presidents and Congresses, continued the party's commitment to high tariffs despite complaints that the tariffs increased consumer prices at home by restricting foreign imports and thereby relieving American manufacturers of the need to keep their prices down. Farmers in the South and Midwest resented tariffs because, while they had to sell their crops in an open world market, they had to buy manufactured goods whose prices were artificially high because of tariffs.

During the Civil War, Congress passed other key pieces of legislation related to the economy. The Legal Tender Act of 1862 authorized the federal government to issue paper money ("greenbacks") to help pay for the war. Having a uniform paper currency was essential to a modern national economy. To that end, the National Banking Act (1863) created national banks authorized to issue greenbacks, which discouraged state banks from continuing to issue their own paper money.

Congress also took steps to tie the new states and territories of the West into the national economy. In the Homestead Act of 1862, Congress provided free 160-acre (or even larger) homesteads to settlers in the West. By encouraging western settlement, the Homestead Act created new markets for goods and services and spurred railroad construction to connect frontier communities with major cities.

The Morrill Land Grant Act of the same year transferred to each state 30,000 acres of federal land for each member of Congress the state had. The sale of those lands provided funds for states to create colleges of "agriculture and mechanic arts," such as Iowa State University and Kansas State University. The "land grant" universities were created specifically to support economic growth by providing technical training needed by farmers and rapidly growing industries such as mining, steel, petroleum, transportation, forestry, and construction (engineering).

LAISSEZ-FAIRE Equally important in propelling the postwar economic boom was what government did *not* do. In 1870, historian Henry Adams expressed concern that there "was no authority" capable of restraining the

Homesteaders An African American family poses outside their log and sod cabin in 1889.

leaders of the nation's largest corporations. At the time, the federal government did not regulate the activities of big businesses, impose high corporate taxes, or provide any meaningful oversight of business operations or working conditions.

In general, both Congress and the presidents opposed government interference in the economy and accepted the economic doctrine of **laissez-faire**, a French phrase meaning "let them do as they will." Business leaders spent time—and money—ensuring that government officials stayed out of their businesses. For their part, the politicians were usually eager to help the titans of industry in exchange for campaign contributions—or bribes for looking the other way.

AN INDUSTRIAL SOCIETY

Industrialization transformed not only the economy and the workplace, but also the nation's social life. Class divisions became more visible. The growing gap between rich and poor was like "social dynamite," said the Reverend Josiah Strong in 1885. Massachusetts reformer Lydia Maria Child reported that the rich "do not intermarry with the middle classes; the middle classes do not intermarry with the laboring class," nor did different classes "mix socially."

THE WAYS OF THE WEALTHY

The financiers and industrialists who dominated social, economic, and political life in post–Civil War America amassed so much fabulous wealth and showed it off so publicly that the period is still called the "Gilded Age."

The name derived from a popular novel by Mark Twain and Charles Dudley Warner, *The Gilded Age: A Tale of Today*, which mocked the crooked dealings of political leaders and the business elite. In 1861, there were only a few dozen millionaires in the United States. By 1900, there were more than 4,000. Most of them were white Protestants who voted Republican, except for a small number of wealthy southern Democrats.

Many of the *nouveaux riches* (French for "newly rich") indulged in what came to be called "conspicuous consumption," competing to host the fanciest parties and live in the most extravagant houses. One tycoon gave a lavish dinner honoring his dog and presented it with a $15,000 diamond necklace. At a party at New York's Delmonico's restaurant, the guests smoked cigarettes wrapped in $100 bills. Mrs. Bradley Martin received such a torrent of criticism after spending $368,000 on a banquet that she and her husband fled to England.

When they were not attending parties, the rich were relaxing in monumental mansions overlooking the cliffs at Newport, Rhode Island, atop Nob Hill in San Francisco, along Chicago's Lake Shore Drive and New York City's Fifth Avenue, and down the "Main Line" in suburban Philadelphia. "Who knows how to be rich in America?" asked E. L. Godkin, editor of the *Nation* magazine. "Plenty of people know how to get money, but . . . to be rich properly is, indeed, a fine art. It requires culture, imagination, and character."

A Growing Middle Class

It was left to the fast-growing middle class to display good "character" by practicing such traditional virtues as self-discipline and restraint, simplicity and frugality. The term *middle class* had first appeared in the 1830s and had become commonplace by the 1870s, as more and more Americans came to view themselves as members of a distinct social class between the ragged and the rich. The middle class, explained the Chicago writer George Ade in an 1895 essay, "The Advantage of Being 'Middle Class,'" meant those people who "work either with hand or brain, who are neither poverty-stricken nor offensively rich."

Accompanying the spread of huge corporations after the Civil War was a rapidly growing middle class enjoying a rising standard of living. While the rich were getting richer, many other people were also becoming better off in terms of their income and quality of life. Most middle-class Americans working outside the home were salaried employees of large businesses who made up a new class of "white-collar" professionals: editors, engineers, accountants, supervisors, managers, marketers, and realtors. Others, mostly unmarried women, were a growing share of the total: clerks, secretaries, salespeople, and government employees, including teachers and librarians. During the 1870s, the number of office clerks quadrupled, and the number of accountants and bookkeepers doubled. At the same time, the number of attorneys, physicians, professors, journalists, nurses, and social workers rose dramatically.

MIDDLE-CLASS WOMEN The growing presence of middle-class women in the workforce partly reflected the increasing number of women who were gaining access to higher education. Dozens of women's colleges were founded after the Civil War, and many formerly all-male colleges began admitting women. By 1900, a third of college students were women. "After a struggle of many years," a New York woman boasted, "it is now pretty generally admitted that women possess the capacity to swallow intellectual food that was formerly considered the diet of men exclusively."

College women By the end of the century, women made up more than a third of college students. Here, an astronomy class at New York's Vassar College is underway in 1880.

To be sure, college women were often steered into home economics classes and "finishing" courses intended to perfect their housekeeping or social skills. Still, the doors of the professions—law, medicine, science, and the arts—were at least partially opened.

Middle-class women also took advantage of other public venues for interaction: charitable associations, women's clubs, literary societies, and church work. "If there is one thing that pervades and characterizes what is called the 'woman's movement,'" E. L. Youmans, a prominent science writer, remarked, "it is the spirit of revolt against the home, and the determination to escape from it into the outer spheres of activity."

NEURASTHENIA Women who tried to escape the "cult of domesticity" and pursue careers outside the home often paid a high price. Many contracted a peculiar affliction, which male physicians called *neurasthenia*, a draining psychological and physical disorder whose symptoms usually included insomnia, hysteria, headaches, depression, and a general state of fatigue. Although neurasthenia plagued both sexes, it most often affected college-educated, middle-class women.

Some prominent doctors sought to use the prevalence of neurasthenia to force women back into the "cult of domesticity." George M. Beard, a neurologist who popularized the term *neurasthenia*, concluded—incorrectly—that women were "more nervous, immeasurably, than men," and that female neurasthenics tended to be "overly active" outside the home. This explanation led one doctor to insist that the malady provided the best "argument against higher education of women."

Many women objected to such self-serving male arguments. Charlotte Perkins Gilman, for instance, wrote her short story "The Yellow Wallpaper" to expose the horrors of the "rest cure" she was subjected to at age twenty-seven. A doctor had ordered her to "live as domestic a life as possible; have your child with you all the time; lie down an hour after each meal; have but two hours intellectual life a day; and *never touch pencil, brush, or pen as long as you live.*" This regimen, Gilman explained, took her "as near lunacy as one can, and come back."

JANE ADDAMS Social worker Jane Addams also struggled with neurasthenia and the dominant male notions of women's roles. After graduating in 1881 from Rockford College in Illinois, she found few opportunities to use her degree and lapsed into a state of depression during which she developed an intense "desire to live in a really *living* world." Middle-class women, she charged, were "so besotted with our [sentimental] novel reading that we have lost the power of seeing certain aspects of life with any sense of reality because we are continually looking for the possible romance."

Addams's desire to engage "real life" eventually led her to found Hull House in Chicago. There, she and other social workers helped immigrants adapt to American life and mentored young women to "learn of life from life itself."

Addams and others helped convince many middle-class women to enter the "real" world. By 1890, a magazine called the *Arena* would urge progressive-minded people to recognize the traditional view of "women as homebodies" for what it was: "hollow, false, and unreal." Upon returning from England to America in 1904, the illustrious writer Henry James reported that the predominance of "new" women and their struggle for autonomy had become "the sentence written largest in the American sky."

The Working Class

The continuing demand for unskilled workers by railroads, factories, mills, mines, slaughterhouses, and sweatshops attracted new groups to the workforce: immigrants above all, but also growing numbers of women and children.

In addition, millions of rural folk, especially young people, formed a migratory stream from the agricultural regions of the South and Midwest to cities and factories across the country.

Although wage levels rose overall during the Gilded Age, there was a great disparity in pay for skilled and unskilled workers. During the recessions and depressions that occurred about every six years, unskilled workers were the first to be laid off or to have their wages slashed. In addition, working conditions were difficult and often dangerous for those at the bottom of the occupational scale.

The average workweek was fifty-nine hours, or nearly six 10-hour days. American industry had the highest rate of workplace accidents and deaths in the world, and there were virtually no safety regulations or government inspections. Few machines had safety devices; few factories or mills had fire escapes. Respiratory diseases were common in mines and unventilated buildings, especially textile mills. Between 1888 and 1894, there were 16,000 railroad workers killed and 170,000 maimed in on-the-job accidents. The United States was also the only industrial nation with no insurance program to cover medical expenses for on-the-job injuries.

WORKING WOMEN Industrial development after the Civil War transformed the nature of the workplace. Mills, mines, factories, and large businesses needed far more unskilled workers than skilled ones. Employers often recruited women and children for the unskilled jobs because they were willing to work for lower wages than men received. In addition to operating sewing machines or tending to textile machines spinning yarn or thread, millions of women worked as maids, cooks, or nannies. In the manufacturing sector, women's wages averaged $7 a week, compared to $10 for unskilled men.

A social worker reported that it was widely assumed in many factories that a married woman would accept lower wages because she "has a man to support her," which was not always the case. The number of women working outside the home tripled between 1870 and 1900, when 5 million women (17 percent of all women) held full-time jobs.

In a letter to the editor of the *Nation* in 1867, a "working woman" described the changing nature of gender roles in American life. Most middle-class women, she acknowledged, still lived in a "world of love, of a sweet and guarded domesticity, of drawing-rooms and boudoirs, of dainty coquetries, of quiet graces, where they flourish like fair flowers in a south window." But each year "thousands of women" were entering a different world "of mud, carts, ledgers, packing-boxes, counting-houses, paste, oils, leather, iron, boards, committees, big boots, and men who . . . meet women on a cool, business level of dollars and cents."

CHILD LABOR Most young people had always worked in America; farms required everyone to pitch in. In the late nineteenth century, however, millions of children took up work outside the home, sorting coal, stitching clothes, shucking oysters, peeling shrimp, canning food, blowing glass, tending looms, and operating other kinds of machinery. **Child labor** increased as parents desperate for income felt forced to put their children to work. By 1880, one of every six children under age fourteen was working full-time; by 1900, the United States had almost 2 million child laborers.

In Pennsylvania, West Virginia, and eastern Kentucky, soot-smeared boys worked in the coal mines. In New England and the South, children labored in dusty textile mills where, during the night shift, they had water thrown in their faces to keep them awake. In the southern mills, a fourth of the employees were below the age of fifteen, and children as young as eight worked alongside adults twelve hours a day, six days a week. As a result, they received little or no education.

Factories, mills, mines, and canneries were especially dangerous places for children, who suffered three times as many accidents as adult workers and suffered higher rates of respiratory diseases. A child working in a southern textile mill was only half as likely to reach the age of twenty as a child who did not work in a mill.

THE "DREADFUL CHILL OF CHANGE"

When novelist Henry James returned to the United States in the early twentieth century after a long stay in England, he was shocked by the "dreadful chill of change." Urban-industrial development and western expansion had generated unparalleled prosperity, but the United States, he feared, had lost much of its social stability and cohesion. In 1885, another writer said that the working poor were unleashing "a seismic shock, a cyclonic violence" that threatened to tear society apart.

ORGANIZED LABOR The efforts of the working poor to form unions to improve their pay and working conditions faced formidable obstacles during the Gilded Age. Many executives fought against unions. They "blacklisted" union organizers by circulating their names to keep them from being hired, fired labor leaders, and often hired "scabs" (nonunion workers) to replace workers who went on strike. Another factor impeding the growth of unions was that much of the workforce was made up of immigrants who spoke different languages and often distrusted people from other ethnic groups.

Nonetheless, with or without unions, workers began to stage strikes that often led to violence. Perhaps at no time before or since have class tensions—both social and cultural—been so bitter.

THE MOLLY MAGUIRES During the early 1870s, violence erupted in the eastern Pennsylvania coalfields, when a secret Irish American group called the Molly Maguires took economic justice into their own hands. The Mollies took their name from an Irish patriot who had led the resistance against the British. Outraged by dangerous working conditions in the mines and the owners' brutal efforts to suppress union activity, the Mollies used intimidation, beatings, and killings to avenge the wrongs done to Irish workers.

Their terrorism reached its peak in 1874–1875, prompting mine owners to hire men from the Pinkerton Detective Agency (commonly referred to as "Pinkertons") to stop the movement. One of the agents who infiltrated the Mollies uncovered enough evidence to have the leaders indicted for the coalfield murders. In 1876, twenty-four Molly Maguires were convicted by a non-Irish jury; ten were hanged.

THE GREAT RAILROAD STRIKE (1877) After the financial panic of 1873, the major rail lines, fearful of a recession, had slashed workers' wages. In 1877, the companies announced another 10 percent wage cut, which led most of the railroad workers at Martinsburg, West Virginia, to walk off the job.

The strike spread to hundreds of other cities and towns. Tens of thousands of workers walked off the job, and the resulting violence left more than 100 people dead and millions of dollars in damaged property. In Pittsburgh, thousands of striking workers burned thirty-nine buildings and destroyed more than 1,000 railcars and locomotives. The violence was not directed solely at employers, either. Workers who refused to join the strike or participate in the riots were harassed and beaten.

The **Great Railroad Strike** became one of the most spectacular incidents of widespread violence in American history and revealed how polarized the working poor and business elites had become. Local and state officials interpreted the growing insurgency as evidence of Communist ideology born in Europe. Governors mobilized state militia units to suppress the rioters, but looting and burning continued until President Rutherford Hayes dispatched federal troops. Eventually the disgruntled workers, lacking organized bargaining power, had little choice but to return to work. The strike had failed.

For many Americans, the railroad strike raised the possibility of what a Pittsburgh newspaper saw as "a great civil war in this country between labor and capital." Many workers felt that violence was their only option. "The working people everywhere are with us," a unionist told a reporter. "They know what it is to bring up a family on ninety cents a day, to live on beans and corn meal week in and week out, to run in debt at the [company] stores until you cannot get trusted any longer, to see the wife breaking down . . . and the children growing sharp and fierce like wolves day after day because they don't get enough to eat."

THE SAND-LOT INCIDENT In California, the national railroad strike indirectly gave rise to a working-class political movement. In 1877, a meeting held in a sandy San Francisco lot to express sympathy for the railroad strikers ended with attacks on passing Chinese workers. In the aftermath of the so-called Sand-Lot Incident, white mobs attacked Chinatown. The Chinese were handy scapegoats for frustrated white laborers who believed the Asians had taken their jobs.

Soon an Irish immigrant, Denis Kearney, had organized the Workingmen's Party of California, whose platform called for the United States to stop Chinese immigration. Kearney lectured the "sand-lotters" about the "foreign peril" and blasted the railroad barons for exploiting the poor. The Workingmen's movement peaked in 1879, when it elected a number of state legislators and the mayor of San Francisco. Although Kearney failed to build a lasting movement, his anti-Chinese theme became a national issue. In 1882, Congress voted to prohibit Chinese immigration for ten years.

THE NATIONAL LABOR UNION As the size and power of corporations increased, efforts to build a national labor union movement gained momentum. During the Civil War, because of the increased demand for skilled labor, so-called "craft unions" made up of workers expert at a particular handicraft grew in strength and number. Yet there was no overall connection among such groups until 1866, when the **National Labor Union (NLU)** convened in Baltimore.

The NLU was more interested in advocating for improved workplace conditions than in bargaining with employers about wages and hours. The group promoted an eight-hour workday, workers' cooperatives (in which workers, collectively, would create and own their own large-scale manufacturing and mining operations), "greenbackism" (the printing of paper money to inflate the currency and thereby relieve debtors), and equal voting rights for women and African Americans.

Like most such organizations in the nineteenth century, however, the NLU did not allow women as members. The NLU also discriminated against African American workers, who were forced to organize black-only unions. After the NLU's head, William Sylvis, died suddenly in 1869, its support declined, and by

Knights of Labor This national union was the most egalitarian union during the Gilded Age.

1872 the union had disbanded. The NLU was not a total failure, however. It was influential in persuading Congress to enact an eight-hour workday for federal employees and to repeal the 1864 Contract Labor Act, which had been passed to encourage the importation of laborers by allowing employers to pay for the passage of foreign workers to America. In exchange, the workers were committed to labor for a specified number of years. Employers had taken advantage of the Contract Labor Act to recruit foreign laborers willing to work for lower wages than their American counterparts.

THE KNIGHTS OF LABOR In 1869, another national labor group emerged: the Noble Order of the **Knights of Labor**. The union grew slowly at first, but as other unions collapsed during the depression of the 1870s, it spread more rapidly.

The Knights of Labor endorsed most of the reforms advanced by previous workingmen's groups, including the creation of bureaus of labor statistics and mechanics' lien laws (to ensure payment of wages), the elimination of convict-labor competition, the establishment of the eight-hour day and worker cooperatives, and the use of paper currency. One reform the group advocated was far ahead of the times: equal pay for equal work by men and women.

The Knights of Labor allowed as members all who had ever worked for wages, except lawyers, doctors, bankers, and those who sold liquor. Such inclusiveness was both a strength and a weakness. By recruiting all types of workers, the Knights grew very large, but they also struggled with internal tensions between skilled and unskilled workers.

In 1879, Terence V. Powderly, the thirty-year-old mayor of Scranton, Pennsylvania, became head of the Knights of Labor. Born of Irish immigrant parents, Powderly had started working for a railroad at age sixteen. Frail, sensitive to criticism, and indecisive, he was in many ways unsuited to the job. He was opposed to strikes, and when they did occur, he did not always support the groups involved. Yet the Knights owed their greatest growth to strikes that occurred under his leadership. In the early 1880s, the Knights increased their membership from about 100,000 to more than 700,000.

ANARCHISM One of the many challenges facing the labor union movement during the Gilded Age was hostility from middle-class Americans who came to view unionized workers, especially those involved in clashes with police, as "radicals" or "anarchists." Anarchists believed that government—any government—was a device used by powerful capitalists to oppress and exploit the working poor. They dreamed of the elimination of government altogether, and some were willing to use bombs and bullets to achieve their revolutionary goal.

Many European anarchists immigrated to the United States during the last quarter of the nineteenth century. Although most of them disavowed violence, the terrorists among them ensured that the label "anarchist" provoked frightening images in the minds of many Americans.

Labor-related violence increased during the 1880s as the gap between the rich and working poor widened. Between 1880 and 1900, some 6.6 million hourly workers participated in more than 23,000 strikes nationwide. Chicago was a hotbed of labor unrest and a magnet for immigrants, especially German and Irish laborers, some of whom were socialists or anarchists who endorsed violence. The Chicago labor movement's foremost demand was for an eight-hour workday, and what came to be called the **Haymarket riot** grew indirectly out of prolonged agitation for this goal.

THE HAYMARKET RIOT (1886) In 1886, some 40,000 Chicago workers went on strike in support of an eight-hour workday. On May 3, violent clashes between strikers and nonunion "scabs" hired to replace striking workers erupted outside the McCormick Harvesting Machine Company plant. The police arrived, shots rang out, and two strikers were killed. The killings infuriated the leaders of the tiny but outspoken anarchist movement in Chicago. August Spies, a German-born anarchist leader, printed leaflets in English and

German demanding "Revenge!" and calling "Workingmen, to Arms!" A mass protest was planned for the following night at Haymarket Square.

On the evening of May 4, after listening to speeches complaining about low wages and long working hours, the crowd of angry laborers was beginning to break up when police arrived and ordered them to disperse. At that point, someone threw a bomb that left dozens of maimed and dying policemen scattered in the street. The police then fired into the fleeing crowd, resulting in more casualties. Seven policemen were killed and sixty more wounded in what journalists called America's first terrorist bombing.

The next day, Chicago's mayor banned all labor meetings in the city, and newspapers printed sensational headlines about anarchists terrorizing Chicago. One New York newspaper demanded stern punishment for "the few long-haired, wild-eyed, bad-smelling, atheistic, reckless foreign wretches" who promoted such unrest.

During the summer of 1886, seven anarchist leaders, all but one of them German speakers, were sentenced to death despite the lack of evidence linking them to the bomb thrower, whose identity was never determined. After being sentenced to be hanged, Louis Lingg declared that he was innocent but was "in favor of using force" to end the abuses of the capitalist system. Lawyers for the anarchists appealed the convictions to the Illinois Supreme Court.

Meanwhile, petitioners from around the world appealed for clemency. One of the petitioners was Samuel Gompers, the founding president of the American Federation of Labor (AFL). "I abhor anarchy," Gompers stressed, "but I also abhor injustice when meted out even to the most despicable being on earth."

On November 10, 1887, Louis Lingg committed suicide in his cell. That same day, the governor commuted the sentences of two of the convicted conspirators to life imprisonment. The next day, as armed police and soldiers surrounded the Cook County Jail, the four remaining condemned men were hanged. Some 200,000 people lined the streets of Chicago as the caskets of those executed were taken for burial. To labor militants around the world, the executed anarchists were working-class martyrs; to the police and the economic elite in Chicago, they were demonic assassins.

A BACKLASH AGAINST UNIONS After the Haymarket riot, tensions between workers and management reached a fever pitch. In 1886 alone, there were 1,400 strikes across the country involving 700,000 workers. But the violence in Chicago had also triggered widespread hostility to the Knights of Labor and labor groups in general. Despite his best efforts, union leader Terence Powderly could never separate in the public mind the Knights from the anarchists, since one of those convicted of conspiracy in the bombing was a member of the union.

Powderly clung to leadership until 1893, but after that the union evaporated. Yet the Knights did attain some lasting achievements, among them an 1880 federal law providing for the arbitration of labor disputes, and the creation of the federal Bureau of Labor Statistics in 1884. Another of their successes was the Foran Act of 1885, which, though poorly enforced, penalized employers who imported immigrant workers. By their example, the Knights also spread the idea of unionism and initiated a new type of organization: the industrial union, which included all skilled and unskilled workers within a particular industry, such as railroad workers or miners.

GOMPERS AND THE AFL The craft unions, representing skilled workers, generally opposed efforts to unite with industrial unionism. Leaders of the craft unions feared that joining with unskilled laborers would mean a loss of their identity and bargaining power. Thus, in 1886, delegates from twenty-five craft unions organized the **American Federation of Labor (AFL)**. Its structure differed from that of the Knights of Labor in that it was a federation of many separate national unions, each of which was largely free to act on its own in dealing with business owners.

Samuel Gompers served as president of the AFL from its founding until his death, in 1924, with only one year's interruption. Born in England, Gompers came to the United States as a teenager, joined the Cigar Makers' Union in 1864, and became president of his New York City local union in 1877. Unlike Terence Powderly and the Knights of Labor, Gompers focused on concrete economic gains—higher wages, shorter hours, and better working conditions.

The AFL at first grew slowly, but by the turn of the century, it claimed 500,000 members in affiliated unions. In 1914, on the eve of World War I, it had 2 million, and in 1920, it reached a peak of 4 million. But even then, the AFL embraced less than 15 percent of the nation's nonagricultural workers. In fact, all unions, including the so-called railroad brotherhoods unaffiliated with the AFL, accounted for little more than 18 percent of those workers.

Organized labor's strongholds were in transportation and the building trades. Most of the larger manufacturing industries—including steel, textiles, tobacco, and meatpacking—remained almost untouched. Gompers never opposed industrial unions, and several became important affiliates of the AFL: the United Mine Workers, the International Ladies Garment Workers, and the Amalgamated Clothing Workers. But the AFL had its greatest success in organizing skilled workers.

Two incidents in the 1890s stalled the emerging industrial-union movement: the **Homestead Steel strike** of 1892 and the **Pullman strike** of 1894. These violent labor conflicts were the climactic economic events of the Gilded Age and represented a test of strength for the organized labor movement. They also served to reshape the political landscape.

THE HOMESTEAD STEEL STRIKE The Amalgamated Association of Iron and Steel Workers, founded in 1876, was the nation's largest craft union. At the massive steel mill at Homestead, Pennsylvania, along the Monongahela River near Pittsburgh, the union had enjoyed friendly relations with Andrew Carnegie's company until Henry Clay Frick became chief executive in 1889.

A showdown was delayed until 1892, however, when the union contract came up for renewal. Carnegie, who had previously expressed sympathy for the union, went on a lengthy hunting trip in his native Scotland, intentionally leaving the rigid Frick to handle the difficult negotiations.

Carnegie knew what was in the works: a cost-cutting reduction in the number of highly paid skilled workers through the use of labor-saving machinery, even though the corporation was enjoying high profits. It was a deliberate attempt to smash the union. As negotiations dragged on, the company announced on June 25 that it would stop negotiating with the 3,800 workers on June 29 unless an agreement was reached. A strike—or, more properly, a lockout, in which management closed down the mill to try to force the union to make concessions—would begin on that date.

Frick ordered construction of a twelve-foot-high fence around the plant and equipped it with watchtowers, searchlights, barbed wire, and high-pressure water cannons. He also hired a private army of 316 Pinkerton agents to protect what was soon dubbed Fort Frick. Before dawn on July 6, 1892, the "Pinkertons" floated up the Monongahela River on two barges pulled by a tugboat.

Thousands of unionists and their supporters were waiting on shore. A fourteen-hour battle broke out in which seven workers and three Pinkertons were killed, and dozens wounded. In the end, the Pinkertons surrendered. A week later, the Pennsylvania governor dispatched 4,000 state militiamen to Homestead, where they surrounded the steel mill and dispersed the picketing workers. Frick then hired strikebreakers to operate the mill. He refused to resume negotiations: "I will never recognize the union, never, never!"

The strike dragged on until November, but by then the union was dead and its leaders had been charged with murder and treason. The union cause was not helped when Alexander Berkman, a Lithuanian anarchist, tried to assassinate Frick on July 23, shooting him twice in the neck and stabbing him three times. Despite his wounds, Frick fought back and, with the help of staff members, subdued the would-be assassin.

Much of the local sympathy for the strikers evaporated after the attack on Frick. Penniless and demoralized, the defeated workers ended their walkout on November 20 and accepted the company's harsh wage cuts. Only a fifth of the strikers were hired back; the rest were "blacklisted" to prevent other steel mills from hiring them. Carnegie and Frick, with the support of local, state, and national government officials, had eliminated the union. After the strike, none of Carnegie's steel plants employed unionized workers.

THE PULLMAN STRIKE The Pullman strike of 1894 was even more notable, as it paralyzed the economies of the twenty-seven states and territories in the western half of the nation. It involved a dispute at Pullman, Illinois, a "model" industrial suburb of Chicago owned by the Pullman Palace Car Company, which made passenger train cars (called "Pullmans" or "sleeping cars").

Employees were required to live in the town's 1,400 cottages, which had been built to high standards, with gas heat and indoor plumbing. With 12,000 residents, the town also boasted a library, a theater, a school, parks and playgrounds, and a glass-roofed shopping mall owned by the company. There were no saloons, social clubs, newspapers, or private property not owned by the company. No political activities were allowed.

As a "company town," Pullman was of much higher quality than the villages in the South owned by textile mills, and the death rate was less than half of that in neighboring communities. Yet over time, many workers complained that they did not like living under the thumb of the company's owner, George Pullman.

During the depression of 1893, Pullman laid off 3,000 of his 5,800 employees and cut wages 25 to 40 percent for the rest, but did not lower rents for housing or the price of food in the company store. In the spring of 1894, desperate workers joined the American Railway Union, founded the previous year by Eugene V. Debs.

The charismatic Debs was a child of working-class immigrants who had quit school at age fourteen to work for an Indiana railroad. By the early 1890s, he had become a tireless spokesman for labor radicalism, and he worked to organize all railway workers—skilled or unskilled—into the American Railway Union, which soon became a powerful organization. He quickly turned his attention to the Pullman controversy, urging the workers to obey the laws and avoid violence. After George Pullman fired three members of a workers' grievance committee, the workers went on strike on May 11, 1894.

Eugene V. Debs Founder of the American Railway Union, and later the presidential candidate for the Socialist Party of America.

In June, after Pullman refused Debs's plea for a negotiated settlement, the Railway Union workers stopped handling trains containing Pullman railcars. By the end of July, they had shut down most of the railroads in the Midwest and cut off all traffic through Chicago. To keep the trains running, railroad executives hired strikebreakers, and the U.S. attorney general, a former attorney for railroad companies, swore in 3,400 special deputies to protect them. Angry workers assaulted strikebreakers and destroyed property.

Finally, on July 3, President Grover Cleveland sent 2,000 federal troops into the Chicago area, claiming it was his duty to ensure delivery of the mail. Meanwhile, the attorney general convinced a federal judge to sign an *injunction* (an official court decree) prohibiting the labor union from interfering.

On July 13, the union called off the strike. A few days later, a court cited Debs for violating the injunction; he served six months in jail. The Supreme Court upheld the decree in the case of *In re Debs* (1895) on broad grounds of national sovereignty: "The strong arm of the national government may be put forth to brush away all obstructions to the freedom of interstate commerce or the transportation of the mails."

Debs emerged from jail a socialist who would later run for president. In 1897, George Pullman died of a heart attack, and the following year, the city of Chicago annexed the town of Pullman.

ECONOMIC SUCCESS AND EXCESS

For all of the stress and strain caused by swift industrialization, American productivity soared in the late nineteenth century. By 1900, the United States was producing a third of the world's goods, and millions of immigrants from around the world continued to risk all in hopes of chasing the American Dream. Corporate empires generated enormous fortunes for a few and real improvements in the quality of life for many. The majority of American workers now labored in factories and mines rather than on farms. "One can hardly believe," observed philosopher John Dewey, "there has been a revolution in history so rapid, so extensive, so complete."

The urban-industrial revolution and the gigantic new corporations it created transformed the size, scope, and power of the American economy, for good and for ill. As the twentieth century dawned, an unregulated capitalist economy had grown corrupt and recklessly out of balance—and only government intervention could restore economic fairness and social stability.

CHAPTER REVIEW

SUMMARY

- **The Causes of Industrial Growth**   During the late nineteenth century, agricultural and industrial production increased sharply. The national railroad network grew to nearly 200,000 miles, the most extensive in the world. The surge of industrialization expanded use of electrical power and the application of scientific research to industrial processes. The *Bessemer converter* allowed for the mass production of steel, which was used to construct railroads, ships, bridges, and buildings.

- **The Rise of Big Business**   Many businesses grew to enormous size and power, often ignoring ethics and the law in doing so. Entrepreneurs like John D. Rockefeller, Andrew Carnegie, and J. Pierpont Morgan were extraordinarily skilled at gaining control of particular industries. Companies such as *Standard Oil* and *Carnegie Steel* practiced both *vertical integration*, through which they controlled all the enterprises needed to produce and distribute their products, and *horizontal integration*, in which they absorbed or eliminated their competitors. To consolidate their holdings and sidestep laws prohibiting *monopolies*, they created *trusts* and eventually *holding companies*. *J. Pierpont Morgan and Company*, an investment bank, pioneered methods for consolidating corporations and eliminating competition, all in an effort to bring "order and stability" to the marketplace.

- **The Alliance of Business and Politics**   The federal government encouraged economic growth after the Civil War by imposing high *tariffs* on imported products, granting public land to railroad companies and settlers in the West, establishing a stable currency, and encouraging the creation of universities to spur technical innovation and research. Equally important, local, state, and federal governments made little effort to regulate the activities of businesses. This *laissez-faire* policy allowed entrepreneurs to experiment with new methods of organization, but also created conditions for rampant corruption and abuse.

- **A Changed Social Order**   While the business and financial elite showed off their new wealth with extravagant homes and parties, the urban and industrial workforce was largely composed of unskilled workers, including recent immigrants, former farmers, and growing numbers of women and children. *Child labor* sometimes involved children as young as eight working twelve-hour days. Business owners and managers showed little concern for workplace safety, and accidents and work-related diseases were common. With industrialization and the rise of Big Business also came an increase in the number of people who considered themselves middle class. Growing numbers of women went to college, took business and professional jobs, and participated in other public activities.

- **Organized Labor**   It was difficult for unskilled workers to organize effectively into unions, in part because of racial and ethnic tensions among laborers, language barriers, and the efforts of owners and supervisors to undermine unionizing efforts. Business owners often hired "strikebreakers," usually desperate immigrant workers who were willing to take jobs at the prevailing wage. Nevertheless, several unions did advocate for workers' rights at a national level. The *National Labor Union* and the *Knights of Labor* organized strikes and lobbied for workers in the 1870s and 1880s, but both groups eventually fell apart. After the violence associated with the *Haymarket riot*, the *Homestead Steel strike*, and the *Pullman strike*, many Americans grew fearful of unions and viewed them as politically radical. Craft unions made up solely of skilled workers became more successful at organizing, as the *American Federation of Labor* focused on better working conditions and avoided involvement in politics.

CHRONOLOGY

1859	First oil well is struck in Titusville, Pennsylvania
1861	Congress creates the Morrill Tariff
1869	First transcontinental railroad is completed at Promontory Summit, Utah
1876	Alexander Graham Bell patents his telephone
1877	Great Railroad Strike
1879	Thomas A. Edison makes the first successful incandescent lightbulb
1882	John D. Rockefeller organizes the Standard Oil Trust
1886	Haymarket riot
	American Federation of Labor is organized
1892	Homestead Steel strike
1894	Pullman strike
1901	J. Pierpont Morgan creates the U.S. Steel Corporation

KEY TERMS

Standard Oil Company p. 633

horizontal integration p. 633

monopoly p. 633

vertical integration p. 634

trust p. 634

holding company p. 634

Bessemer converter p. 635

Carnegie Steel Company p. 636

J. Pierpont Morgan and Company p. 636

tariff p. 638

laissez-faire p. 640

child labor p. 645

Great Railroad Strike of 1877 p. 646

National Labor Union (NLU) p. 647

Knights of Labor p. 648

Haymarket riot p. 649

American Federation of Labor (AFL) p. 651

Homestead Steel strike p. 652

Pullman strike p. 652

 INQUIZITIVE

Go to InQuizitive to see what you've learned—and learn what you've missed—with personalized feedback along the way.

18 The New South and the New West

1865–1900

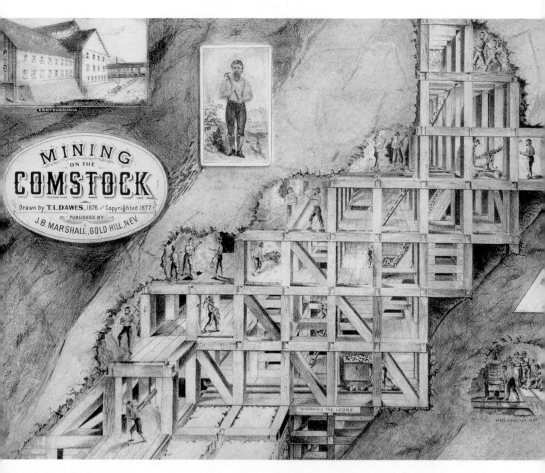

***Mining on the Comstock* (1877)** The Comstock Lode was one of the largest gold and silver mines in America, yielding more than $300 million over two decades. This illustration shows a cutaway of the Comstock Lode, revealing the complex network of shafts and supports, as well as the various tasks performed by miners within its tunnels.

After the Civil War, the devastated South and the untamed West provided enticing frontiers for economic enterprise. The South had to be rebuilt, while the sparsely settled territories and states west of the Mississippi River were ripe for the development of farms, businesses, railroads, and towns. Bankers and financiers in America and in Europe took advantage of these conditions to invest heavily in both regions, but especially in the far western region between the Mississippi River and California.

The Great Plains had long been viewed as a barren landscape suitable only for Indians and animals. Half of Texas, for instance, was still not settled at the end of the Civil War. After 1865, however, the federal government encouraged western settlement and economic development in what was then called "Indian Country." Two-thirds of Native Americans in 1865 lived on the Great Plains, often warring with one another over "hunting rights" to vast buffalo herds.

The construction of transcontinental railroads, the military conquest of the Indians, and the policy of distributing government-owned lands at low cost to settlers, ranchers, miners, and railroads combined to lure millions of pioneers and enterprising capitalists westward. Charles Goodnight, a Texas cattle rancher, recalled that "we were adventurers in a great land . . . fresh and

focus questions

1. In what ways did a "New South" emerge economically in the late nineteenth century?

2. What was the crop-lien system that emerged in the South and how did it shape the region after the Civil War?

3. How and why did white southerners take away African Americans' right to vote and adopt "Jim Crow" segregation laws at the end of the nineteenth century?

4. Who were the various groups of migrants to the West after the Civil War? Why did they move there?

5. What were the experiences of miners, farmers, ranchers, and women in the West in the late nineteenth century?

6. How did the federal government's post–Civil War policies in the West affect Native Americans?

7. How did the South and West change by 1900?

full of the zest of darers." By 1900, a New West and a New South had emerged, and eleven new states had been created out of the western territories.

The Myth of the New South

After the war between the states, the South fought an inner civil war over the future of the region. Many white southerners embraced the "Lost Cause," a romanticized interpretation of the war that painted the Confederates as noble defenders of their distinctive way of life against a tyrannical federal government headed by Abraham Lincoln. Southerners were haunted by a lingering nostalgia for the mythic Old South of white-columned plantations, white supremacy, and cotton-generated wealth produced by armies of enslaved blacks. As one southerner said, his native region remained "old-fashioned, medieval, [and] provincial, worshipping the dead."

At the same time, no region has inspired a more tenacious pride of place, a localism anchored in family life enlivened by visions of a mythic past. Mississippi writer Eudora Welty once explained that in the South, "feelings are bound up with place." *Home* and *history* are two of the most revered words in southern life. Nineteenth-century southerners did not simply live in the present and dream of the future. They were forever glancing backward in the process of moving forward. As William Faulkner recognized in his novel *Intruder in the Dust*, "The past isn't dead. It's not even past."

Other prominent southerners, however, looked more to the future. They called for a New South, where the region's predominantly agricultural economy would be diversified by an expanded industrial sector. The tireless champion of the New South ideal was Henry Woodfin Grady (1850–1889), the powerful managing editor of the *Atlanta Constitution*.

In 1886, Grady told a New York City audience that there had been an Old South "of slavery and secession—that South is dead. There is now a New South of union and freedom—that South, thank God, is living, breathing, and growing every hour." The Old South, he added, "rested everything on slavery and agriculture, unconscious that these could neither give nor maintain healthy growth."

Grady saw the New South becoming "a perfect democracy" of small farms complemented by mills, mines, factories, and cities. The postwar South, Grady claimed, would become a real democracy, no longer run by the planter aristocracy or dependent upon slave labor.

Many southerners shared Grady's vision. The Confederacy, they concluded, had lost the war because it had relied too much upon King Cotton—

and slavery. In the future, the New South must follow the North's example ("out-Yankee the Yankees") and develop a strong industrial sector to go with its agricultural foundation. New South advocates also stressed that more-efficient farming, using the latest machinery and technical expertise, was essential; that widespread vocational training was urgently needed; and that racial harmony built upon the acceptance by blacks of white supremacy (a peculiar form of a "perfect democracy") would provide a stable social environment for economic growth.

TEXTILE MILLS The chief accomplishment of the New South's effort to industrialize was a dramatic expansion of the region's **textile industry**, which produced thread and cotton bedding and clothing. From 1880 to 1900, the number of cotton mills in the South grew from 161 to 400, the number of mill workers (most of whom were white, with women and children outnumbering men) increased fivefold, and the demand for cotton products went up eightfold.

Thousands of dirt-poor farm folk rushed to take jobs in the mill villages that arose after the war. Seventy percent of southern mill workers were under the age of twenty-one, and many were under the age of fourteen. A dawn-to-dusk job in a mill paying fifty cents a day "was much more interesting than one-horse farming," noted one worker, "because you can meet your bills." Those bills were usually paid to the mill owner, who provided housing and supplies to the workers in his village—for a fee. By 1900, the South had surpassed New England as the largest producer of cotton fabric in the nation.

THE TOBACCO INDUSTRY Tobacco growing and cigarette production also soared in the New South. Essential to the rise of the tobacco industry was the Duke family of Durham, North Carolina. At the end of the Civil War, Washington Duke took his barn load of tobacco and, with the help of his two sons, hitched two mules to his wagon and traveled across the state, selling tobacco in small pouches as he went. By 1872, the Dukes had a cigarette factory producing 125,000 pounds of tobacco annually.

Washington's son, James Buchanan Duke, wanted even greater success, however. He spent millions on advertising schemes and perfected the mechanized mass production of cigarettes. Duke also undersold competitors and cornered the supply of ingredients needed to make cigarettes. Eventually, his primary competitors agreed to join forces with him, and in 1890 Duke brought most of them into the **American Tobacco Company**, which controlled 90 percent of the nation's cigarette production.

OTHER NEW SOUTH INDUSTRIES Effective use of other natural resources helped revitalize the South along the Appalachian chain from West Virginia to Alabama. Coal production grew from 5 million tons in 1875 to 49 million tons by 1900. At the southern end of the mountains, Birmingham, Alabama, sprang up during the 1870s in large part because of the massive deposits of iron ore in the surrounding ridges, leading boosters to label the steelmaking city the "Pittsburgh of the South."

Urban and industrial expansion as well as rapid population growth created a need for housing, and after 1870 lumbering became the fastest growing industry in the South. Northern investors bought up vast forests of yellow pine and set about clear-cutting them and hauling the logs to new sawmills, where they were milled into lumber for the construction of homes and businesses. By 1900, lumber had surpassed textiles in annual economic value. Still, for all of its advances, the South continued to lag behind the rest of the nation in industrial development.

THE REDEEMERS Henry Grady's vision of a New South celebrated the **Redeemers**, the conservative, pro-business, white politicians in the Democratic party who had embraced the idea of industrial progress grounded in white supremacy. Their supporters referred to them as Redeemers because they supposedly saved ("redeemed") the South from Yankee domination and "black rule" during Reconstruction.

The Redeemers included a rising class of lawyers, merchants, railroad executives, and entrepreneurs who wanted a more diversified economy. They also sought cuts in state taxes and expenditures, including those for the public-school systems started after the war. "Schools are not a necessity," claimed a Virginia governor. Louisiana cut school funding so much that the percentage of its residents unable to read and write actually increased between 1880 and 1900. Black children in particular suffered from such cutbacks. But the Redeemers did not want educated African Americans. "What I want here is Negroes who can make cotton," explained a white planter, "and they don't need education to help them make cotton."

The Failings of the New South

Despite the development of mills and factories, the South in 1900 remained the least industrial, least urban, least educated, and least prosperous region in the nation. Per capita income in the South in 1900 was only 60 percent of the national average. The typical southerner was less likely to be tending a textile loom or a steel furnace than, as the saying went, facing the eastern end of a westbound mule while plowing a field. The South was still dependent on the North for investment capital and manufactured goods.

Cotton remained king after the Civil War, although it never regained the huge profitability it had generated in the 1850s. By the 1880s, southern farmers were producing as much cotton as they had before the war but were earning far less money because the world price for cotton had declined.

SOUTHERN POVERTY Henry Grady also hoped that growing numbers of southern farmers would own their own land by the end of the nineteenth century. But the opposite occurred. Many actually *lost* ownership of the land that they worked each year. A prolonged decline in crop prices during the last third of the nineteenth century made it more difficult than ever to buy and own land. By 1900, an estimated 70 percent of farmers did not own the land they worked, and in no southern state were more than half of farmers landowners.

THE CROP-LIEN SYSTEM Because most southern communities had no banks after the Civil War, people had to find ways to operate with little or no cash. Many rural areas adopted a barter economy in which a "crossroads" or "furnishing" merchant would provide food, clothing, seed, fertilizer, and

"Free slaves" Sharecroppers painstakingly pick cotton while their white overseer watches them from atop his horse.

other items to poor farmers "on credit" in exchange for a share (or "lien") of their crops when harvested.

Southern farmers, white and black, who participated in the **crop-lien system** fell into three distinct categories: small farm owners, sharecroppers, and tenants. The farms owned by most southerners were small and did not generate much cash income. As a result, even those who owned their own farms had to pledge a portion of their future crop to the local merchant in return for supplies purchased "on credit."

Sharecroppers, mostly blacks who had nothing to offer but their labor, worked an owner's land in return for shelter, seed, fertilizer, mules, supplies, food—and a share of the crop, generally about half. **Share tenants**, mostly white farmers who were barely better off, might have their own mule or horse, a plow and tools, and a line of credit with the country store, but they still needed to rent land to farm. A few paid their rent in cash, but most, like sharecroppers, pledged a share of the harvested crops to the landowner.

Usually, the tenant farmers were able to keep a larger share of the crop (about 60 percent) than allowed to the sharecroppers, which meant that landowners preferred to rent to "croppers" rather than tenants. And many African American sharecroppers worked for the same planter who had owned them as slaves. "The colored folks," said a black Alabama sharecropper, "stayed with the old boss man and farmed and worked on the plantations. They were still slaves, but they were free slaves." Eighty percent of southern blacks lived on farms in the late nineteenth century.

The crop-lien system was self-destructive. The overwhelming focus on planting cotton or tobacco year after year stripped the soil of its fertility and stability. This led to disastrous erosion of farmland during rainstorms as soil washed into nearby creeks, collapsing riverbanks and creating ever-deepening gullies. In addition, landowners required croppers and tenants to grow only a "cash crop," usually cotton or tobacco. This meant that the landless farmers could not grow their own vegetable gardens; they had to get their food from the local merchant in exchange for promised cotton.

Because most farmers did not own the land they worked, the cabins they lived in, or the tools they used, they had little incentive to enrich the soil or maintain buildings and equipment. "The tenant," explained a study of southern agriculture in 1897 written by Matthew B. Hammond, a South Carolina–born economist, "is interested only in the crop he is raising, and makes no effort to keep up the fertility of the land." The tenant system of farming, Hammond concluded, had been "more wasteful and destructive than slavery was anywhere."

The crop-lien system was a post–Civil War version of economic slavery for poor whites as well as for blacks. The landowner or merchant (often the same person) decided what crop would be planted and how it would be cultivated, harvested, and sold. In good times, croppers and tenants barely broke even; in bad times, they struggled to survive. Sharecroppers and share tenants were among the poorest people in the nation. Most of them had little or no education, rarely enough healthy food, and little hope for a better future.

Those who worked the farms developed an intense suspicion of their landlords, who often swindled workers by not giving them their fair share of the crops. Landlords kept the books, handled the sale of the crops, and gave the cropper or tenant his share of the proceeds after deducting for all the items supplied during the year, plus interest that ranged, according to one newspaper, "from 24 percent to grand larceny." Often, the cropper or tenant received nothing at the end of a harvest but a larger debt to be rolled over to the next year's crop. Over time, the high interest charged on the credit offered by the local store or landowner, coupled with sagging prices for cotton and other crops, created a hopeless cycle of debt among small farmers, sharecroppers, and share tenants.

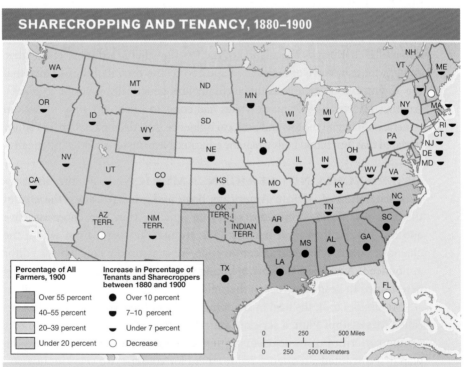

SHARECROPPING AND TENANCY, 1880–1900

Percentage of All Farmers, 1900
- Over 55 percent
- 40–55 percent
- 20–39 percent
- Under 20 percent

Increase in Percentage of Tenants and Sharecroppers between 1880 and 1900
- ● Over 10 percent
- ▼ 7–10 percent
- ▾ Under 7 percent
- ○ Decrease

0   250   500 Miles

0   250   500 Kilometers

- Why was there a dramatic increase in sharecropping and tenancy in the late nineteenth century?
- Explain why the South had more sharecroppers than other parts of the country.

FALLING COTTON PRICES As cotton production soared during the last quarter of the nineteenth century, largely because of dramatic growth in Texas cultivation, the price paid for raw cotton fell steadily. In the 1870s, annual production of cotton was about 2.6 billion pounds, which brought an average price of 11.77 cents per pound. In the 1880s, the average annual production was 3 billion pounds at 10.44 cents per pound. By 1896, the average price of cotton was down to 7.72 cents.

The average annual income of white southerners in 1900 was about half that of Americans outside the South. Eleven percent of whites in the South were illiterate, twice the national average. The region's poorest people were the 9 million former slaves and their children. Per capita black income in 1900 was a third of that of southern whites, and the black illiteracy rate in the South was nearly 50 percent, almost five times higher than that of whites.

RACE RELATIONS DURING THE 1890S

The desperate plight of southern farmers in the 1880s and 1890s affected race relations—for the worse. During the 1890s, white farmers and politicians demanded that blacks be stripped of their voting rights and other civil rights. In part, the new wave of racism was spurred by the revival of the old idea that the Anglo-Saxon "race" was intellectually and genetically superior to blacks. Another reason was that many whites had come to resent any signs of African American financial success and political influence. An Alabama newspaper editor declared that "our blood boils when the educated Negro asserts himself politically."

DISFRANCHISING AFRICAN AMERICANS By the 1890s, a new generation of African Americans born and educated since the end of the Civil War was determined to gain true equality. They were more assertive and less patient than their parents. "We are not the Negro from whom the chains of slavery fell a quarter century ago, most assuredly not," a black editor announced. A growing number of young white adults, however, were equally determined to keep "Negroes in their place."

Mississippi took the lead in stripping blacks of their voting rights. The so-called **Mississippi Plan**, a series of state constitutional amendments in 1890, set the pattern of disfranchisement that nine more states would follow. The plan first instituted a residence requirement for voting—two years in the state, one year in a local election district. This was aimed at African American tenant farmers who were in the habit of moving yearly in search of better economic opportunities. Second, Mississippi disqualified blacks from voting if they had committed certain crimes. Third, in order to vote, people had to have paid all of their taxes on time, including a so-called poll tax specifically for voting—a restriction that hurt both poor blacks and poor whites. Finally, all voters had to be able to read or at least "understand" the U.S. Constitution. White registrars decided who satisfied this requirement, and they often discriminated against blacks.

Other states added variations on the Mississippi Plan. In 1898, Louisiana inserted into its state constitution the "grandfather clause," which allowed illiterate whites to vote if their fathers or grandfathers had been eligible to vote on January 1, 1867, when African Americans were still disenfranchised. By 1910, Georgia, North Carolina, Virginia, Alabama, and Oklahoma had incorporated the grandfather clause. Every southern state created a Democratic primary process to select candidates, and most of these primaries excluded African American voters.

When such "legal" means were not enough to ensure their political dominance, white candidates used fraud and violence. Benjamin Tillman, the white supremacist who was South Carolina's governor from 1890 to 1894, maintained that his state's problems were caused by white farmers renting their land to "ignorant lazy negroes." His use of such racist explanations gained him the support of poor whites in his crusade to oust the ruling Redeemers.

To ensure his election, Tillman and his followers effectively eliminated the black vote. He admitted that "we have done our level best [to prevent blacks from voting]. . . . We stuffed ballot boxes. We shot them. We are not ashamed of it." The whites had regained control of the state government, he concluded, and they were determined to maintain their supremacy.

By the end of the nineteenth century, widespread racial discrimination—segregation of public facilities, political disfranchisement, and vigilante justice—had elevated government-sanctioned bigotry to an official way of life in the South. Tillman bluntly declared in 1892 that blacks "must remain subordinate or be exterminated."

The efforts to suppress the black vote succeeded throughout the South. In 1896, Louisiana had 130,000 registered black voters; by 1900, it had only 5,320. In Alabama in 1900, the census reported that 121,159 black men were literate; only 3,742, however, were registered to vote. By that year, black voting across the South had declined by 62 percent, the white vote by 26 percent.

THE SPREAD OF SEGREGATION At the same time that southern blacks were being shoved out of the political arena, they were also being segregated socially. The symbolic first target was the railroad passenger car. In 1885, novelist George Washington Cable noted that in South Carolina, blacks "ride in first-class [rail] cars as a right" and "their presence excites no comment." From 1875 to 1883, in fact, any local or state law requiring racial segregation violated the federal Civil Rights Act (1875).

By 1883, however, many northern whites endorsed the resegregation of southern life. In that year, the U.S. Supreme Court ruled that the Civil Rights Act of 1875 was unconstitutional. The judges explained that private individuals and organizations could engage in acts of racial discrimination because the Fourteenth Amendment specified only that "no State" could deny citizens equal protection of the law.

The Court's interpretation in what came to be called the Civil Rights Cases (1883) left as an open question the validity of state laws requiring racially segregated public facilities under the principle of "separate but equal," a slogan popular in the South in the late nineteenth century. In the 1880s, Tennessee and Mississippi required railroad passengers to ride in segregated cars.

When Louisiana followed suit in 1890 with a similar law, blacks challenged it in *Plessy v. Ferguson* (1896). The case originated in New Orleans when Homer Plessy, an octoroon (a person having one-eighth African ancestry), refused to leave a whites-only railroad car and was convicted of violating the law. In 1896, the Supreme Court ruled that states had a right to create laws segregating public places such as schools, hotels, and restaurants. Justice John Marshall Harlan, a Kentuckian who had once owned slaves, was the only member of the Court to dissent. He stressed that the Constitution is "color-blind, and neither knows nor tolerates classes among citizens. In respect of civil rights, all citizens are equal before the law." He feared that the Court's ruling would plant the "seeds of race hate" under "the sanction of law."

That is precisely what happened. The Court's ruling in the *Plessy* case legitimized the widespread practice of racially **"separate but equal"** facilities in virtually every area of southern life. In 1900, the editor of the *Richmond Times* insisted that "God Almighty drew the color line, and it cannot be obliterated. The negro must stay on his side of the line, and the white man must stay on his side, and the sooner both races recognize this fact and accept it, the better it will be for both."

The new regulations came to be called "Jim Crow" laws. The name derived from "Jump Jim Crow," an old song-and-dance caricature of African Americans. During the 1890s, the term *Jim Crow* became a derisive expression meaning "Negro." Signs reading "white only" or "colored only" above restrooms and water fountains emerged as hallmarks of the Jim Crow system, and racist customs dating back before the Civil War were revived. If whites walked along a sidewalk, blacks were expected to step aside and let them pass. There were even racially separate funeral homes, cemeteries, and churches. When a white deacon in a Mississippi Baptist church saw a black man in the sanctuary, he asked: "Boy, what you doin' in there? Don't you know this is a white church?" The black man replied: "Boss, I'm here to mop the floor." The white man paused and said, "Well, that's all right then, but don't let me catch you prayin'."

The lynching of Henry Smith Despite lack of evidence, Smith was convicted of murdering a white girl in Paris, Texas. A large crowd assembled to watch her family torture Smith on a platform labeled "Justice." After Smith was burned alive, the townspeople kept his charred teeth and bones as souvenirs.

Widespread racist violence accompanied the Jim Crow laws. From 1890 to 1899, the United States averaged 188 racial lynchings per year, 82 percent of which occurred in the South. Lynchings usually involved a black man (or men) accused of a crime, often rape. White mobs would seize, torture, and kill the accused, always in ghastly ways. Participating whites viewed lynchings as forms of outdoor recreation. Large crowds, including women and children, would watch amid a carnival-like atmosphere. The governor of Mississippi declared that "if it is necessary that every Negro in the state will be lynched, it will be done to maintain white supremacy."

MOB RULE IN NORTH CAROLINA White supremacy was violently imposed in the thriving coastal port of Wilmington, North Carolina, then the largest city in the state, with about 20,000 residents. In 1894 and 1896, black voters, by then a majority in the city, elected African Americans to various municipal offices, infuriating the city's white elite.

On the morning of November 10, 1898, some 2,000 well-armed white men and teens rampaged through the streets of Wilmington. Almost 100 blacks were killed. The mob then stormed the city hall and forced the African

American business leaders and elected officials to board northbound trains. The new, self-appointed all-white city government issued a "Declaration of White Independence" that stripped blacks of their jobs and voting rights. Desperate black residents appealed for help to the governor as well as President William McKinley, but received none.

The Wilmington insurrection marked the first time in history that a lawfully elected municipal government had been overthrown in the United States. Two years later, in the 1900 statewide elections, white supremacist Democrats cemented their control of the political process, when the Democratic party won by a landslide.

THE BLACK RESPONSE

By the end of the nineteenth century, white supremacy had triumphed across the South. Some African Americans chose to leave in search of equality and opportunity. Those who stayed and resisted white supremacy—even in self-defense—were ruthlessly suppressed. In the face of such overwhelming discrimination and abuse, most African Americans had no choice but to accommodate themselves to the realities of white supremacy and segregation. "Had to walk a quiet life," explained James Plunkett, a Virginian. "The least little thing you would do, they [whites] would kill ya."

Yet accommodation did not mean surrender, as African Americans constructed their own lively culture. A young white visitor to Mississippi in 1910 noticed that nearly every black person had "two distinct social selves, the one he reveals to his own people, the other he assumes among the whites."

Ida B. Wells While raising four children, Wells sustained her commitment to ending racial and gender discrimination and lynching.

IDA B. WELLS One of the most outspoken African American activists of the time was Ida B. Wells. Born into slavery in 1862 in Mississippi, she attended a school staffed by white missionaries. She moved in 1880 to Memphis, where she taught in segregated schools and gained entrance to the social life of the city's African American middle class.

In 1883, after being denied a seat on a railroad car because she was black, Wells became the first African American to file suit against such discrimination. The circuit court decided in her favor and fined the railroad, but the Tennessee Supreme Court overturned the ruling. Wells thereafter discovered "[my] first and [it] might be said, my only love"—journalism—and, through it, a weapon with which to wage her crusade for justice. She became editor of *Memphis Free Speech*, a newspaper that focused on African American issues.

In 1892, when three of her friends were lynched by a white mob, Wells launched a crusade against lynching. Angry whites responded by destroying her office and threatening to lynch her. She moved to New York, where she continued to criticize Jim Crow laws and demand that blacks have their voting rights restored. She helped found the National Association for the Advancement of Colored People (NAACP) in 1909 and worked for women's suffrage.

In promoting racial equality, Wells often found herself in direct opposition to Booker T. Washington, the most influential African American leader of the time.

BOOKER T. WASHINGTON
Born a slave in Virginia, in 1856, the son of a black mother and a white father, Booker T. Washington at sixteen had enrolled at Hampton Normal and Agricultural Institute, one of several colleges for ex-slaves created during Reconstruction. There he met the school's founder, Samuel Chapman Armstrong, who preached moderation and urged the students: "Be thrifty and industrious," "Command the respect of your neighbors by a good record and a good character," "Make the best of your difficulties," and "Live down prejudice." Washington listened and learned well.

Nine years later, Armstrong received a request from a group in northern

Booker T. Washington Founder of the Tuskegee Institute, a historically black vocational training school. He went on to become the nation's most prominent African American leader.

Alabama to start a black college called Tuskegee Institute. The college needed a president, and Armstrong urged them to hire Washington. Although only twenty-five years old, Washington was, according to Armstrong, "a very capable mulatto, clear headed, modest, sensible, polite, and a thorough teacher and superior man."

Young Washington quickly went to work. He became a skilled fundraiser, gathering substantial gifts from wealthy whites, most of them northerners. The complicated racial dynamics of the late nineteenth century required him to walk a tightrope between being candid and being an effective college president. He learned that he needed to be like a fox rather than a lion if he hoped to maintain the support of the white community. As the years passed, Tuskegee Institute became celebrated for its dedication to discipline and vocational training, and Booker T. Washington became a source of inspiration and hope to millions.

Washington's recurring message to black students focused on the importance of gaining "practical knowledge." In part to please his white donors, he argued that African Americans should not focus on fighting racial segregation. They should instead work hard and remain silent; their priority should be self-improvement rather than social change. Washington told young African Americans to begin "at the bottom" as well-educated, hard-working farmers, not as social activists.

In a famous speech at the Cotton States and International Exposition in Atlanta in 1895, Washington urged the African American community to "Cast down your bucket where you are— cast it down in making friends . . . of the people of all races by whom we are surrounded. Cast it down in agriculture, mechanics, in commerce, in domestic service, and in the professions." Any effort at "agitation" in the white-dominant South would, he warned, backfire. African Americans first needed to become self-sufficient economically. Civil rights would have to wait.

W. E. B. Du Bois A fierce advocate for black education and civil rights.

W. E. B. DU BOIS Other African American leaders disagreed with Booker T. Washington's "accommodationist" strategy. W. E. B. Du Bois emerged at the turn of the century as Washington's foremost rival. A native of Massachusetts, Du Bois first experienced racial prejudice as a student at Fisk University in Nashville, Tennessee. Later he became the first African American to earn a doctoral degree from Harvard (in history and sociology). In addition to promoting civil rights, he left a distinguished record as a scholar, authoring more than twenty books.

Du Bois had a flamboyant personality and a combative spirit. Not long after he began teaching at Atlanta University in 1897, he launched a public assault on Washington's strategy for improving the quality of life for African Americans.

Du Bois called Washington's celebrated 1895 speech "the **Atlanta Compromise**" and said that he would not "surrender the leadership of this race to cowards." Washington, Du Bois argued, "accepted the alleged inferiority of the Negro" so blacks could "concentrate all their energies on industrial education, the accumulation of wealth, and the conciliation of the South." Du Bois stressed that African American leaders should adopt a strategy of "ceaseless agitation" directed at ensuring the right to vote and winning civil equality. The education of blacks, Du Bois maintained, should not be merely vocational but comparable to that enjoyed by the white elite. Black education should help develop bold leaders willing to challenge Jim Crow segregation and discrimination.

The dispute between Washington and Du Bois came to define the tensions that would divide the twentieth-century civil rights movement: militancy versus conciliation, separatism versus assimilation, social justice versus economic opportunities. What Du Bois and others did not know was that Washington secretly worked to finance lawsuits challenging segregation and disfranchisement, to stop the brutal culture of race lynching, and to increase funding for public schools. He acted privately because he feared that public activism would trigger violence against Tuskegee and himself.

THE SETTLING OF THE NEW WEST

Like the South, the West has always been a region wrapped in myths and stereotypes. The vast land west of the Mississippi River contains remarkable geographic extremes: majestic mountains, roaring rivers, deep-sculpted canyons, searing deserts, grassy plains, and dense forests. For most western Americans, the Civil War and Reconstruction were remote events that hardly touched the lives of the Indians, Mexicans, Asians, farmers, ranchers, trappers, miners, and Mormons scattered through the plains, valleys, and mountains. In the West, the relentless march of white conquest, settlement, and exploitation continued, propelled by a special sense of "manifest destiny," a lust for land, a hope for quick fortunes, and a restless desire to improve one's lot in life.

Between 1870 and 1900, Americans settled more land in the West than they had in the centuries before 1870. By 1900, a third of the nation lived west of the Mississippi River. The post–Civil War West came to symbolize economic opportunity and personal freedom. On another level, however, the economic exploitation of the West was a story of irresponsible behavior and reckless abuse of nature that scarred the land, decimated its wildlife, and nearly exterminated much of Native American culture.

THE WESTERN LANDSCAPE After midcentury, farmers and their families began spreading west to the Great Plains—western Kansas, Nebraska, Oklahoma, northern Texas, the Dakotas, eastern Colorado, Wyoming, and Montana. From California, miners moved eastward through the mountains to Utah and Nevada, drawn by one new strike after another. From Texas, nomadic cowboys annually migrated with herds of cattle northward onto the plains and even across the Rocky Mountains, into the Great Basin of Utah and Nevada.

The settlers in the West encountered challenges markedly different from those they had left behind. The Great Plains had little rainfall and few rivers. The scarcity of water and timber rendered useless the familiar trappings of the pioneer—the ax, the log cabin, the rail fence—as well as traditional methods of tilling the soil.

For a long time, the region had been called the Great American Desert, unfit for human habitation and therefore, in the minds of most Americans, the perfect refuge for Indians who refused to embrace the white way of life. But that view changed in the last half of the nineteenth century. The discovery of gold, silver, copper, iron, and coal; the completion of the transcontinental railroads; the collapse of Indian resistance; and the rise of the buffalo hide and range-cattle industries convinced many Americans, as well as the federal government, that economic development of the West held the key to national prosperity. Capitalists made huge profits investing in western mines, cattle, railroads, and commercial farms. With the use of what water was available, new techniques of dry farming and irrigation could make the vast western lands fruitful after all.

THE MIGRATORY STREAM During the second half of the nineteenth century, an unrelenting stream of migrants flowed into what had been the largely Indian and Hispanic West. As millions of Anglo-Americans, Native Americans, African Americans, Mexicans, South Americans, and European and Chinese immigrants intermingled, they transformed western life and culture. Most of the settlers were white, native-born farm folk. Three quarters of the post–Civil War western migrants were men, but they often traveled with wives and children.

The largest number of foreign immigrants to the West came from northern Europe and Canada. In the northern plains, Germans, Scandinavians, and Irish were especially numerous. In Nebraska in 1870, a quarter of the 123,000 residents were foreign-born. In North Dakota in 1890, immigrants composed 45 percent of the residents.

Compared with European immigrants, those from China and Mexico were much less numerous but nonetheless significant. More than 200,000 Chinese arrived in California between 1876 and 1890, joining some 70,000 others who had come earlier to build railroads and work in mining communities. The Chinese were frequently discriminated against and denied citizenship rights, and they became scapegoats whenever there was an economic downturn. In 1882, Congress passed the Chinese Exclusion Act, effectively banning further immigration from China.

THE AFRICAN AMERICAN MIGRATION In the aftermath of the collapse of Radical Republican rule in the South, some blacks decided to found their own towns in Kansas, Oklahoma, and Mississippi. Others had larger communities in mind. Thousands of African Americans began migrating westward; some 6,000 southern blacks arrived in Kansas in 1879, and as many as 20,000 followed the next year. These migrants came to be known as **Exodusters** because they were making their exodus from the South in search of a haven from racism and poverty.

The foremost promoter of black migration to the West was Benjamin "Pap" Singleton. Born a slave in Tennessee in 1809, he escaped and made his way to Michigan. After the Civil War, he returned to Tennessee and decided that African Americans could never gain equal treatment if they stayed in the former Confederacy. When he learned that land in Kansas could be had for $1.25 an acre, he led a party of 200 colonists to the state in 1878, bought 7,500 acres that had been an Indian reservation, and established the Dunlop community.

Over the next several years, thousands of African Americans followed Singleton to Kansas, leading many southern leaders to worry about the loss of black laborers. In 1879, white southerners closed access to the Mississippi River and threatened to sink all boats carrying blacks to the West. An army officer reported to President Rutherford B. Hayes that "every river landing is blockaded by white enemies of the colored exodus; some of whom are mounted and armed, as if we are at war."

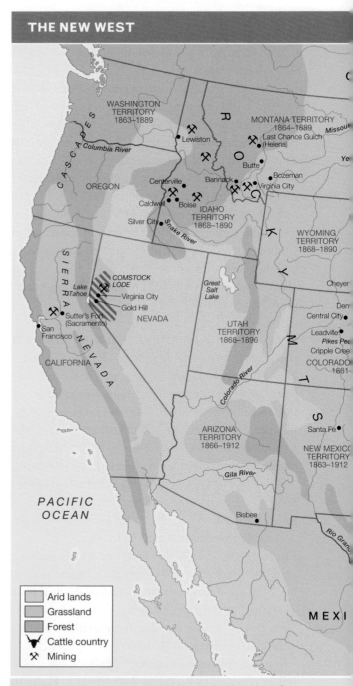

THE NEW WEST

WASHINGTON TERRITORY 1863–1889

MONTANA TERRITORY 1864–1889

ROCKY

Missouri

Lewiston

Last Chance Gulch (Helena)

Columbia River

CASCADES

Butte

Ye

Bozeman

OREGON

Centerville

Bannack

Virginia City

Caldwell

Boise

IDAHO TERRITORY 1868–1890

Silver City

Snake River

WYOMING TERRITORY 1868–1890

Cheyer

SIERRA

Lake Tahoe

COMSTOCK LODE

Virginia City

Gold Hill

Great Salt Lake

Den

Central City

Sutter's Fort (Sacramento)

San Francisco

NEVADA

UTAH TERRITORY 1868–1896

Leadville

Pikes Pea

Cripple Cree

NEVADA

CALIFORNIA

COLORADO 1861

Colorado River

M

PACIFIC OCEAN

ARIZONA TERRITORY 1866–1912

Santa Fé

NEW MEXICO TERRITORY 1863–1912

T

S

Gila River

Bisbee

Rio Gran

Arid lands

Grassland

Forest

Cattle country

Mining

MEXI

- What were the main industries of the New West?
- How did mining transform its ecology?

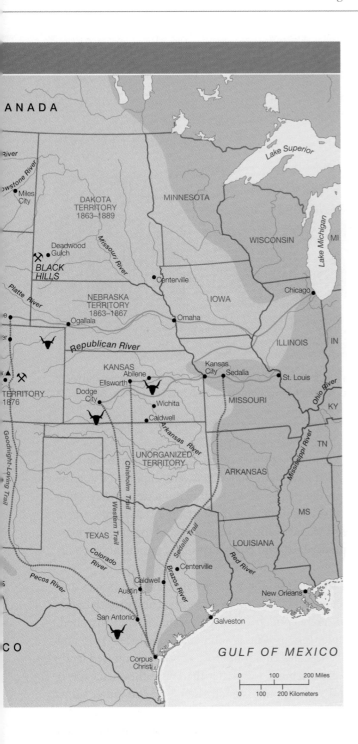

CANADA

River

Yellowstone River

Miles
City

DAKOTA
TERRITORY
1863–1889

MINNESOTA

Lake Superior

WISCONSIN

MI

Lake Michigan

Deadwood
Gulch

BLACK
HILLS

Missouri River

Centerville

NEBRASKA
TERRITORY
1863–1867

Platte River

Ogallala

Omaha

IOWA

Chicago

Republican River

KANSAS
Abilene

Ellsworth

Kansas
City   Sedalia

ILLINOIS   IN

St. Louis

TERRITORY
1876

Dodge
City

Wichita

Caldwell

MISSOURI

Ohio River

KY

Arkansas River

Goodnight-Loving Trail

Chisholm Trail

Western Trail

UNORGANIZED
TERRITORY

ARKANSAS

Mississippi River

TN

TEXAS

Colorado River

Sedalia Trail

Centerville

MS

LOUISIANA

Red River

Pecos River

Caldwell

Austin

Brazos River

San Antonio

Galveston

New Orleans

Corpus
Christi

GULF OF MEXICO

CO

| 0 | 100 | 200 Miles |
| 0 | 100 | 200 Kilometers |

Nicodemus, Kansas By the 1880s, this African American colony had become a thriving town of Exodusters. Here, its residents are photographed in front of the First Baptist Church and general store.

By the early 1880s, however, the exodus of black southerners to the West had petered out. Many African American settlers were unprepared for the harsh living conditions on the plains. Their Kansas homesteads were often not large enough to be self-sustaining, and most of the black farmers were forced to supplement their income by hiring themselves out to white ranchers. Drought, grasshoppers, prairie fires, and dust storms led to frequent crop failures and bankruptcy.

The sudden influx of so many southern blacks also taxed resources and patience. There were not enough houses, stores, or construction materials; few government services; and rarely enough water. Disappointed and frustrated, many African American pioneers in Kansas soon abandoned their land and moved to the few cities in the state. The frontier was not the "promised land" that they had been led to expect, but it was better than what they had experienced in the South. As an Exoduster minister stressed, "We had rather suffer and be free."

By 1890, some 520,000 African Americans lived west of the Mississippi River. As many as 25 percent of the cowboys who participated in the Texas cattle drives were African Americans, and many federal horse soldiers in the West were black.

WESTERN MINING   After the Civil War, the dream of striking it rich by finding gold or silver continued to be the most powerful lure to the West. But the nature of mining had changed drastically. Like much of western agriculture, mining had become a mass-production industry as individual prospectors gave way to large mining companies.

Many prospectors who had hoped to "strike it rich" turned into wage laborers working for mining corporations. Eventually, many of those mine workers formed unions to represent their interests in negotiations with mine owners, in part because of low pay ($3 a day) and in part because deep-shaft mining was so dangerous. In the western "hard-rock" mines, on-the-job accidents disabled one out of every thirty miners and killed one out of eighty. Overall, some 7,500 workers were killed and 20,000 maimed in mine accidents during the late nineteenth century.

The first wave of miners who rushed to California in 1849 had sifted gold dust and nuggets out of riverbeds by means of "placer" mining, or "panning." But once the placer deposits were exhausted, efficient mining required large-scale operations, massive machinery, and substantial capital investment. Companies shifted from surface digging to hydraulic mining, dredging, or deep-shaft hard-rock mining.

Industrial miners used huge hydraulic cannons to strip canyon walls of rock and topsoil in a search for veins of gold or silver. The tons of dirt and debris unearthed by the water cannons covered rich farmland downstream and created sandbars that clogged rivers and killed fish. All told, some 12 billion tons of earth were blasted out of the Sierra Nevada and washed into local rivers.

MINING BOOMTOWNS   Throughout the region, mining camps and towns sprouted like mushrooms in the second half of the century. Initially, the miners lived in crude tents and shacks they built themselves. They worked a nine- to ten-hour day, six days a week, and usually took Sunday off. As—or if—a camp grew, it became a town with cabins, stores, and saloons providing modern services and conveniences.

Tombstone, Arizona, only thirty miles from the Mexican border, was a major silver mining site in the 1870s. By only its fourth year of existence, it was the fastest-growing **boomtown** in the Southwest. It boasted a bowling alley, four churches, a school, two banks, three newspapers, and an ice cream parlor alongside 110 saloons, fourteen gambling halls, and numerous dance halls and brothels.

Some of the other largest and most famous mining boomtowns included Virginia City in Nevada, Cripple Creek and Leadville in Colorado, and

Deadwood in the Dakota Territory. They were male-dominated communities with a substantial population of immigrants: Chinese, Chileans, Peruvians, Mexicans, French, Germans, Scots, Welsh, Irish, and English.

Ethnic prejudice was as common as violence in mining towns. The Chinese, for example, were usually prohibited from laboring in the mines but were allowed to operate laundries and work in boardinghouses. Mexicans were often treated the worst. "Mexicans have no business in this country," a Californian insisted. "The men were made to be shot at, and the women were made for our purposes."

Most of the boomtowns lasted only a few years. Once the mines played out, the people moved on, leaving ghost towns behind. In 1870, Virginia City, then called the richest city in America, had a population of 20,000. Today, it has fewer than 1,000 residents.

New discoveries of gold and silver kept occurring throughout the late nineteenth century. The **Comstock Lode** was found near Gold Hill, Nevada, on the eastern slope of the Sierra Nevadas near the California border. Henry Comstock, a Canadian-born fur trapper, gave the new discovery (actually made by other prospectors in 1859) his name. The Comstock Lode, a seam of gold and silver more than fifty feet wide and thousands of feet deep, was the most profitable mine in history to that point.

The rapid growth of mining spurred the creation of territorial governments and cries for statehood. But after Colorado's admission in 1876, there was a long pause in admitting new states because of party divisions in Congress; Democrats refused to create states out of territories that were dominated by Republicans. After the sweeping Republican victory in the 1888 legislative races, however, Congress admitted North and South Dakota, Montana, and Washington as states in 1889, and Idaho and Wyoming in 1890. Utah entered the Union in 1896 (after the Mormons agreed to abandon the practice of polygamy), and Oklahoma in 1907; and in 1912 Arizona and New Mexico became the forty-seventh and forty-eighth contiguous states. (The final two states, Alaska and Hawaii, were added fifty years later.)

LIFE IN THE NEW WEST

In the 1880s, James H. Kyner, a railroad builder in Oregon, witnessed "an almost unbroken stream of emigrants from horizon to horizon." These "hardy, optimistic folk" traveled west in wagons, on horses, and on foot, "going west to seek their fortunes and to settle an empire." Most of them thought little about forcing out the Native Americans, Chinese workers, and Hispanic cowboys who were there first. Americans claimed a special "destiny" to settle, develop, and dominate the entire continent.

To encourage new settlers in the West, the federal government generously helped finance construction of four transcontinental railroads, dispatched troops to conquer and relocate Indians to designated reservations, and sold government-owned land at low prices—or gave it to railroad companies as a means of rapidly populating areas served by trains. The transcontinental railroads received some 200 million acres of land. Over time, the railroads sold much of the land to create towns and ranches along the rail lines. The New West of ranchers and farmers was largely the product of the railroads; the arrival of trains was the lifeblood of the western economy.

The surge of western migration had many of the romantic qualities so often depicted in novels, films, and television shows. Those who braved harsh conditions and uncertain circumstances were indeed courageous and tenacious. Cowboys and Indians; outlaws and vigilantes; farmers, ranchers, and herders populated the plains, while miners and trappers led more nomadic lives in the hills and backwoods.

These familiar images of western life tell only part of the story, however. Drudgery and tragedy were as commonplace as adventure and success. In contrast to the Hollywood versions of the West, the people who settled the trans-Mississippi frontier were a diverse lot: they included women as well as men, African Americans, Hispanics, Asians, and European immigrants. The feverish quest for quick profits also helped fuel a boom/bust economic cycle that injected chronic instability into the society and politics of the region.

While the West was being taken from the Indians, cattle were herded into the grasslands where the buffalo had roamed. For many years, wild cattle first brought to America by the Spanish had competed with buffalo in the borderlands of Texas and Arizona. Breeding them with Anglo-American domesticated cattle produced the hybrid Texas longhorns. Tough, lean, and rangy, they were noted more for speed and endurance than for yielding choice steak. They had marginal value, moreover, because the largest urban markets for beef were so far away—until the railroads arrived.

THE CATTLE BOOM Once the rail lines reached Kansas, Joseph G. McCoy, an Illinois livestock dealer, recognized the possibilities of driving vast herds of cattle raised in Texas northward to Kansas, where they would be loaded onto freight cars and sent to the rest of the nation. In 1867, in tiny Abilene, "a small, dead place" in eastern Kansas, McCoy bought 250 acres and built a stockyard, barn, an office building, livestock scales, a hotel, and a bank. He then sent an agent to Texas to convince the owners of herds bound north to go through Abilene. Once the Texas herds reached Abilene, cattle by the thousands were loaded onto rail cars and shipped to the Chicago stockyards, where they were slaughtered and then sent (as sides of beef) to cities around the nation.

Herding cattle Cowboys on horseback herd cattle into a corral beside the Cimarron River in 1905.

Abilene flourished as the first successful Kansas cow town. By 1871, there were 700,000 steers passing through it every year. Soon, other western territories and states—Colorado, Wyoming, Dakota, and Montana—followed the Kansas example and had cattle drives and railheads of their own. The thriving cattle industry spurred rapid population growth. The population of Kansas increased from 107,000 in 1860 to almost 1 million by 1880. Nebraska witnessed similar increases.

The ability to ship huge numbers of cattle by rail transformed ranching into a major national industry. Before long, however, the flush times of the cow towns passed, and the cattle drives ended because they were unprofitable. The dangers of the trail, the wear and tear on men and cattle, the charges required by Indians to cross their reservation lands, and the carving out of farms whose fences cut across the trails convinced cattlemen that they could operate best near railroads.

Like miners, cattle ranchers were forced to develop their own code of laws and ways of enforcing them. As cattle often wandered onto other ranchers' land, cowboys would "ride the line" to keep the animals off the adjoining ranches. In the spring they would "round up" the herds, which invariably got mixed up, and sort out ownership by identifying the distinctive ranch symbols "branded," or burned, into the cattle.

All that changed in 1873, when Joseph Glidden, an Illinois farmer, developed the first effective form of barbed-wire fencing, which ranchers used to fence off their lands at relatively low cost. Soon the **open range**—owned by all, where a small rancher could graze his cattle anywhere—was no more. Barbed-wire fences triggered "range wars," where small ranchers, called fence cutters, fought to retain the open range. Fencing put a lot of ranchers out of business.

FARMING ON THE PLAINS Farming on the Great Plains was made harder by the region's unforgiving environment, bitterly cold winters, and scorching summers. A New York newspaper publisher traveling to California described the Great Plains as "a treeless desert" that baked during daylight and was "chill and piercing" cold at night. Still, people made the dangerous trek, lured by inexpensive federal land and misleading advertisements celebrating life on the plains. Between 1870 and 1900, homesteaders, ranchers, miners, railroad operators, and commercial farmers took control of 430 million acres of land west of the Mississippi River.

HOMESTEADERS The first homesteaders in the Great Plains were mostly landless folk eager to try their hand at farming. Many of them had never used a hoe or planted a seed. "I was raised in Chicago without so much as a back yard to play in," said a Montana homesteader, "and I worked 48 hours a week for $1.25. When I heard you could get 320 acres just by living on it, I felt that I had been offered a kingdom."

Yet the farmers faced a grim struggle. Although land was essentially free as a result of the Homestead Act (1862), horses, livestock, wagons, wells, lumber, fencing, seed, machinery, and fertilizer were not. Freight rates and interest rates were criminally high. Declining crop prices produced chronic indebtedness, leading strapped farmers to embrace virtually any plan to increase the money supply and thus pay off their debts with inflated currency. The virgin land itself, although fertile, resisted planting; the heavy sod woven with tough grass roots broke many a plow. Since wood and coal were rare on the prairie, pioneer families initially had to use buffalo chips (dried dung from buffaloes and cattle) for fuel.

Farm families also fought a constant battle with the elements: tornadoes, hailstorms, droughts, prairie fires, blizzards, and pests. Swarms of locusts often clouded the horizon; a Wichita newspaper reported in 1878 that they devoured "everything green . . . destroying every plant that is good for food or pleasant to the eyes." In the late 1880s, a prolonged drought forced many

Innovative farming Powered by over a dozen horses and driven by two men, this early nineteenth-century "combine" machine could cut, thresh, bag, and weigh wheat all at the same time.

homesteaders to give up. In the end, two-thirds of the people who gained land under the Homestead Act failed to become self-sustaining farmers.

COMMERCIAL FARMING Eventually, as the railroads brought piles of lumber from the East, farmers could upgrade their houses built of sod ("Kansas brick") into more comfortable wood-framed dwellings. New machinery and equipment, for those who could afford them, improved productivity. In 1868, James Oliver, a Scottish immigrant living in Indiana, made a sturdy chilled-iron "sodbuster" plow that greatly eased the task of preparing land for planting. At the same time, new threshing machines, hay mowers, planters, manure spreaders, and other equipment lightened the burden of farm labor but often deepened the debts that farmers owed.

In Minnesota, the Dakotas, and central California, wealthy capitalists created gigantic "bonanza farms" that became the marvels of the age. On one bonanza farm in North Dakota, a single field of wheat encompassed 13,000 acres. Wheat became for farmers in the High Plains what cotton had been for southern planters: a perennial cash crop. American-grown wheat was exported around the world. Another bonanza farm in South Dakota employed more than 1,000 migrant workers to tend 34,000 acres. Such agribusinesses were the wave of the future. Thomas Jefferson's dream of an America primarily made up of small farmers continued to give way to industrial agriculture and bonanza farms.

While the overall value of farmland and farm products increased in the late nineteenth century, small farmers did not keep up. Their numbers grew in size but decreased in proportion to the population at large. Wheat in the Western states, like cotton in the antebellum South, was the great export crop that spurred economic growth. For a variety of reasons, however, including an inability to afford new machinery, few small farmers prospered. By the 1890s, they were in open revolt against the "system" of corrupt processors (middlemen) and "greedy" bankers who they believed conspired against them.

WOMEN IN THE WEST The West remained a largely male society throughout the nineteenth century. Many mining towns had a male-to-female ratio as high as nine to one. In both mining and farming communities, women were prized as spouses, in part because farming required help. In 1900, an estimated 98 percent of the women in Nebraska were married. But the women pioneers continued to face the same legal barriers and social prejudices prevalent in the East. A wife could not sell property without her husband's approval, for example. Texas women could not sue except for divorce, nor could they serve on juries, act as lawyers, or witness a will.

The constant fight for survival west of the Mississippi, however, made men and women more-equal partners than in the East. Many women who lost their mates to the deadly toil of "sod busting" assumed complete responsibility for their farms. In general, women on the prairie became more independent than women leading domestic lives back East.

It was not coincidental, then, that the new western territories and states were among the first to allow women to vote and hold office—in the hopes that by allowing women to vote, they would attract more women settlers. In 1890, Wyoming was admitted to the Union as the first state that allowed women to vote in all elections. Utah, Colorado, and Idaho followed soon thereafter.

THE FATE OF WESTERN INDIANS

As settlers spread across the continent, some 250,000 Native Americans, many of them originally from east of the Mississippi, were forced into what was supposed to be their last refuge, the Great Plains and mountain regions of the Far West. The 1851 Fort Laramie Treaty, in which the chiefs of the Plains Indians agreed to accept definite tribal borders and allow white emigrants to travel across their lands, worked for a while. Fighting resumed, however, as Indians continued their ancient practice of following the buffalo herds and as Americans began to settle on Indian lands.

INDIAN RELATIONS IN THE WEST From the early 1860s until the late 1870s, the trans-Mississippi West, often called "Indian Country," raged with the so-called **Indian wars**. Although the U.S. government had signed numerous treaties with Indian nations giving them ownership of reservation lands for "as long as waters run and the grass shall grow," those commitments were repeatedly violated by buffalo hunters, miners, ranchers, farmers, railroad surveyors, and horse soldiers.

In the 1860s, the federal government ousted numerous tribes from lands they had been promised "forever." The U.S. Army's central mission in the West was to protect pioneers traveling on the major Overland Trails, ensure that Native Americans stayed on the reservations, and keep Americans from trespassing on Indian lands.

Americans, however, repeatedly violated the treaty provisions. The result was simmering frustration punctuated by outbreaks of violence. In the summer of 1862, Sioux warriors killed 644 white traders, settlers, government officials, and soldiers in the Minnesota Valley. It was the first of many clashes between American settlers and miners and the Indians living on reservations in the Great Plains.

THE SAND CREEK MASSACRE Two years later, a horrible incident occurred in the Colorado Territory as a result of the influx of white miners. After Indians murdered a white family near Denver, John Evans, the territorial governor, called on whites to "kill and destroy" the "hostile Indians on the plains." At the same time, Evans persuaded "friendly Indians" (mostly Cheyenne and Arapaho) to gather at "places of safety" such as Fort Lyon, in southeastern Colorado near the Kansas border, where they were promised protection.

Despite that promise, at dawn on November 29, 1864, Colonel John M. Chivington's 700 militiamen attacked a camp of Cheyennes and Arapahoes along Sand Creek, about forty miles from Fort Lyon. Black Kettle, the chief, frantically waved first an American flag and then a white flag, but the attacking soldiers paid no heed. Over seven hours, the Colorado militiamen slaughtered, scalped, and mutilated 165 peaceful Indians—men, women, children, and the elderly. Chivington, a former abolitionist and Methodist minister (the "Fighting Parson") who had preached against the brutalities of slavery, had told his men to "kill and scalp all [Indians], big and little, you come across."

In his report on the lopsided bloodbath to army officials, Chivington lied, claiming a great victory against 1,000 entrenched Cheyenne warriors. The bloodthirsty colonel was greeted as a hero back in Denver. "Colorado soldiers have again covered themselves in glory," the *Rocky Mountain News* initially proclaimed.

Then the truth about Sand Creek began to come out. Captain Silas Soule witnessed the massacre but, along with his company of soldiers, had disobeyed orders to join the attack: "I refused to fire and swore [to my men] that none but a coward" would shoot unarmed women and children.

Three weeks after the massacre, Soule wrote a letter revealing in graphic detail what had actually happened at Sand Creek: "Hundreds of women and children were coming toward us, and getting on their knees for mercy," he noted, only to be murdered and "have their brains beat out by men professing to be civilized." Far from being a hero, Soule added, Chivington encouraged the slaughter through his *lack* of leadership: "There was no organization among our troops, they were a perfect mob—every man on his own hook." Soule predicted that "we will have a hell of a time with Indians this winter" because of what had happened at Sand Creek.

Congress and the army launched lengthy investigations, and the congressional report concluded that Chivington had "deliberately planned and executed a foul and dastardly massacre," murdering "in cold blood" Indians who "had every reason to believe they were under [U.S.] protection." An army general described the Sand Creek Massacre as the "foulest and most unjustifiable crime in the annals of America."

The **Sand Creek Massacre** did as Soule had predicted: it ignited warfare that raged across the central plains for the next three years. Arapaho, Cheyenne, and Sioux war parties attacked scores of ranches and stagecoach stations, killing hundreds of white men and kidnapping many white women and children. The federal government responded by authorizing the recruitment of soldiers from among Confederate military prisoners (called "white-washed Rebels") and the creation of African American cavalry regiments.

In 1866, Congress established two "colored" cavalry units and dispatched them to the western frontier. The Cheyenne nicknamed them "buffalo soldiers" because they "fought like a cornered buffalo; who, like a buffalo, had suffered wound after wound, yet had not died; and who, like a buffalo, had a thick and shaggy mane of hair."

The buffalo soldiers were mostly Civil War veterans from Louisiana and Kentucky. They built and maintained forts, mapped vast areas of the Southwest, strung hundreds of miles of telegraph lines, protected railroad construction crews, subdued hostile Indians, and captured outlaws and rustlers. Eighteen of the buffalo soldiers won Congressional Medals of Honor for their service.

INDIAN RELOCATION With other scattered battles erupting, a congressional committee in 1865 gathered evidence on the grisly Indian wars and massacres. Its 1867 "Report on the Condition of the Indian Tribes" led to the creation of an Indian Peace Commission charged with removing the causes of the Indian wars. Congress decided that this would be best accomplished by persuading nomadic Indians yet again to move to out-of-the-way federal reservations, where they would take up farming that would "civilize" them. They were to give up their ancestral lands in return for peace so that the whites could move in. In 1870, Indians outnumbered whites in the Dakota Territory by two to one; by 1880, whites, mostly gold prospectors, would outnumber Indians by more than six to one. The U.S. government had decided it had no choice but to gain control of the region—by purchase if possible, by force if necessary.

In 1867, a conference at Medicine Lodge, Kansas, ended with the Kiowas, Comanches, Arapahoes, and Cheyennes reluctantly agreeing to move to land in western Oklahoma. The following spring, the western Sioux, the Lakotas, signed the Treaty of Fort Laramie (1868), in which they agreed to settle within the huge Black Hills Reservation in southwestern Dakota Territory, in part because they viewed the Black Hills as holy ground.

GRANT'S INDIAN POLICY In his inaugural address in 1869, President Ulysses S. Grant urged Congress to adopt more-progressive policies toward Native Americans: "The proper treatment of *the original inhabitants of this land*" should enable the Native Americans to become *citizens* with all the rights enjoyed by every other American."

Grant's noble intentions, however, ran afoul of longstanding prejudices against Native Americans and the unrelenting efforts of miners, farmers, and ranchers to trespass on Indian lands and reservations. The president recognized the challenges he faced. Indians, he admitted, "would be harmless and peaceable if they were not put upon by whites."

Periodic clashes brought vengeful demands for military action. William T. Sherman, commanding general of the U.S. Army, directed General Philip Sheridan, who was in charge of the military effort in the West, to "kill and punish the hostiles [Indian war parties], capture and destroy the ponies" of the "Cheyennes, Arapahoes, and Kiowas." Sherman then declared that "the more we kill this year, the less we will have to kill next year."

Neither Sherman nor Sheridan agreed with Grant's "peace policy." In their view, the president's naive outlook was shaped by the distance between the Great Plains and Washington, D.C. Fairness and understanding were not the correct weapons against Indian warriors. Sherman ordered Sheridan to force all "nonhostile" Indians onto federal reservations, where they would be provided land for farming, immediate rations of food, and supplies and equipment (a promise that was rarely kept).

Some Native Americans refused to be moved again. In the southern plains of New Mexico, north Texas, Colorado, Kansas, and Oklahoma, the Native Americans, dominated by the Comanches, the greatest horse-borne warriors in America, focused on hunting buffalo. Armed clashes occurred with increasing frequency until the Red River War of 1874–1875, when Sheridan's soldiers won a series of battles in the Texas Panhandle. He boasted that it was "the most successful of any Indian Campaign in this country since its settlement by the whites." The defeated Comanches, Cheyennes, Kiowas, and Arapahoes were forced onto reservations.

CUSTER AND THE SIOUX Meanwhile, trouble was brewing again in the northern plains. White prospectors searching for gold were trespassing on Sioux hunting grounds in the Dakotas despite promises that the army would keep them out. Ohio senator John Sherman warned that nothing would stop the mass migration of Americans across the Mississippi River: "If the whole Army of the United States stood in the way, the wave of emigration would pass over it to seek the valley where gold was found."

The massive gold rush in the Black Hills convinced some Indians to make a last stand. As Red Cloud, a Sioux chief, said, "The white men have crowded the Indians back year by year, and now our last hunting ground, the home of my people, is to be taken from us. Our women and children will starve, but for my part I prefer to die fighting rather than by starvation." Another prominent Sioux war chief, Sitting Bull, told Indians living on the Black Hills reservation that "the whites may get me at last, but I will have good times till then."

In 1875, Lieutenant Colonel George Armstrong Custer, a veteran Indian fighter driven by reckless ambition and courage, led 1,000 soldiers in the Seventh Cavalry regiment into the Black Hills, where he announced the discovery of gold on French Creek near present-day Custer, South Dakota. The news set off a massive gold rush, and within two years, the mining town of Deadwood overflowed with 10,000 miners. The undermanned army units in the area could not keep the miners from violating the rights guaranteed the Sioux by federal treaties. President Grant and federal authorities tried to convince the Sioux to sell the Black Hills to the government. Sitting Bull told the American negotiator to tell "the Great Father [Grant] that I do not want to sell any land to the government."

With that news, Custer was sent back to the Black Hills, this time to find roving bands of Sioux and Cheyenne warriors and force them back onto reservations. If they resisted, he was to kill them.

The colorful, free-spirited Custer, strikingly handsome with golden curly hair, loved war and the thrill of combat. An army officer said Custer was one of the few soldiers who fought for the fun of it; to him, war was "glorious." Custer was a natural warrior whose goal was "not to be wealthy, not to be learned, but to be great."

For all of his flamboyance, however, Custer was also a talented cavalry officer with remarkable endurance. During the Civil War, he had been promoted to general at the age of twenty-three (reporters dubbed him the "Boy General") and had played an important role in the Union victory at Gettysburg. Now he was in charge of an expedition to attack the wandering bands of Sioux hunting parties, even though he recognized that intruding American miners had caused the renewal of warfare. As Custer told newspaper reporters, "We are goading the Indians to madness by invading their hallowed [hunting] grounds."

What became the **Great Sioux War** was the largest military campaign since the end of the Civil War. The war lasted fifteen months and entailed fifteen battles in present-day Wyoming, Montana, South Dakota, and Nebraska. In June 1876, after several indecisive encounters, Custer found a large encampment of Sioux and their Northern Cheyenne and Arapaho allies on the Little Bighorn River in the southeast corner of the Montana Territory.

On June 25, Custer ordered his exhausted men to attack the Indian camp. "Hurrah boys, we've got them," he shouted, not realizing how vastly outnumbered they were. Within minutes, they were surrounded by as many as 2,500 warriors led by the fierce Crazy Horse.

After a half hour of desperate fighting, Custer and his 210 men were all dead. Afterwards, Cheyenne women pierced Custer's eardrums with sewing

Battle of Little Bighorn, 1876 Amos Bad Heart Bull, an Oglala Sioux artist and historian, painted this scene from the Battle of Little Bighorn.

needles because he had failed to listen to their warnings to stay out of their ancestral lands. Custer's death echoed a line from his favorite Shakespeare play, *Julius Caesar*: "I shall have glory by this losing day."

The Sioux had won their greatest battle, but in doing so they helped ensure that they would lose the war. Upon learning of the Battle of Little Bighorn ("Custer's Last Stand"), President Grant and Congress abandoned the "peace policy" and dispatched more troops ("Custer's Avengers") to the plains.

Under General Sheridan's aggressive leadership, the army quickly regained the offensive and relentlessly pursued the Sioux and Cheyenne across Montana. Warriors were slain, villages destroyed, and food supplies burned. Forced back onto reservations, the remaining Native Americans soon found themselves struggling to survive. Many of them died of starvation or disease. By the end of 1876, the chiefs living on the Dakota reservation agreed to sell the Black Hills to the U.S. government. In the spring of 1877, Crazy Horse and his people surrendered. The Great Sioux War was over.

THE DEMISE OF THE BUFFALO Over the long run, the collapse of Indian resistance resulted as much from the decimation of the buffalo herds as from the actions of federal troops. In 1750, an estimated 30 million buffalo traveled the plains; by 1850, there were fewer than 10 million; by 1900, only a few hundred were left. What happened to them?

The conventional story focuses on intensive harvesting of buffalo by white commercial hunters after the Civil War. The construction of railroads allowed them to ship huge numbers of hides each year to cities in the East, where consumers developed a voracious demand for buffalo robes and buffalo leather. The average commercial hunter killed 100 animals a day.

The story is more complicated, however. The buffalo disappeared for a variety of health and environmental reasons, notably a prolonged drought during the late 1880s into the 1890s that severely reduced the grasslands upon which the animals depended. At the same time, the buffalo had to compete for food with other grazing animals; by the 1880s, more than 2 million horses were roaming buffalo lands.

The Plains Indians themselves, empowered by horses and rifles and spurred by the profits reaped from selling hides and meat to white traders, accounted for much of the devastation of the buffalo herds. If there had been no white hunters, the buffalo would probably have lasted only another thirty years because their numbers had been so greatly reduced by other factors.

THE LAST RESISTANCE In the Rocky Mountains and west to the Pacific Ocean, the same story of courageous yet hopeless resistance to white intruders was repeated again and again.

The Blackfeet and Crows had to leave their homes in Montana. In a war along the California-Oregon boundary, the Modocs held out for six months in 1871–1872 before they were overwhelmed. In 1879, the Utes were forced to give up their vast territories in western Colorado. In Idaho, the peaceful Nez Perce bands refused to surrender land along the Salmon River, and prolonged fighting erupted there and in eastern Oregon.

In 1877, Joseph, a Nez Perce chief, led some 650 of his people on a 1,300-mile journey through Montana in hopes of reaching safety in Canada. Just before reaching the border, they were caught by U.S. soldiers. As he surrendered, Joseph delivered an eloquent speech that served as an epitaph to the Indians' efforts to withstand the march of the American empire: "I am tired of fighting. Our chiefs are killed. . . . The old men are all dead. . . . I want to have time to look for my children, and see how many of them I can find. . . . Hear me, my chiefs! I am tired. My heart is sick and sad. From where the sun now stands I will fight no more forever." The Nez Perce requested that they be allowed to return to their ancestral lands in western Idaho, but they were forced to settle in the Indian Territory (Oklahoma), where many died of malaria.

A generation of Indian wars virtually ended in 1886 with the capture of Geronimo, a powerful chief of the Chiricahua Apaches, who had outridden, outwitted, and outfought American forces in the Southwest for fifteen years. Once, the Apaches captured a group of settlers, tied them to their wagon wheels, and roasted them alive. General Nelson A. Miles, commander of the soldiers who captured Geronimo, called him "one of the brightest, most resolute, determined-looking men that I have ever encountered."

THE GHOST DANCE   The last major clash between Indians and American soldiers occurred near the end of the nineteenth century. Late in 1888, Wovoka (or Jack Wilson), a Paiute in western Nevada, fell ill. In a delirium, he imagined being in the spirit world, where he learned of a deliverer coming to rescue the Indians and restore their lands. To hasten their deliverance, he said, the Indians must perform a ceremonial dance that would make them bulletproof against white soldiers. The Ghost Dance craze fed upon old legends of the dead reuniting with the living and bringing prosperity and peace.

The **Ghost Dance movement** spread rapidly. In 1890, the western Sioux adopted it with such passion that it alarmed white authorities. They banned the Ghost Dance on Lakota reservations, but the Indians defied the order, and a crisis erupted.

On December 29, 1890, a bloodbath occurred at Wounded Knee, South Dakota, after nervous soldiers fired into a group of Indians who had surrendered. Nearly 200 Indians, men, women, and children, and 25 soldiers died in the Battle of Wounded Knee.

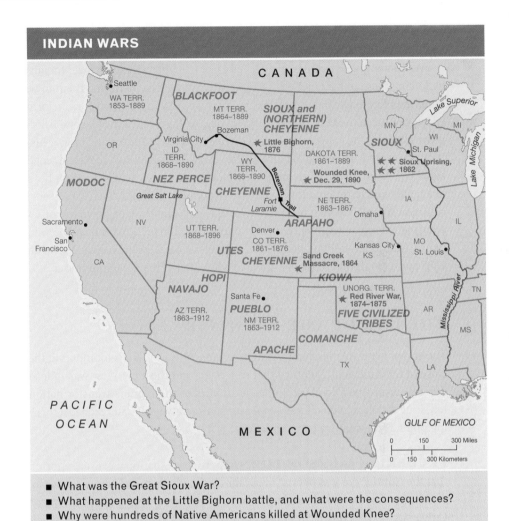

INDIAN WARS

- What was the Great Sioux War?
- What happened at the Little Bighorn battle, and what were the consequences?
- Why were hundreds of Native Americans killed at Wounded Knee?

The Indian wars had ended with characteristic brutality and misunderstanding. General Philip Sheridan, commander of U.S. troops in these conflicts, was acidly candid in summarizing how whites had treated the Indians: "We took away their country and their means of support, broke up their mode of living, their habits of life, introduced disease and decay among them, and it was for this and against this that they made war. Could anyone expect less?"

Many politicians and religious leaders condemned the persistent mistreatment of Indians. In his annual message of 1877, President Rutherford B. Hayes joined the protest: "Many, if not most, of our Indian wars have had their origin in broken promises and acts of injustice on our part." Helen Hunt Jackson, a novelist and poet, focused attention on the Indian cause in *A Century of*

Dishonor (1881), a book that powerfully detailed the sad history of America's exploitation of Native Americans over the centuries.

Well-intentioned but biased white reformers sought to "Americanize" Indians by forcing them to become self-reliant farmers rather than allowing them to be members of nomadic bands or tribes holding property in common. Such reform efforts produced the **Dawes Severalty Act** of 1887 (also called the General Allotment Act), the most sweeping policy directed at Native Americans in U.S. history. Sponsored by Senator Henry L. Dawes of Massachusetts, the act divided tribal lands and "allotted" them to individuals, granting 160 acres to each head of a family and lesser amounts to others. White Bear, a Kiowa chief, expressed a common complaint when he said that he did "not want to settle down in houses you [the federal government] would build for us. I love to roam over the wild prairie. There I am free and happy." But his preferences were not heeded. Between 1887 and 1934, Indians lost an estimated 86 million of their 130 million acres.

THE END OF THE FRONTIER

The end of Native American resistance was one of several developments at the close of the nineteenth century that suggested that the New West was indeed different from the Old West. Other indicators of the region's transformation led some scholars to conclude that American society itself had reached a turning point as the century came to a close.

FREDERICK JACKSON TURNER The 1890 national census reported that the frontier era was over; Americans by then had spread across the entire continent. This news led Frederick Jackson Turner, a young historian at the University of Wisconsin, to announce his "frontier thesis" in 1893, in which he argued that, more than slavery or any other single factor, "the existence of an area of free land, its continuous recession, and the advance of American settlement westward, explain American development." The experience of taming and settling the frontier, he added, had shaped the national character in fundamental ways. It was

> to the frontier [that] the American intellect owes its striking characteristics. That coarseness and strength combined with acuteness and acquisitiveness; that practical, inventive turn of mind, quick to find expedients; that masterful grasp of material things, lacking in the artistic but powerful to effect great ends; that restless, nervous energy; that dominant individualism, working for good and for evil, and withal that

buoyancy and exuberance which comes with freedom—these are traits of the frontier, or traits called out elsewhere because of the existence of the frontier.

Now, however, Turner stressed, "the frontier has gone and with its going has closed the first period of American history."

Turner's view of the frontier—as the westward-moving source of the nation's democratic politics, open society, unfettered economy, and rugged individualism—gripped the popular imagination. But his frontier thesis left out much of the story of American development. The frontier experience that Turner described was in many respects a self-serving myth involving only Christian white men and devoid of towns and cities, which in fact grew along with the frontier, not after it had been tamed. He virtually ignored the role of women, African Americans, Native Americans, Hispanics, and Asians. Moreover, Turner's frontier was always the site of heroism, triumph, and progress. He downplayed the evidence of greed, exploitation, and failure in the settling of the West.

Turner also implied that America would be fundamentally different after 1890 because the frontier experience was essentially over. In many respects, however, the West has retained the qualities associated with the rush for land, gold, timber, and water rights. The mining frontier, as one historian has recently written, "set a mood that has never disappeared from the West: the attitude of every extractive industry—get in, get rich, get out."

DISCONTENTED FARMERS By 1900, both the South and West were quite different socially and culturally from what they had been in 1865. In both cases, dramatically changed economic conditions spurred the emergence of a New South and a New West. In the West, the widespread use of mechanized commercial agriculture changed the dynamics of farming. By the end of the nineteenth century, many homesteaders had been forced to abandon their own farms and become wage-earning laborers—"migrant workers" moving with the seasons to different states to harvest different crops produced on large commercial farms or ranches. They were often treated as poorly as the white and black sharecroppers in the South.

As discontent rose among farmers and farmworkers in the South and the West, many of them joined the People's party, whose followers were known as Populists, a grassroots social and political movement that was sweeping the poorest rural regions of the nation. The Populist movement would tie the South and West together in an effort to wrest control of the political system from Republicans in the Northeast and Midwest. That struggle would come to define the 1890s and determine the shape of the twentieth century.

CHAPTER REVIEW

SUMMARY

- **The New South**   Many southerners embraced the vision of the *New South* promoted by Henry Grady and others, who called for a more diverse economy with greater industrialization, more vocational training, and a widespread acceptance of white supremacy in social relations. The cotton *textile industry* grew to surpass that of New England, iron manufacturing increased, and the *American Tobacco Company* became the world's largest manufacturer of cigarettes. But agriculture—and especially the growing of cotton—still dominated the southern economy, much as it had before the Civil War. Under the *crop-lien system*, large landowners rented land to cash-poor tenant farmers or *sharecroppers* (the latter usually African Americans) in return for a "share" of the cotton they grew each year. The crop-lien system kept millions in long-term debt and limited where they could live and how they could make a living.

- **Jim Crow Policies in the South**   During the 1890s, southern states disfranchised the vast majority of African American voters and instituted a series of policies known as Jim Crow laws segregating blacks and whites in public facilities. Starting with the *Mississippi Plan*, state governments passed a series of comprehensive measures that included poll taxes, grandfather clauses, literacy tests, and residency requirements, making voting nearly impossible for most African Americans, and some poor whites. Disfranchisement was followed by legalized segregation, ruled constitutional by the Supreme Court in the 1896 *Plessy v. Ferguson* decision. African Americans who resisted were often the target of violence at the hands of whites, the worst form being organized lynching.

- **Western Migrants**   Life in the West was often harsh and violent, but the promise of cheap land or wealth from mining drew settlers from the East. Although most westerners were white Protestant Americans or immigrants from Germany and Scandinavia, Mexicans, African Americans (the *Exodusters*), and Chinese, as well as many other nationalities, contributed to the West's diversity. About three-fourths of those who moved to the West were men.

- **Miners, Farmers, Ranchers, and Women**   Many migrants to the West were attracted to opportunities to mine, ranch, farm, or work on the railroads. Miners were drawn to the discovery of precious minerals such as silver at the *Comstock Lode* in Nevada in 1861. But most miners and cattle ranchers did not become wealthy, because mining and raising cattle, particularly after the development of barbed wire and the end of the *open range*, became large-scale enterprises. Farmers on the Great Plains were able to produce wheat for export, but declining grain prices and the need for expensive machinery and transportation meant that only large-scale farms owned by a wealthy few could sustain real profits.

- **Indian Wars and Policies**   By 1900, Native Americans were no longer free to roam the plains, as the influx of miners, ranchers, farmers, and soldiers had curtailed their traditional way of life. Instances of armed resistance, such as the *Great Sioux*

War, were crushed. Beginning in 1887, with the *Dawes Severalty Act*, the American government's Indian policy shifted. It now forced Indians to relinquish their traditional culture and adopt the "American way" of individual landownership.

- **The South and West in 1900**   By 1900, the West resembled the South where agricultural resources were concentrated in the hands of a few. In the 1890s, poor farmers in the West joined with tenant farmers in the South to support the People's party or the Populist movement, which sought to wrest control of the political and economic system from the powerful East and return it to the "plan" folk. This contest would dominate the nation's politics in the 1890s and set its course for the twentieth century.

CHRONOLOGY

1862	Congress passes the Homestead Act
1864	Sand Creek Massacre
1873	Joseph Glidden invents barbed wire
1876	Battle of the Little Bighorn
1880s	Henry Grady spreads the New South idea
1886	Surrender of Geronimo marks the end of the Indian wars
1887	Congress passes the Dawes Severalty Act
1890	Battle of Wounded Knee
	James Duke forms the American Tobacco Company
1893	Frederick J. Turner outlines his "frontier thesis"
1896	*Plessy v. Ferguson* mandates "separate but equal" racial facilities

KEY TERMS

textile industry p. 661

American Tobacco Company p. 661

Redeemers p. 662

crop-lien system p. 664

sharecroppers p. 664

share tenants p. 664

Mississippi Plan (1890) p. 666

"separate but equal" p. 668

Atlanta Compromise (1895) p. 673

Exodusters p. 675

boomtown p. 679

Comstock Lode p. 680

open range p. 683

Indian wars p. 686

Sand Creek Massacre (1864) p. 687

Great Sioux War p. 690

Ghost Dance movement p. 692

Dawes Severalty Act (1887) p. 694

 INQUIZITIVE

Go to InQuizitive to see what you've learned—and learn what you've missed—with personalized feedback along the way.

19 Political Stalemate and Rural Revolt

1865–1900

***Wet Night on the Bowery* (1911)** This scene of early twentieth-century life in New York City by John Sloan captures people of all walks of life converging on a rainy night: a smartly dressed society woman (left), a prostitute (center), and drunks stumbling about farther down the block. Running overhead is the elevated train, while an electric trolley gleams from the wet street.

W ithin three decades after the Civil War, American life had experienced a stunning transformation. An agricultural society long rooted in the soil and little involved in global issues had become an urban and industrialized nation deeply entwined in world markets and international politics.

The period from the end of the Civil War to the beginning of the twentieth century was an era noted for the widening social and economic gap between the powerful and the powerless, the haves and have-nots. It was sardonically labeled the **Gilded Age** for its greed and vulgarity, marked by conspicuous consumption by the newly rich as they flaunted their enormous personal wealth—the same wealth that financed extensive political and corporate corruption. While the Gilded Age brought dramatic changes to lives of citizens across all socioeconomic classes, the resulting shifts to social and cultural life could hardly be considered "gilded" to average Americans or recent immigrants.

URBAN AMERICA

During the late nineteenth century, the United States became a nation dominated by rapidly growing cities. Between 1865 and 1900, the urban population skyrocketed from 8 million to 30 million. In 1865, fewer than twenty

focus questions

1. What were the effects of urban growth during the Gilded Age? What problems did it create?

2. Who were the "new immigrants" of the late nineteenth century? How were they viewed by American society?

3. How did urban growth and the increasingly important role of science influence leisure activities, cultural life, and social policy in the Gilded Age?

4. How did the nature of politics during the Gilded Age contribute to political corruption and stalemate?

5. How effective were politicians in developing responses to the major economic and social problems of the Gilded Age?

6. Why did the money supply become a major political issue, especially for farmers, during the Gilded Age? How did it impact American politics?

cities had populations of more than 50,000; by 1900, there were four times that many. Millions of European and Asian immigrants, as well as migrants from America's rural areas, streamed into cities, attracted by the plentiful jobs and excitements they offered.

The growth of cities brought an array of problems, among them widespread poverty, unsanitary living conditions, and new forms of political corruption. How to feed, shelter, and educate the new city dwellers taxed the imaginations and resources of government officials. Even more challenging was the development of neighborhoods divided by racial and ethnic background as well as social class. At the same time, researchers were making discoveries that improved public health, economic productivity, and communications. Advances in modern science stimulated public support for higher education, but also opened up doubts about many long-accepted "truths" and religious beliefs.

POLITICAL CULTURE Political life during the Gilded Age was shaped by three main factors: the balance of power between Democrats and Republicans, the high level of public participation in everyday politics, and the often corrupt alliance between business and political leaders at all levels of government.

The most important political issue of the Gilded Age, however, was the growing conflicts between city and country, industry and agriculture. Millions of financially distressed farmers felt ignored or betrayed by the political process. While industrialists and large commercial farmers prospered, small farmers struggled with falling crop prices, growing indebtedness to banks and railroads, and what they considered big-city greed and exploitation.

By the 1890s, discontented farmers would channel their frustrations into political action and enliven a growing movement to expand ("inflate") the nation's money supply as a way to relieve economic distress. The election of 1896 symbolized the central conflict of the Gilded Age: the clashing cultural and economic values of two Americas, one older, small-scale, and rural, the other newer, large-scale, and urban.

AMERICA'S MOVE TO TOWN Americans moved to towns and cities after the Civil War, many of which evolved into major metropolitan areas. People from rural areas were attracted by the jobs and excitements of city life. Many had been pushed off the land by new agricultural machinery that sharply reduced the need for farmworkers. Four men could now perform the labor that earlier had required fourteen. Immigrants especially congregated in the cities along the Atlantic and Pacific coast where they arrived on ships from Europe or Asia. "The greater part of our population must live in cities," announced Josiah Strong, a prominent Congregationalist minister, in 1898. "There was no resisting the trend."

While the Far West had the greatest proportion of urban dwellers, concentrated in cities such as San Francisco and Denver, the Northeast and Midwest held far more people in huge cities—New York, Boston, Philadelphia, Pittsburgh, Chicago, Cincinnati, St. Louis, and others. More and more of these city dwellers had little or no money and nothing but their labor to sell. By 1900, more than 90 percent of the people in New York City's most densely populated borough, Manhattan, lived in rented houses or in congested, low-cost buildings called **tenements**, where residents, many of them immigrants, were packed like sardines in poorly ventilated and poorly lit apartments.

GROWTH IN ALL DIRECTIONS Several advances in technology helped city buildings handle the surging populations. In the 1870s, heating innovations, such as steam radiators, enabled the construction of much larger apartment buildings, since coal-burning fireplaces and chimneys, expensive to build, were no longer needed in each apartment. In 1889, the Otis Elevator Company installed the first electric elevator, which made it possible to construct much taller buildings; before the 1860s, few structures had been more than five or six stories. During the 1880s, engineers also developed cast-iron and steel-frame construction techniques that allowed for taller structures—"skyscrapers."

Cities grew out as well as up, as horse-drawn streetcars and commuter railways let people live farther away from their downtown workplaces. In 1873, San Francisco became the first city to use cable cars that clamped onto a moving underground cable driven by a central power source. Some cities ran steam-powered trains on elevated tracks, but by the 1890s electric trolleys were preferred. Mass transit received an added boost from underground subway train systems built in Boston, New York City, and Philadelphia.

The commuter trains and trolleys allowed a growing middle class of business executives and professionals (accountants, doctors, engineers, sales clerks, teachers, store managers, and attorneys) to retreat from crowded downtowns to quieter, tree-lined "streetcar suburbs." But the working poor, many of them immigrants or African Americans, could rarely afford to leave the inner cities. As their populations grew, cities became dangerously congested and plagued with fires, violent crimes, and diseases.

CROWDS, DIRT, AND DISEASE The wonders of big cities—electric lights, streetcars, telephones, department stores, theaters, and many other

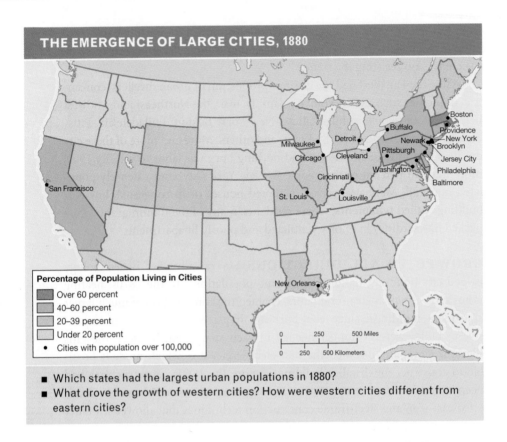

THE EMERGENCE OF LARGE CITIES, 1880

Percentage of Population Living in Cities
- Over 60 percent
- 40–60 percent
- 20–39 percent
- Under 20 percent
- Cities with population over 100,000

- Which states had the largest urban populations in 1880?
- What drove the growth of western cities? How were western cities different from eastern cities?

attractions—were magnetic lures for rural youth bored by the routines of isolated farm life. Thousands moved to the cities in search of economic opportunity and personal freedom.

Yet in doing so they often traded one set of problems for another. In New York City in 1900, some 2.3 million people—two-thirds of the city's population—were living in overcrowded, often filthy tenement housing. Such urban growth frequently occurred with little planning or regulation. Rapidly expanding cities often suffered from poor housing, unhealthy living conditions, and frequent infectious diseases and fires. "The only trouble with New York City," said writer Mark Twain, "is that it is too large. You cannot accomplish anything in the way of business . . . without devoting a whole day to it. The distances are too great."

Tenement buildings were usually six to eight stories tall, lacked elevators, and were jammed so tightly together that most of the apartments had little or no natural light or fresh air. They typically housed twenty-four to thirty-two

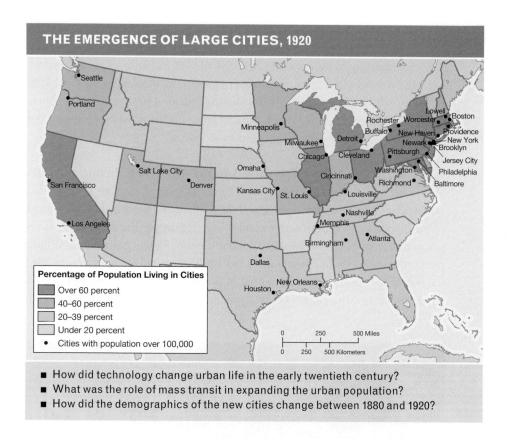

THE EMERGENCE OF LARGE CITIES, 1920

Percentage of Population Living in Cities
- Over 60 percent
- 40–60 percent
- 20–39 percent
- Under 20 percent
- Cities with population over 100,000

- How did technology change urban life in the early twentieth century?
- What was the role of mass transit in expanding the urban population?
- How did the demographics of the new cities change between 1880 and 1920?

families, usually with lots of children who had few places to play except in the streets. On average, there was only one toilet (called a *privy*) for every twenty people.

Late nineteenth-century cities were dirty, smelly, and disease-ridden. The child-mortality rate in many tenements was as high as 40 percent. Streets were filled with contaminated water, horse urine and manure, and roaming pigs. Garbage and raw sewage were carelessly dumped into streets and waterways, causing epidemics of infectious diseases such as cholera, typhoid fever, and yellow fever.

So-called sanitary reformers—public health officials and engineers— eventually created regulations requiring more space per resident as well as more windows and plumbing facilities. Reformers also pushed successfully for new water and sewage systems and for regular trash collection. They lobbied to ban slaughterhouses and the raising of hogs and cattle within city limits, and to replace horse-drawn trolleys with electric-powered streetcars or trolleys.

THE NEW IMMIGRATION

America's roaring prosperity and promise of political and religious freedom attracted waves of immigrants from every part of the globe after the Civil War. By 1900, nearly 30 percent of the residents of major cities were foreign-born. These newcomers provided much-needed labor for the growing economy, but their arrival also sparked racial and ethnic tensions.

A SURGE OF NEWCOMERS FROM EUROPE Immigration has always been one of the most powerful forces shaping American history. This was especially true between 1860 and 1900, as more and more immigrants, most of them poor, arrived from eastern and southern Europe. The number of immigrants rose from just under 3 million annually in the 1870s to more than 5 million per year in the 1880s, and reached nearly 9 million annually in the first decade of the twentieth century. In 1890, four out of five New Yorkers were foreign-born, a higher proportion than in any other city in the world. Chicago was not far behind.

Ellis Island To accommodate the soaring numbers of immigrants passing through New York City, Congress built a reception center on Ellis Island, near the Statue of Liberty. Pictured here is its registry room, where immigrants awaited close questioning by officials.

The so-called "old immigrants" who came before 1880 were mainly Protestants and Roman Catholics from northern and western Europe. This pattern began to change, however, as the proportion of immigrants from southern and eastern Europe, especially Russia, Poland, Greece, and Italy, rose sharply. After 1890, these **"new immigrants"** made up a clear majority of the newcomers. Their languages and cultural backgrounds were markedly different from those of most old immigrants or of most native-born Americans. The dominant religions of the new immigrants, for example, were Judaism, Eastern Orthodox, and Roman Catholicism, whereas Protestants still formed a large majority of the U.S. population.

In 1907, Congress appointed the bipartisan Dillingham Commission to examine the changes in immigration patterns. In its forty-one-volume report, released in 1911, the Commission concluded that the "new" immigrants were

> far less intelligent than the old, approximately one-third of all those over 14 years of age when admitted being illiterate. Racially, they are for the most part essentially unlike the British, German and other peoples who came during the prior period to 1880, and generally speaking they are actuated in coming by different ideals, for the old immigration came to be a part of the country, while the new in a large measure, comes with the intention of profiting, in a pecuniary way, by the superior advantages of the new world and then returning to the old country.

Immigrants were usually desperately poor and needed to find jobs—quickly. Many were greeted at the docks by family and friends, others were met by representatives of immigrant-aid societies or by company agents offering low-paying and often dangerous jobs in mines, mills, sweatshops, and on railroads.

Since most immigrants knew little if any English and nothing about American employment practices, they were easy targets for exploitation. Many unwittingly lost a healthy percentage of their wages to unscrupulous hiring agents in exchange for a bit of whiskey and a job. Companies eager for workers gave immigrants train tickets to inland cities such as Buffalo, Pittsburgh, Cleveland, Chicago, Milwaukee, Cincinnati, and St. Louis.

As strangers in America, most immigrants naturally wanted to live in neighborhoods populated by people from their homeland. The largest cities had vibrant immigrant districts with names such as Little Italy, Little Hungary, and Chinatown, where immigrants practiced their native religions and customs, and spoke and read newspapers in their native languages. But they paid a price for such community solidarity. When new immigrants moved into an area, the previous residents often moved out, taking with them whatever

Mulberry Street, 1900 This photograph captures the many Italian immigrants who made Mulberry Street in downtown New York City their home at the turn of the century. Horse-drawn carts weave through people shopping, socializing, and people-gazing.

social prestige and political influence they had achieved. Living conditions often quickly deteriorated as housing and sanitation codes went unenforced.

THE NATIVIST RESPONSE Then, as now, many native-born Americans saw the newest immigrants as a threat to their jobs and way of life. Many "**nativists**" were racists who believed that "Anglo-Saxon" Americans—people of British or Germanic background—were superior to the Slavic, Italian, Greek, and Jewish newcomers. A Stanford University professor called immigrants from southern and eastern Europe "illiterate, docile, lacking in self-reliance and initiative, and not possessing the Anglo-Teutonic conceptions of law, order, and government." Many were illiterate, but others only appeared so because they could not speak or read English. Some resorted to crime to survive, fueling suspicions that European nations were sending their criminals to America.

Throughout American history, Congress has passed laws regulating immigration; largely, these statutes have been inconsistent in their goals and frequently motivated by racial and ethnic prejudice. During the late nineteenth century, such prejudice took an especially ugly turn against the Chinese.

By 1880, some 75,000 Chinese formed about a ninth of the population of California. They were the first non-European and non-African group to migrate in large numbers to America. Chinese immigrants were easy targets for discrimination; they were not white, they were not Christian, and many could not read or write. Whites resented them for supposedly taking their jobs, although in many instances the Chinese were willing to do menial work that whites refused to do.

In 1882, anti-Chinese sentiment in Congress prompted passage of the **Chinese Exclusion Act**, the first federal law to restrict the immigration of free people on the basis of race and class. The act, which barred unskilled Chinese laborers from entering the country for ten years, was periodically renewed before being extended indefinitely in 1902. With the Chinese Exclusion Act, the golden door welcoming foreigners to the United States began to close. Not until 1943 were barriers to Chinese immigration finally removed.

Chinese Exclusion Act The Chinese caricature "John Chinaman" is escorted out of America by Lady Liberty with his ironing board and opium pipe, while other accepted minorities look on.

The Chinese were not the only group targeted. In 1887, Protestant activists in Iowa formed the American Protective Association (APA), a secret organization whose members pledged never to employ or vote for a Roman Catholic. Working often within local Republican party organizations, the APA quickly enlisted 2.5 million members and helped shape the 1894 election results in Ohio, Wisconsin, Indiana, Missouri, and Colorado.

In 1891, nativists in New England formed the Immigration Restriction League to save the Anglo-Saxon "race" from being "contaminated" by "alien" immigrants, especially Roman Catholics and Jews. The League sought to convince Congress to ban immigrants who were illiterate. Three presidents vetoed bills banning illiterate immigrants: Grover Cleveland in 1897, William H. Taft in 1913, and Woodrow Wilson in 1915 and 1917. The last time, however, Congress overrode the veto, and the restriction of illiterate immigrants became law.

CULTURAL LIFE

The flood of people into cities brought changes in recreation and leisure. Middle- and upper-class families, especially those in streetcar suburbs, often spent free time together at home, singing around a piano, reading novels, or playing games. In congested urban areas, politics as a form of public entertainment attracted large crowds, and saloons became even more popular social centers for working-class men. New forms of mass entertainment—movie theaters, music halls, vaudeville shows featuring singers, dancers, and comedians; art museums, symphony orchestras, sporting events, and circuses—drew a broad cross-section of residents. In large cities, new streetcar transit systems allowed people to travel easily to sporting events, and rooting for the home team helped unify a city's ethnic and racial groups and social classes. By the end of the century, sports of all kinds had become a major part of popular culture.

Urbanization and technological progress also contributed to the prestige of modern science. By encouraging what one writer called a "mania for facts," scientists generated changes throughout social, intellectual, and cultural life. Scientific research led to transformational technologies such as electric power and lights, telephones, phonographs, motion pictures, bicycles, and automobiles.

Although only men could vote in most states, both men and women flocked to hear candidates speak at political meetings. In the largest cities, membership in a political party offered many social benefits. As labor unions became increasingly common, they too took on social roles for working-class men.

Vaudeville For as little as 1¢ for admission, vaudeville shows aimed to please the tastes of their wildly diverse audience with a great range of entertainment.

SALOONS Still, the most popular leisure destinations for the urban working class were **saloons**, beer gardens, and dance halls. By 1900, the United States had more saloons (over 325,000) than grocery stores and meat markets. New York City alone had 10,000 saloons, 1 for every 500 residents.

Saloons were the workingman's social club and were especially popular among male immigrants seeking companionship in a strange land. In cities such as New York, Boston, Philadelphia, and Chicago, the customers were disproportionately Irish, German, and Italian Catholics. Politics was often the topic of intense discussions in saloons; in fact, in New York City in the 1880s, saloons doubled as polling places, where patrons could cast their votes in elections. One journalist called the saloon "the social and intellectual center of the neighborhood."

Men also went to saloons to check job postings, engage in labor union activities, cash paychecks, mail letters, read newspapers, and gossip. Because saloons were heated and offered public restrooms, they served as refuges for the homeless, especially in the winter. Patrons could play chess, billiards, darts, cards, dice, or even handball, since many saloons included gymnasiums.

Although the main barroom was for men only, women and children were allowed to enter a side door to buy a pail of beer to carry home (a task called "rushing the growler"). Some saloons also provided "snugs," separate rooms for women customers. "Stall saloons" included "wine rooms" where prostitutes worked.

LEISURE FOR WOMEN Married working-class women had even less leisure time than working-class men. Many were working for pay themselves, and even those who were not were frequently overwhelmed by housework and child-rearing responsibilities. As a social worker noted, "The men have the saloons, political clubs, trade-unions or [fraternal] lodges for their recreation . . . while the mothers have almost no recreation, only a dreary round of work, day after day, with occasionally doorstep gossip to vary the monotony of their lives." Married working-class women often used the streets as their public space. Washing clothes, supervising children at play, or shopping at the local market provided opportunities for socializing.

Single women, many of whom worked as domestic servants ("maids") and had more leisure time than working mothers, flocked to dance halls, theaters, amusement parks, and picnic grounds. With the advent of movie theaters, the cinema became the most popular form of entertainment for working women. As an advertisement promised, "If you are tired of life, go to the movies. If you are sick of troubles rife, go to the picture show. You will forget your unpaid bills, rheumatism and other ills, if you stow your pills and go to the picture show."

The Impact of Darwinism

Virtually every field of thought felt the impact of natural scientist Charles Darwin's controversial *On the Origin of Species* (1859), one of the most influential books ever written. Basing his conclusions on extensive yet "imperfect" field research, Darwin showed how the chance processes of evolution give energy and unity to life. At the center of his concept was what Darwin called "natural selection." He demonstrated that most organisms produce many more offspring than can survive. Those offspring with certain favorable characteristics adapt and live, while others die from starvation, disease, or predators.

This "struggle for existence" in a crowded world drove the process of natural selection, Darwin said. Over many millions of years, modern species "evolved" from less complex forms of life; individuals and species that had characteristics advantageous for survival reproduced, while others fell by the wayside. As Darwin wrote, "the vigorous, the healthy, and the happy survive and multiply."

Darwin's theory of biological evolution was shocking because most people still embraced a literal interpretation of the biblical creation story, which claimed that all species were created at the same moment by God and remained the same thereafter. Although Darwin had trained for the ministry and was reluctant to be drawn into religious controversy, his biological findings suggested to many, then and since, that there was no providential God controlling the universe. People were no different from plants and animals; they too evolved by trial and error rather than by God's purposeful hand. What came to be called *Darwinism* spelled the end of a God-given world.

Charles Darwin Darwin's scientific theories and influenced more than a century of political and social debate.

Many Christians charged that Darwin's ideas led to atheism, a denial of the existence of God, while others found their faith severely shaken not only by evolutionary theory but also by new scientific standards of scholarly analysis that were being applied to the Bible. Most of the faithful, however, came to reconcile science and religion.

They decided that the process of evolutionary change in nature must be God's doing.

SOCIAL DARWINISM Although Darwin's theory of evolution applied only to biological phenomena, many applied it to human society. Englishman Herbert Spencer, a leading social philosopher, was the first major prophet of what came to be called **social Darwinism**.

Spencer argued that human society and its institutions, like the organisms studied by Darwin, evolved through the same process of natural selection. The "survival of the fittest," in Spencer's chilling phrase, was the engine of social progress. By encouraging people, ideas, and nations to compete with one another for dominance, society would generate "the greatest perfection and the most complete happiness."

Darwin dismissed Spencer's social theories as "unconvincing." He did not believe that the evolutionary process in the natural world had any relevance to human social institutions. Others, however, eagerly endorsed social Darwinism. E. L. Youmans, founding editor of *Popular Science Monthly*, became the foremost champion of Spencer's ideas in America. He claimed that in the United States, Darwinism really meant Spencerism, the "anti-philanthropic, anti-meddling side" of Spencer's philosophy. If, as Spencer believed, society naturally evolved for the better through "survival of the fittest," then interference with human competition in the marketplace was a serious mistake because it would help "unfit" people survive, and thereby hinder progress.

Social Darwinism implied the need for hands-off, laissez-faire government policies; it argued against the regulation of business or of required minimum standards for sanitation and housing. To Spencer, the only acceptable charity was voluntary, and even that was of dubious value. Spencer warned that "fostering the good-for-nothing [people] at the expense of the good, is an extreme cruelty" to the health of civilization.

For Spencer and his many American supporters, successful businessmen and corporations provided proof of the concept of "survival of the fittest." If the unregulated process of capitalist development led to small businesses being destroyed or acquired by huge corporate monopolies, it was simply a necessary phase of the evolutionary process.

In 1872, Spencer's chief academic disciple, William Graham Sumner, began teaching at Yale University, where he preached the gospel of natural selection. Sumner's most lasting contribution, made in his book *Folkways* (1907), was to argue that it would be a mistake for government to try to promote equality, since doing so would interfere with the "survival of the fittest."

REFORM DARWINISM Sumner's efforts to use Darwinism to promote "rugged individualism" and oppose government regulation of business prompted an alternative use of Darwinism in the context of human society. What came to be called **reform Darwinism** found its major advocate in Lester Frank Ward, a government employee who fought his way up from poverty and never lost his empathy for the underdog. Ward's *Dynamic Sociology* (1883) singled out one aspect of evolution that both Darwin and Spencer had neglected: the human brain. True, as Sumner claimed, people, like animals, compete. But, as Ward explained, people also collaborate. Unlike animals, people can plan for a distant future; they have minds capable of shaping and directing social change. Far from being the helpless object of irresistible evolutionary forces, Ward argued, humanity could actively control social evolution through long-range planning.

Ward's reform Darwinism held that *cooperation*, not *competition*, would better promote social progress. Government, in Ward's view, should pursue two main goals: alleviating poverty, which impeded the development of the mind, and promoting the education of the masses. Intellect, informed by science, could foster social improvement. Reform Darwinism would prove to be one of the pillars of the "progressive" movement during the late nineteenth century and after.

REALISM IN LITERATURE AND ART

Before the Civil War, Romanticism had dominated American literature and painting. Romantics such as the transcendentalists in New England believed that fundamental truths rested in the unseen world of ideas and spirit. The most prominent writers and artists were more concerned with romantic or biblical themes than with depicting everyday life.

During the second half of the nineteenth century, however, a new generation calling themselves "realists" began to challenge the Romantic tradition. A writer in *Putnam's Monthly* noted in 1854 a growing emphasis on "the real and the practical." This emphasis on "realism" matured into a full-fledged cultural force, as more and more writers and artists focused on depicting the actual aspects of urban-industrial America: scientific research and technology, factories and railroads, cities and immigrants, labor unions and social tensions.

For many Americans, the horrors of the Civil War had led to a less romanticized and more realistic view of life. An editor attending an art exhibition in 1865 sensed "the greater reality of feeling developed by the war. We have grown more sober, perhaps, and less patient of romantic idealism."

Another factor contributing to the rise of realism was the impact of modern science. "This is a world of reality," admitted a Romantic writer, "and romance breaks against the many hard facts." The "stupendous power of

Science," announced one editor, will rid American thought of "every old-time idea, every trace of old romance and art, poetry and romantic or sentimental feeling" and wash away the "ideal . . . and visionary."

Realism, as writer Fanny Bates stressed, appealed especially to people living in busy, swarming cities, people "whose lives are crowded with a variety of interests." The worship of money was the most common theme in realistic novels and short stories during the Gilded Age. In William Dean Howells's *The Rise of Silas Lapham* (1885), Bromfield Corey announces that money "is the romance, the poetry of our age." Lily Bart, the heroine of Edith Wharton's *The House of Mirth* (1905), declares that she "must have a great deal of money" to be happy.

City streets, sidewalks, and parks provided countless scenes of *real* life to depict on canvas and in works of fiction. Novelist Henry James said that the daily urban scene unleashed a "flood of the real" to study and portray. John Sloan, a New York City painter, chose his subjects by spying on people from his Manhattan studio. He confided in his diary that he was addicted to "*watching every bit* of human life" through his windows and along the sidewalks.

Stag at Sharkey's **(1909)** New York painter George Bellows witnessed such fierce boxing matches across the street from his studio, at the saloon of retired heavyweight boxer, "Sailor" Sharkey. Bellows is one of the most famous artists from the Ashcan School, which was committed to capturing the gritty reality of the urban scene.

Others shared Sloan's "spectatorial" sensibility. "My favorite pastime," writer Theodore Dreiser remembered, "was to walk the city streets and view the lives and activities of others." In his influential novel *Sister Carrie* (1900), Carrie Meeber uses her "gift of observation" to view strangers through the open windows of shops, offices, and factories, imagining what "they deal with, how they labored, to what end it all came."

The realists' emphasis on closely observing everyday life grew out of the scientific spirit. Just as scientists observed visible and verifiable facts and transformed them into knowledge, cultural realists studied the world and made it into art and literature. Like a gust of fresh air, they made Americans aware of the significance of their everyday surroundings, in all their beauty and ugliness.

Gilded Age Politics

The Gilded Age was an era of more political corruption than political innovation. In 1879, Woodrow Wilson, then a young college graduate, described the political system as having "no leaders, no principles."

The real movers and shakers of the Gilded Age were not the men in the White House or Congress but the owners of giant corporations. These "captains of industry" regularly used their wealth to "buy" elections and favors at all levels of government. Jay Gould, one of the most aggressive railroad tycoons, admitted that he elected "the [New York] legislature with my own money."

"Special interests," businesses that bought favors from government officials, dominated Gilded Age politics. By the end of the nineteenth century, however, new movements and parties were pushing to reform the excesses and injustices created by a political system that had grown corrupt in its efforts to support the "special interests" promoted by Big Business.

LOCAL POLITICS AND PARTY LOYALTIES Perhaps the most important feature of Gilded Age politics was its local focus. Most political activity occurred at the state and local levels. Unlike today, the federal government was an insignificant force in the daily lives of most citizens, in part because it was so small. In 1871, the entire federal civilian workforce totaled 51,000 (most of them postal workers), of whom only 6,000 actually worked in Washington, D.C. Not until the twentieth century did the importance of the federal government begin to surpass that of local and state governments.

Americans during the Gilded Age were intensely loyal to their political party, which they joined as much for the fellowship and networking connections as for its positions on issues. Unlike today, party members paid dues to join, and party leaders regularly demanded large campaign contributions from the captains of industry and finance. Collis Huntington, a California railroad tycoon, admitted that bribery in the form of campaign contributions was expected: "If you have to pay money to have the right thing done, then it is only just and fair to do it." Roscoe Conkling, a powerful Republican senator from New York, was equally candid: "Of course, we do rotten things in New York. . . . Politics is a rotten business." Democrat Horatio Seymour, a presidential candidate in 1868, explained that "our people want men in office who will not steal, but who will not interfere with those who do."

In cities crowded with new immigrant voters, politics was usually controlled by "rings"—small groups who shaped policy and managed the nomination and election of candidates. Each ring typically had a powerful "boss" who used his "machine"—a network of neighborhood activists and officials—to govern.

The party in power expected the government employees it appointed to become campaign workers and to do the bidding of **party bosses**. They helped

"COMING OUT" FOR HARRISON.

"'Coming Out' – For Harrison" This 1888 cartoon depicts efforts by employers to force the working class to vote for the Republican party ticket, including presidential nominee Benjamin Harrison.

settle local disputes, provided aid for the poor, and distributed jobs and con-tracts to loyal followers and corporate donors through the **patronage** system. The jobs given to party loyalists covered a wide range, from cabinet posts to courthouse clerk positions. The largest single source of political jobs was the postal service, which accounted for half of all federal civilian employees. Those who were awarded government jobs were expected to contribute a percentage of their salary to the political party.

The corruption associated with the patronage system eventually drew crit-icism from "civil service reformers," who pushed through legislation designed to limit such patronage and introduced a "merit system" for government employment based on ability and experience.

NATIONAL POLITICS Several factors gave national politics during the Gilded Age its distinctive texture. Most important was the close division between Republicans and Democrats in Congress. Because neither party was dominant after the revival of the Democratic party in 1876, they both avoided controversial issues or bold initiatives for fear of losing a close election. Yet, paradoxically, voter intensity at all levels peaked during the Gilded Age. Voter turnout was commonly about 70 to 80 percent. (By contrast, the turnout for the 2012 U.S. presidential election was 58 percent.)

During the Gilded Age, most voters cast their ballots for the same party year after year. Party loyalty was often an emotional choice. In the 1870s and 1880s, for example, people continued to fight the Civil War during political campaigns. Republican candidates regularly "waved the bloody shirt," accus-ing Democrats of having caused "secession and civil war," while Republicans took credit for abolishing slavery and saving the Union.

Democrats, especially in the South, where they monopolized political power after 1877, responded by reminding voters that they stood for limited government, states' rights, and white supremacy. Republicans tended to favor high tariffs on imports, but many Democrats also supported tariffs if they benefited the dominant businesses in their districts or states. Third political parties, such as the Greenbackers, Populists, and Prohibitionists, appealed to specific interests and issues, such as currency inflation, railroad regulations, or legislation to restrict alcohol consumption.

Party loyalties reflected religious, ethnic, and geographic divisions. After the Civil War, the Republican party remained strongest in New England, upstate New York, Pennsylvania, Ohio, and the Midwest. Republicans tended to be Protestants of English or Scandinavian descent. As the party of Abraham Lincoln (the "Great Emancipator") and Ulysses S. Grant, Republicans could also rely upon the votes of African Americans in the South (until their right to vote was taken away) and the support of a large bloc of Union veterans of the Civil War, who were organized into a powerful national interest group called the Grand Army of the Republic.

The Democrats were a more diverse coalition of conservative southern whites, northern Catholics of German or Irish Catholic backgrounds, and others repelled by the Republicans' claim to be the "party of morality." As one Chicago Democrat explained, "A Republican is a man who wants you t' go t' church every Sunday. A Democrat says if a man wants to have a glass of beer on Sunday he can have it."

During the 1880s, Protestant Republicans infuriated many immigrants and Catholics of Irish, Italian, or German background by promoting efforts to limit or prohibit the consumption of alcoholic beverages. Republicans considered saloons the central social evil around which all others revolved, and they associated these evils with the ethnic groups that frequented saloons. They also pushed for nativist policies to restrict immigration and the employment of foreigners.

Between 1869 and 1913, from the first term of Ulysses S. Grant through the election of William Howard Taft, Republicans monopolized the White House except for two nonconsecutive terms of New York Democrat Grover Cleveland. Otherwise, national politics was remarkably balanced. Between 1872 and 1896, *no* president won a majority of the popular vote. In each of those presidential elections, sixteen states invariably voted Republican and fourteen, including every southern state, voted Democratic, leaving six "swing" states to determine the outcome. Two of those states, New York and Ohio, decided the election of eight presidents from 1872 to 1908.

Hayes to Harrison

Both Republicans and Democrats had their share of officials willing to buy and sell government jobs or legislative votes. Yet as early as the 1870s, in response to the corruption uncovered in the Grant administration, each party developed factions promoting honesty in government. The struggle for "clean" government became one of the foremost issues of the Gilded Age.

Hayes and Civil Service Reform

President Rutherford B. Hayes brought to the White House in 1877 both a lingering controversy over the disputed election results (critics called him "His Fraudulency" or "His Accidency") and an uprightness that was in sharp contrast to the barely concealed graft of the Grant era. Hayes appointed a Democrat as postmaster general in an effort to clean up an office infamous for trading jobs for political favors.

The son of an Ohio farmer, Hayes was wounded four times in the Civil War. He went on to serve in Congress and as governor of Ohio. Honest and conservative, he was, said a Republican journalist, a "third-rate nonentity" whose only virtue was that he was "obnoxious to no one."

Hayes had been the compromise presidential nominee of two factions fighting for control of the Republican party, the so-called Stalwarts and Half-Breeds, led, respectively, by Senators Roscoe Conkling of New York and James G. Blaine of Maine. The Stalwarts had been "stalwart" in their support of President Grant during the furor over the misdeeds of his cabinet members. Further, they had mastered the patronage system (spoils system) of distributing political jobs to party loyalists. The Half-Breeds supposedly were only half loyal to Grant and half committed to reform of the spoils system. But in the end, the two factions existed primarily to advance the careers of Conkling and Blaine, who detested each other.

To his credit, President Hayes tried to stay above the petty bickering. He joined the growing public outrage over corruption, admitting that his party "must mend its ways" by focusing on Republican principles rather than fighting over the spoils of office. "He serves his party best who serves his country best," Hayes declared. It was time "for **civil service** [government jobs] **reform**." He appointed a committee to consider a "merit system" for hiring government employees, as used in some European countries. In a dramatic gesture, Hayes also fired Chester A. Arthur, a Stalwart Republican who ran the New York Customs House, because Arthur had abused the patronage system in ways, according to Hayes, that promoted "ignorance, inefficiency, and corruption."

Hayes's commitment to cleaning up politics enraged Republican leaders. In 1879, Ohio congressman James Garfield warned Hayes that "if he wishes to hold any influence" with fellow Republicans, he "must abandon some of his notions of Civil Service reform." For his part, Hayes confessed that he had little hope of success because he was "opposed by . . . the most powerful men in my party."

On economic issues, Hayes held to a conservative line that would guide his successors—from both parties—for the rest of the century. His answer to demands for expansion of the nation's money supply (which would become one of the leading issues of the late nineteenth century) was a resounding no: he vetoed the Bland-Allison Act (1878), a bipartisan effort to increase the supply of silver coins. (More money in circulation was generally believed to raise farm prices and help those trying to pay off debts.) Hayes believed only in "hard money"—gold coins.

When the Democrat-controlled Congress convinced many Republicans to help overturn Hayes's veto, the president confided in his diary that he had become a president without a party. In 1879, with a year still left in his term, Hayes was ready to leave the White House. "I am now in my last year of the Presidency," he wrote a friend, "and look forward to its close as a schoolboy longs for the coming vacation."

GARFIELD, ARTHUR, AND THE PENDLETON ACT

With Hayes choosing not to pursue a second term, the Republican presidential nomination in 1880 was up for grabs. Former president Grant wanted the nomination but was unwilling to campaign for it. In the end, the Stalwarts and Half-Breeds were forced to select a compromise candidate, Congressman James A. Garfield.

Garfield had been a minister, a lawyer, and a college president before serving in the Civil War as a Union army general. In an effort to please the Stalwarts and also win the crucial swing state of New York, the Republicans named Chester A. Arthur, whom Hayes had fired as head of the New York Customs House, as their candidate for vice president.

The Democrats, even more divided than the Republicans, selected Winfield Scott Hancock, a retired Union general who had distinguished himself at the Battle of Gettysburg but had done little since. In large part, Hancock was chosen to help deflect the Republicans' "bloody-shirt" attacks on Democrats as the party of the Confederacy. Yet Hancock undermined that effort by supporting southern efforts to strip blacks of voting rights. In an election marked by widespread bribery, Garfield eked out a popular-vote plurality of only 39,000, or 48.5 percent. He won a more comfortable margin of 214 to 155 in the electoral college. Republicans took control of Congress as well.

Embedded in the voting, however, was a worrisome pattern: the Democrats won all the southern states, and the Republicans won all the northern states. Politically, the Civil War was not over. Moreover, in future presidential elections, if the Republicans lost New York State, they would lose the White House. Securing the nation's most-populous state thus became central to Republican strategy.

A PRESIDENCY CUT SHORT In his inaugural address, President Garfield gave an impassioned defense of civil rights, arguing that the "elevation of the negro race from slavery to the full rights of citizenship is the most important political change we have known since the adoption of the Constitution of 1787." The end of slavery, he said, "has added immensely to the moral and industrial forces of our people. It has liberated the master as well as the slave from a relation which wronged and enfeebled both." But he also confirmed that the Republicans had ended efforts to reconstruct the former Confederacy. Southern blacks were on their own now; they had been "surrendered to their own guardianship."

Garfield would have no time to prove himself as president, however. On July 2, 1881, after only four months in office, he was walking through the Washington, D.C., railroad station, headed to a vacation in Vermont, when he was shot in the arm and back by Charles Guiteau, a former Republican who had been turned down for a federal job. As a policeman wrestled the assassin to the ground, Guiteau shouted: "Yes! I have killed Garfield! [Chester] Arthur is President of the United States. I am a Stalwart!"—a declaration that would eventually destroy the Stalwart wing of the Republican party.

On September 19, after seventy-nine days, Garfield died of complications resulting from inept medical care. During a sensational ten-week trial, Guiteau said that God had ordered him to kill the president. The jury refused to believe that he was insane and pronounced him guilty of murder. On June 30, 1882, Guiteau was hanged; an autopsy revealed that his brain was diseased.

THE CIVIL SERVICE COMMISSION People saw little potential in the new president, Chester A. Arthur, who had been Roscoe Conkling's trusted lieutenant. Yet Arthur surprised most political observers by distancing himself from Conkling and the Stalwarts and becoming a civil service reformer. Throughout his presidency, he kept a promise not to remove any federal office holder purely for political reasons. He also made cabinet appointments based on merit rather than partisanship. One of Arthur's former New York associates, a Stalwart, grumbled that "he has done less for us than Garfield, or even Hayes."

Very little is known about President Arthur. Just before he died, he had all of his official papers and correspondence burned. Why he did so remains a mystery. Unlike most presidents, there is no library or museum dedicated to Arthur's career. He wanted obscurity, and he got it.

In 1883, momentum against the spoils system generated by Garfield's assassination enabled George H. Pendleton, a Democratic senator from Ohio, to convince Congress to establish a Civil Service Commission, the first federal regulatory agency. Because of the Pendleton Civil Service Reform Act, at least 15 percent of federal jobs would now be filled on the basis of competitive tests (the "merit system") rather than political favoritism. In addition, federal employees running for office were prohibited from receiving political contributions from other government workers.

The Pendleton Act was a limited first step in cleaning up the patronage process. It was sorely needed, in part because the federal government was expanding rapidly. By 1901, there would be 256,000 federal employees, five times the number in 1871. A growing number of these federal workers were women.

The Campaign of 1884

Chester Arthur's efforts to clean up the spoils system might have attracted voters, but they did not please Republican leaders. So in 1884 the Republicans dumped the ailing Arthur (he had contracted a kidney disease) and chose as their nominee James Gillespie Blaine of

Senator James Gillespie Blaine of Maine The Republican presidential candidate in 1884.

Maine, the handsome, colorful secretary of state, former senator, and longtime leader of the Half-Breeds.

Blaine inspired the party faithful with his electrifying speeches, and he knew how to wheel and deal in the backrooms. One critic charged that Blaine "wallowed in spoils like a rhinoceros in an African pool." Newspapers soon uncovered evidence of his corruption in the so-called Mulligan letters, which revealed that, as Speaker of the House, Blaine had secretly sold his votes on measures favorable to a railroad corporation. Nobody proved that he had committed any crimes, but the circumstantial evidence was powerful: his senatorial salary alone could not have built either his mansion in Washington, D.C., or his palatial home in Augusta, Maine.

During the presidential campaign, more embarrassing letters surfaced linking Blaine to shady deal-making. In one of them, Blaine told the recipient: "Burn this letter!" For the reform element of the Republican party, this was too much, and many independent-minded Republicans refused to endorse Blaine's candidacy. "We are Republicans but we are not slaves," said one of the independents. He insisted that the party of Lincoln must recommit itself to "retrenchment, purity and reform." Party regulars scorned such critics as "goo-goos"—the "good-government" crowd who were outraged by the corrupting influence of money in politics. The editor of a New York newspaper jokingly called the anti-Blaine Republicans **Mugwumps**, after an Algonquian Indian word meaning "big chief."

Grover Cleveland As president, Cleveland made the issue of tariff reform central to the politics of the late 1880s.

The Mugwumps, a self-appointed group of reformers dedicated to promoting honest government, saw the election as a "moral rather than political" contest. Centered in the large cities and major universities of the northeast, the Mugwumps were mostly professors, editors, and writers who included in their number the most famous American of the time, writer and humorist Mark Twain. Like the Liberal Republicans before them, the Mugwumps sought to reform the patronage system by declaring that *all* federal jobs would be filled solely on the basis of merit. Their break with the Republican party over patronage testified to the depth of their convictions.

The rise of the Mugwumps, as well as growing national concerns about political corruption, prompted the Democrats to nominate New Yorker Grover Cleveland. Cleveland had first attracted national attention in 1881, when he was elected mayor of Buffalo on an anti-corruption platform. He was elected governor of New York in 1882, and he continued to build a reform record by fighting New York City's corrupt Tammany Hall ring. As mayor and as governor, he repeatedly vetoed bills that he felt served private interests at the expense of the public good. He supported civil service reform, opposed expanding the money supply, and preferred free trade to high tariffs.

Although Cleveland was known for his honesty and integrity, he was hurt by two personal issues: the discovery that he had paid for a substitute to take his place in the Union army during the Civil War, and a juicy sex scandal that erupted when a Buffalo newspaper revealed that Cleveland, a bachelor, had befriended an attractive widow named Maria Halpin, who named him the father of her baby born in 1874. Cleveland had discreetly provided financial support for the child.

The escapades of Blaine and Cleveland inspired some of the most colorful battle cries in political history: "Blaine, Blaine, James G. Blaine, the continental liar from the state of Maine," Democrats chanted. Republicans countered with "Ma, ma, where's my pa?" Democrats also paraded through the streets chanting, "Burn this letter!"

Near the end of the nasty campaign, Blaine and his supporters committed two fateful blunders in the crucial state of New York. The first occurred at New York City's fashionable Delmonico's restaurant, where Blaine went to a private dinner with 200 of the nation's wealthiest business leaders to ask them to help finance his campaign. Accounts of the unseemly event appeared in the newspapers for days afterward. One headline blared: "Blaine Hobnobbing with the Mighty Money Kings!" The article explained that the banquet was intended to collect contributions for a "Republican corruption fund."

Blaine's second blunder occurred when a Protestant minister visiting Republican headquarters in New York referred to the Democrats as the party of "rum, Romanism, and rebellion [the Confederacy]." Blaine, who was present, let pass the implied insult to Catholics—a fatal oversight, since he had cultivated Irish American support with his anti-English talk and repeated references to his mother being a Catholic. Democrats claimed that Blaine was, at heart, anti-Irish and anti-Catholic.

The two incidents may have tipped the 1884 presidential election. The electoral vote was 219 to 182 in Cleveland's favor, but the popular vote ran far closer: Cleveland's plurality was fewer than 30,000 votes out of 10 million cast. Cleveland won New York by only 1,149 votes out of 1,167,169 cast. At long last, a Democrat was back in the White House.

CLEVELAND'S REFORM EFFORTS During his first few months in office, President Cleveland struggled to keep Democratic leaders from reviving the self-serving patronage system. Democratic newspapers heaped scorn on him for refusing to award federal jobs to his supporters. One accused Cleveland of "ingratitude" toward those who had "delivered the vote." Despite the president's best efforts, about two-thirds of the 120,000 federal jobs went to Democrats as patronage during his administration.

Cleveland was an old-style Democrat who believed in minimal government activity. During his first term, he vetoed over 400 acts of Congress, more than twice as many as all previous presidents combined. In 1887, he illustrated his "do as little as possible" philosophy by vetoing a congressional effort to provide desperate Texas farmers with seeds in the aftermath of a terrible drought. "Though the people support the government, the government should not support the people," Cleveland asserted.

RAILROAD REGULATION For all of his commitment to limited government intervention, President Cleveland urged Congress to adopt an important new policy: federal regulation of the rates charged by interstate railroads (those whose tracks crossed state lines) to ship goods, crops, or livestock. He believed that railroads were charging unfairly high freight rates. States had adopted laws regulating railroads since the late 1860s, but in 1886 the Supreme Court declared in *Wabash, St. Louis, and Pacific Railroad Company v. Illinois* that no state could regulate the rates charged by railroads engaged in interstate traffic. Because most railroads crossed state lines, Cleveland urged Congress to close the loophole.

Congress followed through, and in 1887, Cleveland signed an act creating the **Interstate Commerce Commission (ICC)**, the first federal regulatory agency. The law empowered the ICC's five members to ensure that railroad freight rates were "reasonable and just." But one senator called the new agency "a delusion and a sham" because its members tended to be former railroad executives. Moreover, the commission's actual powers proved to be weak when challenged in the courts by railroads. Over time, the ICC came to be ignored, and the railroads continued to charge high rates while making secret pricing deals with large shippers.

TARIFF REFORM AND THE ELECTION OF 1888 President Cleveland's most dramatic challenge to Big Business focused on **tariff reform**. During the late nineteenth century, the government's high-tariff policies, shaped largely by the Republican party, had favored American manufacturers by effectively shutting out foreign imports, thereby enabling U.S. corporations to dominate the marketplace and charge higher prices for their products. Tariffs on some 4,000 imported items had also brought in more revenue from foreign manufacturers than the federal government spent. As a result, the tariff revenues were producing an annual government surplus, which proved to Cleveland and the Democrats that the rates were too high.

In 1887, Cleveland argued that Congress should reduce both the tariff rates ("the vicious, inequitable and illogical source of unnecessary taxation . . . [and] a burden upon the poor") and the number of imported goods subject to tariffs to enable European companies to compete in the American marketplace. His outspoken stance set the stage for his reelection campaign in 1888.

To oppose Cleveland, the Republicans, now calling themselves the GOP (Grand Old Party) to emphasize their longevity, turned to the obscure Benjamin Harrison, a Civil War veteran whose greatest attributes were his availability and the fact that he was from Indiana, a pivotal state in presidential elections. The grandson of President William Henry Harrison, he had a modest political record; he had lost a race for governor and had served one term in the U.S. Senate (1881–1887). In the eyes of the party leadership, however, Harrison had the most important attribute: he would do as he was told.

The Republicans accepted Cleveland's challenge to make tariffs the chief issue in the campaign. They enjoyed a huge advantage in campaign funding, as business executives contributed generously to their campaign.

Still, the outcome was incredibly close. Cleveland won the popular vote by the thinnest of margins—5,540,329 to 5,439,853—but Harrison carried crucial New York State and the electoral college by 233 to 168. "Providence," said the new president, "has given us the victory." Matthew Quay, the powerful Republican boss of Pennsylvania who managed Harrison's campaign, knew better. Harrison, he muttered, "ought to know that Providence hadn't a damned thing to do with it! [A] number of men were compelled to approach the penitentiary to make him President."

Quay's decision to distribute campaign money in key states and to promise federal jobs to loyalists also helped Republicans gain control of the House and the Senate. As the Republicans prepared for the inauguration, *Frank Leslie's Illustrated Newspaper*, co-edited by Harrison's son Russell, made clear the new president's priorities: "This is to be a businessman's Administration," and "businessmen will be thoroughly well content with it."

REPUBLICAN ACTIVISM UNDER HARRISON

The Republicans took advantage of their control of the presidency and both houses of Congress to pass a cluster of significant legislation in 1890: the Sherman Anti-Trust Act, the Sherman Silver Purchase Act, the McKinley Tariff Act, and the admission of Idaho and Wyoming as new states, which followed the admission of North and South Dakota, Montana, and Washington in 1889.

The Sherman Anti-Trust Act, named for Ohio senator John Sherman, prohibited powerful corporations from "conspiring" to establish monopolies or "restrain trade" in their industries. It made the United States the first nation in the world to outlaw monopolistic business practices.

"King of the World" Reformers targeted the growing power of monopolies, such as that of John D. Rockefeller's Standard Oil.

Though badly needed, the Sherman Anti-Trust Act was a toothless hoax intended to make it appear that Congress was clamping down on the gigantic corporations dominating more and more industries. That it passed without any opposition suggested that the bill was mostly for show. Critics called it the "Swiss Cheese Act" because it had so many holes in its language. As the *New York Times* recognized in 1890, the "so-called Anti-Trust law" was passed "to deceive the people" and prepare the way for a much higher tariff bill. Senator Sherman, the article added, supported this "humbug" of a law so that party spokesmen "might say 'Behold! We have attacked the trusts. The Republican Party is the enemy of all such rings.'"

The Sherman Anti-Trust Act was rarely enforced, in large part because of its vague definitions of "trusts" and "monopolies." From 1890 to 1901, only eighteen lawsuits were instituted, four of which were filed against labor unions rather than corporations, claiming that striking workers were "conspiring" to "restrain trade."

The Sherman Silver Purchase Act (1890), which required the Treasury to purchase 4.5 million ounces of silver each month to convert into dollar coins, was an effort by the Republicans to please the new western states with numerous silver mines. The bill's sponsor, Senator John Sherman, admitted that he proposed the bill only to defuse cries for the "unlimited coinage" of silver. "I voted for it," he confessed, "but the day it became law I was ready to repeal it." The Sherman act helped set the stage for the currency issue to eclipse all others during the financial panic that would sweep the country in 1893.

As for tariff policy, Republicans viewed their victory as a mandate to reward the support of large corporations by raising tariff rates even higher. Piloted through Congress by Ohio representative William McKinley, the McKinley Tariff Act of 1890 raised duties (taxes) on imported manufactured goods to their highest level ever and added many agricultural products to the tariff list to appease farmers. Its passage encouraged many businesses to raise prices, because their European competitors were now effectively shut out of the U.S. market.

The Republican efforts to reward Big Business backfired, however. In the November 1890 congressional elections, Democrats won big, regaining control of the House by a three to one margin. William McKinley, who had sponsored the tariff bill, lost his seat (although the following year he would be elected Ohio's governor). In the Senate, the Republican majority was reduced to four. Republicans were "astounded and dazed" by the shellacking in the election. Even more worrisome was the emergence of the Populists, a new political party representing disgruntled farmers and wage laborers. Revolution was in the air.

Farmers and the "Money Problem"

More than tariffs, trusts, and efforts to clean up political corruption, national politics during the Gilded Age was preoccupied with monetary issues. The nation's money supply had not grown along with the expanding economy. From 1865 to 1890, the amount of money in circulation (both coins and paper currency) actually *decreased* about 10 percent.

Such currency deflation raised the cost of borrowing money as the shrinking money supply enabled lenders to hike interest rates on loans. Creditors—bankers and others who loaned money—supported a "sound money" policy limiting the currency supply as a means of increasing their profits. By contrast, farmers, ranchers, miners, and others who had to borrow money to make ends meet claimed that the "sound money" policy lowered prices for their crops and herds and drove them deeper into debt. Farmers in the Midwest, Great Plains, and South, and miners in the West, demanded more paper money and the increased coinage of silver, which would inflate the currency supply, raise commodity prices, and provide them with more income.

All six western states admitted to the Union in 1889 and 1890 had substantial silver mines, and their new congressional delegations—largely Republican—wanted the federal government to buy more silver for minting as coins.

AGRICULTURAL UNREST The 1890 congressional elections revealed a deep-seated unrest in the farming communities of the South, on the plains of Kansas and Nebraska, and in the mining towns of the Rocky Mountain region. Over the previous twenty years, corn prices had fallen by a third, wheat by more than half, cotton by two-thirds. The drastic decline in prices was caused by overproduction and growing international competition in world food markets. The vast new lands brought under cultivation in the plains as a result of the extension of rail lines and the use of new farm machinery poured an ever-increasing supply of grains into world markets, driving prices down.

Meanwhile, farmers in the South and West had become increasingly indebted to local banks or merchants who loaned them money at high interest rates to buy seed, fertilizer, tools, and other supplies. As prices for their crops dropped, however, so did the income the farmers received, thus preventing them from paying their debts on time.

In response, most farmers had no choice but to grow even more wheat, cotton, or corn, but the increased supply pushed down prices and incomes even further. High tariffs on imported goods also hurt farmers because they allowed U.S. companies to raise the prices of manufactured goods needed by farm families.

Besides bankers, merchants, and high tariffs, struggling farmers blamed the railroads, warehouse owners, and food processors—the so-called "middlemen"—who helped get their crops and livestock to market. Farmers especially resented that railroads, most of which had a monopoly over the shipping of grains and animals, charged such high rates to ship their agricultural products.

At the same time that farm income was dropping, successive years of parched summers and bitterly cold winters had destroyed harvests in many states. "This season is without parallel in this part of the country," reported the editor of a Nebraska agricultural journal in 1891. "The hot winds burned up the entire crop, leaving thousands of families wholly destitute" and vulnerable to the "money loaners and sharks" charging criminal rates of interest. In a slap at the cutthroat capitalism justified by the heartless logic of social Darwinism, the editor dismissed the popular slogan "survival of the fittest" as a "satanic creed" that means "slavery to millions."

In drought-devastated Kansas in 1890, Populists won five congressional seats from Republicans. In early 1891, the newly elected Populists and Democrats took control of Congress just as an acute economic crisis appeared on the horizon: farmers' debts were mounting as crop prices continued to fall.

THE GRANGER MOVEMENT   When the Department of Agriculture sent Oliver H. Kelley on a tour of the South in 1866, he was struck by the social isolation of people living on small farms. To address the problem, Kelley helped found the National Grange of the Patrons of Husbandry, better known as the Grange (an old word for places where crops were stored).

The Grange grew quickly, reaching a membership of 858,000 men and women by 1875. It started out offering social events and educational programs for farmers and their families, but as it grew, it began to promote "cooperatives" where farmers could join together to store and sell their crops to avoid the high fees charged by brokers and other middlemen.

In five Midwest states, Grange chapters persuaded legislatures to pass "Granger laws" to regulate the prices charged by railroads and grain warehouses (called "elevators"). Railroad and warehouse owners challenged the laws, but in *Munn v. Illinois* (1877), the Supreme Court ruled that states had the right to regulate property that operated in the public interest. Nine years later, however, the Court threw out the *Munn* ruling, finding in *Wabash v. Illinois* that only Congress could regulate industries involved in interstate commerce.

FARMERS' ALLIANCES   The Granger movement failed to address the foremost concerns of struggling farmers: declining crop prices and the inadequate amount of money in circulation. As a result, people shifted their alle-

"I Feed You All!" (1875) The farmer is the cornerstone of American society, according to this Granger-inspired poster. Without the food he produces, no man in any occupation can do his job—including the railroad magnate (left) and warehouse owners who try to exploit him.

giance to a new organization called the Farmers' Alliance. Like the Grange, the Farmers' Alliances organized social and recreational activities for small farmers and their families while also emphasizing political action and economic cooperation to address the hardships caused by chronic indebtedness, declining crop prices, and droughts.

Emerging first in Texas, the Alliance movement swept across the South, Kansas, Nebraska, and the Dakotas. In 1886, a white minister in Texas responded to the appeals of African American farmers by organizing the Colored Farmers' National Alliance. By 1890, the white Alliance movement had about 1.5 million members, and the Colored Farmers' National Alliance claimed more than 1 million members. Most white Alliance members refused to integrate their efforts with blacks, not only because of racism but also because most black farmers were tenants and sharecroppers rather than landowners.

In the states west of the Mississippi River, political activism intensified after record blizzards in 1887, which killed most of the cattle and hogs across the northern plains, and a prolonged drought two years later that destroyed millions of acres of corn, wheat, and oats. Distressed farmers lashed out against what they considered to be a powerful conspiracy of eastern financial and industrial interests, which they variously called "monopolies," "the money power," or "Wall Street." As William Jennings Bryan, a Democratic congressman from Nebraska, explained: "We simply say to the East: take your hands out of our pockets and keep them out."

The Alliances called for the federal government to take ownership of the railroads and create an income tax on wealthy Americans. They also organized economic "cooperatives." In 1887, Charles W. Macune, the Southern Alliance president, urged Texas farmers to create their own Alliance Exchange to free themselves from dependence on commercial warehouses, grain elevators, food processors, and banks. Members of the Alliance Exchange would act collectively, pooling their resources to borrow money from banks and purchase their goods and supplies from a new corporation created by the Alliance in Dallas. The exchange would also build warehouses to store and market members' crops. With these crops as collateral, members would receive cash loans to buy household goods and agricultural supplies. Once the farmers sold their crops, they would pay back the loans provided by the Alliance warehouse.

This *cooperative* scheme collapsed when Texas banks refused to accept paper money. Undaunted, Alliance members then focused on what Macune called a "subtreasury plan," whereby farmers would store their crops in *government*-run warehouses and obtain cash loans for up to 80 percent of the crops' value. This would free them from their traditional dependence on banks that charged high interest rates. Besides providing immediate credit, the subtreasury plan would allow farmers the option of storing a crop in hopes of getting a better price later. The plan would also promote inflation of the money supply because the loans to farmers would be made in new paper money. Monetary inflation was popular with farmers because it allowed them to repay their debts with cheaper money.

Despite the strong support from farmers, however, Congress nixed the subtreasury plan in 1890. Its defeat, as well as setbacks to other Alliance proposals, convinced many farm leaders that they needed more political power to secure the reforms necessary to save the agricultural sector: railroad regulation, currency inflation, state departments of agriculture, anti-trust laws, and more accessible farm-based credit (loans).

NEW THIRD PARTIES The Alliances called for third-party political action to address their concerns. In 1890, farm activists in Colorado joined with miners and railroad workers to form the Independent party, and Nebraska farmers formed the People's Independent party. Leonidas Polk, a former Confederate general who was the head of the North Carolina Alliance, traveled to Kansas and was so impressed by the size of the open-air farm rallies that he declared that farmers across the nation "have risen up and inaugurated a movement such as the world has never seen."

In the South, the Alliance movement forced Democrats to nominate candidates who supported its farm program and succeeded in electing four of them as governors, forty-four as congressmen, and several as U.S. senators, as well as seven pro-Alliance state legislatures. Among the most respected

Mary Elizabeth Lease A charismatic leader in the farm protest movement.

of the southern Alliance leaders was Thomas E. Watson, a lawyer from Georgia. The son of prosperous slaveholders who had lost everything after the Civil War, Watson took the lead in urging black and white tenant farmers to join forces. "You are [racially] kept apart," he told blacks and whites, "that you may be separately fleeced of your earnings." He insisted on cooperation by black and white farmers to resist the power of the wealthy political elite in the South.

In Kansas, Mary Elizabeth Lease emerged as a fiery speaker for the farm protest movement. Born in Pennsylvania to Irish immigrants, Lease migrated to Kansas, taught school, raised a family, and failed at farming in the mid-1880s. She then studied law and became one of the state's first female attorneys.

Like so many Alliance supporters, Lease viewed Eastern financiers as the enemy. "Wall Street owns the country. The great common people of this country are slaves," she shouted, "and monopoly is the master." She declared that the Alliances wanted to abolish "loan-shark" banks and replace them with subtreasury warehouses that would make loans to farmers backed up by their stored crops. The people, she warned, were rising up: "let the bloodhounds of money who have dogged us thus far beware."

THE ELECTION OF 1892 In 1892, Alliance leaders organized a convention in Omaha, Nebraska, at which they formed the **People's party (Populists)**. The delegates approved a platform that called for unlimited coinage of silver, a "progressive" income tax whose rates would rise with income levels, and federal ownership of the railroads. They also endorsed the eight-hour workday and new laws restricting immigration, for fear that foreigners were taking Americans' jobs.

The Populist party's platform turned out to be more exciting than its presidential candidate: Iowa's James B. Weaver, a former Union army officer who had headed the Greenback party ticket twelve years earlier. The major parties renominated the same candidates who had run in 1888: Democrat Grover Cleveland and Republican president Benjamin Harrison. Each major candidate received more than 5 million votes, but Cleveland won a majority of the electoral college. Weaver received more than 1 million votes and carried Colorado, Kansas, Nevada, and Idaho. Alabama was the banner Populist state of the South, with 37 percent of its vote going to Weaver.

THE DEPRESSION OF 1893 AND THE "FREE SILVER" CRUSADE

While farmers were funneling their discontent into politics, a fundamental weakness in the economy was about to cause a major collapse and a social rebellion. Just ten days before Grover Cleveland was inaugurated in the winter of 1893, the Philadelphia and Reading Railroad declared bankruptcy, setting off a national financial crisis, now called the **Panic of 1893**. It grew into the worst depression the nation had ever experienced.

Other overextended railroads collapsed, taking many banks with them. European investors withdrew their funds from America. A quarter of unskilled urban workers lost their jobs, many others had their wages cut, and by the fall of 1893, more than 600 banks had closed and 15,000 businesses had failed. Farm foreclosures soared in the South and West, and by 1900, a third of all American farmers rented their land rather than owned it.

By 1894, the nation's economy had reached bottom. But the depression lasted another four years, with unemployment hovering at 20 percent. In New York City, the rate was close to 35 percent.

President Cleveland's response was recklessly conservative: he convinced Congress to return the nation's money supply to a gold standard by repealing the Sherman Silver Purchase Act of 1890, a move that made the depression worse. The weak economy needed *more* money in circulation, not *less*. Investors rushed to exchange their silver dollars for gold, further constricting the money supply.

Hard times triggered a wave of labor unrest. In 1894, some 750,000 workers went on strike. Railroad construction workers, laid off in the West, began tramping east and talked of marching on Washington, D.C.

One protest group, called Coxey's Army, was led by "General" Jacob S. Coxey, a wealthy Ohio quarry owner turned Populist who demanded that the federal government provide the unemployed with meaningful work. Coxey, his wife, and their son, Legal Tender Coxey, rode in a carriage ahead of some 400 protesters who marched hundreds of miles to Washington, D.C., where police arrested Coxey for walking on the grass. Although his ragtag army dispersed peacefully, the march, as well as the growing strength of Populism, struck fear into the hearts of many conservatives.

Republicans portrayed Populists as "tramps" and "hayseed socialists" whose election would endanger the capitalist system. The Populists responded by charging that Americans were divided into "tramps and millionaires."

In this climate of class warfare and social anxiety, the 1894 congressional elections devastated President Cleveland and the Democrats, who were blamed for the economic crisis. The Republicans gained 118 seats in the House, the largest increase ever. Only in the solid Democratic South did the party retain its advantage. The Populists emerged with six senators and seven representatives, and they expected the festering discontent in rural areas to carry them to national power in 1896. Their hopes would be dashed, however.

SILVERITES VERSUS GOLDBUGS Cleveland's decision to repeal the Sherman Silver Purchase Act created an irreparable division in his party. One pro-silver Democrat labeled the president a traitor. Politicians from western states with large silver mines increased their demands for the "unlimited" coinage of silver, presenting a strategic dilemma for Populists: should the party promote the long list of reforms it had originally advocated, or should it try to ride the silver issue into power?

Although flooding the economy with silver currency would probably not have provided the benefits its advocates claimed, the "free silver" crusade had taken on powerful symbolic overtones. Over the protests of more-radical members, Populist leaders decided to hold their 1896 nominating convention *after* the two major-party conventions, confident that the Republicans and Democrats would at best straddle the silver issue and enable the Populists to lure away pro-silver advocates from both.

The major parties, however, took opposite positions on the currency issue. The Republicans, as expected, nominated William McKinley, a former congressman and governor of Ohio, on a platform committed to gold coins as the only form of currency. A small but vocal group of "Silver Republicans" from western states, led by Senator Henry Teller of Colorado, were so upset that they stormed out of the convention. After the convention, a friend told McKinley that the **"money question"** would determine the election. He was right.

William Jennings Bryan His "cross of gold" speech at the 1896 Democratic Convention roused the delegates and secured him the party's presidential nomination.

The Democratic convention, held in Chicago, was one of the great turning points in political history. The pro-silver, largely rural delegates surprised the party leadership and the "Gold Democrats," or "goldbugs," by capturing control of the convention.

WILLIAM JENNINGS BRYAN Thirty-six-year-old William Jennings Bryan of Nebraska gave the final speech before the balloting began. A fiery evangelical moralist, Bryan was a two-term congressman who had lost a race for the Senate in 1894, when Democrats by the dozens were swept out of office. In the months before the convention, he had traveled throughout the South and West, speaking passionately for the unlimited coinage of silver, attacking Cleveland's "do-nothing" response to the depression, and endorsing both Democrats and Populists who embraced the cause of "free silver."

Bryan was a compelling speaker, a crusading preacher in the role of a Populist politician. In his carefully crafted and well-rehearsed speech, he claimed that two ideas about the role of government were competing for the American voter. The Republicans, he said, believed "that if you just legislate to make the well-to-do prosperous, that their prosperity will leak through on those below." The Democrats, by contrast, believed "that if you legislate to make the masses prosperous their prosperity will find its way up and through every class that rests upon it." For his part, Bryan spoke for the "producing masses of this nation" against the eastern "financial magnates" who had "enslaved" them by manipulating the money supply to ensure high interest rates.

As Bryan brought his electrifying twenty-minute speech to a climax, he fused Christian imagery with Populist anger:

> I come to speak to you in defense of a cause as holy as the cause of liberty—the cause of humanity. . . . We have petitioned, and our petitions have been scorned. . . . We have begged, and they have

mocked when our calamity came. We beg no longer; we entreat no more; we petition no more. We defy them!

Bryan then identified himself with Jesus Christ. Sweeping his fingers across his forehead, he shouted: "You shall not press down upon the brow of labor this crown of thorns. You shall not crucify mankind upon a cross of gold!"—at which point he extended his arms straight out from his sides, as if he were being crucified. His riveting performance worked better than even he could have imagined. As he strode triumphantly off the stage, the delegates erupted in wild applause.

The next day, Bryan won the presidential nomination on the fifth ballot, but in the process the Democratic party was fractured. Disappointed Democrats who had supported Grover Cleveland dismissed Bryan as a fanatic and a socialist. They were so alienated by his positions and his rhetoric that they walked out of the convention and nominated their own candidate, Senator John M. Palmer of Illinois. "Fellow Democrats," Palmer announced, "I will not consider it any great fault if you decide to cast your vote for William McKinley."

When the Populists gathered in St. Louis for their nominating convention two weeks later, they faced an impossible choice. They could name their own candidate and divide the pro-silver vote with the Democrats, or they could endorse Bryan and probably lose their identity. In the end, they backed Bryan but chose their own vice-presidential candidate, Thomas E. Watson, and invited the Democrats to drop their vice-presidential nominee. Bryan refused the offer.

Presidential campaign badges
On the left wings of the "goldbug" and "silverite" badges are McKinley (top) and Bryan (bottom), with their running mates on the right.

THE ELECTION OF 1896 The election of 1896 was one of the most dramatic in history, in part because of the striking contrast between the candidates and in part because the terrible depression made the stakes so high. Bryan was the first major candidate since Andrew Jackson to champion the poor, the discontented, and the oppressed. He excited struggling farmers, miners, and union members. And he was the first leader of a major party to call for the expansion of the federal government to help the working class.

No one loved campaigning more than Bryan. He traveled some 18,000 miles by train, visiting 26 states and 250 cities and towns, delivering impassioned speeches. His populist crusade was for whites only, however. Like so many otherwise progressive Democratic leaders, Bryan never challenged the practices of racial segregation and violence against blacks in the solidly Democratic South. And he alienated many working-class Catholics in northern states by supporting prohibition of alcoholic beverages.

McKinley, meanwhile, stayed at home and kept his mouth shut, letting other Republicans speak for him. He knew he could not compete with Bryan as a speaker, so he conducted a "front-porch campaign," welcoming supporters at his home in Canton, Ohio, and giving only prepared statements to the press. McKinley's brilliant campaign manager, Marcus "Mark" Hanna, shrewdly portrayed Bryan as a "Popocrat," a radical whose "communistic spirit" would ruin the capitalist system and stir up a class war. Hanna convinced the Republican party to declare that it was "unreservedly for sound money"—meaning gold coins.

By appealing to such fears, the Republicans raised vast sums of money from corporations and wealthy donors to finance an army of 1,400 speakers who traveled the country promoting McKinley. It was the most sophisticated—and expensive—presidential campaign in history to that point.

In the end, Bryan won the most votes of any candidate in history— 6.5 million—but McKinley won even more: 7.1 million. The better-organized and better-financed Republicans won the electoral college vote by 271 to 176.

Bryan carried most of the West and all of the South but found little support in the North and East. In the critical Midwest, from Minnesota and Iowa eastward to Ohio, he did not win a state. His evangelical Protestantism repelled many Roman Catholic voters, who were normally drawn to the Democrats. Farmers in the Northeast, moreover, were less attracted to radical reform than were farmers in the West and South. Workers in the cities found it easier to identify with McKinley's focus on reviving the industrial economy than with Bryan's farm-based, free-silver evangelism. Of the nation's twenty largest cities, Bryan carried only New Orleans.

Although Bryan lost, he launched the Democratic party's shift from pro-business conservatism to its eventual twentieth-century role as a party of liberal reform. The Populist party, however, virtually disintegrated. Having won a million votes in 1896, it collected only 50,000 in 1900. Conversely, McKinley's victory climaxed a generation-long struggle for political control of an industrialized urban America. The Republicans would be dominant for sixteen years.

THE ELECTION OF 1896

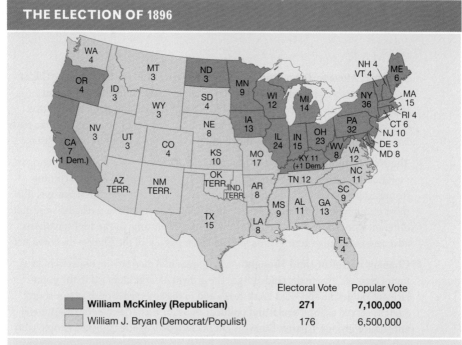

	Electoral Vote	Popular Vote
William McKinley (Republican)	271	7,100,000
William J. Bryan (Democrat/Populist)	176	6,500,000

- How did Bryan's "cross of gold" speech divide the Democratic party?
- How did McKinley's campaign strategy differ from Bryan's?
- Why was Bryan able to carry the West and the South but unable to win in cities and the Northeast?

By 1897, when McKinley was inaugurated, economic prosperity was returning. Part of the reason was inflation of the currency, which bore out the arguments of the Greenbackers and silverites that the nation's money supply had been inadequate during the Gilded Age. But inflation came, in one of history's many ironies, not from more greenbacks or silver dollars but from a flood of gold discovered in South Africa, northwest Canada, and Alaska. In 1900, Congress passed, and McKinley signed, a bill affirming that the nation's money supply would be based only on gold.

Even though the Populist movement faded after William Jennings Bryan's defeat, most of the ideas promoted by Bryan Democrats and Populists, dismissed as too radical in 1896, would be implemented over the next two decades by a more diverse coalition of Democrats and Republicans who would call themselves "progressives."

CHAPTER REVIEW

SUMMARY

- **America's Move to Town** America's cities grew in all directions during the *Gilded Age*. Electric elevators and steel-frame construction allowed architects to extend buildings upward, and mass transit enabled the middle class to retreat to suburbs. Crowded *tenements* bred disease and crime and created an opportunity for urban *party bosses* to accrue power, in part by distributing to the poor various forms of assistance.

- **The New Immigration** By 1900, an estimated 30 percent of Americans living in major cities were foreign-born, with the majority of "*new immigrants*" coming from eastern and southern Europe rather than western and northern Europe, like most immigrants of generations past. Their languages, culture, and religion were quite different from those of native-born Americans. Beginning in the 1880s, *nativists* advocated restrictive immigration laws and won passage of the *Chinese Exclusion Act*.

- **Changes in Culture and Thought** Many areas of American life underwent profound changes during the Gilded Age. The growth of large cities led to the popularity of vaudeville and Wild West shows and to the emergence of spectator sports. *Saloons* served as local social and political clubs for men, despite the disapproval of anti-liquor groups. Charles Darwin's *On the Origin of Species* shocked people who believed in a literal interpretation of the Bible's account of creation. Proponents of *social Darwinism* applied Darwin's theory of evolution to human society by equating economic and social success with "survival of the fittest" and arguing that government should not try to promote equality or protect the less successful. *Reform Darwinism* held that collective efforts and social reform could guide human progress.

- **Gilded Age Politics** Huge corporations corrupted politics and used their money to buy political influence. Political activity was still concentrated at the state and local levels. Americans were intensely loyal to the two major parties, whose local "bosses" and "machines" won votes by distributing *patronage* jobs and contracts to members, as well as charitable relief. Party loyalties reflected regional, ethnic, and religious differences. Although Republicans almost always held the presidency, the overall strength of the major parties was so balanced that neither wanted to risk alienating voters by taking bold stands.

- **Corruption and Reform** National politics during the Gilded Age focused on tariffs, the regulation of corporations, and *civil service reform*. The passage of the Pendleton Civil Service Reform Act in 1883 began the professionalization of federal workers. In the 1884 presidential election, Republicans favoring reform, the *Mugwumps*, helped elect Democrat Grover Cleveland. Cleveland signed the 1887 act creating the *Interstate Commerce Commission (ICC)* to regulate railroads. In 1890, under President Benjamin Harrison, Republicans passed the Sherman Anti-Trust Act, the Sherman Silver Purchase Act, and the McKinley Tariff Act. The first proved ineffective; the third, which raised tariff rates, proved unpopular and led to Cleveland's return to the White House in the 1892 election.

- **Inadequate Currency Supply and Unhappy Farmers** Over the course of the late nineteenth century, the *"money question"* had become a central political issue. The supply of money had not increased as the economy had grown. Many farmers believed that the coinage of silver, rather than a gold standard system, would result in inflation, which in turn would increase the value of their crops and reduce their debts. Farmers and others unsatisfied with the Republican and Democratic parties formed a series of political parties and alliances, one of which, the *People's party*, briefly operated as a national third party. In the election of 1896, the Democratic party nominated William Jennings Bryan, who adopted the coinage of silver as his crusade. He was opposed by Republican William McKinley, who supported the gold standard. McKinley, better organized and better financed, won the election in part by appealing to the growing number of city dwellers and industrial workers.

Chronology

1859	Charles Darwin's *On the Origin of Species* is published
1881	President James A. Garfield is assassinated
1882	Congress passes the Chinese Exclusion Act
1883	Congress passes the Pendleton Civil Service Reform Act
1886	Supreme Court issues *Wabash, St. Louis, and Pacific Railroad Company v. Illinois* decision
1887	Interstate Commerce Commission is created
1890	Congress passes the Sherman Anti-Trust Act, the Sherman Silver Purchase Act, and the McKinley Tariff

Key Terms

Gilded Age p. 699

tenements p. 701

"new immigrants" p. 705

nativists p. 706

Chinese Exclusion Act (1882) p. 707

saloons p. 709

social Darwinism p. 711

reform Darwinism p. 712

party bosses p. 715

patronage p. 716

civil service reform p. 718

Mugwumps p. 721

Interstate Commerce Commission (ICC) p. 724

tariff reform p. 724

People's party (or Populists) p. 731

Panic of 1893 p. 732

"money question" p. 733

 INQUIZITIVE

Go to InQuizitive to see what you've learned—and learn what you've missed—with personalized feedback along the way.

part six

MODERN AMERICA

The United States entered the twentieth century on a wave of unrelenting change, not all of it beneficial. The nation was on the threshold of modernity, which both excited and scared Americans. Old truths and beliefs clashed with unsettling scientific discoveries and social practices. People debated the legitimacy of Darwinism, the existence of God, the dangers of jazz, and the federal effort to prohibit the sale of alcoholic beverages. The advent of automobiles and airplanes helped shrink distance, and such communications innovations as radio and film helped strengthen the sense that America now had a *national* culture.

Spurred by its growing industrial power, the United States began to emerge from its isolationist shell. Previously, presidents and statesmen had sought to isolate America from the intrigues and conflicts of European powers. As early as 1780, John Adams had warned against U.S. involvement in Europe's affairs. "Our business with them, and theirs with us," he wrote, "is commerce, not politics, much less war."

With only a few exceptions, statesmen during the nineteenth century followed such advice. Noninvolvement in foreign wars and nonintervention in the internal affairs of foreign governments formed the pillars of U.S. foreign policy. During the 1890s, however, expanding commercial interests led Americans to broaden their concerns.

Imperialism was the focus of the major European powers, and a growing number of expansionists demanded that the United States join in the hunt for new territories and markets. Others believed the United States should support democratic ideals abroad. Such mixed motives helped spark the Spanish-American War (the War of 1898) and helped justify the resulting acquisition of colonies outside the continental United States. Entangling alliances with European powers soon followed.

The outbreak of the Great War in Europe in 1914 posed an even greater challenge to America's tradition of nonintervention. The prospect of a German victory over the French and British threatened the European balance of power, which had long ensured the security of the United States. By 1917, it appeared that Germany might emerge triumphant and begin to menace the Western Hemisphere. As German submarines began sinking American merchant ships, President Woodrow Wilson's patience finally ran out, and in April 1917, the United States entered the war.

Wilson's crusade to transform international affairs in accordance with his idealistic principles dislodged American foreign policy from its isolationist moorings. It also spawned a prolonged debate about the nation's role in world affairs—a debate that World War II would resolve (for a time) on the side of internationalism.

While the United States was becoming a formidable military power, it was also settling in as a great industrial nation. Cities and factories sprouted across the landscape, and an abundance of new jobs and affordable farmland attracted millions of foreign immigrants. They were not always welcomed, nor were they readily assimilated. Ethnic and racial strife grew, as did labor agitation.

In the midst of such social turmoil and unparalleled economic development, reformers made their first sustained attempt to adapt political and social institutions to the realities of the industrial age. The worst excesses and injustices of urban-industrial development—corporate monopolies, child labor, political corruption, hazardous working conditions, urban ghettos—were finally  addressed in a comprehensive way. During the Progressive Era (1890–1917), local, state, and federal governments sought to rein in the excesses of industrial capitalism and develop a more rational and efficient public policy.

A conservative Republican resurgence challenged the notion of the new regulatory state during the 1920s, and free enterprise and corporate capitalism witnessed a dramatic revival. But the stock market crash of 1929 helped propel the United States and the world into the worst economic downturn in history. The unprecedented severity of the Great Depression renewed demands for federal programs to protect the general welfare. The many New Deal initiatives and agencies instituted by President Franklin Delano Roosevelt and his Democratic administration created the framework for a welfare state that has since served as the basis for public policy.

The New Deal revived public confidence and put people back to work, but it took a second world war to end the Great Depression and restore full employment. The necessity of mobilizing the nation to support the Second World War also accelerated the growth of the federal government, and the unparalleled scope of the war helped catapult the United States into a leadership role in world politics. The use of atomic bombs ushered in a new era of nuclear diplomacy that held the fate of the world in the balance. For all the new creature comforts associated with modern life, Americans in 1945 found themselves living amid an array of new anxieties.

20 Seizing an American Empire

1865–1913

The Charge of the Rough Riders of San Juan Hill **(1898)** Before Frederic Remington pursued art professionally, he had unsuccessful forays into hunting, ranching, and even the saloon business in the West. His intimacy with the Western way of life, along with his technical skill and keen sense of observation, were not lost on Theodore Roosevelt, who invited Remington to travel with the Rough Riders during the Spanish-American War.

After the Civil War, a mood of isolationism—a desire to stay out of conflicts elsewhere in the world—dominated American public opinion. The nation's geographic advantages encouraged this isolationist attitude: oceans to the east and west, and militarily weak neighbors in the Western Hemisphere. That the powerful British navy protected the shipping lanes between the United States and the British Isles gave Americans a heightened sense of security.

By the end of the nineteenth century, however, a dramatic transformation occurred in America's outlook. People grew increasingly aware that the country was a world power with global responsibilities and imperial ambitions. As a Kentucky newspaper editor proclaimed in 1893, the United States was "the most advanced and powerful" nation in the world, an "imperial Republic" destined to shape the "future of the world." The *Washington Post* agreed, revealing that "the Taste of Empire is in the mouth of the people."

While still wanting to stay out of European conflicts, a growing number of Americans urged officials to acquire additional territory outside North America. The old idea of "manifest destiny"—that the United States had been blessed by God ("destined") to expand its territory westward across the continent—was enlarged to include extending American control into other regions of the Western Hemisphere, and even to the Pacific and Asia. Americans embraced a new form of expansionism that sought distant territories as "colonies," with no intention of admitting them to the nation as equal states. The new manifest destiny, in other words, became a justification for imperialism.

focus questions

1. What factors motivated America's new imperialism after the Civil War?

2. How and why did America expand its influence in the Pacific before the Spanish-American War (War of 1898)?

3. What were the causes of the Spanish-American War (War of 1898)? What were its major events?

4. What were the consequences of the Spanish-American War (War of 1898) for American foreign policy?

5. What reasons were behind Theodore Roosevelt's rapid rise to the presidency? What were the main elements of his foreign policies?

In *The Law of Civilization and Decay* (1895), historian Brooks Adams argued that for the United States to survive and prosper, it had to keep pushing beyond its borders. As historian Frederick Jackson Turner had proclaimed in 1893, the continental "frontier" was gone, so Americans needed new frontiers in which to exercise their "expansive character" and to spread their democratic ideals, capitalist investments, and Christian beliefs.

Manifest destiny also took on racial meaning; many Americans agreed with future president Theodore Roosevelt that the United States needed to expand "on behalf of the *destiny* of the [Anglo-Saxon] race." Roosevelt and others believed that the Americans and British were at the top of the racial pyramid, superior to all others in intellect, ambition, and creativity.

Political and business leaders argued that America's rapid industrial development required the nation to acquire foreign territories—by conquest if necessary—to gain easier access to vital raw materials such as rubber, tin, copper, palm oil, and various dyes. At the same time, manufacturers and commercial farmers had become increasingly dependent on international trade, which required an expanded force of warships to protect the merchant vessels. And a modern, steam-powered navy needed ocean bases in the Caribbean and Pacific, where its ships could replenish their supplies of coal and water.

For these and other reasons, America expanded its military presence and territorial possessions both within and beyond the Western Hemisphere. During just a few months in 1898, as the result of a one-sided war against Spain, the United States, born in a revolution against British colonial rule, would itself become an imperial ruler of colonies around the world.

Toward the New Imperialism

The United States was a latecomer to **imperialism**. By the 1880s, the British, French, Belgians, Italians, Dutch, Spanish, and Germans had conquered most of Africa and Asia. Each imperial nation dispatched missionaries to convert conquered peoples to Christianity. By 1900, some 18,000 Protestant and Catholic missionaries were scattered around the world. Writing in 1902, the British economist J. A. Hobson declared that imperialism was "the most powerful factor in the current politics of the Western world."

A small yet influential group of public officials aggressively encouraged the idea of expansion beyond North America. In addition to Theodore Roosevelt, they included naval captain Alfred Thayer Mahan, president of the U.S. Naval War College, and Senators Albert J. Beveridge of Indiana and Henry Cabot

Lodge of Massachusetts. Referring to European imperialism, Lodge said, "We must not be left behind."

In 1890, Mahan published *The Influence of Sea Power upon History, 1660–1783*, in which he argued that national greatness flowed from naval power. Mahan insisted that industrial development required a powerful navy centered on huge battleships, a strong merchant marine, foreign commerce, colonies to provide raw materials and new markets for American products, and global naval bases.

Mahan urged leaders to "look outward" beyond the continental United States. He championed America's "destiny" to control the Caribbean Sea, build a canal across Central America to connect the Atlantic and Pacific Oceans, acquire Hawaii and the Philippine Islands, and spread American values and investments across the Pacific. His ideas were widely circulated, and by 1896 the United States had built eleven new battleships, making its navy the third most powerful in the world, behind Great Britain and Germany.

Claims of racial superiority reinforced the new imperialist spirit. Many Americans and Europeans readily assumed that some races were dominant (Anglo-Saxons) and some inferior (Indians, Africans). Such racist notions were given "scientific" authority by researchers at universities throughout Europe and America.

Prominent Americans used the arguments of social Darwinism to justify economic exploitation and territorial conquest abroad and racial segregation at home. Among nations as among individuals, they claimed, only the strongest survived. John Fiske, a Harvard historian, proclaimed the superior character of "Anglo-Saxon" institutions and peoples. The English-speaking "race," he argued, was destined to dominate the globe and transform the institutions, traditions, language, and even the blood of the world's "backward" races.

EXPANSION IN THE PACIFIC

For John Fiske and other imperialists, Asia offered an especially attractive target. In 1866, Secretary of State William H. Seward had predicted that the United States must inevitably impose its economic domination "on the Pacific Ocean, and its islands and continents." Eager for American manufacturers to take advantage of the huge Asian markets, Seward believed that the nation first had to remove all foreign powers from its northern Pacific coast and gain access to the region's valuable ports. To that end, he tried to acquire the English colony of British Columbia, sandwiched between Russian-owned Alaska and the Washington Territory.

Late in 1866, while encouraging business leaders and civil authorities in British Columbia to consider becoming a U.S. territory, Seward learned of Russia's desire to sell Alaska. He leaped at the opportunity, thinking the purchase might influence British Columbia to join the union. In 1867, the United States bought Alaska for $7.2 million, thus removing the threat of Russian imperialism in North America. Critics scoffed at "Seward's folly," but the purchase of Alaska proved to be the biggest bargain since the Louisiana Purchase, in part because of its vast deposits of gold and oil.

Seward's successors at the State Department sustained his expansionist vision. Acquiring key ports in the Pacific Ocean was the major focus of overseas activity throughout the rest of the nineteenth century. Two island groups occupied especially strategic positions: Samoa and Hawaii (the Sandwich Islands). Both had major harbors, Pago Pago and Pearl Harbor, respectively. In the years after the Civil War, American interest in those islands deepened.

SAMOA In 1878, the Samoans signed a treaty with the United States that granted a naval base at Pago Pago and extraterritoriality for Americans (meaning that in Samoa, Americans remained subject only to U.S. law), exchanged trade concessions, and called for the United States to help resolve any disputes with other nations. The Senate ratified this accord, and in the following year the German and British governments worked out similar arrangements with other islands in the Samoan group. There matters rested until civil war broke out in Samoa in 1887. A peace conference in Berlin in 1889 established a protectorate over Samoa, with Germany, Great Britain, and the United States in an uneasy partnership.

HAWAII Seward and other Americans also wanted the Hawaiian Islands. The islands, a unified kingdom since 1795, had a sizable population of American missionaries and a profitable crop, sugarcane. In 1875, Hawaii had signed a reciprocal trade agreement with the United States through which Hawaiian sugar would enter the country duty free in exchange for Hawaii's promise that none of its territory would be leased or granted to a third power.

This agreement led to a boom in sugar production based on cheap immigrant labor, mainly Chinese and Japanese, and white American sugar planters soon formed an economic elite. By the 1890s, the native Hawaiian population had been reduced to a minority by smallpox and other foreign diseases, and Asians became the largest ethnic group.

Beginning in 1891, Queen Liliuokalani, the Hawaiian ruler, tried to restrict the growing political power exercised by American planters in the islands. Two years later, however, Hawaii's white population (called *haoles*) overthrew the monarchy with the help of U.S. Marines brought in by John L. Stevens,

"Our New Senators" Mocking the Alaska Purchase, this political cartoon shows President Andrew Johnson and Secretary of State Seward welcoming two new senators from Alaska: an Eskimo and a Penguin.

the U.S. ambassador. Within a month, a committee representing the *haoles* came to Washington, D.C., to ask the United States to annex the islands. President Benjamin Harrison sent an annexation treaty to the Senate just as he was leaving the presidency.

To investigate the situation, the new president, Grover Cleveland, sent a special commissioner to Hawaii, who reported that the Americans there had acted improperly and that most native Hawaiians opposed annexation. Cleveland tried to restore the queen to power but met resistance from the *haoles*. On July 4, 1894, the government they controlled created the Republic of Hawaii, which included in its constitution a provision for American annexation.

In 1897, when William McKinley became president, he was looking for an excuse to annex the islands. "We need Hawaii," he claimed. "It is [America's] manifest destiny." The United States annexed Hawaii in the summer of 1898 over the protests of native Hawaiians.

THE SPANISH-AMERICAN WAR (THE WAR OF 1898)

The annexation of Hawaii set in motion a series of efforts to create an American presence in Asia. Ironically, this imperialist push originated in Cuba, a Spanish colony ninety miles south of Florida. Even more ironically, the chief motive for American intervention in Cuba was outrage at Spain's brutal imperialism.

"**FREE CUBA**" Throughout the second half of the nineteenth century, Cubans had repeatedly revolted against Spanish rule, only to be ruthlessly suppressed. As one of Spain's oldest colonies, Cuba was a major market for Spanish goods. Yet powerful American sugar and mining companies had also invested heavily in Cuba. In fact, the United States traded more with Cuba than Spain did, and American owners of sugar plantations in Cuba had grown increasingly concerned about the security of their investments.

On February 24, 1895, Cubans began another guerrilla war against Spanish troops. During what became the Cuban War for Independence (1895–1898), tens of thousands of Cuban peasants died of combat wounds as well as disease and starvation in Spanish detention camps.

Americans followed the conflict through the newspapers. Two newspapers locked in a fierce competition for readers, William Randolph Hearst's *New York Journal* and Joseph Pulitzer's *New York World*. Both worked to outdo the other with sensational headlines about Spanish atrocities in Cuba, real or invented. Hearst explained that the role of newspapers was to shape public opinion and legislation. Newspapers, he claimed, had the power to "declare wars." Hearst's efforts to manipulate public opinion came to be called **yellow journalism**. Editors sent their best reporters to Cuba and encouraged them to distort, exaggerate, or even make up stories to attract more readers.

THE POLITICAL PATH TO WAR   At the outset of the Cuban War for Independence, President Grover Cleveland tried to protect U.S. business interests while avoiding military involvement. Mounting public sympathy for the rebel cause prompted concern in Congress, however. By concurrent resolutions on April 6, 1896, the House and Senate endorsed granting official recognition to the Cuban rebels. After his inauguration in March 1897, President William McKinley continued the official policy of neutrality while taking a sympathetic stance toward the rebels. McKinley, a Civil War veteran, did not want war. "I have been through one war," he said. "I have seen the dead piled up, and I do not want to see another." Later that year, Spain offered Cubans autonomy (self-government without formal independence) in return for ending the rebellion, but the Cubans rejected the offer.

Early in 1898, events pushed Spain and the United States into a war that neither wanted. On January 25, the **U.S. battleship *Maine*** docked in Havana, the Cuban capital, supposedly on a courtesy call. On February 9, the *New York Journal* released the text of a letter from Dupuy de Lôme, Spanish ambassador to the United States, to a friend in Havana, summarizing McKinley's annual message to Congress. In the **de Lôme letter**, the Spaniard called McKinley "weak and a bidder for the admiration of the crowd, besides being a would-be politician who tries to leave a door open behind himself while keeping on good terms with the jingoes [warmongers] of his party."

Six days later, at 9:40 on the night of February 15, the *Maine* mysteriously exploded. Within minutes, its ruptured hull filled with water. Sailors, most of whom were asleep, struggled frantically in the dark, only to drown as the ship sank. Of the 350 sailors on board, 260 died. Years later, the sinking was ruled an accident resulting from a coal explosion, but in 1898 those eager for war with Spain saw no need to delay judgment. Theodore Roosevelt, the thirty-nine-year-old assistant secretary of the navy, called the sinking "an act of dirty treachery" and told a friend that he "would give anything if President McKinley would order the fleet to Havana tomorrow."

Congress authorized $50 million to prepare for combat with Spain, but McKinley, who assumed that the sinking was an accident, did his best to resist demands for war while negotiating with the Spanish and gauging the public mood. He also avoided interacting with Roosevelt, whom he said was "too pugnacious." As the days passed, Roosevelt told his war-hungry friends that the president had "no more backbone than a chocolate éclair." With Roosevelt's encouragement, the public's antagonism toward Spain grew behind the popular saying "Remember the *Maine*, to Hell with Spain!"

In the weeks following the sinking, the Spanish government grudgingly agreed to virtually every American demand regarding Cuba, but the weight of public opinion, the cry of revenge from Democratic leaders, and the influence of Republican jingoists eroded McKinley's neutrality. As a senator explained, "the current was too strong, the demagogues too numerous, the fall elections too near" for McKinley to hold out against war.

On April 11, McKinley asked Congress for authority to use the armed forces to end the fighting in Cuba. On April 20, Congress declared Cuba independent from Spain and demanded the withdrawal of Spanish forces. The Spanish government quickly broke diplomatic ties with the United States and, after U.S. ships began blockading Cuban ports, declared war on April 24. The next day, Congress passed its own declaration of war. The **Teller Amendment** to the war resolution denied any U.S. intention to annex Cuba.

President McKinley called for 125,000 volunteers to supplement the 28,000 men already serving in the U.S. Army. Among the first to enlist was Theodore Roosevelt, who resigned from his government post and told his tailor to make him a dashing army uniform.

Never has an American war generated such unexpected and far-reaching consequences. Although McKinley had gone to war reluctantly, he soon saw it as an opportunity to acquire overseas territories. "While we are conducting war and until its conclusion," he wrote privately, "we must keep all we get; when the war is over we must keep what we want." A war to free Cuba became a way to gain an empire. (What had long been called the Spanish-American War has been renamed the War of 1898 because it involved not just Spanish and American combatants, but Cubans, Filipinos, and Puerto Ricans.)

"A Splendid Little War"

The war with Spain lasted only 114 days, but it set the United States on a course toward overseas imperialism that would transform America's role in the world. The conflict was barely under way before the U.S. Navy produced a spectacular victory 7,000 miles away from Cuba, in the Pacific, at Manila Bay in the Philippine Islands, a colony controlled by the Spanish for more than 300 years. Just before war was declared, Roosevelt, who was still assistant secretary of the navy, had taken advantage of his boss being away from the office one afternoon to order Commodore George Dewey, commander of the U.S. Asiatic Squadron, to engage Spanish forces in the Philippines in case of war in Cuba.

Dewey arrived in Manila Bay on April 30 with six modern warships, which quickly destroyed or captured the outdated Spanish vessels there. Almost 400 Spaniards were killed or wounded. One overweight American sailor died—of heatstroke. An English reporter called it "a military execution rather than a real contest." News of the battle set off wild celebrations in America.

Dewey was now in possession of Manila Bay but had no soldiers to go onshore. He and his warships stayed for several months waiting for reinforcements while German and British warships cruised offshore like watchful vultures, ready to seize the Philippines if the United States did not.

In the meantime, Emilio Aguinaldo, the leader of the Filipino nationalist movement, declared the Philippines independent on June 12, 1898. With Aguinaldo's help, Dewey's forces entered Manila on August 13 and accepted the surrender of the Spanish troops, who had feared revenge if they surrendered to the Filipinos. News of the American victory sent President McKinley in search of a map of Asia to locate the islands.

THE CUBAN CAMPAIGN At the start of the war, the Spanish army in Cuba was five times as large as the entire U.S. Army. But McKinley's call for volunteers inspired nearly a million men to enlist. The new recruits, including some 10,000 African American soldiers (mostly northerners eager to "show our loyalty to our land") had to be equipped and trained before they would be ready for battle. In the "Jim Crow" South, however, blacks were less eager to enlist because, as a Richmond newspaper editor observed, they suffered "a system of oppression as barbarous as that which is alleged to exist in Cuba."

In the meantime, the U.S. Navy blockaded the Spanish fleet inside Santiago Harbor while some 17,000 American troops hastily assembled at Tampa,

Colonel Roosevelt With one hand on his hip, Roosevelt rides with the Rough Riders in Cuba. Most of his regiment was culled from Arizona, New Mexico, and Texas because the Southwestern climate resembled that of Cuba.

Florida. One prominent unit was the First Volunteer Cavalry, better known as the Rough Riders, a special regiment made up of former Ivy League athletes; ex-convicts; western cowboys; Texas Rangers; and Cherokee, Choctaw, Chickasaw, Pawnee, and Creek Indians. All were "young, good shots, and good riders." The Rough Riders are best remembered because Theodore Roosevelt was second in command. One of the Rough Riders said that Roosevelt was "nervous, energetic, virile [manly]. He may wear out some day, but he will never rust out."

When the 578 Rough Riders, accompanied by a gaggle of reporters and photographers, landed on June 22, 1898, at the undefended southeastern tip of Cuba, chaos followed. Except for Roosevelt's horse, Little Texas, almost all of the other horses and mules had been mistakenly sent elsewhere, leaving the Rough Riders to become the "Weary Walkers." Nevertheless, land and sea battles on the southern coast around Santiago quickly broke Spanish resistance.

On July 1, about 7,000 U.S. soldiers took the fortified village of El Caney. While a much larger force attacked San Juan Hill, a smaller unit, led by Roosevelt on horseback and including the Rough Riders on foot, seized nearby Kettle Hill. Thanks to widespread newspaper coverage, much of it exaggerated, Roosevelt became a home-front legend for his headlong gallop toward the Spanish defenders. The *New York Times* reported that he had led the charge with "bulldog ferociousness," acting in a "grand drama for the world to watch and admire."

SPANISH DEFEAT AND CONCESSIONS   On July 3, the Spanish navy trapped at Santiago made a gallant run to evade the American fleet blockading the harbor. "The Spanish ships," reported Captain John Philip, commander of the U.S. warship *Texas*, "came out as gaily as brides to the altar." But they were quickly destroyed. The casualties were as one-sided as those at Manila: 474 Spaniards were killed or wounded, while only 1 American was killed and 1 wounded. Spanish officials in Santiago surrendered on July 17. On July 25, an American force moved into Spanish-held Puerto Rico ("wealthy port" in English), meeting only minor resistance.

The next day, July 26, the Spanish government sued for peace. A ceasefire agreement was signed on August 12. In Cuba, the Spanish forces formally surrendered to the U.S. commander and then sailed for home; excluded from the ceremony were the Cubans, for whom the war had supposedly been fought. On December 10, 1898, the United States and Spain signed the Treaty of Paris.

Under its terms, Cuba was to become independent, and the United States was to annex Puerto Rico and continue to occupy Manila, pending a transfer of power in the Philippines. Thus the Spanish Empire in the Americas, initiated by the voyages of Christopher Columbus some four centuries earlier, came to a humiliating end. Now the United States was ready to create its own empire.

During the four-month War of 1898, more than 60,000 Spanish soldiers and sailors died of wounds or disease—mostly malaria, typhoid, dysentery, or yellow fever. Some 10,500 Cubans died. Among the Americans who served in the war, 5,462 died, but only 379 in battle; most died from disease. At such a cost, the United States was launched onto the world scene as a great power, with all the benefits—and burdens—that came with being an imperial nation.

Halfway through the conflict in Cuba, John Hay, the U.S. ambassador to Great Britain, who would soon become secretary of state, wrote a letter to Roosevelt, calling the conflict "a splendid little war, begun with the highest motives, carried on with magnificent intelligence and spirit, favored by that fortune which loves the brave." The Spaniards, in contrast, called the war "The Disaster," as the humiliating defeat brought into question their country's status as a major world power.

CONSEQUENCES OF VICTORY

Victory in the War of 1898 boosted American self-confidence and reinforced the self-serving belief, influenced by racism and social Darwinism, that the United States had a "manifest destiny" to reshape the world in its own image.

In 1885, the Reverend Josiah Strong wrote a best-selling book titled *Our Country* in which he used a Darwinian argument to strengthen the appeal of manifest destiny. The "wonderful progress of the United States," he boasted, was an illustration of Charles Darwin's concept of "natural selection," since Americans had demonstrated that they were the world's "superior" civilization, "a race of unequaled energy" who represented "the largest liberty, the purest Christianity, the highest civilization" in the world, a race of superior people destined to "spread itself over the earth." Strong asserted that the United States had a Christian duty and economic opportunity to expand "Anglo-Saxon" influence. A growing international trade, he noted, would emerge from America's missionary evangelism and racial superiority.

ANNEXING THE PHILIPPINES

The United States had liberated most of Spain's remaining colonies, yet it soon substituted its own imperialism for Spain's. If war with Spain had saved many lives by ending the insurrection in Cuba, it had also led the United States to take many lives in suppressing another anti-colonial insurrection, in the Philippines. The acquisition of America's first imperial colonies created a host of long-lasting moral and practical problems, from the difficulties of imposing U.S. rule on native peoples to the challenges of defending far-flung territories.

McKINLEY'S MOTIVES   The Treaty of Paris had left the political status of the Philippines unresolved. American business leaders wanted the United States to keep the islands so that they could more easily penetrate the vast markets of nearby China. As Mark Hanna, McKinley's top adviser, stressed, controlling the Philippines would enable the United States to "take a large slice of the commerce of Asia." American missionary organizations, mostly Protestant, also favored annexation; they viewed the Philippines as a base from which to bring Christianity to "the little brown brother." Not long after the United States took control, American authorities ended the Roman Catholic Church's status as the Philippines' official religion and made English the official language, thus opening the door for Protestant missionaries in the region.

These factors helped convince President McKinley of the need to annex "those darned islands" making up the Philippines. He explained that

> one night late it came to me this way—I don't know how it was, but it came: (1) that we could not give them back to Spain—that would be cowardly and dishonorable; (2) that we could not turn them over to France or Germany—our commercial rivals in the Orient—that would be bad business and discreditable; (3) that we could not leave them to themselves—they were unfit for self-government—and they would soon have anarchy and misrule over there worse than Spain's was; and (4) that there was nothing left for us to do but to take them all, and to educate the Filipinos, and uplift and civilize and Christianize them, and by God's grace do the very best we could by them, as our fellowmen for whom Christ also died. And then I went to bed, and went to sleep and slept soundly.

In this brief statement, McKinley had summarized the motivating ideas of American imperialism: (1) national glory, (2) commerce, (3) racial superiority, and (4) evangelism. American negotiators in Paris finally offered Spain $20 million for the Philippines, Puerto Rico, and Guam, a Spanish-controlled island between Hawaii and the Philippines that would serve as a coaling station for ships headed across the Pacific.

Meanwhile, the nation took other expansive steps. In addition to annexing Hawaii in 1898, the United States also claimed Wake Island, between Guam and Hawaii, which would become a vital link in a future transpacific telegraph cable. Then, in 1899, Germany and the United States agreed to divide the Samoa Islands.

DEBATING THE TREATY By early 1899, the Treaty of Paris had yet to be ratified in the Senate because of growing opposition to the idea of a global American empire. Anti-expansionists argued that taking control of former Spanish colonies would violate the longstanding American principle embodied in the Constitution that people should be self-governing.

The opposition might have killed the treaty had not the most prominent Democratic leader, William Jennings Bryan, argued that ending the war would open the way for the future independence of the Philippines. His position convinced enough Senate Democrats to support the treaty on February 6, 1899, by the narrowest of margins: only one vote more than the necessary two thirds.

President McKinley, however, had no intention of granting independence to the Philippines. Although he privately told a friend that "if old Dewey had just sailed away when he smashed that Spanish fleet, what a lot of trouble he would have saved us," he publicly insisted that the United States take control of the islands as an act of "benevolent assimilation" of the native population. A California newspaper gave a more candid explanation, however. "Let us be frank," the editor exclaimed. "WE DO NOT WANT THE FILIPINOS. WE WANT THE PHILIPPINES."

Many Filipinos had a different vision. In January 1899, they declared again their independence and named twenty-nine-year-old Emilio Aguinaldo president. The following month, an American soldier outside Manila fired on soldiers in Aguinaldo's nationalist forces, called *insurrectos*, killing two. The next day, the U.S. Army commander, without investigating the cause of the shooting, ordered his troops to assault the *insurrectos*, beginning a full-scale armed conflict that continued for weeks. General Elwell S. Otis rejected Aguinaldo's proposals for a truce, saying that "fighting, having begun, must go on to the grim end." He would accept only the unconditional surrender of the Filipino forces.

On June 2, 1899, the Philippine Republic declared war against the United States. Since the *insurrectos* more or less controlled the Philippines outside Manila, what followed was largely an American war of conquest at odds with the founding principle of the United States: that people have the right to govern themselves. The war would rob the Filipinos of the chance to be their own masters.

Turmoil in the Philippines Emilio Aguinaldo (seated third from right) and other leaders of the Filipino insurgence.

THE PHILIPPINE-AMERICAN WAR (1898–1902) The effort to crush Filipino nationalism lasted three years and involved some 126,000 U.S. troops, four times as many as had been sent to liberate Cuba. It cost the American government $600 million and took the lives of 200,000 Filipinos (most of them civilians) and 4,234 American soldiers.

It was an especially brutal conflict fought in tropical heat and humidity, with massacres committed by both sides and racism contributing to numerous atrocities by the Americans, many of whom referred to the Filipinos as "niggers." U.S. troops burned villages, tortured and executed prisoners, and imprisoned civilians in overcrowded concentration camps, and both sides used torture to gain information.

A favorite method employed by Americans was the "water cure," a technique to simulate drowning developed in the Spanish Inquisition during the sixteenth century. (Today it is called waterboarding.) A captured insurgent would be placed on his back on the ground. While soldiers stood on his outstretched arms and feet, they pried his mouth open and held it in place with a bamboo stick. They then poured salt water into the captive's mouth and nose until his stomach was bloated, whereupon the soldiers would stomp on his abdomen, forcing the water, now mixed with gastric juices, out of his mouth. This process would be repeated until the captive told the soldiers what they wanted to know—or died. Theodore Roosevelt was convinced that "nobody was seriously damaged" by the "water cure," whereas "Filipinos had inflicted terrible tortures upon our own people."

Thus did the United States destroy a revolutionary movement modeled after America's own struggle for independence. Organized Filipino resistance had collapsed by the end of 1899. On April 1, 1901, Aguinaldo swore an oath accepting the authority of the United States over the Philippines and pledging his allegiance to the U.S. government.

Against the backdrop of this nasty guerrilla war, the great debate over imperialism continued in the United States. In 1899, several anti-imperialist groups combined to form the **American Anti-Imperialist League**. Andrew Carnegie footed the bills for the League and even offered $20 million to buy independence for the Filipinos. Other prominent anti-imperialists included union leader Samuel Gompers, who feared the competition of cheap Filipino labor, college presidents Charles Eliot of Harvard and David Starr Jordan of Stanford, and social reformer Jane Addams. Even former presidents Grover Cleveland and Benjamin Harrison urged President McKinley to withdraw U.S. forces from the Philippines.

The drive for imperialism in Asia, said Harvard philosopher William James, had caused the United States to "puke up its ancient soul." Of the Philippine-American War, James asked, "Could there be any more damning indictment of that whole bloated ideal termed 'modern civilization'?" Senator George Frisbie Hoar led the opposition to annexation of the Philippines. Under the Constitution, he pointed out, "no power is given the Federal government to acquire territory to be held and governed permanently as colonies" or "to conquer alien people and hold them in subjugation."

ORGANIZING THE NEW COLONIES

In the end, the imperialists won the debate over the status of the territories acquired from Spain. Senator Albert J. Beveridge boasted in 1900: "The Philippines are ours forever. And just beyond the Philippines are China's illimitable markets. We will not retreat from either. . . . The power that rules the Pacific is the power that rules the world." He added that the U.S. economy was producing "more than we can consume, making more than we can use. Therefore we must find new markets for our produce." American-controlled colonies would make the best new markets. Without acknowledging it, Beveridge and others were using many of the same arguments that England had used in founding the American colonies in the seventeenth century.

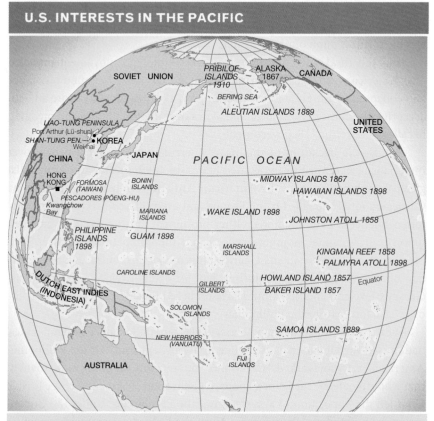

Dates indicate year of acquisition or occupation by the United States.
■ Why was President McKinley eager to acquire territory in the Pacific and the Caribbean?
■ What kind of political system did the U.S. government create in Hawaii and in the Philippines?
■ How did Filipinos and Hawaiians resist the Americans?

On July 4, 1901, the U.S. military government in the Philippines came to an end, and William Howard Taft became the civil governor. In 1902, Congress passed the Philippine Government Act, which declared the islands an "unorganized territory." In 1917, the Jones Act affirmed America's intention to grant the Philippines independence, but that would not happen until 1946.

Closer to home, Puerto Rico had been acquired in part to serve as a U.S. outpost guarding the Caribbean Sea. On April 12, 1900, the Foraker Act established a government on the island, and its residents were declared citizens of Puerto Rico; they were not made citizens of the United States until 1917.

In Cuba, the United States finally fulfilled the promise of independence after restoring order, organizing schools, and improving sanitary conditions. The problem of widespread disease prompted the work of Dr. Walter Reed, who made an outstanding contribution to health in tropical regions around the world. Named head of the Army Yellow Fever Commission in 1900, he proved that mosquitoes carry yellow fever. The commission's experiments led the way to effective control of the disease worldwide.

In 1900, on McKinley's order, Cubans drafted a constitution modeled on that of the United States. The Platt Amendment, added to an army appropriations bill in 1901, sharply restricted the Cuban government's independence, however. The amendment required that Cuba never impair its independence by signing a treaty with a third power, that it keep its debt within the government's power to repay it out of ordinary revenues, and that it acknowledge the right of the United States to intervene whenever it saw fit. Finally, Cuba had to sell or lease to the United States lands to be used for coaling or naval stations, a stipulation that led to a U.S. naval base at Guantánamo Bay that still exists today.

"Well, I hardly know which to take first!" With a growing appetite for foreign territory, Uncle Sam browses his options: Cuba Steak, Puerto Rico Pig, Philippine Floating Islands, and others. An expectant President McKinley waits to take his order.

IMPERIAL RIVALRIES IN EAST ASIA

While the United States was conquering the Philippines, other nations were threatening to carve up China. After Japan defeated China in the First Sino-Japanese War (1894–1895), European nations set out to exploit the weakness of the huge, virtually defenseless nation. By the end of the century, Russia, Germany, France, and Great Britain had each established spheres of influence in China—territories that they (rather than the Chinese government) controlled but did not formally annex.

In 1898 and again in 1899, the British asked the American government to join them in preserving the territorial integrity of China against further imperialist actions. Both times, however, the Senate rejected the request because the United States as yet had no strategic investment in the region. The American outlook changed with the defeat of Spain and the acquisition of the Philippines. Instead of acting jointly with Great Britain, though, the U.S. government decided to act alone.

What came to be known as the **Open Door policy** was outlined in Secretary of State John Hay's Open Door Note, dispatched in 1899 to his European counterparts. Without consulting the Chinese, Hay announced that China should remain an "Open Door" to European and American trade and that other nations should not try to take control of Chinese ports or territory. None of the European powers except Britain accepted Hay's principles, but none rejected them, either. So Hay announced that all major powers involved in China had accepted the policy.

The Open Door policy was rooted in the desire of American businesses to exploit and ultimately dominate Chinese markets. However, it also appealed to those who opposed imperialism because it pledged to keep China from being carved up by powerful European nations.

The policy had little legal standing, however. When the Japanese became concerned about growing Russian influence in the disputed region of Manchuria in northeast China and asked how the United States intended to enforce the policy, Hay replied that America was "not prepared . . . to enforce these views." So the situation would remain for forty years, until continued Japanese military expansion in China would bring about a diplomatic dispute with America that would lead to war.

THE BOXERS A new Asian crisis arose in 1900 when a group of Chinese nationalists known to the Western world as Boxers—they called themselves the "Fists of Righteous Harmony"—rebelled against foreign involvement in China, especially Christian missionary efforts, and laid siege to foreign embassies in

Peking (now known as Beijing). An expedition of British, German, Russian, Japanese, and American soldiers was organized to rescue the international diplomats and their staffs. Hay, fearful that the intervention might become an excuse for other nations to dismember China, took the opportunity to refine the Open Door policy. The United States, he said, sought a solution that would "preserve Chinese territorial and administrative integrity" as well as "equal and impartial trade with all parts of the Chinese Empire." Six weeks later, the foreign military expedition reached Peking and ended the Boxer Rebellion.

ROOSEVELT'S "BIG-STICK" DIPLOMACY

On September 6, 1901, President McKinley was shaking hands at the Pan-American Exposition in Buffalo, New York, when a twenty-eight-year-old unemployed laborer named Leon Czolgosz (pronounced chol-GOTS), an anarchist who did not believe in governments or rulers, approached him with a concealed gun and fired twice at point-blank range. One bullet was deflected by the president's coat button and breastbone, but the other tore through his stomach and lodged in his back. For several days, the attending doctors issued optimistic reports about the president's condition, but after a week, McKinley knew he was dying. "It is useless, gentlemen," he told the doctors and nurses. "I think we ought to have a prayer." Theodore Roosevelt, his vice president, became the new president and soon launched a new era in national development.

More than any other American of his time, Roosevelt transformed the role of the United States in world affairs. The nation had emerged from the War of 1898 a world power with major international responsibilities. To ensure that Americans accepted their new global role, Roosevelt stretched both the Constitution and executive power to the limit. In the process, he pushed a reluctant nation onto the center stage of world affairs.

A "ROCKET" RISE TO PROMINENCE

Born in 1858, "Teedie" Roosevelt had grown up in New York City in an upper-class family. He visited Europe as a child, studied with a personal tutor, spoke German fluently, and graduated from Harvard with honors in 1880. A frail and sickly boy, nearly blind in one eye, he followed his father's advice to "make your own body." He compulsively lifted weights, wrestled, hiked, rowed, swam, boxed, and climbed mountains, all in an effort to build himself into a physical and intellectual athlete. The results were startling. Roosevelt transformed himself into a man of almost superhuman energy who fiercely championed the "strenuous life." He told his children that he would rather see them dead than have them grow up to be "weaklings" and "sissies."

Roosevelt was a fearless "he-man" who also displayed extraordinary intellectual curiosity. He became a voracious reader and talented writer, a natural scientist, a dedicated bird-watcher, a renowned historian and essayist, and a zealous moralist who divided the world into two camps: good and evil. Roosevelt's zest for life and his combative spirit were contagious, and he was ever eager to express an opinion on any subject.

Within two years after graduating from Harvard, Roosevelt, a reform-minded Republican, won election as the youngest member of the New York legislature. Fearlessly independent, he could not be bought. Nor did he tolerate the excesses of the spoils system. "Though I am a strong party man," he warned, "if I find a corrupt public official, I would take off his head."

With the world seemingly at Roosevelt's feet, however, disaster struck. In 1884, his mother, Mittie, only forty-eight years old, died of typhoid fever. Eleven hours later, his "bewitchingly pretty," twenty-two-year-old wife, Alice, died in his arms of kidney failure, having given birth to their only child just two days earlier. The "light has gone out of my life," Roosevelt noted in his diary.

To recover from this "strange and terrible fate," Roosevelt turned his newborn daughter over to his sister, quit his political career, sold the family house, and moved to a cattle ranch in the Dakota Territory, where he threw himself into roping and branding steers, shooting buffalo and bears, capturing outlaws, fighting Indians (whom he called a "lesser race"), and reading novels by the campfire. He was, by his own admission, a poor shot, a bad roper, and an average horseman, but he loved every minute of his western life. Although his time in the West lasted only two years, he never got over being a cowboy. "I owe more than I can express to the West," he wrote in his memoirs.

Back in New York City, Roosevelt remarried and ran unsuccessfully for mayor in 1886. He later served six years as a U.S. Civil Service commissioner and two years as the city's police commissioner. In 1896, he campaigned energetically for William McKinley, and the new president was asked to reward him with the position of assistant secretary of the navy. McKinley resisted at first, saying that Roosevelt was too "hotheaded," but eventually gave in.

Roosevelt took full advantage of the celebrity he had gained with the Rough Riders in Cuba to win the governorship of New York in 1898. By then, he had become the most visible young Republican in the nation. "I have played it in bull luck this summer," he wrote a friend about his recent streak of successes. "First, to get into the war; then to get out of it; then to get elected." Two years later, Republican leaders were urging him to become the vice presidential running mate for McKinley, who was hoping for a second term.

FROM VICE PRESIDENT TO PRESIDENT

In the 1900 presidential contest, the Democrats turned again to William Jennings Bryan, who wanted to make American imperialism the "paramount issue" of the campaign. The Democratic platform condemned the Philippine conflict as "an unnecessary war" that had placed the United States "in the false and un-American position of crushing with military force the efforts of our former allies to achieve liberty and self-government."

The Republicans renominated McKinley and named Roosevelt, now known as "Mr. Imperialism," their candidate for vice president. Roosevelt, who despised Bryan, crisscrossed the nation condemning Bryan's "communistic and socialistic doctrines" promoting higher taxes and the unlimited coinage of silver. In the end, McKinley and Roosevelt won by 7.2 million to 6.4 million popular votes and 292 to 155 electoral votes. Bryan even lost Nebraska, his home state.

On September 14, 1901, McKinley died, and Theodore Roosevelt was elevated to the White House. Six weeks short of his forty-third birthday, Roosevelt was the youngest man ever to become president. But he had more experience in public affairs than most new presidents, and perhaps more vitality than any. One observer compared his boundless personality and energy to Niagara Falls—"both great wonders of nature." Roosevelt's glittering spectacles, glistening teeth, and overflowing enthusiasm were like divine gifts to political cartoonists, as was his famous motto, an old African proverb: "Speak softly, and carry a big stick."

Roosevelt's unshakable self-righteousness led him to cast nearly every issue in moral and patriotic terms. He was the first truly activist president. The presidency was, as he put it, a "bully pulpit"—a wonderful platform for delivering fist-pumping speeches on the virtues of honesty, courage, and civic duty.

Nowhere was Roosevelt's forceful will more evident than in his handling of foreign affairs. Like many of his political friends and associates, he was convinced that the "civilized" and "barbarian" people of the world faced inevitable conflict, not unlike the fate of the Native Americans pushed off their ancestral lands by Americans. In 1899, Roosevelt argued that the United States, as a "great civilized power," needed to take control of other regions of the world to bring "law, order, and righteousness" to "backward peoples." He believed that American imperialists would be missionaries of civic virtue rather than colonial masters, spreading the merits of their superior "race."

U.S. INTERESTS IN THE CARIBBEAN

■ Why did America want to build the Panama Canal?

■ How did the U.S. government interfere with Colombian politics in an effort to gain control of the Canal Zone?

■ What was the Roosevelt Corollary?

THE PANAMA CANAL After the War of 1898, as the United States became more deeply involved in the Caribbean, one issue overshadowed every other: the proposed Panama Canal. By enabling ships to travel from the Pacific Ocean to the Gulf of Mexico, such a canal would cut the travel distance between San Francisco and New York City by almost 8,000 miles.

Two treaties loomed as obstacles to the construction of a canal, however. The Bidlack Treaty (1846) with Colombia (then called New Granada) guaranteed Colombia's control over Panama. In the Clayton-Bulwer Treaty (1850), the British had agreed to acquire no more Central American territory, and the United States joined them in agreeing to build or fortify a canal only by mutual consent.

Secretary of State John Hay asked the British ambassador for consent to build a canal, and the outcome was the Hay-Pauncefote Treaty of 1901. Other obstacles remained, however. From 1881 to 1887, a French company led by Ferdinand de Lesseps, who had engineered the Suez Canal in Egypt, had already spent nearly $300 million and some 20,000 lives to dig a canal a third of the way across Panama, which was still under Colombian control. The company asked that the United States purchase the partially completed canal, which it did.

Meanwhile, Hay had opened negotiations with Ambassador Tomás Herrán of Colombia. In return for acquiring a canal zone six miles wide, the United States agreed to pay $10 million. The U.S. Senate ratified the Hay-Herrán Treaty in 1903, but the Colombian Senate held out for $25 million. As President Roosevelt raged against the "foolish and homicidal corruptionists in Bogotá," the Panamanians revolted against Colombian rule. Philippe Bunau-Varilla, an employee of the French canal company, assisted them and reported, after visiting Roosevelt and Hay in Washington, D.C., that U.S. warships would arrive at Colón, Panama, on November 2.

Colombian troops, who could not penetrate the overland jungle separating them from the Canal Zone, found the U.S. ships blocking the sea-lanes to the area. On November 13, the Roosevelt administration received its first ambassador from the newly independent Panama: Bunau-Varilla, who eagerly signed a treaty that extended the Canal Zone from six to ten miles wide.

For a $10 million down payment and $250,000 a year, the United States received "in perpetuity the use, occupation and control" of the fifty-mile-long Canal Zone. The U.S. attorney general, asked to supply a legal opinion upholding Roosevelt's actions, responded wryly, "No, Mr. President, if I were you I would not have any taint of legality about it." Roosevelt later explained, "I took the Canal Zone and let Congress debate; and while the debate goes on the [construction of the] Canal does also."

Building the Panama Canal was one of the greatest engineering feats in history. Over ten years, some 60,000 mostly unskilled workers from Europe, Asia, and the Caribbean used dynamite and steam shovels to gouge out the canal from dense jungle. Almost a third of the workers died. "People get killed and injured almost every day," a worker reported in his journal. "And all the bosses want is to get the canal built." With great fanfare, the canal opened on August 15, 1914, two weeks after the outbreak of the Great War in Europe.

ROOSEVELT AND LATIN AMERICA Theodore Roosevelt's "theft" of the Panama Canal Zone created ill will throughout Latin America that would last for generations. Latin Americans were also upset by constant interference

THE BIG STICK IN THE CARIBBEAN SEA

Big Stick diplomacy President Theodore Roosevelt wields "the big stick," symbolizing his aggressive diplomacy. As he stomps through the Caribbean, he drags a string of American warships behind him.

from both the United States and European countries in their internal affairs. A frequent excuse for intervention was to promote a safe and stable environment for American businesses, including the collection of debts owed by Latin American governments. The Latin Americans responded with the Drago Doctrine (1902), named after Argentinian foreign minister Luis María Drago, which prohibited armed intervention by other countries to collect debts.

In December 1902, however, German and British warships blockaded Venezuela to force repayment of debts in defiance not only of the Drago Doctrine but also of the Monroe Doctrine, the U.S. policy dating to 1823 that prohibited European intervention in the Western Hemisphere. Roosevelt decided that if the United States were to keep European nations from intervening militarily in Latin America, "then sooner or later we must keep order [there] ourselves."

In 1904, a crisis over the debts of the Dominican Republic prompted Roosevelt to send two warships to the island nation and issue what came to be known as the **Roosevelt Corollary** to the Monroe Doctrine: the principle, in short, that in certain circumstances, the United States was justified in intervening in Latin American nations to prevent Europeans from doing so. Thereafter, U.S. presidents would repeatedly use military force to ensure that Latin American nations paid their debts to U.S. and European banks.

RELATIONS WITH JAPAN

While wielding a "big stick" in Latin America, Roosevelt was playing the role of peacemaker in East Asia. The principle of equal trading rights represented by the Open Door policy was tested in 1904 when the long-standing rivalry between Russia and Japan flared into the Russo-Japanese war over Japan's attempts to expand its influence in China and Korea.

On February 8, Japanese warships devastated the Russian fleet. The Japanese then occupied the Korean peninsula and drove the Russians back into Manchuria. When the Japanese signaled that they would welcome a negotiated settlement, Roosevelt sponsored a peace conference in Portsmouth, New Hampshire. In the Treaty of Portsmouth, signed on September 5, 1905, Russia acknowledged Japan's "predominant political, military, and economic interests in Korea." (Japan would annex the kingdom in 1910.) Both powers agreed to leave Manchuria.

Japan's show of strength against Russia raised concerns among U.S. leaders about the security of the Philippines. During the Portsmouth talks, Roosevelt sent William Howard Taft to meet with the Japanese foreign minister in Tokyo. They negotiated the Taft-Katsura Agreement of July 29, 1905, in which the United States accepted Japanese control of Korea in exchange for Japan acknowledging U.S. control of the Philippines. Three years later, the Root-Takahira Agreement, negotiated by Secretary of State Elihu Root and the Japanese ambassador to the United States, reinforced the Open Door policy by supporting "the independence and integrity of China" and "the principle of equal opportunity for commerce and industry in China."

Behind the outward appearances of goodwill, however, lay mutual distrust. For many Americans, the Russian threat in East Asia now gave way to concerns about the "yellow peril" (a term apparently coined by Kaiser Wilhelm II of Germany). Racial conflict on the West Coast, especially in California, helped sour relations with Japan. In 1906, San Francisco's school board ordered students of Asian descent to attend a separate public school. When the Japanese government protested, President Roosevelt persuaded the school board to change its policy, but only after making sure that Japanese authorities would stop encouraging unemployed Japanese "laborers" to go to America. This "Gentlemen's Agreement" of 1907, the precise terms of which have never been revealed, halted the influx of Japanese immigrants to California and relieved some of the racial tension.

THE GREAT WHITE FLEET

After Roosevelt's election to a full term as president in 1904, he celebrated America's rise as a world power. Since his youth, he had retained a boyish enthusiasm for ships and sea power. In 1907, he sent the entire U.S. Navy, by then second in strength only to Britain's Royal Navy, on a grand fourteen-month tour around the world as a demonstration of America's power.

At every port of call—down the Atlantic coast of South America, then up the Pacific coast, out to Hawaii, and down to New Zealand and Australia— the "Great White Fleet" of sixteen gleaming battleships received a rousing welcome. The triumphal procession continued to Japan, China, the Philippines, then Egypt through the Suez Canal, and across the Mediterranean Sea before steaming back to Virginia in early 1909, just in time to close Roosevelt's presidency on a note of triumph.

Roosevelt's success in expanding U.S. power abroad would have mixed consequences, however, because underlying his imperialism was a militantly racist view of the world. Roosevelt and others believed that the world was made up of "civilized" societies, such as the United States, Japan, and the nations of Europe, and those they described as "barbarous," "backward," or "impotent." It was the responsibility of the "civilized" nations to exercise control of the "barbarous" peoples, by force if necessary. Roosevelt called warfare the best way to promote "the clear instinct for race selfishness" and insisted that "the

Japanese immigration Japanese immigrants are vaccinated aboard a steamship on their way to Hawaii. By 1900, about 40 percent of Hawaii's population was Japanese.

most ultimately righteous of all wars is a war with savages." Such belligerent, self-righteous bigotry defied American ideals of equality and would come back to haunt the United States.

TAFT'S "DOLLAR DIPLOMACY"   Republican William Howard Taft, who succeeded Roosevelt as president in 1909, continued to promote America's economic interests abroad, practicing what Roosevelt called **"dollar diplomacy."** Taft used the State Department to help American companies and banks invest in foreign countries, especially East Asia and the less developed nations of Latin America and the Caribbean. To ensure the stability of those investments, Taft did not hesitate to intervene in nations experiencing political and economic turmoil. In 1909, he dispatched U.S. Marines to support a revolution in Nicaragua. Once the new government was formed, Secretary of State Philander C. Knox helped U.S. banks negotiate loans to prop it up. Two years later, Taft again sent American troops to restore political stability. This time they stayed for more than a decade.

WILSON'S INTERVENTIONISM   In 1913, the new Democratic president, Woodrow Wilson, attacked dollar diplomacy as a form of economic imperialism. He promised to treat Latin American nations "on terms of equality and honor." Yet Wilson, along with William Jennings Bryan, his secretary of state, dispatched American military forces to Latin America more often than Taft and Roosevelt combined.

Wilson argued that the United States must intervene to stabilize weak governments in the Western Hemisphere to keep European nations from doing so. During his two presidential terms, Wilson sent U.S. troops into Cuba once, Panama twice, and Honduras five times.

In 1915, when the Dominican Republic refused to sign a treaty that would have given the United States a "special" role in governing the island nation, Wilson sent U.S. Marines, who established a military government and fought a nasty guerrilla war against anti-American rebels. That same year, Wilson intervened in Haiti, next door to the Dominican Republic. He admitted that his actions were "high-handed" but argued that they were justified because the "necessity for exercising control there is immediate, urgent, imperative." Others disagreed. As the *New York Times* charged, Wilson's frequent interventions made Taft's dollar diplomacy look like "ten cent diplomacy."

THE UNITED STATES IN MEXICO   Mexico was a much thornier problem. In 1910, long-suffering Mexicans had revolted against the dictatorship of Porfirio Díaz, who had given foreign corporations a free rein in developing the nation's economy. After revolutionary armies occupied Mexico City in 1911, the victorious rebels began squabbling among themselves. The leader of the rebellion, Francisco Madero, was overthrown by his chief of staff, General Victoriano Huerta, who assumed power in early 1913 and then had Madero and thirty other political opponents murdered.

A shocked President Wilson refused to recognize "a government of butchers." Huerta ignored Wilson's criticism and established a dictatorship. Wilson decided that Huerta must be removed and ordered U.S. warships to halt shipments of foreign weapons to the new government. Meanwhile, several rival revolutionary Mexican armies, the largest of which was led by Francisco Pancho Villa, began trying to unseat Huerta.

On April 9, 1914, nine American sailors were arrested in Tampico, Mexico, while trying to buy supplies. Mexican officials quickly released them and apologized to the U.S. naval commander. There the incident might have ended, but the imperious U.S. admiral demanded that the Mexicans fire a twenty-one-gun salute to the American flag. After they refused, Wilson sent U.S. troops ashore at Veracruz on April 21, 1914. They occupied the city at a cost of 19 American lives; at least 300 Mexicans were killed or wounded.

Intervention in Mexico U.S. Marines enter Veracruz, Mexico, in 1914.

The use of military force in Mexico played out like many previous American interventions in the Caribbean and Central America. Congress readily supported the decision because American honor was supposedly at stake, and Wilson was sure that most Mexicans would welcome U.S. intervention since his intentions were so "unselfish." But his strategy backfired. Instead of welcoming the Americans as liberators, Mexicans viewed them as invaders. For seven months, the Americans governed Veracruz. They left in late 1914 after Huerta was overthrown by Venustiano Carranza.

Still, the troubles south of the border continued. In 1916, rebel leader Pancho Villa launched raids into Texas and New Mexico in a deliberate attempt to trigger U.S. intervention. On March 9, he and his men attacked Columbus, New Mexico, just three miles across the border. Villa shouted "Kill all the Gringos!" as his army of 500 peasant revolutionaries burned the town and killed seventeen Americans. A furious Wilson sent General John J. Pershing to Mexico with 6,000 U.S. soldiers. For nearly a year, Pershing's troops chased Villa's army through the rugged mountains of northern Mexico. As Pershing muttered, "It's like trying to chase a rat in a cornfield." In 1917, the American troops were ordered home. The elusive Villa, meanwhile, named his mule "President Wilson." By then, however, Wilson paid little notice, for he was distracted by a much greater threat: massive war in Europe.

CHAPTER REVIEW

SUMMARY

- **Toward the New Imperialism**   Near the end of the nineteenth century, the popular idea that America had a "manifest destiny" to expand its territory abroad, combined with industrialists' desire for new markets for their goods, helped fuel America's "new *imperialism*." White Americans believed that their advanced industrial development proved their racial superiority, and by conquering "backward peoples," the United States was simply carrying out the theory of survival of the fittest. Evangelical Protestants also thought they had a duty to Christianize and "uplift" people throughout the world.

- **Expansion in the Pacific**   Business leaders hoped to extend America's commercial reach across the Pacific to exploit vast Asian markets. American planters in the Kingdom of Hawaii developed a thriving sugar industry, which increased Hawaii's commercial connections to the United States. In 1894, Hawaii's minority white population, ousted the native Hawaiian queen, declared a republic, and requested that Hawaii be annexed by the United States. In 1898, President William McKinley agreed to annex the Hawaiian Islands.

- **The Spanish-American War (The War of 1898)**   When Cubans revolted against Spanish colonial rule in 1895, many Americans supported their independence. *Yellow journalism* further aroused Americans' sympathy. Early in 1898, the publication of the *de Lôme letter*, followed by the mysterious explosion that sank the *U.S. battleship* Maine in Havana Harbor, helped propel America into war with Spain. The war lasted only 114 days. Under the Treaty of Paris ending the war, Cuba became independent and the United States annexed Spain's other Caribbean possession, Puerto Rico. In the Philippine Islands, America's Pacific Fleet under Commodore George Dewey defeated the Spanish in the Battle of Manila Bay.

- **Consequences of Victory**   A vicious guerrilla war followed in the Philippines, as Filipinos rebelled against American control. The rebellion was suppressed, and President McKinley announced that the United States would annex the Philippines. The *Anti-Imperialist League* and others to argue that acquiring overseas territories violated American principles of self-determination and independence. But the imperialists won the debate, and Congress set up a government in the Philippines and in Puerto Rico. In the Pacific region, the United States annexed Hawaii, Guam, Wake Island, and some of the Samoa Islands. In East Asia, Secretary of State John Hay promoted the *Open Door policy* of preserving China's territorial integrity and equal access by all nations to trade with China.

- **Theodore Roosevelt and Big-Stick Diplomacy**   Theodore Roosevelt pursued an imperialist foreign policy that confirmed the United States' new role as a world power. He helped negotiate the treaty that ended the Russo-Japanese War, seized control of the Panama Canal, and sent the navy's fleet of new battleships around the world as a symbol of American might. He also proclaimed the *Roosevelt Corollary* to the Monroe Doctrine, asserting that the United States would intercede in Latin America as necessary to prevent European intervention.

- **Taft and Wilson's Interventionism Abroad**   William H. Taft and Woodrow Wilson continued Roosevelt's pattern of intervening in the internal affairs of other nations, especially in Latin America and the Caribbean. What Taft called *"dollar diplomacy"* involved fostering American investments in less-developed nations. Wilson's frustrations at the instability of the Mexican government led him to send troops there twice. In both cases, the presence of U.S. soldiers only deepened resentment of "Yankee imperialism" throughout Latin America.

CHRONOLOGY

1894	Republic of Hawaii is proclaimed
1898	U.S. battleship *Maine* explodes in Havana Harbor
	The Spanish-American War (War of 1898)
	United States annexes Hawaii
1899	U.S. Senate ratifies the Treaty of Paris, ending the War of 1898
1899–1902	Insurgents resist U.S. conquest of the Philippines
1905	Russo-Japanese War
1914	Panama Canal opens
1909–1917	U.S. military interventions in Mexico and Latin America

KEY TERMS

imperialism p. 746

yellow journalism p. 750

U.S. battleship *Maine* p. 751

de Lôme letter p. 751

Teller Amendment p. 752

American Anti-Imperialist League p. 759

Open Door policy p. 762

Roosevelt Corollary p. 768

"dollar diplomacy" p. 771

 INQUIZITIVE

Go to InQuizitive to see what you've learned—and learn what you've missed—with personalized feedback along the way.

21 The Progressive Era

1890–1920

"Votes For Us When We Are Women!" Parades organized by women's suffrage groups attracted women of all ages and social classes. Here, from a patriotically outfitted automobile, some young suffragists ask their many spectators for "votes for us when we are women."

Theodore Roosevelt's emergence as a national political leader coincided with the onset of what historians have labeled the Progressive Era (1890–1920), an extraordinary period of social activism and political innovation during which compelling public issues forced profound changes in the role of government and presidential leadership. Millions of "progressives" believed that America was experiencing a "crisis of democracy" because of the urban-industrial revolution. Widespread inner-city poverty; countless children working in unregulated mines and factories; tainted food; and miserable, unsafe working conditions required bold action by churches, charitable organizations, experts, and individuals—and an expanded role for governments.

Progressives argued that the United States had been changing so rapidly since the end of the Civil War that the nation was at risk of imploding, and the widening gap between rich and poor during the Gilded Age had become a major concern. The growth of new industries like railroading, steel, coal, and oil had attracted waves of poor farm folk and foreign immigrants to cities whose basic social services—food, water, housing, education, sanitation, transportation, and medical care—could not keep pace with the rate of urban growth.

Between 1890 and 1920, armies of progressive reformers attacked the problems created by unregulated industrialization and unplanned urbanization. Most of all, they insisted that something must be done to control the large, powerful corporations that dominated America's economy and corrupted its political life.

focus questions

1. What were the various motives of progressive reformers?

2. Which various sources of thought and activism contributed to the progressive movement?

3. What were the specific goals of progressive reformers? In what ways did they pursue these public goals?

4. What contributions did Presidents Theodore Roosevelt and William Howard Taft make to the progressive movement? How and why did these two men come to disagree about how best to advance progressive ideals?

5. Which policies of President Woodrow Wilson were influenced by the progressive movement? How and why did these differ from the policies of Presidents Roosevelt and Taft?

By the beginning of the twentieth century, progressivism had become the most dynamic social and political force in the nation. In 1910, Woodrow Wilson, then president of Princeton University, told a gathering of clergymen that progressivism had generated "an extraordinary awakening in civic consciousness."

THE PROGRESSIVE IMPULSE

Progressives were liberals, not revolutionaries. They wanted to reform and regulate capitalist society, not destroy it. Most were Christian moralists who felt that politics had become a contest between good and evil, honesty and corruption. What they all shared was the assumption that governments—local, state, and national—must take a more active role in addressing the problems created by rapid urban and industrial growth.

Progressivism was more a widespread impulse supported by elements of both major political parties than it was a single movement with a common agenda. Republican Theodore Roosevelt called it the "forward movement" because it emphasized modernizing "old-fashioned" ways of doing things. He and other reformers stood "for the cause of progress, for the cause of the uplift of humanity and the betterment of mankind."

To make governments more responsive and "efficient" and businesses more honest and safe, progressives drew upon the new "social sciences"—sociology, political science, psychology, public health, and economics—being developed at research universities. The progressive approach was to enable "experts" to "investigate, educate, and legislate." Florence Kelley, a tireless activist, voiced the era's widespread belief that once people knew "the truth" about social ills, "they would act upon it."

Unlike populism, whose grassroots appeal was largely confined to rural regions in the South and Midwest, progressivism was a national movement, centered in large cities but also popular in rural areas among what came to be called Populist progressives. Progressive activists came in all stripes: men and women; Democrats, Republicans, Populists, and Socialists; labor unionists and business executives; teachers, engineers, editors, and professors; social workers, doctors, ministers, and journalists; farmers and homemakers; whites and blacks; clergymen, atheists, and agnostics. Whatever their motives and methods, their combined efforts led to significant improvements.

Yet progressivism also displayed inconsistencies and hypocrisies. Progressives often armed themselves with Christian moralism, but their "do-good" perspective was often limited by the racial and ethnic prejudices of the day, as well as by social and intellectual snobbery. The goals of upper-class white progressives rarely included racial equality. Many otherwise "progressive" people, including Theodore Roosevelt and Woodrow Wilson, believed in the supremacy of the "Anglo-Saxon race" and their own superiority to the working poor. They assumed that the workings of modern society were too complicated for the uninformed masses to understand, much less improve, without direction by those who knew better.

THE VARIED SOURCES OF PROGRESSIVISM

During the last quarter of the nineteenth century, political progressives at the local and state levels began to attack corrupt political bosses and irresponsible corporate barons. They sought more honest and more efficient government, more effective regulation of big businesses ("the trusts"), and better lives for the working poor. Only by expanding the scope of local, state, and federal governments, they believed, could these goals be attained.

ECONOMIC DEPRESSION AND DISCONTENT More than any other factor, the devastating depression of the 1890s ignited the progressive spirit of reform. By 1900, the U.S. population numbered 82 million; at the turn of the new century, an estimated 10 million Americans were living in poverty with annual incomes barely adequate to provide the minimum necessities of life. The devastating effects of the depression prompted many upper-middle-class urban people—lawyers, doctors, executives, social workers, teachers, professors, journalists, and college-educated women—to organize efforts to reform society, both to help those in need and to keep them from becoming revolutionaries.

POPULISM Populism, with its roots in the rural South and West, was another thread in the fabric of progressivism. The Populist party platforms of 1892 and 1896 included reforms intended to give more power to "the people," such as the direct election of U.S. senators by voters rather than by state legislatures. Although William Jennings Bryan's loss in the 1896 presidential campaign ended the Populist party as a serious political force, many reforms pushed by the Populists were implemented by progressives.

"HONEST GOVERNMENT" The Mugwumps—"gentlemen" reformers who had fought the patronage system and insisted that government jobs be awarded on the basis of merit—supplied progressivism with another key goal: the "honest government" ideal. Over the years, the good-government movement expanded beyond ending political corruption to addressing persistent urban issues such as crime, access to electricity, clean water and municipal sewers, mass transit, and garbage collection.

SOCIALISM Another significant "progressive" force was the growing influence of socialist ideas. The Socialist Party of America, supported mostly by militant farmers and immigrant Germans and Jews, served as the radical wing of progressivism. Unlike European socialists, most American socialists did not call for the government to take ownership of large corporations. They focused instead on improving working conditions and closing the widening income gap between rich and poor through "progressive" taxation. Most progressives were capitalist reformers, not socialist radicals. They rejected the extremes of both socialism and laissez-faire individualism, preferring a new, regulated capitalism "softened" by humanitarianism.

MUCKRAKING JOURNALISM Progressivism depended upon newspapers and magazines to inform the public about political corruption and social problems. The so-called **muckrakers** were America's first investigative journalists. Their aggressive reporting played a crucial role in educating the upper and middle classes about political and corporate wrongdoing and revealing "how the other half lives"—the title of Danish immigrant Jacob Riis's pioneering 1890 work of photojournalism about life in the sordid slums of New York City, where some 1.2 million people, mostly immigrants, lived in poverty amid killing diseases.

The muckrakers got their nickname from Theodore Roosevelt, who said that crusading journalists were "often indispensable to . . . society, but only if they know when to stop raking the muck." By uncovering political corruption and writing about social ills in newspapers

Cover of *McClure's* magazine, 1902 This issue features Ida Tarbell's muckraking series investigating the Standard Oil Company.

and popular monthly magazines such as *McClure's*, *Munsey's*, and *Cosmopolitan*, the muckrakers changed the face of journalism and gave it a new political role. Roosevelt, both as governor of New York and as president, frequently used muckrakers to drum up support for his policies; he corresponded with them, invited them to the White House, and used their popularity to help shape public opinion.

Religious Activism

Social justice progressives believed that society had an ethical obligation to help its poorest and most vulnerable members. Others were inspired by the **social gospel**, a newer, specifically Protestant belief that Christians should help the poor to bring about the "Kingdom of God" on earth.

In many respects, the progressive movement as a whole represented a new, energetic form of public outreach that incorporated religious (and nonreligious) groups and focused not so much on saving souls as on social action. More and more Christians adopted the mission of social reform. "We believe," a social gospel organization said, "that the age of sheer individualism is past, and the age of social responsibility has arrived."

THE SOCIAL GOSPEL During the last quarter of the nineteenth century, a growing number of churches and synagogues began emphasizing community service and the care of the unfortunate. New organizations made key contributions to the movement. The Young Men's Christian Association (YMCA) and a similar group for women, the YWCA, both entered the United States from England in the 1850s and grew rapidly after 1870. The Salvation Army, founded in London in 1878, came to the United States a year later.

The YMCA and YWCA combined nondenominational religious evangelism with social services and fitness training in community centers (segregated by race and gender) across the country. Intended to provide low-cost housing and healthful exercise in a "safe Christian environment" for young men and women from rural areas or foreign countries, the YMCA/YWCA centers often included libraries, classrooms, and kitchens. "Hebrew" counterparts—YMHAs and YWHAs—provided many of the same facilities in cities with large Jewish populations. Salvation Army centers offered "soup kitchens" to feed the poor and day nurseries for the children of working mothers.

The major forces behind the social gospel movement were Protestants and Catholics who feared that Christianity had become too closely associated with the upper and middle classes and was losing its appeal to the working poor. In 1875, Washington Gladden, a prominent pastor in Springfield, Massachusetts, invited striking shoe-factory workers to his church, but they refused because the factory owners and managers were members of the congregation. Gladden, heartbroken that Christianity was dividing along class lines, responded by writing *Working People and Their Employers* (1876), which argued that true Christianity was based on the principle that "thou shalt love thy neighbor as thyself." Gladden rejected the view of social Darwinists that the poor deserved their fate and should not be helped. He became the first prominent religious leader to support the rights of workers to form unions. He also spoke out against racial segregation and efforts to discriminate against immigrants.

Walter Rauschenbusch, a German American Baptist minister serving immigrant tenement dwellers in the Hell's Kitchen neighborhood of New York City, became the greatest champion of the social gospel. In 1907, he published *Christianity and the Social Crisis*, in which he argued that "whoever uncouples the religious and social life has not understood Jesus." The Christian emphasis on personal salvation, he added, must be linked with an equally passionate commitment to social justice. Churches must embrace "the social aims of Jesus," he stressed, for Christianity was intended to be a "revolutionary" faith.

In Rauschenbusch's view, religious life needed the social gospel to revitalize it and make it socially relevant: "We shall never have a perfect social life, yet we must seek it with faith." Like the muckrakers, Rauschenbusch sought to expose the realities of poverty in America and convince statesmen to deal with the crisis. His message resonated with Theodore Roosevelt, Woodrow Wilson, and many other progressives in both political parties. Years later, Rev. Martin Luther King Jr. spoke for three generations of radicals and reformers when he said that *Christianity and the Social Crisis* "left an indelible imprint on my thinking."

Rauschenbusch, Gladden, and other "social gospelers" sought to expand the "Kingdom of God" by following Christ's example by serving the poor and powerless. Rugged individualism may have been the path to wealth, they argued, but "Christian socialism" offered hope for unity among all classes. "Every religious and political question," said George Herron, a religion professor at Grinnell College, "is fundamentally economic." And the solution to economic tensions was social solidarity. As progressive economist Richard Ely put it, America could only truly thrive when it recognized that "our true welfare is not an individual matter purely, but likewise a social affair."

SETTLEMENT HOUSES Among the most visible soldiers in the social gospel movement were those who volunteered in innovative community centers called settlement houses. At the Hull House settlement on Halsted Street in a working-class Chicago neighborhood, two women from privileged backgrounds, Jane Addams and Ellen Gates Starr, addressed the everyday needs of the working poor, especially newly arrived European immigrants.

Addams and Starr were driven by an "impulse to share the lives of the poor" and to make social service "express the spirit of Christ." Their staff of two dozen women served thousands of people each week. Besides a nursery for the infant children of working mothers, Hull House also sponsored health clinics, lectures, music lessons and art studios, men's clubs, an employment bureau, job training, a gymnasium, a coffeehouse, and a savings bank. By the early twentieth century, there were hundreds of settlement houses in cities across the United States, most of them in the Northeast and Midwest.

Jane Addams By the end of the century, thanks to the efforts of Jane Addams and others, religious groups were joining the settlement house movement.

To Addams, the social gospel driving progressive reformers reflected their "yearning sense of justice and compassion." She and other settlement house leaders soon realized, however, that their work in the rapidly spreading immigrant slums was like bailing out the ocean with a teaspoon. They thus added political reform to their already lengthy agenda and began lobbying for new laws and regulations to improve the living conditions in poor neighborhoods.

As her influence in Chicago grew, Addams was appointed to prominent governmental and community boards where she focused on improving public health and food safety. She pushed for better street lighting and police protection in poor neighborhoods, and sought to reduce the population's misuse of narcotics. An ardent pacifist and outspoken advocate for suffrage (voting rights) for women, Addams would become the first American woman to win the Nobel Peace Prize.

The Woman Suffrage Movement

From 1880 to 1910, the number of employed women tripled from 2.6 million to 7.8 million. As women, especially college-educated women, became more involved in the public world of work and wages, the women's rights movement grew. Immediately after the Civil War, women in the movement had hoped that the Fifteenth Amendment, which guaranteed voting rights for African

American men, would aid their own efforts to gain the vote. The majority of men, however, still insisted that women stay out of politics because it would corrupt their moral purity.

In 1869 the Wyoming Territory became the first place in the United States to extend equal voting rights to women. In that year, the women's rights movement split over the issue of whether to concentrate solely on gaining the vote or to adopt a broader agenda. Susan B. Anthony and Elizabeth Cady Stanton founded the National Woman Suffrage Association (NWSA) to promote a **woman suffrage** amendment to the Constitution, but they considered it only one among many feminist causes to be championed. For example, they also campaigned for new laws requiring higher pay for women workers and making it easier for abused wives to get divorces. Other suffrage activists insisted that pursuing multiple issues hurt their cause. In 1869, they formed the American Woman Suffrage Association (AWSA), which focused single-mindedly on voting rights.

East meets West San Francisco suffragists marched across the country in 1915 to deliver a petition calling for a constitutional amendment with more than 500,000 signatures to Congress in Washington, D.C. Along the way, they were warmly received by other suffragists, like those of New Jersey, pictured here.

In 1890, the rival groups united as the National American Woman Suffrage Association (NAWSA). That same year, Wyoming was admitted as a state, the first with full voting rights for women. It was in the territories and states west of the Mississippi River that the suffrage movement had its earliest successes. In those areas, women were more engaged in grassroots political activities than they were in the East.

Between 1890 and 1896, the suffrage cause won three more victories in western states—Utah, Colorado, and Idaho. The movement then stalled for a time until proposals for voting rights at the state level easily won a Washington State referendum in 1910 and carried California by a close majority in 1911. The following year three more western states—Arizona, Kansas, and Oregon—joined in to make a total of nine western states with full suffrage. In 1913, Illinois granted women voting rights in presidential and municipal elections. Yet not until New York acted in 1917 did a state east of the Mississippi River allow women to vote in all elections.

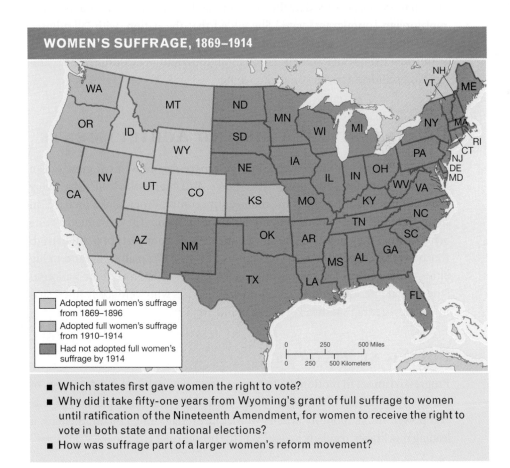

WOMEN'S SUFFRAGE, 1869–1914

Legend:
- Adopted full women's suffrage from 1869–1896
- Adopted full women's suffrage from 1910–1914
- Had not adopted full women's suffrage by 1914

- Which states first gave women the right to vote?
- Why did it take fifty-one years from Wyoming's grant of full suffrage to women until ratification of the Nineteenth Amendment, for women to receive the right to vote in both state and national elections?
- How was suffrage part of a larger women's reform movement?

Many advocates for women's suffrage argued that the right to vote and hold office was a matter of simple justice: women were just as capable as men of exercising the rights and responsibilities of citizenship. Others insisted that women were morally superior to men and therefore would improve the quality of the political process.

Women voters and politicians, advocates argued, would promote the welfare of society as a whole, creating a powerful engine for progressive social change. One activist explicitly linked women's suffrage with the social gospel, declaring that women followed the teachings of Christ more faithfully than men. If they were elected to public office, they would "far more effectively guard the morals of society and the sanitary conditions of cities."

Yet the women's suffrage movement was not free from social, ethnic, and racial prejudices. Carrie Chapman Catt, who became president of the National American Woman Suffrage Association in 1900, warned of the danger that "lies in the votes possessed by the males in the slums of the cities, and the ignorant foreign [immigrant] vote." She added that the nation, with "ill-advised haste," had given "the foreigner, the Negro and the Indian" the vote but still withheld it from white women. Throughout the country, most suffrage organizations excluded African American women.

Progressives' Aims and Achievements

The impulses and groups comprising the progressive movement grew out of what Theodore Roosevelt called the "fierce discontent with evil" that many Americans felt at the turn of the nineteenth century. Progressives focused on many different goals and used many different methods. They assaulted a wide array of what they saw as social and political evils, from corrupt politicians to too-powerful corporations, from economic distress on small farms and in big cities to the general feeling that "the people" had lost control of the nation to "the special interests"—businesses and their leaders who were solely interested in "money-getting" at the expense of public welfare.

Political Reforms

Progressivism set in motion the two most important political developments of the twentieth century: the rise of direct democracy and the expansion of federal power. In his monthly articles in *McClure's* magazine, Lincoln Steffens, a leading muckraker, regularly asked: "Will the people rule? Is democracy possible?"

Steffens and other progressives often answered that the way to improve America's democracy was to make it even more democratic.

To empower citizens to clean up the corrupt political system, progressives pushed to make the political process more open and transparent. One process was the *direct primary*, which would allow all members of a political party to vote on the party's nominees, rather than the traditional practice in which an inner circle of party leaders chose the candidates. In 1896, South Carolina became the first state to adopt a statewide primary, and within twenty years nearly every state had done so.

Progressives also developed other ways to increase public participation in the political process ("direct democracy") so as to curb the power of corporate giants over state legislatures. In 1898, South Dakota became the first state to adopt the *initiative* and *referendum*, procedures that allowed voters to create laws directly rather than having to wait for legislative action. Citizens could sign petitions to have a proposal put on the ballot (the initiative) and then vote it up or down (the referendum). Still another progressive innovation was the recall, whereby corrupt or incompetent elected officials could be removed by a public petition and vote. By 1920, nearly twenty states had adopted the initiative and referendum, and nearly a dozen had sanctioned the recall procedure.

Progressives also fought to change the way that U.S. senators were elected. Under the Constitution, state legislatures elected senators, a process frequently corrupted by lobbyists and vote buying. In 1900, for example, Senate investigators revealed that a Montana senator had given more than $100,000 in secret bribes to members of the legislature that chose him. In 1913, thanks to the efforts of progressives, the **Seventeenth Amendment**, providing for the direct election of senators, was ratified by enough states to become law.

The Efficiency Movement

A second major theme of progressivism was the "gospel of efficiency." Louis D. Brandeis, a Kentucky attorney who became Woodrow Wilson's progressive adviser and later a justice of the Supreme Court, believed that "efficiency is the hope of democracy."

The champion of progressive efficiency was Frederick Winslow Taylor, a Philadelphia-born industrial engineer who during the 1890s became a celebrated business consultant, helping mills and factories implement "scientific management." The nation's first "efficiency expert," Taylor showed employers how to cut waste and improve productivity. By breaking down work activities (filling a wheelbarrow, driving a nail, shoveling coal) into a sequence of mechanical steps and using stopwatches to measure the time it took each worker to perform each step, Taylor established detailed performance standards (and cash rewards) for each job classification, specifying how fast people should work and when they should rest. His celebrated book, *The Principles of Scientific Management* (1911), influenced business organizations for decades.

The goal of what came to be called **Taylorism** was to usher in a "mental revolution" in business management that would improve productivity and profits, raise pay for the most efficient workers, and reduce the likelihood of worker strikes. As Taylor wrote, "Men will not do an extraordinary day's work for an ordinary day's pay."

Many workers, however, resented Taylor's innovations, seeing them as just a tool to make people work faster. Yet his approach to industrial management became one of the most important contributions to capitalist economies in the twentieth century and brought concrete improvements in productivity.

Political progressives applied Taylorism to the operations of government by calling for the reorganization of state and federal agencies to eliminate duplication, the establishment of clear lines of authority, and the replacement of political appointees with trained specialists. By the early twentieth century, many complex functions of government had come to require specialists with technical expertise. As Woodrow Wilson wrote, progressive ideals could be achieved only if government at all levels was "informed and administered by experts." Many cities set up "efficiency bureaus" to identify government waste and apply more cost-effective "best practices."

MUNICIPAL REFORM Two Taylorist ideas for reform of city and county governments emerged in the first decade of the new century. One, the commission system, was first adopted in 1901 by the city of Galveston, Texas, after the local government collapsed following a devastating hurricane and tidal wave that killed more than 8,000—the greatest natural disaster in American history. The commission system placed ultimate authority in a board composed of commissioners who combined both legislative and executive powers in heading up city departments (sanitation, police, utilities, and so on). Houston, Texas, created a commission system in 1906. Dallas and Des Moines, Iowa, followed in 1907, as did Memphis in 1909.

Even more popular than the commission system was the city-manager plan, under which an appointed professional administrator ran a city or county government in accordance with policies set by the elected council and mayor. Staunton, Virginia, adopted the first city-manager plan in 1908. Five years later, the inadequate response of municipal officials to a flood led Dayton, Ohio, to become the first large city to adopt the plan.

Yet the efforts to make local governments more "business-like" and professional had a downside. Shifting control from elected officials representing individual neighborhoods to at-large commissioners and nonpartisan specialists separated local government from party politics, which for many working-class voters had been the main way they could have a voice in how they were governed locally. In addition, running a city like a business led commissioners and managers to focus on reducing expenses rather than expanding services, even when such expansion was clearly needed.

THE WISCONSIN IDEA At the state level, the ideal of efficient government run by nonpartisan experts was pursued most notably by progressive Republican governor Robert M. La Follette of Wisconsin. "Fighting Bob" La Follette declared war on "vast corporate combinations" and political corruption by creating a nonpartisan state government that would become a "laboratory for democracy." He established a Legislative Reference Bureau, which provided elected officials with nonpartisan research, advice, and help in drafting legislation. La Follette used the bureau's reports to enact such reforms as the direct primary, stronger railroad regulation, the conservation of natural resources, and workmen's compensation programs to support people injured on the job.

The "Wisconsin idea" was widely publicized and copied by other progressive governors. La Follette explained that the Wisconsin idea was a commitment to use government power to make "a happier and better state to live in, that its institutions are more democratic, that the opportunities of all its people are more equal, that social justice more nearly prevails."

REGULATION OF BUSINESS Of all the problems facing American society at the turn of the century, one towered above all: the regulation of giant corporations. The threat of corporate monopolies increased during the depression of the 1890s as struggling companies were gobbled up by larger ones. Between 1895 and 1904, some 157 new holding companies gained control of 1,800 different businesses. Almost fifty of these giant holding companies controlled more than 70 percent of the market in their respective industries. In 1896, fewer than a dozen companies other than railroads were worth $10 million or more. By 1903, that number had soared to 300.

Concerns over the concentration of economic power in trusts and other forms of monopolies had led Congress to pass the Sherman Anti-Trust Act in 1890, but it proved ineffective. In addition, government agencies responsible for regulating businesses often came under the influence of those they were supposed to regulate. Retired railroad executives, for instance, were appointed to the Interstate Commerce Commission (ICC), which had been created to regulate railroads. The issue of regulating the regulators has never been fully resolved.

Social Justice

Another important focus of the progressive movement was greater social justice for the working poor, the jobless, and the homeless. In addition to their work in settlement houses and other areas, many progressives formed advocacy organizations such as the National Consumers' League, which educated consumers about harsh working conditions in factories and mills and the widespread use of child workers.

Other organizations, such as the General Federation of Women's Clubs, insisted that civic life needed the humanizing effect of female leadership. Women's clubs across the country sought to clean up filthy slums by educating residents about personal and household hygiene ("municipal housekeeping"), urging construction of sewer systems, and launching public-awareness campaigns about the connection between unsanitary conditions and disease. Women's clubs also campaigned for child-care centers; kindergartens; government inspection of food processing plants; stricter housing codes; laws protecting women in the workplace; and more social services for the poor, sick, disabled, and abused. Still others addressed prostitution and alcohol abuse.

THE CAMPAIGN AGAINST DRINKING Middle-class women reformers, most of them motivated by strong religious convictions, were the driving force behind the social justice movement. Among the most powerful campaigns was that of the Women's Christian Temperance Union (WCTU). Founded in 1874 in Cleveland, Ohio, by 1900 the WCTU had grown into the largest women's group in the nation, boasting 300,000 members. While some of them were motivated by Protestant beliefs that consuming any alcohol was a sin, most saw excessive drinking, especially in saloons, as a threat to social progress and family stability.

By attacking drunkenness and closing saloons, reformers hoped to (1) improve family life by preventing domestic violence by husbands and fathers, (2) reduce crime in the streets, and (3) remove one of the worst tools of corruption—free beer on Election Day—in an effort to "buy" votes among the working class. As a Boston sociologist concluded, the saloon had become "the enemy of society because of the evil results produced upon the individual."

Initially, WCTU members met in churches to pray and then marched to nearby saloons to try to convince their owners to close. As its name suggests, the Women's Christian Temperance Union advocated *temperance*—the reduction of alcohol consumption. But the WCTU also urged individuals to embrace *abstinence* and refuse to drink any alcoholic beverages.

Under the leadership of Frances Willard, president of the WCTU between 1879 and 1898, the organization moved beyond moral persuasion of saloon-keepers and drinkers and began promoting legislation to ban alcohol ("prohibition"). Willard also pushed the WCTU to lobby for other progressive reforms important to women, including an eight-hour workday, the regulation of child labor, government-funded kindergartens, the right to vote, and federal inspections of the food industry. More than anything else, however, the WCTU continued to campaign against drinking.

The battle against alcoholic beverages took on new strength in 1893 with the formation of the Anti-Saloon League, an organization based in local churches that pioneered the strategy of the single-issue political pressure group. Describing itself as "the Protestant church in action against the saloon," the bipartisan League, like the WCTU, initially focused on closing down saloons rather than abolishing alcohol. Eventually, however, it decided to force the prohibition issue into the forefront of state and local elections. At its "Jubilee Convention" in 1913, the League endorsed an amendment to the Constitution prohibiting the manufacture, sale, and consumption of alcoholic beverages, which Congress approved in 1917.

LABOR LEGISLATION In 1890, almost half of the nation's wage workers toiled up to twelve hours a day—sometimes seven days a week—in unsafe, unsanitary, and unregulated conditions for extremely low wages. Legislation to ensure better working conditions and limit child labor was perhaps the most significant reform to emerge from the drive for progressive social justice.

At the end of the nineteenth century, fewer than half of working families lived solely on the husband's earnings. Many married women engaged in "homework"—making clothes, selling flower arrangements, preparing food for others, and taking in boarders. Parents in poor families also frequently took their children out of school and put them to work in factories, shops, mines, mills, and canneries, and on farms. In 1900, some 1.75 million children between the ages of ten and fifteen were working outside the home.

Many progressives argued that children, too, had rights in a democracy. The National Child Labor Committee campaigned for laws prohibiting the employment of children. Within ten years, most states had passed such laws, although some were lax in enforcing them.

Progressives who focused on children's issues also demanded that cities build more parks and playgrounds. Further, reformers made a concerted effort to regulate the length of the workday for women, in part because some of them were pregnant and others had children at home with inadequate supervision.

Child labor Child workers shuck oysters in 1913 at the Varn & Platt Canning Company in Bluffton, South Carolina.

Spearheaded by Florence Kelley, the first president of the National Consumers' League, progressives convinced many state governments to ban the hiring of children below a certain age, and to limit the hours that both women and children could work.

It took a tragic disaster, however, to spur meaningful government regulation of dangerous workplaces. On March 25, 1911, a fire broke out at the Triangle Shirtwaist factory (called a "sweatshop" because of its cramped and unventilated work areas) in New York City. Escape routes were limited because the owner kept the stairway door locked to prevent theft, and 146 workers trapped on the upper floors of the ten-story building died or leaped to their deaths. The victims were mostly young, foreign-born women in their teens, almost all of them Jewish, Italian, or Russian immigrants. In the fire's aftermath, dozens of new city and state regulations dealing with fire hazards, dangerous working conditions, and child labor were enacted across the nation.

THE "PROGRESSIVE" INCOME TAX Progressives also addressed America's growing economic inequality. One way to redistribute wealth was through a "progressive" federal income tax—so called because the tax rates "progress," or rise, as income levels rise, thus forcing the rich to pay more. Such a "graduated" or "progressive" tax system was the climax of the progressive movement's commitment to a more equitable distribution of wealth.

The progressive income tax was an old idea. In 1894, William Jennings Bryan had persuaded Congress to approve a 2 percent tax on annual incomes of more than $4,000. When millionaires responded by threatening to leave America, Bryan exclaimed, "If some of our 'best people' prefer to leave the country rather than pay the tax . . . let them depart." Soon after the tax became law, however, the Supreme Court declared it unconstitutional on a technicality.

Progressives continued to believe, however, that a "graduated" tax would help slow the concentration of wealth in the hands of the richest Americans. In 1907, President Theodore Roosevelt announced his support. Two years later, his successor, William Howard Taft, endorsed a constitutional amendment allowing such a tax, and Congress agreed. Finally, in 1913, the **Sixteenth Amendment** was ratified by enough states to become law.

Progressivism under Roosevelt and Taft

Most progressive legislation originated at the state and local levels. Federal reform efforts began in earnest only when Theodore Roosevelt became president in 1901. During his rapid rise to national fame and leadership, Roosevelt had grown more progressive with each passing year. "A great democracy," he said, "has got to be *progressive* or it will soon cease to be great or a democracy."

Roosevelt was a boundless force of nature, an American original, a "steam engine in trousers" with an oversized intellect and ego. His exuberance, charm, and humor, however, made him an irresistible personality. Even his political opponent, Woodrow Wilson, was smitten after meeting Roosevelt in person: "You can't resist the man."

Roosevelt transformed the presidency and the role of the federal government by breaking with the Gilded Age tradition in which presidents had deferred to Congress. In his view, the problems caused by explosive industrial growth required powerful responses, and he was unwilling to wait for Congress to act. Only an activist president armed with new regulatory agencies and laws could counterbalance the power of the corporations and trusts. "I believe in a strong executive," Roosevelt asserted. "I believe in power." During his administration, the White House became the focus of policy-making.

Square Deal This 1906 cartoon likens Roosevelt to the Greek legend Hercules, who as a baby strangled snakes sent from hell to kill him. Here, the serpents are pro-corporation senator Nelson Aldrich and Standard Oil's John D. Rockefeller.

TAMING BIG BUSINESS Roosevelt was the first president to use executive power to rein in Big Business. As governor of New York, he had pushed for legislation regulating sweatshops, instituting state inspections of factories and slaughterhouses, and limiting the workday to eight hours. Roosevelt believed in capitalism and the accumulation of wealth, but he was willing to adopt radical methods to ensure that the social unrest caused by the insensitivity of business owners to the rights of workers and the needs of the poor did not mushroom into a revolution.

Roosevelt applauded the growth of American industrial capitalism but declared war on corruption and on cronyism—the awarding of political appointments, government contracts, and other favors to politicians' personal friends. He endorsed a **Square Deal** for "every man, great or small, rich or poor." His Square Deal program featured what was called the "Three Cs": greater government *control* of corporations, enhanced *conservation* of natural resources, and new regulations to protect *consumers* against contaminated food and medications.

CURBING THE TRUSTS In December 1901, just a few months after entering the White House, Roosevelt declared that it was time to deal with the "grave evils" resulting from huge corporations exercising dominance over their industries and the nation's economic life. In his view, the federal government had the right and the obligation to curb the excesses of Big Business on behalf of the public good.

Roosevelt's version of progressivism centered on the belief that governments must ensure fairness. He would wage war against the robber barons who displayed "swinish indifference" to the public good and the "unscrupulous politicians" whose votes were regularly bought and sold by corporate lobbyists.

Early in 1902, just five months into his presidency, Roosevelt shocked the business community when he ordered the U.S. attorney general to break up the Northern Securities Company, a vast network of railroads and steamships in the Pacific Northwest organized by J. Pierpont Morgan.

Morgan could not believe the news. The world's most powerful capitalist and wealthiest man rushed from New York City to the White House and told the president: "If I have done anything wrong, send your man to my man and they can fix it up." But the attorney general, who was also at the meeting, told Morgan: "We don't want to 'fix it up.' We want to stop it." Turning to Roosevelt, Morgan then asked if the president planned to attack his other trusts, such as U.S. Steel and General Electric. "Certainly not," Roosevelt replied, "unless we find out that . . . they have done something wrong."

After Morgan left, the president told the attorney general to file the anti-trust paperwork. In 1904, the Supreme Court would rule in a 5–4 decision that the Northern Securities Company was indeed a monopoly and must be dismantled, thereby opening the way for more aggressive enforcement of the Sherman Anti-Trust Act. Roosevelt fully recognized the benefits of large-scale capitalism, and he thought that the rise of Big Business was the inevitable result of the industrial era. He did not want to destroy the titans of industry and finance, but he did insist that they be regulated for the public good.

Altogether, Roosevelt approved about twenty-five anti-trust suits against oversized corporations. He also sought stronger regulation of the railroads. By their very nature, railroads often exercised a monopoly over the communities they served, enabling them to charge customers whatever they wanted. In 1903, Congress passed the Elkins Act, making it illegal for railroads to give secret rebates (cash refunds) on freight charges to high-volume business customers. That same year, Congress approved Roosevelt's request that a federal Department of Commerce and Labor be formed, within which a Bureau of Corporations would monitor the activities of big businesses.

THE 1902 COAL STRIKE In everything he did, Roosevelt acted forcefully. On May 12, 1902, for example, some 150,000 members of the United Mine Workers (UMW) labor union walked off the job at coal mines in Pennsylvania and West Virginia. The miners were seeking a wage increase, a shorter work day, and official recognition of the union by the mine owners, who refused to negotiate. Instead, the owners shut down the mines.

By October, the ongoing shutdown had caused the price of coal to soar, and hospitals and schools reported empty coal bins as winter approached. In many northern cities, the poor had run out of coal for heating. Pastor Washington Gladden led a petition drive urging Roosevelt to step in to mediate the strike.

The president decided upon a bold move: he invited leaders of both sides to a conference in Washington, D.C., where he appealed to their "patriotism, to the spirit that sinks personal considerations and makes individual sacrifices for the public good." The mine owners in attendance, however, refused even to speak to the UMW leaders.

Roosevelt was infuriated by what he called the "extraordinary stupidity and temper" of the "wooden-headed" owners, saying he wanted to grab their spokesman "by the seat of his breeches" and "chuck him out" a window. He threatened to declare a national emergency so that he could take control of the mines and use soldiers to run them. When a congressman questioned the constitutionality of such a move, Roosevelt roared, "To hell with the Constitution when the people want coal!"

The threat worked: the strike ended on October 23. The miners won a nine-hour workday and a 10 percent wage increase. Roosevelt was the first president to use his authority to referee a dispute between management and labor.

Roosevelt's Reelection

Roosevelt's forceful leadership won him friends and enemies. As he prepared to run for reelection in 1904, he acknowledged that the "whole Wall Street crowd" would do all they could to defeat him. Nevertheless, he won the Republican nomination.

The Democrats, having lost twice with William Jennings Bryan, essentially gave the election to Roosevelt and the Republicans by nominating the virtually unknown Alton B. Parker, chief justice of the New York Supreme Court. Parker was the dullest—and most forgettable—presidential candidate in history. One journalist dubbed him "the enigma from New York." The most interesting item in his official campaign biography was that he had trained pigs to come when called by name.

The Democrats suffered their worst election defeat in thirty-two years. After winning the popular vote by 7.6 million to 5.1 million and the electoral vote 336 to 140, Roosevelt told his son it was his "greatest triumph." Having succeeded to the presidency after William McKinley's assassination, he had now won election on his own and, in his view, had a popular mandate to do great things. On the eve of his inauguration in March 1905, he announced: "Tomorrow I shall come into office in my own right. Then watch out for me!"

PROGRESSIVE REGULATION Now elected in his own right, Roosevelt launched his second term with an even stronger commitment to regulating corporations and their corrupt owners (the "criminal rich") who exploited their workers and tried to eliminate competition. His comments irked many of his corporate contributors and congressional Republican leaders. Said the

Pittsburgh steel baron Henry Frick, "We bought the son of a bitch and then he did not stay bought."

To promote the "moral regeneration of business," Roosevelt first took aim at the railroads. In 1906, he persuaded Congress to pass the Hepburn Act, which for the first time gave the federal Interstate Commerce Commission the power to set maximum freight rates for the railroad industry.

Under Roosevelt's Square Deal programs, the federal government also assumed oversight of key industries affecting public health: meat packers, food processors, and makers of drugs and patent medicines. Muckraking journalists had revealed all sorts of unsanitary and dangerous activities in the preparation of food and drug products by many companies. Perhaps the most powerful blow against these abuses was struck by Upton Sinclair's novel *The Jungle* (1906), which told the story of a Lithuanian immigrant working in a filthy Chicago meatpacking plant:

> It was too dark in these storage places to see well, but a man could run his hand over these piles of meat and sweep off handfuls of the dried dung of rats. These rats were nuisances, and the packers would put

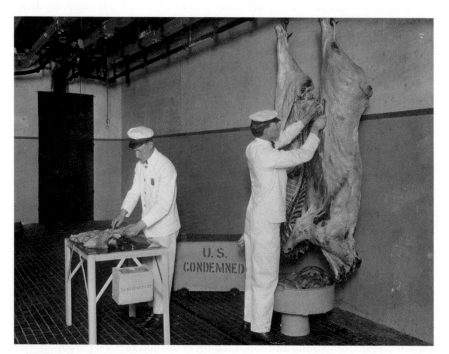

Bad meat Government inspectors closely examine tainted sides of beef at a meatpacking plant.

poisoned bread out for them, they would die, and then rats, bread, and meat would go into the hoppers [to be ground up] together.

After reading *The Jungle*, Roosevelt urged Congress to pass the Meat Inspection Act of 1906. It required the Department of Agriculture to inspect every hog and steer whose carcass crossed state lines—both before and after slaughter. The Pure Food and Drug Act (1906), enacted the same day, required the makers of prepared food and medicines to host government inspectors, too.

ENVIRONMENTAL CONSERVATION Theodore Roosevelt was the first president passionately committed to environmental conservation. An avid outdoorsman and naturalist, he feared that unregulated logging and mining companies were destroying the nation's landscape "by their reckless extermination of all useful and beautiful wild things." Roosevelt championed efforts to protect wilderness areas and manage and preserve the nation's natural resources for the benefit of future generations. He created fifty federal wildlife refuges, approved five new national parks and fifty-one federal bird sanctuaries, and designated eighteen national monuments, including the Grand Canyon.

In 1898, Roosevelt had endorsed the appointment of his friend Gifford Pinchot, the nation's first professionally trained forest manager, as head of the U.S. Department of Agriculture's Division of Forestry. Pinchot, like Roosevelt, believed in economic growth as well as environmental preservation. Roosevelt and Pinchot used the Forest Reserve Act (1891) to protect 172 million acres of federally owned forests from being logged. Lumber companies were furious, but the president held firm, declaring, "I hate a man who skins the land." Overall, Roosevelt set aside more than 234 million acres of federal land for conservation purposes and created forty-five national forests in eleven western states. As Pinchot recalled, "Launching the conservation movement was the most significant achievement of the T.R. Administration, as he himself believed."

ROOSEVELT AND RACE Roosevelt's most significant failure as a progressive, as it was for so many of his successors, was his refusal to confront the movement's major blind spot: racism. Like Populists, progressives worked to empower "the people." For many of them, however, "the people" did not include African Americans, Native Americans, or some immigrant groups. Most white progressives shared the prevailing racist attitudes of the time. They ignored or even endorsed the passage of Jim Crow laws in the South that prevented blacks from voting and subjected them to rigid racial separation.

By 1901, nearly every southern state had prevented almost all African Americans from voting or holding political office by disqualifying or terrorizing

Theodore Roosevelt and Booker T. Washington Roosevelt addresses the National Negro Business League in 1900 with Washington seated to his left.

them. Hundreds of African Americans were being lynched each year across the South, where virtually no blacks were allowed to serve on juries or work as sheriffs or policemen. A white candidate for governor in Mississippi in 1903 announced that he believed "in the divine right of the white man to rule, to do all the voting, and to hold all the offices, both state and federal." The South, wrote W. E. B. Du Bois, then a young sociologist at Atlanta University, "is simply an armed camp for intimidating black folk."

At the same time, few progressives raised objections to the many informal and private patterns of segregation and prejudice in the North and West. "The plain fact is," muckraking journalist Ray Stannard Baker admitted in 1909, "most of us in the North do not believe in any real democracy between white and colored men." Roosevelt confided to a friend in 1906 his belief that "as a race and in the mass," African Americans "are altogether inferior to whites."

Yet the president made a few exceptions. On October 16, 1901, Roosevelt invited Booker T. Washington, the nation's most prominent black leader, to the White House to discuss presidential appointments in the South. Upon learning of the meeting, white southerners exploded with fury. The *Memphis Scimitar* screamed that inviting a "nigger" to dine in the White House was "the most damnable outrage that has ever been perpetrated by a citizen of the United States." South Carolina senator Benjamin R. Tillman threatened that "a thousand niggers in the South will have to be killed to teach them 'their place' again." A stunned Roosevelt insisted that he had done nothing wrong, but he never again would host a black leader.

THE BROWNSVILLE RIOT The following year, 1906, brought a violent racial incident in Brownsville, Texas, where a dozen or so members of an African American army regiment from a nearby fort got into a shootout with whites who had been harassing them outside a saloon. One white bartender was killed, and a police officer was seriously wounded. Both sides claimed the other started the shooting. An investigation concluded that the soldiers were at fault, but no one could identify any of the shooters and none of the soldiers was willing to talk.

Roosevelt responded by dishonorably discharging the entire regiment of 167 soldiers, several of whom had been awarded the Congressional Medal of Honor for their service in Cuba during the War of 1898. Critics flooded the White House with angry telegrams. Secretary of War William H. Taft urged the president to reconsider his decision, but Roosevelt refused to show any mercy to "murderers, assassins, cowards, and comrades of murderers." (Sixty years later, the U.S. Army "cleared the records" of all the black soldiers.) Disheartened black leaders predicted that Roosevelt's harsh language would ignite "race hatred and violence" against innocent African Americans.

Taft and Retrenchment

After his 1904 election victory, Roosevelt had decided he would not run for president again, in part because he did not want to be the first president to serve the equivalent of three terms. It was a noble gesture but a blunder that would have momentous political consequences. For now, however, he urged Republicans to nominate his long-time friend, Secretary of War William Howard Taft, whom the Republican Convention endorsed on its first ballot in 1908.

The Democrats again chose William Jennings Bryan, who still retained a faithful following, especially in the South. Taft promised to continue Roosevelt's policies, and the Republican platform endorsed the president's progressive program. The Democratic platform echoed the Republican emphasis on regulation of business but called for a lower tariff. Bryan struggled to attract national support and was defeated for a third time, as Taft swept the electoral college, 321 to 162.

A LIFE OF PUBLIC SERVICE William Howard Taft was superbly qualified to be president. Born in Cincinnati in 1857, he was the son of a prominent attorney who had served in President Grant's cabinet. He had graduated second in his class at Yale and gone on to become a leading legal scholar, serving on the Ohio Supreme Court. In 1900, President McKinley had appointed him the first American governor-general of the Philippines, and three years later Roosevelt named him secretary of war. Until becoming president, Taft had never held an elected office.

Unlike the robust, athletic Roosevelt, Taft struggled most of his life with obesity, topping out at 332 pounds and earning the nickname "Big Bill." Roosevelt, he explained, "loves the woods, he loves hunting; he loves roughing it, and I don't." Although good-natured and easygoing, Taft as president never managed—even in his own mind—to escape the shadow of his charismatic predecessor. "When I hear someone say 'Mr. President,'" he confessed, "I look around expecting to see Roosevelt."

Taft vowed to preserve capitalism by protecting "the right of private property" and the "right of liberty." In practice, this meant that he was even more determined than Roosevelt to support "the spirit of commercial freedom" against monopolistic trusts, but he was not interested in pushing for additional reforms or exercising extraordinary presidential power. Taft viewed himself as a judge-like administrator, not an innovator, and was reluctant to exercise presidential authority. (After leaving the White House, he got the job he had always wanted: chief justice of the U.S. Supreme Court.) Taft proved neither as energetic nor as wide-ranging as Roosevelt in his role as a reformer president—a difference that would lead to a fateful break between the two men.

TAFT AND THE TARIFF President Taft displayed his credentials as a progressive Republican by supporting *lower* tariffs on imports; he even called a special session of Congress to address the matter. But he proved less skillful than Roosevelt in dealing with Congress. Taft also discontinued Roosevelt's practice of using interviews with journalists to influence congressmen by using his "big stick through the press."

In the end, Taft's failure of leadership enabled Congress to pass the flawed Payne-Aldrich Tariff (1909), which did little to change federal policies. Tariff policies continued to favor the industrial Northeast. Taft's failure to gain real reform and his lack of a "crusading spirit" angered progressive, pro-Roosevelt Republicans, whom Taft called "assistant Democrats." Spurned by the progressive members of his party, Taft gravitated to the "Old Guard" Republican conservatives. Roosevelt was not happy.

THE BALLINGER–PINCHOT CONTROVERSY In 1910, the split between the conservative and progressive Republican factions was widened by what came to be called the Ballinger-Pinchot controversy. Taft's new secretary of the interior, Richard A. Ballinger, opened to commercial development millions of acres of federal lands that Roosevelt had ordered protected. As chief of forestry, Gifford Pinchot complained about the "giveaway," but Taft refused to intervene. When Pinchot made his opposition public early in 1910, Taft fired him, labeling him a "fanatic." In doing so, Taft set in motion a feud with Roosevelt that would eventually end their friendship—and cost him his reelection.

THE TAFT–ROOSEVELT FEUD In 1909, soon after Taft became president, Roosevelt and his son Kermit sailed to Africa, where they would spend nearly a year hunting big-game animals. (When he heard about the extended safari, business tycoon J. Pierpont Morgan expressed the hope that "every lion would do its duty.") Roosevelt had left the White House assuming that Taft would continue to pursue a progressive agenda. But by filling the cabinet with corporate lawyers and firing Gifford Pinchot, Taft had, in Roosevelt's view, failed to "carry out my work unbroken."

Roosevelt's rebuke of Taft was in some ways undeserved. Taft had at least attempted tariff reform, which Roosevelt had never dared. Although Taft had fired Pinchot, he had replaced him with another conservationist. Taft's administration actually preserved more federal land in four years than Roosevelt's had in nearly eight, and it filed twice as many anti-trust suits, including the one that led to the breakup of the Standard Oil Company in 1911. Taft also supported giving women the right to vote and workers the right to join unions.

None of that satisfied Roosevelt, however. On August 31, 1910, the angry former president, eager to return to the political spotlight, gave a speech at Osawatomie, Kansas, in which he announced his latest progressive principles and proposals—his "New Nationalism." Roosevelt explained that he wanted to go beyond ensuring a "Square Deal" in which corporations were forced to "play by the rules"; he now promised to "change the rules" to force large corporations to promote social welfare and to serve the needs of working people.

To save capitalism from the threat of a working-class revolution, Roosevelt called for tighter federal regulation of "arrogant" corporations that too often tried to "control and corrupt" politics; for a federal income tax (the Sixteenth Amendment had still not become law); and for federal laws regulating child labor. It was a sweeping agenda that would greatly expand the power of the federal government over economic and political life.

Then, on February 24, 1912, Roosevelt abandoned his earlier pledge and announced his entry into the race for the 1912 Republican presidential nomination. He dismissed the "second-rate" Taft as a "hopeless fathead" who had "sold the Square Deal down the river." Taft responded by calling Roosevelt a "dangerous egotist" and a "demagogue." They began a bitter war in which Roosevelt had the better weapons, not the least of which was his love of a good fight.

By 1912, a dozen or so "progressive" states were letting citizens vote for presidential candidates in party primaries instead of following the traditional practice in which a state's party leaders chose the nominee. Roosevelt decided that if he won big in the Republican primaries, he could claim to be "the people's choice." But even though he won all but two primaries, including the one in Taft's home state of Ohio, his personal popularity was no match for Taft's authority as party leader. In the thirty-six states that still chose candidates by conventions dominated by party bosses, the Taft Republicans prevailed. At the Republican National Convention, Taft was easily nominated for reelection.

Sideshow Ted This 1912 cartoon criticizes the Bull Moose Party for being just a sideshow (with suffragists selling lemonade outside) and points out the menacing ego of Roosevelt himself.

Roosevelt was furious. He denounced Taft and his supporters as thieves and stormed out of the convention along with his delegates—mostly social workers, teachers, professors, journalists, and urban reformers, along with a few wealthy business executives.

THE PROGRESSIVE PARTY Six weeks later, Roosevelt urged the breakaway faction of Republicans to reconvene in Chicago to create the **Progressive party**. They enthusiastically nominated him as their candidate. He assured the delegates that he felt "fit as a bull moose," leading journalists to nickname the Progressives the "Bull Moose party."

When Roosevelt closed his acceptance speech by saying, "We stand at Armageddon [the climactic encounter between Christ and Satan], and we battle for the Lord," the delegates stood and burst into the hymn "Onward, Christian Soldiers." One reporter wrote that the "Bull Moose" movement was not so much a party as it was a political religion, and Roosevelt was its leading evangelist. Progressives loved him because he showed what a government dedicated to the public good might achieve. And he loved to campaign because it enabled him to engage the people in the democratic process. "The first duty of the American citizen," he stressed, "is that he shall work in politics."

The Progressive party platform, audacious for its time, revealed Roosevelt's growing liberalism. It supported a minimum "living wage" for hourly workers, women's suffrage, campaign finance reform, and a system of "social security" insurance to protect people against sickness, unemployment, and disabilities. It also pledged to end the "boss system" governing politics and destroy the "unholy alliance between corrupt business and corrupt politics." Conservative critics called Roosevelt "a socialist," a "revolutionist," "a virtual traitor to American institutions," and a "monumental egotist."

WOODROW WILSON: A PROGRESSIVE SOUTHERNER

The fight between William Howard Taft and Theodore Roosevelt gave hope to the Democrats, whose presidential nominee, New Jersey governor Woodrow Wilson, had enjoyed remarkable success in his brief political career. Until his nomination and election as governor in 1910, Wilson had been a college professor and then president of Princeton University; he had never run for political office or worked in business. He was a man of ideas who had a keen intellect, an analytical temperament, a tireless work ethic, an inspiring speaking style, and a strong conviction that he knew what was best for the nation.

TO SERVE HUMANITY Born in Staunton, Virginia, in 1856, the son, grandson, nephew and son-in-law of Presbyterian ministers, Thomas Woodrow Wilson had grown up in Georgia and the Carolinas during the Civil War and Reconstruction. The South, he once said, was the only part of the nation where nothing had to be explained to him. Tall and slender, with a long, chiseled face, he developed an unquestioning religious faith. Driven by a consuming sense that God had destined him to "serve" humanity, he often displayed an unbending self-righteousness and a fiery temper, qualities that would prove to be his undoing as president.

Wilson graduated from Princeton in 1879. After law school at the University of Virginia, he briefly practiced law in Atlanta, but he found legal work "dreadful drudgery" and soon enrolled at Johns Hopkins University to study history and political science, earning one of the nation's first doctoral degrees.

He became an expert in constitutional government and taught at several colleges before being named president of Princeton in 1902.

Eight years later, Wilson accepted the support of New Jersey Democrats for the 1910 gubernatorial nomination. And he already harbored higher ambitions. If he could become governor, he reflected, "I stand a very good chance of being the next President of the United States." Like Roosevelt, Wilson was an intensely ambitious and idealistic man who felt destined to preside over America's emergence as the greatest world power.

Wilson proved a surprisingly effective campaigner and won a landslide victory. The professor-turned-governor then persuaded the state legislature

Woodrow Wilson The only president to hold a PhD degree.

to adopt an array of progressive reforms to curb the power of political party bosses and corporate lobbyists. "After dealing with college politicians," Wilson joked, "I find that the men who I am dealing with now seem like amateurs."

Governor Wilson soon attracted the attention of national Democratic leaders. At the 1912 Democratic convention, he faced stiff competition from several veteran party leaders for the presidential nomination. But with the support of William Jennings Bryan, he won on the forty-sixth ballot. It was, Wilson said, a "political miracle."

THE 1912 ELECTION The 1912 presidential campaign was one of the most exciting in history. It involved four distinguished candidates: Democrat Woodrow Wilson, Republican William Howard Taft, Socialist Eugene V. Debs, and Progressive Theodore Roosevelt. For all of their differences in personality and temperament, the candidates shared a basic progressive assumption that modern social problems could be resolved only through active governmental intervention.

No sooner did the formal campaign open than Roosevelt's candidacy almost ended. While on his way to deliver a speech in Milwaukee, Wisconsin, he was shot by John Schrank, a lunatic who believed that any president seeking a third term should be shot. The bullet went through Roosevelt's

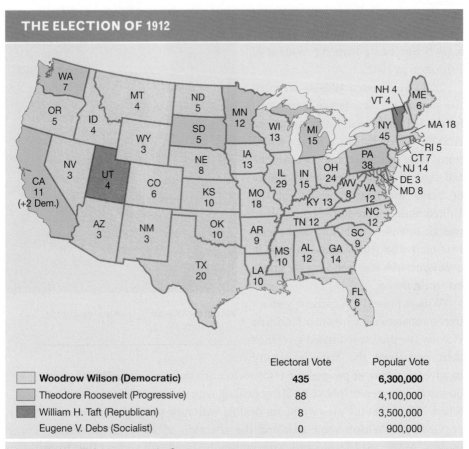

THE ELECTION OF 1912

	Electoral Vote	Popular Vote
Woodrow Wilson (Democratic)	**435**	**6,300,000**
Theodore Roosevelt (Progressive)	88	4,100,000
William H. Taft (Republican)	8	3,500,000
Eugene V. Debs (Socialist)	0	900,000

■ Why was Taft so unpopular?
■ How did the division between Roosevelt and Taft give Wilson the presidency?
■ Why was Wilson's victory in 1912 especially significant?

thick overcoat, a steel eyeglass case, and fifty-page speech, then fractured a rib before nestling just below his right lung, an inch from his heart. Refusing medical attention, Roosevelt demanded that he be driven to the auditorium to deliver an eighty-minute speech to 10,000 supporters. In a dramatic gesture, he showed the audience his bloodstained shirt and punctured text and vowed, "It takes more than this to kill a bull moose."

As the campaign developed, Taft quickly lost ground. "There are so many people in the country who don't like me," he lamented. The contest settled into a debate over the competing programs touted by the two front-runners: Roosevelt's New Nationalism and Wilson's **New Freedom**. The New Freedom, designed by Louis Brandeis, aimed to restore economic competition by eliminating all trusts rather than simply regulating them. Where Roosevelt admired the power and efficiency of law-abiding corporations, no matter how large, Brandeis and Wilson were convinced that huge, "heartless" industries needed to be broken up.

On Election Day, Wilson won handily, collecting 435 electoral votes to 88 for Roosevelt and only 8 for Taft. After learning of his election, the self-righteous Wilson told the chairman of his campaign committee that "I owe you nothing. God ordained that I should be the next president of the United States. Neither you nor any other mortal could have prevented that."

Had the Republicans not divided their votes between Taft and Roosevelt, however, Wilson would have lost. His was the victory of a minority candidate over a divided opposition. Since all four candidates called themselves progressives, however, the president-elect expressed his hope "that the thoughtful progressive forces of the nation may now at last unite."

The election of 1912 profoundly altered the character of the Republican party. The defection of the Bull Moose Progressives had weakened its progressive wing. As a result, when Republicans returned to power in the 1920s, they would be more conservative in tone and temperament.

EUGENE DEBS The real surprise of the 1912 election was the strong showing of the Socialist party candidate, Eugene V. Debs, running for the fourth time. The tall, blue-eyed idealist had devoted his adult life to fighting against the "monstrous system of capitalism" on behalf of the working class, first as a labor union official, then as a socialist promoting government ownership of railroads and the sharing of profits with workers.

Debs became the unifying symbol of a diverse movement that united West Virginia coal miners, Oklahoma sharecroppers, Pacific Northwest lumberjacks, and immigrant workers in New York City sweatshops. One newspaper described "The Rising Tide of Socialism" in 1912, as some 1,150 Socialists won election to local and state offices across the nation, including eighteen mayoral seats.

To many voters, the Socialists, whose 118,000 dues-paying members in 1912 were double the number from the year before, offered the only real alternative to a stalemated political system in which the two major parties had few real differences. But fear of socialism was also widespread. Theodore Roosevelt warned that the rapid growth of the Socialist party was "far more ominous than any Populist or similar movement in the past."

In 1912, with few campaign funds, Debs crisscrossed the nation giving fiery speeches. He dismissed Roosevelt as "a charlatan, mountebank [swindler], and fraud" whose progressive promises were nothing more than "the mouthings of a low and utterly unprincipled self-seeker and demagogue." Debs's untiring efforts brought him more than 900,000 votes, more than twice as many as he had received four years earlier.

A BURST OF REFORM BILLS

On March 4, 1913, a huge crowd surrounded the Capitol in Washington, D.C., to watch Wilson's inauguration. The new president declared it "a day of dedication." He promised to lower "the stiff and stupid" Republican tariff, create a new national banking system, strengthen anti-trust laws, and establish an administration "more concerned about human rights than about property rights."

Roosevelt had been a strong president by force of personality. Wilson became a strong president by force of conviction. Like Roosevelt, Wilson was an activist president; he was the first to speak to the nation over the radio and to host weekly press conferences. He frequently spoke to Congress and visited legislators in their offices.

As a political scientist, Wilson was an expert at the processes of government. During his first two years, he pushed through Congress more new bills than any previous president. Like "most reformers," however, Wilson "had a fierce and unlovely side," according to the president of Harvard University. He found it hard to understand—much less work with—people who disagreed with him.

Wilson's victory, coupled with Democratic majorities in the House and Senate, gave his party effective national power for the first time since the Civil War. It also gave southerners a significant role in national politics for the first time since the war. Five of Wilson's ten cabinet members were born in the South.

THE TARIFF AND THE INCOME TAX Like Taft, Wilson pursued tariff reform, but with much greater success. By 1913, the federal tariff included hundreds of taxes on different imported goods, from oil to nails. The president believed that U.S. corporations were misusing the tariff to keep out foreign competitors and create American monopolies that kept consumer prices artificially high.

To attack high tariff rates, Wilson took a bold step: he summoned Congress to a special session that lasted eighteen months, the longest in history, and he addressed its members in person—the first president to do so since John Adams. The new tariff bill passed the House easily. The crunch came in the Senate, the traditional graveyard of tariff reform, where swarms of industry lobbyists grew so thick, Wilson said, that "a brick couldn't be thrown without hitting one of them." The president finally won approval there by publicly criticizing the "industrious and insidious" tariff lobby.

The Underwood-Simmons Tariff Act (1913) lowered tariff rates on almost 1,000 imported products. To compensate for the reduced tariff revenue, the bill created the first income tax allowed under the newly ratified Sixteenth Amendment: the initial tax rates were 1 percent on income more than $3,000

($4,000 for married couples) up to a top rate of 7 percent on annual income of $50,000 or more. Most Americans (99 percent) paid no income tax because they earned less than $3,000 a year.

THE FEDERAL RESERVE ACT No sooner had the new tariff passed the Senate than the administration proposed the first major banking reform since the Civil War. Ever since Andrew Jackson had killed the Second Bank of the United States in the 1830s, the nation had been without a central bank. Instead, the money supply was chaotically "managed" by thousands of local and state banks.

Such a decentralized system was unstable and inefficient because, during financial panics, fearful depositors, eager to withdraw their money, would create "runs" that often led to the failure of smaller banks. The primary reason for a new central bank was to prevent more such panics, which had occurred five times since 1873. Wilson believed that the banking system needed a central reserve agency that, in a crisis, could distribute emergency cash to banks threatened by runs. But he insisted that any new banking system must be overseen by the government rather than by bankers themselves (the "money power"). He wanted a central bank that would benefit the entire economy, not just the large banks headquartered on Wall Street in New York City.

After much dickering, Congress passed the **Federal Reserve Act** on December 23, 1913. It created a national banking system with twelve regional districts, each of which had its own Federal Reserve Bank owned by member banks in the district. Nationally chartered banks, which agreed to regulation by a Federal Reserve Bank in exchange for the right to issue money, had to be members of the Federal Reserve System. State-chartered banks—essentially unregulated—did not (and, indeed, two-thirds of the nation's banks chose not to become members of the Federal Reserve System). The twelve regional Federal Reserve banks were supervised by a central board of directors in Washington, D.C.

The overarching purpose of the Federal Reserve System was to adjust the nation's currency supply to promote economic growth and ensure the stability and integrity of member banks. When banks were short of cash, they could borrow from the Federal Reserve ("the Fed"), using their loans as collateral. Each of the new regional banks issued Federal Reserve notes (currency) to member banks in exchange for their loans. The Federal Reserve board required member banks to have a certain percentage of their total deposits in cash on hand ("reserve") at all times. The new system soon proved its worth. The Federal Reserve Act was the most significant new program of Wilson's presidency.

ANTI-TRUST ACTIONS President Wilson made "trust-busting" the central focus of his New Freedom program. Giant corporations had continued to grow despite the Sherman Anti-Trust Act and the Bureau of Corporations, the federal watchdog agency created by Theodore Roosevelt.

Wilson decided to make a strong **Federal Trade Commission (FTC)** the cornerstone of his anti-trust program. Created in 1914, the five-member FTC replaced the Bureau of Corporations and assumed new powers to define "unfair trade practices" and issue "cease and desist" orders when it found evidence of such practices.

Like Roosevelt, Wilson also supported efforts to strengthen and clarify the Sherman Anti-Trust Act. Henry D. Clayton, a Democrat from Alabama, drafted an anti-trust bill in 1914. The **Clayton Anti-Trust Act** declared that labor unions were not to be viewed as "monopolies in restraint of trade," as courts had maintained since 1890. It also prohibited corporate directors from serving on the boards of competing companies and further clarified the meaning of various "monopolistic" activities.

WILSON DECLARES VICTORY

In November 1914, just two years after his election, President Wilson announced that he had accomplished the major goals of progressivism. He had fulfilled his promises to lower the tariff, create a national banking system, and strengthen anti-trust laws. The New Freedom was now complete, he wrote.

Wilson's declaration, however, bewildered many progressives, especially those who had long advocated additional federal social-justice legislation that Wilson had earlier supported. Herbert Croly, the influential editor of the *New Republic* magazine, wondered how the president could assert "that the fundamental wrongs of a modern society can be easily and quickly righted as a consequence of [passing] a few laws." Wilson's about-face, he concluded, "casts suspicion upon his own sincerity [as a progressive] or upon his grasp of the realities of modern social and industrial life."

PROGRESSIVISM FOR WHITES ONLY African Americans continued to resent the racial conservatism displayed by most progressives. Carter Glass, the Virginia senator who was largely responsible for developing the Federal Reserve Act in 1913, was an enthusiastic supporter of his state's efforts to disfranchise black voters. When questioned by a reporter about being a racist progressive, Glass embraced the label: "Discrimination! Why that is exactly what we propose. To remove every Negro voter who can be gotten rid of."

Similarly, Woodrow Wilson showed little concern about the discrimination and violence that African Americans faced. In fact, he shared many of the racist attitudes common at the time. As a student at Princeton, he had expressed his disgust at the Fifteenth Amendment, which had guaranteed voting rights for black men after the Civil War, arguing that whites must resist domination by "an ignorant and inferior race." As a politician, Wilson did court African American voters, but he rarely consulted black leaders and largely avoided associating with them.

Wilson's cabinet secretaries racially segregated the employees in their agencies. The president endorsed the policy, claiming that racial segregation "is not humiliating but a benefit." To him, "separate but equal" was the best way to resolve racial tensions. He was the first

New freedom, old rules Woodrow Wilson and the First Lady ride in a carriage with African American drivers.

president since the Civil War who openly endorsed discrimination against African Americans.

THE VOTE FOR WOMEN Activists for women's suffrage also were disappointed in President Wilson. Despite having two daughters who were suffragists, he insisted that the issue of women's voting rights should be left to the states rather than embodied in a constitutional amendment.

Wilson's lack of support led some leaders of the suffrage movement to revise their tactics. In 1910, Alice Paul, a New Jersey–born Quaker and social worker, returned from working with the militant suffragists of England, where she had participated in various forms of civil disobedience to generate attention and

support. After Paul joined the National American Woman Suffrage Association (NAWSA), she urged activists to use more aggressive tactics: picket state legislatures, target and "punish" politicians who failed to endorse suffrage, chain themselves to public buildings, incite police to arrest them, and undertake hunger strikes.

In March 1913, Paul organized 5,000 suffragists to protest at Wilson's inauguration. Four years later, having broken with the NAWSA and formed the National Woman's Party, Paul decided that suffragists must do something even more dramatic: picket the

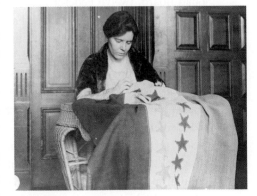

Alice Paul Sewing a suffrage flag—orange and purple, with stars—that she and other suffragists often waved at strikes and protests.

White House. Beginning on January 11, 1917, Paul and her followers took turns carrying signs all day, five days a week, for months, until the president ordered their arrest. Some sixty suffragists were jailed.

Paul was sentenced to seven months in prison. She then went on a hunger strike, leading prison officials to force-feed her raw eggs through a tube inserted in her nose. She later recalled that "it was shocking that a government of men could look with such extreme contempt on a movement that was asking nothing except such a simple little thing as the right to vote." Under an avalanche of negative press coverage and public criticism, Wilson finally pardoned Paul and the other activists.

PROGRESSIVISM RENEWED By 1916, Wilson's determination to win reelection revived his commitment to progressive activism. The president nominated Bostonian Louis D. Brandeis, the "people's attorney," to the Supreme Court. Brandeis was not just a famed defender of unions against big businesses; he would also be the first Jewish member of the Supreme Court. Progressives viewed the nomination as a "landmark in the history of American democracy." Others disagreed. Former president Taft dismissed Brandeis as "a muckraker, an emotionalist for his own purposes, a socialist . . . who is utterly unscrupulous." The Senate, however, confirmed Brandeis's appointment.

FARM LEGISLATION President Wilson also urged Congress to pass the first federal legislation directed at assisting farmers. He first supported a proposal to set up rural banks to provide long-term farm loans. The Federal Farm Loan Act became law in 1916. Under the control of the Federal Farm Loan Board, twelve Federal Land banks offered loans to farmers for five to forty years at low interest rates. Farmers could borrow up to 50 percent of the value of their land. At about the same time, a dream long advocated by Populists—federal loans to farmers on the security of their crops stored in warehouses—finally came to fruition when Congress passed the Warehouse Act of 1916. These crop-security loans were available to sharecroppers, tenant farmers, and to farmers who owned the land that they worked.

Farmers also benefited from the Smith-Lever Act of 1914, which provided federal programs to educate farmers about new machinery and new ideas related to agricultural efficiency, and the Smith-Hughes Act (1917), which funded agricultural and mechanical education in high schools. Farmers with the newfangled automobiles had more than a passing interest as well in the Federal Highways Act of 1916, which helped finance new highways, especially in rural areas.

LABOR LEGISLATION One of the long-standing goals of many progressive Democrats was a *federal* child-labor law. When Congress passed the

Keating-Owen Act in 1916, banning products made by child workers under fourteen from being shipped across state lines, Wilson expressed doubts about its constitutionality but eventually signed it.

Another landmark law was the eight-hour workday for railroad workers. The Adamson Act of 1916 resulted from a threatened strike by railroad unions demanding an eight-hour day and other concessions. Wilson, who objected to some of the unions' demands, nevertheless asked Congress to approve the Adamson Act. It required time-and-a-half pay for overtime work beyond eight hours and appointed a commission to study working conditions in the railroad industry.

ASSESSING PROGRESSIVISM

Progressivism reached its peak during Woodrow Wilson's two terms as president. After decades of political upheaval and social reform, progressivism had shattered the traditional "laissez-faire" notion that government had no role in protecting the public welfare by regulating the economy. The courage and compassion displayed by progressives demonstrated that people of good will could make a difference in improving the quality of life for all.

Progressivism awoke people to the evils and possibilities of modern urban-industrial life. Most important, progressives established the principle that governments—local, state, and federal—had a responsibility to ensure that Americans were protected from abuse by powerful businesses and corrupt politicians. Yet on several fronts, progressivism fell short of its supporters' hopes and ideals. It would take the Great Depression during the 1930s to lead to the passage of a national minimum wage and the creation of a government-administered pension program for retirees and disabled workers (Social Security).

Like all great historic movements, progressivism produced unexpected consequences. For all of its efforts to give more power to "the people," voter participation actually fell off during the Progressive Era. Probably the main reason for the decline of party loyalty and voter turnout was that, by the twentieth century, people had many more activities to distract them. New forms of recreation like movies, cycling, automobiles, and spectator sports competed with politics for time and attention. Also, people showed less interest in political parties and public issues in part because of the progressive emphasis on government by appointed specialists and experts rather than elected politicians.

Ultimately, progressivism faded as an organized political movement because international issues pushed aside domestic concerns. By 1916, the optimism of a few years earlier was challenged by the distressing slaughter occurring in Europe in the Great War. The twentieth century, which had dawned with such bright hopes for social progress, held in store episodes of unprecedented brutality that led people to question whether "progress" was even possible anymore.

CHAPTER REVIEW

SUMMARY

- **The Progressive Impulse**   Progressives were mostly middle-class idealists in both political parties who promoted reform and government regulation to ensure social justice. Many progressives wished to restrict the powers of local political machines and establish honest and efficient government. They also called for legislation to end child labor, promote workplace safety, ban the sale of alcoholic beverages, regulate or eliminate trusts and other monopolies, and grant *woman suffrage*.

- **The Varied Sources of Progressivism**   Many religious reformers, such as those involved in the *social gospel* movement, urged their fellow Protestants to reject social Darwinism and do more to promote a better life for the urban poor. The settlement house movement sprang from this idea and spread through urban America as educated middle-class women formed community centers in poverty-stricken neighborhoods. Progressives drew inspiration from the women's suffrage movement, as more women became involved in social reform efforts and in the workplace. Many progressive ideas arose from the ongoing efforts of reformers to end political corruption. Progressives, while not radicals, also responded to the growing socialist movement and its calls for economic justice for the working class. *Muckrakers*—investigative journalists who exposed political and corporate corruption—further fueled the desire of progressive reformers to address abuses of power in American society.

- **Progressives' Aims and Achievements**   Progressives focused on stopping corruption in politics. They advanced political reforms such as the direct primary; the initiative, referendum, and recall at the state level; and the direct election of U.S. senators through the passage of the *Seventeenth Amendment*. Other progressives focused on incorporating new modes of efficiency and scientific management in business, known as *Taylorism*, into government. Their efforts inspired many cities and counties to adopt the commission system and the city-manager plan. Still other progressives, who saw regulation of Big Business as the overriding issue facing the nation, focused on legislation and bureaucratic oversight to control or eliminate trusts and other forms of monopolies.

- **Progressivism under Roosevelt and Taft**   The administrations of Theodore Roosevelt and William H. Taft increased the power of the presidency and the federal government to regulate corporate power and improve the lives of many Americans. Roosevelt promoted his progressive *Square Deal* program, which included regulating trusts through the creation of the Bureau of Corporations, arbitrating the 1902 coal strike, persuading Congress to regulate the railroads through the Elkins and Hepburn Acts, and to clean up the meat and drug industries with the Meat Inspection and Pure Food and Drug Acts. Roosevelt also initiated an environmental conservation campaign to manage and preserve the nation's natural resources.

- **Woodrow Wilson's Progressivism**   Wilson's *New Freedom* program included the Underwood-Simmons Tariff Act, the *Federal Reserve Act*, the *Clayton Anti-Trust Act*, and the *Federal Trade Commission*. But he initially opposed federal efforts to promote social justice, and he withheld support for a bill to regulate child labor and a constitutional amendment guaranteeing women's suffrage. A southerner, he believed blacks were inferior and he supported increased segregation in the federal workforce.

CHRONOLOGY

1901	William McKinley is assassinated; Theodore Roosevelt becomes president
	Galveston, Texas, adopts the commission system of city government
1902	Justice Department breaks up Northern Securities Company
1903	Congress passes the Elkins Act and creates the Bureau of Corporations
1906	Upton Sinclair's *The Jungle* is published
	Congress passes the Meat Inspection Act and the Pure Food and Drug Act
1909	William Howard Taft inaugurated
1911	Triangle Shirtwaist fire
	Frederick Taylor's *The Principles of Scientific Management* is published
1912	Woodrow Wilson wins four-way presidential election
1913	Alice Paul and 5,000 suffragists protest Wilson's inauguration
	Sixteenth and Seventeenth Amendments ratified
	Underwood-Simmons Tariff and Federal Reserve Act passed
1914	Congress passes the Clayton Anti-Trust Act

KEY TERMS

muckrakers p. 780

social gospel p. 781

woman suffrage p. 784

Seventeenth Amendment (1913) p. 787

Taylorism p. 788

Sixteenth Amendment (1913) p. 793

Square Deal p. 794

Progressive party p. 803

New Freedom p. 806

Federal Reserve Act (1913) p. 809

Federal Trade Commission (FTC) (1914) p. 810

Clayton Anti-Trust Act (1914) p. 810

 INQUIZITIVE

Go to InQuizitive to see what you've learned—and learn what you've missed—with personalized feedback along the way.

22 America and the Great War

1914–1920

Make American History In this U.S. Navy recruiting poster in New York City, a sailor encourages a young man to play an active role in the Great War.

T hroughout the nineteenth century, the Atlantic Ocean had protected America from the major land wars on the continent of Europe. During the early twentieth century, however, the nation's century-long isolation from European conflicts ended. Ever-expanding world trade meant that U.S. interests were becoming deeply entwined with the global economy. In addition, the development of steam-powered ships and submarines meant that foreign navies could directly threaten American security.

At the same time, the election of Woodrow Wilson in 1912 brought to the White House a self-righteous moralist determined to impose his standards on what he saw as renegade nations. This combination of circumstances made the outbreak of the "Great War" in Europe in 1914 a profound crisis for the United States. The war would become the defining event of the early twentieth century.

For almost three years, President Wilson maintained America's stance of "neutrality" in the war while providing increasing amounts of food and supplies to Great Britain and France. In 1917, however, German submarine attacks on U.S. ships forced Congress into declaring war. The decision would turn the tide in the fighting and reshape America's international role as a dominant world power.

focus questions

1. What caused the outbreak of the Great War, and why was the United States drawn into it? What was distinctive about the fighting on the Western Front?

2. How did the Wilson administration mobilize the home front? How did these mobilization efforts shape American society?

3. What were the major events of the war after the United States entered the conflict? How did the American war effort contribute to the defeat of the Central Powers?

4. How did Wilson promote his plans for a peaceful world order as outlined in his Fourteen Points?

5. What were the consequences of the war at home and abroad?

AN UNEASY NEUTRALITY

Woodrow Wilson once declared that he had "a first-class mind," and he was indeed highly intelligent, thoughtful, principled, and courageous. For all of his accomplishments and abilities, however, the president had no experience or expertise in international relations before he was elected president. He confessed that "it would be an irony of fate if my administration had to deal chiefly with foreign affairs"—a topic he did not even mention in his 1913 inaugural address. But from the summer of 1914, when war erupted in Europe, Wilson was forced to shift his attention from the New Freedom's progressive reforms to foreign affairs.

Wilson saw himself as being directed by God to help create a new world order governed by morality and ideals rather than by selfish national interests. Both Wilson and William Jennings Bryan, his secretary of state, believed that America had a duty to promote democracy and Christianity around the world. "Every nation of the world," Wilson declared, "needs to be drawn into the tutelage [guidance] of America."

THE GREAT WAR

Woodrow Wilson faced his greatest challenge beginning in the summer of 1914, when a war that few wanted yet no one could stop broke out in Europe. The "dreadful conflict" erupted suddenly, like "lightning out of a clear sky," a North Carolina congressman said. Wilson admitted that he was shocked by "this incredible European eruption." Unfortunately, it coincided with a sharp decline in the health of his wife Ellen, who died on August 6. "God has stricken me," the president wrote a friend, "almost beyond what I can bear."

Wilson would also have trouble bearing the accelerating horrors of the war in Europe. Its scope and destruction shocked everyone. Lasting for more than four years, from 1914 to 1918, it would become known as the Great War because it would involve more nations and cause greater destruction than any previous war: 20 million military and civilian deaths, and 21 million more wounded. The Great War would topple monarchs, destroy empires, create new nations, and set in motion a series of events that would lead to an even greater war in 1939.

CAUSES The Great War resulted from complex and long-simmering national rivalries and ethnic conflicts in central Europe. At the core of the tensions was the Austro-Hungarian Empire, an unstable collection of eleven nationalities that was determined to stop the expansionism of its neighbor and longstanding enemy, Serbia, in the Balkan Peninsula. Serbia had long hoped to create "Yugoslavia," a nation encompassing all Serbs from throughout the Austro-Hungarian Empire.

At the same time, a recklessly militaristic Germany, led by Kaiser (Emperor) Wilhelm II, sought to assert its dominance against its old enemies, the Russian Empire and France, while expanding its navy to challenge the British Empire's supremacy on the seas.

FIGHTING ERUPTS War erupted after Gavrilo Princip, a nineteen-year-old Serbian nationalist in Sarajevo (the capital of Austrian Bosnia), shot and killed the heir to the Austro-Hungarian throne, 50-year-old Archduke Franz Ferdinand, and his pregnant wife Sophie, on June 28, 1914. The killings in Sarajevo set Europe on fire.

To avenge the murders, Austria-Hungary, with Germany's unconditional approval, sought to bully and humiliate Serbia by demanding a say in its internal affairs. Serbia gave in to virtually all of the demands, but Austria-Hungary declared war anyway. In turn, Russia mobilized its army to defend Serbia, which triggered reactions by a complex set of European military alliances: the Triple Alliance, or **Central Powers** (Germany, Austria-Hungary, and Italy), and the Triple Entente, or **Allied Powers** (France, Great Britain, and Russia).

Germany, expecting a limited war and quick victory, declared war on Russia on August 1, 1914, and on France two days later. Germany then invaded neutral Belgium, murdering hundreds of civilians. Events spiraled out of control. The "rape of Belgium" brought Great Britain into the war against Germany on August 4 on the **Western Front**, the line of fighting in northern France and Belgium. Despite the Triple Alliance, Italy at first declared its neutrality before joining the Allies in return for a promise of territory taken from Austria-Hungary.

On the Eastern Front, Russian armies began clashing with German and Austro-Hungarian forces as well as those of the Turkish (Ottoman) Empire. Within five weeks of the assassination in Sarajevo, a "great war" had consumed all of Europe. (It would not be called the First World War until the second one came along in 1939.)

An Industrial War

The Great War was the first industrial war, involving the total mobilization of the economy and civilians as well as warriors. Of the approximately 70 million soldiers and sailors who fought on both sides, more than half were

THE GREAT WAR IN EUROPE, 1914

Central Powers (Triple Alliance)
Allied Powers (Triple Entente)
Neutral countries

- How did the European system of military alliances spread conflict across all of Europe?
- How was the Great War different from previous wars?
- How did the war in Europe lead to ethnic tensions in the United States?

killed, wounded, imprisoned, or unaccounted for. New weapons dramatically changed the nature of warfare. Machine guns, submarines, aerial bombing, poison gas, flame throwers, land mines, mortars, long-range artillery, and armored tanks produced appalling casualties and widespread destruction, a slaughter on a scale unimaginable to this day. An average of 900 Frenchmen and 1,300 Germans died *every* day on the Western Front.

TRENCH WARFARE The early weeks of the war involved fast-moving assaults as German armies swept across Belgium and northeastern France. The casualties were appalling. On a single day, August 22, 1914, the French army lost 27,000 men. But the war on the Western Front soon bogged down into hellish **trench warfare**, in which often inept generals sent masses of brave soldiers (German generals referred to the British army as "lions led by donkeys") out of waterlogged, zigzagging trenches—some of them 40 feet deep and swarming with rats—that had been dug along the Western Front some 450 miles from the coast of Belgium across northeastern France to the border of Switzerland.

On either side, the attackers were usually at a disadvantage as they slogged across muddy acres of devastated "no-man's-land" between the opposing entrenchments, where they encountered corpse-filled shell holes, webs of barbed wire, and constant gunfire and artillery shelling. From 1914 to 1918, the opposing armies in northeastern France attacked and counterattacked but gained little ground, while casualties rose into the millions. By 1918, the Allies (France, Great Britain, Italy, Russia, and the United States, among others), had suffered 5.4 million killed and 7 million wounded.

Charles de Gaulle, a young French lieutenant who forty years later would become his nation's president, said the conflict had become a "war of extermination." A British army chaplain described the war as a senseless "Waste of Muscle, Waste of Brain, Waste of Patience, Waste of Pain . . . Waste of Glory, Waste of God."

The object in such a war of attrition was not so much to gain ground as to keep inflicting death and destruction on the enemy until its manpower and resources were exhausted. In one assault against the Germans at Ypres in Belgium, the British lost 13,000 men in three hours of fighting—during which time they gained 100 meaningless yards. As the war ground on, nations on both sides found themselves using up their available men, resources, courage, and cash.

An American journalist reported that the massive casualties changed the way men looked at war. In earlier conflicts, soldiers were eager to fight and confident they would return unscathed. Now, the new recruits seemed to have "left hope behind" and were confident that they were "going to their death." By 1915, the great powers were engaged in a global war with no end in sight.

INITIAL AMERICAN REACTIONS

Disbelief in the United States over the bloodbath in Europe mingled with relief that a wide ocean stood between America and the killing fields. President Wilson, an avowed pacifist, maintained that the United States "was too proud to fight" in Europe's war, "with which we have nothing to do, whose causes cannot touch us." He repeatedly urged Americans to remain "neutral in thought as well as in action." Privately, however, Wilson sought to ensure that the United States could provide Great Britain and France as much financial assistance and supplies as possible.

That most Americans wanted the nation to stay out of the fighting did not keep them from choosing sides. More than a third of the nation's citizens were first- or second-generation immigrants still loyal to their homelands. Eight million German-born Americans lived in the United States in 1914, and most of the 4 million Irish-born Americans detested England, which had ruled the Irish for centuries. For the most part, these groups supported the Central Powers, while other Americans, largely of British origin, supported the Allied Powers.

SUPPORTING THE ALLIES By the spring of 1915, the Allied Powers' need for food and supplies had generated an economic windfall for American businesses, bankers, and farmers. Exports to France and Great Britain quadrupled from 1914 to 1916. To finance their record-breaking purchases of American supplies, the Allies, especially Britain and France, needed loans from U.S. banks and "credits" from the U.S. government that would allow them to pay for their purchases later.

Early in the war, Secretary of State William Jennings Bryan took advantage of Wilson's absence from Washington after the death of his wife to tell J. Pierpont Morgan, the world's richest banker, that loans to any nations at war were "inconsistent with the true spirit of neutrality."

Upon his return, an angry Wilson reversed Bryan's policy by removing all restrictions on loans to the warring nations ("belligerents"). American banks and other investors would eventually send more than $2 billion to the Allies before the United States entered the fighting, and only $27 million to Germany. What Bryan feared, and what Wilson did not fully realize, was that as Britain and France borrowed and purchased more from the United States, it became harder for America to remain neutral.

"The Sandwich Man" To illustrate America's biased brand of neutrality, this political cartoon shows Uncle Sam wearing a sandwich board that advertises the nation's conflicting desires.

Despite the disproportionate financial assistance provided to the Allies, the Wilson administration maintained its official neutrality for thirty months. In particular, Wilson tried valiantly to defend the age-old principle of "freedom of the seas." As a neutral nation, the United States, according to international law, should have been able to continue to trade with all the nations at war.

On August 6, 1914, Bryan urged the warring nations to respect the rights of neutral nations to ship goods across the Atlantic. The Central Powers agreed, but the British refused. In November 1914, the British ordered the ships of neutral nations to submit to searches to discover if cargoes were bound for Germany. A few months later, the British announced that they would seize any ships carrying goods to Germany.

NEUTRAL RIGHTS AND SUBMARINE ATTACKS With its warships bottled up by a British blockade, the German government announced a "war zone" around the British Isles. All ships in those waters would be attacked by submarines, the Germans warned, and "it may not always be possible to save crews and passengers." The Germans' use of submarines, or **U-boats** (*Unterseeboot* in German), violated the long-established wartime custom of stopping an enemy vessel and allowing the passengers and crew to board lifeboats before sinking it. During 1915, German U-boats sank 227 British ships in the Atlantic Ocean and the North Sea.

The United States called the submarine attacks "an indefensible violation of neutral rights," and Wilson warned that he would hold Germany to "strict accountability" for the loss of American lives and property. Then, on May 7, 1915, a German submarine sank the **Lusitania**, an unarmed British luxury liner. Of the 1,198 persons on board who died, 128 were Americans.

The sinking of the *Lusitania*, asserted former president Theodore Roosevelt, was mass murder that called for a declaration of war. Wilson at first urged patience: "There is such a thing as a man being too proud to fight. There is such a thing as a nation being so right that it does not need to convince others by force that it is right."

Critics scolded Wilson for his bloodless response. Roosevelt dismissed it as "unmanly," called the president a "jackass," and threatened to "skin him alive if he doesn't go to war." Wilson privately admitted that he had misspoken. The timid language, he said, had "occurred to me while I was speaking, and I let it out. I should have kept it in."

Wilson's earlier threat of "strict accountability" now required a tough response. On May 13, Secretary of State Bryan demanded that the Germans stop unrestricted submarine warfare, apologize, and pay the families of those killed on the *Lusitania*. The Germans countered that the ship was armed (which was false) and secretly carried rifles and ammunition (which was true). On June 9, Wilson dismissed the German claims and reiterated that the United States was "contending for nothing less high and sacred than the rights of humanity." Bryan resigned as secretary of state in protest of Wilson's pro-British stance.

Stunned by the global outcry over the *Lusitania*, the German government told its U-boat captains to quit attacking passenger vessels. Despite the order, however, a German submarine sank the British liner *Arabic*, and two Americans on board were killed. The Germans paid a cash penalty to their families and issued what came to be called the *Arabic* Pledge on September 1, 1915: "Liners will not be sunk by our submarines without warning and without safety of the lives of non-combatants, provided that the liners do not try to escape or offer resistance."

In early 1916, Wilson sent his closest adviser, Colonel Edward M. House, to London, Paris, and Berlin in hopes of stimulating peace talks, but the mission failed. On March 24, 1916, a U-boat sank the French passenger ferry *Sussex*, killing eighty passengers and injuring two Americans. After Wilson threatened to end relations with Germany, its leaders renewed their promise not to sink merchant and passenger ships. The *Sussex* Pledge implied the virtual abandonment of submarine warfare. Colonel House noted in his diary that Americans were "now beginning to realize that we are on the brink of war and what war means."

PREPARING FOR WAR The sinking of U.S. passenger vessels led to efforts to strengthen the army and navy in case the nation was forced into war. On December 1, 1914, a "preparedness" movement, led by Theodore Roosevelt and Henry Cabot Lodge, created the National Security League to convince Congress and the president to begin preparing for war.

Wilson, too, believed in preparedness. After the *Lusitania* sinking, he directed the War and Navy Departments to develop plans for a $1 billion military expansion. His efforts were controversial, however. Many Americans—pacifists, progressives, and non-interventionists—opposed the "preparedness" effort, seeing it as simply a propaganda campaign to benefit defense industries ("war traffickers") that made weapons and other military equipment.

Despite such opposition, Congress in 1916 passed the National Defense Act, which provided for the expansion of the U.S. Army from 90,000 to 223,000 men over the next five years. While Bryan and others complained that Wilson wanted to "drag this nation into war," the reverse was actually true. Wilson told an aide that he was determined not to "be rushed into war, no matter if every damned congressman and senator stands up on his hind legs and proclaims me a coward."

THE 1916 ELECTION

As the 1916 election approached, Theodore Roosevelt hoped to become the Republican nominee. But his decision in 1912 to run as a third-party candidate had alienated many powerful Republicans, and his eagerness to enter the European war scared many voters. So instead, the Republicans nominated Supreme Court Justice Charles Evans Hughes, a progressive who had served as governor of New York from 1907 to 1910.

The Democrats, staying with Wilson, adopted a platform centered on social-welfare legislation and prudent military preparedness. The peace theme, refined in the slogan "He kept us out of war," became the campaign's rallying cry, although the president now acknowledged that the United States could no longer refuse to play the "great part in the world which was providentially cut out for her. . . . We have got to serve the world." Colonel House was more blunt. He told Secretary of State Robert Lansing that they "could not permit the Allies to go down in defeat, for if they did, we would follow."

Both Wilson and Hughes were sons of preachers; both were attorneys and former professors; both had been progressive governors; both were known for their integrity. Hughes called for higher tariffs, attacked Wilson for being hostile to Big Business, and implied that Wilson was not neutral enough in responding to the war. Theodore Roosevelt, who was devastated that his party did not nominate him, called the bearded Hughes a "whiskered Wilson." Wilson, however, proved to be the better campaigner—barely.

By midnight on election night, Wilson went to bed assuming that he had lost. Roosevelt was so sure Hughes had won that he sent him a congratulatory telegram. At 4 A.M., however, the results from California were tallied. Wilson had eked out a victory in that state by only 4,000 votes, and thus had become the first Democrat to win a second consecutive term since Andrew Jackson in 1832. His pledge of "peace, prosperity, and progressivism" won him the western states, Ohio, and the Solid South.

AMERICA GOES TO WAR

After his reelection, Wilson again urged the warring nations to negotiate a peace settlement, but to no avail. On January 31, 1917, desperate German military leaders renewed unrestricted submarine warfare in the Atlantic. All vessels from the United States headed for Britain, France, or Italy would be sunk without warning. "This was practically ordering the United States off the Atlantic," said an angry William McAdoo, Wilson's secretary of the Treasury.

The German decision, Colonel House wrote in his journal, left Wilson "sad and depressed," for the president knew it meant war. For their part, the

Germans greatly underestimated the American reaction. The United States, the German military newspaper proclaimed, "not only has no army, it has no artillery, no means of transportation, no airplanes, and lacks all other instruments of modern warfare." When his advisers warned that German submarines might cause the United States to enter the war, Kaiser Wilhelm scoffed, "I don't care."

THE ZIMMERMANN TELEGRAM On February 3, President Wilson informed Congress that the United States had formally ended diplomatic relations with the German government. Three weeks later, on February 25, Wilson learned that the British had intercepted a message from a German official, Arthur Zimmermann, to the Mexican government, urging the Mexicans to invade the United States. In exchange, Germany would give Mexico "lost territory in Texas, New Mexico, and Arizona." On March 1, newspapers broke the news of the so-called **Zimmermann telegram**. Infuriated Americans called for war against the Germans, whose attacks on American vessels increased.

AMERICA ENTERS THE WAR In March 1917, German submarines torpedoed five U.S. ships in the North Atlantic. For Wilson, this was the last straw. On April 2, he called on Congress to declare war against Germany.

In one of his greatest speeches, Wilson insisted that "the world must be made safe for democracy." He warned that waging war in Europe would require mobilizing "all the material resources of the country" and he called for 500,000 men to bolster the armed forces. The United States, he asserted, was entering the war to lead a "great crusade" not simply to defeat Germany but to end wars forever. Congress greeted Wilson's message with thunderous applause. On April 4, the Senate passed the war resolution by a vote of 82 to 6. The House followed, 373 to 50, and Wilson signed the measure on April 6.

America's long embrace of isolationism was over. The nation had reached a turning point in its relations with the world that would test all of President Wilson's political and diplomatic skills—and his stamina.

MOBILIZING A NATION

In April 1917, the U.S. Army remained small, untested, and poorly armed. With only 107,000 men, it was only the seventeenth largest army in the world. Now the Wilson administration needed to recruit, equip, and train an army of millions and transport them across an ocean infested with German submarines.

Mobilizing the nation for war led to an unprecedented expansion of federal authority. The government drafted millions of men between the ages of twenty-one and thirty into the armed services, forced the conversion of industries and farms to wartime needs, took over the railroads, and in many other respects assumed control of national life.

Soon after the U.S. declaration of war, President Wilson called for complete economic mobilization and created new federal agencies to coordinate the effort. Fighting in the Great War would cost the U.S. government $30 billion, which was more than thirty times the entire federal budget in 1917.

The War Industries Board (WIB), established in 1917, soon became the most important of all the federal mobilization agencies. Bernard Baruch, a savvy financier, headed the WIB, which had the authority to ration raw materials, construct new factories, and set prices.

Wilson appointed Republican Herbert Hoover to head the new Food Administration, whose slogan was "Food will win the war." Its purpose was to increase agricultural production while reducing civilian food consumption, since Great Britain and France needed massive amounts of American corn and wheat. Hoover organized a huge group of volunteers who fanned out across the country to urge housewives and restaurants to participate in "Wheatless" Mondays, "Meatless" Tuesdays, and "Porkless" Thursdays and Saturdays.

A NEW LABOR FORCE Removing 4 million men from the workforce to serve in the armed forces created an acute labor shortage. To meet it, women were encouraged to take jobs previously held mostly by men. One government poster shouted: "Women! Help America's Sons Win the War: Learn to Make Munitions." Another said, "For Every Fighter, a Woman Worker."

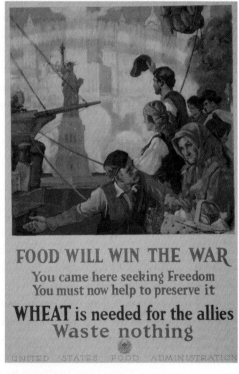

FOOD WILL WIN THE WAR
You came here seeking Freedom
You must now help to preserve it
WHEAT is needed for the allies
Waste nothing
UNITED STATES FOOD ADMINISTRATION

The immigrant effort This Food Administration poster emphasizes that "wheat is . . . for the allies," an important message to immigrants who hailed from Central Powers nations such as Germany and Austria.

Initially, women had supported the war effort mostly in traditional ways. They helped organize fund-raising drives, donated canned food and war-related materials, volunteered for the Red Cross, and joined the army nurse corps. As the scope of the war widened, however, women were recruited to work on farms, loading docks, and railway crews, as well as in the armaments industry, machine shops, steel and lumber mills, and chemical plants. "At last, after centuries of disabilities and discrimination," said a speaker at a Women's Trade Union League meeting in 1917, "women are coming into the labor [force] and festival of life on equal terms with men."

But the changes in female employment were limited and brief. About 1 million women participated in "war work," but most were young and single and already working outside the home, and most returned to their previous jobs once the war ended. In fact, after the war, male-dominated unions encouraged women to go back to domestic roles. The Central Federated Union of New York insisted that "the same patriotism which induced women to enter industry during the war should induce them to vacate their positions after the war."

The Great War also generated dramatic changes for many members of minority groups. Hundreds of thousands of African American men enlisted or were drafted into the military, where they were required to serve in racially segregated units commanded by white officers, as in the Civil War half a century earlier.

On the home front, northern businesses sent recruiting agents into the southern states, which were still largely rural and agricultural, to find workers for their factories and mills. For the first time, such efforts were directed at African Americans as well as whites. More than 400,000 southern blacks, mostly farmers, joined what came to be known as the **Great Migration**, a mass movement that would continue through the 1920s and change the political and social chemistry of northern cities such as St. Louis, Chicago, Detroit, New York, and Philadelphia. By 1930 the number of African Americans living in the North was triple that of 1910.

Recruiting agents and newspaper editors, both black and white, portrayed the North as the "land of promise" for southern blacks. Northern factory jobs were plentiful and high paying by southern standards, and racism was less obvious and violent—at least at first. A black migrant from Mississippi wrote home from Chicago in 1917 that he wished he had moved north twenty years earlier. "I just begin to feel like a man [here]," he explained. "It's a great deal of pleasure in knowing that you have some privilege. My children are going to the same school with the whites, and I don't have to be humble to no one."

Many Mexican Americans found similar opportunities during the war and after. Between 1917 and 1920, some 100,000 Mexicans crossed the border into

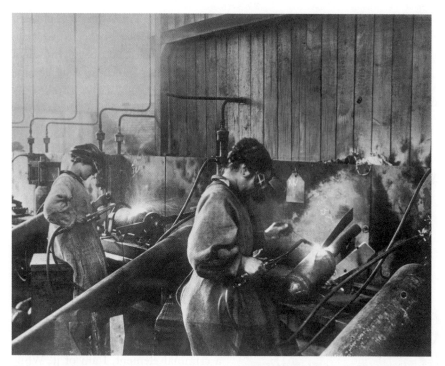

At the munitions factory Women on both sides played crucial roles in the war effort, from building airplanes to cooking for soldiers overseas. Here, American women use welding torches to build bombs.

the United States. Some joined the military. The economic expansion caused by the war enabled migrant farmworkers already living in states such as Texas, New Mexico, Arizona, and California to take better jobs in factories and mills in rapidly growing cities such as Phoenix, Los Angeles, and Houston, where they moved into Spanish-speaking neighborhoods called *barrios*.

But the newcomers, whether Latinos or blacks, were often resented. J. Luz Saenz, a Mexican American from Texas, noted in his diary that it took only three days after he was discharged from the army to have whites "throw us out from restaurants and deny us service as human beings." In 1917, more than forty African Americans and nine whites were killed during a riot in a weapons plant in East St. Louis, Illinois. Two years later, a Chicago race riot left twenty-three African Americans and fifteen whites dead.

A LOSS OF CIVIL LIBERTIES Once war was declared, Americans often equated anything German with disloyalty. German Americans were publicly harassed and discriminated against. Many Americans quit drinking beer because most breweries were owned by German Americans. Symphonies refused to perform music by Bach and Beethoven, schools canceled German language classes, and grocers renamed *sauerkraut* "liberty cabbage." President Wilson had predicted as much. "Once [we] lead this people into war," he said, "they'll forget there ever was such a thing as tolerance." What Wilson did not say was that he himself would lead the effort to suppress civil liberties, for, as he claimed, subversive forces in a nation at war must be "crushed out."

Under the Espionage and Sedition Acts, Congress prohibited any criticism of government leaders and war policies. The Espionage Act of 1917 called for twenty years in prison for anyone who helped the enemy; encouraged insubordination, disloyalty, or refusal of duty in the armed services; or interfered with the war effort in other ways.

During the war, 1,055 people were convicted under the Espionage Act. Most were simply critics of the war. Socialist leader Eugene V. Debs, a militant pacifist, was convicted simply for opposing the war and was sentenced to ten years in prison. He told the court he would always criticize wars imposed by the "master" class: "While there is a lower class, I am in it. While there is a criminal element, I am of it. While there is a soul in prison, I am not free."

The Sedition Act of 1918 broadened the Espionage Act to those who tried to impede the sale of war bonds or promoted cutbacks in production; it even outlawed saying, writing, or printing anything "disloyal, profane, scurrilous, or abusive" about the American form of government, the Constitution, or the army and navy.

The Supreme Court endorsed the Espionage and Sedition Acts in two rulings issued just after the war ended. *Schenck v. United States* (1919) reaffirmed the conviction of Charles T. Schenck, head of the Socialist party, for circulating leaflets opposing the war among members of the armed forces. Justice Oliver Wendell Holmes wrote the unanimous court opinion

Keep out of it In this 1918 war poster, the Kaiser—with his famous moustache and spiked German helmet—is depicted as a spider, spinning an invisible web to catch the stray words of Allied civilians.

that freedom of speech did not apply to words that represented "a clear and present danger to the safety of the country." In *Abrams v. United States* (1919), the Court upheld the conviction of a man who had distributed pamphlets opposing military intervention in Russia to remove the Bolsheviks, who had seized power in 1917.

THE AMERICAN ROLE IN THE WAR

In 1917, America's war strategy focused on helping the struggling French and British armies on the Western Front. The Allied leaders stressed that they needed at least a million American troops (called "doughboys") to defeat the Germans, but it would take months to recruit, equip, and train that many new soldiers. On December 21, 1917, French premier Georges Clemenceau urged the Americans to rush their army, called the American Expeditionary Force, to France. "A terrible blow is imminent," he told an American journalist about to leave Paris. "Tell your Americans to come quickly." Clemenceau was referring to the likelihood of a massive German attack, made more probable by the end of the fighting on the Eastern Front following the Bolshevik Revolution in Russia in November 1917.

THE BOLSHEVIK REVOLUTION Among the many casualties of the Great War, none was greater in scale than the destruction of the backward Russian Empire and its monarchy. It was the first nation to crack under the stress and strain of the Great War. On March 15, 1917, bumbling Tsar Nicholas II, having presided over a war that had ruined the Russian economy and the nation's transportation system, abdicated his throne and turned the nation over to the "provisional government" of a new Russian republic committed to continuing the war.

The fall of the tsar gave Americans the illusion that all the major Allied powers were now fighting for the ideals of constitutional democracy—an illusion that was shattered after the Germans in April helped exiled radical Vladimir Ilyich Lenin return to Russia from Switzerland. The Germans hoped that he would cause turmoil in his homeland. He did much more than that.

As Lenin observed, power in war-weary Russia was lying in the streets, waiting to be picked up. To do so, he mobilized the Bolsheviks, a group of ruthless Communist revolutionaries who were convinced that they were in the vanguard of the irresistible force of history. During the night of November 6, the Bolsheviks seized power from the provisional government, established a dictatorship, and called for a quick end to the war.

Lenin banned political parties and all organized religions (atheism became the official belief), eliminated civil liberties and the free press, and killed or imprisoned opposition leaders, including the tsar and his family. In short, he imposed his totalitarian blueprint of the perfect society on the Russian people. In 1918, Lenin instructed Bolshevik leaders to crack down on peasants who resisted the revolution: "Comrades! Hang (hang without fail, so that people will see) no fewer than one hundred kulaks, rich men, bloodsuckers. Yours, Lenin."

The Bolshevik Revolution triggered a prolonged civil war throughout Russia. President Wilson sent 20,000 American soldiers to Siberia to support the anti-Communist Russian forces, but they were unsuccessful.

FOURTEEN POINTS Woodrow Wilson was determined to ensure that the Great War would be the last world war. In September 1917, he asked Colonel Edward House to organize a group of 150 experts in politics, history, geography, and foreign policy, called the Inquiry, to draft a peace plan, since America, according to Wilson, had no selfish goals; it was simply "one of the champions of the rights of mankind." Drawing upon their advice, Wilson developed what would come to be called the **Fourteen Points**, which he presented to Congress on January 8, 1918, calling it "the only possible program" for peace.

The first five of the fourteen points endorsed the open conduct of diplomacy rather than secret treaties, the recognition of neutral nations' right to continue maritime commerce in time of war ("freedom of the seas"), the removal of international trade barriers, the reduction of armaments, and the transformation of colonial empires.

Most of the other points dealt with territorial claims. In redrawing the map of Europe, Wilson demanded that the victors follow the difficult principle of "self-determination," allowing overlapping nationalities and ethnic groups to develop their own independent nations. Point thirteen called for a new nation for Poland, long dominated by the Russians on the east and the Germans on the west. Point fourteen, the capstone of Wilson's postwar scheme, called for the creation of a "league" of nations to preserve global peace. When the Fourteen Points were made public, African American leaders asked the president to add a fifteenth point: an end to racial discrimination. Wilson did not respond. Overall, reaction to the speech was positive. The headline for the *New York Times* editorial proclaimed: "The President's Triumph."

As the war ground on, the battling nations grew weary of the costs and shortages of food, clothing, and gasoline. But no diplomatic solution was in sight. In Germany, food and fuel shortages led to growing discontent. Workers went on strike, and servicemen mutinied and deserted. "The Monarchy," said a German official, "is lurching toward the edge of the abyss."

RUSSIA SURRENDERS Conditions were even worse in Russia. After taking power, Lenin declared that the world would be freed from war only by a global revolution in which capitalism was replaced by communism. To that end, he wanted Russia out of the Great War as soon as possible. On March 3, 1918, Lenin signed a humiliating peace agreement with Germany, the Treaty of Brest-Litovsk. The treaty forced Russia to transfer vast territories to Germany and Turkey and to recognize the independence of the Ukraine region, thereby depriving Russia of much of its population, coal and wheat production, and heavy industry. In addition, Russia had to pay $46 million to Germany. Lenin was willing to accept such a harsh peace because he needed to concentrate on his internal enemies in the ongoing Russian civil war.

With Russia out of the war, the Germans could focus on the Western Front. Erich Ludendorff, the German army commander, said that the ability to move hundreds of thousands of soldiers from the Russian front to France would give

Meuse-Argonne Offensive American soldiers of the 23rd Infantry, 2nd Division, fire machine guns at the Germans from what was left of the Argonne Forest in France.

him numerical superiority for the first time and enable him to "deal an annihilating blow to the British before American aid can become effective."

AMERICANS ON THE WESTERN FRONT On March 21, the Germans began the first of several offensives in France and Belgium designed to win the war before the American soldiers arrived in force. By May, the German armies had advanced within fifty miles of Paris, and the British Fifth Army was destroyed.

The massive German offensive nearly defeated the Allies. In early April, however, the Germans suddenly lost their momentum. On April 5, the German commander called a halt because so many soldiers were exhausted and demoralized, convinced, as one officer admitted, that their "hope [for victory] had been dashed" by their inability to sustain the supply lines needed for such a widespread advance.

In May, French and British leaders pressed Wilson to hurry American troops into the fighting. By the end of the month, some 650,000 American soldiers were in Europe. In June, they were ready to fight. At the month-long Battle of Belleau Wood, which began on June 2, U.S. forces commanded by General John J. Pershing joined the French in driving the Germans back. A French officer watching the high-spirited, if untrained, American soldiers remarked that they were providing "a wonderful transfusion of blood" for the Allied cause.

Pershing was determined to use U.S. troops to break the stalemate on the Western Front. During the ferocious fighting, a French officer urged an American unit to retreat. In a famous exchange, U.S. Marine Captain Lloyd W. Williams refused the order, saying: "Retreat? Hell, we just got here."

In a massive Allied offensive, begun on September 26, 1918, American troops joined British and French armies in a drive toward Sedan, France, and its strategic railroad, which supplied the German army occupying northern France. With 1.2 million U.S. soldiers involved, including some 200,000 African Americans, it was the largest American action of the war, and it resulted in 117,000 American casualties, including 26,000 dead. But along the entire French-Belgian front, the outnumbered Germans were in retreat during the early fall of 1918. "America," wrote German General Erich Ludendorff, "became the decisive power in the war."

On October 6, the German government asked Wilson for peace negotiations based on his Fourteen Points. British and French leaders accepted the Fourteen Points as a basis of negotiations, but with two significant reservations: the British insisted on the right to discuss limiting freedom of the seas to preserve their naval dominance, and the French demanded massive reparations (payments) from Germany and Austria for war damages.

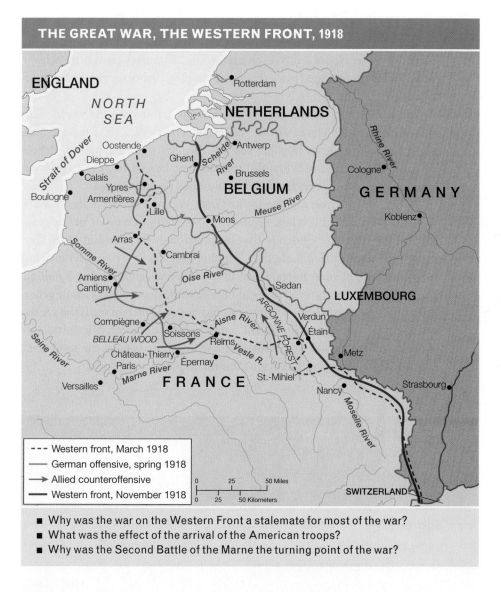

THE GREAT WAR, THE WESTERN FRONT, 1918

- - - Western front, March 1918
—— German offensive, spring 1918
→ Allied counteroffensive
■■■ Western front, November 1918

0   25   50 Miles
0   25   50 Kilometers

- Why was the war on the Western Front a stalemate for most of the war?
- What was the effect of the arrival of the American troops?
- Why was the Second Battle of the Marne the turning point of the war?

THE GERMAN COLLAPSE By the end of October 1918, Germany was on the verge of collapse. Revolutionaries rampaged through the streets. Sailors mutinied. Germany's allies (Bulgaria, Turkey, and Austria-Hungary) dropped out of the war, and panicked military leaders demanded that the civilian government ask for an armistice (cease-fire agreement). On November 9, the German Kaiser resigned, and a republic was proclaimed. Early on the morning of November 11, an armistice was signed in which the Germans were assured that Wilson's Fourteen Points would be the basis for the peace conference.

Six hours later, at the eleventh hour of the eleventh day of the eleventh month, and after 1,563 days of terrible warfare, the killing ended. From Europe, Colonel House sent Wilson a telegram: "Autocracy [government by an individual with unlimited power] is dead; long live democracy and its immortal leader."

The end of fighting led to wild celebrations throughout the world. "The nightmare is over," wrote African American activist W. E. B. Du Bois. "The world awakes. The long, horrible years of dreadful night are passed. Behold the sun!" Wilson was not as joyful. The Great War, he said, had dealt a grievous injury to civilization "which can never be atoned for or repaired."

During its nineteen months in the Great War, the United States had lost 53,000 servicemen in combat. Another 63,000 died of diseases, largely casualties of the influenza epidemic that swept through the world in 1918. Germany's war dead totaled more than 2 million, including civilians; France lost nearly 1.4 million combatants, Great Britain 703,000, and Russia 1.7 million. The war also ruined the economies of Europe while decimating a whole generation of young men. The new Europe would be very different from the prewar version: much poorer, more violent, more polarized, more cynical, less sure of itself, and less capable of decisive action. The United States, for good or ill, emerged from the war as the world's dominant power.

Armistice Night in New York **(1918)** George Luks, known for his vivid paintings of urban life, captured the unbridled outpouring of patriotism and joy that extended into the night of Germany's surrender.

THE POLITICS OF PEACE

On June 25, 1918, Colonel Edward House wrote President Wilson from France, urging him to take charge of the peacemaking process. "It is one of the things with which your name should be linked during the ages." House was right. Woodrow Wilson and the peace agreement ending the Great War would be forever linked, but not in a positive light.

In the making of the peace agreement, Wilson showed himself both at his best and worst. His Fourteen Points embodied his vision of a better world governed by fairer principles. He felt guided "by the hand of God." His vision of a peacekeeping "League of Nations" was, in his view, the key element to a "secure and lasting peace" and was the "most essential part of the peace settlement." If the diplomats gathering to draft the peace treaty failed to follow his ambitious plans to reshape the world in America's image, he warned, "there will be another world war" within a generation.

WILSON'S KEY ERRORS

Whatever the merits of President Wilson's peace plan, his efforts to implement it proved clumsy. He made several key decisions that would come back to haunt him. First, against the advice of his staff and of European leaders, he decided to attend the peace conference in Paris that opened on January 18, 1919. Never before had an American president left the nation for such a prolonged period (six months). During his months abroad, Wilson lost touch with political developments at home.

Wilson's second error of judgment involved politics. In the congressional elections of November 1918, Wilson defied his advisers and political tradition by urging voters to elect a Democratic Congress as a sign of approval of his policies in handling the war—and the peace. He "begged" the public not to "repudiate" his leadership. Prior to that time, presidents had remained neutral during congressional elections and abstained from campaigning.

Republicans, who for the most part had backed Wilson's war measures, were not pleased. Theodore Roosevelt, whose son Kermit, a pilot, had been killed in the war, called Wilson's self-serving appeal for votes "a cruel insult to every Republican father or mother whose sons have entered the Army or Navy." Voters were not impressed, either. In the elections, the Democrats lost control of both houses of Congress, which was a bad omen for Wilson's peacemaking efforts, since any treaty to end the war would have to be approved by at least two-thirds of the Senate, now controlled by Republicans.

Meanwhile, Wilson had dispatched Colonel House and several aides to Europe to begin convincing Allied leaders to embrace the Fourteen Points.

The lopsided defeat of Wilson and the Democrats in the elections, said House, "made his difficulties enormously greater."

Wilson further weakened support for his peacemaking efforts when, in a deliberate slight, he refused to appoint a prominent Republican to the American delegation to the peace conference. Although House had urged him to appoint Theodore Roosevelt or Senator Henry Cabot Lodge, the president's archenemy and the leading Republican in Congress, Wilson refused. In the end, he appointed Harry White, an obscure Republican, to join the delegation. Former president William Howard Taft groused that Wilson's real intention in going to Paris was "to hog the whole show." He almost did.

Wilson's participation in the Paris Peace Conference would be the climactic event of his career, an opportunity for him to convince Europe to follow his impassioned idealism in creating a very different postwar world. Ray Stannard Baker, a muckraking journalist, wrote at the time that the president "has yet to prove his greatness. The fate of a drama lies in its last act, and Wilson is now coming to that."

Wilson's last act would indeed be dramatic—tragically so. Initially, however, his entrance on the European stage was triumphant in December 1918. The cheering crowds in London, Paris, and Rome verged on hysteria. Millions of grateful Europeans greeted him as an almost mystical hero, even a savior. An Italian mayor described Wilson's visit as the "second coming of Christ." The ecstatic welcome led Wilson to think he truly was being directed by God to save the world. In a sign of his growing egotism, he claimed that he was now "at the apex of my glory in the hearts of these people." He was determined to shape a peace treaty and postwar world based on principles of justice, fairness, and self-determination.

From such a height, there could only be a fall. Although popular with the European people, Wilson had to negotiate with tough-minded, wily European statesmen who shared neither his lofty goals nor his ideals. In fact, they resented his efforts to forge a peace settlement modeled on American values. That Wilson had not bothered to consult them about his Fourteen Points peace proposal before announcing it to the world did not help. In the end, the European leaders would force him to abandon many of his ideals.

THE PARIS PEACE CONFERENCE

The Paris Peace Conference lasted from January to June 1919. The participants had no time to waste. The German, Austro-Hungarian, and Ottoman thrones and empires were in ruins. Across much of Europe, food was scarce and lawlessness rampant. The threat of revolution hung over central Europe as Communists in the defeated nations threatened to take control.

The peace conference dealt with immensely complex and controversial issues (including creating new nations and redrawing the maps of Europe and the Middle East) that required both political statesmanship and technical expertise. The British delegation alone included almost 400 members, many of them specialists in political geography or economics. The peacemakers met daily, debating, arguing, and compromising.

THE BIG FOUR From the start, the Paris Peace Conference was controlled by the Big Four: the prime ministers of Britain, France, and Italy, and the president of the United States. Georges Clemenceau, the seventy-seven-year-old French premier known as "The Tiger," had little patience with President Wilson's preaching. In response to Wilson's declaration that "America is the only idealistic nation in the world," Clemenceau grumbled that talking with Wilson was like talking to Jesus Christ. "God gave us the Ten Commandments and we broke them," the French leader sneered. "Wilson gave us the Fourteen Points—we shall see."

The Big Four fought in private and in public. The French and the British, led by Prime Minister David Lloyd George, insisted that Wilson agree to their harsh provisions to weaken Germany, while Vittorio Orlando, prime minister of Italy, focused on gaining territories from defeated Austria.

THE LEAGUE OF NATIONS Although suffering from chronic health issues, including hypertension and blinding headaches, Wilson lectured the other statesmen about the need to embrace his beloved **League of Nations**, which he insisted must be the "keystone" of any peace settlement. He believed that a world peace organization would abolish war by settling international disputes and mobilizing united action against aggressors. Article X of the charter, which Wilson called "the heart of the League," allowed member nations to impose military and economic sanctions, or penalties, against military aggressors. The League, Wilson predicted, would have such moral influence that it would make military action to preserve peace unnecessary. These unrealistic expectations became, for Wilson, a self-defeating crusade.

On February 14, 1919, Wilson presented the final draft of the League covenant to the Allies and left Paris for a ten-day visit home, where he faced growing opposition among Republicans. The League of Nations, Theodore Roosevelt complained, would revive German militarism and undermine American morale. "To substitute internationalism for nationalism," Roosevelt argued, "means to do away with patriotism." Henry Cabot Lodge, chairman of the Senate Foreign Relations Committee, dismissed the League of Nations because he feared it would involve the U.S. military in foreign conflicts without Senate approval.

THE TREATY OF VERSAILLES

When Wilson returned to Paris in the spring of 1919, he had lost his leverage with the British and French because it was increasingly uncertain that the U.S. Senate would approve any treaty he endorsed. Although a skilled debater, Wilson was forced to concede many controversial issues to ensure that the Europeans would approve his League of Nations.

Wilson yielded to French demands that Germany transfer vast territories to France on its west and to Poland on its east and north. In other territorial matters, Wilson had to abandon his principle of national self-determination, whereby every ethnic group would be allowed to form its own nation. As Secretary of State Robert Lansing correctly predicted, allowing each ethnic group to determine its own fate "will raise hopes which can never be realized."

The issue of reparations—payments by the vanquished to the victors—triggered especially bitter arguments. The British and the French (on whose soil much of the war was fought) wanted Germany to pay the entire financial cost of the war, including their veterans' pensions. On this point, Wilson made perhaps his most fateful concessions. Although initially opposed to reparations, he eventually agreed to a crucial clause in the peace treaty by which Germany was forced to accept responsibility for the war and its entire expense. The "war guilt" clause, written by American John Foster Dulles, a future secretary of state, so offended Germans that it became a major factor in the rise of the Nazi party during the 1920s. Wilson himself privately admitted that if he were a German, he would refuse to sign the flawed treaty.

Colonel House, the president's closest confidante, privately blamed Wilson for many problems associated with the treaty. He found the president "so contradictory that it is hard to pass judgment on him." He "speaks constantly of teamwork but seldom practices it." Wilson was "becoming stubborn and angry, and he never was a good negotiator." House worried that Wilson was too "unreasonable" about the League of Nations, "which does not make for solutions." It was an eerily accurate prediction of what was in store.

On May 7, 1919, the victorious powers presented the treaty to the German delegates, who returned three weeks later with 443 pages of criticism. Among other things, they noted that Germany would lose 13 percent of its territory, 10 percent of its population, and all of its colonies in Asia and Africa.

A few minor changes were made, but when the Germans still balked, the French threatened to launch a new military attack. Finally, on June 28, the Germans gave up and signed the treaty in the glittering Hall of Mirrors at Versailles, the magnificent palace built by King Louis XIV in the late seventeenth century. Thereafter, the agreement was called the **Treaty of Versailles**.

None of the peacemakers was fully satisfied. As France's Clemenceau observed, "it was not perfect," but it was, after all, the "result of human beings. We did all we could to work fast and well." A British official reversed Wilson's claim that it had been a "war to end all wars" by saying it was a "peace to end peace"—as turned out to be the case.

When Adolf Hitler, a young German soldier who had been wounded in the war, learned of the treaty's provisions, he vowed revenge. "It cannot be that two

EUROPE AFTER THE TREATY OF VERSAILLES, 1918

Legend:
- 1914 boundaries
- New nations
- Plebiscite areas
- Occupied area

0   250   500 Miles
0   250   500 Kilometers

■ Why was self-determination so difficult to apply in Central Europe?
■ How did territorial concessions weaken Germany?

million Germans have fallen in vain," he screamed during a speech in Munich in 1922. "We demand vengeance!"

THE TREATY DEBATE On July 8, 1919, Wilson arrived back in Washington, D.C., to begin working for approval of the treaty by the Senate, where the Republicans outnumbered the Democrats. Before leaving Paris, he had assured a French diplomat that he would not allow any changes to the treaty. "I shall consent to nothing," he vowed. "The Senate must take its medicine." Thus began one of the most brutally partisan and bitterly personal disputes in American history.

On July 10, Wilson became the first president to enter the Senate and deliver a treaty to be voted on. He called upon senators to accept their "great duty" and ratify the treaty, which had been guided "by the hand of God." Wilson then grew needlessly confrontational. He dismissed critics of the League of Nations as "blind and little provincial people." The world, he claimed, was relying on the United States to sign the treaty: "Dare we reject it and break the heart of the world?"

Yes, answered Senate Republicans, who had decided that Wilson's commitment to the League was a reckless threat to America's independence. Henry Cabot Lodge denounced the treaty's "scheme of making mankind suddenly virtuous by a statute or a written constitution." Lodge's strategy was to stall approval of the treaty in hopes that public opposition would grow. He took six weeks simply reading aloud the lengthy text to his Foreign Relations committee. He then organized a parade of expert witnesses, most of them opposed to the treaty, to appear at the hearings on ratification.

In the Senate, a group of "irreconcilables," fourteen Republicans and two Democrats, refused to support American membership in the League. They were mainly western and midwestern progressives, isolationists who feared that such sweeping foreign commitments would threaten domestic reforms.

Lodge himself belonged to a larger group called the "reservationists," who insisted upon limiting American participation in the League in exchange for approving the treaty. The only way to get Senate approval was for Wilson to meet with Lodge and others and agree to revisions, the most important of which was the requirement that Congress authorize any American participation in a League-approved war. Colonel House urged the president to "meet the Senate in a conciliatory spirit." Wilson replied that he had long ago decided that you "can never get anything in this life that is worthwhile without fighting for it." House courageously disagreed, reminding the president that American civilization was "built on compromise." It was the last time the two men would speak to or see each other.

As Republican senator Frank B. Kellogg of Minnesota noted, the proposed changes were crafted not by enemies of the treaty but by friends who wanted to save it. Republican senator James Watson of Indiana told Wilson that he had no choice but to accept some revisions: "Mr. President, you are licked. There is only one way you can take the United States into the League of Nations."

But the self-righteous president was temperamentally incapable of compromising. He refused to negotiate, declaring that "if the Treaty is not ratified by the Senate, the War will have been fought in vain."

LET THE PEOPLE DECIDE In September 1919, after a summer of fruitless debate, an exhausted Wilson decided to bypass his Senate opponents by speaking directly to voters. On September 2, against his doctor's orders and his wife's advice, he left Washington for a grueling railroad tour through the Midwest to the West Coast, intending to visit twenty-nine cities and deliver forty speeches on behalf of the treaty.

No president had ever made such a strenuous effort to win public support. In St. Louis, Wilson said that he had returned from Paris "bringing one of the greatest documents of human history," which was now in danger of being rejected by the Senate. He pledged to "fight for a cause . . . greater than the Senate. It is greater than the government. It is as great as the cause of mankind. . . ."

Wilson traveled and spoke, sometimes as many as four times a day, despite suffering from pounding headaches. By the time the president's train reached Spokane, Washington, the president was visibly fatigued. But he kept going through Oregon and California. Some 200,000 people greeted him in Los Angeles. In all, he had covered 10,000 miles in twenty-two days and given thirty-two major speeches.

Then disaster struck. After delivering an emotional speech on September 25, 1919, in Pueblo, Colorado, Wilson collapsed from headaches so severe that he had to cancel the trip. On the train heading back, as he looked out the window with tears rolling down his cheeks, he told his doctor that he had suffered the "greatest disappointment of [his] life."

A STRICKEN PRESIDENT Back in Washington, D.C., a week later, the president suffered a crushing stroke (cerebral hemorrhage) that left him paralyzed on his left side; he could barely speak or see. Only his secretary, his doctor, and his wife, Edith, knew his true condition. For five months at the end of 1919 and in early 1920, Wilson lay flat on his back while his doctor issued reassuring medical bulletins. If a document needed Wilson's signature, his wife guided his trembling hand. Lansing urged the president's aides to declare him disabled and appoint Vice President Thomas Marshall in his place; they angrily refused. Soon thereafter, Lansing was replaced.

The stroke made Wilson even more arrogant and stubborn and paralyzed his administration as well. He became emotionally unstable, at times crying uncontrollably and displaying signs of paranoia. For the remaining seventeen months of his term, his protective wife, along with aides and trusted cabinet members, kept him isolated from all but the most essential business. When a group of Republican senators visited the White House, one of them said: "Well, Mr. President, we have all been praying for you." Wilson replied, "Which way, Senator?"

THE TREATY UNDER ATTACK Such presidential humor was rare, however. Wilson's hardened arteries seemed to have hardened his political judgment as well. For his part, Lodge pushed through the Senate fourteen changes (the number was not coincidental) in the draft of the Treaty of Versailles. The exiled Colonel House became so concerned that he wrote Edith Wilson a letter in which he said how "vital" it was for some form of the treaty to be approved: The president's "place in history is in the balance." He pleaded for Wilson to negotiate a compromise. The First Lady refused to share his concerns with her husband.

In the end, Wilson rejected any proposed changes to the treaty. As a result, his supporters in the Senate were thrown into an unlikely alliance with the irreconcilables, who opposed the treaty under any circumstances. The final Senate vote in 1920 on Lodge's revised treaty was 39 in favor and 55 against. On the question of approving the original treaty without changes, the irreconcilables and the reservationists, led by Lodge, combined to defeat ratification, with 38 for and 53 against.

Woodrow Wilson's grand effort at global peacemaking had failed miserably. (Although, he did receive the Nobel Peace Prize for his efforts.) When told of the final Senate vote, he said it "would have been better if I had died last fall."

After refusing to ratify the treaty, Congress tried to declare an official end to American involvement in the war by a joint resolution on May 20, 1920, which Wilson vetoed in a fit of spite. It was not until July 2, 1921, four months after he had left office and almost eighteen months after the fighting had stopped, that another joint resolution officially ended the state of war with Germany and Austria-Hungary. Separate peace treaties with Germany, Austria, and Hungary were ratified on October 18, 1921, but by then Warren G. Harding was president.

The U.S. failure to ratify the Versailles Treaty or to exercise strong world leadership would prove to have long-range consequences. With Great Britain and France too exhausted and too timid to keep Germany weak and isolated, a dangerous power vacuum would emerge in Europe, one which Adolf Hitler and the Nazis would fill.

STUMBLING FROM WAR TO PEACE

After the war, most Americans were far more concerned with domestic issues than with the Treaty of Versailles, as celebration over the war's end soon gave way to widespread inflation, unemployment, labor unrest, socialist and Communist radicalism, race riots, terrorist bombings, and government tyranny. With millions of servicemen returning to civilian life, war-related industries shutting down, and wartime price controls ending, unemployment and prices for consumer goods spiked.

Bedridden by his stroke, the president became increasingly distant, depressed, and peevish. Wilson, observed David Lloyd George, the British prime minister, was "as much a victim of the war as any soldier who died in the trenches." His administration was in disarray, he had never been so unpopular, and the Democratic party was floundering along with him.

SUFFRAGE AT LAST   One of the few benefits of the Great War was the momentum it gave to American women demanding a constitutional guarantee of their right to vote. After six months of delay, debate, and failed votes,

Their first votes Women of New York City's East Side vote for the first time in the presidential election of 1920.

Congress passed the **Nineteenth Amendment** in the spring of 1919 and sent it to the states for ratification.

Tennessee's legislature was the last of thirty-six state assemblies to approve the amendment, and it did so in dramatic fashion. The initial vote was 48–48. Then a twenty-four-year-old Republican legislator named Harry T. Burn changed his vote to yes at the insistence of his mother.

The Nineteenth Amendment became official on August 18, 1920, making the United States the twenty-second nation to allow women's suffrage. It was a climactic achievement of the Progressive Era. Suddenly, 9.5 million women were eligible to vote in national elections; in the 1920 presidential election, they would make up 40 percent of the electorate.

ECONOMIC TURBULENCE As consumer prices rose, discontented workers, released from wartime controls on wages, grew more willing to go out on strike. In 1919, more than 4 million hourly wage workers, 20 percent of the U.S. workforce, participated in 3,600 strikes. Most of them wanted nothing more than higher wages and shorter workweeks, but their critics linked them with the worldwide Communist movement. Charges of a Communist conspiracy were greatly exaggerated, however. In 1919, fewer than 70,000 Americans nationwide belonged to the Communist party.

The most controversial labor dispute was in Boston, where most of the police went on strike on September 9, 1919. Massachusetts governor Calvin Coolidge mobilized the National Guard to maintain order. After four days, the striking policemen offered to return, but instead Coolidge ordered that they all be fired. When labor leaders appealed for their reinstatement, Coolidge responded in words that made him an instant national hero: "There is no right to strike against the public safety by anybody, anywhere, any time."

RACE RIOTS The summer of 1919 also brought a wave of deadly race riots. As more and more African Americans, including many of the 367,000 who were war veterans, moved out of the South to different parts of the country, developed successful careers, and asserted their civil rights, resentful whites reacted with an almost hysterical racism. In 1919 alone, seventy-six African Americans, including nine military veterans, were killed by southern whites.

What African American leader James Weldon Johnson called the Red Summer (*red* signifying blood) began in July, when a mob of whites invaded the black neighborhood in Longview, Texas, angry over rumors of interracial dating. They burned shops and houses and ran several African Americans out of town. A week later, in Washington, D.C., exaggerated and false reports of black assaults on white women stirred up white mobs, and gangs of white and black rioters waged a race war in the streets until soldiers and driving rains ended the fighting.

The worst was yet to come. In late July, 38 people were killed and 537 injured in five days of race rioting in Chicago, where some 50,000 blacks, mostly from the rural South, had moved during the war, leading to tensions with local whites over jobs and housing. White unionized workers especially resented blacks who were hired as strikebreakers. Altogether, twenty-five race riots erupted in 1919, and eighty African Americans were lynched, including eleven war veterans.

The race riots of 1919 were a turning point for many African Americans. "We made the supreme sacrifice," a black veteran told poet-journalist Carl Sandburg. "Now we want to see our country live up to the Constitution and the Declaration of Independence." Another ex-soldier noted how much the war experience had changed the outlook of blacks: "We were determined not to take it anymore."

Safe, briefly Escorted by a police officer, an African American family moves its belongings from their home, likely destroyed by white rioters, and into a protected area of Chicago.

THE RED SCARE With so many people convinced that the strikes and riots were inspired by Communists and anarchists (two very different groups who shared a hatred for capitalism), a New York journalist reported that Americans were "shivering in their boots over Bolshevism, and they are far more scared of Lenin than they ever were of the [German] Kaiser. We seem to be the most frightened victors the world ever saw."

Fears of revolution were fueled by the violent actions of a few militants. In early 1919, the Secret Service discovered a plot by Spanish anarchists to kill President Wilson and other government officials. In April 1919, postal workers intercepted nearly forty homemade mail bombs addressed to government officials. One mail bomb, however, blew off the hands of a Georgia senator's maid. In June, another bomb damaged U.S. Attorney General A. Mitchell Palmer's house. Palmer, who had ambitions to succeed Wilson as president, concluded that a "Red Menace," a Communist "blaze of revolution," was "sweeping over every American institution of law and order."

That August, Palmer appointed a twenty-four-year-old attorney named J. Edgar Hoover to lead a new government division created to collect information on radicals. Hoover and others in the Justice Department worked with a network of 250,000 informers in 600 cities, all of them members of the American Protective League, which had been founded during the war to root out "traitors" and labor radicals.

On November 7, 1919, federal agents rounded up 450 alien "radicals," most of whom were law-abiding Russian immigrants. All were deported to Russia without a court hearing. On January 2, 1920, police in dozens of cities arrested 5,000 more suspects.

What came to be called the **First Red Scare** (another would occur in the 1950s) represented one of the largest violations of civil liberties in American history. In 1919, novelist Katharine Fullerton Gerould announced in *Harper's Magazine* that, as a result of the government crackdown, America "is no longer a free country in the old sense." Panic about possible foreign terrorists erupted across the nation as vigilantes took matters into their own hands. At a patriotic pageant in Washington, D.C., a sailor shot a spectator who refused to rise for "The Star-Spangled Banner"; the crowd cheered. In Hammond, Indiana, a jury took only two minutes to acquit a man who had murdered an immigrant for yelling "To hell with the U.S." In Waterbury, Connecticut, a salesman was sentenced to six months in jail for saying that Vladimir Lenin was "one of the brainiest" of the world's leaders.

By the summer of 1920, the Red Scare had begun to subside. Although Attorney General Palmer kept predicting more foreign-inspired terrorism, it never came. But the Red Scare left a lasting mark by strengthening the conservative crusade for "100 percent Americanism" and new restrictions on immigration.

EFFECTS OF THE GREAT WAR

The extraordinary turbulence in 1919 and 1920 was an unmistakable indication of how the Great War had changed the shape of modern history: it was a turning point after which little was the same. It had destroyed old Europe—not only many of its cities, people, economies, and four grand empires, but also its self-image as the center of civilized Western culture. Winston Churchill, the future British prime minister, called postwar Europe "a crippled, broken world."

Peace did not bring stability. Most Germans and Austrians believed they were the victims of a harsh peace, and many wanted revenge. At the same time, the war had hastened the already simmering Bolshevik Revolution that caused Russia to exit the war, abandon its western European allies, and, in 1922, reemerge as the Union of Soviet Socialist Republics (USSR). Thereafter, Soviet communism would be one of the most powerful forces shaping the twentieth century.

Postwar America was a much different story. For the first time, the United States had decisively intervened in a major European war. The American economy had emerged from the war largely unscathed, and bankers and business executives were eager to fill the vacuum created by the destruction of the major European economies. The United States was now the world's dominant power. What came to be called the "American Century" was at hand.

CHAPTER REVIEW

SUMMARY

- **An Uneasy Neutrality**   The Wilson administration declared the nation neutral but allowed businesses to extend loans to the warring nations, principally the Allies (Britain, France, and Russia), to purchase food and military supplies. Americans were outraged by the Germans' use of submarine (*U-boat*) warfare, especially the sinking of the *Lusitania*. In 1917, submarine attacks and the publication of the *Zimmermann telegram*, which revealed that Germany had tried to encourage Mexico to wage war against the United States, led America to enter the Great War.

- **Mobilizing a Nation**   The Wilson administration drafted young men into the army and created new agencies such as the War Industries Board and the Food Administration to coordinate industrial production and agricultural consumption. As white workers left their factory jobs to join the army, hundreds of thousands of African Americans migrated from the rural South to the urban North as part of the *Great Migration*. Many southern whites and Mexican Americans also migrated to industrial centers. One million women participated in war work but were encouraged to leave these jobs as soon as the war ended. The federal government severely curtailed civil liberties, and the Espionage and Sedition Acts of 1917 and 1918 criminalized virtually any public opposition to the war.

- **The American Role in Fighting the War**   Communists seized power in November 1917 in Russia and negotiated a separate peace treaty with Germany, thus freeing the Germans to focus on the Western Front. By 1918, however, the arrival of millions of American troops turned the tide of the war. German leaders sued for peace, and an armistice was signed on November 11, 1918. Woodrow Wilson insisted that the United States wanted a new, democratic Europe. His *Fourteen Points (1918)* speech outlined his ideas for a League of Nations to promote peaceful resolutions to future conflicts.

- **The Fight for the Peace**   At the Paris Peace Conference, President Wilson was only partially successful. The *Treaty of Versailles (1919)* did create a *League of Nations* but included a "war guilt clause" that forced Germany to pay reparations for war damages to France and Britain. In the end, Wilson's illness following a stroke, his refusal to compromise on the terms of the treaty, and his alienation of Republican senators resulted in the Senate voting against ratification.

- **Lurching from War to Peace**   The United States struggled to come to terms with its new status as the leading world power and with changes at home. As wartime industries shifted to peacetime production, wage and price controls ended. As former soldiers reentered the workforce, unemployment rose, and consumer prices increased, provoking labor unrest in cities across the nation. Many Americans believed these problems were part of a Bolshevik plot. Several incidents of domestic terrorism provoked what would be known as the *First Red Scare (1919–1920)*, during which the Justice Department illegally arrested and deported many suspected radicals, most of whom were immigrants. At the same time, race riots broke out as resentful white mobs tried to stop African Americans from exercising their civil rights. The summer of 1919 also brought the ratification of the *Nineteenth Amendment (1919)* to the Constitution, which gave women the right to vote.

CHRONOLOGY

1914	The Great War (World War I) begins in Europe
1915	The *Lusitania* is torpedoed by a German U-boat
March 1917	Germany announces unrestricted submarine warfare in the Atlantic
April 1917	United States enters the Great War
January 1918	Woodrow Wilson delivers Fourteen Points speech
November 11, 1918	Representatives of warring nations sign armistice
1919	Paris Peace Conference convenes
	Race riots break out during the Red Summer
	First Red Scare leads to arrests and deportations of suspected radicals
	Woodrow Wilson suffers stroke
1920	The Senate rejects the Treaty of Versailles
	The Nineteenth Amendment is ratified

KEY TERMS

Central Powers p. 819

Allied Powers p. 819

Western Front p. 819

trench warfare p. 821

U-boats p. 823

Lusitania p. 823

Zimmermann telegram p. 826

Great Migration p. 828

Fourteen Points (1918) p. 832

League of Nations p. 839

Treaty of Versailles (1919) p. 840

Nineteenth Amendment (1920) p. 846

First Red Scare (1919–1920) p. 848

 INQUIZITIVE

Go to InQuizitive to see what you've learned—and learn what you've missed—with personalized feedback along the way.

23 A Clash of Cultures
1920–1929

Nightclub **(1933)** With all its striking sights and sounds, the roar of the twenties subsided for some at the heart of it all. In this painting by American artist Guy Pène du Bois, flappers and their dates crowd into a fashionable nightclub, yet their loneliness amid the excitement is deafening.

The decade between the end of the Great War and the onset of the Great Depression at the end of 1929 was perhaps the most dynamic in American history, a period of rapid urbanization, technological innovation, widespread prosperity, social rebelliousness, cultural upheaval, and political conservatism. Women were at last allowed to vote in all states (although most African American women—and men—in the South were prevented from doing so) and to experience many freedoms previously limited to men. At the same time, the Eighteenth Amendment outlawed alcoholic beverages in 1920 ("Prohibition"), setting off an epidemic of lawbreaking—by citizens, police, and public officials.

Cultural conflicts resulted largely from explosive tensions between rural and urban ways of life. For the first time in the nation's history, more people lived in cities than in rural areas. While the urban middle class prospered, farmers suffered as the wartime boom in exports of grains and livestock to Europe ground to a halt. Four million people moved from farms to cities during the twenties, in part because of the better quality of life and in part because of the prolonged agricultural recession.

Amid this massive rural/urban population shift, bitter fights erupted as modernists and traditionalists waged a cultural civil war that continues today, with one group looking to the future for inspiration and the other looking to the past for guidance. All of the changes created what one historian called a "nervous generation" of Americans "groping for what certainty they could find."

The scope and pace of societal changes were bewildering, as the emergence of national radio networks, talking motion pictures, mass ownership of automobiles, and national chain stores, combined with the soaring popularity of

focus questions

1. Assess the consumer culture that emerged in America in the 1920s. What are the factors that contributed to its growth?

2. What were the other major new social and cultural trends and movements that became prominent during the twenties? How did they challenge traditional standards and customs?

3. What does "modernism" mean in intellectual and artistic terms? How did the modernist movements influence American culture in the early twentieth century?

spectator sports and the rise of mass marketing and advertising, transformed America into the world's leading consumer society. The culture of mass consumption fueled the explosive growth of middle-class urban life while assaulting traditional virtues such as frugality, prudence, and religiosity.

In the political arena, reactionaries and rebels battled for control. The brutal fight between Woodrow Wilson and the Republican-led Senate over the Treaty of Versailles, coupled with the administration's crackdown on dissenters and socialists, had weakened an already fragmented and disillusioned progressivism. As reformer Amos Pinchot bitterly observed, President Wilson had "put his enemies in office and his friends in jail." By 1920, many progressives had grown skeptical of any politician claiming to be a reformer or an idealist. Social reformer Jane Addams sighed that the 1920s were "a period of political and social sag."

The desire to restore traditional values and social stability led voters to elect Republican Warren G. Harding president in 1920. He promised to return America to "normalcy." Both major parties still included progressive wings, but they were shrinking. The demand for honest, efficient government and public services remained strong; the impulse for social reform, however, shifted into a drive for moral righteousness and social conformity. By 1920, many veteran progressives had withdrawn from public life.

Mainstream Americans were also shocked by new, "modernist" forms of artistic expression and sexual liberation. Mabel Dodge Luhan, a leading promoter of modern art and literature, said that the generation of young literary and artistic rebels that emerged during and after the war was determined to overthrow "the old order of things."

In sum, postwar life in America and Europe was fraught with turbulent changes, contradictory impulses, superficial frivolity, and seething tensions. As French painter Paul Gauguin acknowledged, the upheavals of cultural modernism and the chaotic aftermath of the war produced "an epoch of confusion" and a riotous clash of irreverent new ideas with traditional manners and morals.

A "New Era" of Consumption

America experienced so many dramatic changes during the twenties that people referred to it as a "New Era." The robust U.S. economy became the envy of the world. Following the brief postwar recession in 1920–1921, economic growth soared to record levels. Jobs were plentiful, and average income rose throughout the decade. The nation's total wealth almost doubled between 1920 and 1930, while wage workers enjoyed record-breaking increases in average income. By 1929, the United States enjoyed the highest standard of living in the world.

Construction led the way. The war had caused people to postpone building offices, plants, homes, and apartments. By 1921, however, a building boom was under way that would last the rest of the decade. At the same time, the remarkable growth of the automotive industry created an immediate need for roads and highways. New construction and new cars stimulated other industries such as lumber, steel, concrete, rubber, gasoline, and furniture.

Technology also played a key role in the prosperity of the twenties. Manufacturing grew more mechanized and efficient. Powerful new machines (electric motors, steam turbines, dump trucks, tractors, bulldozers, steam shovels) and more-efficient ways of operating farms, factories, plants, mines, and mills generated dramatic increases in production.

A GROWING CONSUMER CULTURE

In the late nineteenth century, the U.S. economy had been driven by commercial agriculture and large-scale industrial production—the building of railroads and bridges, the manufacturing of steel, and the construction of housing and businesses in cities. During the twenties, the dominant aspect of the economy involved an explosion of new consumer goods.

The success of mass production made mass consumption more important than ever. A 1920 newspaper editorial insisted that, with the war over, the American's "first importance to his country is no longer that of citizen but that of *consumer.*" To keep factory production humming required converting once-frugal people into enthusiastic shoppers. "People may ruin themselves by saving instead of spending," warned one economist.

The new **consumer culture** encouraged carefree spending. "During the war," a journalist noted in 1920, "we accustomed ourselves to doing without, to buying carefully, to using economically. But with the close of the war came reaction. A veritable orgy of extravagant buying is going on. Reckless spending takes the place of saving, waste replaces conservation." As paying with cash and staying out of debt came to be seen as needlessly "old-fashioned" practices, consumer debt almost tripled during the twenties.

Advertising, first developed in the late nineteenth century, grew into a huge enterprise. Zelda Sayre Fitzgerald, the writer and wife of the wildly popular novelist F. Scott Fitzgerald, recalled that "we grew up founding our dreams on the infinite promises of American advertising." New weekday radio programs popular with middle-class women, for example, were often sponsored by

Does the Home You Love Love You?

Westinghouse

A modern home This 1925 Westinghouse advertisement urges homemakers to buy its "Cozy Glow, Jr." heater and "Sol-Luk Luminaire" lamp, among other new electrical appliances that would "do anything for you in return."

national companies advertising laundry detergent and hand soap—hence the term "soap operas." Because women purchased two-thirds of consumer goods, advertisers targeted them.

The consumer culture generated bewildering changes in everyday life. The huge jump in the use of electricity was a revolutionary new force. In 1920, only 35 percent of homes had electricity; by 1930, the number was 68 percent. Similar increases occurred in the number of households with indoor plumbing, washing machines, and automobiles. Moderately priced creature comforts and conveniences such as flush toilets, electric irons and fans, handheld cameras, wristwatches, cigarette lighters, vacuum cleaners, and linoleum floors, became more widely available, especially among the urban middle class. As always, the poor, with little discretionary income, remained on the margins of the consumer culture.

THE RISE OF MASS CULTURE

The powerful consumer culture helped create a marketplace of retail stores and national brands (Kellogg's Corn Flakes, General Electric toasters, etc.) in which local and regional businesses were increasingly squeezed out by giant national "chain" stores. By the 1920s, Woolworth's, for example, had 1,500 stores scattered across the country; Walgreen's had 525. National retailers bought goods in such large quantities that they were able to get discounted prices that they passed on to consumers.

Mass advertising and marketing campaigns promoting national products increasingly led to a *mass culture*: more and more Americans now saw the same advertisements and bought the same products at the same stores. They also read the same magazines, listened to the same radio programs, drove the same cars, adored the same sports stars and celebrities, and watched the same movies.

MOVIE-MADE AMERICA In 1896, a New York audience viewed the first moving-picture show. By 1924, the movie business had become the nation's chief form of mass entertainment. Hollywood, California, became the international center of movie production, grinding out cowboy Westerns, crime dramas, murder mysteries, and the timeless comedies of Mack Sennett's Keystone Company. Movie attendance during the 1920s averaged 80 million people a week, more than half the national population, and attendance surged even more after 1927 with the appearance of "talkies," movies with sound.

Charlie Chaplin An English-born actor who rose to international fame as the "Tramp," pictured above in the 1921 silent film *The Kid*.

But movies did much more than entertain. They helped expand the consumer culture by feeding the desires of moviegoers, setting standards and tastes in fashion, music, dancing, and hairstyles. They also helped stimulate the sexual revolution. A researcher concluded that movies made young Americans in the twenties more "sex-wise, sex-excited, and sex-absorbed" than previous generations.

RADIO Radio broadcasting enjoyed even more spectacular growth. In 1920, station WWJ in Detroit began transmitting news bulletins, and KDKA in Pittsburgh began broadcasting regularly scheduled programs. The first radio commercial aired in New York in 1922. By the end of that year, there were 508 stations. In 1926, the National Broadcasting Company (NBC), a subsidiary of the Radio Corporation of America (RCA), began linking its stations into a national network; the Columbia Broadcasting System (CBS) entered the field the next year.

The widespread ownership of radios changed the patterns of everyday life. At night after dinner, families gathered around the radio to listen to live music, political speeches, news broadcasts, weather forecasts, baseball and football games, boxing matches, and comedy shows. One ad claimed that the radio "is your theatre, your college, your newspaper, your library." Calvin Coolidge was the first president to address the nation by radio, and his monthly talks paved the way for Franklin Delano Roosevelt's influential "fireside chats" during the thirties.

FLYING MACHINES Advances in transportation were as significant as the impact of commercial radio and movies on popular culture. In 1903, Wilbur and Orville Wright, owners of a bicycle shop in Dayton, Ohio, had built and flown the first "flying machine" over the beach at Kitty Hawk, North Carolina.

The development of airplanes advanced slowly until the outbreak of war in 1914, when Europeans began using the airplane as a military weapon. When the United States entered the war, it had no combat planes; American pilots flew British or French warplanes. An American aircraft industry arose during the war but collapsed in the postwar demobilization. Under the Kelly Act of 1925, however, the federal government began to subsidize the industry through airmail contracts. The Air Commerce Act of 1926 provided federal funds for the advancement of air transportation and navigation, including the construction of airports.

The aviation industry received a huge psychological boost in 1927 when twenty-six-year-old Charles A. Lindbergh Jr., a St. Louis–based mail pilot, made the first *solo* transatlantic flight, traveling from New York City to Paris in thirty-three and a half hours through severe storms and dense fog. When Lindbergh, known as the "Lone Eagle," landed in France, 100,000 people greeted him with thunderous cheers. The New York City parade celebrating his accomplishment surpassed the celebration of the end of the Great War. (When Lindbergh met Britain's King George V soon after his long flight, the monarch asked him, "How did you pee?" In paper cups, the pilot answered.)

THE CAR CULTURE By far the most significant economic and social development of the early twentieth century was the widespread ownership of automobiles. In 1924, when asked about the changes transforming American life, a resident of Muncie, Indiana replied: "I can tell you what's happening in just four letters: A-U-T-O."

The first motorcar ("horseless carriage") had been manufactured for sale in 1895, but the founding of the Ford Motor Company in 1903 revolutionized the infant industry. The first cars were handmade, expensive, and designed for the wealthy. Henry Ford changed all that by building "a car for the multitude." He vowed that "When I'm through, everybody will be able to afford one, and about everyone will have one." Ford's Model T, the celebrated "Tin Lizzie," came out in 1908 at a price of $850 (about $22,000 today). By 1924, as a result of Ford's efficient production techniques, the same car sold for $290 (less than $4,000 today).

Other automakers followed Ford's mass production/low-priced model. In 1920, there were more than 8 million registered vehicles; in 1929, there were more than 23 million. The automobile revolution was in part propelled by the discovery of vast oil fields in Texas, Oklahoma, Wyoming, and California. By 1920, the United States produced two-thirds of the world's oil and gasoline.

The automobile industry also became the leading example of modern mass-production techniques. Ford's Highland Park plant outside Detroit used a moving conveyor system that pulled the chassis down an assembly line of sequential work stations. Each worker performed a single task, such as installing a fender or a wheel, as the car-in-process moved down the line. Through this technique, a new car could be pieced together in ninety-three minutes.

Such efficiency enabled Ford to lower the price of his cars, thereby increasing the number of people who could afford them. His high profits helped him pay his workers the highest wages in the industry. Although Ford was a notorious taskmaster—he prohibited his workers from talking, sitting, smoking, or singing while on the job—his methods worked. During the twenties, the United States built ten times more automobiles than all of Europe combined.

Just as the railroad helped transform the pace and scale of life in the second half of the nineteenth century, the automobile changed social life during the twentieth century. Americans literally developed a love affair with cars. In the words of one male driver, young people viewed the car as "an incredible engine of escape" from parental control and a safe place to "take a girl and hold hands, neck, pet, or . . . go the limit."

Cars and networks of new roads enabled people to live farther away from their workplaces, thus encouraging suburban sprawl. Cars also helped fuel the economic boom of the 1920s by creating tens of thousands of new jobs and a huge demand for steel, glass, rubber, leather, oil, and gasoline. The car culture stimulated road construction, sparked a real estate boom in Florida and California, and dotted the landscape with gasoline stations, traffic lights, billboards, and motor hotels ("motels"). By 1929, the federal government was constructing 10,000 miles of paved highways each year.

SPECTATOR SPORTS During the 1920s, automobile ownership and rising incomes changed the way people spent their leisure time. Americans fell in love with spectator sports; people in cities could drive into the countryside, visit friends and relatives, and go to ballparks, stadiums, or boxing rinks to see baseball or football games and prizefights.

Baseball, created in the 1870s, had become the "national pastime" by the 1920s. With larger-than-life heroes such as New York Yankee greats George Herman "Babe" Ruth Jr. and Henry Louis "Lou" Gehrig, professional teams attracted intense loyalties and huge crowds. In 1920, more than a million spectators attended Ruth's games.

Two years later, the Yankees built a new stadium, called the "house that Ruth built," and went on to win World Series championships in 1923, 1927,

Ford Motor Company's Highland Park plant, 1913 Gravity slides and chain conveyors contributed to the mass production of automobiles.

and 1928. More than 20 million people attended professional baseball games in 1927, the year that Ruth, the "Sultan of Swat," set a record by hitting sixty home runs. Because baseball remained a segregated sport in the 1920s, so-called Negro Leagues were organized for African Americans.

Football, especially at the college level, also attracted huge crowds. It, too, benefited from outsized heroes such as running back Harold Edward "Red" Grange of the University of Illinois, the first athlete to appear on the cover of *Time* magazine. In a game against the University of Michigan, the "Galloping Ghost" scored a touchdown the first four times he carried the ball. After Illinois won, students carried Grange on their shoulders for two miles across the campus. When he signed a contract with the Chicago Bears in 1926, he single-handedly made professional football competitive with baseball as a spectator sport.

What Ruth and Grange were to their sports, William Harrison "Jack" Dempsey was to boxing. Like Babe Ruth, Dempsey, who won the world heavyweight title in 1919 by defeating the hulking Jess Willard, was especially popular with working-class men, for he too had been born poor. In 1927, when James Joseph "Gene" Tunney defeated Dempsey, more than 100,000 people attended, including 1,000 reporters, ten state governors, and numerous Hollywood celebrities. Some 60 million people listened to the fight over the radio.

The "Jazz Age"

While the masses of Americans devoted their free time to spectator sports, radio programs, and movies, many young people, especially college students, focused their energies on social and cultural rebellion. F. Scott Fitzgerald, a boyishly handsome Princeton University dropout, was labeled "the voice of his generation" after his first novel, *This Side of Paradise* (1920), became a best seller with its colorful account of rowdy student life at Princeton. Fitzgerald fastened upon the **"Jazz Age"** as a label for the spirit of rebelliousness and spontaneity he observed among many young Americans.

Duke Ellington and his band Jazz emerged in the 1920s as a uniquely American expression of the modernist spirit. African American artists bent musical conventions to give freer rein to improvisation and sensuality.

THE BIRTH OF JAZZ

Fitzgerald's Jazz Age label referred to the popularity of jazz music, a dynamic blend of several musical traditions. It had first emerged as piano-based "ragtime" at the end of the nineteenth century. Thereafter, African American musicians such as Jelly Roll Morton, Duke Ellington, Louis Armstrong, and Bessie Smith (the "Empress of the Blues") combined the energies of ragtime with the emotions of the blues to create *jazz*, originally an African American slang term meaning sexual intercourse. With its improvisations, variations, and sensual spontaneity, jazz appealed to people of all ethnicities and ages because it was all about pleasure and immediacy, letting go and enjoying the freedom of the moment.

Louis Armstrong, an inspired trumpeter with a uniquely froggy voice, was the Pied Piper of jazz, an inventive and freewheeling performer who reshaped the American music scene. Born in a New Orleans shack in 1900, the grandson of slaves, he was abandoned by his father and raised by his prostitute mother, who was fifteen when he was born. As a youth, he saw the mean and ugly side of America. "I seen everythin' from a child comin' up," he said once. "Nothin' happen I ain't never seen before." Then he found music, using his natural genius to explore the fertile possibilities of jazz.

As a teen, he sneaked into music halls to watch Joe "King" Oliver and other early jazz innovators. In 1922, Armstrong moved to Chicago, where he delighted audiences with his passionate trumpet performances and open-hearted personality. Throughout the twenties, Armstrong and his band crisscrossed the United States, spreading the gospel of jazz.

The culture of jazz quickly spread from its origins in New Orleans, Kansas City, Memphis, and St. Louis to the African American neighborhoods of Harlem in New York City and Chicago's South Side. Large dance halls accommodated the demand for jazz music and the new dances it inspired, like the

Charleston and the Black Bottom. Affluent whites flocked to the dance halls as well as to "black" nightclubs and "jazz joints." During the 1920s, people commonly spoke of *jazzing* something up" (invigorating it) or "jazzing around" (acting youthfully and energetically).

Many Americans, however, were not fans of jazz or the sexually suggestive dances it inspired. Dr. Francis E. Clark, a Christian moralist, denounced "indecent dance" as "an offense against womanly purity." Princeton professor Henry van Dyke dismissed jazz as "merely an irritation of the nerves of hearing, a sensual teasing of the strings of physical passion." Such criticism, however, failed to stem the popularity of jazz, which swept across Europe as well as America. Europeans, including modernist painters Henri Matisse and Pablo Picasso, grew infatuated with the inventive energies of jazz music.

A SEXUAL REVOLUTION?

What most shocked old-timers during the Jazz Age was a defiant sexual revolution among young people, especially those on college campuses. "None of the Victorian mothers—and most of the mothers were Victorian—had any idea how casually their daughters were accustomed to being kissed," wrote F. Scott Fitzgerald in *This Side of Paradise* (1920).

During the twenties, Americans learned about the hidden world of "flaming youth" (the title of a popular novel): wild "petting parties," free love, speakeasies, "joyriding," and skinny-dipping. A promotional poster for the 1923 silent film *Flaming Youth* asked: "How Far Can a Girl Go?" Other ads claimed the movie appealed especially to "neckers, petters, white kisses, red kisses, pleasure-mad daughters, [and] sensation-craving mothers."

THE IMPACT OF SIGMUND FREUD The increasingly frank treatment of sex resulted in part from the influence of Sigmund Freud, the Austrian founder of modern psychoanalysis. Freud, trained as a physician, insisted that the human mind was mysteriously "conflicted" by often unconscious efforts to repress powerful irrational impulses and sexual desires ("libido").

In 1899, Freud had published *The Interpretation of Dreams*, a pathbreaking book that stressed the crucial role of the subconscious in shaping behavior and moods. He also highlighted the significance of dreams as providing the "royal road to the unconscious," for dreams revealed "repressed" sexual yearnings, many of which resulted from early childhood experiences. Women and men, Freud argued, are endowed with equal sexual energy, and human behavior is driven by a variety of intense sexual desires and efforts to release pent-up aggression. These natural human conflicts cause unhappiness because people desire more pleasures than they can attain.

It did not take long for Freud's ideas to penetrate society at large. Books, movies, and plays included frequent references to Freud's ideas, and some of the decade's most popular magazines—*True Confessions, Telling Tales,* and *True Story*—focused on romance and sex. Likewise, the most popular female movie stars—Madge Bellamy, Clara Bow, and Joan Crawford—projected images of sensual freedom, energy, and independence.

Advertisements for new movies reinforced the self-indulgent images of the Jazz Age: "brilliant men, beautiful jazz babies, champagne baths, midnight revels, petting parties in the purple dawn, all ending in one terrific climax that makes you gasp." Traditionalists were shocked by the behavior of rebellious young women. "One hears it said," lamented a Baptist magazine, "that the girls are actually tempting the boys more than the boys do the girls, by their dress and conversation."

Freud's emphasis on unruly sexual desires swirling about in the subconscious fascinated some people and scared others. For many young Americans, Freud seemed to provide scientific justification for rebelling against social conventions and indulging in sex. Some oversimplified his theories by claiming that sexual pleasure was essential for emotional health, that all forms of sexual activity were good, and that all inhibitions about sex were bad.

MARGARET SANGER AND BIRTH CONTROL   Perhaps the most controversial women's issue of the Jazz Age was birth control. Christians—both Protestants and Catholics—opposed it as a violation of God's law. Others saw it differently. Margaret Sanger, a nurse and midwife in the tenements of Manhattan, saw many young mothers struggling to provide for their growing families. Born in 1883, one of eleven children of Irish immigrants, she understood the poverty often experienced by large immigrant families.

As a nurse and midwife, Sanger witnessed firsthand the consequences of unwanted pregnancies, tragic miscarriages, and amateur abortions. To her, there was an obvious solution: *birth control,* a term she and friends coined in 1914. Sanger began to distribute birth-control information to working-class women and resolved to spend the rest of her life helping women gain control of their bodies.

In 1921, Sanger organized the American Birth Control League, which in 1942 changed its name to Planned Parenthood. The Birth Control League distributed information to doctors, social workers, women's clubs, and the scientific community. In the 1920s, however, Sanger alienated supporters of birth control by endorsing sterilization for the mentally incompetent and for people with certain hereditary conditions. Birth control, she stressed, was "the most constructive and necessary of the means to racial health."

The "new woman" of the 1920s Two risk-taking flappers dance atop the Hotel Sherman in Chicago, 1926.

Although Sanger did not succeed in legalizing the distribution of contraceptives and contraceptive information through the mail, she laid the foundation for such efforts. In 1936, a federal court ruled that physicians could prescribe contraceptives—a vital step in Sanger's efforts to realize her slogan, "Every child a wanted child."

THE "NEW WOMEN" New clothing fashions reflected the rebellion against traditional female roles in an especially powerful way. The emancipated "new women" of the twenties seized the right to vote while eagerly discarding the confining wardrobe of their mothers' generation—pinched-in corsets, layers of petticoats, and floor-length dresses. In 1919, skirts were typically six inches above the ground; by 1927, they were at the knee.

The shortest skirts were worn by the so-called **flappers**, pleasure-seeking young women who—in defiance of proper prewar standards—drove automobiles, "bobbed" their hair (cut it short, requiring the invention of the "bobby pin"), and wore minimal underclothing, gauzy fabrics, sheer stockings, dangling necklaces, and plenty of makeup, especially rouge and lipstick. They often joined young men in smoking cigarettes, drinking, gambling, and dancing to jazz music.

The flappers wanted more than marriage and motherhood. Their carefree version of feminism was fun-loving, defiant, self-indulgent, and often self-destructive, and their antics shocked and scared observers. A Catholic priest in Brooklyn complained that the feminism of the 1920s had provoked a "pandemonium of powder, a riot of rouge, and a moral anarchy of dress."

NOT SO NEW WOMEN Most women in the 1920s were not flappers, however. Lillian Symes, a longtime activist, stressed that her "generation of feminists" had little in common with the "spike-heeled, over-rouged flapper of today. We grew up before the postwar disillusionment engulfed the youth of the land." Although more middle-class women attended college in the 1920s than ever before, a higher percentage of them married soon after graduation than had been the case in the nineteenth century.

The conservative political mood helped to steer women who had worked for the war effort back into their traditional roles as homemakers, and college curricula began to shift accordingly. At Vassar College, an all-women's school outside of New York City, students took courses such as "Husband and Wife," "Motherhood," and "The Family as an Economic Unit." At the same time, fewer college-educated women pursued careers: the proportion of physicians who were women fell during the twenties from 6 to 4 percent, and similar reductions occurred among dentists, architects, and chemists. A student at all-female Smith College in Massachusetts expressed frustration "that a woman must choose between a home and her work, when a man may have both. There must be a way out, and it is the problem of our generation to find the way."

As before, most women who worked outside the home labored in unskilled, low-paying jobs. Only 4 percent of working women in the 1920s were salaried professionals. Some women moved into new vocations created by the growing consumer culture, such as accounting assistants and department-store clerks. The number of beauty shops soared from 5,000 in 1920 to 40,000 in 1930, creating jobs for hair stylists, manicurists, and cosmeticians.

But the majority of women were still either full-time wives and mothers or household servants. Fortunately, the growing availability of electricity and electrical appliances—vacuum cleaners, toasters, stoves, refrigerators, washing machines, irons—made housework easier. Likewise, "supermarkets" offered year-round access to fruits, vegetables, and meats, which greatly reduced the traditional tasks of food preparation—canning, baking bread, and plucking chickens. African American and Latino women faced the greatest challenges. As a New York City newspaper observed, they were forced to do "work which white women will not do." Women of color usually worked as maids, laundresses, or seamstresses, or on farms.

THE COLOR LINE In addition to sexism, racism also continued to limit the freedom of women. For example, in 1919, an interracial couple from Ayer, Massachusetts, Mabel Puffer, a wealthy college graduate, and Arthur Hazzard, a handyman and leader within the local black community, decided to get married in Concord, New Hampshire. They checked into separate rooms in a hotel, then met in the lobby and walked three blocks to the courthouse to apply for a marriage license, only to be told that there was a five-day waiting period. So they waited. The mayor of Concord agreed to perform the service, and Hazzard's siblings and mother made plans to attend.

When news of the interracial couple strolling the streets of Concord reached the Boston newspapers, the first headline, in the *Boston Traveller,* read: "Will Marry Negro in 'Perfect Union': Rich Ayer Society Woman Determined to Wed Servant Although Hometown Is Aflame with Protest." The next day, the *Boston Evening Globe* ran the provocative story on its front page. The headline was sensational: "Hope to Prevent White Woman Wedding Negro: Two Friends of Mabel E. Puffer Have Gone to Concord, N.H."

Suddenly, the mayor of Concord reversed himself and announced he could not perform the wedding. The betrothed couple, after being turned down several times, finally found a minister willing to marry them. The night before the wedding was to occur, the Ayer police chief arrived, arrested Hazzard on a charge of "enticement," and took Puffer into custody because she had been deemed "insane." In reporting the story, the Concord newspaper concluded that the community "gazed after their departing dust with no regrets." The nation that Woodrow Wilson had led into World War I to "make the world safe for democracy" remained an unsafe place for those bold enough to cross the color line.

African American Life

The most significant development in African American life during the early twentieth century was the **Great Migration** northward from the South. The mass movement of blacks began at the start of the twentieth century but accelerated in 1915–1916, when rapidly expanding war industries in the northern states needed new workers, and continued throughout the twenties.

Between 1920 and 1930, almost a million African Americans, mostly sharecroppers, joined the exodus from the South. Many landed in New York City, Chicago, Detroit, Cleveland, Washington, D.C., Philadelphia, and other large cities. The Great Migration continued in fits and starts throughout the twentieth century, producing dramatic social, economic, and political changes. In 1900, only 740,000 African Americans lived outside the South, just 8 percent of the nation's black population. By 1970, more than 10.6 million African Americans lived outside the South, 47 percent of the nation's total.

The African Americans making up the Great Migration were lured by what writer Richard Wright called the "warmth of other suns"—better living conditions and better-paying jobs. In the North, for the most part, they were able to speak more freely and were treated more equally than in the South. Educational opportunities for children were also much better in the northern states. Collectively, blacks gained more political leverage by settling in populous states like New York, Pennsylvania, Ohio, and Illinois, with many electoral votes. The political effects of the Great Migration were evident in 1928 when a Chicago Republican, Oscar De Priest, became the first black elected to Congress since Reconstruction and the first ever from a northern district.

The Great Migration was fraught with challenges, however. Black newcomers from the Jim Crow South were not always welcomed. They sometimes clashed with local ethnic groups, especially Irish and Italians who feared that the newcomers would take their jobs. Many southern blacks, ignorant of city ways, were taken advantage of by white landlords, realtors, and bankers, forced into substandard and segregated housing, and paid lower wages than whites.

But northern discrimination still paled beside the ferocious injustices in the segregated South. The Missouri-born black poet Langston Hughes spoke for many when he wrote that he was "fed up With Jim Crow laws, / People who are cruel And afraid, / Who lynch and run, / Who are scared of me And me of them."

THE NAACP The mass migration of southern blacks northward helped spur the creation of the **National Association for the Advancement of Colored People (NAACP)**, founded in 1910 by black activists and white progressives. Black NAACP members came mainly from the Niagara movement, a group formed in 1905 to fight racial discrimination nationwide. W. E. B. Du Bois became the organization's director of publicity and research and the editor of its journal, *Crisis*.

Politically, the NAACP focused on legal action to bring the Fourteenth and Fifteenth Amendments back to life. One early victory came with *Guinn v. United States* (1915), in which the Supreme Court struck down Oklahoma's efforts to deprive African Americans of the vote. In *Buchanan v. Worley* (1917), the Court invalidated a residential segregation ordinance in Louisville, Kentucky. In 1919, the NAACP launched a national campaign against lynching, then a still-common form of vigilante racist violence. An anti-lynching bill to make mob murder a federal crime passed the House in 1922 but was defeated by southerners in the Senate.

THE HARLEM RENAISSANCE So many blacks converged in New York City during the twenties that they inspired the **Harlem Renaissance**, the nation's first black literary and artistic movement. It started in the fast-growing African American community of Harlem in northern Manhattan. In 1890, one in seventy people in Manhattan had been African American; by 1930, it was one in nine.

The "great, dark city" of Harlem, in poet Langston Hughes's phrase, contained more blacks per square mile than any other urban neighborhood in the nation. Such rapid population growth generated a sense of common identity, growing power, and distinctive self-expression that transformed Harlem into

Into Bondage This painting by Aaron Douglas exemplifies how black artists in the Harlem Renaissance used their African roots and collective history as artistic inspiration.

the cultural capital of African American life. Writer James Weldon Johnson described a "Black Manhattan" as a "typically Negro" community of 175,000 in that it featured "movement, color, gaiety, singing, dancing, boisterous laughter, and loud talk." Dotted with lively taverns, lounges, supper clubs, dance halls, and saloons ("speakeasies"), Harlem became what journalists called the "Nightclub Capital of the World." Alain Locke, the first black Rhodes Scholar, announced that the Harlem Renaissance was led by a self-confident "new Negro" who no longer felt subservient to white culture.

In poetry and prose, Harlem Renaissance writers celebrated African American culture, including jazz and the blues. As Hughes wrote, "I am a Negro—and beautiful. . . . The night is beautiful. So [are] the faces of my people." But while Hughes loved Africa and its cultural heritage, his outlook emphatically "was not Africa. I was [shaped by] Chicago and Kansas City and Broadway and Harlem."

Women, both black and white, were active in the Harlem Renaissance. In January 1925, a thirty-four-year-old African American woman named Zora Neale Hurston arrived in Harlem from Eatonville, an all-black community in rural central Florida. She was an aspiring writer and inventive storyteller in search of the "New Negro Movement." With only $1.50 in her purse, "no job, no friends and a lot of hope," she became the first African American to enroll at Barnard College, the woman's college of Columbia University on the edge of Harlem, where she majored in cultural anthropology.

A brassy, flamboyant woman, Hurston had mastered the art of survival by learning to reinvent herself as the need arose. Motherless at nine, a runaway at fourteen, she became a calculating opportunist blessed with remarkable willpower. The spirited Hurston said she came to Harlem to immerse herself in the "clang and clamor" of city life.

Within a few months, Hurston was behaving, in her words, as the queen of the Harlem Renaissance, writing short stories and plays about the "Negro furthest down" on the social scale while positioning herself at the center of the community's raucous social life. ("How can any deny themselves the pleasure of my company! It's beyond me.") She reveled in the black pride and cultural confidence enlivening Harlem. Her outspokenness invited controversy, as when she claimed that she "did not belong to the sobbing school of Negrohood who hold that nature somehow has given them a lowdown dirty deal and whose feelings are all hurt about it." Hurston went on to become a leading anthropologist, folklorist, and novelist, expert at describing the ways in which African Americans in the Lower South forged cohesive communities in the face of white bigotry and violence.

The Harlem Renaissance also celebrated the distinctive contributions of poor African Americans to American culture. James Weldon Johnson coined the term "Aframerican" to designate Americans with African ancestry and to emphasize that blacks were no longer divided by their heritage; they were proud to be Americans who happened to have an African ancestry. Aframericans, he insisted, were "conscious collaborators" in the creation of American society and culture.

By 1930, Harlem Renaissance writers had produced dozens of novels and volumes of poetry; several Broadway plays; and a flood of short stories, essays, and films. A people capable of producing such great art and literature, Johnson declared, should never again be "looked upon as inferior."

GARVEYISM The celebration of black culture found much different expression in what came to be called **Negro nationalism**, which promoted black separatism from mainstream American life. Its leading spokesman was Marcus Garvey, who claimed to speak for all 400 million blacks worldwide. In 1916, Garvey brought to Harlem the headquarters of the Universal Negro Improvement Association (UNIA), which he had started in his native Jamaica two years before.

Garvey insisted that blacks had *nothing* in common with whites. In passionate speeches and in editorials in the UNIA's popular newspaper, the *Negro World*, Garvey urged African Americans to remove themselves from the surrounding white culture and to cultivate black solidarity and "black power."

The UNIA quickly became the largest black political organization in the nation. By 1923, Garvey, who often wore gaudy military uniforms and feather-plumed hats, claimed the UNIA had as many as 4 million members served by 800 offices. His goal was to build an all-black empire in Africa. To that end, he began calling himself the "Provisional President of Africa," raising funds to send Americans to Africa, and expelling any UNIA member who married a white.

Garvey's message of black nationalism and racial solidarity appealed especially to poor blacks in northern cities, but he also had supporters across the

Marcus Garvey The Jamaican-born founder of the Universal Negro Improvement Association and leading spokesman for "Negro nationalism" in the 1920s.

rural South. Garveyism, however, appalled some black leaders, especially those leading the NAACP. W. E. B. Du Bois labeled Garvey "the most dangerous enemy of the Negro race. . . . He is either a lunatic or a traitor." An African American newspaper pledged to help "drive Garvey and Garveyism in all its sinister viciousness from the American soil."

Garvey's eccentric crusade collapsed in 1923 when he was convicted of fraud for overselling shares of stock in a steamship corporation, the Black Star Line, which he founded to transport American blacks to Africa. Sentenced to a five-year prison term, he was pardoned in 1927 by President Calvin Coolidge on the condition that he be deported to Jamaica, where he received a hero's welcome. Garvey died in obscurity in 1940, but the memory of his movement kept alive an undercurrent that would reemerge in the 1960s under the slogan "black power."

THE MODERNIST REVOLT

The dramatic changes in society and the economy during the twenties were spurred by transformations in science and the arts during the previous two decades. Since the eighteenth-century Enlightenment, conventional wisdom had held that the universe was governed by basic underlying laws of time and energy, light and motion. This rational world of order and certainty disintegrated in the early twentieth century, thanks to the discoveries of European physicists.

ALBERT EINSTEIN

During a century remarkable for its scientific discoveries and technological advances, one genius stands out: Albert Einstein, a scientific rebel with an unrivaled imagination. Many of his greatest discoveries emerged not from research but from his remarkable ability to *picture* in his mind the strange effects of natural forces, from the infinitesimally small to the infinitely large.

In 1905, Einstein, a twenty-six-year-old German-born physicist working in Switzerland, published several papers that changed science forever. In the first paper, which would earn him the Nobel Prize in 1921, Einstein revealed that light was not simply a wave of continuous energy but a stream of tiny particles, called *quanta* (now called *photons*). This breakthrough would provide the theoretical basis for quantum physics and new electronic technologies such as television, laser beams, and semiconductors used to make computers.

In his second paper, Einstein confirmed the existence of molecules and atoms by showing how their random collisions explained the jerky motions of tiny particles in water.

Einstein's third paper introduced the special theory of relativity, which argues that no matter how fast one is moving toward or away from a source of light, the speed of that light beam will appear the same, a constant 186,000 miles per second. But space and time will appear relative to the speed of light. So if a train were traveling at the speed of light, time would slow down from the perspective of an observer, and the train itself would get shorter and heavier.

In 1916, Einstein unveiled his *general theory of relativity*, which maintained that the fundamental concepts of space, time, matter, and energy are not distinct, independent things with stable dimensions, as Sir Isaac Newton had assumed in the eighteenth century, but that they are interacting elements constantly changing one another. As a beam of light travels through space-time, gravity causes it to curve. Likewise, the hands of a clock traveling at high speeds move more slowly than those of a stationary clock.

Nothing is fixed or absolute in Einstein's bewildering universe; everything is *relative* to the location and motion of the observer and the distorting effects of gravity, which warp space and time. Things are big or little, long or short, slow or fast, light or heavy only by comparison to something else. Einstein also explained that all matter is a special form of energy, and that a very small amount of material could yield enormous energy if its atomic structure were disrupted.

By showing that much more was going on in the universe than had long been assumed, Einstein's discoveries revolutionized the way scientists perceived the natural world. A British newspaper said the general theory of relativity was "one of the most momentous . . . pronouncements of human thought." In 1919, after astronomers had spent three years testing Einstein's theories, the *New York Times* announced: "Einstein's Theory Triumphs."

Einstein was so influential in deciphering the forces of the cosmos that his ideas became impossible to ignore—and almost as difficult to explain. Many of his complex discoveries entered popular culture as people oversimplified his theory of relativity by claiming that there were no absolute standards; all was "relative." During the twenties, the idea of "relativity" emerged in popular discussions of topics such as sexuality, the arts, and politics; there was less faith in absolutes. Notions of relativity shaped many of the intellectual, cultural, and social currents of the twentieth century.

MODERNIST ART AND LITERATURE

The scientific breakthroughs associated with Sigmund Freud, Albert Einstein, and other scientists helped to inspire a "modernist" cultural revolution. **Modernism** as a recognizable movement appeared first in the capitals of Europe (London, Paris, Berlin, and Vienna) in the 1890s. By the second decade of the twentieth century, it had spread to the United States, especially New York City and Chicago.

Put most simply, modernism was the widespread awareness that new ideas and ways of doing things were making a sharp break with tradition. The modernist point of view arose out of recognition that new technologies, modes of transportation and communication, and scientific discoveries were transforming the nature of everyday life as well as the way people "saw" the world.

The horrors of the Great War served to accelerate and expand the appeal of modernism—and helped explain why modernists cared little for established standards of good taste or for history. To be "modern" was to break free of tradition, take chances, violate artistic rules and moral restrictions, and behave in deliberately shocking ways. "Art," said a modernist painter, "is meant to disturb."

As an experimental cultural movement, modernism was loosely based on three unsettling assumptions: (1) God did not exist; (2) "reality" was not rational, orderly, or obvious; and, in the aftermath of the Great War, (3) social progress could no longer be taken for granted.

Modernists were artistic revolutionaries who delighted in the madness of the unexpected and refused to be conventional. In its simplest sense, modernism was a disrespectful war of new values against old ones. Experimental poet Ezra Pound provided the slogan for the modernist movement: "Make It New!"

Much about modernism provoked, perplexed, and upset people. Until the twentieth century, most writers and artists had taken for granted an accessible "real" world that could be readily observed, scientifically explained, and accurately represented in words or paint or even music. The modernists, however, applied Einstein's ideas about relativity to a world in which "reality" no longer had an objective or recognizable basis. They agreed wholeheartedly with Freud that reality, in fact, was an intensely inward and subjective experience—

something deeply personal and even unrecognizable by others, something to be imagined and expressed by one's innermost being rather than observed and reproduced. Walter Pach, an early American champion of modern art, explained that modernism resulted from the discovery of "the role played by the unconscious in our lives."

THE ARMORY SHOW The crusade to bring European-inspired modernism to the United States reached a climax in the **Armory Show** of 1913, the most scandalous event in the history of American art. To house the 1,200 modernist works collected from more than 300 painters and sculptors in America and Europe, the two dozen young painters who organized the show leased the vast 69th Regiment Armory in New York City.

The Armory Show, officially known as the International Exhibition of Modern Art, opened on February 17, 1913. It created an immediate sensation. For many, modern art became the thing that they loved to hate. Modernism, grumbled a prominent critic, "is nothing else than the total destruction of the art of painting." The *New York Times* warned visitors that they would enter "a stark region of abstractions" at the "lunatic asylum" show that was "hideous to our unaccustomed eyes."

The experimentalist ("*avant-garde*") artists whose works were on display (including paintings by Vincent Van Gogh, Paul Gauguin, and Henri Matisse, as well as Cezanne and Picasso) were "in love with science but not with objective reality," the *Times* critic complained, and had produced paintings "revolting in their inhumanity." Former president Theodore Roosevelt dismissed the show as "repellent from every standpoint."

Yet the show also generated excited praise. "A new world has arisen before our eyes," announced an American art magazine. "To miss modern art," an art critic stressed, "is to miss one of the few thrills that life holds." From New York, the show went on to Chicago and Boston, where it aroused similarly strong responses and attracted more huge crowds.

***Russian Ballet* (1916)** Jewish American artist Max Weber's painting is a modernist take on a traditional subject. Splicing the scene of the performance into overlapping planes of jarring colors, this painting exemplifies the impact of psychoanalysis and the theory of relativity on the arts.

After the Armory Show, modern art became one of the nation's favorite topics of debate. Many found a new faith in the disturbing powers of art. "America in its newness," predicted Walt Kuhn, a painter who helped organize the exhibition, "is destined to become the coming center" of modernism. Indeed, the Museum of Modern Art, founded in New York City in 1929, came to house the world's most celebrated collection of avant-garde paintings and sculpture.

POUND, ELIOT, AND STEIN The leading American champions of modern art and literature lived not in Chicago or in New York but in England and Europe: Idaho-born Ezra Pound and St. Louis–born T. S. Eliot in London, and Californian Gertrude Stein in Paris. Working separately but spreading their influence together, they were self-conscious revolutionaries deeply concerned with creating strange, new, and often beautifully difficult forms of modernist expression. They found more inspiration and more receptive audiences in Europe than in the United States.

As the foreign editor of the Chicago-based *Poetry* magazine, Pound became the cultural impresario of modernism, the conduit through which many experimental American poets gained publication and exposure. In bitter poems and earnest essays denouncing war and commercialism, he displayed an incessant, uncompromising urgency to transform the literary landscape. An English poet called him a "solitary volcano." T. S. Eliot claimed that Pound was single-handedly responsible for the modernist movement in poetry.

Pound recruited, edited, published, and reviewed the best among the new generation of modernist writers, improving their writing, bolstering their courage, and propelling their careers. In his own poetry, he expressed the feeling of many that the war had wasted a whole generation of young men who died in defense of a "botched civilization."

One of the young American writers Pound took under his wing was Eliot, who had recently graduated from Harvard. Within a few years, Eliot surpassed Pound to become the leading American modernist. Eliot declared that traditional poetry "was stagnant to a degree difficult for any young poet to imagine."

Eliot's epic 433-line poem *The Waste Land* (1922), which Pound edited, became a monument of modernism. It expressed a sense of postwar disillusionment and melancholy that had a powerful effect on other writers. As a poet and critic for the *Criterion,* which he founded in 1922, Eliot became the arbiter of modernist taste in Anglo-American literature.

Gertrude Stein was the self-appointed champion of the American modernists who chose to live in Paris. Long regarded as simply the literary eccentric who wrote, "Rose is a rose is a rose is a rose," Stein was in fact one of the chief promoters of the triumphant subjectivity undergirding modernist expression. She sought to capture in words the equivalent of abstract painting and its self-conscious revolt against portraying recognizable scenes from "real" life. Stein, who declared that literature that "tells about what happens [in life] is of no interest to anybody," became famous for hosting a cultural salon in Paris that became a gathering place for American and European modernists.

THE "LOST GENERATION"   Along with the shock of modernism, the arts and literature of the twenties were also greatly influenced by the horrors of the Great War. F. Scott Fitzgerald wrote in *This Side of Paradise* that the "sad young men" who had fought in Europe to "make the world safe for democracy" had "grown up to find all Gods dead, all wars fought, all faiths in man shaken."

Cynicism had displaced idealism in the wake of the war's horrific senselessness. As Fitzgerald asserted, "There's only one lesson to be learned from life anyway. . . . That there's no lesson to be learned from life." Frederic Henry, a character in Ernest Hemingway's novel *A Farewell to Arms* (1929), declares that "abstract words such as *glory, honor, courage* . . . were obscene" in the context of the war's colossal casualties.

Fitzgerald, Hemingway, and other young modernists were labeled the **Lost Generation**—those who had lost faith in the values and institutions of Western civilization and were frantically looking for new gods to worship. It was Gertrude Stein who in 1921 told Hemingway that he and his friends who had served in the war "are a lost generation." When Hemingway objected, she held her ground. "You are [lost]. You have no respect for anything. You drink yourselves to death."

In his first novel, *The Sun Also Rises* (1926), Hemingway used the phrase "lost generation" in the book's opening quotation. The novel centers on Jake Barnes, a young American journalist castrated by a war injury. His despairing impotence leads him to wander the cafes and nightclubs of postwar Europe with his unhappy friends, who acknowledge that they are all wounded and sterile in their own way: they have lost their innocence, their illusions, and their motivation to do anything with their lives.

Fitzgerald, the earliest chronicler of the "lost generation," blazed up brilliantly and then quickly flickered out, like many of the characters in his novels. His works centered on self-indulgent and self-destructive people who drank and partied too much. A friend and fellow writer called Fitzgerald "our darling, our genius, our fool." What gave depth to the best of his work was what a character in *The Great Gatsby* (1925), his finest novel, called "a sense of the fundamental decencies" amid all the surface gaiety—and a sense of impending doom in a world that had lost its meaning through the disorienting discoveries of modern science and the horrors of world war.

CHAPTER REVIEW

SUMMARY

- **A "New Era" of Consumption**   The American economy grew at its fastest rate in history during the 1920s, led by an explosion in mass production and sales of new consumer goods. Innovations in production, advertising, and financing, and a jump in the use of electricity, enabled and encouraged millions of Americans to purchase automobiles, radios, and other electrical appliances. The automobile industry was at the center of these changes, as Ford Motor Company pioneered mass production using moving assembly lines, a highly efficient method that helped make its cars affordable for a majority of Americans. The new *consumer culture* valued leisure, self-expression, and self-indulgence. During the twenties, consumer debt tripled. Innovations in communications (especially the growth in radio ownership), transportation, finance, and advertising also brought about a mass culture, as more and more Americans purchased national brand-name items from retail chain stores, listened to the same radio shows, watched the same movies, and followed the lives and careers of national celebrities and superstars.

- **The "Jazz Age"**   Other new social and cultural trends and movements rapidly challenged the traditional order. The carefree fads and attitudes of the 1920s, perhaps best represented by the frantic rhythms of jazz music, led writer F. Scott Fitzgerald to call the decade the *Jazz Age*. A "new woman" appeared, best represented by *flappers*—young women who challenged prewar restrictions with their short hemlines, drinking, smoking, and open discussions of sex. The majority of women, however, remained full-time housewives and mothers or domestic servants, and fewer young women pursued professional careers. With the Great Migration continuing, African Americans in northern cities felt freer to speak out against racial injustice and express pride in their race. The *Harlem Renaissance* movement gave voice to African American literature and music. Racial separatism and black nationalism grew popular under the leadership of Marcus Garvey, while other African Americans joined white supporters in the *National Association for the Advancement of Colored People (NAACP)* and supported its efforts to undo racism through education, legislation, and court challenges.

- **The Modernist Revolt**   Many American artists and intellectuals were attracted to modernism, a movement that had begun in Europe before the Great War and reflected new developments in science, particularly Albert Einstein's theory of relativity and Sigmund Freud's exploration of how the subconscious mind shapes human behavior. To be "modern" meant to break free of tradition, to violate restrictions, to shock the public, and to make one's works difficult to explain or interpret. Americans were first exposed to modern art in a substantial way with the *Armory Show* of 1913.

CHRONOLOGY

1903	Wright Brothers fly first motorized airplane
	Ford Motor Company is founded
1910	National Association for the Advancement of Colored People (NAACP) is founded
1913	Armory Show introduces Americans to modern art
1916	Marcus Garvey brings Universal Negro Improvement Association to New York
1920	Prohibition begins
	F. Scott Fitzgerald's *This Side of Paradise* is published
	Warren G. Harding is elected president
1921	Albert Einstein receives Nobel Prize in physics
1922	First radio commercial is aired
1927	Charles A. Lindbergh Jr. makes first solo transatlantic airplane flight

KEY TERMS

consumer culture p. 855

"Jazz Age" p. 861

flappers p. 864

Great Migration p. 866

National Association for the Advancement of Colored People (NAACP) p. 867

Harlem Renaissance p. 867

Negro nationalism p. 869

modernism p. 872

Armory Show p. 873

Lost Generation p. 875

INQUIZITIVE

Go to InQuizitive to see what you've learned—and learn what you've missed—with personalized feedback along the way.

24 The Reactionary Twenties

Black Tuesday In this photograph, panic-stricken crowds take to Wall Street as news of the plummeting stock market spread on the morning of Tuesday, October 29, 1929. An account of the crash in the *New York Times* wrote that "the streets were crammed with a mixed crowd—agonized little speculators, . . . sold-out traders, . . . inquisitive individuals and tourists seeking . . . a closer view of the national catastrophe. . . . Where was it going to end?"

T he self-indulgent excesses of the "lost generation" and the frivolities of the Jazz Age made little sense to the vast majority of Americans during the twenties. Most people still led traditional lives; they aggressively defended established values, old certainties, and the comfort of past routines, and they were shocked by the decade's social turmoil and cultural rebelliousness. They traced the germs of dangerous radicalism to the multiethnic cities teeming with immigrants and foreign ideas such as socialism, communism, and anarchism. The reactionary conservatism of the 1920s fed on the popularity of **nativism**, the fear of and prejudice against immigrants from countries outside of western Europe, and a militant Protestantism that sought to restore the primacy of traditional Christian morality.

REACTIONARY CONSERVATISM AND IMMIGRATION RESTRICTION

The United States has opened its borders and ports to more people from more countries than any other nation. But newcomers have never been universally welcomed or embraced. After the end of the Great War, masses of people emigrated from Europe to the United States. Between 1919 and 1924, more than 600,000 people from southern and eastern Europe, most of them Italians, entered the United States, along with 150,000 Poles and 50,000 Russians. At the same time, some 150,000 Mexicans crossed the border; most of them landed in the Southwest and California. In the early 1920s, more than half of the white men and a third of the white women working in mines, mills, and factories

focus questions

1. How did the reactionary conservatism during the 1920s manifest itself in social life and governmental policies?

2. To what extent did the policies of the Republican party dominate the federal government during the twenties? In what ways were these policies a rejection of progressivism?

3. How did Herbert Hoover emerge as the most popular political figure during the twenties?

4. What were the major causes of the Great Depression?

5. How did the Great Depression impact the American people?

were immigrants, some of whom had a passion for socialism or anarchism—as well as a willingness to use violence to achieve their political goals.

Fears of an invasion of foreign radicals led Congress to pass the Emergency Immigration Act of 1921, which limited total immigration to 150,000 a year and restricted newcomers from each European country to 3 percent of the total number of that nationality represented in the 1910 census. Three years later, after people complained that too many eastern and southern Europeans were still being admitted, Congress passed the **Immigration Act of 1924**. It reduced the number of admitted Europeans to 2 percent of the 1890 census, so as to include fewer "new" immigrants from southern and eastern Europe.

The immigration laws targeted particular groups. For example, they banned immigrants from Japan or China. The Immigration Act of 1924, however, allowed newcomers from countries in the Western Hemisphere. An unintended result was that people of Latin American descent (chiefly Mexicans, Puerto Ricans, and Cubans) became the fastest-growing ethnic minority during the twenties.

The number of Mexicans living in Texas increased tenfold between 1900 and 1930 in response to the needs of Texas farmers for "stoop" laborers. "Cotton picking suits the Mexican," was the common assertion among Texas growers. Because Mexican migrant workers were mostly homeless nomads willing to move with the seasons, farm owners came to prefer them over black and white tenants and farm laborers.

SACCO AND VANZETTI The nativism embedded in the new immigration laws reinforced the connection between European immigrants and political radicalism. That connection erupted in the most widely publicized criminal case of the twenties.

On May 5, 1920, two Italian immigrants who described themselves as revolutionary anarchists eager to topple the American government, shoemaker Nicola Sacco and fish peddler Bartolomeo Vanzetti, were arrested outside Boston, Massachusetts, for stealing $16,000 from a shoe factory and killing the paymaster and a guard. Both men were armed with loaded pistols when arrested, both lied to police, and both were identified by eyewitnesses. The stolen money, however, was never found, and several people claimed that they were with Sacco and Vanzetti far from the scene of the crime when it occurred.

The **Sacco and Vanzetti case** occurred at the height of Italian immigration to the United States and against the backdrop of numerous terror attacks by anarchists, some of which Sacco and Vanzetti had participated in. The charged atmosphere, called "the Red hysteria" by one journalist, ensured that the men's trial would be a public spectacle.

In July 1921, Sacco and Vanzetti were convicted and sentenced to death. Their legal appeals lasted six years before they were electrocuted on August 23, 1927, still claiming their innocence. To millions of workers and liberals around the world, Sacco and Vanzetti became martyrs, victims of capitalist injustice. People still debate their guilt or innocence.

THE NEW KLAN The most violent of the reactionary movements during the twenties was a revived Ku Klux Klan, the infamous post–Civil War group of anti-black racists that had re-created itself in 1915. The old Klan had died out in the 1870s once white Democrats regained control of the former Confederate states after Reconstruction. The new Klan—The Invisible Empire of the Knights of the Ku Klux Klan—was, by 1920, a *nationwide* organization devoted to "the maintenance of White Supremacy" and "100 percent Americanism"; only "natives"—white Protestants born in the United States—could be members. At its peak, the new Klan numbered over 4 million members, making it the largest far-right movement in history.

Shrouded in secret signs and codes, practicing weird rituals, and costumed in white sheets and spooky hats, the Klan called for militant patriotism, restrictions on immigration and voting, and strict personal morality. It

Ku Klux Klan rally In 1925, the KKK marched down Pennsylvania Avenue in Washington, D.C.

opposed bootleg liquor and labor unions, and it preached hatred against not only African Americans but Roman Catholics, Jews, immigrants, Communists, atheists, prostitutes, and adulterers. The United States was no melting pot, shouted Imperial Wizard William J. Simmons: "It is a garbage can! . . . When the hordes of aliens walk to the ballot box and their votes outnumber yours, then that alien horde has got you by the throat."

In Texas, the Klan focused on imposing its severe view of righteous Protestant morality on others. Members used the instruments of terrorism—harassment, intimidation (often in the form of burning crosses), beatings, and "tar and feathers"—to discipline alcoholics, gamblers, adulterers, and other sinners. In the spring of 1922 alone, the Dallas Klan flogged sixty-eight men.

The reborn Klan, headquartered in Atlanta, grew rapidly across the nation, and especially in the rural Midwest. During the twenties, 40 percent of its "Anglo-Saxon" members were in three midwestern states: Illinois, Indiana, and Ohio. Recruiters, called Kleagles, were told to "play upon whatever prejudices were most acute in a particular area." In Texas, the Klan fed on prejudice against Mexicans; in California, hatred focused on Japanese Americans; in New York, the enemy was primarily Jews and Catholics.

Most Klan members were small farmers, sharecroppers, or wage workers, but the organization also attracted clergymen, engineers, doctors, lawyers, accountants, business leaders, and teachers. As a prominent southern journalist observed, the new Klan was "anti-Negro, anti-alien, anti-red, anti-Catholic, anti-Jew, anti-Darwin, anti-Modern, anti-Liberal; Fundamentalist, vastly Moral, militantly Protestant." African Americans grew increasingly concerned. The Chicago *Defender*, the black newspaper with the widest circulation in the nation, urged its readers to fight back against Klansmen trying to "win what their fathers [in the Civil War] lost by fire and sword."

By 1923, the Klan's membership had surpassed 4 million, including judges, mayors, sheriffs, state legislators, six governors, and three U.S. senators. The Grand Dragon, an Indiana con man named David C. Stephenson, grew so influential in electing local and state officials (the "kluxing" of America, as he called it) that he boasted, "I am the law in Indiana!"

The Klan's influence, both in Indiana and nationwide, suddenly crumbled, however, after Stephenson, who had planned to run for president, was arrested and sentenced to life in prison in 1925 for kidnapping and raping a twenty-eight-year-old woman who then committed suicide. Membership tumbled, and Klan organizations splintered or shut down altogether. Several states passed anti-Klan laws, and others banned the wearing of masks and burning of crosses. By 1930, nationwide membership had dwindled to 100,000, mostly southerners.

Yet the impulse underlying the Klan lived on, fed by deep-seated fears and hatreds that have yet to disappear.

FUNDAMENTALISM

While fighting "growing immorality" and the "alien menace," the Klan also defended "old-time religion" against dangerous ideas circulating in "progressive" or "liberal" Protestant churches. The most threatening ideas were that the Bible was not literally the word of God and that Charles Darwin's theories of biological evolution were true. Conservative Protestants embraced a militant fundamentalism, distinctive for its hostility toward new "liberal" beliefs and its insistence on the literal truth of the Bible.

The result was a religious civil war, often called the modernist–fundamentalist conflict. It divided congregations and whole denominations. A burst of Protestant fundamentalism swept the country, largely as a reaction to the spread of modernism in mainline Protestantism, which sought to accommodate Christian teaching with modern science.

Among national leaders, however, only the "Great Commoner," William Jennings Bryan, the former Democratic congressman, secretary of state, and three-time presidential candidate, had the support, prestige, and eloquence to transform fundamentalism into a popular crusade. Bryan was a strange bird, a liberal progressive and pacifist populist in politics and a right-wing religious crusader. He remained a firm believer in the literal truth of the Bible.

Bryan backed new state laws banning the teaching of evolution in public schools. He condemned Darwin's theory of evolution, which suggested that human beings over millions of years had evolved from monkeys and apes, with the same passion he had once directed against Republican presidential candidates.

THE SCOPES TRIAL During the 1920s, anti-evolution bills were introduced in numerous state legislatures, but the dramatic high point of the fundamentalist war on Darwinism came in Tennessee, where in 1925 the legislature outlawed the teaching of evolution in public schools and colleges. In the mining town of Dayton, in eastern Tennessee, civic leaders eager to create publicity for their depressed economy persuaded John T. Scopes, a twenty-four-year-old substitute high-school science teacher, to become a test case against the new law. He was arrested for "teaching" Darwin's theory of evolution. The **Scopes Trial** did indeed bring worldwide publicity to Dayton, but not the kind town leaders had hoped for.

Monkey trial In this snapshot of the courtroom, Scopes (far left) clasps his face in his hands and listens to one of his attorneys (second from right). Darrow (far right), too, listens on, visibly affected by the sweltering weather.

Before the start of the twelve-day trial on July 10, 1925, the sweltering streets of Dayton overflowed with evangelists, atheists, hot-dog and soda-pop peddlers, and some 200 newspaper and radio reporters. Main Street merchants festooned their shop windows with pictures of apes and monkeys lampooning Darwinian evolution. One store urged visitors, "Don't monkey around when you come to Dayton—come to us." A man tattooed with Bible verses preached on a street corner while a live monkey was paraded about town.

The two warriors pitting science against fundamentalism were both national celebrities: Bryan, who had offered his services to the prosecution, and Chicagoan Clarence Darrow, the nation's most famous defense attorney, a tireless defender of the rights of the working class who had volunteered to defend Scopes and evolution.

Bryan insisted that the trial was about a state's right to determine what was taught in the public schools. It was a "contest between evolution and Christianity, a duel to the death." Darrow, who viewed the law as a blood sport, countered: "Scopes is not on trial. Civilization is on trial." His goal was to prevent "bigots and ignoramuses from controlling the education of the United States" by proving that America was "founded on liberty and not on narrow, mean, intolerable and brainless prejudice of soulless religio-maniacs."

On July 20, the seventh day of the trial, the defense called Bryan as an "expert" witness on biblical interpretation. Darrow began by asking him about biblical stories. Did he believe that Jonah was swallowed by a whale and that Joshua made the sun stand still? Yes, Bryan replied. All things were possible with God. Darrow pressed on relentlessly, even cruelly. What about the great flood and Noah's ark? Was Eve really created from Adam's rib? Bryan hesitated and fumbled to reply.

The crowd grew uneasy as the hero of fundamentalism crumpled in the heat. Bryan appealed to the judge for relief, claiming that the Bible was not on trial, only to have Darrow yell: "I am examining you on your fool ideas that no intelligent Christian on earth believes." A humiliated Bryan claimed that Darrow was insulting Christians. Darrow, his thumbs clasping his colorful suspenders, shot back: "You insult every man of science and learning in the world because he does not believe in your fool religion." At one point, Darrow and Bryan, their patience exhausted, lunged at each other, prompting the judge to adjourn court.

As the trial ended, the judge said that the only question for the jury was whether John T. Scopes had taught evolution, and no one had denied that he had done so. The jurors did not even sit down before deciding, in nine minutes, that Scopes was guilty. But the Tennessee Supreme Court, while upholding the anti-evolution law, waived Scopes's $100 fine on a technicality. Both sides claimed victory.

Five days after the trial ended, Bryan, still in Dayton, died in his sleep at age sixty-five. Scopes left Dayton to study geology at the University of Chicago; he became a petroleum engineer.

For all of its comic aspects, the Scopes Trial symbolized the waning of an old order in America and the rise of a *modern* outlook—more pluralistic, diverse, and skeptical, more tolerant of controversial ideas, and less obsessed with intellectual control. Still, the debate between fundamentalism and modernism continues today.

PROHIBITION

William Jennings Bryan died knowing that one of his crusades had succeeded: the distribution of alcoholic beverages had been outlawed nationwide. The movement to prohibit the sale of beer, wine, and liquor forged an unusual alliance between rural and small-town Protestants and urban political progressives—between believers in "old-time religion," who opposed drinking as sinful, and progressive social reformers, mostly women, who were convinced that **Prohibition** would reduce prostitution and alcohol-related violence.

What connected the two groups were the ethnic and social prejudices that many members shared. The head of the Anti-Saloon League, for example, declared that German Americans "eat like gluttons and drink like swine." For many anti-alcohol crusaders, in fact, the primary goal of prohibition seemed to be policing the behavior of the foreign-born, the working class, and the poor, just as fundamentalists sought to enforce their religious beliefs on others.

During the Great War, the need to use grain for food rather than for making booze, combined with a grassroots backlash against beer brewers because of their German background, also transformed the cause of Prohibition into a virtual test of American patriotism. On December 18, 1917, Congress sent to the states the Eighteenth Amendment. Ratified on January 16, 1919, it banned "the manufacture, sale, and transportation of intoxicating liquors," effective one year later.

As the most ambitious social reform ever attempted in the United States, however, Prohibition proved to be a colossal and costly failure. It did not suddenly persuade people to quit drinking. Instead, it compelled millions to break—or stretch—the law. In 1923, a federal agent said it would take a visitor in any city less than thirty minutes to find a drink. In New Orleans, he added, it would only take thirty-five seconds.

The National Prohibition Act of 1919 (commonly called the Volstead Act) outlined the rules and regulations needed to enforce the Eighteenth Amendment. It had so many loopholes that it virtually guaranteed failure, however. Technically, it never said that *drinking* alcohol was illegal, only the manufacture, distribution, and sale of alcoholic beverages.

In addition, individuals and organizations were allowed to keep and drink any liquor owned on January 16, 1919. Not surprisingly, people stocked up before the law took effect. Farmers were allowed to "preserve" their fruits through the process of fermenting them, which resulted in barns stockpiled with "hard cider" and homemade wine. So-called medicinal liquor was also still allowed, which meant that physicians (and even veterinarians) wrote numerous prescriptions for "medicinal" brands such as Old Grand-Dad and Jim Beam whiskies.

Thousands of people set up home breweries to make their own beer, producing 700 million gallons in 1929 alone. Wine was made just as easily, and "bathtub gin" was the easiest of all, requiring little more than a one-gallon still and some fruit, grain, or potatoes. Liquor crossed the nation's 18,700-mile-long borders more easily than people did. Two-thirds of the illegal liquor came from Canada, most of the rest from Mexico or overseas.

The new law was too sweeping to enforce and too inconveniencing for most Americans to respect. It also had unexpected consequences. The loss of liquor taxes cost the federal government 10 percent of its annual revenue, and the closing of breweries, distilleries, and saloons eliminated thousands of jobs.

An even greater weakness of Prohibition was that Congress never supplied adequate funding to enforce it. Given the public thirst for alcohol and the profits to be made in making and selling it illegally ("bootlegging") it would have taken armies of agents to police the nation, and jail cells would have overflowed with violators. New York's mayor said it would take 250,000 policemen to enforce Prohibition in his city alone. In working-class and ethnic-rich Detroit, the bootleg industry was second in size only to the auto industry, and New York City's police commissioner estimated in 1929 that there were 32,000 illegal bars ("speakeasies") in the city.

Moreover, a huge number of prominent Americans regularly broke the law. President Warren G. Harding drank and served bootleg liquor in the White House, explaining that he was "unable to see this as a great moral issue," and the largest bootlegger in Washington, D.C., reported that "a majority of both houses" of Congress were regular customers.

The efforts to defy Prohibition generated widespread police corruption and boosted organized crime. Many of the activities and images associated with the Roaring Twenties were fueled by bootleg liquor supplied by crime syndicates and sold in speakeasies, which local policemen often ignored in exchange for bribes. Well-organized crime syndicates behaved like giant corporations; they controlled the entire stream of liquor's production, pricing, distribution, and sales. As a result, the Prohibition era was a fourteen-year orgy of unparalleled criminal activity. By 1930, more than one-third of Americans in federal prison were Prohibition violators.

All fair in drink and war Torpedoes filled with malt whiskey were discovered in the New York harbor in 1926, an elaborate attempt by bootleggers to smuggle alcohol during Prohibition. Each "torpedo" had an air compartment so it could be floated to shore.

The most famous Prohibition-era gangster was Alphonse "Scarface" Capone. In 1927, his Chicago-based bootlegging, prostitution, and gambling empire brought him an annual income of $60 million and involved an army of 700 gangsters. Capone was a larger-than-life hero to many. He gave huge tips to waiters and hatcheck girls and provided a soup kitchen for Chicago's poorest residents. When criticized, he claimed to be providing the public with the goods and services it demanded: "Some call it bootlegging. Some call it racketeering. I call it business. They say I violate the prohibition law. Who doesn't?"

Capone neglected to add that he had also beaten to death several police officers; ordered the execution of dozens of rivals; and bribed mayors, judges, and policemen. Law-enforcement officials led by FBI agent Eliot Ness began to smash Capone's bootlegging operations in 1929. In the end, he was tried and convicted on charges of tax evasion and sentenced to eleven years in prison.

A REPUBLICAN RESURGENCE

In national politics, the small-town backlash against the immorality of modern city life—whether represented by fears of immigrant radicals plotting revolution, liberal churches not taking the Bible literally, or jazzed-up flappers swilling cocktails—was mirrored by a Republican resurgence determined to reverse the progressivism of Theodore Roosevelt and Woodrow Wilson.

By 1920, the progressive coalition had fragmented. Roosevelt had died in 1919 at the age of sixty, just as he was beginning to campaign for the 1920 Republican presidential nomination. Wilson's health problems had forced him to retire as well. Many Americans preferred other candidates anyway. Organized labor resented the Wilson administration's crackdown on striking workers in 1919–1920, and farmers in the Great Plains and the West thought that wartime price controls on wheat and corn had discriminated against them. Liberal intellectuals became disillusioned with grassroots democracy because of popular support for Prohibition, the Ku Klux Klan, and religious fundamentalism.

By 1920, the growing middle class had become preoccupied with ushering in a "new era" of prosperity based on mass production and mass consumption. Voters turned away from progressivism in part because it had accomplished its major goals: the Eighteenth Amendment, which outlawed alcoholic beverages, and the Nineteenth Amendment, which allowed women to vote nationwide.

Progressivism did not simply disappear, of course. The impulse for honest, efficient government and greater regulation of big businesses remained strong, especially at the state and local levels, where movements for better roads, education, public health, and social-welfare programs gained momentum during the decade. At the national level, however, Republican conservatives returned to power.

HARDING AND "NORMALCY" After the Great War and the furious debate over the League of Nations, most Americans were weary of Woodrow Wilson's crusading idealism. Wilson himself recognized the shifting public mood. "It is only once in a generation," he remarked, "that a people can be lifted above material things. That is why conservative government is in the saddle two-thirds of the time."

In 1920, Republican leaders turned to a likeable mediocrity as their presidential candidate: Warren G. Harding, a dapper, silver-haired U.S. senator from Ohio. Harding was selected not for his abilities or experience (which were minimal) but because he was from a key state and looked presidential.

Harding set the conservative tone of his campaign when he told a Boston audience that it was time to end Wilson's progressivism and internationalism: America did not need "heroics, but healing; not nostrums, but normalcy; not revolution, but restoration; not agitation, but adjustment; not surgery, but serenity; not the dramatic, but the dispassionate." Harding pledged to "safeguard America first . . . to exalt America first, to live for and revere America first."

The Democrats were initially encouraged by the Republicans' decision to nominate Harding, but they also had to find a candidate of their own. At their convention, the divided delegates finally chose another Ohioan, James Cox, a former newspaper publisher and three-term governor of the state. For vice president, the convention chose New Yorker Franklin Delano Roosevelt, only thirty-eight years old, who as assistant secretary of the navy occupied the same position his Republican cousin Theodore Roosevelt had once held. Handsome, vigorous, and a stirring speaker, he would deliver more than 1,000 speeches during the campaign.

But Cox's campaign was disorganized and underfunded, and the Democrats struggled against the conservative postwar mood. In the words of progressive journalist William Allen White, Americans were "tired of issues, sick at heart of ideals, and weary of being noble." The Republicans took the offensive, blaming Wilson and the Democrats for the nation's troubles.

Harding won big, getting 16 million votes to 9 million for Cox, who carried no state outside the Solid South. "It wasn't a landslide," a Democratic organizer contended. "It was an earthquake." The lopsided victory increased the Republican majority in both houses of Congress. Franklin Roosevelt predicted that his party could not hope to return to power until the Republicans led the nation "into a serious period of depression and unemployment." He was right.

"JUST A PLAIN FELLOW" Harding's vanilla promise of a **"return to normalcy"** reflected his unexceptional background and limited abilities. One of his own speechwriters admitted that his boss was both "indolent" and "ignorant of most of the big questions that would confront him." A farmer's son and newspaper editor, Harding described himself as "just a plain fellow" who was "old-fashioned and even reactionary in matters of faith and morals" and had pledged "total abstinence" from alcohol.

In fact, however, Harding was a hell-raiser. He drank outlawed liquor in the White House, smoked and chewed tobacco, hosted twice-weekly poker games, and had numerous extramarital affairs and even fathered children with women other than his domineering wife, Florence Harding, whom he called "the Duchess." His dalliances brought him much grief. One of the women blackmailed him, demanding money for her silence—which she received.

The public was virtually unaware of Harding's escapades. Voters saw him as a handsome, charming politician who looked the part of a leader. Yet Harding privately worried about his own limitations. "I am not fit for this office and should never have been here," he once admitted. "I cannot hope to be one of the great presidents, but perhaps I may be remembered as one of the best loved." Tart-tongued Alice Roosevelt Longworth, daughter of Theodore Roosevelt, said Harding "was not a bad man. He was just a slob."

ANDREW MELLON AND THE ECONOMY The Harding administration inherited a slumping economy burdened by high wartime taxes and a national debt that had ballooned from $1 billion in 1914 to $27 billion in 1920 because of the expenses associated with the war. Unemployment was at nearly 12 percent.

To generate economic growth, Secretary of the Treasury Andrew Mellon, at the time the third-richest man in the world behind John D. Rockefeller and Henry Ford, developed what came to be called the Mellon plan, which called for reducing federal spending and lowering tax rates. Mellon persuaded Congress to pass the landmark Budget and Accounting Act of 1921, which created a Bureau of the Budget to streamline the process of preparing an annual federal budget to be approved by Congress. The bill also created a General Accounting Office to audit spending by federal agencies. This act fulfilled a long-held progressive desire to bring greater efficiency and nonpartisanship to the budget preparation process.

Mellon also proposed a series of tax reductions. By 1918, the tax rate on the highest income bracket had risen to 73 percent. Mellon believed that such high rates were pushing wealthy Americans to avoid paying taxes by investing their money in foreign countries or in tax-free government bonds. His policies systematically reduced tax rates while increasing tax revenues. The top tax rate was cut from 73 percent in 1921 to 24 percent in 1929. Rates for individuals with the lowest annual incomes were also cut substantially, helping the working poor.

By 1926, those with incomes of $300,000 or more were the source of 65 percent of federal income tax revenue. In 1921, less than 20 percent had come from this group. During this same period, the overall tax burden on those with incomes of less than $10,000 dropped from $155 million to $32.5 million. By 1929, barely 2 percent of American workers had to pay any income tax at all.

At the same time, Mellon helped Harding reduce the federal budget from its wartime highs. Government expenditures fell, as did the national debt, and the economy soared. Unemployment plummeted to 2.4 percent in 1923. Mellon's supporters labeled him the greatest secretary of the Treasury since Alexander Hamilton in the late eighteenth century.

REDUCED REGULATION The Republican economic program also sought to dismantle or neutralize many progressive regulatory laws and agencies. Harding appointed commissioners to these federal agencies who would promote "regulatory capitalism" and policies "friendly" to business interests.

In addition, Harding's four Supreme Court appointments were all conservatives, including Chief Justice William Howard Taft, the former president, who announced that he had been "appointed to reverse a few decisions." During the 1920s, the Taft court struck down a federal child-labor law and a minimum-wage law for women and issued numerous injunctions against striking unions.

RACIAL PROGRESSIVISM In one area, however, President Harding proved to be more progressive than Woodrow Wilson: civil rights. He reversed the Wilson administration's policy of excluding African Americans from federal government jobs and spoke out against the vigilante racism that had flared up across the country. In his first speech to Congress in 1921, Harding attacked the Ku Klux Klan for fomenting "hatred and prejudice and violence" and urged Congress "to wipe the stain of barbaric lynching from the banners of a free and orderly, representative democracy." Southern Democrats in the Senate, however, stopped an anti-lynching bill from becoming law.

SETBACKS FOR UNIONS Urban workers shared in the affluence of the 1920s. "A workman is far better paid in America than anywhere else in the world," a French visitor wrote in 1927, "and his standard of living is enormously higher." Nonfarm workers gained about 30 percent in real wages between 1921 and 1928, while farm income rose only 10 percent. Yet organized labor suffered in the 1920s. Although President Harding endorsed collective bargaining and tried to reduce the twelve-hour workday and the six-day work-week to give the working class "time for leisure and family life," he ran into stiff opposition in Congress. The widespread strikes of 1919 had created fears that unions promoted radical socialism.

Between January 1920 and August 1921, the unemployment rate jumped from 2 percent to 14 percent, and industrial production fell by 23 percent as the economy made the transition from war to peace. The brief postwar depression so weakened the unions that in 1921 business groups in Chicago designated the **open shop** to be the "American plan" of employment. Unlike the closed shop, which forced businesses to hire only union members, the open shop gave an employer the right to hire anyone. A labor organizer identified another reason for the weakness of unions in the New Era: "The Ford car has done an awful lot of harm to the unions. . . . As long as men have enough money to buy a second-hand Ford and tires and gasoline, they'll be out on the road and paying no attention to union meetings."

Employers often required workers to sign "yellow-dog" contracts, which forced them to agree not to join a union. Owners also used labor spies, blacklists, and intimidation to block unions. Some employers, such as Henry Ford, tried to kill the unions with kindness by introducing programs of "industrial democracy," guided by company-sponsored unions, or various schemes of "welfare capitalism," such as profit sharing, bonuses, pensions, health programs, and recreational activities.

The result was that union membership dropped from about 5 million in 1920 to 3.5 million in 1929 as industrial production soared and joblessness fell to 3 percent. But the anti-union effort, led by businesses that wanted to keep wages low and unions weak, helped to create a "purchasing-power crisis" whereby the working poor were not earning enough income to buy the abundance of goods being churned out by ever more-productive industries. Productivity increased by 43 percent in the Roaring Twenties, but wages barely rose. In fact, large groups of hourly workers, such as miners and textile mill hands, saw their income *drop*. Executives used company profits to pay dividends to stockholders, invest in new equipment, and increase their own salaries, while doing little to help wage earners. In 1929, an estimated 5 percent of the nation's workforce (executives) received one-third of the nation's income.

In other words, the much-trumpeted "new economy" was not benefiting enough working-class Americans to be sustainable. The gap between income levels and purchasing power would be a major cause of the Great Depression, as the Republican formula of high tariffs, low wages, low taxes, little regulation, and anti-unionism would eventually implode.

ISOLATIONISM IN FOREIGN AFFAIRS

In addition to the Senate's rejection of American membership in the League of Nations, the postwar spirit of isolation found other expressions. George Jean Nathan, a drama critic, expressed the sentiments of many Americans when he announced that the "great problems of the world—social, political, economic and theological—do not concern me in the slightest. . . . What concerns me alone is myself, and the interests of a few close friends."

Yet the desire to stay out of foreign wars did not mean that the United States could ignore its expanding global interests. As a result of the Great War, the United States had become the world's chief banker, and American investments and loans enabled foreigners to purchase U.S. exports.

WAR DEBTS AND REPARATIONS Probably nothing did more to heighten America's isolationism—and anti-American feelings among Europeans—than the complex challenge facing America's allies: paying off their huge war debts to the United States. Beginning in 1917, when France and Great Britain ran out of money for military supplies, the U.S. government had advanced them massive loans, first for the war effort and then, after the war, for reconstruction projects.

Most Americans, including Treasury Secretary Andrew Mellon, expected the debts to be repaid, but the Europeans thought otherwise. The British noted that after the American Revolution, the United States had refused to pay old debts to British merchants. The French likewise pointed out that they had never been repaid for helping the Americans win the Revolutionary War.

But the most difficult challenges in the 1920s were the practical problems of repayment. To get U.S. dollars to pay their war-related debts, European nations had to sell their goods to the United States. However, rising American tariff rates greatly reduced imported European goods, thus making it even harder for the Allies to repay their debts.

The French and British insisted that they could repay only by collecting the $33 billion in war reparations owed them by Germany, whose economy was in chaos. Twice during the 1920s, American bankers had to provide loans so that Germany could pay its obligations to Britain and France, thereby enabling them to pay their debts to the United States.

ATTEMPTS AT DISARMAMENT After the Great War, many Americans decided that the best way to keep the peace was to limit the size of armies and navies. The United States had no intention of maintaining a large army after 1920, but under the shipbuilding program begun in 1916, it had constructed a powerful navy second only to that of Great Britain. Although neither the British nor the Americans wanted a naval armaments race, both were worried about the growth of Japanese power.

To address the problem, President Harding in 1921 invited diplomats from eight nations to a peace conference in Washington, D.C., at which Secretary of State Charles Evans Hughes made a blockbuster proposal. The only way out of an expensive naval arms race, he declared, "is to end it now" by eliminating scores of existing warships. He pledged that America would junk 30 battleships and cruisers and then named 36 British and Japanese warships that would also be destroyed. It was one of the most dramatic moments in diplomatic history. The stunned audience of diplomats, ambassadors, admirals, and senators stood and roared its approval. In less than fifteen minutes, one journalist reported, Hughes had destroyed more warships "than all the admirals of the world have sunk in a cycle of centuries."

Following Hughes's lead, delegates from the United States, Britain, Japan, France, and Italy signed the Five-Power Treaty (1922), which limited the size of their navies. It was the first disarmament treaty in history. The agreement also, in effect, divided the world into regions: U.S. naval power became supreme in the Western Hemisphere, Japanese power in the western Pacific, and British power from the North Sea to Singapore.

THE HARDING SCANDALS

As time passed, President Harding found himself increasingly distracted by scandals in his administration. Early in 1923, the head of the Veterans Bureau resigned when faced with an investigation for stealing medical and hospital supplies intended for former servicemen. A few weeks later, the legal adviser to the bureau killed himself. Soon thereafter, Jesse Smith, a colleague of Attorney General Harry M. Daugherty who was illegally selling federal paroles, pardons, and judgeships from his Justice Department office, was found shot dead in a hotel room after he had threatened to "quit the racket." Then, Daugherty himself was accused of selling for personal gain German assets seized after the war. When asked to testify about the matter, he refused on the grounds that doing so might incriminate him.

The most serious of the scandals was called the "**Teapot Dome Affair**." The Teapot Dome was a government-owned oil field in Wyoming that provided reserve fuel for warships. After Harding moved administrative control of the oil field from the Department of the Navy to the Department of the Interior, Secretary of the Interior Albert B. Fall, deeply in debt and eight years overdue in paying his taxes, began signing overly generous federal contracts with close friends who were executives of petroleum companies that wanted access to the oil. In doing so, Fall took bribes of about $400,000 from an oil tycoon. Fall was convicted of conspiracy and bribery and sentenced to a year in prison, the first former cabinet official to serve time because of misconduct in office.

How much Harding knew of the scandals remains unclear, but he knew enough to be troubled. "My God, this is a hell of a job!" he confided to a journalist. "I have no trouble with my enemies; I can take care of my enemies all right. But my damn friends, my Goddamn friends. . . . They're the ones that keep me walking the floor nights!"

Teapot Dome scandal In this 1924 political cartoon, Republican officials try to outrun the Teapot Dome scandal, represented by a giant steamrolling teapot, on an oil-slicked highway.

In 1923, Harding left on what would be his last journey, a speaking tour to the West Coast and a trip to the Alaska Territory. While in Seattle, he suffered an attack of food poisoning from which he never fully recovered. Soon thereafter, he died in San Francisco. He was fifty-seven years old.

Largely as a result of Harding's corrupt associates, his administration came to be viewed as one of the worst in history. More recent assessments, however, suggest that the scandals obscured Harding's accomplishments. He led the nation out of the turmoil of the postwar years and helped create the economic boom of the 1920s. He endorsed diversity and civil rights and was a forceful proponent of women's rights. Still, even Harding's foremost scholarly defender admits that he lacked good judgment and "probably should never have been president."

COOLIDGE CONSERVATISM

The news of Harding's death reached Vice President Calvin Coolidge when he was visiting his father in the isolated village of Plymouth Notch, Vermont, his birthplace. There, at 2:47 A.M. on August 3, 1923, Colonel John Coolidge, a farmer and merchant, issued the presidential oath of office to his son.

Calvin Coolidge, born on the fourth of July in 1872, was a throwback to an earlier era. A puritan in his personal life, he was horrified by the jazzed-up Roaring Twenties. He sincerely believed in the ideals of personal integrity and

Calvin Coolidge "Silent Cal" was so inactive as president that when he died in 1933, American humorist Dorothy Parker remarked, "How could they tell?"

devotion to public service, and, like Harding, he was an evangelist for capitalism and minimal government regulation of business.

AN INACTIVE PRESIDENT Although Coolidge had won every political race he had entered, beginning in 1898, he had never loved the limelight. Shy and awkward, he was a man of famously few words—hence, his nickname, "Silent Cal." Voters liked his uprightness, his straight-talking style, and his personal humility. He was a simple, direct man of strong principles and intense patriotism who championed self-discipline and hard work.

As a state senator in Massachusetts, Coolidge had often aligned himself with Republican progressives. He voted for women's suffrage, a state income tax, a minimum wage for female workers, and salary increases for public school teachers. By the time he entered the White House, however, he had abandoned most of those causes.

Coolidge was determined *not* to be an activist president. Walter Lippmann, the foremost political journalist of the twenties, wryly observed that "it is a grim, determined, alert inactivity, which keeps Mr. Coolidge occupied constantly." To Coolidge, activist presidents created more problems than solutions. Unlike Theodore Roosevelt and Woodrow Wilson, he knew he was "not a great man." Nor did he have an ambitious program to push through Congress. "Four-fifths of our troubles," Coolidge believed, "would disappear if we would sit down and keep still." Following his own logic, he insisted on twelve hours of sleep *and* a lengthy afternoon nap.

EVANGELIST FOR CAPITALISM Americans embraced the unflappability and unstained integrity of Silent Cal. He was simple and direct, a self-righteous man of strong principles, intense patriotism, pinched frugality, and few words. President Coolidge, said a critic, "can be silent in five languages." Yet he promoted his regressive conservatism with a ruthless consistency. Even more than Harding, Coolidge linked the nation's welfare with the success of big business. "The chief business of the American people is business," he preached. "The man who builds a factory builds a temple. The man who works there worships there." Coolidge famously declared that "wealth is the *chief* end of man."

With the help of Treasury Secretary Mellon and Republican-controlled Congresses, Coolidge continued Harding's efforts to lower income tax rates. Where Harding had sought to balance the interests of labor, agriculture, and industry, Coolidge focused on promoting industrial development by limiting federal regulation of business and industry and reducing taxes. He was also "obsessed" with reducing federal spending, even to the point of issuing government workers only one pencil at a time—and only after they turned in the stub of the old pencil. His fiscal frugality and pro-business stance led the *Wall Street Journal* to exult: "Never before, here or anywhere else, has a government been so completely fused with business." The nation had too many laws, Coolidge insisted, and "we would be better off if we did not have any more." True to his word, he vetoed fifty acts of Congress. As a journalist said, "In a great day of yes-men, Calvin Coolidge was a no-man."

THE ELECTION OF 1924 Coolidge restored the dignity of the presidency while capably managing the warring Republican factions. He easily gained the party's 1924 presidential nomination.

Meanwhile, the Democrats again fell to fighting among themselves, prompting humorist Will Rogers's classic statement that "I am a member of no organized political party. I am a Democrat." The party's fractiousness reflected the ongoing divisions between urban and rural America, North and South. The nominating convention split down the middle on a proposal to express disapproval of Ku Klux Klan bigotry. It then took 103 ballots to decide on a presidential candidate: former ambassador John W. Davis, a prominent Wall Street lawyer from West Virginia who could nearly outdo Coolidge in his limited-government conservatism.

While the Democrats bickered, rural populists and urban progressives decided to abandon both major parties, as they had done in 1912. Reorganizing the old Progressive party, they nominated Robert M. "Fighting Bob" La Follette for president. As a Republican senator, La Follette had voted against the 1917 declaration of war against Germany. Now, in addition to the Progressives, he won the support of the Socialist party and the American Federation of Labor.

In the 1924 election, Coolidge swept both the popular and the electoral votes by decisive majorities. Davis and the Democrats took only the solidly Democratic South, and La Follette carried only Wisconsin, his home state.

The popular vote went 15.7 million for Coolidge, 8.4 million for Davis, and 4.8 million for La Follette—the largest popular vote ever polled by a third-party candidate up to that time.

Coolidge's big victory represented the height of postwar political conservatism. Business executives interpreted the Republican victory as an endorsement of their influence on government, and Coolidge saw the economy's surging prosperity as confirmation of his aggressive support of the interests of business.

THE RISE OF HERBERT HOOVER

During the twenties, the drive for industrial efficiency, which had been a prominent theme among progressives, powered the wheels of mass production and consumption and became a cardinal belief of Republican leaders. Herbert Hoover, secretary of commerce in the Harding and Coolidge cabinets, was himself a remarkable success story.

Born into an Iowa farm family in 1874, orphaned at age eight, and raised by Quaker uncles in Iowa and Oregon, he was a shy but industrious "loner" who graduated from Stanford University and became a world-renowned mining engineer, oil tycoon, financial wizard, and multimillionaire before the age of forty. His meteoric success and genius for managing difficult tasks bred in him a self-confidence that bordered on conceit. Short-tempered and quick to take offense, Hoover had to have complete control of any project he managed. In his twenties, he was already planning to be president of the United States.

A PROGRESSIVE CONSERVATIVE After applying his managerial skills to the Food Administration during the Great War, Hoover served with the U.S. delegation at the Versailles peace conference. He idolized Woodrow Wilson and supported American membership in the League of Nations. A young Franklin Roosevelt, then assistant secretary of the navy, was dazzled by Hoover, the man he would eventually defeat in the presidential election of 1932. In 1920, Roosevelt said that Hoover was "certainly a wonder [boy], and I wish we could make him President of the United States."

Hoover, however, soon disappointed Roosevelt by declaring himself a Republican "progressive conservative." In a book titled *American Individualism* (1922), Hoover wrote of an "ideal of *service*" that went beyond "rugged individualism" to promote the greater good. He wanted government officials to encourage business leaders to forgo "cutthroat competition" and engage in "voluntary cooperation" by forming trade associations that would share information and promote standardization and efficiency.

As secretary of commerce during the 1920s, Hoover transformed the small Commerce Department into the government's most dynamic agency. He looked for new markets for business, created a Bureau of Aviation to promote the new airline industry, and established the Federal Radio Commission.

THE BUSINESS OF FARMING During the 1920s, agriculture remained the weakest sector in the economy. The wartime boom fed by agricultural exports and sales abroad lasted into 1920 before commodity prices collapsed as European agricultural production returned to prewar levels. Overproduction brought lower prices for crops that persisted into 1923, and after that, improvement was spotty. A bumper cotton crop in 1926 resulted only in a price collapse and an early taste of depression in much of the South, where foreclosures and bankruptcies spread.

Yet the most successful farms, like the most successful corporations, were getting larger, more efficient, and more mechanized. By 1930, about 13 percent of all farmers had tractors; the proportion was even higher on the western plains. Better plows, harvesters, combines, and other machines accompanied improved crop yields, fertilizers, and methods of animal breeding.

Most farmers, however, were still struggling to survive. They asked for political help, and in 1924, Senator Charles L. McNary of Oregon and Representative Gilbert N. Haugen of Iowa introduced the first McNary-Haugen bill, which sought to secure "equality for agriculture in the benefits of the protective tariff." The proposed bill called for surplus American crops to be sold on the world market to raise prices in the home market. The goal was to achieve "parity"—that is, to raise domestic prices so that farmers would have the same purchasing power relative to the prices they had enjoyed between 1909 and 1914, a time viewed as a golden age of American agriculture.

The McNary-Haugen bill passed both houses of Congress in 1927 but was vetoed by President Coolidge, who dismissed it as unsound and unconstitutional. The process was repeated in 1928. In a broader sense, however, McNary-Haugenism did not fail. The debates over the bill made the "farm problem" a national policy issue and defined it as a matter of surpluses. Moreover, the evolution of the McNary-Haugen plan revived the idea of a political alliance between the rural South and the West, a coalition that in the next decade would have a dominant influence on national farm policy.

THE 1928 ELECTION: HOOVER VERSUS SMITH On August 2, 1927, while on vacation in the Black Hills of South Dakota, President Coolidge suddenly announced, "I do not choose to run for President in 1928." His decision surprised the nation and cleared the way for Hoover to win the Republican

Herbert Hoover "I have no fears for the future of our country," Hoover told the nation at his inauguration in 1929.

nomination. The party's platform took credit for the nation's longest period of sustained prosperity, the government's cost cutting, debt and tax reduction, and the high tariffs ("as vital to American agriculture as . . . to manufacturing") designed to "protect" American businesses from foreign competition.

The Democratic nomination went to four-term New York governor Alfred E. Smith, called the "Happy Warrior" by Franklin D. Roosevelt in his nominating speech. The candidates presented sharply different images: Hoover, the successful businessman and bureaucratic manager from an Iowa farm, and Smith, a professional Irish American politician from New York City's Lower East Side. To working-class Democrats in northern cities, Smith was a hero, the poor grandson of Irish Catholic immigrants who had worked himself up to governor of the most populous state. His outspoken criticism of Prohibition also endeared him to the Irish, Italians, and others who wanted to have a drink at a saloon.

On the other hand, as the first Roman Catholic nominated for president by a major party, a product of New York's machine-run politics, and a "wet" on Prohibition (in direct opposition to his party's platform), Smith represented all that was opposed by southern and western rural Democrats—as well as most rural and small-town Republicans. A Kansas newspaper editor declared that the "whole puritan civilization, which has built a sturdy, orderly nation, is threatened by Smith." The Ku Klux Klan issued a "Klarion Kall for a Krusade" against him, mailing thousands of postcards proclaiming that "Alcohol" Smith, the Catholic New Yorker, was the Antichrist.

While Hoover stayed above the fray, reminding Americans of their unparalleled prosperity and promising a "job for every man," Smith was forced to deal with constant criticism. He denounced his opponents for injecting "bigotry, hatred, intolerance and un-American sectarian division" into the campaign.

But no Democrat could have beaten Hoover in 1928. The nation was prosperous and at peace, and Hoover seemed the best person to sustain the good times. He was perhaps the best-trained economic mind ever to run for president, and he was widely viewed as the brilliant engineer "who never failed."

On Election Day, Hoover, the first Quaker to be president, won in a landslide, with 21 million popular votes to Smith's 15 million and an electoral college majority of 444 to 87. He even penetrated the Democrats' Solid South, winning Virginia, North Carolina, Tennessee, Florida, and Texas, leaving Smith only six Deep South states plus Massachusetts and Rhode Island. Republicans also kept control of both houses of Congress.

Hidden in the results, however, was a glimpse of hope for Democrats. Overall, Smith's vote total, especially strong in the largest cities, doubled that of John Davis four years earlier. In 1932, Franklin D. Roosevelt would build upon that momentum to win back the presidency for the Democrats.

But for now, Hoover was in command. Coolidge, however, was skeptical that Hoover could sustain the good times. He quipped that the "Wonder Boy" had offered him "unsolicited advice for six years, all of it bad." Coolidge's doubts about Hoover's political abilities would prove all too accurate, as the new president would soon be struck by an economic earthquake that would test all of his skills—and expose his weaknesses as a leader.

THE CAUSES OF THE GREAT DEPRESSION

Herbert Hoover's election in 1928 boosted the hopes of investors in what had come to be called "the Great Bull Market." Since 1924, the prices of stock shares invested in U.S. companies had steadily risen. Beginning in 1927, prices soared further on wings of reckless speculation driven by a mass mania unmatched in history. In 1919, some 317 million shares of stock changed hands; in 1929, the number was more than a billion.

Much of the nation's total capital was sucked into the stock market. Treasury Secretary Andrew W. Mellon's tax reductions had given people more money to spend or invest, and much of it went into the stock market. In some respects, the stock market had become the economy. In April 1929, Hoover voiced concern about the "orgy of mad speculation" in the stock market and urged investors to be more cautious—while privately telling his own broker to sell many of his stock holdings.

THE STOCK MARKET What made it so easy for hundreds of thousands of people to invest in stocks was the common practice of buying "on margin"—that is, an investor could make a small cash down payment (the "margin") on shares of stock and borrow the rest from a stockbroker, who held the stock certificates as security in case the price plummeted. If stock prices rose, as they did in 1927, 1928, and most of 1929, the investor made enough profits to pay for the "margin loan" and reinvest the rest.

But if the stock price declined and the buyer failed to meet a "margin call" for cash to pay off the broker's loan, the broker could sell the stock at a much lower price to cover the loan. By August 1929, stockbrokers were lending investors more than two-thirds of the face value of the stocks they were buying. Yet few people seemed concerned, and stock prices kept rising.

Despite the soaring stock market, there were signs that the economy was weakening. By 1927, steel production, residential construction, and automobile sales were slowing, as was the rate of consumer spending. By mid-1929, industrial production, employment, and other measures of economic activity were also declining. Still, the stock market rose.

Then, in early September 1929, the speculative bubble burst when the stock market fell sharply. By the middle of October, world markets had gone into a steep decline. Still, most investors remained upbeat. The nation's foremost economist, Irving Fisher of Yale University, told investors on October 17 that "stock prices have reached what looks like a permanently high plateau." Five days later, a leading bank president assured reporters that there was "nothing fundamentally wrong with the stock market or with the underlying business and credit structure."

THE CRASH The next week, however, stock market values wobbled, then tumbled again, triggering a wild scramble among terrified investors. As they rushed to sell their shares, the decline in stock prices accelerated. On Black Tuesday, October 29—the worst day in the stock market's history to that point—widespread panic set in. Stock prices went into free fall, and brokers found themselves flooded with stocks they could not sell. On that day, investors lost $15 billion. By the end of the month, they had lost $50 billion.

An atmosphere of gloom settled over the financial community. "Life would no longer be, ever again, all fun and games," comedian Harpo Marx sighed as he anticipated the onset of the worst depression in history. Even the zany Marx Brothers movies during the thirties could not "laugh the big bad wolf of the Depression out of the public mind."

The carefree pleasure-seeking of the Jazz Age ended not with a whimper but with the booming crash on Wall Street. Fear and uncertainty spread like a virus across the nation and the world.

Wild rumors circulated of fortunes lost and careers ruined. Investors who had borrowed heavily to buy stocks were now forced to sell their holdings at huge losses so they could pay their debts. Some stockbrokers and investors committed suicide. In New York, the president of a bankrupt cigar company jumped off the ledge of a hotel, and two business partners joined hands and leaped to their deaths from the Ritz Hotel. Room clerks in Manhattan hotels began asking guests at registration if they wanted a room for jumping or sleeping.

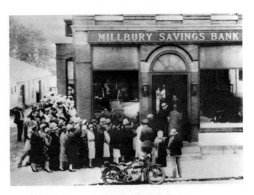

The national economy began to sputter and stumble. In 1930, at least 26,355 businesses shut down; even more failed the following year. The resulting slowdown in economic growth, called a *recession*, became so severe and long-lasting that it came to

Bank run As news of the Great Crash spread across the world, people rushed to banks to withdraw their deposits. The line for this Millbury, Massachusetts, savings bank wraps around the building.

be known as the **Great Depression**. But the collapse of the stock market did not *cause* the Great Depression. Rather, it revealed that the prosperity of the 1920s had been built on weak foundations.

The stock market crash had the added effect of creating a psychological panic that accelerated the economic decline. Frightened of losing everything, people rushed to take their money out of banks and out of the stock market. Such behavior only made things worse. By 1932, more than 9,000 banks had closed as the nation's formerly robust economy experienced a shocking collapse.

WHY THE ECONOMY COLLAPSED

What were the underlying *causes* of the Great Depression? Most scholars emphasize a combination of interrelated elements.

The economy had actually begun to fall into a recession months *before* the stock market crash. Put most simply, the once roaring economy fell victim to *overproduction* and *underconsumption*. During the twenties, manufacturing production increased 43 percent, but the purchasing power of consumers did not grow nearly as fast. In essence, the economy was producing more and more products that consumers could not afford to buy, and too many people had been borrowing too much money for unproductive purposes, such as speculating in the stock market.

Too many business owners had taken large profits while denying wage increases to employees. By plowing profits into business expansion, executive salaries, and stock dividends rather than wage increases, employers created a growing imbalance between production and consumption, supply and demand. Because union membership plummeted during the twenties, organized labor no longer exerted as much leverage with management over wage increases. Two-thirds of families in 1929 earned less than $2,000 annually, an amount said by economists to provide "only basic necessities."

At the same time that the stock market was crashing, factories were reducing production or shutting down altogether. From 1929 to 1933, U.S. economic output (called *gross domestic product*, or GDP) dropped almost 27 percent. By 1932, one-quarter of the workforce was out of work. As the financial and industrial sectors collapsed, the farm sector stagnated. Farm incomes had soared during the Great War because the European nations needed American grains, beef, and pork. Eager to sustain their prosperity, farmers took out mortgages to buy more acreage or equipment to boost output. Increasing production during the twenties, however, led to lower prices for grains and livestock. To make matters worse, record harvests in the summer and fall of 1929 caused prices for corn, wheat, and cotton to fall precipitously, pinching the income of farmers with mounting debts.

GOVERNMENT'S ROLE Government policies also contributed to the Depression. High tariffs hurt the economy by reducing foreign trade. Like most Republican presidents, Herbert Hoover supported congressional efforts to raise tariffs on imported goods to keep out foreign competition. The Smoot-Hawley Tariff of 1930, authored by Republicans Reed Owen Smoot and Willis C. Hawley, was intended to help the farm sector by raising tariff barriers on farm products imported into the United States. But a swarm of corporate lobbyists convinced Congress to add hundreds of new imported manufactured items to the tariff bill.

More than 1,000 economists urged Hoover to veto the tariff bill because its logic was flawed: by trying to "protect" American farmers from foreign competition, the bill would actually raise prices on most raw materials and consumer products. And by reducing European imports into the United States, the bill would make it much harder for France and Great Britain to repay their war debts. Hoover signed the bill anyway, causing another steep drop in the stock market. The Smoot-Hawley Tariff also prompted other countries to retaliate by passing tariffs of their own, thereby making it more difficult for American farms and businesses to sell their products abroad. U.S. exports plummeted, worsening the Depression.

Another factor contributing to the Great Depression was the stance of the Federal Reserve Board ("the Fed"), the government agency that served as a "central bank" by managing the nation's money supply and interest rates.

Instead of expanding the money supply to generate growth, the Federal Reserve did the reverse, reducing the money supply out of concern for possible inflation in consumer prices. Between 1929 and 1932, the money supply shrank by a third, leading almost 10,000 small banks to close—and take millions of their depositors with them into bankruptcy.

THE IMPACT OF EUROPE A final cause of the Depression was the chaotic state of the European economy, which had never fully recovered from the Great War. During the late 1920s, nations such as Great Britain, France, Spain, and Italy slowed their purchases of American goods as their economies began slowly recovering. Meanwhile, the German economy continued to flounder.

A related factor was the inability of European nations to pay their war debts to each other—and to the United States. The American government insisted that the $11 billion it had loaned the Allies be repaid, but Great Britain and France had no money. They were forced to borrow huge sums ($5 billion) from U.S. banks, which only increased their overall indebtedness. After the stock market crash in October 1929, American banks could no longer prop up the European economies.

The Federal Reserve's tighter monetary policy also drastically slowed the amount of American capital (money) going abroad. The German economy, which had grown dependent on loans from American banks, was devastated as American money dried up. Then the Smoot-Hawley Tariff made it even more difficult for European nations to sell their products in the United States. So as the European economy sputtered, it dragged the American economy deeper into depression.

THE HUMAN TOLL OF THE DEPRESSION

The Depression came to be called "Great" because its effects were so severe and long lasting. By 1932, perhaps a quarter of the U.S. population could not afford housing or adequate food. The carefree optimism of the twenties disappeared; grassroots protests erupted as the Depression worsened. Hungry people looted grocery stores, angry mobs stopped local sheriffs from foreclosing on farms, and judges were threatened at bankruptcy hearings.

Some talked of revolution and radical change. "Folks are restless," Mississippi governor Theodore Bilbo told reporters in 1931. "Communism is gaining a foothold. . . . In fact, I'm getting a little pink myself." Yet for all the radical talk, few Americans embraced communism. "There was anger and rebellion among a few," recounted an Iowa farmer, but most people lived in "helpless despair and submission."

UNEMPLOYMENT AND "RELIEF" As the economy spiraled downward between 1930 and 1933, growing numbers of workers were fired or had their wages cut. Unemployment soared to 4 million in 1930, then 8 million in 1931, and to 12 million by 1932.

Desperate unemployed city dwellers became street-corner merchants. Some 6,000 jobless New Yorkers sold apples on street corners to survive. They could buy a crate of apples grown in the Pacific Northwest for $1.75. If they sold a crate of sixty apples at a nickel apiece, they could pocket $1.25. The motto of the apple sellers was, "Buy an apple a day and eat the Depression away."

Many struggling business executives and professionals—lawyers, doctors, dentists, accountants, stockbrokers, teachers, nurses, and engineers—went without food and medical care to save money and avoid the humiliation of "going on relief." The sense of shame cut across class lines. In *The Grapes of Wrath* (1939), John Steinbeck's best-selling novel about the victims of the Depression, a poor but proud woman is disgraced by accepting "charity" from the Salvation Army: "We was hungry. They made us crawl for our dinner. They took our dignity."

HUNGER Hard-pressed families went without fruit and most vegetables. Surveys of children in the nation's public schools in 1932 showed that one-quarter suffered from malnutrition. The U.S. Public Health Service revealed that the families of unemployed workers had 66 percent more illnesses than the families of employed workers. In 1931, New York City hospitals reported about 100 cases of death by starvation.

Hungry people by the millions lined up at "soup kitchens," where churches and charities distributed minimal amounts of food and water. Others rummaged through trash cans or garbage dumps. In Detroit, "we saw the city at its worst," wrote Louise V. Armstrong. "One vivid, gruesome moment of those dark days we shall never forget. We saw a crowd of some fifty men fighting over a barrel of garbage which had been set outside the back door of a restaurant. American citizens fighting over scraps of food like animals!"

HOMELESSNESS The contraction of the economy especially squeezed debtors who had monthly mortgages to pay. A thousand Americans per day lost their homes to foreclosure, and millions were forced to move in with relatives or friends. At first, the poor made homeless by the Depression were usually placed in almshouses, also called *poorhouses* or *workhouses*. By 1933, however, the homeless overwhelmed the small number of public facilities; more than 40 percent of home mortgages were in default. People were forced to live in culverts, under bridges, on park benches, and in doorways and police stations. To make matters worse, the poor were subject to frequent abuse and arrest. The constitutions of fourteen states even banned paupers from voting.

Millions of homeless people, mostly men, took to living on the road or the rails. These hobos, or *tramps*, walked, hitchhiked in cars, or sneaked onto empty railway cars and rode from town to town. One railroad, the Missouri Pacific, counted 200,000 vagrants living in its empty boxcars in 1931. The following year, the Southern Pacific Railroad reported that it had evicted 683,457 people from its freight trains. A black military veteran recalled life as a hobo: "Black and white, it didn't make any difference who you were, 'cause everybody was poor. . . . They didn't have no mothers or sisters, they didn't have no home; they were dirty, they had overalls on, they didn't have no food, they didn't have anything."

The morning news in a Chicago shantytown In response to the economic devastation of the Great Depression, numerous shantytowns emerged in cities across the country to house the recently-homeless; here, a man reads a newspaper outside his makeshift dwelling in Chicago.

DESPERATE RESPONSES As always, those hardest hit were the most disadvantaged groups—immigrants, women, farmers, the urban unemployed, Native Americans, and African Americans. Desperate conditions led desperate people to do desperate things. Crime soared, as did street-corner begging, homelessness, and prostitution.

Although the divorce rate dropped during the decade, in part because couples could not afford to live separately or pay the legal fees to obtain a divorce, many jobless husbands simply deserted their wives and children. "You don't know what it's like when your husband's out of work," a woman told a reporter. "He's gloomy and unhappy all the time. Life is terrible. You must try all the time to keep him from going crazy." With their future so uncertain, married couples often decided not to have children, and birthrates plummeted. Many struggling parents sent their children to live with relatives or friends. Some 900,000 children simply left home and joined the growing army of homeless "tramps." During the Great Depression, for the first time ever, more people left the United States than arrived as immigrants.

PLIGHT OF WORKING WOMEN The Depression put women in a peculiar position. By 1932, an estimated 20 percent of working women were unemployed, a slightly lower percentage than men. Because women held a dis-

Just dropping off a résumé In October 1938, the federal government opened six custodian positions and 15,000 African American women lined up overnight to turn in their applications. Pictured here is a policeman leaping over a hedge to keep the crowd under control.

proportionate number of the lowest-paying jobs, they were often able to keep them. Even so, many women also had the added burden of keeping their families together emotionally with their husbands out of work. Magazines published numerous articles about the challenge of maintaining households when the husband had been "unmanned" by losing his job.

As the Depression deepened, however, married women in the workforce became the primary targets of layoffs. Some twenty-six states passed laws prohibiting their employment. The reasoning was that a married woman—who presumably had a husband to take care of her—should not "steal" a job from a man supporting a family. It was acceptable for single women to find jobs because these were usually considered "women's work": salesgirls, beauticians, schoolteachers, secretaries, and nurses. The job market for African American women was even more restricted, with most of them working as maids, cooks, or laundresses.

MINORITIES Most African Americans still lived in the eleven southern states of the former Confederacy, where the farm-dominated economy was depressed before 1929 and worsened during the Great Depression. African Americans in the South earned their meager livelihoods from farming, as tenants and sharecroppers. Pervasive racial discrimination kept blacks out of the few labor unions in the South and consigned them to the most-menial, lowest-paying jobs.

They also continued to be the victims of violence and intimidation. Most blacks were still excluded from voting and were segregated in public places like hotels and trains. Already living in poverty, they were among the hardest hit by the Depression. As a blues song called "Hard Times Ain't Gone Nowhere" revealed, "Hard times don't worry me; I was broke when it first started out." Some 3 million rural blacks in the South lived in cramped cabins without electricity, running water, or bathrooms.

In many mills, factories, mines, and businesses, the philosophy of "last hired, first fired" meant that the people who could least afford to be jobless were fired first. Blacks who had left the South to take factory jobs in the North were among the first to be laid off. Blacks had the highest rate of joblessness in the early years of the Great Depression. "At no time in the history of the Negro since slavery," reported the Urban League, "has his economic and social outlook seemed so discouraging." Churches and other charity organizations gave aid, but some refused to provide support for blacks, Mexicans, and Asians.

Impoverished whites found themselves competing with local Hispanics and Asians for seasonal farmwork in the cotton fields or orchards of large corporate farms. Many Chinese, Japanese, and Filipino farm laborers moved to cities. Mexicans, who had come to the United States during the 1920s, were also mostly migrant farmworkers, traveling from farm to farm to work during harvest and planting seasons of different crops. They settled in California, New Mexico, Arizona, Colorado, Texas, and the midwestern states. As economic conditions worsened, government officials called for the deportation of Mexican-born Americans to avoid the cost of providing them with public services. By 1935, more than 500,000 Mexican Americans (250,000 from Texas alone) and their American-born children were deported to Mexico.

Everywhere one looked in the early 1930s, people were suffering. City, county, and state governments quickly proved incapable of managing the spreading misery. As Americans turned to the federal government for ideas and answers, Herbert Hoover, the "Great Engineer," struggled to provide adequate responses to the unprecedented crisis of the Great Depression.

CHAPTER REVIEW

SUMMARY

- **The Reactionary Twenties**   With the end of the Great War, a renewed surge of immigration led to a wave of *nativism*. To Americans who feared that many immigrants were political radicals, the *Sacco and Vanzetti case* confirmed their suspicions. Nativists persuaded Congress to restrict future immigration, particularly from eastern and southern Europe, in the *Immigration Act of 1924*. Other reactionary movements reflected the feeling of many white Protestants that their religion and way of life were under attack. A revived Ku Klux Klan promoted hatred of Catholics, Jews, immigrants, Communists, and liberals, as well as African Americans. Fundamentalist Protestants campaigned against teaching evolution in public schools. Their efforts culminated in the 1925 *Scopes Trial* in Dayton, Tennessee, where a high school teacher was convicted of violating a state law prohibiting the teaching of evolution. Along with progressive reformers, conservative Protestants also supported the nationwide *Prohibition* of alcoholic beverages that had gone into effect in 1920, despite widespread disregard for the law and the increased criminal activity and violence associated with it. Union membership declined in the 1920s as businesses adopted new techniques (such as the so-called *open shop*) to resist unions, a conservative Supreme Court rolled back workers' rights, and workers themselves lost interest in organizing amid the general prosperity of the decade.

- **Republican Resurgence**   Although the Eighteenth Amendment (paving the way for Prohibition) and the Nineteenth Amendment (guaranteeing women's right to vote) marked the culmination of progressivism at the national level, the movement lost much of its appeal as disillusionment with the Great War and its results created a public preference for disarmament and isolationism, stances reflected in the Five-Power Treaty of 1922. Warren G. Harding's landslide presidential victory in 1920 was based on his call for a *"return to normalcy."* Harding and his fellow Republicans, including his vice president and successor, Calvin Coolidge, followed policies advocated by Secretary of the Treasury Andrew Mellon that emphasized lowering taxes and government spending as well as raising tariffs to protect domestic industries. The plan succeeded spectacularly in reviving the economy. Harding died suddenly in 1923, soon after news broke about the *Teapot Dome Affair* involving a government-owned oil field in Wyoming, one of many incidents of corruption growing out of Harding's appointments. Coolidge, an austere, frugal man who identified with the interests of business, restored trust in the presidency and won reelection in a landslide in 1924. In the 1928 presidential election, Herbert Hoover, secretary of commerce under Harding and Coolidge, won a third straight decisive victory for the Republicans as Democratic candidate Al Smith.

- **The Great Depression**   The 1929 stock market crash revealed the structural flaws in the economy, but it was not the only cause of the *Great Depression (1929–1941)*. During the twenties, business owners did not provide adequate wage increases for workers, thus preventing consumers' "purchasing power" from keeping up with increases in production. The nation's agricultural sector also suffered from overproduction throughout the decade. Government policies—such as high tariffs that helped to reduce international trade and the reduction of the nation's money supply as a means of dealing with the financial panic—exacerbated the emerging economic depression.

- **The Human Toll of the Depression** Thousands of banks and businesses closed, and millions of homes and jobs were lost. By the early 1930s, many people were homeless and hopeless, begging on street corners and sleeping in doorways. Many state laws and business practices discouraged the employment of married women, and discrimination against African Americans, Native Americans, Hispanics, and Asian Americans in hiring was widespread.

CHRONOLOGY

1920	Prohibition begins
	Nicola Sacco and Bartolomeo Vanzetti trial
	Warren G. Harding is elected president
1921	Washington Naval Conference and Five-Power Treaty
	Congress passes Emergency Immigration Act
1923	Teapot Dome scandal becomes public
	President Harding dies in office and is succeeded by Calvin Coolidge
1924	Congress passes Immigration Act
	Coolidge is reelected president
1925	Scopes "monkey trial"
1927	Sacco and Vanzetti are executed
1928	Herbert Hoover is elected president
1929	Stock market crashes in late October

KEY TERMS

nativism p. 879

Immigration Act of 1924 p. 880

Sacco and Vanzetti case p. 880

Scopes Trial p. 883

Prohibition p. 886

"return to normalcy" p. 889

open shop p. 892

Teapot Dome Affair p. 894

Great Depression (1929–1941) p. 903

 INQUIZITIVE

Go to InQuizitive to see what you've learned—and learn what you've missed—with personalized feedback along the way.

25 The Great Depression

1929–1939

***Construction of a Dam* (1939)** One of the most famous and controversial of the artists commissioned by the New Deal's Works Progress Administration was William Gropper, who painted this mural displayed in the Department of the Interior building in Washington, D.C. Based on his observations of dam construction on the Columbia and Colorado Rivers, Gropper illustrates the triumph and brotherhood that emerged from the New Deal's massive public projects during the Great Depression.

The year 1929 dawned with high hopes. Rarely had a new president entered office with greater expectations. In fact, Herbert Hoover, a man of boundless self-confidence, was worried that people viewed him as "a superman; that no problem is beyond my capacity." He was right to be concerned. People did consider him a superman—"the man who had never failed"—a dedicated public servant whose engineering genius and business savvy would ensure continued prosperity. In 1929, more Americans were working than ever before and earning record levels of income. But that was about to change.

The **Great Depression**, which began at the end of 1929, brought the worst of times. No business slump had been so deep, so long, or so painful. By 1932, one of every four Americans was unemployed; in many large cities, nearly *half* of the adults were out of work. Millions of others saw their working hours and wages reduced. Some 500,000 people had lost homes or farms because they could not pay their mortgages. Over 4,000 banks failed in the first two months of 1933, with more than $3.6 billion in lost deposits. For middle-class Americans, nothing was more devastating than losing their life savings. Record numbers of people were out of work, out of money, and out of hope. One California woman wrote that she was the "mother of seven children, and utterly heart broken, in that they are hungry, have only 65¢ in money. The father is in Los Angeles trying to find something to do."

What made the Great Depression so severe and so lasting was its global nature. In 1929, Europe was still reeling from the Great War. Once the American economy tumbled, it sent shock waves throughout the world. Economic distress fed the rise of totalitarian regimes—fascism and Nazism in Italy and Germany, communism in the Soviet Union. "Capitalism is dying," theologian Reinhold Niebuhr proclaimed. "Let no one delude himself by hoping for reform from within."

focus questions

1. How did the Hoover administration respond to the Great Depression?

2. What were the goals and accomplishments of the First New Deal?

3. What were the major criticisms of the New Deal?

4. How did the New Deal evolve? How did it transform the role of the federal government in American life?

Yet that is exactly what Franklin Delano Roosevelt sought to do in 1932 as he assumed the presidency. He would save capitalism by transforming it. Like his hero, his cousin Theodore Roosevelt, he believed that the basic problem of twentieth-century life was the excessive power of large corporations. Only the federal government could regulate corporate capitalism for the public benefit.

Few leaders have taken office in more dire circumstances. Yet within days of becoming president, Roosevelt took dramatic steps that forever changed the scope and role of the federal government. He believed that America's democratic form of government had the ultimate responsibility to help people who were in distress, not out of a sense of charity but out of a sense of obligation. Along with a supportive Congress, he set about enacting dozens of bold measures to relieve human suffering and promote economic recovery.

Roosevelt was an inspiring personality, overflowing with cheerful strength, strong convictions, and an unshakeable confidence in himself and in the resilience of the American people. He was also a pragmatist willing to try different approaches. His program for recovery, the New Deal, was therefore a series of trial-and-error actions rather than a comprehensive scheme. None of the well-intentioned but often poorly planned initiatives worked perfectly, and some failed miserably. Yet their combined effect was to restore hope and energy to the nation.

FROM HOOVERISM TO THE NEW DEAL

The Great Depression revealed Herbert Hoover to be a brilliant mediocrity. His initial response to the economic disaster was denial: there was no crisis, he insisted. All that was needed, he and others in his administration argued, was to let the economy cure itself. The best policy, Treasury Secretary Andrew Mellon advised, would be to do nothing. Letting events run their course, he claimed, would "purge the rottenness out of the [capitalist] system." But Mellon's do-nothing approach did not work. Falling wages and declining land and home values made it even harder for struggling farmers, businesses, and households to pay their bills. With so many people losing jobs and income, consumers and businesses simply could not buy enough goods and services to reenergize the economy.

HOOVER'S EFFORTS AT RECOVERY

As the months passed, President Hoover proved less willing than Andrew Mellon to sit by and let events take their course. As the "Great Engineer," he in fact did more than any previous president in addressing such calamitous economic circumstances. He invited business, labor, government, and agricultural leaders to a series of White House conferences in which he urged companies to maintain employment and wage levels, asked union leaders to end strikes, and pleaded with state governors to accelerate planned construction projects so as to keep people working. He also formed committees and commissions to study various aspects of the economic calamity, and he cut the income tax. Yet nothing worked. Unemployment continued to rise, and wage levels continued to fall.

SHORT-SIGHTED TAX INCREASES The Great Depression was the greatest national emergency since the Civil War, and the nation was woefully unprepared to deal with it. As personal income plummeted, so did government tax revenues. President Hoover insisted on trying to balance the federal budget by raising taxes and cutting budgets—precisely the wrong prescription for a sick economy. He pushed through Congress the Revenue Act of 1932, the largest—and most poorly timed—peacetime tax increase in history. By taking money out of consumers' pockets, the higher taxes accelerated the economic slowdown. People had less money to spend when what the struggling economy most needed was increased consumer spending.

Hooverville Of the many Hoovervilles set up in Seattle, Washington, alone, this particular shantytown near the shipyards was the largest. It lasted nine years.

Young and hungry A toddler begs for change in one of the homeless camps.

HOOVER'S REACTION TO THE SOCIAL CRISIS By the fall of 1930, many cities were buckling under the strain of lost revenue and human distress. The federal government had no programs to deal with homelessness and joblessness. State and local governments cut spending, worsening the economic situation. All across the country, shantytowns sprouted in vacant lots. People erected shacks out of cardboard and scrap wood and metal. They called their makeshift villages *Hoovervilles* to mock the president. To keep warm, they wrapped themselves in newspapers, calling them *Hoover blankets*. As their numbers rose, more and more people called for government to step in. Frustrated by his critics, Hoover dismissed the concerns of "calamity mongers and weeping men."

Hoover feared that the nation would be "plunged into socialism" if the government provided direct support to the poor. His governing philosophy, rooted in America's mythic commitment to rugged individualism and free enterprise, set firm limits on emergency government action. The president still trumpeted the virtues of "self-reliance" and individual initiative, claiming that government assistance would rob people of the desire to help themselves.

Hoover hoped that the "natural generosity" of the American people and charitable organizations would be sufficient, and he believed that volunteers (the backbone of local charity organizations) would relieve the social distress caused by the Depression. But his faith in traditional "voluntarism" was misplaced. Local and state relief agencies were overwhelmed by the magnitude of the social crisis, as were churches and charitable organizations like the Salvation Army and the Red Cross.

RISING CRITICISM OF HOOVER

That the economic collapse was so unexpected made people all the more insecure and anxious, and President Hoover increasingly became the target of their frustration. The Democrats shrewdly exploited his predicament. In

November 1930, they gained their first national election victory since 1916, winning a majority in the House and a near majority in the Senate.

Hoover refused to see the Republican election losses as a warning. Instead, he grew more resistant to calls for federal intervention in the struggling economy. By 1932, 15 million people were unemployed. The *New York Times* concluded that Hoover had "failed as a party leader. He has failed as an economist. . . . He has failed as a business leader. . . . He has failed as a personality because of [his] awkwardness of manner and speech and lack of mass magnetism."

CONGRESSIONAL INITIATIVES With a new Congress in session in 1932, demands for federal action forced Hoover to do more. That year, Congress set up the **Reconstruction Finance Corporation (RFC)** to make emergency loans to banks, life-insurance companies, and railroads. But if the federal government could help bail out huge banks and railroads, asked New York Democratic senator Robert F. Wagner, why not "extend a helping hand to that forlorn American, in every village and every city of the United States, who has been without wages since 1929?" Hoover still held back, however, and signed only the Emergency Relief Act (1932), which authorized the RFC to make loans to the states for construction projects. Critics called the RFC a "breadline" for businesses while the unemployed went hungry.

FARMERS AND VETERANS IN PROTEST Meanwhile, the average *annual* income of families working the land during the early 1930s was $240. Prices for agricultural products fell so low that farmers lost money if they took them to market. Thousands of midwestern farmers protested the low prices by dumping milk, vegetables, and fruits on the highways.

Fears of organized revolt arose when thousands of unemployed military veterans converged on the nation's capital in the spring of 1932. The "**Bonus Expeditionary Force**," made up of veterans of the American Expeditionary Force (AEF) that fought in Europe in the Great War, pressed Congress to pay the cash bonuses owed to nearly 4 million veterans. The House passed a bonus bill, but the Senate voted it down because it would have forced a tax increase. Most of the disappointed veterans went home. The rest, along with their wives and children, having no place to go, camped in vacant federal buildings and in a shantytown within sight of the Capitol.

Eager to remove the homeless veterans, Hoover persuaded Congress to pay for their train tickets home. More left, but others stayed even after Congress adjourned, hoping to meet with the president. Late in July, Hoover ordered the government buildings cleared. In doing so, a policeman panicked, fired into the crowd, and killed two veterans. The secretary of war then dispatched 700 soldiers to remove the "Bonus Army." The soldiers, commanded by army chief of staff General Douglas MacArthur, dispersed the unarmed veterans and their families. Then, exceeding orders, the soldiers burned their makeshift camp. Fifty-five veterans were injured and 135 arrested. Widespread news coverage of the incident led even more people to view Hoover and the Republicans as heartless. (The veterans were finally paid their "bonus" in 1936.)

The disheartened, angry mood of the Bonus Army matched that of the country and of President Hoover himself. He worked hard, but the stress sapped his health and morale. "I am so tired," he said, "that every bone in my body aches." When aides urged him to be more of a public leader, he replied, "I have no Wilsonian qualities." He hated giving speeches, and when he did his remarks came across as cold and uncaring. The man who in 1928 had promised Americans "permanent prosperity" failed because he never understood or acknowledged the seriousness of the nation's economic problems.

THE 1932 ELECTION In June 1932, glum Republicans gathered in Chicago to nominate President Hoover for a second term. By contrast, the Democrats arrived in Chicago for their convention a few weeks later confident that they would nominate the next president. Fifty-year-old New York governor Franklin Delano Roosevelt won on the fourth ballot.

Roosevelt broke precedent by traveling to Chicago to accept the nomination in person. The stakes were high, he said, because Hoover and the Republicans had failed to address the economic disaster. "I pledge you, I pledge myself to a *new deal* for the American people" that would "break foolish traditions" and create a new, enlightened administration "of competence and courage."

Roosevelt first had to defeat Hoover, however. The race, he said, would be "more than a political campaign; it is a call to arms." It was a vague but uplifting message of hope at a time when many people were slipping into despair. In contrast to Hoover, Roosevelt exuded energy and confidence. His campaign song was "Happy Days Are Here Again."

Throughout the campaign, Roosevelt repeatedly promised a "New Deal" for the American people, stressing that a revitalized economy required new ideas and aggressive action. "The country needs, and, unless I mistake its temper, the country demands bold, persistent experimentation," he said. "Above all, try something."

Roosevelt's proposals, Hoover warned, "would destroy the very foundations of our American system." The election, he stressed, was more than a contest between two men and two political parties; it was a battle "between two philosophies of government" that would decide "the direction our nation will take over a century to come."

THE ELECTION OF 1932

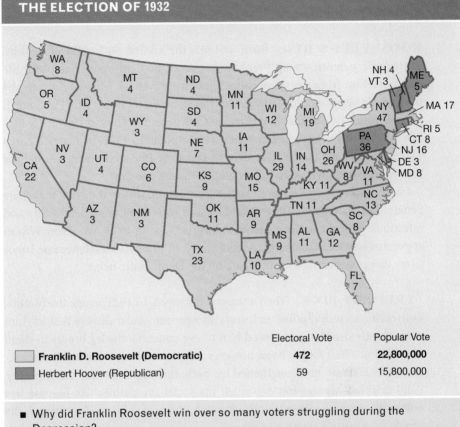

	Electoral Vote	Popular Vote
Franklin D. Roosevelt (Democratic)	472	22,800,000
Herbert Hoover (Republican)	59	15,800,000

- Why did Franklin Roosevelt win over so many voters struggling during the Depression?
- What were Herbert Hoover's criticisms of Roosevelt's New Deal?
- During the 1932 presidential campaign, what did Roosevelt pledge to fight the Depression?

Hoover lost decisively. Americans swept Roosevelt into office with 23 million votes to Hoover's 16 million. In 1928, Hoover had carried 40 states; four years later, he won but six.

ROOSEVELT'S NEW DEAL

Franklin Roosevelt promised voters a "New Deal," and within hours of being inaugurated, he and his aides set about creating a "new order of competence and courage." For better or worse, the federal government assumed responsibility for national economic planning and for restoring prosperity and ensuring social security—for all. What Roosevelt called the "forgotten man" would no longer be forgotten.

ROOSEVELT'S RISE   Born in 1882, the adored only child of wealthy, aristocratic parents, young Franklin Roosevelt had enjoyed a pampered life that freed him from worrying about a job or a paycheck. He was educated by tutors at Springwood, his father's Hudson River estate near Hyde Park, north of New York City. He attended Harvard College and Columbia University Law School. (He did not graduate.) While a law student in 1905, he married Anna Eleanor Roosevelt, the favorite niece of Theodore Roosevelt, then president of the United States, who was also Franklin's distant cousin.

In 1910, Franklin Roosevelt won a Democratic seat in the New York State Senate. Tall, handsome, athletic, and blessed with a sparkling personality and infectious smile, he seemed destined for greatness. In 1913, Woodrow Wilson appointed him assistant secretary of the navy. In 1920, Roosevelt became James Cox's vice presidential running mate on the Democratic ticket.

"TRIAL BY FIRE"   Then a tragedy occurred. In 1921, at age thirty-nine, Roosevelt contracted polio, an infectious neuromuscular disease that left him permanently disabled and forced him to use cumbersome leg braces to stand or walk. Roosevelt fought back, however. For seven years, aided by his remarkable wife, Eleanor, he strengthened his body to compensate for his disability. Polio crippled his legs but expanded his social sympathies. He became less pompous, more considerate, more focused, and more able to identify with the problems of people facing hard times.

Roosevelt had a remarkable ability to make people feel at ease and express concern about their troubles. The aristocrat had developed the common touch as well as a great talent for public relations, but he also was vain and calculating and a clever manipulator. In other words, he was a consummate politician.

A PEOPLE'S PRESIDENT   Roosevelt was neither a masterful administrator nor a deep thinker. One of his closest aides said the president never "read a serious book." But Roosevelt had many virtues: courage, good instincts, optimism, and charm. He loved talking to people, and he was determined to help those who could not help themselves. Colonel Edward House, the veteran Democratic counselor, explained that his former boss, Woodrow Wilson, "liked humanity as a whole and disliked people individually." Roosevelt, by contrast, was "genuinely fond of people and shows it."

THE 1933 INAUGURATION   Inaugurated in March 1933, Franklin Delano Roosevelt assumed leadership during a crisis that threatened the foundations of American capitalism. "The situation is critical, Franklin," the prominent journalist Walter Lippmann warned. "You may have to assume dictatorial powers"—as had already happened in Germany, Italy, and the Soviet Union.

Roosevelt did not become a dictator, but he did take extraordinary steps while assuring Americans "that the only thing we have to fear is fear itself." He confessed in his inaugural address that he did not have all the answers, but he did know that "this nation asks for action, and action now." He asked Congress for "a broad Executive power to wage a war against the emergency" just as "if we were in fact invaded by a foreign foe." Roosevelt's uplifting speech won rave reviews. Nearly 500,000 Americans wrote letters to the new president, and even the pro-Republican *Chicago Tribune* praised his "courageous confidence."

THE FIRST HUNDRED DAYS In March 1933, President Roosevelt confronted four major challenges: reviving the industrial economy, relieving the widespread human misery, rescuing the ravaged farm sector, and reforming those aspects of the capitalist system that had helped cause the Depression. He quickly addressed all of those challenges—and more.

The new president admitted that he would try several different "experiments." Some would succeed, and others would fail, but the important thing was to do something bold—and fast. It was no time for timid leadership or paralyzing doubts. The defining characteristic of Roosevelt's approach to presidential leadership was *action*. He had a genius for leading others—even when he did not know for sure where he was taking them. To advise him, Roosevelt assembled a "brain trust" of brilliant specialists who feverishly developed fresh ideas to address the nation's urgent problems.

Roosevelt and his advisers initially settled on a three-pronged strategy to revive the economy. First, they addressed the immediate banking crisis and provided short-term emergency relief for the jobless. Second, the New Dealers—men and women (professors, journalists, economists, social workers, and political appointees) who swarmed to Washington during the winter of 1933—encouraged agreements between management and unions. Third, they attempted to raise depressed commodity prices by paying farmers "subsidies" to *reduce* the sizes of their crops and herds so that prices would *rise* and thereby increase farm income.

The new Congress was as ready to take action as was the new president. From March 9 to June 16, the so-called First Hundred Days, Congress approved fifteen major pieces of legislation proposed by Roosevelt. Several of these programs comprised what came to be called the **First New Deal** (1933–1935).

Shoring Up the Financial System

Money is the lubricant of capitalism, and money was fast disappearing from circulation by 1933. Ever since the stock market crash of 1929, panicky depositors

Franklin Delano Roosevelt Preparing to deliver the first of his popular "fireside chats" to a national radio audience. This message focused on measures to reform the American banking system.

had been withdrawing their money from banks and the stock market. Taking so much money out of circulation worsened the Depression and brought the banking system to the brink of collapse. Throughout the twenties, an average of almost 700 banks a year failed. After 1929, that number doubled and then tripled.

BANKING REGULATION On his second day in office, March 9, 1933, Roosevelt called Congress into special session to pass the Emergency Banking Relief Act, which declared a four-day bank holiday to allow the financial panic to subside. (Herbert Hoover criticized the move as a step toward "gigantic socialism.") For the first time in history, all U.S. banks closed their doors.

Roosevelt's financial experts worked all night drafting a bill to restore confidence in the banks. On March 12, in the first of his radio-broadcast "fireside chats" to the nation, the president assured the 60 million listeners that it was safer to "keep your money in a reopened bank than under the mattress." The following day, people took their money back to the banks. "Capitalism was saved in eight days," said one of Roosevelt's advisers.

A few weeks later, on June 16, Roosevelt signed the Glass-Steagall Banking Act of 1933, part of which created the **Federal Deposit Insurance Corporation (FDIC)**, which guaranteed customer accounts in banks up to $2,500, thus reducing the likelihood of future panics. The banking crisis had ended, and the administration was ready to pursue a broader program of economic recovery.

REGULATING WALL STREET Before the Great Crash in 1929, there was little government oversight of the securities (stocks and bonds) industry. In 1933, the Roosevelt administration developed two important pieces of legislation intended to regulate the operations of the stock market and eliminate fraud and abuses. The Securities Exchange Act of 1933 was the first major federal legislation to regulate the sale of stocks and bonds. It required corporations that issued stock for public sale to "disclose" all relevant information about the operations and management of the company so that purchasers could know what they were buying. The second bill, the Securities Exchange Act of 1934, established the **Securities and Exchange Commission**, a federal agency to enforce the new laws and regulations governing the issuance and trading of stocks and bonds.

THE FEDERAL BUDGET Roosevelt next convinced Congress to pass an Economy Act (1933) allowing him to cut government workers' salaries, reduce payments to military veterans for non-service-connected disabilities, and reorganize federal agencies to help reduce government expenses. He then took the dramatic step of ending Prohibition, in part because it was being so widely violated, in part because most Democrats wanted it ended, and in part because he wanted to regain the federal tax revenues from the sale of alcoholic beverages. The Twenty-First Amendment, ratified by the states on December 5, 1933, ended the "noble experiment" of Prohibition.

HELPING THE UNEMPLOYED AND HOMELESS

Another urgent priority in 1933 was relieving the widespread human distress. Herbert Hoover had stubbornly refused to help the unemployed and homeless, since he assumed that individual self-reliance, acts of charity, and the efforts of local organizations (the Red Cross, churches, and "city missions") would be sufficient.

The Roosevelt administration, however, knew that the numbers of people in need far exceeded the capacity of charitable organizations and local agencies. To address the problem, the president pushed through a series of programs that created what came to be called the "welfare state." He did not believe that the government should give people cash (called a "dole"), but he insisted that the federal government help the unemployed and homeless by getting them jobs. For the first time, the federal government took primary responsibility for assisting the most desperate Americans.

PUTTING PEOPLE TO WORK The Federal Emergency Relief Administration (FERA), headed by Harry L. Hopkins, was Roosevelt's first major effort to deal with unemployment. It sent grants to the states to spend on the unemployed and homeless. After the state-sponsored programs funded by the FERA proved inadequate, Congress created the Civil Works Administration (CWA) in November 1933. It marked the first large-scale *federal* experiment with work relief by putting people directly on the government payroll at competitive wages: 40¢ an hour for unskilled workers, $1 for skilled.

The CWA provided 4 million federal jobs during the winter of 1933–1934 and organized a variety of useful projects: repairing 500,000 miles of roads, laying sewer lines, constructing or improving more than 1,000 airports and 40,000 public schools, and providing 50,000 teaching jobs that helped keep small rural public schools open. As the number of people employed by the CWA soared, however, the program's costs skyrocketed to more than $1 billion. Roosevelt balked at such high costs and worried that the people hired would become dependent upon federal jobs. So in the spring of 1934, he ordered the CWA dissolved. By April, some 4 million workers were again unemployed.

THE CCC The most successful of the New Deal jobs programs was the Civilian Conservation Corps (CCC), managed by the War Department. It built 2,500 camps to house up to half a million unemployed, unmarried young men ages seventeen to twenty-seven. They worked as "soil soldiers" in national forests, parks, and recreational areas, and on soil-conservation projects. The CCC also recruited 150,000 unemployed military veterans and 85,000 Native Americans, housing them in separate camps.

CCC workers had to be between 60 and 78 inches tall, weigh more than 107 pounds, and have at least six teeth. They were to be paid $1 a day for no more than nine months so as to make room for others. Congress passed the bill only after Oscar De Priest, an African American legislator from Illinois, introduced an amendment requiring that the agency not discriminate on account of race, color, or creed.

Federal relief programs Civilian Conservation Corps enrollees in 1933, on a break from work. Directed by army officers and foresters, the CCC camps were operated like military bases.

CCC workers cleared brush; built trails, roads, bridges, campgrounds, fire towers, fish hatcheries, and 800 parks; planted 3 *billion* trees; taught farmers how to control soil erosion; and fought fires. The enrollees, supervised by soldiers, were given shelter, clothing, and food, and took classes to learn to read and earn high-school diplomas. Women were excluded from the CCC, and African Americans and Native Americans were housed in segregated facilities.

Roosevelt loved to visit the CCC camps. After sharing a meal with one group, he said: "I wish I could spend a couple of months here myself." By 1942, when the CCC was dismantled, some 3 million young men had passed through the program.

REVIVING THE INDUSTRIAL SECTOR   The centerpiece of the New Deal's efforts to revive the industrial economy was the National Industrial Recovery Act (NIRA) of 1933. One of its two major sections created massive public-works construction projects funded by the federal government as a means of creating jobs. The NIRA started the Public Works Administration (PWA), granting $3.3 billion for the construction of government buildings, highways, bridges, dams, port facilities, and sewage plants.

The second, and more controversial, part of the NIRA created the **National Recovery Administration (NRA)**, which represented a radical shift in the federal government's role in the economy. Never before in peacetime had Washington bureaucrats taken charge of setting prices, wages, and standards for working conditions.

The primary purpose of the NRA was to promote economic growth by ignoring anti-trust laws and allowing executives of competing businesses to negotiate among themselves and with labor unions to create "codes of fair competition" that would set prices, production levels, minimum wages, and maximum hours within each industry, no matter how small. In New York City, for example, women who made their living as burlesque show strippers agreed to an NRA code limiting the number of performers on stage and the number of performances they could provide each night.

In exchange for allowing companies to "cooperate" rather than compete, the NRA codes included "fair labor" policies long sought by unions and social progressives: a national forty-hour work week, minimum weekly wages of $13 ($12 in the South, where living costs were lower), and a ban on the employment of children under the age of sixteen. The NRA also included a provision that guaranteed the right of workers to organize unions.

These were landmark changes, and, for a time, the downward spiral of wages and prices subsided. But as soon as economic recovery began, small business owners complained that the larger corporations dominated the NRA, whose price-fixing robbed small producers of the chance to compete. And because the NRA wage codes excluded agricultural and domestic workers (at the insistence of southern Democrats), most African Americans derived no direct benefit from the program. When the Supreme Court declared the NRA unconstitutional in May 1935, few regretted its demise.

The NRA experiment did, however, have lasting effects. It set new work-place standards, such as the forty-hour work week, created a national minimum wage, and helped end the abuse of child labor. Its endorsement of collective bargaining between workers and owners spurred the growth of unions. Yet, as 1934 ended, industrial recovery was still nowhere in sight.

AGRICULTURAL ASSISTANCE In addition to rescuing the banks and providing jobs to the unemployed, Roosevelt created the Farm Credit Administration to help farmers deal with their crushing debts and lower their mortgage payments to avoid bankruptcy.

The **Agricultural Adjustment Act** of 1933 created a new federal agency, the Agricultural Adjustment Administration (AAA), which sought to raise prices for crops and herds by paying farmers to cut back production. The money for such payments came from a tax levied on the "processors" of certain basic commodities—cotton gins, flour mills, and slaughterhouses.

By the time the AAA was created, however, the spring growing season was already under way. The prospect of another bumper cotton crop forced the AAA to organize a "plow-under" program in which farmers were paid to kill their fledgling crops. Moreover, in an effort to raise pork prices, some 6 million baby pigs were slaughtered and buried. By the end of 1934, the AAA's efforts had worked: wheat, cotton, and corn production had declined, and prices had risen. Farm income increased by 58 percent between 1932 and 1935.

At the end of the First Hundred Days of Roosevelt's presidency, the principle of an activist federal government had been established. While conservative critics warned that Roosevelt was leading America toward fascism or communism, the president had become the most popular man in the nation.

DUST BOWL MIGRANTS At the same time that the agricultural economy was struggling, a terrible drought created an ecological catastrophe known as the **Dust Bowl**. Colorado, New Mexico, Kansas, Nebraska, Texas, Arkansas, and Oklahoma were hardest hit. Crops withered, and income plummeted. Strong winds swept across the treeless plains, scooping up tons of parched topsoil into billowing dark clouds, called black blizzards, that engulfed farms and towns. By 1938, topsoil had disappeared from more than 25 million acres of prairie land.

Parched farmers could not pay their debts, and banks foreclosed on family farms. Suicides soared, and millions of people abandoned their farms. Many uprooted farmers and their families from the South and the Midwest headed toward California, where jobs were said to be plentiful. Frequently lumped together as "Okies" or "Arkies," most of the Dust Bowl refugees were from cot-

Okies on the run A sharecropping family reaches its destination of Bakersfield, California, in 1935, after "we got blowed out in Oklahoma."

ton belt communities in Arkansas, Texas, Missouri, and Oklahoma. During the 1930s and 1940s, some 800,000 people, mostly whites, headed to the Far West.

Without money to pay rent or a mortgage, homeless migrants set up squatter camps, often called "Little Oklahomas" alongside highways or close to towns where they could get food and supplies. When one crop was harvested, the migrants moved on to the next, carrying their belongings with them.

Most people uprooted by the Dust Bowl went to California's urban areas—Los Angeles, San Diego, or San Francisco. Others moved into the San Joaquin Valley, the state's agricultural heartland. There they discovered that California was no paradise. Only a few could afford to buy land. Most had to work as farm laborers. Living in tents or crude cabins, migrant workers suffered from exposure to the elements, poor sanitation, and social abuse. As an Okie reported, when the big farmers "need us they call us *migrants*, and when we've picked their crop, we're *bums* and we got to get out."

THE TENNESSEE VALLEY AUTHORITY Early in his presidency, Franklin Roosevelt declared that the "South is the nation's No. 1 economic problem." Indeed, since the end of the Civil War, the economy and quality of life in the southern states had lagged far behind the rest of the nation. That gap only widened during the Depression.

To help the blighted South, Roosevelt created one of the most innovative programs of the First New Deal: the Tennessee Valley Authority (TVA), which would bring electrical power, flood control efforts, and jobs to Appalachia, the desperately poor mountainous region that stretched from West Virginia through western Virginia and North Carolina, Kentucky, eastern Tennessee, and northern Georgia and Alabama.

By 1940, the TVA, a public corporation, had constructed twenty-one hydroelectric dams which created the "Great Lakes of the South" and produced enough electricity to power the entire region, at about half the average national rate. The TVA also dredged rivers to allow for boat and barge traffic, promoted soil conservation and forestry management, drew new industries to the region, encouraged the formation of labor unions, and improved schools and libraries. It gave 1.5 million farms access to electricity and indoor plumbing for the first time.

During Roosevelt's first year in office, his programs and his personal charm generated widespread support, and the First New Deal gave Americans a sense of renewed faith in the future. In the congressional elections of 1934, the Democrats increased their dominance in Congress with an almost unprecedented midterm victory for a party in power.

Eleanor Roosevelt Intelligent, principled, and a political figure in her own right, she is pictured here addressing the Red Cross Convention in 1934.

ELEANOR ROOSEVELT One of the reasons for Franklin Roosevelt's popularity was his energetic wife, Eleanor Roosevelt, who would prove to be one of the most influential leaders of the time. She ceaselessly prodded her husband about social justice issues and sometimes scolded him, yet she always supported his ambitions and decisions.

Born in 1884 in New York City, Eleanor married her distant cousin Franklin in 1905. All too quickly, she learned that Franklin's domineering mother, Sara Delano Roosevelt, would always be the most important woman in his life. "He might have been happier with a wife who was completely uncritical," like his mother, Eleanor wrote later. "That I was never able to be, and he had to find it in other people."

During the 1920s, Eleanor, shy and insecure, revealed that at heart she was a creature of conscience. She began a lifelong crusade on behalf of women, blacks, and youth, giving voice to the voiceless. Her tireless compassion resulted in large part from the self-doubt and loneliness she had experienced as the child of an alcoholic father and an aloof mother.

Equally influential in shaping Eleanor's outlook was the sense of betrayal she felt upon discovering in 1918 that her husband had fallen recklessly in love with Lucy Mercer, her friend and secretary. "The bottom dropped out of my own particular world," she recalled.

Eleanor and Franklin decided to maintain their marriage, but as their son James said, it became an "armed truce." Eleanor later observed that she could "forgive, but never forget," but she never truly forgave or forgot. In the White House, the Roosevelts lived entirely apart, rarely seeing each other except for formal occasions and public events.

Eleanor Roosevelt redefined the role of First Lady. Not content just to host social events in the White House, she became a relentless activist: the first woman to address a national political convention, to write a nationally syndicated newspaper column, and to hold regular press conferences. She tirelessly crisscrossed the nation, speaking in support of the New Deal, meeting with African American leaders, supporting women's causes and labor unions, and urging Americans to live up to their humanitarian ideals. In 1933, she convened a White House conference that called on the Federal Emergency Relief Administration (FERA) to "see that women are employed wherever possible." Within six months, some 300,000 women were at work on various federal government projects.

A popular joke in Washington claimed that President Roosevelt's nightly prayer was: "Dear God, please make Eleanor a little tired." In fact, however, he and his success were deeply dependent on her. She was the impatient agitator dedicated to what *should* be done; he was the calculating politician concerned with what *could* be done.

THE NEW DEAL UNDER FIRE

By 1934, Franklin Roosevelt had become the best loved and most hated president of the twentieth century. He was loved because he believed in and fought for the common people, for the "forgotten man" (and woman). And he was loved for what one French leader called his "glittering personality." Roosevelt radiated energy and hope, joy in his work, courage in a crisis, optimism for the future, and a monumental self-assurance bordering on arrogance. His famously arched eyebrows, upturned chin, and twinkling eyes, along with his cigarette holder, itself tilted upward, symbolized his jaunty determination to triumph over the nation's massive problems. "Meeting him," said British prime minister Winston Churchill, "was like uncorking a bottle of champagne." Roosevelt, he added, was "the greatest man I have ever known."

Roosevelt was perhaps the most visible and accessible president who had occupied the White House. Twice a week he held press conferences, explaining new legislation, addressing questions and criticisms, and, in the process, winning over most journalists. Roosevelt also mastered the art of using carefully timed radio addresses ("fireside chats") to speak to the nation.

But Roosevelt was hated, too, especially by business leaders and political conservatives who believed that the New Deal and the higher taxes it required were moving America toward socialism. Some called Roosevelt a "traitor to his class." Even his cousin Alice, Theodore's daughter, accused him of being a dictator. Others, on the left, hated him for not doing enough to end the Depression. By the mid-1930s, the early New Deal programs had slowed the economy's downward slide, but prosperity remained elusive. "We have been patient and long suffering," said a farm leader. "We were promised a New Deal. . . . Instead, we have the same old stacked deck."

In many respects, the conflicting opinions of Roosevelt reflected his own divided personality and erratic management style. He was at the same time a man of idealistic principles and a practical politician prone to snap judgments, capable of both compromise and contradictory actions. He once admitted to an aide that to implement the New Deal he had to "deceive, misrepresent, leave false impressions . . . and trust to charm, loyalty, and the result to make up for it. . . . A great man cannot be a good man."

CONTINUING HARDSHIPS

Although the programs making up the First New Deal helped ease the devastation caused by the Depression, they did not restore prosperity or end the widespread suffering. As late as 1939, some 9.5 million workers (17 percent of the labor force) remained unemployed. Critics stressed that the economy, while stabilized, remained mired in the Depression.

AFRICAN AMERICANS AND THE NEW DEAL However progressive Franklin Delano Roosevelt was on social issues, he showed little interest in the plight of African Americans, even as black voters were shifting from the Republicans (the "party of Lincoln") to the Democrats. Roosevelt, like Woodrow Wilson before him, failed to address long-standing patterns of

"There's no way like the American way" Margaret Bourke-White's famous 1937 photograph of desperate people waiting in a Louisville, Kentucky, disaster-relief line captures the continuing racial divide of the era and the elusiveness of the "American Dream" for many minorities.

racism and segregation in the South for fear of angering conservative southern Democrats in Congress.

As a result, many New Deal programs discriminated against blacks. As Mary White Ovington, the treasurer of the National Association for the Advancement of Colored People (NAACP), stressed, the racism in any agency "varies according to the white people chosen to administer it, but always there is discrimination." The FHA, for example, refused to guarantee mortgages on houses purchased by blacks in white neighborhoods, and both the CCC and the TVA practiced racial segregation. The NAACP waged an energetic legal campaign against racial prejudice throughout the 1930s, but a major setback occurred in the Supreme Court ruling on *Grovey v. Townsend* (1935), which upheld the Texas Democrats' whites-only election primary.

Thanks to relentless pressure from Eleanor Roosevelt, the president did appoint more African Americans to government positions than ever before. One of the most visible was Mary McLeod Bethune, the child of former slaves from South Carolina, who had founded Bethune-Cookman College in Florida and served as head of the NAACP in the 1920s. In 1935, Roosevelt approved her appointment as the director of the Division of Negro Affairs within the National Youth Administration, an agency that provided jobs to unemployed young Americans. Bethune worked with other blacks in New Deal agencies to form an informal "Black Cabinet" to ensure that African Americans had equal access to federal programs.

COURT CASES AND CIVIL LIBERTIES The continuing prejudice against blacks in the South was vividly revealed in a controversial case in Alabama. In 1931, an all-white jury, on flimsy, conflicting testimony, convicted nine black youths, ranging in age from thirteen to twenty-one, of raping two young white women while riding a freight train. Eight of the "Scottsboro Boys" were sentenced to death before cheering whites who packed the courtroom, while 10,000 spectators outside celebrated with a brass band. In his award-winning novel *Native Son* (1940), African American writer Richard Wright recalled the "mob who surrounded the Scottsboro jail with rope and kerosene" after the initial conviction.

The injustice of the Scottsboro case sparked protests throughout the nation and the world. The two white girls, it turned out, had been selling sex to white and black boys on the train. One of the girls eventually recanted the rape charges and began appearing at rallies on behalf of the defendants.

No case in legal history had produced as many trials, appeals, reversals, and retrials as the Scottsboro case. Further, it prompted two important legal inter-

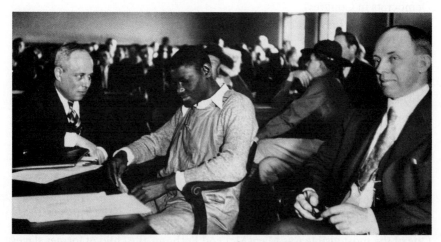

Scottsboro case Haywood Patterson (center), one of the defendants in the case, with his attorney, Samuel Liebowitz (left) in Decatur, Alabama, in 1933.

pretations. In *Powell v. Alabama* (1932), the U.S. Supreme Court overturned the original convictions because the judge had not ensured that the accused were provided adequate defense attorneys. The Court ordered new trials. In another case, *Norris v. Alabama* (1935), the Court ruled that the systematic exclusion of African Americans from Alabama juries had denied the Scottsboro defendants equal protection under the law—a principle that had widespread impact on state courts by opening up juries to blacks. Although the state of Alabama eventually dropped the charges against the four youngest of the Scottsboro defendants and granted paroles to the others, their lives were ruined. The last defendant was released from prison in 1950.

NATIVE AMERICANS AND THE DEPRESSION The Great Depression also ravaged Native Americans. They were initially encouraged by Roosevelt's appointment of John Collier as commissioner of the Bureau of Indian Affairs (BIA). Collier steadily increased the number of Native Americans employed by the BIA and ensured that Native Americans gained access to the various relief programs. Collier's primary objective, however, was passage of the Indian Reorganization Act. Designed to reinvigorate Native American cultural traditions by restoring land to tribes, the proposed law would have granted them the right to start businesses, establish self-governing constitutions, and receive federal funds for vocational training and economic development. The act that Congress passed, however, was a much-diluted version of Collier's original proposal, and the "Indian New Deal" brought only partial improvement to the lives of Native Americans. But it did spur the various tribes to revise their constitutions so as to give women the right to vote and hold office.

CRITICS ASSAULT THE NEW DEAL

For all of their criticisms of the inadequacy of New Deal programs, Native Americans and African Americans still voted in large majorities for Franklin Roosevelt. Other New Deal critics, however, hated Roosevelt the man, as much as they despised his policies. Many Republican business executives were so angered by the president's promotion of a welfare state and the goals of labor unions that they refused to use his name, calling him "that man in the White House."

HUEY LONG Others criticized Roosevelt for not doing enough to help the common people. The most potent of the president's "populist" opponents was Huey Pierce Long Jr., a Democratic senator from Louisiana. A short, colorful man with wild, curly hair, Long, known as "Kingfish," was a theatrical politician (a demagogue) who appealed to the raw emotions of the masses. The swaggering son of a backwoods farmer, he sported pink suits and pastel shirts, red ties, and two-toned shoes. He claimed to serve the poor, arguing that his Louisiana would be a place where "every man [is] a king, but no one wears a crown."

First as Louisiana's governor, then as its most powerful U.S. senator, Long viewed the state as his personal empire. Reporters called him the "dictator of Louisiana." True, he reduced state taxes, improved roads and schools, built charity hospitals, and provided better public services, but in the process, he used bribery, intimidation, and blackmail to get his way.

In 1933, Long arrived in Washington as a supporter of Roosevelt and the New Deal, but he quickly grew suspicious of the NRA's efforts to cooperate with big business. Having developed presidential aspirations, he had also grown jealous of "Prince Franklin" Roosevelt's popularity.

To launch his own presidential candidacy, Long devised a simplistic plan for dealing with the Great Depression that he called the Share-the-Wealth Society. Long wanted to raise taxes on the wealthiest Americans and redistribute the money to "the people"—giving every poor family $5,000 and every worker an annual income of $2,500, providing pensions to retirees, reducing working hours, paying bonuses to military veterans, and enabling every qualified student to attend college. It did not matter that his plan would have spent far more money than would have been raised by his proposed taxes. As he told a group of Iowa farmers, "Maybe somebody says I don't understand it [government finance]. Well, you don't have to. Just shut your damn eyes and believe it. That's all."

By early 1935, Long claimed to have enough support to unseat Roosevelt. "I can take him," he bragged. "He's a phony. . . . He's scared of me. I can outpromise him, and he knows it. People will believe me, and they won't believe him." Long's antics led the president to declare that the Louisiana senator was "one of the two most dangerous men in the country." (The other was General Douglas MacArthur.)

THE TOWNSEND PLAN Another popular critic of Roosevelt was a retired California doctor, Francis E. Townsend. Shocked by the sight of three elderly women digging through garbage cans for food scraps, he began promoting the Townsend Recovery Plan in 1934. Townsend wanted the federal government to pay $200 a month to every American over sixty who agreed to quit working. The recipients would have to spend the money each month.

Townsend claimed that his plan would create jobs for young people by giving older people the means to retire, and it would energize the economy by enabling retirees to buy more products. But like Huey Long's Share-the-

Wealth scheme, the numbers in Townsend's plan did not add up; although it would have served only 9 percent of the population, it would have paid those retirees more than half the total national income.

Townsend, like Long, didn't care about the plan's cost. Not surprisingly, it attracted great support among Americans sixty years of age and older. Thousands of Townsend Clubs sprang up across the nation, and advocates flooded the White House with letters urging Roosevelt to enact it.

FATHER COUGHLIN A third outspoken critic was Father Charles E. Coughlin, a Roman Catholic "radio priest" in Detroit, Michigan. In fiery weekly broadcasts that attracted as many as 40 million listeners, he assailed Roosevelt as "anti-God" and claimed that the New Deal was a Communist conspiracy. During the 1930s, Coughlin became increasingly anti-Semitic, claiming that Roosevelt was a tool of "international Jewish bankers" and relabeling the New Deal the "Jew Deal." He praised Adolf Hitler and the Nazis for killing Jews because he believed that all Jews were Communists who must be hunted down. During the 1940 presidential campaign, the thuggish Coughlin bragged, "When we get through with the Jews in America they'll think the treatment they received in Germany was nothing."

Of Long, Townsend, and Coughlin, Long had the largest political following. A 1935 poll showed that he could draw more than 5 million votes as a third-party candidate for president, perhaps enough to prevent Roosevelt's reelection. Roosevelt decided to "steal the thunder" from his most vocal critics by instituting an array of new programs. "I'm fighting Communism, Huey Longism, Coughlinism, Townsendism," Roosevelt told a reporter in early 1935. He needed "to save our system, the capitalist system" from such "crackpot ideas."

Opposition from the Court

By the mid-1930s, businesses were filing lawsuits against various elements of the New Deal, and some of them made their way to the U.S. Supreme Court.

On May 27, 1935, the Court killed the National Industrial Recovery Act (NIRA) by a unanimous vote. In *Schechter Poultry Corporation v. United States*, the justices ruled that Congress had given too much authority to the president when the NIRA created the National Recovery Administration, giving it the power to bring business and labor leaders together to create "codes of fair competition" for their industries.

Then, on January 6, 1936, in *United States v. Butler*, the Supreme Court declared unconstitutional the Agricultural Adjustment Act's tax on "middle men," the companies that processed food crops and commodities like cotton.

In response, the Roosevelt administration passed the Agricultural Adjustment Act of 1938, which reestablished the earlier crop-reduction payment programs but left out the tax on processors.

By the end of its 1936 term, the Supreme Court had ruled against New Deal programs in seven of nine major cases. The same line of conservative judicial reasoning, Roosevelt warned, might endanger other New Deal programs—if he did not act swiftly to prevent it.

THE SECOND NEW DEAL

To rescue his legislative program from judicial and political challenges, Roosevelt launched in 1935 the second, more radical phase of the New Deal, explaining that "social justice, no longer a distant ideal, has become a definite goal" of his administration. In his effort "to steal Huey Long's thunder," the president called on Congress to pass a cluster of "must" legislation that included a federal construction program to employ the jobless; banking reforms; increased taxes on the wealthy; and "social security" programs to protect people during unemployment, old age, and illness.

THE WPA In the first three months of 1935, dubbed the Second Hundred Days, Roosevelt convinced Congress to pass most of the **Second New Deal's** "must" legislation. The results changed the face of American life. The first major initiative was the $4.8 billion Emergency Relief Appropriation Act. The largest peacetime spending bill in history to that point, it included an array of federal job programs managed by a new agency, the **Works Progress Administration (WPA)**.

The WPA quickly became the nation's largest employer, hiring an average of 2 million people annually over four years. WPA workers built New York City's LaGuardia Airport, restored the St. Louis riverfront, and managed the bankrupt city of Key West, Florida. The WPA also employed a wide range of writers, artists, actors, and musicians in new cultural programs: the Federal Theatre Project, the Federal Art Project, the Federal Music Project, and the Federal Writers' Project.

The National Youth Administration (NYA), also under the WPA, provided part-time employment to students and aided jobless youths. Two future presidents were among the beneficiaries; twenty-seven-year-old Lyndon B. Johnson directed an NYA program in Texas, and Richard M. Nixon, a struggling Duke University law student, found work through the NYA at 35¢ an hour. Although the WPA took care of only 3 million of some 10 million jobless at any one time, it helped some 9 million people before it expired in 1943.

Federal art project A group of WPA artists at work on *Building the Transcontinental Railroad*, a mural celebrating the contributions of foreign newcomers that appears in the immigrants' dining hall on Ellis Island, outside of New York City.

THE WAGNER ACT Another major element of the Second New Deal was the National Labor Relations Act, often called the **Wagner Act** in honor of the New York senator, Robert Wagner, who drafted it and convinced Roosevelt to support it. The Wagner Act was one of the most important pieces of labor legislation in history, guaranteeing workers the right to organize unions and bargain directly with management about wages and other issues. It also created a National Labor Relations Board to oversee union activities.

SOCIAL SECURITY As Francis Townsend had stressed, the Great Depression hit the oldest Americans and those with disabilities especially hard. To address the problems faced by the elderly and disabled, Roosevelt proposed the **Social Security Act** of 1935. Social Security was, he announced, the "cornerstone" and "supreme achievement" of the New Deal.

The basic concept of government assistance to the elderly was not new. Progressives during the early 1900s had proposed a federal system of social security for the aged, poor, disabled, and unemployed. Other nations had already enacted such programs, but not the United States. The hardships caused by the Great Depression revived the idea, however, and Roosevelt masterfully guided the legislation through Congress.

The Social Security Act was designed largely by Secretary of Labor Frances Perkins, the first woman cabinet member in history. Its centerpiece was a self-financed federal retirement fund for people over sixty-five. Beginning in 1937, workers and employers contributed payroll taxes to establish the fund. Most of the collected taxes were spent on pension payments to retirees; whatever was left over went into a trust fund for the future. Roosevelt stressed that Social Security was not intended to guarantee everyone a comfortable retirement. Rather, it was meant to supplement other sources of income and protect the elderly. Only during the 1950s did voters and politicians come to view Social Security as the *primary* source of retirement income for working-class Americans.

The Social Security Act also set up a shared federal–state unemployment-insurance program, financed by a payroll tax on employers. In addition, it committed the national government to a broad range of social-welfare activities based upon the assumption that "unemployables"—people who were unable to work—would remain a state responsibility while the national government would provide work relief for the able-bodied. To that end, the Social Security Act provided federal funding for three state-administered public-assistance programs—old-age assistance, aid to dependent children, and aid for the blind—and further aid for maternal, child-welfare, and public health services.

When compared with similar programs in Europe, the U.S. Social Security system was conservative. It was the only government-managed retirement program in the world financed by taxes on the earnings of workers; most other countries funded such programs out of general government revenues.

The Social Security payroll tax was also a regressive tax because it used a single withholding tax *rate* for everyone, regardless of income level. It thus pinched the poor more than the rich, and it hurt efforts to revive the economy because it removed from circulation a significant amount of money. In addition, the Social Security system, at the insistence of southern Democrats determined to maintain white supremacy, excluded 9.5 million workers who most needed the new program: farm laborers, domestic workers (maids and cooks), and the self-employed, a disproportionate percentage of whom were African Americans.

Roosevelt regretted the act's limitations, but he knew that they were necessary compromises to gain congressional approval and to withstand court challenges. As he told an aide who criticized funding the program out of employee contributions:

I guess you're right on the economics, but those taxes were never a problem of economics. They are politics all the way through. We put those payroll contributions there so as to give the contributors a moral, legal, and political right to collect their pensions and their unemployment benefits. With those taxes in there, no damn politician can ever scrap my Social Security program.

Roosevelt also preferred that workers fund their own Social Security pensions because he wanted Americans to view their retirement checks as an *entitlement*—as something that they had paid for and deserved. Conservatives condemned the Social Security Act as tyrannical and "socialistic." Former president Herbert Hoover refused to apply for a Social Security card because of his opposition to the "radical" program. He received a Social Security number anyway.

TAXING THE RICH Another major bill in the second phase of the New Deal was the Revenue Act of 1935, sometimes called the "Wealth-Tax Act" but popularly known as the "soak-the-rich" tax. It raised tax rates on annual income above $50,000, in part because of stories that many wealthy Americans were not paying taxes. The powerful banker J.P. Morgan confessed to a Senate committee that he had created fictitious sales of stock to his wife that enabled him to pay no taxes.

Morgan and other business leaders fumed over Roosevelt's tax and spending policies. Newspaper tycoon William Randolph Hearst growled that the wealth tax was "essentially communism." Roosevelt countered by stressing that "I am fighting communism. . . . I want to save our system, the capitalistic system." Yet he added that saving capitalism and "rebalancing" its essential elements required a more equal "distribution of wealth."

Social Security A poster distributed by the government to educate the public about the new Social Security Act.

A NEW DIRECTION FOR UNIONS The New Deal reinvigorated the labor union movement. When the National Industrial Recovery Act (NIRA) demanded that every industry code affirm workers' rights to organize, unionists quickly translated it to mean "the president wants you to join the union." John L. Lewis, head of the United Mine Workers (UMW), was among the first to capitalize on the pro-union spirit of the NIRA. He rebuilt the UMW from 150,000 members to 500,000 within a year.

Encouraged by Lewis's success, Sidney Hillman of the Amalgamated Clothing Workers and David Dubinsky of the International Ladies Garment Workers organized workers in the clothing industry. As leaders of industrial unions (composed of all types of workers in a particular industry, skilled or unskilled), which were in the minority by far, they found the smaller, more restrictive craft unions (composed of skilled male workers only, with each union serving just one trade) to be obstacles to organizing workers in the country's basic industries.

In 1935, with the passage of the Wagner Act, industrial unionists formed a Committee for Industrial Organization (CIO). Craft unionists began to fear submergence by the mass unions made up mainly of unskilled workers. Jurisdictional disputes divided them, and in 1936 the American Federation of Labor (AFL) expelled the CIO unions, which then formed a permanent structure, called after 1938 the Congress of Industrial Organizations (also known by the initials CIO). The rivalry spurred both groups to greater efforts.

The CIO focused on organizing the automobile and steel industries. Until the Supreme Court upheld the Wagner Act in 1937, however, companies failed to cooperate with its pro-union provisions. Employers instead used various forms of intimidation to fight the infant unions. Early in 1937, automobile workers spontaneously tried a new tactic, the "sit-down strike," in which they refused to leave a workplace until employers had granted them collective-bargaining rights.

Led by the fiery Walter Reuther, thousands of employees at the General Motors assembly plants in Flint, Michigan, occupied the factories and stopped all production. Company officials called in police to harass the strikers, sent spies to union meetings, and threatened to fire the workers. They also pleaded with President Roosevelt to dispatch federal troops. He refused, while expressing his displeasure with the sit-down strike, which the courts later declared illegal. The standoff lasted more than a month. Then, on February 11, 1937, the company relented and signed a contract recognizing the United Automobile Workers (UAW) as a legitimate union.

Roosevelt's Second Term

On June 27, 1936, Franklin Delano Roosevelt accepted the Democratic party's nomination for a second term. The Republicans chose Governor

Alfred M. Landon of Kansas, a progressive Republican who had endorsed many New Deal programs. "We cannot go back to the days before the depression," he scolded conservative Republicans. "We must go forward, facing our new problems." The Republicans hoped that the followers of Huey Long, Charles E. Coughlin, Francis E. Townsend, and other Roosevelt critics would combine to draw enough Democratic votes away from the president to give Landon a winning margin.

But that possibility faded when an assassin, the son-in-law of a Louisiana judge whom Long had sought to remove, shot and killed the forty-two-year-old senator in 1935. In the 1936 election, Roosevelt carried every state except Maine and Vermont, with a popular vote of 27.7 million to Landon's 16.7 million, the largest margin of victory to that point. Democrats would also dominate the new Congress, by 77 to 19 in the Senate and 328 to 107 in the House.

In winning another landslide election, Roosevelt forged a new electoral coalition that would affect national politics for years to come. While holding the support of most traditional Democrats, North and South, he made strong gains in the West among beneficiaries of New Deal agricultural programs. In the northern cities, he held on to the ethnic groups helped by New Deal welfare policies. Many middle-class voters whose property had been saved by New Deal measures flocked to support Roosevelt, as did intellectuals stirred by the ferment of new ideas coming from the government. The revived labor union movement also threw its support to Roosevelt, and in the most meaningful shift of all, a majority of African Americans voted for a Democratic president. "My friends, go home and turn Lincoln's picture to the wall," a Pittsburgh journalist told black voters. "That debt has been paid in full."

THE COURT-PACKING PLAN Roosevelt's landslide victory convinced him that he could do almost anything and the voters would support him. But one major roadblock stood in the way: the conservative Supreme Court, made up of "nine old men." Lawsuits challenging the constitutionality of the Social Security and Wagner Acts were pending before the Court. Given the Court's conservative bent and its earlier anti–New Deal rulings, Roosevelt feared that the Second New Deal was in danger of being nullified.

For that reason, he hatched a clumsy plan to "reform" the Court by enlarging it. Congress, not the Constitution, determines the size of the Supreme Court, which over the years had numbered between six and ten justices. In 1937, the number was nine. On February 5, 1937, Roosevelt, without consulting congressional leaders or even his own advisers, asked Congress to name up to six new Supreme Court justices, one for each of the current justices over seventy years old, explaining that the aging members of the Court were falling behind in their work and needed help.

But the **"Court-packing" scheme**, as opponents labeled the plan, backfired. It was too manipulative and far too political, and quickly became the most controversial proposal of Roosevelt's presidency. The plan ignited a firestorm of opposition among conservative Republicans and even aroused fears among Democrats that the president was seeking dangerous new powers.

As it turned out, several Court decisions during the spring of 1937 surprisingly upheld disputed provisions of the Wagner and Social Security Acts. In addition, a conservative justice resigned from the Court, and Roosevelt replaced him with a New Dealer, Senator Hugo Black of Alabama.

Despite criticism from both parties, Roosevelt insisted on forcing his Court-packing bill through Congress. On July 22, 1937, the Senate overwhelmingly voted it down. It was the biggest political blunder and greatest humiliation of Roosevelt's career. The episode fractured the Democratic party and damaged the president's prestige. The momentum of his 1936 landslide victory was lost. As Secretary of Agriculture Henry A. Wallace later remarked, "The whole New Deal really went up in smoke as a result of the Supreme Court fight."

A SLUMPING ECONOMY During 1935 and 1936, the economy finally began showing signs of revival. By the spring of 1937, industrial output had risen above the 1929 level. In 1937, however, Roosevelt, worried about federal budget deficits and rising inflation, ordered sharp cuts in government spending. The economy stalled, then slid into a slump deeper than that of 1929. In only three months, unemployment rose by 2 million people. When the spring of 1938 failed to bring economic recovery, Roosevelt reversed himself and asked Congress to adopt a new federal spending program, and Congress voted $3.3 billion in new expenditures. The increase in government spending reversed the economy's decline, but only during World War II would employment again reach pre-1929 levels.

The Court-packing fight, the sit-down strikes, and the 1937 recession all undercut Roosevelt's prestige and power. When the 1937 congressional session ended, the only major New Deal initiatives were the Wagner-Steagall National Housing Act and the Bankhead-Jones Farm Tenant Act. The Housing Act, developed by Senator Robert F. Wagner, set up the federal Housing Authority, which extended long-term loans to cities to build public housing projects in blighted neighborhoods and provide subsidized rents for poor people. Later, during World War II, it financed housing for workers in new defense plants.

The Farm Tenant Act created a new agency, the Farm Security Administration (FSA), which provided loans to keep farm owners from losing their land to bankruptcy. It also made loans to tenant farmers to enable them to purchase farms. In the end, however, the FSA proved to be little more than another relief operation that tided a few farmers over during difficult times. A more effective answer to the problem eventually arrived in the form of national mobilization for war, which landed many struggling tenant farmers in military service or the defense industry, broadened their horizons, and taught them new skills.

In 1938, the Democratic Congress also enacted the Fair Labor Standards Act. It replaced many of the provisions that had been in the NIRA, which had been declared unconstitutional. The federal government established a national minimum wage of 40¢ an hour and a maximum workweek of forty hours. The act, which applied only to businesses engaged in *interstate* commerce, also prohibited the employment of children under the age of sixteen.

SETBACKS FOR THE PRESIDENT   During the late 1930s, the Democrats in Congress increasingly split into two factions, with conservative southerners on one side and liberal northerners on the other. Many white southern Democrats balked at the party's growing dependence on the votes of northern labor unions and African Americans. Senator Ellison "Cotton Ed" Smith of South Carolina and several other southern delegates walked out of the 1936 Democratic party convention, with Smith declaring that he would not support any party that views "the Negro as a political and social equal." Other critics believed that Roosevelt was exercising too much power and spending too much money. Some southern Democrats began to work with conservative Republicans to veto any additional New Deal programs.

Roosevelt now headed a divided party, and the congressional elections of November 1938 handed the administration another setback when the Democrats lost 7 seats in the Senate and 80 in the House. In his State of the Union message in 1939, Roosevelt for the first time presented no new reform programs but instead spoke of the need "to *preserve* our reforms." The conservative coalition of Republicans and southern Democrats had stalemated the president. As one observer noted, the New Deal "has been reduced to a movement with no program, with no effective political organization, with no vast popular party strength behind it."

A HALFWAY REVOLUTION   The New Deal's political momentum petered out in 1939 just as a new world war was erupting in Europe and Asia. Many New Deal programs had failed or were poorly conceived and implemented, but others were changing American life for the better: Social Security, federal regulation of stock markets and banks, minimum wage levels for workers, federally insured bank accounts, the right to join labor unions. Never before had the federal government intervened so directly in the economy or spent so much on social welfare programs. Franklin Roosevelt had also transformed the nation's political dynamics, luring black voters in large numbers to the Democratic party, and he had raised the nation's spirits through his relentless optimism.

Roosevelt had led the nation out of the Depression and changed the role of the federal government. By the end of the 1930s, its power and scope were vastly larger than in 1932. Landmark laws expanded the powers of the national government by establishing new regulatory agencies and laying the foundation of a social welfare system.

Most important of all, the New Deal brought faith and hope to the discouraged and desperate. As a CCC worker recalled late in life, Roosevelt "restored a sense of confidence and morale and hope—hope being the greatest of all." New Deal programs provided stability for tens of millions of people. "We aren't on relief anymore," one woman noted with pride. "My husband is working for the government."

The enduring reforms of the New Deal also constituted a significant change from the progressivism of Theodore Roosevelt and Woodrow Wilson. They had assumed that the function of government was to use aggressive *regulation* of industry and business to ensure that people had an equal opportunity to pursue the American Dream. But Franklin Roosevelt and the New Dealers insisted that the government should provide at least a minimal quality of life for all Americans. The enduring protections afforded by bank-deposit insurance, unemployment benefits, a minimum hourly wage, the Wagner Act, and Social Security pensions gave people a sense of security and protected the nation against future economic crises. (There has not been a similar "depression" since the 1930s.)

The greatest failure of the New Deal was its inability to restore prosperity and end record levels of unemployment. In 1939, 10 million Americans—nearly 17 percent of the workforce—remained jobless. Only the Second World War would finally produce full employment—in the armed forces as well as in factories supporting the military.

Roosevelt's energetic pragmatism was his greatest strength—and weakness. He was flexible in developing new policies and programs; he kept what worked and discarded what failed. He sharply increased the regulatory powers of the federal government and laid the foundation for what would become an expanding system of social welfare programs. Despite what his critics charged, however, Roosevelt was no socialist; he sought to preserve the basic capitalist economic structure while providing protection to the nation's most vulnerable people. In this sense, the New Deal represented a "halfway revolution" that permanently altered the nation's social and political landscape. In a time of peril, Roosevelt created for Americans a more secure future.

CHAPTER REVIEW

SUMMARY

- **Hoover's Failure** The first phase of the federal response to the *Great Depression* included President Hoover's attempts at increasing public works and exhorting unions, businesses, and farmers to cooperate to revive economic growth. His belief in voluntary self-reliance prevented him from using federal intervention to relieve the human suffering and contributed to his underestimation of the financial collapse. Such programs as the *Reconstruction Finance Corporation* were too few and too late. By March 1933, the economy was shattered. Millions of Americans were without jobs, without the basic necessities, and without hope.

- **The First New Deal** In 1933, newly inaugurated president Franklin Delano Roosevelt and his "brain trust" set out to restore the economy and public confidence. During his early months in office, Congress and Roosevelt enacted the *First New Deal*, which propped up the banking industry with the *Federal Deposit Insurance Corporation*, provided short-term emergency work relief in the form of jobs for the unemployed, promoted industrial recovery with the *National Recovery Administration*, and passed the *Agricultural Adjustment Act* intended to raise agricultural prices by encouraging farmers to cut production. Most of the early New Deal programs eased hardships but did not restore prosperity; they helped to end the economy's downward spiral but still left millions unemployed and mired in poverty.

- **New Deal Under Fire** The Supreme Court ruled that many of the First New Deal programs were unconstitutional violations of private property and states' rights. Many conservatives criticized the New Deal for expanding the scope and reach of the federal government so much that it was steering the nation toward socialism. The "radio priest," Father Charles E. Coughlin, charged that the New Deal was a Jewish-atheist-Communist conspiracy. Other critics did not think the New Deal reforms went far enough. Senator Huey Long of Louisiana and Dr. Francis Townsend of California proposed radical plans to reshape the distribution of wealth from the rich to the poor. African Americans criticized the widespread racial discrimination in New Deal policies and agencies.

- **The Second New Deal and the New Deal's Legacy** Roosevelt responded to the criticism and the continuing economic hardship with a *Second New Deal*, which sought to reshape the nation's social structure by expanding the role of the federal government. Many of the programs making up the Second New Deal, such as the *Works Progress Administration*, *Social Security*, and the *Wagner Act*, aimed to achieve greater social justice by establishing new regulatory agencies and laying the foundation of a federal social welfare system. Frustrated by the Supreme Court's opposition to the First New Deal, Roosevelt proposed his "*Court-packing*" *scheme*, but it was rejected by the Senate. Support for the New Deal began to lose steam amid the lingering effects of the Great Depression. However, the New Deal established the idea that the federal government should provide at least a minimal quality of life for all Americans, and it provided people with some security against a future crisis, reaffirming for millions a faith in American capitalism.

CHRONOLOGY

November 1932	Franklin D. Roosevelt is elected president
March 1933	Congress passes the Emergency Banking Relief Act ("Bank Holiday")
	Congress establishes the Civilian Conservation Corps
May 1933	Congress creates the Tennessee Valley Authority and the Agricultural Adjustment Act
June 1933	Congress establishes the Federal Deposit Insurance Corporation (Banking Act) and passes the National Industrial Recovery Act
December 1933	Prohibition repealed with the passage of the Twenty-First Amendment to the Constitution
May 1935	Supreme Court finds National Industrial Recovery Act unconstitutional
1935	President Roosevelt creates the Works Progress Administration
1936	President Roosevelt is reelected in a landslide
1937	Social Security payments begin

KEY TERMS

Great Depression (1929–1941) p. 913

Reconstruction Finance Corporation (RFC) (1933) p. 917

Bonus Expeditionary Force p. 917

First New Deal (1933–1935) p. 921

Federal Deposit Insurance Corporation (FDIC) (1933) p. 922

Securities and Exchange Commission (1934) p. 923

National Recovery Administration (NRA) (1933) p. 925

Agricultural Adjustment Act (1933) p. 926

Dust Bowl p. 926

Second New Deal (1935–1938) p. 936

Works Progress Administration (WPA) (1935) p. 936

Wagner Act (1935) p. 937

Social Security Act (1935) p. 937

"Court-packing" scheme (1937) p. 942

 INQUIZITIVE

Go to InQuizitive to see what you've learned—and learn what you've missed—with personalized feedback along the way.

26 The Second World War

1933–1945

***Raising the Flag on Iwo Jima* (February 23, 1945)** Five members of the United States Marine Corps raise the U.S. flag on Mount Suribachi, during the Battle of Iwo Jima. Three of these Marines would die within days after this photograph was taken. The image earned photographer Joe Rosenthal the Pulitzer Prize. A bronze statue of this scene is the centerpiece of the Marine Corps War Memorial in Virginia.

W hen Franklin Roosevelt became president in 1933, he shared with most Americans a determination to stay out of international disputes. His focus was on combating the Great Depression at home. While the United States had become deeply involved in global trade during the twenties, it had remained aloof from global conflicts. So-called isolationists insisted that there was no justification for America to become embroiled in international affairs. With each passing year during the thirties, however, Germany, Italy, and Japan threatened the peace and stability of Europe and Asia.

The Rise of Fascism in Europe

In 1917, Woodrow Wilson had led the United States into the First World War to make the world "safe for democracy." In fact, though, democracy was in retreat after 1919, while Soviet communism was on the march. So, too, was **fascism**, a radical form of totalitarian government in which a dictator uses propaganda and brute force to seize control of all aspects of national life—the economy, the armed forces, the legal and educational systems, and the press. Fascism in Germany and Italy thrived on a violent ultranationalist patriotism and almost hysterical emotionalism built upon claims of racial superiority and the simmering resentments that grew out of defeat in the First World War.

focus questions

1. How did German and Japanese actions lead to the outbreak of war in Europe and Asia?

2. How did President Roosevelt and Congress respond to the outbreak of wars in Europe and Asia between 1933 and 1941?

3. What were the effects of the Second World War on American society?

4. What were the major factors that enabled the United States and its allies to win the war in Europe?

5. How were the Japanese defeated in the war in the Pacific?

6. How did President Roosevelt and the Allies work to shape the postwar world?

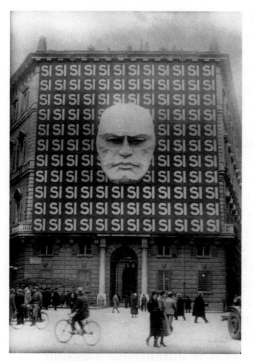

Fascist propaganda Benito Mussolini's headquarters in Rome's Palazzo Braschi, which bore an oversized reproduction of his head.

At the same time, halfway around the world, the Japanese government fell under the control of expansionists eager to conquer China and most of Asia. Japanese leaders were convinced that they were a "master race" with a "mission" to lead a resurgent Asia, just as Adolf Hitler claimed that Germany's "mission," as home of the supposedly superior "Aryan" race, was to dominate Europe. By 1941, there would be only a dozen or so democratic nations left on earth.

ITALY AND GERMANY In 1922, former journalist Benito Mussolini and 40,000 of his black-shirted supporters seized control of Italy, taking advantage of a paralyzed political system incapable of dealing with widespread unemployment, runaway inflation, mass strikes, and fears of communism. By 1925, Mussolini was wielding dictatorial power as "Il Duce" (the Leader). He called his version of antisocialist totalitarian nationalism *fascism*. All political parties except the Fascists were eliminated, and several political opponents were murdered. There was something darkly comical about the strutting, chest-thumping Mussolini, who claimed that "my animal instincts are always right."

There was nothing amusing, however, about Mussolini's German counterpart, the Austrian-born Adolf Hitler. Hitler's remarkable transformation during the 1920s from social misfit to head of the National Socialist German Workers' (Nazi) party startled the world. Hitler and the Nazis claimed that they represented a German ("Aryan") master race whose "purity and strength" were threatened by liberals, Jews, socialists, Communists, homosexuals, Gypsies, and other "inferior" peoples. Hitler promised to make Germany strong again by renouncing the Versailles Treaty, defying the limits on its armed forces, and uniting the German-speaking people of Europe into a Greater German Empire that would give the nation "living space" to expand, dominate "lesser" races, and rid the continent of Jews.

Hitler portrayed himself as Germany's savior from the humiliation of having lost the Great War and the widespread suffering caused by the Great Depression. Appointed chancellor on January 30, 1933, five weeks before Frank-

Adolf Hitler Hitler performs the Nazi salute at a rally. The giant banners, triumphant music, powerful oratory, and expansive military parades were all designed to stir excitement and allegiance among Nazis.

lin Roosevelt was first inaugurated, Hitler, like Mussolini, was idolized by the masses. He declared himself absolute leader, or *Führer*, became president in 1934 and supreme commander of the armed forces, banned all political parties except the Nazis, created a secret police force known as the *Gestapo*, and stripped people of voting rights. There would be no more elections, labor unions, or strikes.

During the mid-1930s, Hitler's brutal Nazi police state cranked up the engines of tyranny and terrorism, propaganda and censorship. Two million brown-shirted, brawling thugs, called "storm troopers," fanned out across the nation, burning books and persecuting, imprisoning, and murdering Communists, Jews, Gypsies—and their sympathizers.

THE EXPANDING AXIS As the 1930s unfolded, a catastrophic series of events in Asia and Europe sent the world hurtling toward disaster. In 1931–1932, some 10,000 Japanese troops had occupied Manchuria in northeast China, a territory rich in raw materials and deposits of iron ore and coal. At the time, China was fragmented by civil war between Communists led by Mao Zedong and Nationalists led by Chiang Kai-shek. The Japanese took advantage of China's weakness to proclaim Manchuria's independence, renaming it the "Republic of Manchukuo." In 1934, Japan began an aggressive military buildup in anticipation of conquering all of east Asia.

The next year, Mussolini launched Italy's reconquest of Ethiopia, a weak nation in eastern Africa that Italy had controlled until 1896. When the League of Nations branded Mussolini an aggressor and imposed economic sanctions on Italy, the racist Italian leader expressed surprise that European leaders would prefer a "horde of barbarian Negroes" in Ethiopia over Italy, the "mother of civilization."

In 1935, Hitler, in flagrant violation of the Versailles Treaty, began rebuilding Germany's armed forces. The next year, he sent 35,000 soldiers into the Rhineland, the demilitarized buffer zone between France and Germany. In a staged vote, 99 percent of the Germans living in the Rhineland approved Hitler's action. The failure of France and Great Britain to enforce the Versailles Treaty convinced Hitler that the western democracies were cowards and would not try to stop him from achieving his goal of German dominance.

The year 1936 also witnessed the outbreak of the Spanish Civil War, which began when Spanish troops loyal to General Francisco Franco, with the support of the Roman Catholic Church, revolted against the fragile new republican government. Hitler and Mussolini rushed troops ("volunteers"), warplanes, and military and financial aid to support Franco's fascist insurgency.

While peace in Europe was unraveling, the Japanese government fell under the control of aggressive militarists. In 1937, a government official announced that the "tide has turned against the liberalism and democracy that once swept over the nation." On July 7, 1937, Japanese and Chinese soldiers clashed at China's Marco Polo Bridge, near Beijing. The incident quickly escalated into a full-scale conflict, the Sino-Japanese War.

By December, the Japanese had captured the Nationalist Chinese capital of Nanjing, whereupon the undisciplined soldiers ran amok, looting the city and mercilessly murdering and raping civilians. As many as 300,000 Chinese were murdered in what came to be called the Rape of Nanjing. Thereafter, the Sino-Japanese War bogged down into a stalemate.

From Isolationism to Intervention

Most Americans responded to the mounting crises abroad by deepening their commitment to isolationism. They were determined to keep the United States out of another European war.

U.S. NEUTRALITY The widespread isolationism led President Roosevelt to sign the first of several **"neutrality laws"** passed by Congress to help avoid the supposed mistakes that had led the nation into the First World War. The Neutrality Act of 1935 prohibited Americans from selling weapons or traveling on ships owned by nations at war. In 1936, Congress revised the Neutrality Act by banning loans to warring nations.

Roosevelt, however, was not so sure that the United States could or should remain neutral. In October 1937, he delivered a speech in Chicago, the heartland of isolationism, in which he called for international cooperation to "quarantine the aggressors" who were responsible for disturbing world peace. But his appeal fell flat.

The Neutrality Act of 1937 allowed Roosevelt to require that nonmilitary American goods bought by warring nations be sold on a cash-and-carry basis—that is, a nation would have to pay cash and then carry the American-made goods away in its own ships. This was intended to preserve America's profitable trade with warring nations without running the risk of being drawn into the fighting.

THE AXIS ALLIANCE In 1937, Japan joined Germany and Italy in establishing the Rome-Berlin-Tokyo **"Axis" alliance**. Hitler and Mussolini vowed to create a "new order in Europe," while the Japanese imperialists pursued their "divine right" to control all of east Asia by creating what they called the Greater East Asia Co-Prosperity Sphere.

ANSCHLUSS AND THE MUNICH PACT (1938) In March 1938, Hitler forced the *Anschluss* (union) of Austria with Germany. Hitler's triumphant return to his native country was greeted by pro-German crowds waving Nazi flags and tossing flowers. Soon, "Jews not Wanted" signs appeared in Austrian cities.

Hitler then threatened to annex the Sudeten territory (Sudetenland), a mountainous region in western Czechoslovakia along the German border where more than 3 million ethnic Germans lived. British and French leaders repeatedly tried to "appease" Hitler, hoping that if they agreed to his demands for the Sudeten territory he would stop his aggressions.

On September 30, 1938, the British prime minister, Neville Chamberlain, and the French prime minister, Édouard Daladier, joined Mussolini and Hitler in signing the notorious Munich Pact, which transferred the Sudetenland to Germany. Six months later, in March 1939, Hitler broke his word when he sent German tanks and soldiers to conquer the remainder of the Czech Republic. The European democracies, having shrunk their armies after the First World War, continued to cower in the face of his ruthless behavior and seemingly unstoppable military.

The rape of Czechoslovakia convinced Roosevelt that Hitler and Mussolini were "madmen" who "respect force and force alone." Throughout late 1938 and 1939, Roosevelt tried to convince Americans, as well as British and French leaders, that the fascists would respond only to force, not words. He also persuaded Congress to increase military spending in anticipation of a possible war.

THE CONQUEST OF POLAND Later in 1939, the insatiable Hitler, having decided that he had "the world in my pocket," turned to Poland, Germany's eastern neighbor. Conquering Poland would give the German army a clear path to invade the Soviet Union, especially the fertile Ukraine region.

To ensure that the Soviets did not interfere with his plans, Hitler camouflaged his anticommunism on August 23, 1939, when he signed the Nazi-Soviet Non-Aggression Pact with Josef Stalin, the antifascist Soviet premier. The announcement of the treaty stunned a world that had understood fascism and communism to be enemies. The two tyrants agreed to divide northern and eastern Europe between them; the Germans took most of Poland, and the Soviet Union claimed a "sphere of interest" in Estonia, Latvia, Finland, and a portion of Lithuania. Just nine days later, at dawn on September 1, an estimated 1.5 million German troops invaded Poland from the north, south, and west. Hitler ordered them "to kill without mercy men, women, and children of the Polish race or language." He also ordered all terminally ill patients in German hospitals killed to make room for soldiers wounded in Poland.

This was the final straw for the western democracies. Having allowed Austria and Czechoslovakia to be seized by Hitler's war machine, Great Britain and France now did an about-face. On September 3, they honored their commitment to defend Poland. Europe, the world's smallest continent, was again embroiled in what would soon become another world war. The nations making up the British Empire and Commonwealth—Canada, India, Australia, New Zealand—joined the war. Americans watched in horror as another world war erupted. "This nation," declared Franklin Roosevelt, "will remain a neutral nation, but I cannot ask that every American remain neutral in thought as well. Even a neutral cannot be asked to close his mind or conscience."

Sixteen days after German troops stormed across the Polish border, the Soviet Union invaded Poland from the east. Pressed from all sides, Poland surrendered after a few weeks, having suffered 70,000 deaths and many more wounded. On October 6, 1939, the Nazis and Soviets divided Poland between them. Over the next five years, millions of Poles were arrested, deported, enslaved, or murdered.

REVISING THE NEUTRALITY ACT In September 1939, President Roosevelt had decided that the United States must do more to stop "aggressor" nations. He summoned Congress into special session to revise the Neutrality Act. "I regret that the Congress passed the Act," the president said. "I regret equally that I signed the Act."

After six weeks of heated debate, Congress passed the Neutrality Act of 1939, which allowed Britain and France to send their ships to the United States to bring back American military supplies. Public opinion supported such measures as long as other nations did the actual fighting.

WAR IN EUROPE The war in Europe settled into a three-month stalemate during early 1940, as Hitler's generals waited out the winter. Then, in the early spring, Germany attacked again. At dawn on April 9, Nazi armies occupied Denmark and landed along the Norwegian coast. German paratroopers, the first ever used in warfare, seized Norway's airports. Denmark fell in a day, Norway within a few weeks. On May 10, German forces invaded the Low Countries—Belgium, Luxembourg, and the Netherlands (Holland). Luxembourg fell the first day, the Netherlands three days later. Belgium lasted until May 28.

AGGRESSION IN EUROPE, 1935–1939

- Keeping in mind the terms of the Treaty of Versailles ending the First World War, explain why Hitler began his campaign of expansion by invading the Rhineland and the Sudetenland.
- Why did the German attack on Poland begin the Second World War, whereas Hitler's previous invasions of Austria and Czechoslovakia did not?

A few days later, German tanks roared into northern France. "The fight beginning today," Hitler declared, "decides the fate of the German nation for the next thousand years!" His brilliant *Blitzkrieg* ("lightning war") strategy centered on speed. Fast-moving columns of tanks, motorized artillery, and truck-borne infantry, all supported by warplanes and paratroopers, moved so fast that they paralyzed their stunned opponents.

British and French troops sent to help the Belgians were forced to make a frantic retreat to the English Channel coast, with the Germans in hot pursuit. On May 26, while German *Panzer* divisions (made up of tanks and other armored vehicles) followed Hitler's surprising order to rest and refuel, Great Britain was able to organize a weeklong evacuation of British and French soldiers from the beaches at Dunkirk, on the northern French coast near the border with Belgium. Despite attacks from German warplanes, some 338,000 defeated and demoralized soldiers escaped to England, leaving behind vast stockpiles of vehicles, weaponry, and ammunition.

While the evacuation was unfolding, German forces decimated the remaining French armies. Tens of thousands of panicked French refugees clogged the roads to Paris. The crumbling French war effort prompted Italy's dictator, Mussolini, to declare war on France and Great Britain, which he dismissed as "the reactionary democracies of the West." On June 14, 1940, German soldiers marched unopposed into Paris. Eight days later, French leaders surrendered, whereupon the Germans established a puppet fascist government in the city of Vichy.

The rapid fall of France stunned the world. In the United States, complacency about the Nazis turned to fear and even panic as people realized the Germans could eventually assault America. The Second World War was but ten months old, yet Germany ruled most of western Europe. Only the "neutral" nations of Spain, Sweden, and Switzerland had avoided the Nazi onslaught. Great Britain now stood alone against Hitler's relentless military power. "The war is won," an ecstatic Hitler bragged to Mussolini. "The rest is only a matter of time."

PREPARING AMERICA FOR WAR As Hitler's armies conquered Europe, the United States found itself in no condition to wage war. After the First World War, the U.S. Army was reduced to a small force; by 1939, it numbered only 175,000. By contrast, Germany had almost 5 million soldiers. In promoting "military preparedness," President Roosevelt in May 1940 called for increasing the size of the army and producing 50,000 combat planes in 1942, a seemingly outlandish goal, since Germany was producing only 15,000 warplanes that year.

Roosevelt also responded to Winston Churchill's repeated requests for assistance by increasing military shipments to Great Britain and promising to provide all possible "aid to the Allies short of war." Churchill was focused on one strategic objective: to convince, coax, bluff, charm, seduce, or frighten the United States into entering the war.

THE MANHATTAN PROJECT Adding to Roosevelt's concerns was the possibility that Germany might have a secret weapon. The famous physicist Albert Einstein, a Jewish Austrian refugee from Nazism, had alerted Roosevelt in the fall of 1939 that the Germans were trying to create atomic bombs. In June 1940, Roosevelt set up the National Defense Research Committee to coordinate military research, including a top-secret effort to develop an atomic bomb—the Manhattan Project—before the Germans did. Almost 200,000 people worked on the Manhattan Project, including Dr. J. Robert Oppenheimer, who led the team of distinguished scientists scattered among thirty-seven secret facilities in thirteen states.

THE BATTLE OF BRITAIN Having conquered western Europe, Hitler began planning the invasion of Great Britain ("Operation Sea Lion"), scheduled for September 1940. The late summer brought the Battle of Britain, as the Germans first sought to destroy Britain's Royal Air Force (RAF). The Nazis deployed some 2,500 warplanes, outnumbering the RAF two to one. "Never has a nation been so naked before its foes," Churchill admitted.

Churchill became the symbol of Britain's determination to stop Hitler. With his bulldog face, ever-present cigar, and "V for Victory" gesture, he urged the British citizenry to make the war "their finest hour." He breathed defiance while preparing for a German invasion, building fortifications, laying mines, digging trenches and fashioning tank traps, and mobilizing the population. The British, he pledged, would confront Hitler's invaders with "blood, toil, tears, and sweat." They would "never surrender."

The London "Blitz" An aerial photograph of London set aflame by German bombing raids in 1940. Winston Churchill responded, "We shall never surrender."

In July and August, 1940, the German air force (*Luftwaffe*) launched day and night bombing raids against military targets across southeast England. The pilots in the Royal Air Force (their average age was twenty-three), with the benefit of radar, a secret new technology, fended off the German assault, ultimately destroying 1,700 German warplanes. Hitler then ordered his bombers to target civilians and cities (especially London) in night raids designed to terrorize British civilians. In what came to be called "the Blitz" during September and October of 1940, the Germans caused massive damage in Britain's major cities, destroying a million homes and killing 40,000 civilians.

The Blitz, however, enraged rather than demoralized the British people. A London newspaper headline summarized the nation's courage and defiant mood: "Is That the Best You Can Do, Adolf?" The British success in the air proved decisive, for in October 1940, Hitler gave up his invasion plans. It was the first battle he had lost, and it was Britain's finest hour.

"ALL AID SHORT OF WAR" During 1940, Franklin Roosevelt began a crucial campaign to convince Americans that isolationism was impractical and even dangerous. His phrase, all "aid short of war," became the label for his efforts to help Great Britain.

Roosevelt and Churchill negotiated a trade on September 2, 1940, called the Destroyers for Bases Agreement, by which fifty old U.S. warships went to the British Royal Navy in return for allowing the United States to build military bases on British island colonies in the Caribbean.

Two weeks later, on September 16, 1940, Roosevelt pushed through a reluctant Congress the first peacetime conscription (military draft) in American history. The Selective Training and Service Act required all 16 million men ages twenty-one to thirty-five to register for the draft at one of 6,500 local draft boards. (The minimum age was later reduced to eighteen.)

A SAVAGE DEBATE The world crisis transformed Roosevelt. Having been stalemated for much of his second term by congressional opposition to the New Deal, he was revitalized by the need to stop Nazism. Yet his efforts to aid Great Britain and prepare America for war outraged isolationists. A prominent Democrat remembered that the dispute between isolationists and so-called interventionists was "the most savage political debate during my lifetime."

Isolationists, mostly midwestern and western Republicans, formed the America First Committee to oppose "military preparedness." Charles Lindbergh, the first man to fly solo across the Atlantic ocean, led the isolationist effort. To Lindbergh, Roosevelt's efforts to help Britain were driven primarily by Jews who owned "our motion pictures, our press, our radio, and our government." Lindbergh assured Americans that Britain was doomed; they should join hands with Hitler.

ROOSEVELT'S THIRD TERM The isolationists sought to make the 1940 presidential campaign a debate about the war. In June, just as France was falling to Germany, the Republicans nominated Wendell L. Willkie of Indiana, a plainspoken corporate lawyer and former Democrat who had voted for Roosevelt in 1932.

Once the campaign started, Willkie warned that Roosevelt was a "warmonger" and predicted that "if you re-elect him you may expect war in April, 1941." Roosevelt responded that he had "said this before, but I shall say it again and again and again: Your boys are not going to be sent into any foreign wars." In November 1940, Roosevelt won an unprecedented third term by 27 million votes to Willkie's 22 million and by an even more decisive margin, 449 to 82, in the electoral college. Winston Churchill wrote Roosevelt that he had "prayed for your success and I am truly thankful for it."

THE LEND-LEASE ACT Once reelected, Roosevelt found an ingenious way to provide more military aid to Britain, whose cash was running out. The **Lend-Lease Act**, introduced in Congress on January 10, 1941, allowed the president to lend or lease military equipment to "any country whose defense the President deems vital to the defense of the United States." It was a bold challenge to the isolationists. As Senator Hiram Johnson of California claimed, "This bill is war."

Roosevelt responded to critics by arguing that "no nation can appease the Nazis. No man can turn a tiger into a kitten by stroking it." The United States, he added, would provide everything the British needed while doing the same for China in its war against Japan, all in an effort to keep Americans from going to war themselves. "We must again be the great arsenal of democracy," Roosevelt explained. Churchill shored up the president's efforts by announcing that Britain did not need American troops to defeat Hitler: "Give us the tools and we will finish the job." In early March, 1941, Congress approved the Lend-Lease Act. "Let not the dictators of Europe or Asia doubt our unanimity now," Roosevelt declared.

Between 1941 and 1945, the Lend-Lease program would ship $50 billion worth of supplies to Great Britain, the Soviet Union, France, China, and other Allied nations. The Lend-Lease was Roosevelt's most emphatic effort to move America from isolationism to interventionism and it gave a huge boost to British morale. Churchill called it the most generous "act in the history of any nation."

GERMANY INVADES THE SOVIET UNION While Americans continued to debate Roosevelt's efforts to help Great Britain, the European war expanded. In the spring of 1941, German troops joined Italian soldiers in Libya, forcing the British army in North Africa to withdraw to Egypt. In April 1941, Nazi forces overwhelmed Yugoslavia and Greece. With Hungary, Romania, and Bulgaria also part of the Axis, Hitler controlled nearly all of Europe. But on June 22, 1941, without warning, Hitler launched "Operation Barbarossa," a shocking invasion of the Soviet Union, his supposed ally. Hitler's objective in turning on Stalin was his long-standing obsession to destroy communism, enslave the vast population of the Soviet Union, open up new lands for German settlement, and exploit Russia's considerable natural resources.

Hitler's foolhardy decision was the defining moment of the European war. The 3 million German soldiers sent to the Soviet Union would eventually be worn down and thrown back. At first, however, the invasion seemed a great success, as the German armies raced across the vast plains of Ukraine and western Russia. Entire Soviet armies and cities were surrounded and destroyed. During the second half of 1941, an estimated 3 million Soviet soldiers, 50 percent of the Soviet army, were captured. For four months, the Soviets retreated in the face of the German blitzkrieg.

During the summer of 1941, German forces surrounded Leningrad, now called St. Petersburg, and began a siege of the city. As weeks passed, food and supplies became scarce. Hunger alone would kill 800,000 people. Desperate people ate cats, dogs, rats, and even sawdust. As the bitterly cold winter set in, corpses were left to freeze in the snow. Still, the soldiers and civilians held out. Leningrad became known as the city that refused to die. By December, 1941, other German armies had reached the suburbs of Moscow, a thousand miles east of Berlin.

To American isolationists, Germany's invasion of Russia confirmed that America should stay out of the war and let two dreadful dictatorships bleed each other to death. Roosevelt, however, insisted on including the Soviet Union in the Lend-Lease agreement; he and Churchill were determined to keep the Russians fighting Hitler so that Hitler could not concentrate on Great Britain.

Gradually, Stalin slowed the Nazi advance by forcing the Russian people to fight—or be killed by their own troops. During the Battle of Moscow, Soviet defenders showed their pitiless resolve by executing 8,000 civilians charged with "cowardice."

Slowly, the tide started to turn against the Germans. By the winter of 1941–1942, Hitler's generals were learning the same bitter lesson that the Russians had taught Napoléon and the French in 1812. Invading armies must contend not only with Russia's ferocious fighters and enormous population but also vast distances, deep snow, and subzero temperatures.

THE ATLANTIC CHARTER By the late summer of 1941, the United States was no longer a "neutral" nation. In August, Roosevelt and Churchill drew up a joint statement of "common principles" known as the **Atlantic Charter**. The agreement pledged that after the "final destruction of the Nazi tyranny," the victors would promote certain common values: the self-determination of all peoples, economic cooperation, freedom of the seas, and a new system of international security to be called the United Nations. Within weeks, eleven anti-Axis nations, including the Soviet Union, had endorsed the Atlantic Charter.

WAR IN THE ATLANTIC No sooner had Roosevelt signed the Atlantic Charter than U.S. warships came under fire. On September 4, 1941, the *Greer* was tracking a German submarine ("U-boat") off the coast of Iceland and sharing the information with British warplanes when it was attacked. Roosevelt seized the opportunity to tell Americans that the ship was the victim of an unprovoked attack. In response, he essentially began an undeclared war in the Atlantic by ordering naval warships to provide protection for convoys all the way to Iceland, allowing them to "shoot on sight" any German submarines.

Six weeks later, on October 17, 1941, a German U-boat sank the American warship *Kearny*. Eleven sailors were killed. "The shooting has started," Roosevelt reported, "and history has recorded who fired the first shot." Two weeks later, the destroyer *Reuben James* was torpedoed and sunk while escorting a convoy near Iceland, with a loss of 115 seamen.

The sinkings spurred Congress to change the 1939 Neutrality Act by allowing merchant vessels to be armed and to enter combat zones and the ports of nations at war ("belligerents"). Step by step, the United States had begun to engage in naval warfare against Nazi Germany. Still, Americans hoped to avoid all-out war.

The Storm in the Pacific

In 1940, Japan and the United States had begun a series of moves that pushed them closer to war. Convinced that they were Asia's "leading race," the Japanese had forced the helpless Vichy French government, under German control, to permit the construction of Japanese airfields in French-controlled Indochina (now Cambodia, Laos, and Vietnam). The United States responded with the Export Control Act of July 2, 1940, which authorized President Roosevelt to restrict the export of military supplies and other strategic materials crucial to Japan. Three weeks later, on July 26, Roosevelt ordered that all Japanese assets in the United States be frozen and that oil shipments be stopped.

THE TRIPARTITE PACT On September 27, 1940, the Imperial Japanese government signed a Tripartite Pact with Nazi Germany and Fascist Italy, by which each pledged to declare war on any nation that attacked any of them. Roosevelt called the pact an "unholy alliance" designed to "dominate and enslave the entire human race." Several weeks later, the United States expanded its trade embargo against Japan to include iron ore, copper, and brass, deliberately leaving oil as the remaining bargaining chip.

Without access to American products, Japan's expansionist plans stalled; more than half of its imports came from the United States. In July 1941, Japan

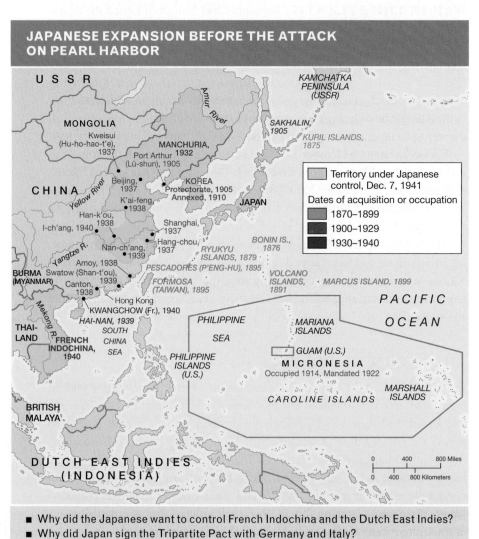

JAPANESE EXPANSION BEFORE THE ATTACK ON PEARL HARBOR

■ Why did the Japanese want to control French Indochina and the Dutch East Indies?
■ Why did Japan sign the Tripartite Pact with Germany and Italy?

announced that it was taking complete control of French Indochina in its effort to expand the "Empire of the Rising Sun" and gain access to the raw materials denied it by the United States. Roosevelt responded by restricting oil exports to Japan. He also closed the Panama Canal to Japanese shipping and merged the Filipino army with the U.S. Army. *Time* magazine claimed that Roosevelt was "waging the first great undeclared war in U.S. history."

THE ATTACK ON PEARL HARBOR On October 16, 1941, Hideki Tōjō became the Japanese prime minister. Viewing war with the United States as inevitable, he ordered a powerful fleet of Japanese warships to prepare for a secret attack on the U.S. bases in Hawaii. The Japanese naval commander, Admiral Isoroku Yamamoto, knew that his country could not defeat the United States in a long war; its only hope was "to decide the fate of the war on the very first day" by launching a "fatal attack" on the U.S. Navy.

On November 5, 1941, the Japanese asked the Roosevelt administration to end its embargo or "face conflict." The American secretary of state, Cordell Hull, responded on November 26 that Japan must remove its troops from China before the United States would lift its embargo. The Japanese then ordered a fleet of warships to begin steaming toward Hawaii. By this time, political and military leaders on both sides considered war inevitable. Yet Hull continued to meet with Japanese diplomats in Washington, privately dismissing them as being as "crooked as a barrel of fish hooks."

In late November, Roosevelt told his "war cabinet" that the United States or Great Britain was "likely to be attacked, perhaps next Monday." He and others expected the Japanese to attack Singapore or the Philippines. The U.S. Navy Department sent an urgent message to its commanders in the Pacific: "Negotiations with Japan . . . have ceased, and an aggressive move by Japan is expected within the next few days."

By the time Roosevelt's message arrived, Japanese warplanes were already headed for U.S. bases in Hawaii. In the early morning of Sunday, December 7, 1941, Japanese planes began bombing the unsuspecting U.S. fleet at **Pearl Harbor**. Of the eight American battleships, all were sunk or disabled, along with eleven other ships. Japanese bombers also destroyed 180 American warplanes. The raid, which lasted less than two hours, killed more than 2,400 American servicemen (mostly sailors) and civilians, and wounded nearly 1,200 more. At the same time that the Japanese were attacking Pearl Harbor, they were assaulting U.S. military facilities in the Philippines and on Guam and Wake islands in the Pacific, as well as British bases in Singapore, Hong Kong, and Malaya.

The surprise attack actually fell short of military success in two important ways. First, the bombers ignored the maintenance facilities and oil storage tanks that supported the U.S. fleet, without which the surviving ships might have been forced back to the West Coast. Second, the Japanese missed the U.S. aircraft carriers that had left port a few days earlier. In the naval war to come, aircraft carriers, not battleships, would prove to be decisive.

In a larger sense, the attack on Pearl Harbor was a spectacular miscalculation, for it brought the American isolationist movement to an abrupt end. Even the Japanese admiral who planned the attack had misgivings amid his officers' celebrations: "I fear that we have only succeeded in awakening a sleeping tiger."

At half past noon on December 8, President Roosevelt delivered his war message to Congress: "Yesterday, December 7, 1941—a date which will live in infamy—the United States of America was suddenly and deliberately attacked by naval and air forces of the Empire of Japan." He asked Congress to declare a "state of war." The Senate approved the resolution twenty-five minutes after Roosevelt finished speaking; the House followed immediately thereafter.

Three days later, on December 11, Germany and Italy declared war on what Hitler called the "half Judaized and the other half Negrified" United States.

Explosion of the USS *Shaw* The destroyer exploded after being hit by Japanese warplanes at Pearl Harbor. The *Shaw* was repaired shortly thereafter and went on to earn eleven battle stars in the Pacific campaign.

After learning of the attack on Pearl Harbor, Hitler shouted that "it is impossible for us to lose the war." The separate wars in Asia, Europe, and Africa had now become one global conflict. Roosevelt told the American people in a radio address that "it will not only be a long war. It will be a hard war." Yet he assured everyone that "we are going to win, and we are going to win the peace that follows."

ARSENAL OF DEMOCRACY

Waging war against Germany and Japan required all of America's immense industrial capacity. On December 18, 1941, Congress passed the War Powers Act, which gave the president far-reaching authority to reorganize government agencies and create new ones, regulate business and industry, and even censor mail and other forms of communication. With the declaration of war, men between the ages of eighteen and forty-five were drafted.

Some 16 million men and several hundred thousand women served in the military during the war. The average American soldier or sailor in the Second World War was twenty-six years old, stood five feet eight, and weighed 144 pounds, an inch taller and eight pounds heavier than the typical recruit in the First World War. Only one in ten had attended college, and only one in four had graduated from high school.

In 1940, Adolf Hitler had scoffed at the idea that the United States could produce 50,000 warplanes a year, claiming that America was nothing but "beauty queens, millionaires, and Hollywood." His ignorance of America's industrial potential proved fatal. By the end of 1942, U.S. war production had already exceeded the *combined* output of Germany, Japan, and Italy. At an Allied planning conference in Iran in 1943, Josef Stalin raised a glass to toast "American production, without which this war would have been lost."

The **War Production Board**, created by Roosevelt in 1942, directed the conversion of industries to war production. In 1941, more than 3 million automobiles were manufactured in the United States; only 139 were built during the next four years, as automobile plants began making tanks, jeeps, trucks, and warplanes.

In making the United States the "great arsenal of democracy," the Roosevelt administration transformed the nation's economy into the world's most efficient military machine. By 1945, the year the war ended, the United States would be manufacturing half of the goods produced in the world. American factories, many running twenty-four hours a day, seven days a week, produced 300,000 warplanes, 89,000 tanks, 3 million machine guns, and 7 million rifles.

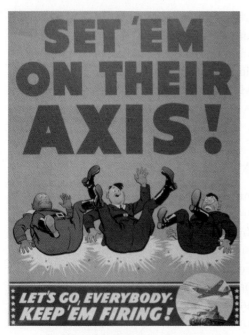

War Production Board This 1942 poster features caricatures of Mussolini, Hitler, and Tōjō, who—according to the poster—will fall on their "axis" if Americans continued their relentless production of military equipment.

FINANCING THE WAR To cover the war's huge cost (more than $3 trillion in today's values), Congress passed the Revenue Act of 1942 (also called the Victory Tax). Whereas in 1939 only about 4 million people (about 5 percent of the workforce) filed tax returns, the new act made most workers (75 percent) taxpayers. By the end of the war, 90 percent of workers were paying income tax. Tax revenues covered about 45 percent of military costs from 1939 to 1946; the government borrowed the rest, mostly through a massive promotional campaign that sold $185 billion worth of government war bonds, which paid interest to purchasers. By the end of the war, the national debt was six times what it had been at the start.

The size of the federal government soared during the war. More than a dozen new federal agencies were created, and the number of civilian federal workers quadrupled from 1 million to 4 million. Jobs were suddenly plentiful as millions quit work to join the military. The nation's unemployment rate plummeted from 14 percent in 1940 to 2 percent in 1943.

People who had long lived on the margins of the economic system, especially women, were now brought into the labor force. Stubborn pockets of poverty did not disappear, but for most civilians, especially those who had lost their jobs and homes in the Depression, the war spelled a better life. Some 24 million Americans moved during the war to take advantage of new job opportunities. Many headed to the West Coast, where shipyards and airplane factories were hiring nonstop.

ECONOMIC CONTROLS The need for the United States not only to equip and feed its own military forces but also provide massive amounts of food, clothing, and weapons to its allies created shortages of virtually all consumer goods that caused sharp price increases. In 1942, Congress responded by authorizing the Office of Price Administration to set price ceilings. With prices frozen, basic goods had to be allocated through rationing, with coupons doled out for limited amounts of sugar, coffee, gasoline, automobile tires, and meat.

The government promoted patriotic conservation by urging every family to become a "fighting unit on the home front." Posters featured slogans such as "Save Your Stuff to Make Us Tough," "Use it up, wear it out, make it do, or do without," and "Save Your Scraps to Beat the Japs." People collected scrap metal and tin foil, rubber, and cardboard for military use. Households were even encouraged to save cooking fat, from which glycerin could be extracted to make explosives.

Businesses and workers often grumbled about the wage and price controls, and on occasion the government seized industries threatened by strikes. Despite these problems, the effort to stabilize wages and prices succeeded. By the end of the war, consumer prices had risen about 31 percent, far better than the 62 percent during the First World War.

The War at Home

The Second World War transformed life at home as it was being fought abroad. Housewives went to work as welders and riveters, and farmers joined industrial unions. Some 3.5 million rural folk from the South left farms for cities. The federal government paid for a national day-care program for young children to enable their mothers to work full-time. The dramatic changes required by the war also caused unexpected changes in many areas of social life, the impact of which would last long after the war's end.

WOMEN IN THE WAR The war marked a watershed in the status of women. With millions of men going into military service, the demand for civilian workers shook up old prejudices about gender roles. During the war, nearly 350,000 women served in the **Women's Army Corps (WAC)**, the navy's equivalent, Women Accepted for Volunteer Emergency Service (WAVES), the Marine Corps, the Coast Guard, and the Army Air Force.

Sidney Hillman, appointed by Roosevelt to find workers for defense plants, announced that "war is calling on the women of America for production skills." More than 8 million women entered the civilian workforce. To help recruit women for traditionally male jobs, the government launched a promotional campaign featuring the story of "Rosie the Riveter," a woman named Rosina Bonavita, who excelled as a riveter at an airplane factory.

Many women were eager to escape the grinding routines of domestic life and earn good wages. A female welder remembered that her wartime job "was the first time I had a chance to get out of the kitchen and work in industry and make a few bucks. This was something I had never dreamed would happen."

Women of the workforce, 1942 At the Douglas Aircraft Company in Long Beach, California, three women assemble the tail section of a Boeing B-17 Flying Fortress bomber.

AFRICAN AMERICANS More than a half million African Americans left the South for better opportunities during the war years, and more than a million blacks nationwide joined the industrial workforce for the first time. Lured by jobs and higher wages in military-related plants and factories, African Americans from Texas, Oklahoma, Arkansas, and Louisiana headed west, where the dramatic expansion of defense-related jobs had significant effects on the region's population. During the war years, the number of African Americans rose sharply in western cities such as Seattle, Portland, and Los Angeles.

At the same time, the war provided a boon to southern textile mills by requiring millions of military uniforms. Manufacturing jobs led thousands of "dirt poor" sharecroppers and tenant farmers, many of them African Americans, to leave the land for steady work in new mills and factories. Sixty of the 100 army camps created during the war were in southern states, further transforming local economies. During the war, the U.S. rural population decreased by 20 percent.

AFRICAN AMERICANS IN UNIFORM The most volatile social issue ignited by the war was African American participation in the military. Although the armed forces were still racially segregated in 1941, African Americans rushed to enlist after the attack on Pearl Harbor. As African American Joe Louis, the world heavyweight boxing champion, put it, "Lots of things [are] wrong with America, but Hitler ain't going to fix them." Altogether, about a million African Americans—men and women—served in the armed forces during the war.

Black soldiers and sailors, assigned to racially segregated units, were initially excluded from combat units. They loaded ships, drove trucks, dug latrines, and handled supplies and mail. Black officers could not command white soldiers or sailors. Henry L. Stimson, the secretary of war, claimed that "leadership is not embedded in the negro race." Military bases had segregated facilities—and experienced frequent racial "incidents."

Bigotry at home During the Detroit Riots of 1943, police officers do nothing when a white thug hits a black man.

Tuskegee Airmen The Tuskegee Airmen were the first African American military pilots. Here, the first graduates are reviewed at Tuskegee, Alabama, in 1941.

In late 1944, however, the need for more troops led the government to revisit its racial policies. Under pressure from the African American community as well as Eleanor Roosevelt, General Dwight Eisenhower, commander of the U.S. forces in Europe, agreed to let black volunteers fight in fifty-two all-black fifty-man platoons commanded by white officers. A black officer said the decision was "the greatest" for African Americans "since enactment of the constitutional amendments following the Civil War."

The black soldiers earned the reputation of being fierce fighters. The same was true of some 600 African American pilots trained in Tuskegee, Alabama. The so-called **Tuskegee Airmen** flew more than 15,000 missions, and their unquestionable excellence spurred military and civilian leaders to desegregate the armed forces after the war. At war's end, however, the U.S. Army reimposed segregation. It would be several more years before the military was truly integrated.

MEXICAN AMERICANS As rural dwellers moved west, many farm counties experienced a labor shortage. In an ironic about-face, local and federal authorities who before the war had forced migrant laborers back across the Mexican border now recruited them to harvest crops on American farms. The Mexican government would not consent to provide the laborers, however, until the United States promised to ensure them decent working and living conditions. The result was the creation of the **bracero program** in 1942, whereby Mexico agreed to provide seasonal farmworkers on year-long contracts. Under the bracero program, some 200,000 Mexican farmworkers entered the western United States, mostly packed in cattle cars on trains. At least that many more crossed the border as undocumented workers.

The rising tide of Mexican Americans in Los Angeles prompted a stream of anti-Mexican editorials and ugly racial incidents. Even though some 300,000 Mexican Americans served in the war and earned a higher percentage of Congressional Medals of Honor than any other minority group, racial prejudices still prevailed. In southern California, there was constant conflict between white servicemen and Mexican American gang members and teenage "zoot-suiters." (Zoot suits were flamboyant clothing worn by some young Mexican American men.) In 1943, several thousand off-duty sailors and soldiers, joined by hundreds of local whites, rampaged through Los Angeles, assaulting Hispanics, African Americans, and Filipinos. The weeklong violence came to be called the "Zoot Suit Riots."

NATIVE AMERICANS IN THE MILITARY Indians supported the war effort more fully than any other group in American society. Almost a third of eligible Native American men served in the armed forces. Many others worked in defense-related industries, and thousands of Indian women volunteered as nurses or joined the WAVES. As was the case with African Americans, Indians benefited from the experiences afforded by the war by gaining vocational skills and a greater awareness of how to succeed within mainstream society.

Why did so many Native Americans fight for a nation that had stripped them of their land and ravaged their heritage?

Navajo code talkers The complex Navajo language made it impossible for the Germans and Japanese to decode American messages. Here, a code talker relays messages for U.S. marines in the Battle of Bougainville in the South Pacific in 1943.

Some felt that they had no choice. Mobilization for the war effort ended many New Deal programs that had provided Indians with jobs. At the same time, many viewed the Nazis and Japanese warlords as threats to their own homeland. Whatever their motivations, Indians distinguished themselves in the military. Unlike their African American counterparts, Indian servicemen were integrated into regular units with whites. Perhaps their most distinctive role was serving as "code talkers": every military branch used Indians, especially Navajos, to encode and decipher messages using Indian languages unknown to the Germans and Japanese.

DISCRIMINATION AGAINST JAPANESE AMERICANS The attack on Pearl Harbor ignited a hunger for vengeance against the nisei—people of Japanese descent living in the United States. Many Americans saw no difference between the Japanese who attacked Pearl Harbor and Japanese Americans. As Idaho's governor declared, "A good solution to the Jap problem would be to send them all back to Japan, then sink the island."

Such hysteria helps explain why the U.S. government sponsored one of the worst violations of civil liberties during the twentieth century, when more than 120,000 nisei were forcibly removed from their homes and transported to ten **"war relocation camps."** Forced to sell their farms and businesses within 48 hours and ordered to bring with them only what they could carry, the internees were sent by train and bus to the barbed-wire enclosed internment camps scattered across remote areas in the West. They lost not only their property but also their liberty.

President Roosevelt initiated the relocation when he issued Executive Order 9066 on February 19, 1942, authorizing the forcible removal of all ethnic Japanese living on the Pacific coast. It was perhaps his worst decision as president. Roosevelt called his action a "military necessity" although not a single incident of espionage involving Japanese Americans was proved. As it turned out, more than 70 percent of those affected were U.S. citizens.

On Evacuation Day, Burt Wilson, a white schoolboy in Sacramento, California, was baffled as soldiers ushered the nisei children out of his school:

> We wondered what had happened. They took somebody out of eighth grade, a boy named Sammy, who drew wonderful cartoons. He was my friend, and one day he was there and the next day he was gone. And that was very difficult for us to understand because we didn't see Sammy or any Japanese American—at least I didn't—as the enemy.

Few if any nisei were disloyal. In fact, 39,000 Japanese Americans served in the armed forces during the war, and others worked as interpreters and translators. But all were victims of fear and racial prejudice. Not until 1983 did

A farewell to civil rights American troops escorted Japanese Americans by gunpoint to remote internment camps, some of which were horse-racing tracks, whose stables served as housing.

the government acknowledge the injustice of the internment policy. Five years later, it granted those nisei still living $20,000 each in compensation, a tiny amount relative to what they had lost during four years of confinement.

THE ALLIED DRIVE TOWARD BERLIN

By mid-1942, the "home front" was hearing good news from Europe. U.S. naval forces had been increasingly successful at destroying German U-boats off the Atlantic coast. Up to that point, German submarines had sunk hundreds of Allied cargo vessels, killing 2,500 sailors. Stopping the submarine attacks was important because the Grand Alliance—Great Britain, the United States, and the Soviet Union—called for the defeat of Germany first. Defeating the Japanese could wait.

WAR AIMS AND STRATEGY

A major consideration for Allied military strategy was the fighting on the vast Eastern Front in the Soviet Union. During 1941–1942, the Nazis and Soviets waged colossal battles. The Soviet population—by far—bore the brunt of the war against the Nazis, leading Josef Stalin to insist that the Americans and British relieve the pressure on his troops by attacking the Germans in western Europe, thereby forcing Hitler to pull units away from the Russian Front.

Franklin Roosevelt and Winston Churchill agreed that they needed to create a second front in western Europe, but they could not agree on the timing or location of an invasion. U.S. military planners wanted to attack the Germans in France before the end of 1942. The British, however, were wary of moving too fast. An Allied defeat on the French coast, Churchill warned, was "the only way in which we could possibly lose this war." Finally, Roosevelt decided to accept Churchill's compromise proposal for a joint Anglo-American invasion of North Africa, which was occupied by German and Italian armies not nearly as strong as those in Europe.

THE NORTH AFRICA CAMPAIGN On November 8, 1942, British and American forces landed in Morocco and Algeria on the North African coast ("Operation Torch"). They were led by an untested, little-known U.S. general, Dwight D. Eisenhower. Farther east, British armies were pushing the Germans and Italians back across Libya.

The Americans lost badly in early battles. In early 1943, however, Eisenhower, soon known by his nickname, "Ike," found an audacious field commander in General George Patton, who said he loved war "more than my life." Armed with ivory-handled pistols and brimming with bravado, Patton showed American troops how to fight a war of speed and daring.

Hammered from all sides and unable to retreat, some 250,000 Germans and Italians surrendered on May 12, 1943, leaving all of North Africa in Allied control. Ernie Pyle, a war correspondent, reported that the U.S. troops "fought like veterans. They were well handled. We had enough of what we needed." But, he added, "the worst was yet to come."

THE CASABLANCA CONFERENCE Five months earlier, in January 1943, Roosevelt, Churchill, and the Anglo-American military chiefs met at a seaside resort near Casablanca, the largest city in French Morocco. It was a historic occasion. No U.S. president had ever flown abroad while in office, and none had ever visited Africa. Stalin chose to stay in the Soviet Union, but he sent a message which again urged the Allies to invade Nazi-controlled western Europe to relieve the pressure on the Russians.

At the Casablanca conference, the British convinced the Americans that they should follow up the anticipated victory in North Africa with an assault on the Italian island of Sicily before attacking Italy itself. Roosevelt and Churchill also decided to step up the bombing of Germany and to increase shipments of military supplies to the Soviet Union and the Nationalist Chinese forces fighting the Japanese.

Before leaving the Casablanca conference, Roosevelt announced, with Churchill's blessing, that the war would end only with the "unconditional surrender" of all enemy nations. This decision was designed to quiet Soviet suspicions that the Americans and British might negotiate separately with Hitler to end the war in western Europe. The announcement also reflected Roosevelt's determination that "every person in Germany should realize that this time Germany is a defeated nation."

THE BATTLE OF THE ATLANTIC While fighting raged in North Africa, the Battle of the Atlantic reached its climax. Great Britain desperately needed more food and military supplies from the United States, but German submarines operating in "wolfpacks" were sinking the British vessels transporting American goods faster than British shipyards could replace them. There could be no invasion of German-occupied France until the U-boat menace was defeated. By July 1942, some 230 Allied ships and almost 5 million tons of war supplies had been lost. "The only thing that ever frightened me during the war," recalled Churchill, "was the U-boat peril."

By the end of 1942, however, the British and Americans had discovered ways to defeat the U-boats. British experts cracked the German naval radio codes, enabling Allied convoys to steer clear of U-boats or to hunt them down with long-range warplanes (called "subchasers") and anti-submarine weapons deployed on warships. New technology also helped, as sonar and radar allowed Allied ships to track submarines. Yet the best tactic against U-boats was to group cargo vessels into tightly bunched convoys so that warships could protect them more effectively. In May 1943, the Allies destroyed forty-one U-boats. Thereafter, the U-boats were on the defensive, and Allied shipping losses fell significantly.

SICILY AND ITALY On July 10, 1943, following the Allied victory in North Africa, about 250,000 British and American troops landed on the coast of Sicily. General Eisenhower called it the "first page of the liberation of the European continent." The island was in Allied hands by August 17, bringing to an end Benito Mussolini's twenty years of fascist rule in Italy.

On July 25, 1943, the Italian king had dismissed Mussolini as prime minister and had him arrested. The new Italian government startled the Allies when it offered not only to surrender but also to switch sides. To prevent them from doing so, Hitler sent German armies into Italy.

The Italian campaign thereafter became a series of stalemated battles that left people wondering if it had been worth the cost. Winter came early to southern Italy, making life even more miserable for the soldiers. The Germans positioned themselves behind formidable defenses and rugged terrain that enabled them to slow the Allied advance to a crawl. "Italy was one hill after another," said a U.S. soldier, "and when it was wet, you were either going up too slow or down too fast, but always the mud. And every hill had a German [machine] gun on it." Allied casualties soared as the stalemate continued.

By February 1944, the two sides were, in the words of U.S. commander Mark W. Clark, like "two boxers in the ring, both about to collapse." Mussolini, plucked from prison by a daring German airborne commando raid, became head of a puppet fascist government in northern Italy as Allied forces finally took control of the rest of the country. On June 4, 1944, the U.S. Fifth Army entered Rome.

THE TEHRAN CONFERENCE Late in the fall of 1943, in Tehran, Iran, Churchill and Roosevelt had their first joint meeting with Josef Stalin. Their discussions focused on the planned invasion of Nazi-controlled France and a simultaneous Russian offensive westward across eastern Europe. The three leaders agreed to create an international organization—the United Nations—to maintain peace after the war. Upon arriving back in the United States, Roosevelt confided to Churchill his distrust of Stalin, saying that it was a "ticklish" business keeping the "Russians cozy with us" because of the tension between communism and capitalism. As General Eisenhower stressed, however, the fate of Britain and the United States depended on the Soviets' survival as an ally. "The prize we seek," he said in 1942, "is to keep 8 million Russians [soldiers] in the war."

THE STRATEGIC BOMBING OF EUROPE Months of preparation went into the long-anticipated Allied invasion of German-occupied France. While waiting for D-day (the day the invasion would begin), the U.S. Army Air Force tried to pound Germany into submission with an air campaign that dropped thousands of bombs and killed some 350,000 civilians. Yet the air offensive failed to shatter either German morale or war-related production. Many bombs missed their targets because of thick clouds, high winds, and inaccurate navigational systems, and many Allied planes were shot down. The bombing campaign, however, did force the Germans to commit precious resources to air-raid defense and eventually wore down their air force. With Allied air supremacy assured by 1944, the much-anticipated invasion of Hitler's "Fortress Europe" could move forward.

PLANNING AN INVASION In early 1944, Dwight D. Eisenhower arrived in London with a new title: Supreme Commander of the Allied Expeditionary Force (AEF) that would invade Nazi-controlled western Europe. Eisenhower faced enormous challenges, ranging from creating an effective command structure to handling disagreements between President Roosevelt and Prime Minister Churchill.

Eisenhower also faced the daunting task of planning **Operation Overlord**, the daring assault on Hitler's "Atlantic Wall," a formidable array of fortifications, mines, machine guns, barbed wire, and jagged beach obstacles along the French coastline. An attack by sea against heavily fortified defenders was the toughest of military operations. The planned invasion gave Churchill nightmares: "When I think of the beaches . . . choked with the flower of American and British youth . . . I see the tides running red with their blood. I have my doubts. I have my doubts."

General Dwight D. Eisenhower
Eisenhower visiting with U.S. paratroopers before they began the D-day assault in Operation Overlord.

For months, Eisenhower, neither an experienced strategist nor a combat commander, dedicated himself to planning the risky invasion and managing the complex political and military rivalries among the Allied leaders. Well-organized and efficient, he was a high-energy perfectionist, often impatient and short-tempered with his staff. He attended to every detail, including the amassing of 5 million tons of military equipment and munitions and thousands of warplanes and ships.

As D-day approached, Eisenhower's chief of staff predicted only a fifty-fifty chance of success. The seaborne invasion was the greatest gamble and most complex military operation in history. "I am very uneasy about the whole operation," admitted Sir Alan Brooke, head of British forces. "It may well be the most ghastly disaster of the whole war." Eisenhower was so concerned that he carried in his wallet a note to be circulated if the Allies failed. It read: "If any blame or fault attaches to the attempt, it is mine alone."

D-DAY AND AFTER Operation Overlord succeeded in part because it surprised the Germans. The Allies made elaborate efforts—including the positioning of British decoy troops and making misleading public statements—to fool the Nazis into believing that the invasion would come at Pas-de-Calais, on

The landing at Normandy D-Day, June 6, 1944. Before they could huddle under a seawall and begin to dislodge the Nazi defenders, U.S. soldiers on Omaha Beach had to cross a fifty-yard stretch that exposed them to machine guns housed in concrete bunkers.

the French-Belgian border, where the English Channel was narrowest. Instead, the landings would occur along fifty miles of shoreline in northern Normandy, a French coastal region almost 200 miles south.

On the blustery evening of June 5, 1944, Eisenhower visited some of the 16,000 American paratroopers preparing to drop behind the German lines in France. The soldiers, their faces blackened by burnt cork and heads shaved to resemble Indian warriors, noticed Eisenhower's concern and tried to lift his spirits. "Now quit worrying, General," one of them said, "we'll take care of this thing for you." A sergeant said, "We ain't worried. It's Hitler's turn to worry." After the planes took off, Eisenhower returned to his car with tears in his eyes. He later confided to an aide: "I hope to God I know what I'm doing." As he got into bed that night, Winston Churchill, with tears running down his cheeks, asked his wife: "Do you know that by the time you wake up in the morning, 20,000 men may have been killed?"

As the planes carrying the paratroopers arrived over France, thick clouds and German anti-aircraft fire disrupted the formations. Some soldiers were dropped miles from their landing sites, some were dropped far out at sea, and some were dropped so low that their parachutes never opened. Yet the U.S. 82nd and 101st Airborne Divisions outfought three German divisions during the chaotic night and prepared the way for the main invasion by destroying bridges and capturing artillery positions and key road junctions.

THE NORMANDY LANDINGS As the gray, misty light of dawn broke on D-day, June 6, 1944, the biggest invasion fleet in history—some 5,300 Allied ships carrying 370,000 soldiers and sailors—filled the horizon off the Normandy coast. Sleepy German soldiers guarding the beaches awoke to see the breathtaking array of ships. "I saw an armada like a plague of locusts," said a German officer. "The number of ships was uncountable."

Major battles often depend on luck. (When asked what kind of generals he preferred, Napoléon said "lucky ones.") Eisenhower was lucky on D-day, for the Germans misinterpreted the Normandy landings as a diversion for the "real" attack at Pas-de-Calais. It helped that the German commander, Field Marshal Erwin Rommel, assuming that the weather was too rough for an invasion, had gone home to Germany to celebrate his wife's June 6 birthday. "How stupid of me," Rommel said when he heard the news. "How stupid of me!" By one in the afternoon, he was racing back to France.

Word that the long-anticipated liberation of Nazi Europe had begun captured the world's attention. People stopped what they were doing to listen to news about the invasion over the radio. Church bells rang across the United States and Great Britain. Stalin cabled Churchill and Roosevelt that the news brought "joy to us all."

Despite Eisenhower's meticulous preparations, however, the huge operation almost failed. Clouds and anti-aircraft fire caused many paratroopers to drift way off course. Bombers dropped their loads too far inland. During the first day, foul weather and rough seas caused injuries and nausea and capsized dozens of landing craft. More than 1,000 men, weighed down by seventy pounds of equipment, drowned as they stepped off landing craft into water up to their necks.

The noise was deafening as shells exploded across the beach and in the surf. The bodies of the killed, wounded, and drowned piled up amid wrenching cries for help. "As our boat touched sand and the ramp went down," Private Harry Parley remembered, "I became a visitor to Hell" as German gunners fired on the attacking soldiers.

The first U.S. units ashore at Omaha Beach, beneath 130-foot-tall cliffs defended by German machine guns and mortars, lost more than 90 percent of their men. In one company, 197 of the 205 men were killed or wounded within ten minutes. Officers struggled to rally the exhausted, bewildered troops.

Inch by inch, backed by waves of reinforcements, the U.S. soldiers pushed across the beach and up the cliffs. By nightfall, 170,000 Allied soldiers—57,000 of them Americans—were scattered across fifty miles of windswept Normandy coastline. So too were the bodies of some 10,724 dead or wounded Allied soldiers.

On June 13, a week after the Normandy landings, Erwin Rommel, the German commander, told his wife that the "battle is not going at all well for us." Within three weeks, the Allies had landed more than 1 million troops, 566,000 tons of supplies, and 171,000 vehicles. "Whether the enemy can still be stopped at this point is questionable," German headquarters near Paris warned Hitler. "The enemy air superiority is terrific and smothers almost every one of our movements. . . . Losses in men and equipment are extraordinary."

Operation Overlord was the greatest seaborne invasion in the annals of warfare, but it was small when compared with the offensive launched by the

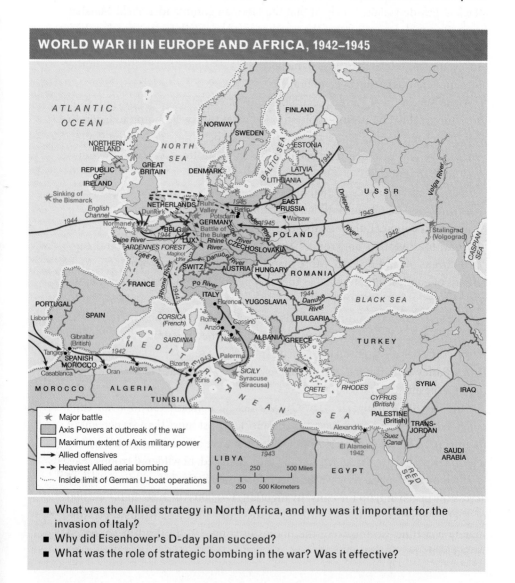

WORLD WAR II IN EUROPE AND AFRICA, 1942–1945

- What was the Allied strategy in North Africa, and why was it important for the invasion of Italy?
- Why did Eisenhower's D-day plan succeed?
- What was the role of strategic bombing in the war? Was it effective?

Soviet army in Russia a few weeks later. Between June and August 1944, the Soviets killed, wounded, or captured more German soldiers (350,000) than were stationed in all of western Europe.

Still, the Normandy invasion was a turning point in the war. With the beachhead secured, the Allied leaders knew that victory was just a matter of time, as Hitler's armies were caught between the Soviets advancing from the east and the Allied forces from the west. "What a plan!" Churchill exclaimed to the British Parliament. Even Stalin applauded the invasion's "vast conception and masterly execution."

THE LIBERATION OF PARIS It would take seven more weeks and 37,000 more lives for the Allied troops to gain control of Normandy; the Germans lost more than twice that many, and some 19,000 French civilians were killed. Then, on July 25, 1944, American armies broke out from Normandy and headed east toward Paris. On August 15, a joint American-French invasion force landed on the Mediterranean coast and raced up the Rhone Valley in eastern France.

German resistance collapsed after only ten weeks of ferocious fighting. On D-day, one German unit, the 21st Panzer Division, boasted 12,000 men and 127 tanks; ten weeks later, having retreated across France, it had 300 men and just 10 tanks. A division of the Free French Resistance, aided by American units, had the honor of liberating Paris on August 25. As U.S. soldiers marched through the cheering crowds, a reporter said that he had never "seen in any place such joy as radiated from the people of Paris this morning."

By mid-September, most of France and Belgium had been cleared of German troops. Meanwhile, the Soviet army moved relentlessly westward along a 1,200-mile front, pushing the Germans out of Russia. Between D-day and the end of the war in Europe a year later, 1.2 million Germans were killed and wounded.

ROOSEVELT'S FOURTH TERM In 1944, amid the largest war in history, the calendar required another presidential election. The Republicans nominated New York governor Thomas E. Dewey, who argued that it was time for a younger man to replace the "tired" Democratic leader. Voters, however, preferred the seasoned Franklin Roosevelt. On November 7, 1944, the president was elected for a fourth term, this time by a popular vote of 25.6 million to 22 million and an electoral vote of 432 to 99.

THE RACE TO BERLIN By the time Franklin Roosevelt was reelected, Allied armies were approaching the German border from the east and west. Churchill, worried that if the Soviets arrived first in Berlin, the German capital,

Stalin would control the postwar map of Europe, urged Eisenhower to beat the Soviets to Berlin. Eisenhower, however, decided it was not worth the estimated 100,000 Americans who would be killed or wounded in such an operation.

THE YALTA CONFERENCE   As the Allied armies converged on Berlin, Stalin hosted Roosevelt and Churchill at the **Yalta Conference** (February 4–11, 1945) in Crimea, on the Black Sea. The leaders agreed that, once Germany surrendered, the Soviets would occupy eastern Germany, and the Americans and British would control western Germany. Berlin, the German capital within the Soviet zone, would be subject to joint occupation. The Americans and British later created a fourth occupation zone in Germany for the French to administer.

Stalin's goals at Yalta were to retrieve former Russian territory transferred to Poland after the First World War and to impose Soviet control over the countries of eastern and central Europe. Roosevelt, exhausted and in failing health, agreed to Stalin's proposals because he needed the Soviets to support the creation of a new international peacekeeping organization, the United Nations, and to help defeat Japan. Military analysts estimated that Japan could hold out for eighteen months after the defeat of Germany unless the Soviets joined the war in the Pacific.

Roosevelt and Churchill got Stalin to sign the Yalta Declaration of Liberated Europe, which called for free and open elections in the liberated nations of eastern Europe. Nevertheless, the wily Stalin would fail to live up to his promises. When the Red Army "liberated" Hungary, Romania, Bulgaria, Czechoslovakia, Poland, and eastern Germany, it plundered and sent back to Russia anything of economic value, dismantling thousands of factories and mills and rebuilding them in the Soviet Union. To ensure control over eastern Europe, the Soviets shipped off to prison anyone who questioned the new Communist governments they created.

Roosevelt viewed the Yalta meeting as a test of whether the wartime alliance between the United States and the Soviet Union would survive once the conflict ended. He staked his hopes for postwar cooperation on the creation of the United Nations (UN).

At Yalta, the "Big Three" agreed to hold organizational meetings for the UN beginning on April 25, 1945. Like Woodrow Wilson, Roosevelt was determined to replace America's "outdated" isolationism with an engaged internationalism. But to get Stalin's approval of the UN, Roosevelt gave in to his demands for territory held by Japan in northeast Asia.

Republicans later savagely attacked Roosevelt for "giving" eastern Europe over to Soviet domination. Some blamed his behavior on his declining health.

(He would die in a few weeks.) But even a robust Roosevelt could not have dislodged the Soviet army from its control of eastern Europe. The course of the war shaped the outcome at Yalta, not Roosevelt's failed diplomacy. The United States had no real leverage. As a U.S. diplomat admitted, "Stalin held all the cards." "I didn't say the result was good," Roosevelt said after returning from the Yalta Conference. "I said it was the best I could do."

The Yalta Conference Churchill, Roosevelt, and Stalin (with their respective foreign ministers behind them) confer on plans for the postwar world in February 1945.

DEATH OF A PRESIDENT By early 1945, Nazi Germany was on the verge of defeat, but sixty-three-year-old Franklin Roosevelt would not live to join the victory celebrations. In the spring of 1945, he went to the "Little White House" in Warm Springs, Georgia, to rest up for the conference that would create the United Nations. On the morning of April 12, 1945, he complained of a headache but seemed to be in good spirits. It was nearly lunchtime when he said to an artist painting his portrait, "Now we've got just about 15 minutes more to work." Then, as she watched him reading some documents, he groaned, saying that he had "terrific pain" in the back of his head. Suddenly he slumped over and fell into a coma. He died two hours later.

Roosevelt's death shocked and saddened the world, in part because few people were aware that he was sick. Even his sharpest critics were devastated. Ohio senator Robert Taft, known as "Mr. Republican," called Roosevelt's death one of the worst tragedies in the nation's history. "The President's death removes the greatest figure of our time at the very climax of his career. . . . He dies a hero of the war, for he literally worked himself to death in the service of the American people." By contrast, Hitler viewed Roosevelt's death as a "great miracle." "The war is not lost," he told an aide. "Read it. Roosevelt is dead!"

THE COLLAPSE OF NAZISM Adolf Hitler's shrinking Nazi empire collapsed less than a month later. In Berlin on April 28, as Soviet troops prepared to enter the city, Hitler married his mistress, Eva Braun, in an underground bunker. That same day, Italian freedom fighters captured Mussolini and his mistress. Despite his plea to "Let me live, and I will give you an empire," Mussolini and his mistress were shot and hung by their heels from a girder above a Milan gas station. On April 30, Hitler and his wife retired to their underground bedroom, where she poisoned herself and he put a bullet in his head. Their bodies were taken outside, doused with gasoline, and burned.

On May 2, Berlin fell. Axis forces in Italy surrendered the same day. Five days later, on May 7, the chief of staff of the German armed forces agreed to unconditional surrender. So ended Nazi domination of Europe, little more than twelve years after Hitler had come to power proclaiming his "Thousand-Year Reich."

On May 8, V-E day ("Victory in Europe") generated massive celebrations. In Paris, an American bomber pilot flew his plane through the Eiffel Tower. In New York City, 500,000 people celebrated in the streets. But the elation was tempered by the ongoing war against Japan and the immense challenges of helping Europe rebuild. The German economy had to be revived, a new democratic government had to be formed, and millions of displaced Europeans had to be clothed, housed, and fed.

THE HOLOCAUST The end of the war in Europe revealed the horrific extent of the **Holocaust**, Hitler's systematic effort to destroy the Jews and other racial, political, sexual, and religious "undesirables," including Communists and prostitutes. Reports of the Nazis' methodical slaughter of Jews had appeared as early as 1942, but the gruesome stories seemed beyond belief until the Allied armies liberated the hundred or so "death camps" where the Germans had imposed their shocking "Final Solution": the wholesale extermination of some 6 million Jews, along with more than 1 million other captured peoples. At the Auschwitz-Birkenau camp in Poland, 865,000 were killed as soon as they arrived, and up to 6,000 were gassed in a single day.

American officials, even some Jewish leaders, had dragged their feet in acknowledging the Holocaust during the war for fear that relief efforts for Jewish refugees might stir up anti-Semitism at home. Under pressure, President Roosevelt had set up a War Refugee Board early in 1944. It managed to rescue about 200,000 European Jews and some 20,000 others. But the president refused appeals to bomb the concentration camp at Auschwitz, arguing that the Nazis would simply build another one. Overall, the Allied response to the Nazi atrocities was inept at best and disgraceful at worst. In 1944, Churchill called the Holocaust the "most horrible crime ever committed in the history of

Holocaust survivors American troops liberate survivors of the Mauthausen concentration camp in May 1945. The Nazis tattooed the prisoners with identification numbers on their wrists or chests, as seen on the man at left.

the world." He did not know at the time that Stalin's death camps killed more people than Hitler's.

THE PACIFIC WAR

For months after the attack on Pearl Harbor at the end of 1941, the news from the Pacific was "all bad," as President Roosevelt acknowledged. With stunning speed, the Japanese captured numerous territories in Asia, including the British colonies of Hong Kong, Burma, Malaya, and Singapore, and the French colony of Indochina. "Everywhere in the Pacific," said Winston Churchill, "we were weak and naked."

THE PHILIPPINES In the Philippines, U.S. forces and their Filipino allies were overwhelmed by Japanese invaders. On April 10, 1942, the Japanese gathered some 12,000 captured American troops along with 66,000 Filipinos and forced them to march sixty-five miles in six days up the Bataan peninsula.

More than 10,000 died along the way. News of the Bataan Death March outraged Americans and contributed to the Pacific war's ferocious emotional intensity and mutual atrocities.

By the summer of 1942, Japan had seized control of a vast Asian empire and was on the verge of assaulting Australia when its naval leaders succumbed to what one admiral called "victory disease." Intoxicated with easy victories and lusting for more, they pushed into the South Pacific, intending to isolate Australia and strike again at Hawaii.

CORAL SEA AND MIDWAY During the spring of 1942, U.S. forces in the Pacific finally had some success. In the Battle of the Coral Sea (May 2–6, 1942), U.S. naval warplanes forced a Japanese fleet headed toward the island of New Guinea to turn back after sinking an aircraft carrier and destroying seventy planes.

A few weeks later, Admiral Yamamoto steered his main Japanese battle fleet of eighty-six warships toward Midway, the westernmost of Hawaii's inhabited islands, from which he hoped to strike Pearl Harbor again. This time, however, the Japanese were taken by surprise. Americans had broken the Japanese military radio code, allowing Admiral Chester Nimitz, commander of the U.S. central Pacific fleet, to learn where Yamamoto's fleet was heading.

The first Japanese attack hit Midway hard on June 4, 1942, but at the cost of about a third of their warplanes. American planes from the *Yorktown* and *Enterprise* then struck back, crippling the Japanese fleet. The **Battle of Midway** was the first major defeat for the Japanese navy in 350 years and the turning point of the Pacific war. The American victory blunted Japan's military momentum, eliminated the threat to Hawaii, and bought time for the United States to organize its massive industrial productivity for a wider war.

MacARTHUR'S PACIFIC STRATEGY American and Australian forces were jointly under the command of the imperious General Douglas MacArthur, a military genius with tremendous willpower and courage who constantly irritated his superiors in Washington with his "unpleasant personality" and his repeated efforts to embellish his image. MacArthur had retired in 1937 but was called back into service in mid-1941, in part because he was such a brilliant strategist. In 1942, he assumed command of the Allied forces in the southwest Pacific.

On August 7, 1942, after first pushing the Japanese back in New Guinea, MacArthur landed 16,000 U.S. Marines on Guadalcanal Island, one of the so-called Solomon Islands, where the Japanese had built an air base. The U.S. commander was optimistic that his undersupplied troops could defeat the entrenched Japanese, even though, he said, there were "a hundred reasons why this operation should fail." But it did not fail. The savage fighting on Guadalcanal lasted through February 1943 but resulted in the Japanese army's first defeat and a loss of 20,000 men, compared to 1,752 Americans.

The Japanese were skilled defensive fighters who rarely surrendered, and they controlled most of the largest islands in the Pacific. Their suicidal intensity led General MacArthur and Admiral Nimitz to adopt a shrewd "leapfrogging" strategy whereby they focused on the most important islands and used airpower and sea power to bypass the others, leaving the isolated Japanese bases to "wither on the vine," as Nimitz put it. For example, when U.S. warplanes destroyed the Japanese airfield at Rabaul in eastern New Guinea, 135,000 Japanese troops were left stranded on the island, cut off from resupply by air or sea. What the Allies did to Rabaul set the pattern for the "island-hopping" strategy in the Pacific.

BATTLES IN THE CENTRAL PACIFIC On June 15, 1944, just days after the D-day invasion, U.S. forces liberated Tinian, Guam, and Saipan, three Japanese-controlled islands. Saipan was strategically important because it allowed the new American B-29 "Superfortress" bombers to strike Japan itself. The struggle for the island lasted three weeks. Some 20,000 Japanese were killed compared to 3,500 Americans. But 7,000 more Japanese soldiers committed suicide upon the order of their commanding general, who killed himself with his sword.

General MacArthur's forces invaded the Japanese-held Philippines on October 20. The Japanese, knowing that the loss of the Philippines would cut them off from essential raw materials, brought in warships from three directions to battle the U.S. fleet.

The four battles fought in the Philippine Sea from October 23 to October 26, 1944, came to be known collectively as the Battle of Leyte Gulf, the largest naval engagement in history and the worst Japanese defeat of the war. Some 216 U.S. warships converged to engage 64 Japanese ships. By the end of the first day, 36 Japanese warships, including 4 aircraft carriers, had been destroyed.

The Battle of Leyte Gulf included the first Japanese *kamikaze* ("divine wind") attacks, in which young suicide pilots deliberately crashed their bomb-laden planes into American warships. From the fall of 1944 to the war's end in the summer of 1945, an estimated 4,000 kamikaze pilots died on suicide missions. One in seven hit an American ship, thirty-four of which were sunk. "Kamikazes just poured at us, again and again," a sailor remembered. "It scared the shit out of us."

As MacArthur waded ashore with the U.S. troops liberating the Philippines, he reminded reporters of his 1942 pledge—"I shall return"—when

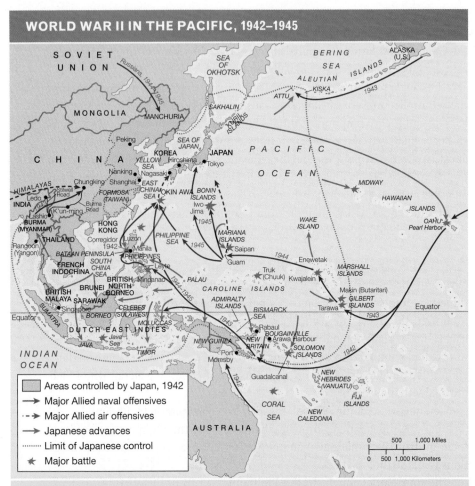

WORLD WAR II IN THE PACIFIC, 1942–1945

Areas controlled by Japan, 1942
→ Major Allied naval offensives
··→ Major Allied air offensives
→ Japanese advances
······ Limit of Japanese control
✳ Major battle

0   500   1,000 Miles
0   500 1,000 Kilometers

- What was MacArthur's "leapfrogging" strategy? Why were the battles in the Marianas a major turning point in the war?
- What was the significance of the Battle of Leyte Gulf?
- How did the battle at Okinawa affect both Japanese and American military strategists thereafter?

he was evacuated from the islands in the face of the Japanese invasion. Now he announced with great fanfare: "People of the Philippines, I have returned! The hour of your redemption is here. . . . Rally to me."

A WAR TO THE DEATH The closer the Allied forces got to Japan, the fiercer the resistance they encountered. While fighting continued in the Philippines, 30,000 U.S. Marines landed on Iwo Jima, a volcanic atoll 760 miles from Tokyo. The Americans thought Iwo Jima was needed as a base for fighter planes to escort bombers over Japan. The Japanese fought with suicidal intensity, and it took nearly six weeks to secure the tiny island at a cost of nearly 7,000 American lives—and 21,000 of the 22,000 Japanese soldiers. In the end, the furious battle was fought for an air base that never materialized.

The assault on the Japanese island of Okinawa, which began on Easter Sunday, April 1, was even bloodier. Only 360 miles from the main Japanese islands, Okinawa was strategically important because it would serve as the staging area for the planned Allied invasion of Japan. The conquest of Okinawa was the largest amphibious operation of the Pacific war, involving some 300,000 troops and requiring almost three months of brutal fighting. More than 150,000 Japanese were killed; the remaining 7,871 were either captured or surrendered. A third of U.S. pilots and a quarter of submariners lost their lives at Okinawa.

As the fighting raged on Okinawa, Allied commanders began planning Operation Downfall—the invasion of Japan itself. To weaken the Japanese defenses, destroy their war-related industries, and erode civilian morale, the Allied command began bombing raids in the summer of 1944. In early 1945, General Curtis Lemay, head of the U.S. Bomber Command, ordered devastating "firebomb" raids upon Japanese cities: "Bomb and burn 'em till they quit."

On March 9, some 300 B-29 bombers dropped napalm bombs on Tokyo. The attack incinerated sixteen square miles of the city and killed some 100,000 people while rendering a million homeless. By then, American military leaders had lost all moral qualms about targeting civilians. The kamikaze attacks, the Japanese savagery toward prisoners of war, the burning of Manila that killed 100,000 civilians, and the "rape" of China had eroded almost all sympathy for the island nation. By August 1945, sixty-six Japanese cities had been firebombed. Secretary of War Henry Stimson called the lack of public outcry in the United States over the raids "appalling."

THE ATOMIC BOMB Still, the Japanese leaders showed no willingness to surrender. In early 1945, new U.S. president Harry S. Truman learned of the first successful test of an atomic bomb in New Mexico. Now that military planners knew the bomb would work, they selected two Japanese cities as targets. The first was **Hiroshima**, a port city and army headquarters in southern Japan. On July 25, 1945, Truman, who knew nothing about the devastating effects of radiation poisoning, ordered that the atomic bomb be used if Japan did not surrender before August 3.

Although an intense debate emerged over the decision to drop the bomb— spurred by Truman's chief of staff, Admiral William D. Leahy, who argued that

Bombing of Nagasaki A 20,000-foot tall mushroom cloud enveloped the city of Nagasaki after the atomic bombing on August 9, 1945.

the "Japanese were already defeated and ready to surrender"—Truman said that he "never had any doubt that it should be used." He later recalled that "we faced half a million casualties trying to take Japan by land. It was either that or the atom bomb, and I didn't hesitate a minute, and I've never lost any sleep over it since."

To Truman and others, the use of atomic bombs seemed a logical next step to end the war. As it turned out, scientists greatly underestimated the physical effects of the bomb. Their prediction that 20,000 people would be killed proved much too low.

In mid-July 1945, the Allied leaders met in Potsdam, Germany, near Berlin. There they issued the Potsdam Declaration. In addition to outlawing Nazism, it demanded that Japan surrender by August 3 or face "prompt and utter destruction." Truman left Potsdam optimistic about postwar relations with the Soviet Union. "I can deal with Stalin," he wrote. "He is honest—but smart as hell." (Truman would soon change his mind about Stalin's honesty.)

The deadline for Japan's surrender passed, and on August 6, 1945, a B-29 bomber named *Enola Gay* (after the pilot's mother) took off at 2:00 A.M. from the island of Tinian and headed for Hiroshima. At 8:15 A.M., flying at 31,600 feet, the *Enola Gay* released the five-ton, ten-foot-long uranium bomb nicknamed "Little Boy."

Forty-three seconds later, the bomb exploded at an altitude of 1,900 feet, creating a blinding flash of light followed by a fireball towering to 40,000 feet. The bomb's incredible shock wave and firestorm killed some 78,000 people, including thousands of Japanese soldiers and 23 American prisoners of war housed in the city. By the end of the year, the death toll would reach 140,000, as people died of injuries or radiation poisoning. In addition, of the city's 76,000 buildings, only 6,000 were left standing, and four square miles of the city were turned to rubble.

Two days after the Hiroshima bombing, an opportunistic Soviet Union, hoping to share in the spoils of victory, hastened to enter the war in the Pacific by sending hundreds of thousands of troops into Japanese-occupied Manchuria along the border between China and the Soviet Union. Truman and his aides, frustrated by the stubborn refusal of Japanese leaders to surrender and fearful that the Soviet Union's entry would complicate negotiations, ordered a second atomic bomb ("Fat Man") to be dropped on Japan. On August 9, the city of Nagasaki, a shipbuilding center, experienced the same nuclear devastation that had destroyed Hiroshima. Five days later, on August 14, 1945, the Japanese emperor accepted the terms of surrender. The formal surrender ceremony occurred on an American warship in Tokyo Bay on September 22, 1945.

A NEW AGE IS BORN

Thus ended the costliest war in history. It was a *total* war in its scope, intensity, and numbers. Including deaths from war-related disease and famine, some 50 million civilians and 22 million combatants died.

The Second World War was more costly for the United States than any other foreign war: 292,000 combat deaths and 114,000 noncombat deaths among soldiers, sailors, airmen, and marines. A million more were wounded, with half of them seriously disabled. In proportion to its population, however, the United States suffered far fewer losses than did the other major Allies or their enemies, and American territory escaped the devastation suffered in so many parts of the world. For every American killed in the Second World War, for example, some fifty-nine Soviets died.

The war was the pivotal event of the turbulent twentieth century. It engulfed five continents, leveled cities, reshaped societies, and transformed international relations. German and Italian fascism as well as Japanese militarism were destroyed. The war set in motion the fall of China to communism in 1949 and the outbreak of the Korean War a year later. Colonial empires in Africa and Asia rapidly crumbled as the conflict unleashed independence movements. The Soviet Union emerged from the war as a new global superpower, while the United States, as Winston Churchill told the House of Commons, stood "at the summit of the world."

WHY DID THE ALLIES WIN? Many factors contributed to the Allied victory. Roosevelt and Churchill were better at coordinating military efforts and maintaining national morale than were Hitler, Mussolini, and the

Japanese emperor, Hirohito. By 1944, Hitler had grown increasingly unstable and unpredictable and more withdrawn from the German people, especially after a failed attempt by high-ranking officers to assassinate him that July.

In the end, however, what turned the tide was the awesome productivity of American industry and the ability of the Soviet Union to absorb the massive German invasion and then push back all the way to Berlin. By the end of the war, Japan had run out of food and Germany had run out of fuel. By contrast, the United States was churning out more of everything. As early as 1942, just a few weeks after the attack on Pearl Harbor, Fritz Todt, a Nazi engineer, told Hitler that the war against the United States was already lost because of America's ability to out-produce all the other warring nations combined.

A TRANSFORMATIONAL WAR Like the First World War, the Second World War had far-reaching effects. It shattered the old world order and created a new international system, and nations such as France, Germany, Great Britain, and Japan were left devastated or impoverished. Henry Luce, the powerful publisher of *Time* magazine, said that the war had demonstrated the "moral and practical bankruptcy of all forms of Isolationism." Internationalism was now the dominant outlook, as most Americans acknowledged that the United States had profound responsibilities for global stability and security. It had emerged from the war with the most powerful military in the world—and as the only nation with atomic weapons.

The expansion of the federal government spurred by the war effort continued after 1945, and presidential authority increased enormously at the expense of congressional and state power. The war also ended the Great Depression and launched a long period of unprecedented prosperity and global economic domination. Big businesses grew into gigantic corporations as a result of huge government contracts for military weapons and supplies. New technologies and products developed for military purposes—radar, computers, electronics, plastics and synthetics, jet engines, rockets, atomic energy—transformed the private sector, as did new consumer products generated from war-related innovations. And the opportunities created by the war for women as well as for African Americans, Mexican Americans, and other minorities set in motion major social changes that would culminate in the civil rights movement of the 1960s and the feminist movement of the 1970s.

In August 1945, President Truman announced that the United States had "emerged from this war the most powerful nation in this world—the most powerful nation, perhaps, in all history." But the Soviet Union, despite its profound human losses and physical destruction, had gained much new territory, built massive armed forces, and enhanced its international influence, making it the greatest power in Eurasia. A little over a century after Frenchman Alexis de Tocqueville had predicted that Europe would eventually be overshadowed by the United States and Russia, his prophecy had come to pass.

CHAPTER REVIEW

SUMMARY

- **Fascism and the Start of the War**   In Italy, Benito Mussolini assumed control by promising law and order. Adolf Hitler rearmed Germany in defiance of the Treaty of Versailles. By March 1939, Nazi Germany had annexed Austria and seized Czechoslovakia. Hitler then invaded Poland with the *blitzkrieg* strategy in September 1939, after signing a nonaggression pact with the Soviet Union. The British and French governments declared war.

- **America Goes to War**   The United States issued *"neutrality laws"* to avoid being drawn into wars in Europe and Asia, but with the fall of France, Roosevelt accelerated military aid to Great Britain through the *Lend-Lease Act*. In the summer of 1941, the United States and Great Britain signed the *Atlantic Charter*, announcing their aims in the war. After Japan joined with Germany and Italy to form the *"Axis" alliance*, President Roosevelt froze Japanese assets in the United States and restricted oil exports to Japan, which frustrated the Japanese, who decided to launch a surprise attack at *Pearl Harbor*, Hawaii.

- **The Second World War and American Society**   The war had profound social effects. Americans—white, black, and brown—migrated west to take jobs in defense industry factories; unemployment was soon a thing of the past. Farmers recovered, supported by Mexican labor through the *bracero program*. The federal government, through agencies such as the *War Production Board*, took control of managing the economy. Many women took nontraditional jobs. About 1 million African Americans served in the military in segregated units. More than 100,000 Japanese Americans were forcibly interned in "*war relocation camps*."

- **Road to Allied Victory in Europe**   By 1943, the Allies had defeated the German and Italian armies occupying North Africa. From there, they launched attacks on Sicily and then the mainland of Italy. Stalin, meanwhile, demanded a full-scale Allied attack on the Atlantic coast of France to ease pressure on the Russian Front, but *Operation Overlord* was delayed until June 6, 1944. German resistance slowly crumbled. The "Big Three" Allied leaders—Roosevelt, Churchill, and Stalin—met at the *Yalta Conference* in February 1945, where they decided that a conquered Germany would be divided into four occupation zones. In May, Soviet forces captured Berlin, and Germany surrendered. After the war, Allied forces discovered the extent of the *Holocaust*—the Nazis' systematic effort to exterminate the Jews.

- **The Pacific War**   The Japanese advance across the Pacific was halted in June 1942 with the *Battle of Midway*. Fierce Japanese resistance at Iwo Jima and Okinawa and Japan's refusal to surrender after the firebombing of Tokyo led the new president, Harry S. Truman, to order the use of atomic bombs on the cities of *Hiroshima* and Nagasaki.

- **Postwar World**   The Soviet Union and the United States emerged from the war as global superpowers, with the United States possessing the world's strongest economy. The opportunities for women and minorities during the war also increased their aspirations and would contribute to the emergence of the civil rights and feminist movements.

CHRONOLOGY

1933	Adolf Hitler becomes chancellor of Germany
1937	War between China and Japan begins
1939	Non-Aggression pact between Germany and the Soviet Union
September 1939	German troops invade Poland
1940	Battle of Britain
June 1941	Germany invades Soviet Union
August 1941	United States and Great Britain sign the Atlantic Charter
December 7, 1941	Japanese launch surprise attack at Pearl Harbor, Hawaii
June 1942	Battle of Midway
January 1943	Roosevelt and Churchill meet at Casablanca
November 1943	Roosevelt and Churchill meet Stalin in Tehran
June 6, 1944	D-day
February 1945	Yalta Conference
April 1945	Roosevelt dies; Hitler commits suicide
May 8, 1945	Nazi Germany surrenders; V-E day
August 1945	Atomic bombs dropped on Hiroshima and Nagasaki
September 2, 1945	Japan surrenders; V-J day

KEY TERMS

fascism p. 949

"neutrality laws" p. 952

"Axis" alliance p. 953

Lend-Lease Act (1945) p. 959

Atlantic Charter (1941) p. 961

Pearl Harbor p. 963

War Production Board p. 965

Women's Army Corps (WAC) p. 967

Tuskegee Airmen p. 970

bracero program p. 971

"war relocation camps" p. 972

Operation Overlord p. 977

Yalta Conference (1945) p. 982

Holocaust p. 984

Battle of Midway p. 986

Hiroshima p. 989

 INQUIZITIVE

Go to InQuizitive to see what you've learned—and learn what you've missed—with personalized feedback along the way.

part seven

THE AMERICAN AGE

The United States emerged from the Second World War as the dominant nation on the planet, the world's preeminent military and economic power, and the only nation to possess atomic weapons. The war changed things in ways no one could have imagined. Some changes came immediately; others emerged more slowly. But their combined effect was truly transformational.

While much of Europe and Asia struggled to recover from the devastation of the war, the United States was virtually unscathed, its economic infrastructure intact and operating at peak efficiency. Jobs that had been scarce in the 1930s were now available for the taking. By 1955 the United States, with only 6 percent of the world's population, was producing half of the world's goods. American capitalism became a dominant cultural force as U.S. products, fashion, and forms of entertainment attracted international attention.

In 1941, Henry Luce, the publisher of *Time* and *Life* magazines, proclaimed that the twentieth century had become the "American century." The ideal of America, he explained, included "a love of freedom, a feeling for the equality of opportunity, a tradition of self-reliance and independence." America seemed free and unshackled, its potential unlimited.

The deepening cold war between democratic and Communist nations cast a cloud of anxiety and fear over postwar life. The tense ideological contest with the Soviet Union produced numerous crises and sparked a witch hunt for Communists in the United States. After 1945, Republican and Democratic presidents aggressively sought to "contain" the spread of communism. This bedrock assumption embroiled the United States in costly wars in Korea and in Southeast Asia.

A backlash against the Vietnam War (1964–1973) also inflamed a rebellious "countercultural" movement at home in which young idealists not only opposed the war but also provided much of the energy for many overdue social reforms, including racial equality, gay rights, feminism, and environmentalism. The anti-war movement destroyed Lyndon Johnson's presidency in 1968 and provoked a conservative counterattack. President Richard Nixon's paranoid reaction to his critics led to the Watergate affair and the destruction of his presidency.

Through all of this turmoil, however, the expanding role of the federal government that Franklin Roosevelt and his New Deal programs had initiated remained essentially intact. With only a few exceptions, both Republicans and Democrats after 1945 acknowledged that the federal government must assume greater responsibility for the welfare of individuals. This fragile consensus, however, had largely broken down by the late 1980s amid stunning international developments and social changes at home. The surprising collapse of the Soviet Union in 1989 and the disintegration of European communism left the United States as the only superpower.

The end of the cold war and the dissolution of the Soviet Union lowered the threat of nuclear war and reduced public interest in foreign affairs. Yet numerous ethnic, nationalist, and separatist conflicts brought constant international instability. The United States found itself drawn into political and military crises in faraway lands such as Bosnia, Somalia, Afghanistan, Iraq, Ukraine, and Syria.

Throughout the 1990s, the United States waged a difficult struggle against many groups engaged in organized terrorism. The challenges of tracking the movements of foreign terrorists became tragically evident in 2001. At 8:46 on the morning of September 11, 2001, the world watched in horror as hijacked commercial airplanes slammed into the World Trade Center in New York City. Seventeen minutes later, a second hijacked plane hit the South Tower.

Officials identified the hijackers as members of al Qaeda (Arabic for "The Base"), a well-financed network of Islamic terrorists led by a wealthy Saudi renegade, Osama bin Laden. President George W. Bush responded by declaring a "war on terror." With the passage of the so-called Patriot Act, Congress gave the president authority to track down and imprison terrorists at home and abroad. The "war on terror" began with assaults first on terrorist bases in Afghanistan and then on Saddam Hussein's dictatorship in Iraq ("Operation Iraqi Freedom"). Yet terrorism proved to be an elusive and resilient foe, and the war in Iraq and the ensuing U.S. military occupation was much longer, more expensive, and less successful than Americans had expected.

The surprising victory of Barack Obama in the 2008 presidential election resulted from people embracing his theme of "hope and change." He pledged to end the wars in Iraq and Afghanistan, unite the nation, and provide jobs to the growing numbers of unemployed. As the first African American president, Obama symbolized the societal changes transforming national life.

Yet no sooner was Obama inaugurated than he inherited the worst economic slowdown since the Great Depression. What came to be called the Great Recession dominated the Obama presidency and, indeed, much of American life, bringing with it a prolonged sense of uncertainty and insecurity. For all of its economic power and military might, the United States in the twenty-first century has not eliminated the threat of terrorism or unlocked the mystery of sustaining prosperity and reducing economic inequality.

27 The Cold War and the Fair Deal

1945–1952

Duck and cover A "duck-and-cover" air-raid drill in 1951 that was commonplace in schools across the country during the cold war. The drills began in 1949, when the Soviet Union set off its first nuclear weapon. Pictured above are American schoolchildren practicing ducking and covering in February 1951.

No sooner did the Second World War end than a prolonged "cold war" between communism and capitalism began. The awkward wartime alliance between the United States and the Soviet Union collapsed during the spring and summer of 1945. With the elimination of their common enemy, Nazism, the two nations became intense global rivals who could not bridge their ideological differences over basic issues such as human rights, individual liberties, democratic elections, and religious freedom.

Mutual suspicion and a race to gain influence over "nonaligned" nations in Asia, Africa, the Middle East, and Central and South America further distanced the two former allies. The defeat of Japan and Germany had created power vacuums in Europe and Asia that sucked the Soviet Union and the United States into an unrelenting war of words fed by clashing strategic interests and political ideologies.

The postwar era also brought an eruption of anti-colonial liberation movements in Asia, Africa, and the Middle East that would soon strip Great Britain, France, the Netherlands, and the United States of their global empires. The Philippines, for example, gained its independence from America in 1946. The next year, Great Britain withdrew from Hindu-dominated India after carving out two new Islamic nations, Pakistan and Bangladesh (originally called East Pakistan). The emergence of Communist China (the People's Republic) in 1949 further complicated global politics and cold war tensions. The advent of atomic weapons made the very idea of warfare unthinkably horrific, which in turn made national leaders more cautious in handling disputes.

focus questions

1. Why and how did the cold war between the United States and the Soviet Union develop after the Second World War?

2. What was the impact of American efforts to contain the Soviet Union and the expansion of communism during Truman's presidency?

3. How did Truman expand the New Deal? How effective was his own "Fair Deal" agenda?

4. What were the major international developments during 1949–1950, and how did they alter U.S. foreign policy?

5. How did the Red Scare emerge after the Second World War? How did it impact American politics and society?

TRUMAN AND THE COLD WAR

In April 1945, less than three months after Harry S. Truman had begun his new role as vice president, Eleanor Roosevelt calmly informed him, "Harry, the President is dead." When Truman asked what he could do to help her, the First Lady replied: "Is there anything we can do for *you*? For you are the one in trouble now."

Truman was largely unknown outside of Washington. What everyone did know, however, was that he was not Franklin Delano Roosevelt. Truman had no wealthy family, had not traveled the world, and had not attended Harvard or Columbia. In fact, he had not gone to college.

Truman was a plain, decent, lovable man who lacked Roosevelt's dash, charm, brilliance, and creativity. On his first full day as president, Truman was awestruck. "Boys, if you ever pray, pray for me now," he told reporters. "I don't know whether you fellows ever had a load of hay fall on you, but when they told me yesterday what had happened, I felt like the moon, the stars and all the planets had fallen on me."

The plain-speaking man from Missouri resembled his hero Andrew Jackson in his decisiveness, bluntness, folksy manner, salty language, and raw courage. Despite his lack of executive experience, Truman was confident and self-assured—and he needed to be. Managing the transition from war to peace both at home and abroad was a monumental task. He was expected to lead America into a postwar era complicated by the cold war and the need to rebuild Europe and Asia.

He ended up doing better than anyone expected. Truman rose above his limitations to do extraordinary things. He never pretended to be something he was not; as he admitted, he was "an ordinary human being who has been lucky." During a visit in 1952, British leader Winston Churchill confessed to Truman that initially he had held him "in very low regard. I loathed your taking the place of Franklin Roosevelt. I misjudged you badly. Since that time, you, more than any other man, have saved Western civilization."

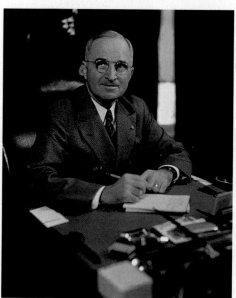

Harry S. Truman The successor to Franklin Roosevelt who led the United States out of the Second World War and into the Cold War.

ORIGINS OF THE COLD WAR Historians have long debated the unanswerable question: Was the United States or the Soviet Union more responsible for the onset of the cold war? The conventional view argues that the Soviets, led by Josef Stalin, a ruthless Communist dictator, set out to dominate the globe after 1945. The United States had no choice but to defend democratic capitalist values. By contrast, "revisionist" historians insist that instead of continuing Roosevelt's efforts to collaborate with the Soviets, President Truman pursued a confrontational foreign policy that aggravated tensions. Yet such an interpretation fails to recognize that Truman inherited a deteriorating relationship with the Soviets. Both sides in the postwar world were captives of a nuclear nightmare of fear, suspicion, and posturing.

In retrospect, the onset of the cold war seems to have been inevitable. America's commitment to capitalism, political self-determination, and religious freedom conflicted dramatically with the Soviet Union's preference for controlling its neighbors, enforcing ideological conformity, and prohibiting religious practices. Insecurity, as much as Communist ideology, drove much of Soviet behavior after the Second World War. Russia, after all, had been invaded by Germany twice in the first half of the twentieth century, and some 23 million people died as a result. Soviet leaders were determined to create loyal nations on their borders for protection. The people of Eastern Europe were caught in the middle.

CONFLICTS WITH THE SOVIETS The wartime military alliance against Nazism disintegrated after 1945 as the Soviet Union violated the promises it had made at the Yalta Conference and imposed military control and the Communist political system on the nations of Eastern Europe it had liberated. On May 12, 1945, four days after victory in Europe, Winston Churchill asked Truman: "What is to happen about Europe? An **iron curtain** is drawn down upon [the Russian] front. We do not know what is going on behind [it]." Churchill and Truman wanted to lift the "iron curtain" and help those nations develop democratic governments. But events during the second half of 1945 dashed those expectations.

As early as the spring of 1945 and continuing for the next two years, the Soviet Union systematically imprisoned half of the European continent. The Soviets systematically installed "puppet" governments across central and Eastern Europe (Albania, Bulgaria, Czechoslovakia, East Germany, Hungary, Poland, Romania, and Yugoslavia). In their ruthless pursuit of total control, the Soviets eliminated all political parties except the Communists, created secret police forces, took control of intellectual and cultural life (including the mass media), undermined the Roman Catholic Church, and organized a process of ethnic cleansing whereby whole populations—12 million Germans, as well as Poles and Hungarians—were relocated from their homes in Eastern Europe, usually to West Germany or to prisons. Anyone who opposed the Soviet-installed regimes was exiled, silenced, executed, or imprisoned.

Stalin's promises at the Yalta Conference to allow open elections in the nations of Eastern Europe controlled by Soviet armies had turned out to be lies. In a fit of candor, he admitted that "a freely elected government in any of these countries would be anti-Soviet, and that we cannot allow."

U.S. secretary of state James F. Byrnes tried to use America's monopoly on atomic bombs to pressure the Soviets to abide by the Yalta accords. In April 1945, he suggested to President Truman that nuclear weapons "might well put us in position to dictate our own terms [with the Soviets] at the end of the war." The Soviets, however, paid little attention, in part because their spies had kept them informed of what American scientists had been doing and in part because they were developing their own atomic bombs.

A few days before the opening of the conference to organize the United Nations in April, Truman met with Soviet foreign minister Vyacheslav Molotov. The Soviets had just put in place a pro-Communist government in Poland in violation of Stalin's pledge at Yalta to allow free elections. Truman directed Molotov to tell Stalin that the United States expected the Soviet leader to live up to his agreements. "I have never been talked to like that in my life," Molotov angrily replied. "Carry out your agreements," Truman snapped, "and you won't get talked to like that."

Later, in July 1945, when Truman met Stalin at the Potsdam Conference, he wrote his mother that he had never seen "such pig-headed people as are the Russians." He later acknowledged that the Soviets broke their promises "as soon as the unconscionable Russian Dictator [Stalin] returned to Moscow!" Truman added, with a note of embarrassment, "And I liked the little son of a bitch."

THE CONTAINMENT POLICY

By the beginning of 1947, relations with the Soviet Union had grown ice cold. A year before, in February 1946, Stalin had proclaimed the superiority of the Communist system and declared that peace was impossible "under the present capitalist development of the world economy." His provocative statement led the State Department to ask for an analysis of Soviet communism from George Frost Kennan, the best-informed expert on the Soviet Union, then working in the U.S. embassy in Moscow.

Kennan responded on February 22, 1946, with a famous 5,000-word "Long Telegram"—the longest in the history of the State Department. He explained that the Soviet Union was founded on a rigid ideology (Marxism-Leninism), which saw a fundamental global conflict between Communist and capitalist nations and helped Soviet rulers justify their amoral actions. They could not imagine "permanent peaceful coexistence" with capitalist nations and were "fanatically" committed to the necessity of perpetual tension and conflict. In this regard, Kennan implied, Franklin Roosevelt had mistakenly assumed that his personal diplomacy with Stalin would ensure that the Soviets behaved. Kennan insisted instead that Stalin needed external enemies to maintain his totalitarian power at home.

The best way for the United States to deal with such an ideological foe, Kennan advised, was through patient, persistent, and firm "strategic" efforts to "contain" Soviet expansionism, without resorting to war. The economic power of capitalist democracies was their greatest asset. Creating "unalterable counterforce" to Communist expansionism, Kennan predicted, would eventually cause "either the breakup or the gradual mellowing of Soviet power" because communism, in Kennan's view, was an inherently unstable system that would eventually collapse. No other American diplomat at the time forecast so accurately what would happen to the Soviet Union some forty years later.

Kennan later acknowledged that his "Long Telegram" suffered from excessive optimism and occasional vagueness. In its broadest dimensions, its call for "firm and vigilant **containment**" echoed the outlook of Truman and his advisers and would guide U.S. foreign policy for decades.

In 1946, civil war broke out in Greece between an authoritarian monarchy backed by the British and a Communist-led insurgency supported by the Soviets. On February 21, 1947, the financially strapped British informed the U.S. government that they could no longer provide economic and military aid to Greece and would withdraw in five weeks. Truman quickly conferred with congressional leaders, one of whom, Republican senator Arthur Vandenburg of Michigan, warned the president that he would need to "scare the hell out of the American people" about the menace of communism to gain public support for his aid program. Truman was eager to do so, for he had grown tired of "babying the Russians."

THE TRUMAN DOCTRINE On March 12, 1947, President Truman gave a national radio speech in which he asked Congress for $400 million for economic and military assistance for Greece and Turkey. More important, the president announced what came to be known as the **Truman Doctrine**. To ensure congressional support, he intentionally exaggerated the danger of a

Communist takeover in Greece. Like a row of dominoes, Truman predicted, the fall of Greece would topple the other nations of the eastern Mediterranean, then Western Europe. To prevent such a catastrophe, he said, the United States must "support free peoples who are resisting attempted subjugation by armed minorities or by outside pressures."

In this single sentence, the president established the foundation of U.S. foreign policy for the next forty years. In essence, he was declaring war on communism everywhere. In Truman's view, shared by later presidents, the assumptions of the "domino theory" made an aggressive "containment" strategy against communism a necessity.

Truman's speech generated widespread public support. The *New York Times* said that his message was clear: "The epoch of isolation is ended. It is being replaced by an epoch of American responsibility." At the State Department, Secretary of State Marshall announced that "we are now concerned with the peace of the entire world."

George Kennan cringed at the president's "grandiose" commitment to "contain" communism *everywhere*. In his view, Truman's "militarized view of the Cold War" was a foolish *crusade*, an open-ended ideological confrontation without limits rather than a *policy* with an accompanying program of steps capable of implementation. Efforts to "contain" communism needed to be selective rather than universal, political and economic rather than military; the United States could not intervene in every "hot spot" around the world. Walter Lippmann, the nation's leading political journalist, characterized Truman's policy of global anti-communism as a "strategic monstrosity" that would entangle the United States in endless international disputes and force it to partner with right-wing dictatorships—as turned out to be the case. Truman and his advisers rejected such concerns. In 1947, Congress approved the president's request for economic and military assistance to Greece and neighboring Turkey.

THE MARSHALL PLAN In the spring of 1947, most of postwar Europe remained broke, shattered, and desperate. Factories had been bombed to rubble; railroads and bridges had been destroyed; millions were homeless, starving, and jobless; and political unrest was growing. By 1947, Socialist and Communist parties were emerging in many European nations, including Italy, France, and Belgium. The crises among the struggling European democracies required bold action.

The United States stepped into the breach. In May 1947, Secretary of State George C. Marshall delivered a speech at Harvard University in which he outlined America's policy toward Europe in nonideological terms. Building upon suggestions given him by George Kennan and others, he called for massive financial and technical assistance to rescue Europe, including the Soviet Union.

What came to be known as the **Marshall Plan** was intended to reconstruct the European economy, neutralize Communist insurgencies, and build up foreign markets for American products. As Truman said, "the American [capitalist] system can survive only if it is part of a world system." But the Marshall Plan was also part of Truman's effort to contain the expansionist tendencies of the Soviet Union by reestablishing a strong Western Europe anchored in American values. The Americans, said a British official, "want an integrated Europe looking like the United States of America."

In December 1947, Truman submitted Marshall's proposal to Congress. Initially, Republican critics dismissed it as "New Dealism" for Europe. However, two months later, on February 25, 1948, a Communist-led coup in Czechoslovakia, the last nation in Eastern Europe with a democratic government, ensured the Marshall Plan's passage.

From 1948 until 1951, the Marshall Plan provided $13 billion to sixteen European nations. The Soviet Union,

"It's the same thing" The Marshall Plan, which distributed massive amounts of economic aid throughout postwar Europe, is represented in this 1949 cartoon as a modern tractor driven by a prosperous farmer. In the foreground a poor, overworked man is yoked to an old-fashioned "Soviet" plow, forced to go over the ground of the "Marshal Stalin Plan," while Stalin himself tries to persuade others that "it's the same thing without mechanical problems."

however, refused to participate and forced the Eastern European countries under its control—Albania, Bulgaria, Poland, Romania, Yugoslavia—to refuse to participate as well.

The Marshall Plan (officially called the European Recovery Plan) worked as hoped. By 1951, Western Europe's industrial production had soared to 40 percent above prewar levels, and its farm output was larger than ever. England's *Economist* magazine called the Marshall Plan "an act without peer in history." It became the most successful peacetime diplomatic initiative in American history.

DIVIDED GERMANY Although the Marshall Plan drew the nations of Western Europe closer together, it increased tensions with the Soviet Union, as Stalin saw it as a way to weaken Soviet influence in the region. The breakdown of the wartime alliance between the United States and the Soviet Union also left the problem of postwar Germany unsettled. In 1945, Berlin, the German capital, had been divided into four sectors, or zones, each governed by one of the four principal allied nations—the United States, France, Great Britain, and the Soviet Union.

The devastated German economy continued to languish, requiring the U.S. Army to provide food and basic necessities to millions of civilians. Slowly, the Allied occupation zones evolved into functioning governments. In 1948, the British, French, and Americans united their three administrative zones into one and developed a common currency to be used in West Germany as well as in West Berlin, a city of 2.4 million people, which was more than 100 miles inside the Soviet occupation zone of East Germany.

The political unification of West Germany and its economic recovery infuriated Stalin, who was determined to keep Germany weak. And the status of divided Berlin had become a powder keg. On June 23, 1948, Stalin ordered the Soviet army occupying eastern Germany to stop all road and rail traffic into West Berlin. The blockade, he hoped, would force the United States and its allies to leave the divided city.

The Americans interpreted Stalin's blockade as a tipping point in the cold war. "When Berlin falls," predicted General Lucius D. Clay, the U.S. Army commander in Germany, "western Germany will be next. Communism will run rampant." The United States thus faced a dilemma: risk a third world war by using force to break the Soviet blockade or begin a humiliating retreat from West Berlin, leaving the residents to be swallowed up by communism.

Truman, who prided himself on his decisiveness ("the buck stops here"), made clear his stance: "We stay in Berlin—period." The United States announced an embargo against all goods exported from Soviet-controlled eastern Germany and began organizing a massive airlift to provide food and supplies to West Berliners.

By October 1948, the U.S. and British air forces were flying in 7,000 tons of food, fuel, medicine, coal, and equipment to West Berlin each day. To support the airlift and prepare for a possible war, thousands of former military pilots were called back into service. Truman revived the military draft, and Congress provided emergency funds to increase military spending.

At times it seemed that the two superpowers were on the verge of war. For all the threats and harsh words, however, the **Berlin airlift** went on for eleven months without any shots being fired. Finally, on May 12, 1949, the Soviets lifted their blockade, in part because bad Russian harvests had made them desperate for food grown in western Germany.

Through the iron curtain German children greet a U.S. cargo plane as it flies into West Berlin to drop off much-needed food and supplies.

The Berlin airlift was the first major "victory" for the West in the cold war, and the unprecedented efforts of the United States and Great Britain to supply West Berliners transformed most of them from defeated adversaries into devoted allies. In May 1949, as the Soviet blockade was ending, the Federal Republic of Germany (West Germany) was founded. In October, the Soviet-controlled German Democratic Republic (East Germany) came into being.

FORMING ALLIANCES The Soviet blockade of Berlin convinced the United States and its allies that they needed to act together to stop further Communist expansion into Western Europe. On April 4, 1949, the North Atlantic Treaty was signed by twelve nations: the United States, Great Britain, France, Belgium, the Netherlands, Luxembourg, Canada, Denmark, Iceland, Italy, Norway, and Portugal. Greece and Turkey joined the alliance in 1952, West Germany in 1955, and Spain in 1982.

The **North Atlantic Treaty Organization (NATO)** declared that an attack against any one of the members would be considered an attack against all. The creation of NATO marked the high point of efforts to "contain" Soviet expansion. In 1949, Congress provided $1 billion in military equipment to NATO members. By joining NATO, the United States—for the first time since its alliance with France during the Revolutionary War—committed itself to go to war on behalf of its allies. Isolationism was dead.

REORGANIZING THE MILITARY The onset of the cold war and the emergence of nuclear weapons led Truman to restructure the way the U.S. armed forces were managed. In 1947, Congress passed the **National Security Act**, which created a Department of Defense to oversee the three military branches—the Army, Navy, and Air Force—and the National Security Council (NSC), an advisory group of the government's top specialists in international relations. The act also established the Central Intelligence Agency (CIA) to coordinate global intelligence-gathering activities.

A JEWISH NATION: ISRAEL At the same time that the United States was helping to form new alliances, it was helping to form a new nation. Palestine, the biblical Holy Land, had been a British protectorate since 1919. For hundreds of years, Jews throughout the world had dreamed of returning to their ancestral homeland of Israel and its ancient capital Zion, a part of Jerusalem. Many Zionists—Jews who wanted a separate Jewish nation—had migrated there. More arrived during and after the Nazi persecution of European Jews. Hitler's effort to exterminate the Jews convinced many that their only hope for a secure future was to create their own nation.

Late in 1947, the United Nations voted to divide ("partition") Palestine into separate Jewish and Arab states. The Jews readily agreed, but the Arabs were fiercely opposed. Palestine was their ancestral home, too; Jerusalem was as holy to Muslims as it was to Jews and Christians. Arabs viewed the creation of a Jewish nation in Palestine as an act of war, and they attacked Israel in early 1948. Hundreds were killed before the Haganah (Jewish militia) won control of most of Palestine. When British oversight of Palestine officially expired on May 14, 1948, David Ben-Gurion, the Jewish leader in Palestine, proclaimed Israel's independence. President Truman officially recognized the new Israeli nation within minutes, as did the Soviet Union.

One million Jews, most of them European immigrants, now had their own nation. Early the next morning, however, the Arab League nations—Lebanon, Syria, Iraq, Jordan, and Egypt—invaded Israel, beginning a period of nearly constant warfare in the Holy Land. Mediators from the UN gradually worked out a truce agreement, restoring an uneasy peace by May 11, 1949, when Israel joined the United Nations. Israel got to keep all its conquered territories, including the whole Palestine coast.

The Palestinian Arabs lost everything. Most of them became stateless refugees who scattered into neighboring Lebanon, Jordan, and Egypt. Stored-up resentments and sporadic warfare between Israel and the Arab states have festered ever since, complicating U.S. foreign policy, which has tried to maintain friendships with both sides but has usually tilted toward Israel.

THE OCCUPATION OF GERMANY AND AUSTRIA

DENMARK

SWEDEN

NORTH
SEA

BALTIC SEA

USSR

To
USSR

EAST
PRUSSIA

To Poland

Danzig
(Gdańsk)

Hamburg

Access
corridor

Annexed
by Poland

NETHERLANDS

Bremen

WEST
GERMANY

Berlin

Joint occupation
by four powers

EAST
GERMANY

Warsaw

POLAND

BELGIUM   Bonn

Lublin

Frankfurt

Iron Curtain

SAAR

LUXEMBOURG

FRANCE

Danube River

CZECHOSLOVAKIA

Munich

Vienna

SWITZERLAND

AUSTRIA

HUNGARY

ITALY

ROMANIA

	French zone		U.S. zone
	British zone		Soviet zone

0   50   100 Miles

0   50 100 Kilometers

YUGOSLAVIA

- How did the Allies decide to divide postwar Germany at the Yalta Conference?
- What was the "iron curtain"?
- Why did the Allies airlift supplies to West Berlin?

EXPANDING THE NEW DEAL

For the most part, Republicans and Democrats in Congress cooperated with President Truman on issues related to the cold war, though often grudgingly. Senator Claude Pepper, a liberal Democrat from Florida, insisted that if Franklin Roosevelt were still alive, "we'd be getting on better with Russia." Republican Senator Robert A. Taft of Ohio accused Truman of "appeasing Russia, a policy which has sacrificed throughout Eastern Europe and Asia the freedom of many nations and millions of people." On domestic issues, however, Truman faced widespread opposition. The cost-cutting Republicans in Congress hoped that they could end the New Deal as the war drew to a close.

FROM WAR TO PEACE In September 1945, Truman called Congress into a special emergency session at which he presented a twenty-one-point program to guide the nation's "reconversion" from wartime back to peacetime. Massive government spending during the war had ended the Great Depression and brought about full employment, but Truman's postwar challenge was to ensure that the peacetime economy absorbed the millions of men and women who had served in the armed forces and were now seeking civilian jobs. During the second half of 1945 and throughout 1946, some 700,000 people in uniform, mostly men, returned to civilian life. By 1947, the armed forces had shrunk from 12 million to 1.5 million.

Fears of massive unemployment in defense-related industries led people to worry about another depression. A *New York Times* headline predicted: "5,000,000 EXPECTED TO LOSE ARMS JOBS!" Truman called for unemployment insurance to cover more workers, a higher minimum wage, construction of massive low-cost public housing projects, regional development projects to put military veterans to work, and much more.

Truman's primary goal was to "prevent prolonged unemployment" while avoiding the "bitter mistakes" that had produced wild price inflation and a recession after the First World War. He also wanted to retain, for a while, the wartime controls on wages, prices, and rents, as well as the rationing of scarce

Drugstore in Bronxville, NY America quickly demobilized after the long war effort, turning its attention to the pursuit of abundance.

food items. Most of all, he wanted to minimize unemployment as workers in defense plants were laid off and millions of military veterans went looking for civilian jobs. Truman called on Congress to *guarantee* every American a job.

Congress refused to go that far. Instead, it approved the Employment Act of 1946, which authorized Truman and the federal government "to promote maximum employment, production, and purchasing power." Liberals were disappointed by the new president's inability to win over legislators. "Alas for Truman," said the *New Repub-*

lic, there was "no bugle note in his voice" to rally public opinion. "What one misses," said Max Lerner, an influential journalist, "is the confident sense of direction that Roosevelt gave, despite all the contradictions of his policy."

Throughout 1946, Republicans and conservative southern Democrats in Congress balked at most of Truman's efforts to revive or expand New Deal programs. The Great Depression was over, critics stressed. Different times demanded different programs—or none at all.

The end of the war caused short-term economic problems but not the postwar depression many had feared. Many women who had been recruited to work in defense industries were shoved out as men took off uniforms and looked for jobs. At a shipyard in California, the foreman gathered the women workers and told them to go welcome the troop ships as they pulled into port. The next day, all of the women were fired to make room for male veterans.

Still, several shock absorbers cushioned the economic impact of demobilization. They included federal unemployment insurance (and other Social Security benefits) and the Servicemen's Readjustment Act of 1944, known as the GI Bill of Rights, under which the federal government spent $13 billion on military veterans for education, vocational training, medical treatment, unemployment insurance, and loans for building houses and starting new businesses.

WAGES, PRICES, AND LABOR UNREST   The most acute economic problem Truman faced was the postwar spike in prices charged for consumer goods. During the war, the government had frozen wages and prices and banned strikes by labor unions. When wartime economic controls were removed, prices for scarce consumer items shot up, spurring labor unions to demand pay increases for their members. When raises were not provided, a record number of postwar strikes erupted in 1945–1946. Workers at General Motors went on strike for almost four months, making it much more difficult for people to buy a car. Never before or since had so many American workers walked off the job in one year.

Labor disputes crippled the crucial coal and railroad industries. Like Theodore Roosevelt before him, Truman grew frustrated with the stubbornness of both management and labor leaders. He took federal control of the coal mines, whereupon the mine owners agreed to union demands. In May 1946, Truman threatened to draft striking railroad workers into the military if they did not go back to work. His threat, probably illegal, did the trick, but it embittered many workers who had long voted Democratic. A leading union official announced that organized labor "is through with Truman."

Truman's efforts to control rising prices were equally controversial. On June 30, 1946, he lifted wartime controls on consumer prices. Within days, prices for groceries skyrocketed, rising in two weeks as much as they had risen in the previous three years. So Truman restored price controls. Ranchers were so upset by the president's change of course that they refused to sell their cattle for slaughter. Suddenly, there was a "beefsteak" crisis as consumers complained that the supply of food was worse than it had been during the war. *Time* magazine's Washington-based political reporter alerted his editor that Truman was so unpopular "he could not carry Missouri now."

On October 14, just three weeks before the midterm congressional elections, Truman announced that he was removing price controls on meat. Steaks and hamburger meat soon appeared on grocery shelves, but prices again soared. A Republican political strategist loved the turn of events, telling his colleagues that "the tide is sweepin' our way." And it was.

POLITICAL COOPERATION AND CONFLICT During the congressional election campaigns in 1946, Republicans adopted a simple, four-word slogan: "Had Enough? Vote Republican!" Using loudspeakers, Republicans drove through city streets saying, "Ladies, if you want meat, vote Republican." A union leader tagged Truman "the No. 1 Strikebreaker," while much of the public, upset by the unions, price increases, food shortages, and the scarcity of automobiles and affordable housing, blamed the strikes on the White House.

Labor unions had emerged from the war with more power than ever before. Some 14.5 million workers, more than a third of the workforce, were now unionized. Members had tended to vote Democratic, but not in the 1946 elections, which gave Republicans majorities in both houses of Congress for the first time since 1928. "The New Deal is kaput," one newspaper editor crowed. The *Chicago Tribune* claimed that Americans had "won the greatest victory for the Republic since Appomattox." The president, taunted the *United States News*, "is a one-termer." Even many Democrats had soured on Truman, circulating a slogan that expressed their frustration: "I'm just Mild about Harry."

The new Republican Congress that convened in early 1947 reflected the national discontent. It curbed the power of unions by passing the **Taft-Hartley Labor Act** of 1947 (officially called the Labor-Management Relations Act). The law allowed employers to campaign against efforts to form unions and outlawed unions from coercing workers to join or refusing to negotiate grievances.

The Taft-Hartley Act also required union leaders to take "loyalty oaths" declaring that they were not members of the Communist party, banned strikes by federal employees, and imposed a "cooling-off" period of eighty days on any strike that the president deemed dangerous to the public welfare. The most troubling element of the bill was a provision that allowed state legislatures to pass "right-to-work" laws which ended the practice of forcing all wage workers at a company to join a union once a majority voted to unionize.

In a show of support for organized labor, Truman vetoed the Taft-Hartley bill, which unions called "the slave-labor act." He denounced the "shocking" bill as "bad for labor, bad for management, and bad for the country." Working-class Democrats were delighted. Many unionists who had gone over to the Republicans in 1946 returned to the Democrats because of Truman's strong support.

Congress, however, overturned the president's veto, and Taft-Hartley became law. The number of strikes dropped sharply thereafter, and representatives of management and labor learned to work together. At the same time, by 1954, fifteen state legislatures, mainly in the South and West, had used the Taft-Hartley Act to pass "right-to-work" laws forbidding union-only workplaces. Those states thereafter recruited industries to relocate because of their low wages and "nonunion" policies.

CIVIL RIGHTS Another of Truman's challenges was the bigotry faced by returning African American soldiers. When one highly decorated black veteran arrived home, he was welcomed by a white neighbor who said: "Don't you forget . . . that you're still a nigger."

The Second World War had changed America's racial landscape in important ways, however. As a *New York Times* editorial explained in early 1946, "This is a particularly good time to campaign against the evils of bigotry, prejudice, and race hatred because we have witnessed the defeat of enemies who tried to found a mastery of the world upon such cruel and fallacious policy."

African Americans had fought in large numbers to overthrow the Nazi regime of government-sponsored racism, and returning veterans were unwilling to put up with racial abuse at home. The cold war also gave political leaders added incentive to improve race relations. The Soviets often compared racism in the United States to the Nazis' brutalization of the Jews. In the ideological contest against capitalism, Communists highlighted examples of American racism to win influence among the newly emerging nations of Africa.

In the fall of 1946, a delegation of civil rights activists urged President Truman to condemn the Ku Klux Klan and the lynching of African Americans. They graphically described incidents of torture and intimidation against blacks in the South. Truman responded by appointing a Commission on Civil Rights to investigate violence against African Americans. A year later, with Truman's endorsement, the Commission issued *To Secure These Rights*, which called for a federal anti-lynching bill, abolition of the poll tax designed to keep poor blacks from voting, a voting rights act, an end to racial segregation in the armed forces, and a ban on racial segregation in public transportation. Southern Democrats were furious at Truman's civil rights liberalism.

On July 26, 1948, Truman banned racial discrimination in the federal government. Four days later, he issued an executive order ending racial segregation in the armed forces. The air force and navy quickly complied, but the army dragged its feet until the early 1950s. By 1960, however, the armed forces were the most racially integrated of all national organizations. Desegregating the military was, Truman claimed, "the greatest thing that ever happened to America."

JACKIE ROBINSON   Meanwhile, racial segregation was being dismantled in a much more public area: professional baseball. In April 1947, the Brooklyn Dodgers roster included the first African American to play major league baseball: Jackie Robinson. He was selected in part because of his abilities and in part because of his personality; he was a strong, quiet warrior of incomparable courage who was capable of not fighting back when provoked. And he was often provoked.

Jackie Robinson Robinson's unfaltering courage and superior athletic skill prompted the integration of sports, drawing African American and Latino spectators to the games. Here, he greets his Dominican fans at Trujillo High School in Santo Domingo.

During the 1947 season, teammates and opposing players viciously baited Robinson. Pitchers threw at him, base runners spiked him, and spectators booed him, even as he led the Dodgers to the National League championship. Hotels refused him rooms, and restaurants denied him service. Hate mail arrived by the bucketful. One sportswriter called Robinson "the loneliest man I have ever seen in sports."

On the other hand, black spectators were electrified by Robinson's courageous example and turned out in droves to watch him play. As time passed, Robinson won over many fans and players with his courage, wit, and talent. Other teams soon began signing black players. Racial attitudes were changing—slowly.

MEXICAN AMERICANS   In the Far West, Mexican Americans (often grouped with other Spanish-speaking immigrants as *Hispanics* or *Latinos*) continued to experience ethnic prejudice. Schools in Arizona, New Mexico, Texas, and California routinely segregated Mexican American children from whites. The 500,000 Latino veterans were especially frustrated that their efforts in the war were not rewarded with equality at home. They were frequently denied access to educational, medical, and housing benefits available to white servicemen. Some mortuaries even denied funeral services to Mexican Americans killed in combat. As a funeral director in Texas explained, "the Anglo people would not stand for it."

To fight such prejudicial treatment, Mexican American war veterans led by Dr. Hector Perez Garcia, a U.S. Army major who had served as a combat surgeon, organized the American GI Forum in Texas in 1948. Soon there were branches across the nation. Garcia, born in Mexico in 1914 and raised in Texas, stressed the importance of formal education to Mexican Americans. The organization's motto read: "Education Is Our Freedom and Freedom Should Be Everybody's Business."

At a time when Mexican Americans in Texas averaged no more than a third-grade education, Garcia and five of his siblings had completed medical school and become physicians. Yet upon his return from the war, he encountered "discrimination everywhere. We had no opportunities. We had to pay [poll taxes] to vote. We had segregated schools. We were not allowed to go into public places."

Garcia and the GI Forum initially focused on veterans' issues but soon expanded the organization's scope to include fostering equal opportunities and equal treatment for all people. The GI Forum lobbied to end poll taxes, sued for the right of Latinos to serve on juries, and developed schools for jobless veterans. In 1984, Garcia received the Presidential Medal of Freedom, the nation's highest civilian honor.

SHAPING THE FAIR DEAL During 1947, after less than three years in the White House, Truman had yet to shake the widespread impression that he was not up to the job. Critics proclaimed that "to err is Truman." The editors of *Time* magazine reflected the national sentiment when they wrote, "Mr. Truman has often faced his responsibilities with a cheerful, dogged courage. But his performance was almost invariably awkward, uninspired, and above all, mediocre." Voters, they added, believed that Truman "means well, but he doesn't do well." Most political analysts assumed that the president would lose his effort to win another term.

Truman, too, feared that he would lose. In July 1947, he met with General Dwight D. Eisenhower as he was preparing to retire as chairman of the Joint Chiefs of Staff. Worried that General Douglas MacArthur, a self-described "right-wing Republican," might be the Republican presidential nominee in 1948, Truman urged Eisenhower to run as the Democratic nominee and even offered to be his vice-presidential running mate. Eisenhower declined, explaining that he was going to become president of Columbia University in New York City.

With the president's popularity sinking, the Democratic party was about to split in two. Southern conservatives resented Truman's outspoken support of civil rights, while the left wing of the party resented the firing of Secretary of Commerce Henry A. Wallace for publicly criticizing the administration's anti-Soviet policies. Wallace had said that the United States had "no more business in the *political affairs* of Eastern Europe than Russia has in the *political affairs* of Latin America." The danger of another world war, he said, "is much less from communism than it is from [American] imperialism." Wallace's comments so outraged the leaders of the State Department that Truman felt he had no choice but to get rid of him.

Despite the gloomy predictions for 1948, Truman mounted an intense reelection campaign. In his 1948 State of the Union message, Truman announced that the programs he would later call his "**Fair Deal**" (to distinguish them from Roosevelt's New Deal) would build upon the efforts of the New Deal to help all Americans. The first goal, Truman said, was to ensure civil rights for all Americans. He added proposals to increase federal aid to education, expand unemployment and retirement benefits, create a comprehensive system of national health insurance, enable more rural people to connect to electricity, and increase the minimum wage.

THE ELECTION OF 1948 The Republican-controlled Congress dismissed Truman's proposals, an action it would later regret. At the Republican convention, New York governor Thomas E. Dewey won the presidential nomination on the third ballot. While the platform endorsed most of the New Deal

Birth of the Dixiecrats Alabama delegates stand to boo Truman's call for civil rights before they walked out of the 1948 Democratic National Convention.

reforms and approved the administration's bipartisan foreign policy, Dewey promised to run things more efficiently.

In July, glum Democrats gathered for their convention in Philadelphia. Some party leaders, including Roosevelt's son James, a California congressman, tried to convince Dwight Eisenhower to accept the nomination, and many others joined the "dump Truman" effort. Eisenhower declined, however, explaining that his refusal was "final and complete."

Delegates who expected to do little more than go through the motions of nominating Truman were doubly surprised, first by the battle on the convention floor over civil rights and then by Truman's endorsement of civil rights for African Americans in his acceptance speech. Liberal Democrats led by Minnesota's Hubert Humphrey commended Truman "for his courageous stand on the issue of civil rights" and declared that the "time has arrived for the Democratic party to get out of the shadow of civil rights." White segregationist delegates from Alabama and Mississippi walked out in protest. The solidly Democratic South had fractured over race.

On July 17, a group of rebellious southern Democrats met in Birmingham, Alabama. While waving Confederate flags and singing "Dixie," they nominated South Carolina's segregationist governor, Strom Thurmond, on a States' Rights Democratic party ticket, quickly dubbed the "Dixiecrat party." The **Dixiecrats** denounced Truman's "infamous" civil rights initiatives and championed states' rights against federal efforts to change the tradition of white supremacy in the South. A few days later, on July 23, the left wing of the Democratic party gathered in Philadelphia to form a new Progressive party and nominate for president Henry A. Wallace, Roosevelt's former secretary of agriculture and vice president, whom Truman had fired as secretary of commerce.

The splits in the Democratic ranks seemed to spell the final blow to Truman, but he refused to give in. He was finally renominated long after midnight. By the time he entered the auditorium, it was 2 A.M., but he aroused the faithful by promising that "I will win this election and make the Republicans like it!" He pledged to bring Congress into special session and demand that it confront the housing crisis and boost the minimum wage.

Within days, an invigorated Truman set out on a 22,000-mile "whistle-stop" train tour, making ten speeches a day scolding the "do-nothing" Eightieth Congress. The plain-talking president attracted huge crowds. The Republicans, he charged, "have the propaganda and the money, but we have the people, and the people have the votes. *That's* why we're going to win." Friendly audiences loved his fighting spirit and dogged courage, shouting, "Pour it on, Harry!" and "Give 'em hell, Harry." Truman responded: "I don't give 'em hell. I just tell the truth and they think it's hell."

The polls predicted a sure win for Dewey, but on Election Day Truman pulled off the biggest upset in history, taking 24.2 million votes (49.5 percent) to Dewey's 22 million (45.1 percent) and winning a thumping margin of 303 to 189 in the electoral college. Democrats also regained control of both houses of Congress. Thurmond and Wallace each received more than 1 million votes, but the revolt of right and left had worked to Truman's advantage. The Dixiecrat rebellion backfired by angering black voters, who turned out in droves to support Truman, and the Progressive party's radicalism made it hard for Republicans to tag Truman as soft on communism. Thurmond carried four southern states (South Carolina, Mississippi, Alabama, and Louisiana).

THE FAIR DEAL REJECTED   Truman viewed his surprising victory as a mandate to expand the social welfare programs established by Franklin Roosevelt. His State of the Union message in early 1949 repeated the agenda he had set forth the year before. "Every segment of our population and every individual," he declared, "has a right to expect from our government a *fair deal.*"

Most of the Fair Deal proposals that gained congressional approval were extensions or enlargements of New Deal programs: a higher minimum hourly wage, expansion of Social Security coverage to 10 million workers not included in the original 1935 bill, and a sizable slum-clearance and public-housing program.

THE ELECTION OF 1948

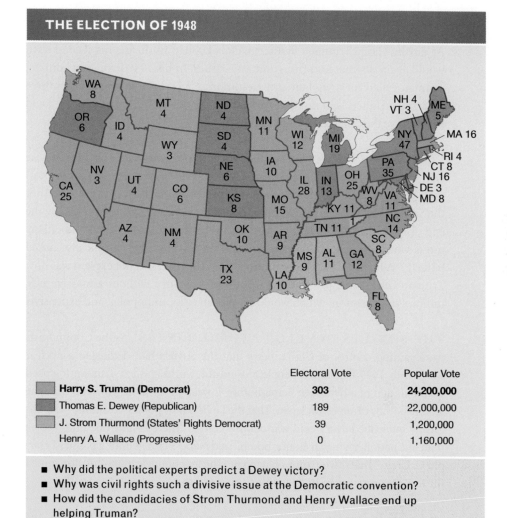

	Electoral Vote	Popular Vote
Harry S. Truman (Democrat)	**303**	**24,200,000**
Thomas E. Dewey (Republican)	189	22,000,000
J. Strom Thurmond (States' Rights Democrat)	39	1,200,000
Henry A. Wallace (Progressive)	0	1,160,000

- Why did the political experts predict a Dewey victory?
- Why was civil rights such a divisive issue at the Democratic convention?
- How did the candidacies of Strom Thurmond and Henry Wallace end up helping Truman?

Despite enjoying Democratic majorities in Congress, however, Truman ran up against the same alliance of conservative southern Democrats and Republicans who had worked against Roosevelt in the late 1930s. The bipartisan conservative coalition nixed most of Truman's new programs. Congress rejected several civil rights bills, national health insurance, federal aid to education, and a new approach to subsidizing farmers. It also turned down Truman's requested repeal of the anti-union Taft-Hartley Act. Yet the Fair Deal was not a complete failure. It laid the foundation for programs that the next generation of reformers would promote.

THE COLD WAR HEATS UP

As during Harry Truman's first term, global concerns during his second term would again distract him from domestic issues. In his 1949 inaugural address, Truman called for a vigilant anti-Communist foreign policy resting on three pillars: the United Nations, the Marshall Plan, and NATO. None of them could help resolve the civil war in China, however.

"LOSING" CHINA   One of the thorniest postwar problems, the Chinese civil war, was fast coming to a head. Chinese Nationalists, led by Chiang Kai-shek, had been fighting Mao Zedong and the Communists since the 1920s. After the Second World War, the Communists won over most of the peasants. By the end of 1949, the Nationalist government was forced to flee to the island of Formosa, which it renamed Taiwan. Truman's critics—mostly Republicans—asked bitterly, "Who lost China to communism?" What they did not explain was how Truman could have prevented a Communist victory without a massive U.S. military intervention, which would have been risky, unpopular, and expensive.

THE SOVIETS DEVELOP ATOMIC BOMBS   As the Communists were gaining control of China, news that the Soviets had detonated a nuclear weapon in 1949 frightened people around the world and led Truman to speed up the design of a hydrogen "superbomb," a weapon far more powerful than the atomic bombs dropped on Japan. That the Soviets now possessed atomic weapons greatly intensified every cold war confrontation. "There is only one thing worse than one nation having an atomic bomb," said Nobel Prize–winning physicist Harold C. Urey. "That's two nations having it." The fear of nuclear annihilation joined the fear of communism in deepening the Red Scare.

NSC-68   In January 1950, President Truman grew so concerned about the Soviets possessing atomic weapons that he asked the National Security Council to assess America's changing role in the cold war world. Four months later, the Council submitted a top-secret report, **NSC-68**. The document called for an even more robust effort to "contain" the spread of communism.

NSC-68 endorsed President Truman's "containment" strategy, calling for "a policy of calculated and gradual coercion" against Soviet expansionism—everywhere. The report claimed that the Soviets, driven to impose their will "on the rest of the world," were becoming increasingly "reckless" and would invade western Europe by 1954, by which time they would have enough nuclear weapons to destroy the United States.

By signing NSC-68, Truman explained that it would mean "doubling or tripling the [military] budget, increasing taxes heavily, and imposing various kinds of economic controls. It meant a great change in our normal peacetime way of doing things." NSC-68 became the essential guidebook for American policy during the cold war.

WAR IN KOREA

By the mid-1950s, tensions between the United States and the Soviet Union in Europe had temporarily eased as a result of the "balance of terror" created by both sides having atomic weapons. In Asia, however, the situation remained turbulent. The Communists had gained control of mainland China and were threatening to destroy the Chinese Nationalists, who had taken refuge on Taiwan.

Japan, meanwhile, was experiencing a dramatic recovery from the devastation caused by U.S. bombing raids during the Second World War. Douglas MacArthur showed deft leadership as the consul in charge of U.S.-occupied Japan. He oversaw the disarming of the Japanese military, the drafting of a democratic constitution, and the nation's economic recovery, all of which were turning Japan into America's friend.

To the east, however, tensions between North and South Korea threatened to erupt into civil war. The Japanese had occupied the Korean Peninsula since 1910, but after they were defeated and withdrew in 1945, the victorious Allies had faced the difficult task of creating an independent Korean nation.

A DIVIDED KOREA   Complicating that effort was the presence of Soviet troops in northern Korea. They had accepted the surrender of Japanese forces above the 38th parallel, which divides the Korean Peninsula, while U.S. forces had overseen the Japanese surrender south of the line. The Soviets quickly organized a Communist government, the Democratic People's Republic of Korea (North Korea). The Americans countered by helping to establish a democratic government in the more populous south, the Republic of Korea (South Korea). By the end of 1948, separate regimes had appeared in the two sectors, Soviet and American forces had withdrawn, and some 2 million North Koreans had fled to South Korea.

WAR ERUPTS   On June 24, 1950, Secretary of State Dean Acheson telephoned President Truman: "Mr. President," he reported, "I have very serious news. The North Koreans have invaded South Korea." With the encouragement of the Soviet Union and Communist China, the Soviet-equipped North Korean People's Army had rapidly forced the South Korean army into a headlong retreat. Within three days, Seoul, the South Korean capital, was captured, and only 22,000 of the 100,000 South Korean soldiers were still capable of combat.

Truman assumed, correctly, that the North Korean attack had been encouraged by the Soviets. "There's no telling what they'll do if we don't put up a fight right now," Truman predicted. He then made a critical decision: without consulting the Joint Chiefs of Staff or the Congress, he decided to wage war through the backing of the United Nations rather than by seeking a declaration of war from Congress. He knew that a congressional debate over a war in Korea would take so long that it may then be too late to stop the Communists.

An emergency meeting of the UN Security Council in late June 1950 censured the North Korean "breach of peace." By sheer coincidence, the Soviet delegate, who held a veto power, was at the time boycotting the council because it would not seat Communist China in place of Nationalist China. On June 27, the Security Council called on UN members to "furnish such assistance to the Republic of Korea as may be necessary to repel the armed attack and to restore international peace and security in the area."

Truman then ordered U.S. air, naval, and ground forces into action and appointed seventy-year-old Douglas MacArthur supreme commander of the UN forces. The attack on South Korea, Truman said, made "it plain beyond all doubt that the international Communist movement is prepared to use armed

Fight and flight American soldiers and Korean civilian refugees march into the Nakdong River region in the south.

invasion to conquer independent nations." Truman's decisive steps gained strong bipartisan approval, but neither the nation nor the administration were united on the objectives of the war or its conduct.

The Korean conflict was the first military action authorized by the United Nations, and some twenty other nations participated. The United States provided the largest contingent by far, some 330,000 troops. The American defense of South Korea set a worrisome precedent: war by order of a president—rather than by a vote of Congress, which the U.S. Constitution requires. Truman dodged the issue by officially calling the conflict a "police action" rather than a war. Critics labeled it "Mr. Truman's War."

TURNING THE TABLES For the first three months, the fighting in Korea went badly for the Republic of Korea (ROK) and the UN forces. By September 1950, the decimated South Korean troops were barely hanging on. Then, in a brilliant maneuver on September 15, General MacArthur staged a surprise amphibious landing behind the North Korean lines at Inch'ŏn, the port city for Seoul. UN troops drove a wedge through the North Korean army, only a quarter of whom (some 25,000 soldiers) managed to flee across the border. Days later, South Korean troops recaptured Seoul.

At that point, MacArthur became overconfident and persuaded Truman to allow U.S. troops to push into North Korea. Containment of communism was no longer enough; MacArthur now sought to rid North Korea of the "red menace," even if this meant expanding the war into China to prevent the Chinese from resupplying their North Korean allies.

THE CHINESE INTERVENE By October 1950, UN forces were about to capture the North Korean capital, P'yŏngyang. President Truman, concerned that MacArthur's move would provoke Communist China to enter the war, flew 7,000 miles to Wake Island to meet with MacArthur. At the meeting on October 15, MacArthur dismissed Chinese threats to intervene, even though they had massed troops on the Korean border. That same day, the Communist government in Beijing announced that China "cannot stand idly by" as its North Korean allies were humiliated. On October 20, UN forces entered the North Korean capital, and on October 26, advance units reached Ch'osan on the Yalu River, North Korea's border with China.

MacArthur predicted total victory by Christmas. On the night of November 25, however, some 300,000 Chinese "volunteers" counterattacked, sending U.S. forces into a desperate retreat. "We ran like antelopes," said an American soldier. By January 15, the Communist Chinese and North Koreans had recaptured Seoul.

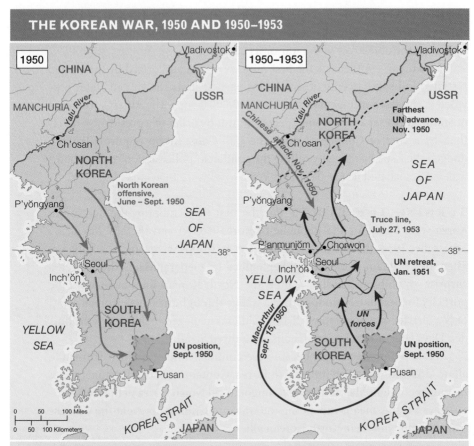

THE KOREAN WAR, 1950 AND 1950–1953

- How did the surrender of the Japanese in Korea during 1945 set up the conflict between Soviet-influenced North Korea and U.S.-influenced South Korea?
- What was General MacArthur's strategy for winning the Korean conflict?
- Why did President Truman remove General MacArthur from command?

MacArthur Crosses the Line The Chinese intervention caught MacArthur wholly unprepared. He now asked for thirty-four atomic bombs and proposed air raids on China. His plans horrified the military leadership in Washington, D.C. It would be, said General Omar Bradley, chairman of the Joint Chiefs of Staff, "the wrong war at the wrong place at the wrong time with the wrong enemy." Truman agreed.

In late 1950, the UN forces rallied. By January 1951, they had secured their lines below Seoul and launched a counterattack. When Truman began negotiations with North Korea to restore the prewar boundary, MacArthur undermined the president by issuing an ultimatum for China to make peace or suffer an attack. On April 5, on the floor of Congress, the Republican minority leader read a letter from MacArthur that criticized the president and said that "there is no substitute for victory." Such open insubordination left Truman only two choices: he could accept MacArthur's aggressive demands, or fire him.

SACKING A HERO On April 11, 1951, with civilian control of the military at stake, Truman removed MacArthur and replaced him with General Matthew B. Ridgway. "I believe that we must try to limit the war to Korea," Truman explained. "A number of events have made it evident that General MacArthur did not agree with that policy. I have therefore considered it essential to relieve General MacArthur so that there would be no doubt or confusion as to the real purpose and aim of our policy."

Truman's sacking of MacArthur, the army's only five-star general, divided the nation. *Time* magazine reported that "seldom had a more unpopular man fired a more popular one." Sixty-six percent of Americans initially opposed Truman's decision. That all of the top military leaders supported Truman's decision deflated much of the criticism. "Why, hell, if MacArthur had had his way," the president warned, "he'd have had us in the Third World War and blown up two-thirds of the world."

A CEASE-FIRE On June 24, 1951, the Soviet representative at the United Nations proposed a cease-fire in Korea along the 38th parallel, the original dividing line between North and South. Secretary of State Acheson accepted the cease-fire (armistice) with the consent of the United Nations. China and North Korea responded favorably.

Truce talks started on July 10, 1951, at Panmunjŏm, only to drag on for two years while sporadic fighting continued. By the time a truce was reached, on July 27, 1953, Truman had retired and Dwight D. Eisenhower was president. No peace treaty was ever signed, and Korea, like Germany, remained divided. The inconclusive war cost the United States more than 33,000 battle deaths and 103,000 wounded or missing. South Korean casualties were about 2 million, and North Korean and Chinese casualties were an estimated 3 million.

THE IMPACT OF THE KOREAN WAR To most Americans, the North Korean attack on South Korea provided concrete proof that there was an international Communist conspiracy guided by the Soviet Union to control the world.

Truman's assumption that Stalin and the Soviets were behind the invasion of South Korea led him to deepen the American commitment to stop communism. "The interests of the United States are global in character," he explained. "A threat to the peace of the world *anywhere* is a threat to our security." Fearful that the Soviets would use the Korean conflict as a diversion to invade Western

Europe, he ordered a major expansion of U.S. military forces in Europe—and around the world. Truman also increased assistance to French troops fighting a Communist independence movement in the French colony of Indochina (which included Vietnam), starting America's deepening military involvement in Southeast Asia.

ANOTHER RED SCARE

The Korean War excited another Red Scare at home, as people grew fearful that Communists were infiltrating American society. Since 1938, the **House Committee on Un-American Activities (HUAC)** had kept up a drumbeat of accusations about supposed Communist agents in the federal government.

On March 21, 1947, President Truman signed an executive order (also known as the Loyalty Order) requiring federal government workers to undergo a background investigation to ensure they were not Communists or even associated with Communists (or other "subversive" groups).

Truman knew that the "loyalty program" violated civil liberties, but he felt he had no choice. He was responding to pressure from FBI director J. Edgar Hoover and Attorney General Tom Clark, both of whom were convinced that there were numerous spies working inside the federal government. Truman was also eager to blunt criticism that he was not doing enough to ensure that Soviet sympathizers were not working in government. Yet Truman thought that the fear about Communist spies was greatly exaggerated. "People are very much wrought up about the communist 'bugaboo,'" he wrote to Pennsylvania governor George Earle, "but I am of the opinion that the country is perfectly safe so far as Communism is concerned."

THE HOLLYWOOD TEN Charges that Hollywood was a "hotbed of communism" led the House Committee on Un-American Activities to launch a full-blown investigation of the motion-picture industry. The HUAC subpoenaed dozens of actors, producers, and directors to testify at its hearings, held in Los Angeles in October 1947. Ten witnesses refused to testify, arguing that the questioning violated their First Amendment rights. All ten were cited for contempt, given prison terms, and blacklisted (banned) from the film industry.

ALGER HISS The spy case most damaging to the Truman administration involved Alger Hiss, president of the Carnegie Endowment for International Peace, who had served in several government agencies. Whittaker Chambers, a former Soviet spy and later an editor of *Time* magazine who reversed himself and became an informer testifying against supposed Communists in the government, told the HUAC in 1948 that Hiss had given him secret documents ten years earlier, when Chambers was spying for the Soviets and Hiss was working in the State Department. Hiss sued for libel, and Chambers produced microfilms of the State Department documents that he said Hiss had passed to him. Although Hiss denied the accusation, he was indicted and, after one mistrial, convicted in 1950. The charge was perjury, but he was convicted of lying about espionage, for which he could not be tried because the statute of limitations on the crime had expired.

ATOMIC SPYING In 1950, the FBI unearthed a spy network involving both American and British Communists who had secretly passed information about the development of the atomic bomb to the Soviet Union. The disclosure led to the arrest of Klaus Fuchs, a German-born English nuclear physicist who had worked in the United States during the war and helped to develop the atomic bomb.

As it turned out, a New York couple, former Communists Julius and Ethel Rosenberg, were part of the same Soviet spy ring. Their claims of innocence were undercut by the confession of Ethel's brother, who admitted he was a spy along with his sister and brother-in-law.

The convictions of Fuchs and the Rosenbergs fueled Republican charges that Truman's administration was not doing enough to hunt down Communist agents. The Rosenberg case, called the crime of the century by J. Edgar Hoover, also heightened fears that a vast Soviet network of spies and sympathizers was operating in the United States—and had "given" Stalin the secret of building atomic weapons. Irving Kaufman, the federal judge who sentenced the Rosenbergs to death, explained that "plain, deliberate murder is dwarfed . . . by comparison with the crime you have committed." They were the first Americans executed for spying.

MCCARTHY'S WITCH HUNT Evidence of Soviet spying encouraged some to exploit fears of the Communist menace. Early in 1950, a little-known Republican senator, Joseph R. McCarthy of Wisconsin, surfaced as the most ruthless manipulator of anti-Communist anxieties.

McCarthy, eager to attract media attention through his "bare-knuckle" tactics, took up the cause of anti-communism with a fiery speech to a women's Republican club in Wheeling, West Virginia, on February 9, 1950, in which he charged that the State Department was infested with Communists. He claimed to have their names, although he never provided them.

McCarthy got what he wanted most: publicity. As the *New York Times* said, "It is difficult, if not impossible, to ignore charges made by Senator McCarthy just because they are usually proved exaggerated or false." During the next four

Joseph R. McCarthy The crusading senator who was determined to identify any Communists serving in the federal government.

years, McCarthy made more wild accusations, initially against many Democrats, whom he smeared as "dupes" or "fellow travelers" of the "Commies," then against officers in the U.S. Army.

McCarthy enjoyed the backing of fellow Republicans eager to hurt Democrats in the 1950 congressional elections by claiming they were not being tough enough on fighting communism. But by the summer of 1951, **McCarthyism** had gotten out of control. McCarthy's excesses were revealed for all to see when he outrageously accused George Marshall, the former secretary of state and war hero, of making "common cause with Stalin" by "being an instrument of the Communist conspiracy." Concerns about truth or fair play did not faze McCarthy; his focus was on creating a reign of terror through groundless accusations. Truman called him a "pathological character assassin."

McCarthy's witch hunt never uncovered a single Communist agent. But his smear campaign, which tarnished many lives and reputations, went largely unchallenged until the end of the Korean War. During the Red Scare, thousands of left-wing Americans were "blacklisted" from employment because of past political associations, real or rumored. Movies with titles like "I Married a Communist" fed the hysteria, and magazine stories warned of "a Red under every bed."

THE McCARRAN ACT Fears of Soviet spies working with American sympathizers led Congress in 1950 to pass the McCarran Internal Security Act over President Truman's veto, making it unlawful "to combine, conspire, or agree with any other person to perform any act which would substantially contribute to . . . the establishment of a totalitarian dictatorship." Communist organizations had to register with the attorney general. Would-be immigrants who had belonged to totalitarian parties in their home countries were barred from entering the United States. And during any future national emergencies, American Communists were to be herded into concentration camps. The McCarran Internal Security Act, Truman said in his veto message, would "put the government into the business of thought control."

A COLD WAR GOVERNMENT The years after the Second World War were unlike any other postwar period in American history. Having taken on global burdens, the United States became committed to a permanently large national military establishment, along with shadowy new government agencies such as the National Security Council (NSC), the National Security Agency (NSA), and the Central Intelligence Agency (CIA).

The federal government—and the presidency—grew larger, more powerful, and more secretive, fueled by the actions of both major political parties as well as by the intense lobbying efforts of what Dwight D. Eisenhower would later call the *military-industrial complex.*

Fears of communism and concerns about a Soviet spy network in the United States mushroomed into politically motivated paranoia. Long-standing prejudices against Jews fed the hysteria; indeed, many Communist sympathizers were Jews from eastern Europe.

The Red Scare also provided a powerful tool for Republicans to claim that Democrats were "soft on Communism." One of the worst effects of the Red Scare was to encourage widespread conformity of thought and behavior. By 1950, it had become dangerous to criticize anything associated with the American way of life.

ASSESSING HARRY TRUMAN On March 30, 1952, Harry Truman announced that he would not seek another presidential term, in part because it was unlikely he could win. Less than 25 percent of voters surveyed said that he was doing a good job, the lowest presidential approval rating in history. Although Americans applauded Truman's integrity and courage, the unrelenting war against communism, at home and abroad, led people to question his strategy. Negotiations to end the war in Korea had bogged down, the "red-baiting" of McCarthyism was expanding, and conservative southern Democrats, members of Truman's own party, had defeated most of his Fair Deal proposals. The war had also brought higher taxes and higher prices for American consumers, many of whom blamed the president. Only years later would people (and historians) fully appreciate how effectively Truman had dealt with so many complex problems.

By the time Truman left the White House in early 1953, the cold war had become an accepted part of the American way of life. But fears about the spread of communism were counterbalanced by the joys of unexpected prosperity. Toward the end of Truman's presidency, the economy began to grow at what would become the fastest rate in history, transforming social and cultural life and becoming the marvel of the world. The booming economy brought with it the "nifty" fifties.

CHAPTER REVIEW

SUMMARY

- **The Cold War** The cold war was an ideological contest between the Western democracies (especially the United States) and the Communist countries. At the end of the Second World War, the Soviet Union established "friendly" governments in the Eastern European countries it occupied behind an *iron curtain* of totalitarian control and secrecy.

- **Containment** President Truman responded to the Soviet occupation of Eastern Europe with the policy of *containment*, the aim of which was to halt the spread of communism by opposing it wherever it emerged. With the *Truman Doctrine* (*1947*), he proposed giving economic and military aid to countries facing Communist insurgencies, such as Greece and Turkey; he also convinced Congress to approve the *National Security Act*, which reorganized the U.S. armed forces and created the Central Intelligence Agency. With the *Marshall Plan*, Truman offered redevelopment aid to all European nations. In 1948, the *Berlin airlift* overcame a Soviet blockade of supplies to West Berlin. In 1949, the United States became a founding member of the *North Atlantic Treaty Organization* (*NATO*), a military alliance of Western democracies united primarily against the Soviet Union.

- **Truman's Fair Deal** Truman's *Fair Deal* was proposed to expand the New Deal despite intense Republican opposition in Congress. Truman could not stop the *Taft-Hartley Act*, a Republican-backed measure to curb the power of labor unions. Truman was more successful in expanding Social Security and, through executive orders, desegregating the military and banning racial discrimination in the hiring of federal employees. After winning a second term in 1948, he proposed a civil rights bill, national health insurance, federal aid to education, and new farm subsidies. Despite the Democrats' majority in Congress, however, conservative Republicans and southern Democrats (*Dixiecrats*) joined forces to defeat these initiatives.

- **The Korean War** Containment policies proved less effective in East Asia, as Communists won a long civil war in China in 1949 and ignited a war in Korea. In response, Truman authorized *NSC-68*, a comprehensive blueprint for American foreign and defense policies that called for a dramatic increase in military spending and nuclear arms. When North Korean troops invaded South Korea in June 1950, Truman quickly decided to go to war under the auspices of the United Nations. After a year of major gains and reverses by both sides and then two years of stalemate, a truce, concluded in July 1953, established a demilitarized zone in Korea.

- **The Red Scare** The onset of the cold war inflamed another Red Scare. Investigations by the *House Committee on Un-American Activities* (*HUAC*) sought to find "subversives" within the federal government. Starting in 1950, Senator

Joseph R. McCarthy exploited fears of Soviet spies infiltrating the highest levels of the U.S. government. *McCarthyism* flourished in the short term because the threat of a world dominated by Communist governments seemed all too real to many Americans.

CHRONOLOGY

November 1946	Republicans win control of both houses of Congress
February 1946	George Kennan urges a containment policy toward the Soviet Union
March 1947	The Truman Doctrine promises financial and military assistance to countries resisting Communist takeover
May 1947	The Marshall Plan provides massive financial assistance to European nations
June 1947	Congress passes the Taft-Hartley Labor Act over Truman's veto
July 1947	National Security Council (NSC) is established
May 1948	Israel is proclaimed an independent nation
July 1948	Truman's executive order ends segregation in the U.S. armed forces
October 1948	United States and Great Britain airlift supplies to West Berlin
November 1948	Truman defeats Dewey in the presidential election
April 1949	North Atlantic Treaty Organization (NATO) is created
October 1949	China "falls" to communism
February 1950	Senator Joseph McCarthy begins his crusade against suspected Communists in the federal government
June 1950	United States and other UN members go to war in Korea

KEY TERMS

iron curtain p. 1003

containment p. 1005

Truman Doctrine (1947) p. 1005

Marshall Plan (1948) p. 1007

Berlin airlift (1948) p. 1008

North Atlantic Treaty Organization (NATO) p. 1009

National Security Act p. 1010

Taft-Hartley Labor Act (1947) p. 1014

Fair Deal (1949) p. 1018

Dixiecrats p. 1019

NSC-68 (1950) p. 1022

House Committee on Un-American Activities (HUAC) p. 1028

McCarthyism p. 1030

 INQUIZITIVE

Go to InQuizitive to see what you've learned—and learn what you've missed—with personalized feedback along the way.

28 Cold War America

1950–1959

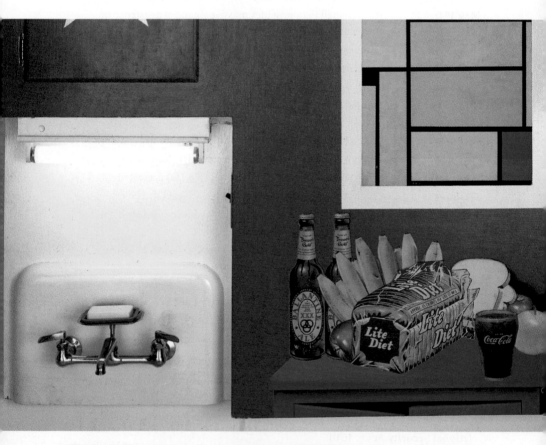

The Art of Consumerism The United States experienced tremendous prosperity after the Second World War, giving many Americans the unprecedented opportunity to engage in carefree consumption during the 1950s—and personal indebtedness. The Pop Art movement reflected the era's materialism. Its artists made use of the newly mass-produced and advertised products to celebrate the consumer culture. One such artist was Tom Wesselmann, whose 1962 collage *Untitled (Still-Life No. 20)* is shown above.

I n the summer of 1959, two young newlyweds spent their honeymoon in an underground bomb shelter in the backyard of their home. *Life* magazine showed them in their twenty-ton, steel and concrete bunker stocked with enough food and water to survive an atomic attack. The image of newlyweds seeking sheltered security in a new age of nuclear terror symbolized how America in the 1950s was awash in contrasting emotions.

The deepening cold war with the Soviet Union cast a frightening shadow over the nation's traditionally sunny optimism. In 1959, two out of three Americans listed the possibility of atomic war as the nation's most urgent threat. Still, Americans emerged from the Second World War proud of their military strength, international stature, and industrial might. It was a time rich with possibilities. As the editors of *Fortune* magazine proclaimed in 1946, "This is a dream era. . . . The Great American Boom is on."

So it was, at least for white, middle-class Americans. During the late 1940s and throughout the 1950s, the United States enjoyed unprecedented economic growth, and most Americans were content. Divorce and homicide rates fell, and people lived longer, on average, thanks in part to medical breakthroughs, including new antibiotics and the vaccine invented by Dr. Jonas Salk that ended the menace of polio. The "happy days" image of America in the fifties as an innocent, prosperous nation awash in good times and enlivened by teenage energies has a kernel of truth. But life was actually much more complicated, even contradictory and hypocritical at times, as many Americans worried about what seemed an uncontrollable future.

focus questions

1. What were President Eisenhower's political philosophy and priorities?

2. What factors contributed to postwar prosperity? To what extent did all Americans benefit from it?

3. What were the criticisms of postwar American society and culture? What were the various forms of dissent and anxiety?

4. What were the goals and strategies of the civil rights movement that emerged in the 1950s? What was its impact?

5. What were President Eisenhower's priorities in conducting the nation's foreign policy? What was his influence on global affairs?

MODERATE REPUBLICANISM

Dwight David Eisenhower dominated the political landscape during the 1950s. The military hero of the Second World War was a model of moderation, stability, and optimism. He was a soldier who hated war, a politician who hated politics. Committed to what he called **moderate Republicanism**, Eisenhower promised to restore the authority of state and local governments and restrain the federal government from engaging in political and social "engineering." In the process, he sought to renew traditional virtues and inspire Americans with a vision of a brighter future.

"TIME FOR A CHANGE" By 1952, the Truman administration was the target of growing public criticism. The conflict in Korea had stalled, the economy was sputtering, and Truman was put on the defensive by the disclosure that corrupt lobbyists had rigged military contracts. The scandal led Truman to fire nearly 250 employees of the Internal Revenue Service, but doubts lingered that he would ever finish the housecleaning. Critics charged that the slogan for his administration was "plunder at home, blunder abroad."

It was, Republicans claimed, "time for a change," and public sentiment turned their way as the 1952 election approached. Beginning in the late 1940s, both Republican and Democratic leaders, including Truman, recruited Eisenhower to be their presidential candidate. The affable Eisenhower, known as "Ike," had displayed remarkable organizational and diplomatic skill in coordinating the Allied invasion of Nazi-controlled Europe. In 1952, after serving as president of Columbia University, he had moved to Paris to become supreme commander of NATO forces in Europe. His decision to run for president as a Republican was wildly popular with voters. Bumper stickers announced simply: "I Like Ike."

Dwight D. Eisenhower His many supporters wore "I Like Ike" hats, pins, and even nylon stockings, speaking to the powerful consumer culture's impact on politics.

Eisenhower was nominated on the first ballot. Republican leaders then tried to reassure party conservatives by balancing the ticket with a youthful, fiercely ambitious running mate: Richard M. Nixon, a thirty-nine-year-old California senator distinctive for his shrewd opportunism and combative temperament. Nixon was an aggressive anti-Communist focused on exposing left-wing "subversives" in the Truman administration. His dogged pursuit of the Alger Hiss spying case had brought him national prominence. The Republican platform declared that the Democratic emphasis on "containing" communism was "negative, futile, and misguided." If elected, Eisenhower would roll back the Communist threat by bringing "genuine independence" to the "captive peoples" of Eastern Europe.

THE ELECTION OF 1952 The presidential campaign featured contrasting personalities. Eisenhower was an international figure and a man of readily acknowledged decency and integrity. His beaming smile and humble greatness won over the masses. Illinois governor Adlai Stevenson, the Democratic candidate, was hardly known outside his home state. Eisenhower pledged to clean up "the mess in Washington." Then, late in the campaign, he promised to travel to Korea to secure "an early and honorable" end to the prolonged conflict.

Stevenson was outmatched. Although brilliant and witty, he came across to most voters as more an "intellectual" than a "leader." Republicans labeled him an "egghead" (meant to suggest a balding professor with more intellect than common sense). Even Truman grumbled that Stevenson "was too busy making up his mind whether he had to go to the bathroom or not."

On election night, Eisenhower triumphed in a landslide, gathering nearly 34 million votes to Stevenson's 27 million. The electoral vote was much more lopsided: 442 to 89. Stevenson even failed to win his home state of Illinois. More important, by securing four southern states, Eisenhower had cracked the solidly Democratic South.

Yet voters liked Eisenhower more than they liked other Republican candidates. In the 1952 election, Democrats kept control of most governorships, lost control in the House by only eight seats, and broke even in the Senate. Throughout his second presidential term, Eisenhower would have to work with a Democratic Congress.

A "MIDDLE WAY" PRESIDENCY Eisenhower was the first professional soldier elected president since Ulysses S. Grant in 1868. He promised to pursue a "middle way between untrammeled freedom of the individual and the demands of the welfare of the whole nation." He saw no need to dismantle all New Deal and Fair Deal programs. Instead, he wanted to end the "excesses"

THE ELECTION OF 1952

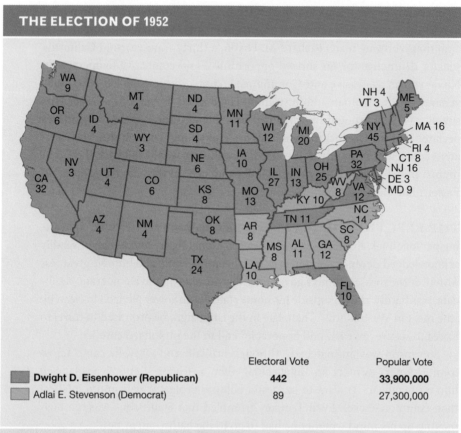

	Electoral Vote	Popular Vote
Dwight D. Eisenhower (Republican)	442	33,900,000
Adlai E. Stevenson (Democrat)	89	27,300,000

- Why was the contest between Adlai Stevenson and Dwight D. Eisenhower so lopsided?
- Why was Eisenhower's victory in several southern states remarkable?

that had resulted from twenty years of Democratic control of the White House. He pledged to shrink the federal bureaucracy and make it more efficient while restoring the balance between the executive and legislative branches.

Eisenhower also promised to reduce the national debt, cut military expenses, balance the federal budget, and trim taxes. At the same time, however, he insisted that workers had a right to form unions and bargain with management. He added that employees needed to be paid enough to afford the comforts of a good life. "We all—workers and farmers, foremen and financiers, technicians and builders—all must produce, produce more, and produce yet more," he said, to make the American Dream a reality and to ensure global stability. Peace would be maintained "not by weapons of war but by wheat and cotton, by milk and wool, by meat and by timber and by rice." He hated the growing arms race because "every gun that is made, every warship launched, every rocket fired signifies, in the final sense, a theft from those who hunger and are not fed, those who are cold and are not clothed."

Eisenhower's cautious personality and genial public face fit the prevailing mood of most voters. He was a unifier, not a divider; he inspired trust, sought consensus, and avoided confrontation. He also championed the nineteenth-century view that Congress should make policy and the president should carry it out.

"DYNAMIC CONSERVATISM" AT HOME Eisenhower labeled his domestic program "dynamic conservatism," by which he meant being "conservative when it comes to money and liberal when it comes to human beings." He kept intact the basic structure of the New Deal, even convincing Congress to establish a federal Department of Health, Education and Welfare and working with Democrats to extend Social Security benefits to millions of workers formerly excluded: white-collar professionals, maids and sales clerks, farmworkers, and members of the armed forces. Eisenhower also approved increases in the minimum wage and public-housing projects for low-income occupants. Conservative Republicans declared that he was being too liberal. He told his brother Edgar in 1954 that if the "stupid" right wing of the Republican party tried "to abolish Social Security and eliminate labor laws and farm programs, you would not hear of that party again in our political history."

TRANSPORTATION IMPROVE-MENTS Under Eisenhower, the federal government launched two huge construction projects: the St. Lawrence Seaway and the Interstate Highway System. The St. Lawrence Seaway (in partnership with Canada) opened the Great Lakes to oceangoing ships.

The **Federal-Aid Highway Act** (1956) created a national network of interstate highways to serve the needs of commerce and defense, as well as the public. The interstate highway system, funded largely by federal gasoline taxes, took twenty-five years to construct and

Drive in, cash in Founded by brothers Maurice and Richard McDonald in southern California, this hugely successful fast food chain started as a carhop drive-in and did not have customer seating until the 1960s.

was the largest federal project in history. It stretched for 47,000 miles and required 55,512 bridges.

Highway construction generated what economists call "multiplier effects": it created jobs; stimulated economic growth; and spurred the tourism, motor hotel ("motel"), billboard, fast-food, and long-haul trucking industries. Interstates transformed the way people traveled and where they lived, and it even created a new form of middle-class leisure—the family vacation by car. In 1956, writer Bernard De Voto exclaimed that "a new highway is not only a measure of progress, but a true index of our culture."

THE END OF McCARTHYISM   Republicans thought their presidential victory in 1952 would curb the often unscrupulous efforts of Wisconsin senator Joseph R. McCarthy to ferret out Communist spies in the federal government. Instead, the publicity-seeking senator's behavior grew even more outlandish, in part because reporters were dazzled by his theatrics. President Eisenhower despised McCarthy but refused to criticize him in public, explaining that he did not want to "get into a pissing contest with that skunk." In March 1954, the president indirectly chastised McCarthy when he told a press conference that "we are defeating ourselves if we use methods [in opposing communism] that do not conform to the American sense of justice."

McCarthy finally committed political suicide when he made the absurd charge that the U.S. Army itself was "soft" on communism. For thirty-six days in the spring of 1954, the Army-McCarthy hearings provided 80 million television viewers with a fantastic spectacle. McCarthy was at his worst, hounding witnesses, seeking publicity, and producing little evidence to back up his charges. He was finally outwitted by the deliberate, reasoned counterattacks of the army's legal counsel, Joseph Welch. When McCarthy tried to smear one of Welch's associates, the attorney was outraged: "Until this moment, Senator, I think I never really gauged your cruelty or your recklessness. . . . Have you no sense of decency, sir, at long last?" When the audience burst into applause, the confused senator was reduced to whispering, "What did I do?"

On December 2, 1954, the Senate voted 67 to 22 to "condemn" McCarthy. Soon thereafter, his political influence collapsed. His crusade against Communists in government had catapulted him into the limelight and captured the nation's attention, but in the process he had trampled upon civil liberties. Now, with unexpected suddenness, his crusade was over. His rapid demise helped the Democrats capture control of both houses of Congress in the 1954 elections. In 1957, at the age of forty-eight, he died of liver inflammation brought on by years of alcohol abuse. His successor, William Proxmire, declared that McCarthy was "a disgrace to Wisconsin, to the Senate, and to America."

A People of Plenty

What most distinguished the United States from the rest of the world after the Second World War was what one journalist called America's "screwball materialism." After a brief postwar recession in 1945–1946, the economy soared to record heights as businesses shifted from wartime production to the construction of new housing and the manufacture of mass-produced consumer goods. In 1953, Eisenhower's first year in office, the United States, with 6 percent of the world's population, was producing two-thirds of the world's manufactured goods. In 1957, *U.S. News and World Report* magazine declared that "never had so many people, anywhere, been so well off."

Postwar Prosperity

Several factors created the nation's prosperity. First, huge federal expenditures during the Second World War and Korean War propelled the economy out of the Great Depression. High government spending continued in the 1950s, thanks to the relentless construction of highways, bridges, airports, and ports, and the global arms race. The military budget after 1945 represented the single most important stimulant to the economy.

The superior productivity of American industries also contributed to economic growth. No sooner was the war over than the federal government turned over to civilian owners many war-related plants, giving them a boost as they retooled for peacetime manufacturing. Military-related research helped stimulate new glamour industries: chemicals (including plastics), electronics, and aviation. By 1957, the aircraft industry was the nation's largest employer.

The economy also benefited from the emergence of new technologies, including the first generation of computers. Factories and industries became increasingly "automated." At the same time, the oil boom in Texas, Wyoming, and Oklahoma continued to provide low-cost fuel to heat buildings and to power cars and trucks.

Another reason for the record-breaking economic growth was the lack of foreign competition. Most of the other major industrial nations—Great Britain, France, Germany, Japan, and the Soviet Union—had been physically devastated during the Second World War, leaving American manufacturers with a virtual monopoly on international trade that lasted well into the 1950s.

The Consumer Culture

The major catalyst for economic expansion after 1945, however, was the unleashing of pent-up consumer demand from the Depression and the war years. What differentiated the postwar era from earlier periods of prosperity

A TV culture The dynamics of American family life changed with the onslaught of new, affordable products. In this 1959 advertisement for TV dinners, the family eats out of disposable containers in front of the television.

was the large number of people who shared in the rising standard of living. Between 1947 and 1960, the average income for the working class increased by as much as it had in the previous *fifty* years. More and more blue-collar Americans, especially automotive and steel workers, moved into the middle class. George Meany, the leading union spokesman during the 1950s, declared in 1955 that his members "never had it so good." Americans had money to spend during the fifties, and they did so with gusto.

THE GI BILL OF RIGHTS In 1944, as Americans grew confident of victory in the Second World War, fear that a sudden influx of veterans into the civilian workforce would produce widespread unemployment led Congress to pass the Servicemen's Readjustment Act, also called the Veterans Act and nick-named the **GI Bill of Rights**. ("GI" meant "government issue," a phrase stamped on military uniforms and equipment that became slang for "serviceman.")

The GI Bill boosted upward social mobility in postwar America. Its package of benefits for veterans included unemployment pay for one year, preference to those applying for federal government jobs, loans for home construction or starting a business, access to government hospitals, and generous subsidies for education. Some 5 million veterans bought homes with the assistance of GI Bill mortgage loans, which required no down payment. Almost 8 million took advantage of $14.5 billion in GI Bill benefits to attend college or enroll in job-training programs.

Overall, the GI Bill was one of the most successful federal programs in history. For African American veterans, however, most colleges and universities remained racially segregated and refused to admit blacks. Those that did often discriminated against them. African Americans attending white colleges or universities were barred from playing on athletic teams, attending social events, and joining fraternities or sororities. Black veterans were also often prevented from buying homes in white neighborhoods. Although women veterans were eligible for GI Bill benefits, there were so few of them that the program had the unintended effect of widening the income gap between men and women.

THE SUBURBAN FRONTIER The second half of the twentieth century brought a mass migration to a new frontier—the suburbs. The acute postwar housing shortage (98 percent of cities reported shortages of houses and apartments in 1945) sparked the suburban revolution. People were eager to escape from inner cities to the sprawling suburbs emerging in the countryside, just outside of city or town limits. Of the 13 million homes built between 1948 and 1958, there were 11 million constructed in the suburbs. Many among the exploding middle-class white population moved to what were called the Sunbelt states—California, Arizona, Florida, Texas, and the southeast region, where rapid population growth and new highways generated an economic boom. As air conditioning became common in the Sunbelt, it greatly enhanced the appeal of living in warmer climates. California led the way. In 1940, it was the fifth most populous state; by 1963, it was first.

Suburbia met an acute need (affordable housing) and fulfilled a common dream—personal freedom and family security within commuting distance of cities. In the half century after the Second World War, the suburban "good life" included a big home with a big yard on a big lot accessed by a big car—or two. During the 1950s, suburbs grew six times as fast as cities, and by 1970 more people lived in suburbs than in cities.

A brassy New York real estate developer, William Levitt, led the suburban revolution. He had made a fortune during the war building housing units on new navy bases and around defense plants, and after the war he put his expertise to use in the suburbs. Between 1947 and 1951, on 6,000 acres of Long Island farmland forty miles east of New York City, he built 17,447 small (750 square feet), sturdy, two-bedroom homes to house more than 82,000 mostly lower-middle-class people.

Levitt believed he was enabling the American Dream. The planned community, called Levittown, included schools, swimming pools, shopping centers,

Levittown Identical mass-produced houses in Levittown, New York, and other suburbs across the country provided veterans and their families with affordable homes.

and playing fields. Levitt encouraged and even enforced uniformity and conformity. The lookalike houses came in different colors but only three styles—the Cape Cod, the Rancher, and the Colonial. All sold for the same low price—$6,990, with no down payments for veterans—and featured the same floor plan and accessories. Each had a living room with a picture window and a television set, a bathroom, two bedrooms, and a kitchen equipped with an electric refrigerator, oven, and washing machine. Trees were planted every twenty-eight feet in the former potato fields; homeowners were required to cut their grass once a week and prohibited from hanging laundry on outside clothes lines during weekends.

When the first houses in Levittown went on sale, people stood in long lines to buy one. In seven days, Levitt sold 707 houses. He soon built three more Levittowns in Pennsylvania, New Jersey, and Puerto Rico. They and other planned suburban communities benefited greatly from government assistance. Federal and state tax codes favored homeowners over renters, and local governments paid for the infrastructure the subdivisions required: roads, water and sewer lines, fire and police protection. By insuring loans for up to 95 percent of the value of a house, the Federal Housing Administration (FHA) made it easy for builders to construct low-cost homes and for people to purchase them.

Levitt and other suburban developers created lily-white communities outside mostly black-populated cities. Initially, the contracts for houses in Levittown specifically excluded "members of other than the Caucasian race." As Levitt explained, "We can solve a housing problem or we can try to solve a racial problem. But we can't combine the two." It wasn't long, however, before the U.S. Supreme Court ruled in *Shelley v. Kraemer* (1948) that such racial restrictions were illegal.

The Court ruling, however, did not end segregated housing practices; it simply made them more discreet. In 1953, when Levittown's population reached 70,000, it was the largest community in the nation without a single African American resident.

MINORITIES ON THE MOVE The mass migration of rural southern blacks to the urban North, Midwest, and West after the Second World War was much larger than their migration after the First World War, and its social consequences were even more dramatic. After 1945, more than 5 million blacks left the South in search of better jobs, higher wages, decent housing, and greater civil rights.

By 1960, for the first time in history, more African Americans were living in urban areas than in rural areas. As blacks moved into northern cities, many white residents moved to the suburbs, leaving behind racial ghettos. Between 1950 and 1960, some 3.6 million whites left the nation's largest cities for suburban neighborhoods, while 4.5 million blacks moved into the cities.

Deeply entrenched racial attitudes outside the South forced blacks to work to counter the hostility they confronted. Through organizations such as the National Association for the Advancement of Colored People (NAACP), the Congress of Racial Equality (CORE), and the National Urban League, they sought to change the hearts and minds of their white neighbors. However, for all of the racism that black migrants encountered, most found their new lives preferable to the enforced segregation and often violent racism in the South. Southern blacks still faced voting discrimination and segregation in theaters, parks, schools, colleges, hospitals, buses, cinemas, libraries, restrooms, beaches, bars, and prisons.

The Second Great Migration African American families, such as the New Jersey–bound family pictured here, moved to northern urban centers in droves following the end of World War II.

Just as African Americans were on the move, so, too, were Mexicans and Puerto Ricans. Congress renewed the *bracero* program, begun during the Second World War, which enabled Mexicans to work as wage laborers in the United States, often as migrant workers moving from farm to farm as needed. Mexicans streamed across the nation's southwest border. By 1960, Los Angeles had the largest concentration of Mexican Americans in the nation.

Mexican Americans, Puerto Ricans, and other Hispanic/Latino minorities who served in the military also benefited from the GI Bill. Many of them—and their families—were able to relocate to the mainland United States because of the educational and housing programs provided veterans through the federal government. Between 1940 and 1960, nearly a million Puerto Ricans, mostly small farmers and agricultural workers, moved into American cities, especially New York City. By the late 1960s, more Puerto Ricans lived in New York City than in San Juan, the capital of Puerto Rico.

SHIFTING WOMEN'S ROLES During the Second World War, millions of women had assumed traditionally male jobs in factories and mills. After the war, those women were encouraged to return to their traditional roles as loving wives, caring mothers, and happy homemakers. A 1945 article in *House Beautiful* magazine informed women that the returning war veteran was "head man again. . . . Your part in the remaking of this man is to fit his home to him, understanding why he wants it this way, forgetting your own preferences."

The prevailing images of middle-class life featured tree-lined suburban streets, kids riding their bikes through beautiful neighborhoods, and women as devoted servants to their husbands. Idealized images of "the happy home-maker" and suburban life in popular television programs like *The Donna Reed Show* or *Leave It to Beaver* also supported the cold war campaign to portray the superiority of capitalism, democracy, freedom, and religion over communism. Russian women were depicted toiling in drudgery in drab factories or on government farms.

During the fifties, the U.S. marriage rate reached an all-time high, and the average age of marriage for women plummeted to nineteen. There was enormous social pressure on teenaged girls to get married quickly; if a woman wasn't engaged or married by her early twenties, she was in danger of becoming an "old maid." In 1956, one-fourth of all white college women wed while still enrolled in school, and most dropped out before receiving a degree. A common joke was that women went to college to get an "M.R.S. degree"—that is, a husband.

Despite this version of the nineteenth century's "cult of domesticity," many women did work outside the home, usually out of necessity. In 1950, women comprised 29 percent of the workforce, and that percentage rose steadily throughout the decade. Some 70 percent of employed women worked in clerical positions—as secretaries, bank tellers, or sales clerks—or on assembly lines or in the service industry (waitresses, laundresses, maids). Less than 15 percent were employed in a professional capacity (teachers, nurses, accountants, social workers). Women represented only 3.5 percent of attorneys and 6 percent of physicians. African American and other minority women had even fewer vocational choices and were mostly delegated to low-paying service jobs such as maids and cooks.

THE CHILD-CENTERED FIF-TIES With the war over, millions of military veterans eagerly returned to schools, jobs, wives, and babies. The record number of Americans born during the postwar period (roughly 1941–1964) composed what came to be known as the "**baby boom** generation," which would shape the nation's social and cultural life throughout the second half of the twentieth century and after.

Postwar babies initially created a surge in demand for diapers, washing machines, and baby food, then required the construction of thousands of new schools—and the hiring of teachers to staff them. Children's needs drove much of the economy's growth, creating a huge market for toys, candy, gum, records, clothes, and other items. In 1958, *Life* magazine reported that four-year-olds were causing a "backlog of business orders that will take two decades to fulfill."

Hollywood homemakers TV shows, movies, and plays in the fifties were outlets for homemakers' anxieties and fantasies. Top: *Father Knows Best* was a popular comedy about a middle-class family in the Midwest. Jane Wyatt portrayed the clan's matriarch Margaret, the unflappable voice of reason who oversaw an idealized suburban home life. Bottom: Domestic bliss was never in reach for African American female characters. In the award-winning Broadway production of *Porgy and Bess* (1959), Dorothy Dandridge plays an addict so lost in the vice of New Orleans that even her self-sacrificing disabled lover (Sidney Poitier) cannot save her.

That so many women were having babies and raising children necessarily shaped societal attitudes toward them—and vice versa. A special issue of *Life* in 1956 featured the "ideal" middle-class woman: a thirty-two-year-old "pretty and popular" white suburban housewife, mother of four, who had married at age sixteen. She was described as an excellent wife, mother, volunteer, and "home manager" who preferred marriage and child-rearing to a career outside the home. She made her own clothes, hosted dozens of dinner parties each year, sang in her church choir, and was devoted to her husband. "In her daily round," *Life* reported, "she attends club or charity meetings, drives the children to school, does the weekly grocery shopping, makes ceramics, and is planning to study French."

The soaring birthrate reinforced the notion that a woman's place was in the home. "Of all the accomplishments of the American woman," *Life* proclaimed, "the one she brings off with the most spectacular success is having babies."

A Religious Nation

After the Second World War, Americans joined churches and synagogues in record numbers. In 1940, less than half the adult population belonged to a church; by 1960, more than 65 percent were members of churches or synagogues. The cold war provided a direct stimulant to Christian evangelism. A godly nation, it was widely assumed, would better withstand the march of "godless" communism.

President Eisenhower promoted a patriotic religious crusade. "Recognition of the Supreme Being," he declared, "is the first, the most basic, expression of Americanism. Without God, there could be no American form of government, nor an American way of life." In 1954, Congress added the phrase "[one nation] under God" to the Pledge of Allegiance. In 1956, it made the statement "In God We Trust" the nation's official motto. Eisenhower ordered that the motto be displayed on all currency. "Today in the United

Roadside service Drive-in churches offered their members the comfort of listening to Sunday Mass from their cars. Here, the pastor of New York's Tremont Methodist Church greets a member of his car-centered congregation.

States," *Time* magazine claimed in 1954, "the Christian faith is back at the center of things."

The prevailing tone of the religious revival was upbeat and soothing. As the Protestant Council of New York City explained to its radio and television presenters, their on-air broadcasts "should project love, joy, courage, hope, faith, trust in God, goodwill. . . . In a very real sense we are 'selling' religion, the good news of the Gospel."

The best salesman for this "good news" was the Reverend Norman Vincent Peale. No speaker was more in demand, and no writer was more widely read. Peale's book *The Power of Positive Thinking* (1952) was a phenomenal best seller—and for good reason. It offered a simple how-to course in personal happiness, which Peale called Practical Christianity. "Flush out all depressing, negative, and tired thoughts," he advised. "Start thinking faith, enthusiasm, and joy." By following this simple formula, he pledged, each American could become "a more popular, esteemed, and well-liked individual." At the height of Peale's popularity, he was reaching 30 million people each week through radio, television, and his weekly newspaper columns.

CRACKS IN THE PICTURE WINDOW

In contrast to Peale's feel-good religion, the fifties also experienced growing anxiety, dissent, and diversity. In *The Affluent Society* (1958), for example, economist John Kenneth Galbraith attacked the prevailing notion that sustained economic growth was solving social problems. He reminded readers that the nation had yet to eradicate poverty, especially among minorities in inner cities; female-led households; Mexican American migrant farmworkers; Native Americans; and rural southerners, both black and white.

POVERTY AMID PROSPERITY Uncritical praise for the "throwaway" culture of consumption masked the chronic poverty amid America's mythic plenty. In 1959, a quarter of the population had *no* financial assets, and more than half had no savings accounts or credit cards. Poverty afflicted nearly half of the African American population, compared to only a quarter of whites. Although by 1950 blacks were earning on average more than four times their 1940 wages, they and other minority groups lagged well behind whites in their *rate* of improvement. At least 40 million people remained "poor" during the 1950s, but their plight was largely ignored.

LITERATURE AS SOCIAL CRITICISM One of the most striking aspects of the fifties was the sharp contrast between the happy public mood and the increasingly bitter social criticism from intellectuals, theologians, novelists, playwrights, poets, and artists who questioned the prevailing attitude about the superiority of the American way of life. Playwright Thornton Wilder labeled the young adults of the fifties the "Silent Generation" because of the smug complacency prevalent among upper-middle-class whites. Writer Norman Mailer was equally disdainful. He said the 1950s was "one of the worst decades in the history of man."

THE BEATS A small but highly visible and controversial group of young writers, poets, painters, and musicians rejected the consumer culture and the traditional expectations and responsibilities of middle-class life. They were known as the **Beats,** a term with multiple meanings: to be "beat" was likened to being "upbeat" and even "beatific," as well as being "on the beat" in "real cool" jazz music. But the Beats also liked the name because it implied "weariness," being "exhausted" or "beaten down," qualities which none of them actually exhibited.

Art ache The Beat community fostered in its members a frenzied desire to experience life in all of its intensity, including the cultural realm. In this 1959 photograph, poet Tex Kleen reads in a bathtub at Venice Beach, California, while artist Mad Mike paints trash cans.

Jack Kerouac, Allen Ginsberg, William Burroughs, Neal Cassady, Gary Snyder, and other Beats rebelled against conventional literary and artistic expression and excelled at outrageous, often criminal behavior. Intensely self-absorbed, the mostly male Beats celebrated, even embodied, lives of breathtaking risk fueled by feverish spontaneity and raw energy. They pursued reckless alcohol- and drug-induced ecstasies and sexual excesses. (Many of them were gay or bisexual during an era when homosexuality was considered a form of deviance requiring psychotherapy.)

The Beat hipsters emerged from the bohemian underground in New York City's Greenwich Village. Enlivened by tequila, marijuana, amphetamines, and heroin, the male Beats were essentially apolitical and self-indulgent chauvinists, more interested in transforming themselves than in reforming the world. Kerouac and the other Beats wanted their art and literature to change consciousness rather than address social ills.

During three feverish weeks, Kerouac typed nonstop (dictated by the "Holy Ghost") the manuscript of his remarkable novel *On the Road* (1957), an account of a series of frenzied cross-country trips he and others made between 1948 and 1950. The Beats were nomadic hipsters, restless and tormented souls whose road to salvation lay in hallucinogenic drugs and lots of alcohol, casual sex, petty crime, gratuitous violence, a passion for up-tempo jazz ("bebop"), fast cars, the street life of urban ghettos, an affinity for Buddhism, and a vagabond spirit. At heart, the Beats were romantics searching for an authentic sense of self in a nation absorbed in consumerism, conformism, and anti-communism. Their tortured rebelliousness set the stage for the more widespread youth revolt of the 1960s.

ROCK 'N' ROLL The millions of children making up the first wave of the baby boomers became adolescents in the 1950s. There were so many of them that people began calling them teenagers. A distinctive teen subculture began to emerge, as did a wave of juvenile delinquency. By 1956, more than a million teens were being arrested each year. One contributing factor was access to automobiles, which enabled teens to escape parental control and, in the words of one journalist, provided "a private lounge for drinking and for petting [embracing and kissing] or sex episodes."

Many blamed teen delinquency on rock 'n' roll, a new form of music that emerged during the 1950s. Alan Freed, a Cleveland disc jockey known as "Moondog," coined the term *rock 'n' roll* in 1951. He had noticed that white teenagers buying rhythm and blues (R&B) records preferred the livelier recordings by African Americans and Hispanic Americans. Freed began playing R&B records on his radio show, but he called the music "rock 'n' roll" (a phrase used in African American communities to refer to dancing and sex). By 1954, Freed had moved to New York City, where his popular program helped bridge the gap between "white" and "black" music. African American singers such as Chuck Berry, Little Richard, and Ray Charles, as well as Hispanic American performers such as Ritchie Valens (Richard Valenzuela), captivated young, white, middle-class audiences.

At the same time, Sam Phillips, a radio disk jockey in Memphis, Tennessee, was searching for a particular type of pop singer. "If I could find a white man with a Negro sound," Phillips said, "I could make a billion dollars."

He found his singer in Elvis Presley, the lanky son of poor Mississippi farmers. In 1956, the twenty-one-year-old Presley, by then a regional star famous for his long, unruly hair, sullen yet sensual sneer, and swiveling hips, released his smash-hit recording "Heartbreak Hotel." Over the next two years, he emerged as the most popular musician in American history, carrying rock 'n' roll across the race barrier and assaulting the bland conformity of fifties culture. Presley's gyrating performances (his nickname was "Elvis the Pelvis") and incomparably rich and raw baritone voice drove young people wild and earned him millions of fans around the world. His movements, said one music critic, "suggest, in a word, sex."

Cultural conservatives were outraged and urged parents to destroy Presley's records because they promoted "a pagan concept of life." A Roman Catholic official denounced Presley as a vile symptom of a teenage "creed of dishonesty, violence, lust and degeneration." Patriotic groups claimed that rock 'n' roll music was part of a Communist plot to corrupt America's youth. Writing in the *New York Times*, a psychiatrist characterized rock 'n' roll as a "communicable disease." The U.S. Senate subcommittee tasked with investigating juvenile delinquency warned that Presley was threatening "to rock-n-roll the juvenile world into open revolt against society. The gangster of tomorrow is the Elvis Presley type of today."

Yet rock 'n' roll flourished in part because it was so controversial. It gave teenagers a self-conscious sense of belonging to a tribal social group. More important, it brought together, on equal terms, musicians (and their audiences) of varied races and backgrounds.

THE CIVIL RIGHTS MOVEMENT

Soon after the cold war began, Soviet diplomats began to use America's racial discrimination against African Americans as a propaganda tool to illustrate the defects of the American way of life. Under the Jim Crow system in the southern states, blacks still risked being lynched if they registered to vote. They were forced to use separate facilities—water fountains, restrooms, hotels, theaters, parks—and to attend segregated schools. In the North, discrimination was not as "official," but it was equally real, especially in housing and employment. President Eisenhower had an opportunity to exercise transformational leadership in race relations; his unwillingness to do so was his greatest failure. As *Time* magazine noted in 1958, Eisenhower "overlooked the fact that the U.S. needed [his] moral leadership in fighting segregation."

EISENHOWER AND RACE Eisenhower had entered the White House committed to civil rights in principle, and he pushed for improvements in some areas. During his first three years, public facilities (parks, playgrounds, libraries, restaurants) in Washington, D.C., were desegregated, and he intervened to end discrimination at military bases in Virginia and South Carolina. He also appointed the first African American to an executive office: E. Frederic Morrow, who was named Administrative Officer for Special Projects. Beyond that, however, Eisenhower refused to make civil rights for African Americans a moral crusade. Pushing too hard, he believed, would "raise tempers and increase prejudices," doing more harm than good. His passive attitude meant that governmental leadership on civil rights would come from the judiciary more than from the executive or legislative branches.

In 1953, Eisenhower appointed former Republican governor Earl Warren of California as chief justice of the U.S. Supreme Court, a decision he later said was the "biggest damn fool mistake I ever made." Warren, who had seemed safely conservative while in elected office, displayed a social conscience and a streak of libertarianism on the bench. Under Warren's leadership (1953–1969), the Supreme Court became a powerful force for social and political change.

AFRICAN AMERICAN ACTIVISM The most-crucial leaders of the civil rights movement came from those whose rights were most often violated: African Americans, Hispanic Americans, Asian Americans, and other minorities. Courageous blacks led what would become the most important social movement in twentieth-century American history. With intelligence, bravery, and dignity, they fought in the courts, at the ballot box, and in the streets.

Although many African Americans moved to the North and West during and after the Second World War, a majority remained in the South, where

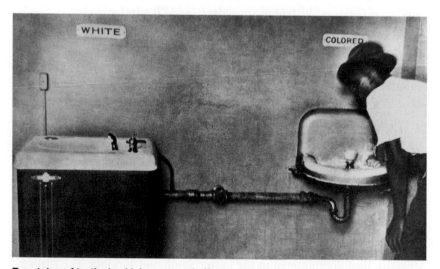

Fountains of truth An Alabama motel offers its white patrons chilled water from a cooler, while its African American guests must use a simple drinking fountain.

they still faced a rigidly segregated society. In the 1952 presidential election, for example, only 20 percent of eligible African Americans were registered to vote. In addition, the public schools, especially in the South, were supposedly racially separate but equal in quality. In fact, however, many all-black schools were underfunded, understaffed, and overcrowded.

In the mid-1930s, the National Association for the Advancement of Colored People (NAACP) challenged the **separate-but-equal** judicial doctrine that had preserved racial segregation since the *Plessy* decision by the Supreme Court in 1896. It took almost fifteen years, however, to convince the courts that racial segregation must end. Finally, in *Sweatt v. Painter* (1950), the Supreme Court ruled that a separate black law school in Texas was *not* equal in quality to the state's whites-only schools. The Court ordered the state to remedy the situation. It was the first step toward dismantling America's tradition of racial segregation.

THE *BROWN* DECISION By the early 1950s, people were challenging state laws mandating racial segregation in the public schools. Five such cases, from Kansas, Delaware, South Carolina, Virginia, and the District of Columbia—usually cited by reference to the first, ***Brown v. Board of Education of Topeka, Kansas***—went to the Supreme Court in 1952. President Eisenhower told the attorney general that he hoped the justices would postpone dealing with the explosive case "until the next Administration took over." When it became obvious that the Court was moving forward, Eisenhower urged Chief Justice Warren to side with segregationists. Warren was not swayed: "You mind your business," he told the president, "and I'll mind mine."

Warren wrote the pathbreaking opinion, delivered on May 17, 1954, in which the Court declared that "in the field of public education the doctrine of 'separate but equal' has no place." The justices used a variety of sociological and psychological findings to show that even if racially separate schools were equal in quality, the very practice of separating students by race caused feelings of inferiority among black children. A year later, the Court directed that the process of racial *integration* should move "with all deliberate speed."

Eisenhower refused to endorse or enforce the Court's ruling. Privately, he grumbled "that the Supreme Court decision set back progress in the South at least fifteen years." Anyone who thinks "you can do these things by force is just plain nuts," he said. Eisenhower had "little faith in the ability of law to change the human heart or eliminate prejudice."

While token racial integration began as early as 1954 in Kentucky and Missouri, hostility mounted in the Lower South and Virginia. The Alabama State Senate and the Virginia legislature both passed resolutions "nullifying" the Supreme Court's decision, arguing that racial integration was an issue of states' rights. Arkansas governor Orval Faubus insisted that the "federal government is a creature of the states. . . . We must either choose to defend our rights or else surrender."

In 1954, Harry F. Byrd, a Virginia senator and former governor, supplied a rallying cry for diehard white racists when he called for "**massive resistance**" against federal efforts to enforce integration in the South. Senator James O. Eastland of Mississippi, a state where African Americans made up 45 percent of the population, pledged that "integration will never come to Mississippi" and denounced the *Brown* decision as an "illegal, immoral, and sinful doctrine." He told the Senate that "the Negro race is an inferior race" and that the South was determined to maintain "white supremacy."

The opponents of court-ordered integration were militantly defiant. In 1956, a Declaration of Constitutional Principles ("Southern Manifesto") was signed by 101 members of Congress, deploring the *Brown* decision as "a clear abuse of judicial power" that had created an "explosive and dangerous condition" in the South. Only three southern Democrats refused to sign. One of them, Senator Lyndon B. Johnson of Texas, would become president seven years later. In six southern states at the end of 1956, two years after the *Brown* ruling, no black children attended school with whites. Some southern politicians threatened to shut down white schools rather than allow racial integration.

THE MONTGOMERY BUS BOYCOTT The *Brown* case did much more than mobilize white resistance. It inspired many blacks (and white activists) by suggesting that the federal government was finally beginning to confront racial discrimination. Yet the essential role played by the NAACP and the courts in the civil rights movement often overshadows the courageous contributions of individual African Americans who took great personal risks to challenge segregation.

For example, in Montgomery, Alabama, on December 1, 1955, Mrs. Rosa Parks, a forty-two-year-old black seamstress who was a fiercely determined activist for racial justice, refused to give up her seat on a city bus to a white man. By doing so, she launched the modern civil rights movement.

Like many southern communities, Montgomery, the "Cradle of the Confederacy," required blacks to sit in the rear seats of buses or trains. They could sit in the front seats designated for whites only if there were empty seats. If a white rider asked a black to move, they were expected to go "to the back of the bus." Parks, however, was "tired of giving in." When the bus driver told her that "niggers must move back" or he would have her arrested, she replied, with quiet courage, "You may do that." Police then arrested her.

The next night, black community leaders met at Dexter Avenue Baptist Church to organize a long-planned boycott of the city's bus system, most of whose riders were African Americans. Student and faculty volunteers from Alabama State University stayed up all night to distribute 35,000 flyers denouncing the arrest of Rosa Parks and urging support for the **Montgomery bus boycott**.

MARTIN LUTHER KING JR. In the Dexter Avenue church's twenty-six-year-old pastor, Martin Luther King Jr., the boycott movement found a brave and charismatic leader. Born in Atlanta, the grandson of a slave and son of a prominent minister, King was intelligent, courageous, and an eloquent and passionate speaker. "We must use the weapon of love," King told supporters. "We must realize so many people are taught to hate us that they are not totally responsible for their hate." To his foes, King warned, "We will soon wear you down by our capacity to suffer, and in winning our freedom we will so appeal to your heart and conscience that we will win you in the process." King preached **nonviolent civil disobedience**, the tactic of defying unjust laws through peaceful actions, but he also valued militancy, for without confrontation with those in power there would be no negotiation or progress.

Civil disobedience Martin Luther King Jr. is roughly arrested for "loitering" in 1958. He would be arrested thirty times in his life for defying racist laws.

The Montgomery bus boycott was a stunning success—but it was not easy. For 381 days, African Americans, women and men, organized carpools, used black-owned taxis, hitchhiked, or simply walked. White supporters also provided rides. A few boycotters rode horses or mules to work. The unprecedented mass protest infuriated many whites; police harassed and ticketed black carpools, and white thugs attacked black pedestrians. Ku Klux Klan members burned black churches and bombed houses owned by King and other boycott leaders. King himself was arrested twice. In trying to calm an angry black crowd, he urged restraint: "Don't get panicky. Don't get your weapons. We want to love our enemies."

On December 20, 1956, the Montgomery boycotters won a federal case they had initiated against racial segregation on public buses. The Supreme Court affirmed that "the separate but equal doctrine can no longer be safely followed as a correct statement of the law." The next day, King and other African Americans boarded the city buses. The success of the boycott showed that well-coordinated, nonviolent black activism could trigger major changes in public policy. Among African Americans, hope replaced resignation, and action supplanted passivity. The boycott also catapulted King into the national spotlight.

And what of Rosa Parks? She and her husband lost their jobs, and hate mail as well as death threats and firebombings forced them to leave Alabama eight months after her arrest. They moved to Detroit, where they remained fully engaged in the evolving civil rights movement.

THE CIVIL RIGHTS ACTS OF 1957 AND 1960 President Eisenhower's timidity in the area of race relations emerged again when he was asked to protect the right of African Americans to vote. In 1956, hoping to exploit divisions between northern and southern Democrats and reclaim some of the black vote for Republicans, congressional leaders agreed to support what became the Civil Rights Act of 1957.

The first civil rights law passed since 1875, it finally got through the Senate, after a year's delay, with the help of majority leader Lyndon B. Johnson, a Texas Democrat who knew that he could never be elected president if he was viewed as just another racist white southerner. The bill was intended to ensure that all Americans, regardless of race or ethnicity, were allowed to vote. Johnson won southern acceptance of the bill by watering down its enforcement provisions. Eisenhower reassured Johnson that the final version represented "the mildest civil rights bill possible."

The Civil Rights Act established the Civil Rights Commission and a new Civil Rights Division in the Justice Department intended to prevent interference with the right to vote. Yet by 1959, the law had not resulted in a single southern black voter being added to the rolls. Neither did the Civil Rights Act of 1960, which provided for federal courts to register African Americans to vote in districts where there was a "pattern and practice" of racial discrimination. This bill, too, lacked teeth and depended upon vigorous presidential enforcement! to achieve any tangible results.

DESEGREGATION IN LITTLE ROCK   A few weeks after the Civil Rights Act of 1957 was passed, Arkansas's Democratic governor, Orval Eugene Faubus, a rabid segregationist eager to win a third term, called a special session of the state legislature to pass a series of bills designed to give him sweeping new powers to close public schools threatened with integration and to transfer funds from public schools facing federally enforced integration to private "segregation academies." Faubus defied a federal court order by using the state's National Guard to prevent nine black students from enrolling at Little Rock's Central High School. The National Guard commander's orders were explicit: "No niggers in the building." When one of the students, fifteen-year-old Elizabeth Eckford, tried to enter the school, a surging mob of jeering whites shrieked, "Lynch her! Lynch her!"

Local authorities removed the black students, and the mayor of Little Rock frantically called the White House to request federal troops, explaining that Faubus was creating "tensions where none existed." At that point, Eisenhower, who had resisted all appeals for federal action, reluctantly dispatched 1,000 army paratroopers of the 101st Airborne Division to protect the brave black students as they entered the school. "Mob rule," he told the nation, "cannot be allowed to overrule the decisions of our courts."

"Lynch her!" Fifteen-year-old Elizabeth Eckford endures the hostile screams of future classmates as she enters Central High School in Little Rock, Arkansas.

It was one of the nation's most painful and momentous confrontations, the first time since the 1870s that federal troops had been sent to the South to protect the rights of African Americans. With television cameras sending images across the country, seasoned paratroopers used bayonets and rifle butts to disperse the angry crowd. Inside Central High School, the nine black students attended their first classes with soldiers patrolling the halls. During lunch hour, two white pupils saw a black student eating alone. They asked: "Would you like to come over to our table?" The grateful boy replied: "Gosh, I'd love to."

The soldiers stayed in Little Rock through the school year. To a man, unyielding southern governors and congressmen furiously lashed out at Eisenhower, charging that he was violating states' rights. Eisenhower had "lit the fires of hate," claimed Senator James Eastland. A South Carolina moderate took a different tack: "Those who believed that integration could be accomplished gradually and peacefully are now convinced that Eisenhower will have to use force all the way."

In the summer of 1958, Governor Faubus, supported by the state legislature, closed the Little Rock high schools rather than allow racial integration. The governor of Virginia did the same in his state. Their actions led Jonathan Daniels, editor of the Raleigh, North Carolina, *News & Observer*, to write that closing public schools is "something beyond secession from the Union; [it] is secession from civilization."

SOUTHERN CHRISTIAN LEADERSHIP CONFERENCE After Little Rock, progress toward greater civil rights seemed agonizingly slow. Frustrated African Americans began blaming the NAACP for relying too much on the courts. "The Negro masses are angry and restless, tired of prolonged legal battles that end in paper decrees," reported black journalist Louis Lomax.

The widespread sense of disappointment gave Martin Luther King's nonviolent civil rights movement even greater visibility. As King explained, "We were confronted with blasted hopes, and the dark shadow of a deep disappointment settled upon us. So we had no alternative except that of preparing for direct action, whereby we would present our very bodies as a means of laying our case before the conscience of the local and national community."

On January 10, 1957, Dr. King invited about sixty black ministers and leaders to Ebenezer Church in Atlanta. Their goal was to form an organization to coordinate and support nonviolent direct action as a method of desegregating bus systems across the South. After a follow-up meeting in New Orleans on February 15, a new organization emerged: the **Southern Christian Leadership Conference (SCLC)**, with Dr. King as its president. Unlike the NAACP, which recruited individual members, SCLC coordinated activities on behalf of a cluster of organizations, mostly individual churches or community groups. Because Dr. King pushed for direct action against the segregated South, only a few African American ministers were initially willing to affiliate with SCLC, for fear of a white backlash.

King persisted, however, and over time SCLC grew into a powerful organization. The activists knew that violence awaited them. Roy Wilkins, head of the NAACP, noted that "the Negro citizen has come to the point where he is not afraid of violence. He no longer shrinks back. He will assert himself, and if violence comes, so be it." Thus began the second phase of the civil rights movement, a phase that would come to fruition in the 1960s as King and other African American activists showed the nation the courage to resist injustice, the power to love everyone, and the strength to endure discouragement and opposition.

FOREIGN POLICY IN THE FIFTIES

The Truman administration's commitment to "contain" communism focused on the Soviet threat to western Europe. During the 1950s, the Eisenhower administration, especially Secretary of State John Foster Dulles, expanded America's objective in the cold war. "Containment" was no longer enough; the United States must develop a "dynamic" foreign policy that would "roll back" communism around the world.

Dulles's goal was to "liberate" those people under Communist rule rather than merely contain Communist expansion. As a cold warrior, Dulles expected every nation to choose sides. "For us," he said, "there are two kinds of people in the world. There are those who are Christians and support free enterprise, and there are the others." He soon discovered, however, that the complexities of world affairs and the realities of Soviet and Communist Chinese power made his moral commitment to manage the destiny of the world unrealistic—and costly.

CONCLUDING AN ARMISTICE In Korea, President Eisenhower faced three choices: increase the war effort, continue the military stalemate, or pursue a negotiated settlement. He chose the third option, but he first had to convince John Foster Dulles that negotiations were warranted. Dulles did not want peace until the Chinese had suffered "one hell of a licking" and the two Koreas had been reunited. In April 1953, Eisenhower told Dulles that he was not willing to prolong the military effort, but he was comfortable using the threat of nuclear weapons and other actions to break the impasse.

In May 1953, Eisenhower took the bold step of intensifying the aerial bombardment of North Korea and let it be known that he would use nuclear weapons if a truce were not forthcoming. Thereafter, negotiations moved quickly toward a cease-fire agreement (called an armistice) on July 26, 1953. It ended "all acts of armed force" and reaffirmed the historical border between the two Koreas just above the 38th parallel until a "final peaceful settlement" could be reached. Other factors in bringing about the armistice were China's rising military losses and the uncertainty and caution felt by the Soviet Communists after the death of Josef Stalin on March 5, 1953.

The Korean War transformed the United States into the world's policeman by convincing political and military leaders that communism was indeed a global threat. Within a few years, the United States would build scores of military bases around the world and organize a permanent "national security" apparatus in Washington to manage its new responsibilities, not the least of which was a growing stockpile of nuclear weaponry.

DULLES AND MASSIVE RETALIATION Like Woodrow Wilson, Secretary of State Dulles was a Presbyterian minister's son whose favorite hymn was "Onward, Christian Soldiers." Self-righteous and humorless, he believed that the United States was "born with a sense of destiny and mission" to defeat communism.

Dulles insisted that the Democratic policy of "containing" communism was "immoral" because it did nothing to free people from oppression. America, he argued, should work toward the "liberation" of the "captive peoples" of Eastern Europe and China. Eisenhower, however, was quick to explain that the "liberation" doctrine would not involve military force. Instead, he would promote the removal of Communist control "by every peaceful means, but only by peaceful means."

Dulles and Eisenhower knew that the United States could not win a ground war against the Soviet Union or Communist China, whose armies had millions more soldiers than did the United States. Nor could the administration afford—politically or financially—to sustain military expenditures at the levels required during the Korean War. So Dulles and Eisenhower crafted a strategy that came to be called "**massive retaliation**," which meant using the threat of nuclear warfare ("massive retaliatory power") to prevent Communist aggression. The strategy, they argued, would provide a "maximum deterrent at bearable cost."

"Massive retaliation" had major weaknesses, however. By the mid-1950s, both the United States and the Soviet Union had developed hydrogen bombs, which were 750 times as powerful as the atomic bombs dropped on Japan in 1945. A single hydrogen bomb would have a devastating global impact, yet war planners envisioned using hundreds of them. "The necessary art," Dulles explained, was in the brinkmanship, "the ability to get to the verge without getting into war. . . . If you are scared to go to the brink, you are lost." The *Milwaukee Journal* found Dulles's "brinkmanship" strategy terrifying: "It is like saying that the closer you get to war the better you serve peace. It is like saying that the destiny of the human race is something to gamble with."

THE CIA'S FOREIGN INTERVENTIONS While Eisenhower and Dulles were publicly promoting the "liberation" of Communist nations and "massive retaliation" as a strategy against the Soviets, they were secretly using the new **Central Intelligence Agency (CIA)** to manipulate world politics in covert ways that produced unintended consequences—all of them bad.

The anti-colonial independence movements unleashed by the Second World War placed the United States in the awkward position of watching nationalist groups around the globe revolt against British and French rule. In Iran in May 1951, the parliament seized control of the nation's British-run oil industry. The following year, a newly elected prime minister, Mohammed Mossadegh, cut all diplomatic ties with Great Britain and insisted that Iran, not Britain, should own, sell, and profit from Iranian oil. Dulles predicted that Iran was on the verge of falling under Communist control. The CIA and the British intelligence service, MI6, then launched Operation Ajax, designed, in the words of the agency's head, Allen Dulles (the secretary of state's brother), to "bring about the fall of Mossadegh."

In 1954, the CIA bribed Iranian army officers and hired Iranian agents to arrest Mossadegh, who was convicted of high treason. He was imprisoned for three years, then put under house arrest until his death in 1967. In return for access to Iranian oil, the U.S. government thereafter provided massive support for the anti-Communist and increasingly authoritarian regime of the shah (king) of Iran, Mohammad Reza Pahlavi, who consolidated power after the removal of Mossadegh. In the end, Operation Ajax proved to be a disaster by reinstating the incompetent and indecisive shah.

The success of the CIA-engineered coup in Iran emboldened Eisenhower to authorize other secret operations to undermine "unfriendly" government regimes, even if it meant aligning with corrupt dictatorships. In 1954, the target was Guatemala, a desperately poor Central American country led by Colonel Jacobo Arbenz Guzman. Arbenz's decision to take over U.S.-owned property and industries convinced Dulles that Guatemala was falling victim to "international communism." Dulles persuaded Eisenhower to approve a CIA operation to organize a secret Guatemalan army in Honduras. On June 18, 1954, aided by CIA-piloted warplanes, 150 paid "liberators" crossed the border and forced Arbenz Guzman into exile in Mexico. The United States then installed a new ruler in Guatemala who eliminated all political opposition.

By secretly overthrowing elected governments to ensure that they did not join the Soviet bloc, however, the CIA operations destabilized Iran and Guatemala and created problems in the Middle East and Central America that would eventually come back to haunt the United States.

INDOCHINA During the 1950s, the United States also became embroiled in Southeast Asia. Indochina, created by French imperialists in the nineteenth century out of the old kingdoms of Cambodia, Laos, and Vietnam, offered a distinctive case of anti-colonial nationalism. During the Second World War, after Japanese troops occupied the region, the Viet Minh (League for the Independence of Vietnam) waged a guerrilla resistance movement led by Ho Chi Minh, a seasoned revolutionary and passionate nationalist. "Uncle Ho," a wispy man weighing barely 100 pounds, worked sixteen hours each day toward a single goal: independence for his country. At the end of the war against Japan, the Viet Minh controlled part of northern Vietnam. On September 2, 1945, Ho Chi Minh proclaimed the creation of a Democratic Republic of Vietnam, with its capital in Hanoi.

The French, like the Americans would later, underestimated the determination of Ho and the Vietnamese nationalists to maintain their independence. In 1946, the First Indochina War began when Ho's fighters resisted French efforts to restore the colonial regime. French forces quickly regained control of the cities, while the Viet Minh controlled the countryside. Ho predicted that his forces would absorb more losses, but the French would give in first. When the Korean War ended, the United States continued its efforts to strengthen French control of Vietnam. By the end of 1953, the Eisenhower administration was paying nearly 80 percent of the cost of the French military effort.

In December 1953, some 12,000 French soldiers parachuted into **Dien Bien Phu**, a cluster of villages in a valley ringed by mountains in northwestern Vietnam. Their plan was to build a well-fortified base to lure Viet Minh guerrillas into the open and then overwhelm them with superior firepower. The French assumed that the surrounding forested hills were impassable. But slowly, more than 55,000 Viet Minh fighters equipped with Chinese Communist weapons took up positions atop the ridges overlooking the French military base. They laboriously dismantled cannons and carried them in pieces up the hills, then dug trenches and tunnels down into the valley. By March 1954, the French paratroopers found themselves surrounded.

As the weeks passed, the French government pleaded with the United States to relieve the pressure on Dien Bien Phu. The National Security Council—Dulles, Vice President Nixon, and the chairman of the Joint Chiefs of Staff—urged Eisenhower to use atomic bombs to aid the trapped French force. Eisenhower snapped back: "You boys must be crazy. We can't use those awful things against Asians for the second time in less than ten years. My God!"

The president opposed U.S. intervention unless the British joined the effort. When they refused, Eisenhower told the French that U.S. military action in

Dien Bien Phu Viet Minh soldiers march French captives to a prisoner camp in Dien Bien Phu on May 7, 1954.

Vietnam was "politically impossible." On May 7, 1954, the Viet Minh fighters overwhelmed the last French resistance. The catastrophic defeat caused the collapse of the French government and signaled the end of French colonial rule in Asia.

On July 20, 1954, representatives of France, Britain, the Soviet Union, the People's Republic of China, and the Viet Minh signed the Geneva Accords, which gave Laos and Cambodia their independence and divided Vietnam in two at the 17th parallel. The Geneva Accords gave the Viet Minh Communists control in the North; the French would remain south of the line until nationwide elections in 1956. American and South Vietnamese representatives refused to sign the Geneva Accords, arguing that the treaties legitimized the Communist victory. After 1954, Ho Chi Minh took complete control of the government in North Vietnam, executing thousands of Vietnamese he deemed opponents.

In South Vietnam, power gravitated to a new premier chosen by the French at American urging: Ngo Dinh Diem, a Catholic nationalist who had opposed both the French and the Viet Minh. In 1954, Eisenhower began providing military and economic aid to Diem. The president remained opposed to the use of U.S. combat troops. Diem's autocratic efforts to eliminate all opposition played into the hands of the Communists, who found eager recruits among the discontented South Vietnamese. By 1957, Communist guerrillas known as the **Viet Cong** were launching attacks on the Diem government. As the warfare intensified, the Eisenhower administration concluded that its only option was to "sink or swim with Diem."

In 1954, Eisenhower had used what he called the **"falling domino" theory** to explain why the United States needed to fight communism in Vietnam: "You have a row of dominos set up, you knock over the first one, and what will happen to the last one is the certainty that it will go over very quickly." If South Vietnam were to fall to communism, he predicted, the rest of Southeast Asia would soon follow.

The domino analogy assumed that communism was a monolithic global movement directed by Soviet leaders in Moscow. Yet anti-colonial insurgencies such as those in Southeast Asia were animated as much by nationalist

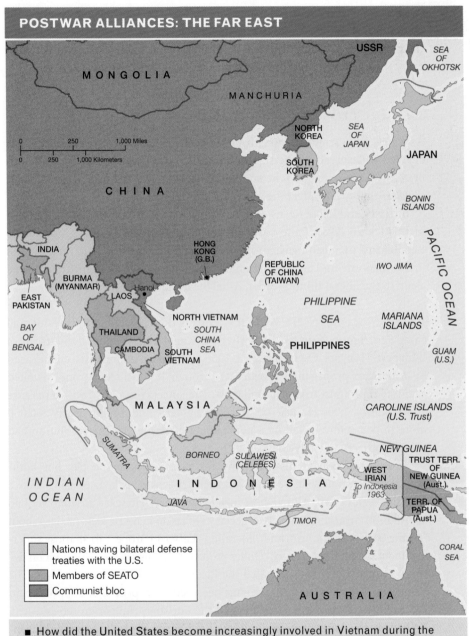

POSTWAR ALLIANCES: THE FAR EAST

Legend:
- Nations having bilateral defense treaties with the U.S.
- Members of SEATO
- Communist bloc

- How did the United States become increasingly involved in Vietnam during the fifties?
- Why did the installation of Ngo Dinh Diem by the French and the Americans backfire and generate more conflict in Vietnam?

motives as by communist ideology. The domino analogy also meant that the United States was assuming that it must police the entire world to ensure that the dominoes, no matter how small, did not begin falling. As a consequence, every insurgency around the world mushroomed into a strategic crisis.

REELECTION AND FOREIGN CRISES

As a new presidential campaign unfolded in 1956, Dwight Eisenhower still enjoyed widespread public support. But his health was beginning to deteriorate. In September 1955, he suffered a heart attack, the first of three major illnesses that would affect the rest of his presidency.

In 1956, the Republicans eagerly renominated Eisenhower and Vice President Richard Nixon. The party platform endorsed Eisenhower's moderate Republicanism, meaning balanced budgets, reduced government intervention in the economy, and an internationalist foreign policy. The Democrats turned again to the liberal Illinois leader, Adlai Stevenson.

REPRESSION IN HUNGARY During the last week of the presidential campaign, fighting erupted along the Suez Canal in Egypt and in the streets of Budapest, Hungary. On October 23, 1956, Hungarian nationalists, encouraged by American propaganda broadcasts through Radio Free Europe, revolted against Communist troops in Budapest. The Soviets responded with a massive attack, killing 2,000 Hungarian "freedom fighters" and forcing nearly 200,000 more to flee before installing a new puppet government. The revolution had been smothered in twelve days.

Eisenhower offered his sympathy for the Hungarian people, but nothing more. His strategy in dealing with such crises was, as he later said, "Take a hard line—and bluff." Although he avoided war over Hungary, Eisenhower had allowed administration officials, especially Dulles, to make reckless pledges about "rolling back" communism and "liberating" Eastern Europe. "To all those suffering under Communist slavery," Dulles promised, "let us say you can count on us."

In Hungary, the Soviets called the Eisenhower administration's bluff. The Hungarian freedom fighters, having been led to expect U.S. support, paid with their lives. As the Soviets crushed the uprising, Hungarian rebels asked, "When are the Americans coming?" Richard Nixon cynically reassured Eisenhower that the Soviet crackdown would be beneficial in showing the world the ruthlessness of communism. The president, however, felt guilty, telling Dulles that "we have excited Hungarians for all these years" and are "now turning our backs on them when they are in a jam." Dulles showed little concern, reminding the president that "we always have been against violent rebellion."

THE SUEZ WAR Eisenhower was more successful in handling an unexpected international crisis in Egypt. In 1952, an Egyptian army officer, Gamal Abdel Nasser, had overthrown the monarchy of King Farouk and set out to become the leader of the Arab world. To do so, he promised to destroy the new Israeli nation, created in 1948, and vowed to end British and French imperialism in the region. Nasser, with Soviet support, first sought to take control of the Suez Canal, the internationally managed waterway in Egypt connecting the Mediterranean and Red Seas.

The canal had opened in 1869 as a joint French–Egyptian venture. From 1882 on, British troops had protected the canal as the British Empire's "lifeline" to oil in the Middle East and to India and its other Asian colonies. When Nasser's regime pressed for the withdrawal of the British forces, Eisenhower and Dulles supported the demand. In 1954, an Anglo–Egyptian treaty provided for the withdrawal of British troops within twenty months.

In 1955, Nasser, adept at playing both sides in the cold war, announced a huge arms deal with the Soviet Union. The United States countered by offering to help Egypt finance a massive hydroelectric dam at Aswan on the Nile River. In 1956, when Nasser increased trade with the Soviet bloc and recognized the People's Republic of China, Dulles abruptly cancelled the Aswan Dam offer.

Unable to retaliate directly against the United States, Nasser seized control of the French-based Suez Canal Company and denied Israel-bound ships access through the canal. The British and French were furious, but they needed a pretext for military action. Israel soon provided one. On September 30, 1956, Israeli, British, and French officials secretly hatched a plan: Israel would invade Egypt and race west to the Suez Canal. The French and British would then send troops to the canal zone, posing as peacekeepers to keep Egypt and Israel separated.

On October 29, 1956, Israeli paratroopers dropped into Egypt. The British and French governments then issued an ultimatum demanding that the fighting cease. When Egypt rejected the ultimatum, British warplanes began bombing Egyptian airfields. On November 5, British and French soldiers invaded the canal zone. Nasser responded by sinking all forty of the international ships then in the Suez Canal. A few days later, Anglo–French commandos and paratroopers took control of the canal.

Eisenhower was furious that the three nations had hatched their scheme and attacked Egypt without informing the American government. He bluntly told Anthony Eden, the British prime minister, that he "flatly reject[ed] the thought of using force" in Egypt. And he resolved to put a stop to the invasion. "How could we possibly support Britain and France," he asked, "if in doing so we lose the whole Arab world?"

Eisenhower demanded that the British and French withdraw and that the Israelis evacuate the Sinai Peninsula—or face severe economic sanctions. That the three aggressor nations grudgingly complied on November 7 testified to Eisenhower's strength, influence, and savvy. The Suez debacle caused the downfall of the British government and hastened the process of independence among its remaining colonies. But perhaps its major result was that the British government realized that never again would it be able to act independently of the United States. Egypt reopened the Suez Canal, and, as Eisenhower had predicted, operated it in a professional, nonpolitical manner.

The **Suez crisis** affirmed the nation's status as *the* global superpower, and it helped Eisenhower win an even more lopsided reelection victory than in 1952. In carrying Louisiana, Eisenhower became the first Republican to win a Lower South state since Reconstruction; nationally, he carried all but seven states and won the electoral vote 457 to 73. Eisenhower's decisive victory, however, failed to swing a congressional majority for his party in either house.

SPUTNIK On October 4, 1957, the Soviets shocked the United States by launching the first communications satellite, called *Sputnik*, a polished aluminum sphere the size of a beach ball. Americans panicked at the news, believing that if the Soviets could put a satellite in orbit, they could also fire a rocket with a nuclear warhead across the Pacific Ocean and detonate it on the West Coast.

The Soviet success in space dealt a severe blow to the prestige of American science and technology, which had seemed unquestionably preeminent since the Second World War. Democrats charged that the Soviets had "humiliated" the United States and launched a congressional investigation to assess the new threat to the nation's security.

"*Sputnik*-mania" led the United States to increase defense spending and establish a crash program to enhance science education. In 1958, Congress created the National Aeronautics and Space Administration (NASA) to coordinate research and development related to outer space. The same year, Congress, with Eisenhower's support, enacted the National Defense Education Act (NDEA), which authorized large federal grants to colleges and universities to enhance education and research in mathematics, science, and modern languages, as well as for student loans and fellowships. The NDEA provided more financial aid to higher education than any other previous legislation.

THE EISENHOWER DOCTRINE In the aftermath of the Suez Crisis, Eisenhower decided that the United States must replace Great Britain and France as the guarantor of Western interests in the Middle East. In 1958, Congress approved what came to be called the Eisenhower Doctrine, a resolution that promised to extend economic and military aid to Arab nations and to use

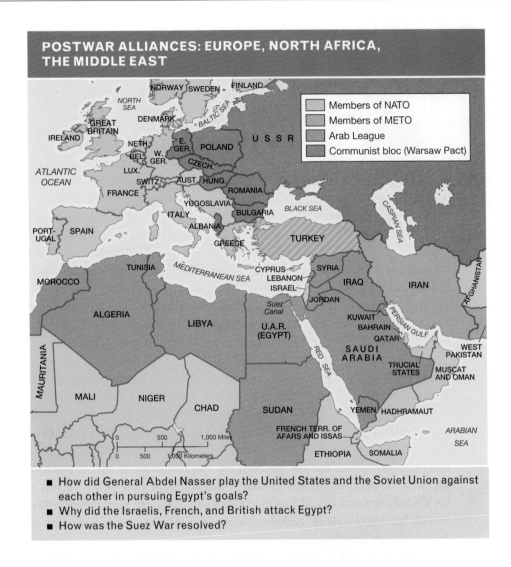

POSTWAR ALLIANCES: EUROPE, NORTH AFRICA, THE MIDDLE EAST

- Members of NATO
- Members of METO
- Arab League
- Communist bloc (Warsaw Pact)

- ■ How did General Abdel Nasser play the United States and the Soviet Union against each other in pursuing Egypt's goals?
- ■ Why did the Israelis, French, and British attack Egypt?
- ■ How was the Suez War resolved?

armed force if necessary to assist any such nation against Communist aggression. When Lebanon appealed to the United States to help fend off an insurgency, Eisenhower ordered 5,000 marines into the country. In October 1958, once the situation had stabilized, U.S. forces (up to 15,000 at one point) withdrew.

CRISIS IN BERLIN Since the Second World War, West Berlin had become an oasis of Western democracy and prosperity in Communist East Germany, while East Berlin continued to be administered by the Soviet Union. West Berlin also served as an enticing alternative to life behind the "iron curtain." Each year, thousands of East Germans escaped to West Berlin. Nikita Khrushchev, the unpredictable Soviet leader, called West Berlin a "bone in his throat."

Nikita Khruschev A fiery speaker, the Soviet premier addresses journalists at a press conference in 1959.

On November 10, 1958, Khrushchev threatened to give East Germany control of East Berlin and of the air lanes into West Berlin. After the deadline he set (May 27, 1959), Western authorities would have to deal with the Soviet-controlled East German government, in effect officially recognizing it, or face the possibility of another blockade of the city.

Eisenhower told Khrushchev that he "would hit the Russians" with every weapon in the American arsenal if they persisted in their efforts to intimidate West Berlin. At the same time, however, Eisenhower also sought a settlement. There was little hope of resolving the conflicting views on Berlin, but the negotiations distracted attention from the May 27 deadline, which passed almost unnoticed. In September 1959, Khrushchev and Eisenhower agreed that the time was ripe for a summit meeting.

THE U-2 SUMMIT The summit meeting literally crashed and burned, however, when on Sunday morning, May 1, 1960, a Soviet rocket brought down a U.S. spy plane (called the U-2) flying over the Soviet Union. Khrushchev, embarrassed by the ability of American spy planes to enter Soviet airspace, then sprang a trap on Eisenhower. The Soviets announced only that the plane had been shot down. The U.S. government, not realizing that the Soviets had captured the pilot, said it was missing a weather plane over Turkey. It was a lie. Khrushchev announced that the Soviets had American pilot Francis Gary Powers "alive and kicking" and also had the photographs Powers had taken of Soviet military installations.

On May 11, Eisenhower abandoned U.S. efforts to cover up the incident. Rather than blame others, he took personal responsibility for the spying program, explaining that such illegally obtained intelligence information was crucial to national security. At the testy summit meeting in Paris five days later, Khrushchev lectured Eisenhower for forty-five minutes before walking out. The U-2 incident set back efforts to reduce cold war tensions. Later, in 1962, Francis Gary Powers would be exchanged for a captured Soviet spy.

EVALUATING THE EISENHOWER PRESIDENCY

During President Eisenhower's second term, Congress added Alaska and Hawaii as the forty-ninth and fiftieth states (1959), while the nation experienced its worst economic slump since the Great Depression. Volatile issues such as civil rights, defense policy, and corrupt aides, including White House chief of staff Sherman Adams, compounded the administration's troubles. The president's desire to avoid divisive issues and maintain public goodwill led him at times to value harmony and popularity over justice. One observer called the Eisenhower years "the time of the great postponement" during which the president left domestic and foreign policies "about where he found them in 1953."

Opinion of Eisenhower's presidency has improved with time, however. He presided with steady self-confidence over a prosperous nation. In dealing with crises, he displayed unusually good judgment and firmness of purpose. He fulfilled his pledge to end the war in Korea, refused to intervene militarily in Indochina, and maintained the peace in the face of explosive global tensions. Eisenhower's greatest decisions were the wars he chose to avoid. After the truce in Korea, not a single American soldier died in combat during his two administrations, something no president since has achieved. For the most part, he acted with poise, restraint, and intelligence in managing an increasingly complex cold war.

If Eisenhower refused to take the lead in addressing social and racial problems, he did balance the budget while sustaining the major reforms of the New Deal. If he tolerated unemployment of as much as 7 percent, he saw to it that inflation remained minimal. Even Adlai Stevenson admitted that Ike's victory in 1952 had been good for America. "I like Ike, too," he said.

Eisenhower's January 17, 1961, farewell address focused on the threat posed to government integrity by "an immense military establishment and a large arms industry." It was all the more striking for Eisenhower, a celebrated military leader, to highlight the dangers of a large "military-industrial complex" exerting "unwarranted influence" in Congress and the White House. "The potential for the disastrous rise of misplaced power exists and will persist," he warned. Eisenhower never promoted warfare as an instrument of foreign policy. Instead, he pledged to "do anything to achieve peace within honorable means. I'll travel anywhere. I'll talk to anyone." His successors were not as successful in keeping war at bay.

CHAPTER REVIEW

SUMMARY

- **Eisenhower's Dynamic Conservatism**   President Eisenhower promoted *moderate Republicanism*, or "dynamic conservatism." While critical of excessive government spending on social programs, he expanded Social Security coverage and launched ambitious public works programs, such as the *Federal-Aid Highway Act* that constructed the Interstate Highway System.

- **Growth of the U.S. Economy**   High levels of federal government spending continued during the postwar period. The *GI Bill of Rights* boosted home buying and helped many veterans attend college and enter the middle class. Consumer demand for homes, cars, and household goods fueled the economy.

- **Critics of Mainstream Culture**   The *Beats* and many other writers and artists rebelled against what they claimed was the suffocating conformity of middle-class life. Adolescents rebelled through acts of juvenile delinquency and a new form of sexually provocative music called rock 'n' roll. Pockets of chronic poverty persisted despite record-breaking economic growth, and minorities did not prosper to the extent that white Americans did.

- **Civil Rights Movement**   During the early 1950s, the NAACP mounted legal challenges in federal courts to states requiring racially segregated public schools. In *Brown v. Board of Education (1954)*, the U.S. Supreme Court nullified the *separate-but-equal* doctrine. Many white southerners adopted a strategy of *"massive resistance"* against court-ordered desegregation. In response, civil rights activists used *nonviolent civil disobedience* to force local and state officials to allow integration, as demonstrated in the *Montgomery bus boycott* in Alabama and the forced desegregation of public schools in Little Rock, Arkansas. Martin Luther King organized the *Southern Christian Leadership Conference (SCLC)* after white violence against activists in Little Rock. In 1957, the U.S. Congress passed a Civil Rights Act intended to stop discrimination against black voters in the South, but it was rarely enforced.

- **American Foreign Policy in the 1950s**   Eisenhower's first major foreign-policy accomplishment was to end the fighting in Korea. Thereafter, he kept the United States out of war and relied on secret *Central Intelligence Agency (CIA)* intervention, financial and military aid, and threats of *massive retaliation* to stem the spread of communism. Though American aid was not enough to save the French at *Dien Bien Phu*, Eisenhower's belief in the *"falling domino" theory* deepened U.S. support for the government in South Vietnam in its war with North Vietnam and the Communist *Viet Cong* insurgents.

CHRONOLOGY

1944	Congress passes the Servicemen's Readjustment Act (GI Bill of Rights)
1951	Alan Freed coins the term *rock 'n' roll*
1952	Eisenhower wins the presidency
July 1953	Armistice is reached in Korea
1954	*Brown v. Board of Education of Topeka, Kansas*
July 1954	Geneva Accords adopted
December 1955	Montgomery, Alabama, bus boycott begins
1956	Congress passes the Federal-Aid Highway Act
	Soviets suppress Hungarian revolt
	In Suez War, Israel, Britain, and France attack Egypt
1957	Federal troops sent to protect students attempting to integrate Central High School in Little Rock, Arkansas
	Soviet Union launches *Sputnik 1* satellite
1960	U-2 incident reveals that the United States is flying spy planes over the Soviet Union

KEY TERMS

moderate Republicanism p. 1036

Federal-Aid Highway Act (1956) p. 1039

GI Bill of Rights (1944) p. 1042

Suburbia p. 1043

baby boom p. 1047

Beats p. 1050

separate-but-equal p. 1054

Brown v. Board of Education (1954) p. 1054

massive resistance p. 1055

Montgomery bus boycott p. 1056

nonviolent civil disobedience p. 1056

Southern Christian Leadership Conference (SCLC) p. 1059

massive retaliation p. 1061

Central Intelligence Agency (CIA) p. 1062

Dien Bien Phu p. 1063

Viet Cong p. 1064

"falling domino" theory p. 1064

Suez crisis p. 1068

 INQUIZITIVE

Go to InQuizitive to see what you've learned—and learn what you've missed—with personalized feedback along the way.

29

A New Frontier and a Great Society

1960–1968

***The Dove* (1964)** African American artist Romare Bearden's collage presents a disjointed vision of a contemporary urban street scene: fragments of black bodies appear in a surreal clash of flesh and pavement, reflecting the upheaval and violence of African American life in the 1960s. At the same time, though, the titular dove presides over the scene, suggesting that a life of peace could still be in reach.

F or those who considered the social and political climate of the fifties dull, the following decade provided a striking contrast. The sixties were years of extraordinary social turbulence and liberal activism, tragic assassinations and painful trauma, cultural conflict and youth rebellion. Assassins killed four of the most important leaders of the time: John F. Kennedy, Malcolm X, Martin Luther King Jr., and Robert F. Kennedy.

The "politics of expectation" that a British journalist said shone brightly in Kennedy's short tenure as president did not die with him in November 1963. Instead, Kennedy's idealistic commitment to improving America's quality of life—for everyone—was given new meaning and momentum by his successor, Texan Lyndon B. Johnson, whose war on poverty and Great Society programs outstripped Franklin Roosevelt's New Deal in their scope and promises.

Johnson's energy and legislative savvy resulted in a blizzard of new federal programs as many social issues that had been ignored or postponed for decades—civil rights for minorities, equality for women, gay rights, medical insurance, federal aid to the poor—forced their way to the forefront of national concerns.

In the end, however, Johnson promised too much. The Great Society programs fell victim to unrealistic hopes, poor execution, and the nation's deepening involvement in Vietnam. The deeply entrenched assumptions of the cold war led the nation into the longest, most controversial, and least successful war in its history to that point.

focus questions

1. What were President John F. Kennedy's efforts to contain communism abroad and pursue civil rights and other social programs at home?

2. What were the strategies and achievements of the civil rights movement in the 1960s? What divisions emerged among its activists during the decade?

3. What were Lyndon B. Johnson's major war on poverty and Great Society initiatives? How did they impact American society?

4. What were Presidents Kennedy and Johnson's motivations for deepening America's military involvement in the Vietnam War?

5. What were the issues that propelled Richard Nixon to victory in the 1968 presidential election?

THE NEW FRONTIER

In his 1960 speech accepting the Democratic presidential nomination, John F. Kennedy showcased the muscular language that would characterize his campaign and his presidency: "We stand today on the edge of a **New Frontier**—the frontier of unknown opportunities and perils—a frontier of unfulfilled hopes and threats." Kennedy and his staff fastened upon the frontier metaphor as the label for their proposed domestic program because they believed that Americans had always been adventurers, eager to conquer and exploit new frontiers. Kennedy promised that if elected he would get the country "moving again" and be a more aggressive cold warrior than Dwight Eisenhower.

KENNEDY VERSUS NIXON In 1960, the presidential election featured two candidates—Vice President Richard M. Nixon and Massachusetts senator John F. Kennedy (JFK)—of similar ages but contrasting personalities and backgrounds. As Eisenhower's partner over successive terms, Nixon was assured the Republican nomination in 1960, although President Eisenhower himself had grave misgivings. When asked by reporters to name a single major accomplishment of his vice president, Ike replied: "If you give me a week, I might think of one."

A native of California, the forty-seven-year-old Nixon had come to Washington after the Second World War eager to reverse the tide of New Deal liberalism. His visibility among Republicans benefited from his leadership of the anti-Communist hearings in Congress during the McCarthy hysteria. All his life, Nixon had clawed and struggled to reach the top. Now he had the presidency within his grasp. But Nixon, graceless, awkward, and stiff, proved to be one of the most complicated and most interesting political figures in American history.

Forty-three-year-old John Kennedy had not distinguished himself in the House or the Senate. More pragmatic than principled, he was handsome, articulate, and blessed with energy and wit. Friends said his charisma was magical. "One of life's great pleasures," his brother-in-law said, "was spending time with that man."

Kennedy had a bright, agile mind, a quick wit, a Harvard education, a record of heroism in the Second World War, a rich and powerful Roman Catholic family, and a beautiful and accomplished young wife. In the words of a southern senator, Kennedy combined "the best qualities of Elvis Presley and Franklin D. Roosevelt"—a combination that played well in the first-ever televised presidential debate, as he began the process of seducing a nation.

The Kennedy–Nixon debates Nixon's decision to debate his less prominent opponent on television backfired.

Some 70 million people tuned in to the debate and saw an obviously uncomfortable Nixon perspiring heavily and looking pale. By contrast, Kennedy looked tanned and confident. He offered crisp answers that made him appear to be qualified for the nation's highest office. The morning after the debate, his approval ratings skyrocketed.

John Kennedy was a relentless presidential campaigner, traveling 65,000 miles, visiting twenty-five states, and making more than 350 speeches, including an address to Protestant ministers in Texas in which he neutralized concerns about his being a Roman Catholic by stressing that the pope in Rome would never "tell the President—should he be a Catholic—how to act." In speech after speech, Kennedy said he was tired of waking up and reading about what Soviet and Cuban leaders were doing. Instead, he wanted to read about what the U.S. president was doing to combat communism. He wanted to develop a foreign policy that would break out of the confining assumptions of the Cold War, but as yet had no clear plan for doing so.

Kennedy also worked to increase the registration of African American voters across the nation. His response to the growing civil rights movement was ambivalent, however. Like Eisenhower, Kennedy believed racial unrest needed to be handled with caution rather than boldness. To him, racial justice was less an urgent moral crusade than a potential barrier to his election. He understood the injustices of bigotry and segregation, but he needed the votes of southern whites to win the presidency.

During the campaign, Kennedy won the hearts of many black voters by helping to get Martin Luther King Jr. out of a Georgia jail after King had been unjustly convicted of "trespassing" in an all-white restaurant. "I've got a suitcase of votes," said King's appreciative father, "and I'm going to take them to Mr. Kennedy and dump them in his lap." On the Sunday before Election Day, a million leaflets describing Kennedy's effort to release King from prison were distributed in African American churches across the nation.

In November, Kennedy and his running mate, powerful Texas senator Lyndon B. Johnson, won one of the closest presidential elections in history. Their margin was only 118,574 votes out of more than 68 million cast. Nixon won more states than Kennedy, but the Democrat captured 70 percent of the black vote, which proved decisive in at least three key states.

A VIGOROUS NEW ADMINISTRATION   John F. Kennedy was the youngest person and first Roman Catholic elected president. He had promised "to get America moving again," and he was eager to begin. His inauguration ceremony on a bitterly cold, sunny January day introduced the nation to his distinctive elegance and flair. In his speech, Kennedy focused almost entirely on foreign affairs. He accepted the responsibility of "defending freedom in its hour of maximum danger" and promised to keep America strong while seeking to reduce friction with the Soviet Union: "Let us never negotiate out of fear, but let us never fear to negotiate."

Kennedy claimed "that the torch has been passed to a new generation of Americans—born in this century, tempered by war, disciplined by a hard and bitter peace," and he dazzled listeners with uplifting words: "Let every nation know, whether it wishes us well or ill, that we shall pay any price, bear any burden, meet any hardship, support any friend, oppose any foe, to assure the survival and success of liberty. . . . And so, my fellow Americans: ask not what your country can do for you—ask what *you* can do for your country."

Such steely optimism heralded a presidency of fresh promise and new beginnings. Yet much of the glamour surrounding Kennedy was cosmetic. Despite his athletic interests and robust appearance, he suffered from ser-

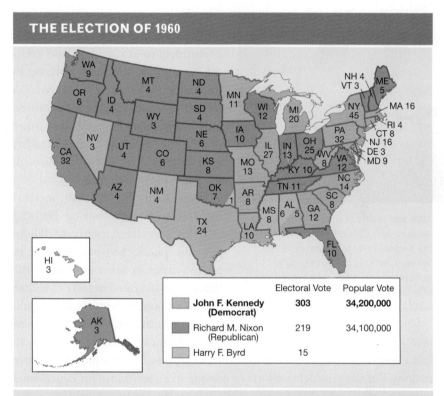

THE ELECTION OF 1960

	Electoral Vote	Popular Vote
John F. Kennedy (Democrat)	**303**	**34,200,000**
Richard M. Nixon (Republican)	219	34,100,000
Harry F. Byrd	15	

- How did the election of 1960 represent a sea change in American presidential politics?
- How did John F. Kennedy win the election in spite of winning fewer states than Richard M. Nixon?

ious medical problems: Addison's disease (a withering of the adrenal glands), venereal disease, chronic back pain resulting from a birth defect, and fierce fevers. He took powerful prescription medicines or injections daily, sometimes hourly, to manage a degenerative bone disease, to deal with anxiety, to help him sleep, and to control his allergies. Like Franklin D. Roosevelt, Kennedy and his associates hid his physical ailments—as well as his often reckless sexual dalliances in the White House with a galaxy of women, including actress Marilyn Monroe and Judith Campbell Exner, the girlfriend of a Chicago mob boss.

Yet Kennedy had a difficult time launching his New Frontier domestic program. His narrow election victory gave him no mandate, and he faced a congressional roadblock in the form of conservative southern Democrats who joined with Republicans to oppose his efforts to increase federal aid to

Jack and Jackie Young, dashing, wealthy, and culturally sophisticated, the Kennedys were instant celebrities. Women imitated the First Lady's famous hairdo, while men craved JFK's effortless "cool" and youthful energy.

education, provide medical insurance for the aged, and create a cabinet-level department of urban affairs and housing to address inner-city poverty. In his first year, Kennedy submitted 355 legislative requests; Congress approved only half of them. He suffered so many defeats that he complained he "couldn't get a Mother's Day resolution through the goddamned Congress."

Legislators did approve increasing the minimum wage, a Housing Act that earmarked nearly $5 billion for new public housing projects in poverty-stricken inner-city areas, the Peace Corps, created in 1961 to recruit idealistic young volunteers who would provide educational and technical service abroad, and the Alliance for Progress, a financial assistance program to Latin American countries intended to blunt the appeal of communism in those nations. But the president's efforts to provide more assistance for educational programs and medical care for the elderly never got out of committees.

Perhaps Kennedy's greatest legislative success was in convincing Congress to commit $40 billion to put an American on the moon within ten years. (It would happen in 1969.) What spurred the start of the program was the news that the Soviets had launched the first manned space flight in 1961. Former president Eisenhower said that Kennedy's "race to the moon for national prestige is nuts." But Vice President Lyndon Johnson assured the president that "dramatic accomplishments in space are being increasingly identified as a major indicator of world leadership." Kennedy explained that he had decided to shoot for the moon not because it is "easy, but because it is hard, because that goal will serve to organize and measure the best of our energies and skills."

CIVIL RIGHTS The most important developments in domestic life during the sixties occurred in civil rights. Throughout the South, racial segregation remained firmly in place. Signs outside public restrooms distinguished between "whites" and "colored"; restaurants declared "Colored Not Allowed," or "Colored Served Only in Rear." Stores prohibited African Americans from trying on clothes before buying them. Despite the *Brown v. Board of Education* ruling in 1954, many public schools across the South remained segregated and unequal in quality.

Like Franklin D. Roosevelt, President Kennedy celebrated racial equality but did little to promote it until forced to do so. His caution reflected his narrow election margin in 1960. He was reluctant to challenge conservative southern Democrats on the explosive issue of segregation. Both he and his brother Robert ("Bobby"), the attorney general and his closest adviser, had to be dragged into actively supporting the civil rights movement. After appointing Harris Wofford, a white law professor and experienced campaigner for racial equality, as the special presidential assistant for civil rights, President Kennedy told him "to make substantial headway against . . . the nonsense of racial discrimination," but to do so with "minimum civil rights legislation [and] maximum Executive action." Such actions led Martin Luther King Jr. to comment that Kennedy had great political skill but no "moral passion" about the need to end racial injustice.

CATASTROPHE IN CUBA Kennedy's performance in foreign relations was spectacularly mixed. Although he had told a reporter that he wanted to "break out of the confines of the Cold War," he quickly found himself reinforcing its confining assumptions. While still a senator, Kennedy had blasted President Eisenhower for not being tough enough with the Soviets and for allowing Fidel Castro and his Communist followers to take over Cuba, just ninety miles from the southern tip of Florida.

Soon after his inauguration, Kennedy learned that a secret CIA operation, which had been approved by Eisenhower, was training 1,500 anti-Castro Cubans in Guatemala, Texas, and Florida to invade their homeland in hopes of triggering a mass uprising against Castro. U.S. military leaders assured Kennedy that the invasion plan (Operation Trinidad) was feasible; CIA analysts predicted that news of the invasion would inspire anti-Castro Cubans to rebel against their Communist dictator.

In reality, the covert operation had little chance of succeeding. Its assumptions were flawed, its strategy faulty, its tactics bungled, and the forces and weapons used inadequate. Kennedy seemed to realize it might fail when he callously said, "If we have to get rid of those 800 men [actually 1,400], it is much better to dump them in Cuba than in the United States."

When the ragtag force of right-wing Cubans, transported on American ships, landed before dawn at the **Bay of Pigs** on Cuba's south shore on April 17, 1961, Castro's forces were waiting for them. Kennedy panicked when he realized the operation was failing and refused desperate pleas from the rebels for "promised" support from U.S. warplanes. General Lyman Lemnitzer, chair of the Joint Chiefs of Staff, said that Kennedy's "pulling out the rug [on the Cuban invaders] was . . . absolutely reprehensible, almost criminal." Some 1,200 rebels were captured; the rest were killed. (Kennedy later paid $53 million to ransom the captured rebels).

The clumsy effort to overthrow the Cuban government was a complete failure. It humiliated Kennedy and elevated Castro in the eyes of the world. To his credit, Kennedy admitted that the Bay of Pigs invasion was a "colossal mistake." Only later did he learn that the planners of the operation had assumed that he would commit American forces once the invasion effort had failed. He said that after the initial disastrous reports from the Bay of Pigs, "we all looked at each other and asked, 'How could we have been so stupid?'" After the failed invasion, Kennedy never again trusted his trigger-happy military and intelligence leaders.

THE VIENNA SUMMIT Just weeks after the Bay of Pigs invasion, Kennedy met Soviet premier Nikita Khrushchev at a summit conference in Vienna, Austria. Khrushchev badgered and bullied the young president, bragged about the superiority of communism, and threatened to take control of all of Berlin, the divided city inside Communist East Germany. A stunned Kennedy told the British prime minister that Khrushchev was "much more of a barbarian" than he had expected. He confided to a journalist that the summit "was awful. Worst thing of my life. He rolled right over me—he thinks I'm a fool—he thinks I'm weak." When asked what he planned to do next, Kennedy replied: "I have to confront them [the Soviets] someplace to show that we're tough."

The first thing Kennedy did upon returning to the White House was to request an estimate of how many Americans might be killed in a nuclear war with the Soviet Union. The answer was chilling: 70 million. Kennedy, desperate not to appear weak in the face of Khrushchev's aggressive actions in Germany, asked Congress for additional spending on defense and called up 156,000 members of the Army Reserve and National Guard to protect West Berlin. He also ordered an armed military convoy to travel from West Germany across East Germany to West Berlin to show the Soviets that he would protect the city with force.

The Soviets responded on August 13, 1961. They stopped all traffic between East and West Berlin and began erecting the twenty-seven-mile-long **Berlin Wall** to separate East Berlin from West Berlin, where thousands of refugees were fleeing communism each week. For the United States, the wall became a powerful propaganda weapon in the Cold War. As Kennedy said, "Freedom has many difficulties and democracy is not perfect, but we have never had to put up a wall to keep our people in."

Severed ties Two West Berliners climb the newly constructed Berlin Wall to talk with a family member at an open window.

The Berlin Wall demonstrated the Soviets' willingness to challenge American resolve in Europe. In response, Kennedy and Secretary of Defense Robert McNamara embarked upon the most intensive arms race in history, increasing the number of nuclear missiles fivefold, adding 300,000 men to the armed forces, and creating the U.S. Special Forces (Green Berets), an elite group of commandos who specialized in guerrilla warfare and could provide a "more flexible response" than nuclear weapons to "hot spots" around the world.

THE CUBAN MISSILE CRISIS Soon after taking office, President Kennedy predicted that "we shall have to test anew" whether a nation "such as ours can endure." It was an accurate prediction. In the fall of 1962, Nikita Khrushchev and the Soviets decided to challenge Kennedy again. To protect Communist Cuba from another American-backed invasion and to show critics at home that he was not afraid of the Americans, Khrushchev approved the secret installation of Soviet missiles on the island nation. The Soviets felt they were justified in doing so because Kennedy, after the Bay of Pigs invasion, had ordered that U.S. missiles with nuclear warheads be installed in Turkey, along the Soviet border.

On October 16, 1962, Kennedy learned that photos taken two days earlier by U.S. spy planes showed some forty Soviet missile sites and twenty-five jet bombers in Cuba. Although the Soviet actions had violated no law or treaty, Kennedy decided that the missiles had to be removed. But how?

Over the next thirteen days, perhaps the most dangerous two weeks in history, Kennedy and the National Security Council (NSC) considered several possible responses, ranging from doing nothing to invading Cuba. The world held its breath as the NSC discussed the unthinkable possibility of a nuclear exchange with the Soviets. The commander of the U.S. Marines at one point reminded the group that the missiles in Cuba were not a true strategic threat; the Soviet Union, he said, "has a hell of a lot better way to attack us than to attack us from Cuba." Yet the group insisted that the missiles be removed for symbolic reasons.

Eventually, the NSC fastened on two options: (1) a "surgical" air strike on the missiles followed, if necessary, by an invasion, or (2) a naval blockade of Cuba in which U.S. warships would stop Soviet vessels and search them for missiles. Although most of the military advisers supported the first option, Kennedy chose the blockade, prompting a general to shout, "You're screwed! You're screwed!"

Kennedy, however, had been burned by overconfident military advisers during the Bay of Pigs operation and was not going to let it happen again. He also feared that an American attack on Cuba would give the Soviets an excuse to take control of West Berlin.

On Monday night, October 22, a grim Kennedy delivered a televised speech of the "highest national urgency" to the world, announcing that the U.S. Navy was establishing a "quarantine" of Cuba to prevent Soviet ships from delivering more weapons to the island nation. He urged the Soviets to "move the world back from the abyss of destruction." The world watched as tensions grew.

Khrushchev replied that Soviet ships would ignore the quarantine and accused Kennedy of "an act of aggression propelling humankind into the abyss of a world nuclear-missile war." Despite such rhetoric, however, on Wednesday, October 24, five Soviet ships, presumably with more missiles aboard, stopped well short of the quarantine line.

Two days later, Khrushchev, knowing that the United States still enjoyed a 5 to 1 advantage in nuclear weapons, offered a deal. The Soviets would agree to remove the missiles already in Cuba in return for a *public* pledge by the United States never to invade Cuba—and a *secret* agreement to remove U.S. missiles from Turkey. Kennedy agreed. Secretary of State Dean Rusk stressed to a newscaster, "Remember, when you report this, [say] that eyeball to eyeball, they [the Soviets] blinked first." The air force chief of staff, General Curtis Lemay, who had urged an air attack on Cuba, called the deal "the greatest defeat in our history."

In the aftermath of the **Cuban missile crisis**, tensions between the United States and the Soviet Union subsided, in part because of several symbolic steps: an agreement to sell the Soviet Union surplus American wheat, the installation of a "hotline" telephone between Washington and Moscow to provide instant contact between the heads of government, and the removal of U.S. missiles from Turkey, Italy, and Britain.

"PEACE FOR ALL TIME" Going to the edge of nuclear war led Kennedy and others in the administration to soften their Cold War rhetoric and pursue other ways to reduce the threat of atomic warfare. As Kennedy told his advisers, "It is insane that two men, sitting on opposite sides of the world, should be able to decide to bring an end to civilization." He told an audience at American University on June 10, 1963, that his new goal was "not merely peace in our time, but peace for all time," which would require reducing the risk of nuclear warfare. "We all inhabit this small planet," he explained. "We all breathe the same air."

Soon after delivering this speech, the president began discussions with Soviet and British leaders to reduce the risk of nuclear war. The discussions resulted in the Test Ban Treaty, ratified in September 1963, which banned the testing of nuclear weapons in the atmosphere. It was the first joint agreement of the Cold War and an important move toward improved relations with the Soviet Union. As Kennedy put it, using an ancient Chinese proverb, "A journey of a thousand miles begins with one step."

VIETNAM As tensions with the Soviet Union eased, a new crisis was growing in Southeast Asia, where events were moving toward what would eventually become the greatest American foreign-policy calamity of the century. Throughout the fifties, U.S. officials increasingly came to view the preservation of South Vietnam as the critical test of American willpower in the Cold War. In 1956, then senator John F. Kennedy described South Vietnam as the "cornerstone of the free world in Southeast Asia."

Yet the situation in South Vietnam had worsened under the corrupt leadership of Premier Ngo Dinh Diem and his family. Diem had backed away from promised social and economic reforms, and his repressive tactics, directed not only against Communists but also against the Buddhist majority and other critics, played into the hands of his enemies.

Kennedy sent even more weapons, money, and some 16,000 military advisers to South Vietnam to help shore up the government. (They were called "advisers" to avoid the impression that U.S. soldiers were doing the fighting.) The Viet Cong, however, were winning the fight, in part because Diem proved to be corrupt and dictatorial.

By the fall of 1963, Kennedy agreed with his top advisers that Diem was "out of touch with his people" and had to be removed—in large part because he refused to follow American orders. On November 1, Vietnamese generals, with the approval of U.S. officials, took control of the Saigon government. They then took a step that Kennedy had neither intended nor expected: they murdered Diem and his brother. The rebel generals, however, soon fell to fighting one another, leaving Vietnam even more vulnerable to the Communist insurgency. Thereafter, unstable South Vietnam essentially became an American colony. The United States put the generals in power, gave the orders, and provided massive financial support, much of which was diverted into the hands of corrupt politicians.

By September 1963, Kennedy had developed doubts about the ability of the United States to defend the South Vietnamese. "In the final analysis," he told aides, "it's their war. They're the ones who have to win it or lose it. We can help them as advisers but they have to win it." Yet only a week later, in a televised interview, Kennedy reiterated the domino theory endorsed by Presidents Truman and Eisenhower, saying that if South Vietnam fell to communism, the rest of Southeast Asia would soon follow. He stressed that "we should stay [in South Vietnam]. We should use our influence in as effective a way as we can, but we should not withdraw."

KENNEDY'S ASSASSINATION What Kennedy would have done in Vietnam has remained a matter of endless discussion, because on November 22, 1963, while riding in an open car through Dallas, Texas, he was shot and killed by Lee Harvey Oswald, a twenty-four-year-old ex-Marine turned Communist. Oswald, who had lived for a time in the Soviet Union, idolized Fidel Castro and hated the United States and its capitalist system. As he fled the scene, he also shot and killed a Dallas policeman.

Debate still swirls about whether Oswald acted alone or as part of a conspiracy, and he did not live long enough to tell his story. As he was being transported to a court hearing, Jack Ruby, a Dallas nightclub owner distraught over Kennedy's death, shot and killed the handcuffed Oswald as a nationwide television audience watched.

Kennedy's shocking assassination and heartrending funeral enshrined the president in the public imagination as a martyred leader cut down in the prime of his life. He came to have a stronger reputation after his death than he enjoyed in life. "That debonair touch, that shock of chestnut hair, that beguiling grin, that shattering understatement—these are what we shall remember," wrote newspaper columnist Mary McGrory. Kennedy's drama-filled, thousand-day presidency had flamed up and out like a comet hitting the earth's atmosphere.

Americans wept in the streets, and the world was on edge as the wounded nation buried its fallen president and welcomed a new and very different one, Lyndon Johnson.

CIVIL RIGHTS

After the Montgomery bus boycott of 1955–1956, Martin Luther King Jr.'s philosophy of militant nonviolence stirred others to challenge the deeply entrenched patterns of racial segregation in the South. During the sixties, King became the face and heart of the civil rights movement. His goal was integration and equality, and he was an uplifting example of fortitude and dignity in confronting brutality and oppression. By nature, he was inspirational and courageous, with an astonishing capacity for forgiveness and a deep understanding of the dynamics of political power and social change. Yet he was also immensely complicated and contradictory, even hypocritical, as the FBI discovered by subjecting him to relentless electronic surveillance and even blackmail.

King was neither a genius nor a saint, but his shortcomings pale into insignificance when compared to his achievements. He was one of the world's most inspiring examples of courage, conviction, and dignity in the face of often violent prejudice and persecution. With the help of those he led and inspired, King changed the trajectory of American history—for the better. Alas, he did not live to see the promised land made possible by his actions.

SIT-INS The civil rights movement gained momentum when four brave African American college students sat down and ordered coffee and doughnuts at an "all-white" Woolworth's lunch counter in Greensboro, North Carolina, on February 1, 1960. The clerk refused to serve them, explaining that blacks had to eat standing up or take their food outside.

The Greensboro Four, as the students came to be called, waited forty-five minutes and then returned the next day with two dozen more students. As they sat for hours, fruitlessly waiting to be served, some read Bibles; others read Henry David Thoreau's famous essay on civil disobedience. They returned every day for a week, patiently tolerating being jeered at, jostled, and spat upon by white hooligans.

Within two months, similar sit-ins—involving 50,000 blacks and whites, men and women, young and old—had occurred in more than 100 cities. Some 3,600 people were arrested nationwide, but the sit-ins worked. By the end of July 1960, officials in Greensboro lifted the whites-only policy. The

Civil rights and its peaceful warriors The Greensboro Four—(listed from left) Joseph McNeil, Franklin McCain, Billy Smith, and Clarence Henderson—await service on day two of their sit-in at the Woolworth's.

civil rights movement had found an effective new, nonviolent tactic against segregation.

In April 1960, some 200 student activists, black and white, converged in Raleigh, North Carolina, to form the **Student Nonviolent Coordinating Committee (SNCC**—pronounced "snick"). The goal of what they called "the movement" was to intensify the effort to dismantle segregation. SNCC expanded the sit-ins to include "kneel-ins" at all-white churches and "wade-ins" at segregated public swimming pools. In many communities, demonstrators were pelted with rocks, burned with cigarettes, and even killed by white racists. As a Florida hog farmer named Holstead "Hoss" Manucy told a journalist, "I ain't got no bad habits. Don't smoke. Don't cuss. My only bad habit is fightin' niggahs."

FREEDOM RIDES In 1961, civil rights leaders decided to focus on integrating public transportation: buses and trains. Their larger goal was to force the Kennedy administration to engage the cause of civil rights in the

Freedom Riders On May 14, 1961, a white mob in Alabama assaulted a Freedom Bus, flinging fire bombs into its windows and beating the activists as they emerged. Here, the surviving Freedom Riders sit outside the burnt shell of their bus.

South. On May 4, the New York–based Congress of Racial Equality (CORE), led by James Farmer, sent a courageous group of eighteen black and white **Freedom Riders**, as they were called, on two public buses traveling from Washington, D.C., through the Lower South to New Orleans. They wanted to test a federal court ruling that banned racial segregation on buses and trains, and in terminals.

On May 14, a mob of white racists in rural Alabama, many of them members of the Ku Klux Klan, surrounded the Greyhound bus carrying the "Freedom Riders." After throwing a firebomb into the bus, the Klan members barricaded its door. "Burn them alive," one of them yelled. "Fry the damned niggers." The riders were able to escape, only to be battered with metal pipes, chains, and clubs.

A few hours later, Freedom Riders on a second bus were beaten after entering whites-only waiting rooms at the bus terminal in Birmingham, Alabama. The police, as it turned out, had encouraged the beatings. Alabama's governor complained that the Freedom Riders were violating "our law and customs." The next day, the Freedom Riders wanted to continue their trip, but the bus drivers refused.

When Diane Nash, a fearless black college student and SNCC leader in Nashville, Tennessee, heard about the violence in Birmingham, she recruited new riders. President Kennedy called her, warning that she would "get killed if you do this," but she refused to back down. "It doesn't matter if we're killed," she told the president. "Others will come—others will come."

On May 17, Nash and ten other students took a bus to Birmingham, where they were arrested. While in jail, they sang "freedom songs": "We'll Never Turn Back," "Ain't Gonna Let Nobody Turn Me Around," "We Shall Overcome." Eugene "Bull" Connor, the city's notoriously racist police chief, grew so frustrated at their joyous rebelliousness that he drove them in the middle of the night to the Tennessee state line and dropped them off to walk. Instead of going back to Nashville, however, the gutsy students returned to Birmingham.

President Kennedy was not inspired by the Freedom Riders. To him, they were a "pain in the ass" threatening to embarrass him and the United States on the eve of his summit meeting with Soviet leader Nikita Khrushchev. He dismissed them as "publicity seekers" who were putting the administration in "a politically painful spot." When Kennedy suggested to several civil rights leaders that they allow things to "cool off," James Farmer replied that blacks had been "cooling off for a hundred years. . . . If we got any cooler, we'd be in the deep freeze." Louis Martin, an influential black newspaper publisher, explained that "Negroes are getting ideas [about securing equal rights] they didn't have before." Kennedy asked where they were getting such ideas. Martin replied: "From you!"

The activists finally forced the president to provide another bus, which enabled them to renew the journey to New Orleans. When the new group of riders reached Montgomery, the capital of Alabama, they too were attacked. The next night, civil rights activists, including Martin Luther King Jr., gathered at a Montgomery church to honor the Freedom Riders. But their meeting was interrupted by a rampaging mob of whites armed with rocks and firebombs.

Ministers made frantic appeals to the White House. Kennedy responded by urging the Alabama governor to intervene. After midnight, national guardsmen arrived to disperse the mob. The Freedom Riders continued into Mississippi, where they were jailed. They never made it to New Orleans.

Still, the courage and principled resistance of the Freedom Riders—and of federal judges whose rulings supported integration efforts—prompted the Interstate Commerce Commission (ICC) in September 1961 to order that all interstate transportation facilities be integrated. Equally important, the Freedom Riders kindled the growth of civil rights groups. The experience of being assaulted and jailed galvanized the participants to become full-time members while attracting more recruits. The freedom rides were thus a crucial turning point in the civil rights movement.

White segregationists, however, remained violently opposed to racial equality. In Birmingham in September 1962, Dr. King was speaking at the annual meeting of the Southern Christian Leadership Conference when a white member of the American Nazi party jumped to the stage and punched him in the face. King simply dropped his hands and allowed the man to punch him again. "Don't touch him," King yelled. "We have to pray for him." His self-control and composure were as remarkable as his bravery. His home was bombed three times, and he was arrested fourteen times, yet he kept telling people to use "the weapon of nonviolence, the breastplate of righteousness, the armor of truth, and just keep marching" toward justice.

JAMES MEREDITH In the fall of 1962, James Meredith, an African American student and air force veteran whose grandfather had been a slave, tried to enroll at the all-white University of Mississippi in Oxford. Ross Barnett, the governor of Mississippi, refused to allow Meredith to register for classes. Attorney General Robert F. Kennedy then dispatched federal marshals to enforce the law.

When the marshals were assaulted with bricks, bottles, and steel pipes by a white mob shouting "Go to Hell, JFK," President Kennedy sent National Guard troops. Their arrival ignited rioting that left two dead and dozens injured. Once the violence subsided, however, Meredith was registered at the university. "Only in America," a reporter noted, "would the federal government send thousands of troops to enforce the right of an otherwise obscure citizen to attend a particular university."

BIRMINGHAM In early 1963, in conjunction with the celebration of the hundredth anniversary of Abraham Lincoln's Emancipation Proclamation, Martin Luther King Jr. defied President Kennedy's wishes by organizing a massive series of demonstrations in Birmingham. Alabama was now led by George Wallace, a feisty racist governor who had vowed to protect "segregation now, segregation tomorrow, segregation forever!" King knew that weeks of public demonstrations would result in thousands of arrests and would likely provoke violence, but a hard-won victory, he felt, would "break the back of segregation all over the nation."

As King and other activists led 2,500 demonstrators through Birmingham streets on May 7, the all-white police force led by "Bull" Connor used snarling dogs, tear gas, electric cattle prods, and high-pressure fire hoses on the protesters. Millions of Americans were outraged when they saw the ugly confrontations on television. "The civil rights movement," President Kennedy observed, "owes Bull Connor as much as it owes Abraham Lincoln." It also owed a lot to the power of television.

More than 3,000 demonstrators were arrested, including Dr. King and several white ministers, both men and women, who were rushing to the cause of civil rights. While in jail, King was inspired to write a "Letter from Birmingham Jail," a stirring defense of **nonviolent civil disobedience** that has become a classic document of the civil rights movement. "One who breaks an unjust law," King stressed, "must do so openly, lovingly, and with a willingness to *accept the penalty*." In a reference to President Kennedy's timid support, King wrote that the most perplexing foe of equal justice was not the southern white bigot but "the white moderate, who is more devoted to 'order' than to justice . . . who constantly says, 'I agree with you in the goal you seek, but I cannot agree with your methods.'"

King's efforts prevailed when Birmingham officials finally agreed to end their segregationist practices. White racists did not change overnight, however. One angry Alabaman sent a letter to King: "This isn't a threat but a promise— your head will be blown off as sure as Christ made green apples."

Throughout 1963, whites in the Lower South continued to defy efforts at racial integration, while blacks and white liberals organized demonstrations in cities and towns across the nation. On June 11, 1963, Alabama governor George Wallace theatrically blocked the door at the University of Alabama as African American students tried to register for classes. Wallace finally stepped aside in the face of insistent federal marshals.

That night, President Kennedy finally decided he needed to lead. In a hastily arranged televised speech, he announced that he would soon submit to Congress a major new civil rights bill that would remove race as a consideration "in American life or law." He stressed that "a great change is at hand," and he was determined to make "that change, that [civil rights] revolution" peaceful and constructive. "We are confronted primarily with a moral issue," the president said. "It is as old as the Scriptures and is as clear as the American Constitution. The heart of the question is whether all Americans are to be afforded equal rights and equal opportunities." He asked "every American, regardless of where he lives," to "stop and examine his conscience," for America, "for all its hopes and all its boasts, will not be fully free until all its citizens are free."

Four hours later, an African American civil rights activist, Medgar Evers, was shot to death in his driveway in Jackson, Mississippi. Such violence aroused the nation's indignation and made civil rights America's most pressing

Bull's dogs Eugene "Bull" Connor ordered Birmingham police to unleash their dogs and clubs on civil rights demonstrators in May 1963.

social issue. Yet southern Democrats in the House of Representatives would block Kennedy's civil rights bill for months.

"I HAVE A DREAM!" The standoff in Congress led African American leaders to take a bold step. On August 28, some 250,000 blacks and whites, many of them schoolchildren brought in on buses, marched arm-in-arm down the Mall in Washington, D.C., chanting "Equality Now!" and singing "We Shall Overcome."

The **March on Washington** for Jobs and Freedom was the largest political demonstration in American history. "When you looked at the crowd," remembered a U.S. Park Service ranger, "you didn't see blacks or whites. You saw America." Prominent entertainers sang protest songs, and civil rights activists gave speeches calling for racial justice.

Then something remarkable happened. Standing on the steps of the Lincoln Memorial, thirty-four-year-old Martin Luther King Jr. began to speak. He started awkwardly. Noticing his nervousness, someone urged him to "tell 'em about the dream."

As if suddenly inspired, King set aside his prepared remarks and delivered an extraordinary speech that resonated around the world. He started slowly and picked up speed, as if he were speaking at a revival, giving poetic voice to the hopes of millions as he stressed the "fierce urgency of now" and the unstoppable power of "meeting physical force with soul force." President Kennedy, who had tried to convince organizers to call off the march, was watching on TV at the White House, just a mile away. As King spoke, the president told an aide that "he's damn good."

King then shared his dream for America:

> In spite of the difficulties and frustrations of the moment, I still have a *dream*. It is a *dream* deeply rooted in the American dream. I have a *dream* that one day this nation will rise up and live out the true meaning of its creed: 'We hold these truths to be self-evident; that all men are created equal.' I have a *dream* that one day . . . the sons of former slaves and the sons of former slaveowners will be able to sit together at the table of brotherhood.

As if at a massive church service, many in the crowd began shouting "Amen!" as King summoned a flawed nation to justice: "So let freedom ring!" he shouted, for "when we allow freedom to ring from every town and every hamlet, from every state and every city, we will be able to speed up the day when *all* God's children—black men and white men, Jews and Gentiles, Protestants and Catholics—will be able to join hands and sing in the words of the old Negro spiritual, *Free at last, free at last, thank God Almighty, we are free at last!*"

As King finished, there was a startling hush, then a deafening ovation. The crowd spontaneously joined hands and began singing "We Shall Overcome." "I have never been so proud to be a Negro," said baseball superstar Jackie Robinson. "I have never been so proud to be an American."

But King's dream remained just that—a dream. Eighteen days later, four Klansmen in Birmingham detonated a bomb in a black church, killing four young girls. The murders sparked a new wave of indignation across the country and the world. The editors of the *Milwaukee Sentinel* stressed that the bombing "should serve to goad the conscience. The deaths . . . in a sense are on the hands of each of us."

FREEDOM SUMMER During late 1963 and throughout 1964, the civil rights movement grew in scope, visibility, and power. Racism, however, remained entrenched in the Lower South, as blacks continued to be excluded from the political process. White officials kept African Americans from voting by charging them expensive poll taxes, forcing them to take difficult literacy tests, making the application process inconvenient, and intimidating them through the use of arson, beatings, and lynchings.

In early 1964, Harvard-educated Robert "Bob" Moses, a black New Yorker who had resigned from the SCLC to head the Student Nonviolent Coordinating Committee (SNCC) office in Mississippi, decided it would take "an army" to force the state to give voting rights to blacks. So he set about recruiting an army of black and white volunteers who would live with rural African Americans, teach them in "freedom schools," and help them register to vote.

Most of the recruits for what came to be called "Freedom Summer" were idealistic white college students, many of whom were Jewish. Mississippi's white leaders prepared for "the nigger-communist invasion" by doubling the state police force and stockpiling tear gas, electric cattle prods, and shotguns. Writer Eudora Welty reported from her hometown of Jackson, Mississippi, that she had heard that "this summer all hell is going to break loose."

It did. In mid-June, the volunteer activists met at an Ohio college to learn about southern racial history, nonviolent civil disobedience, and the likely abuses they would suffer. On the final evening of the training session, Moses pleaded with anyone who feared heading to Mississippi to go home; several did. The next day, the remaining volunteers boarded buses and headed south, fanning out across the state.

In all, forty-one "freedom schools" taught thousands of children math, writing, and history. They also tutored black adults about the complicated process of voter registration. In response, the Ku Klux Klan, local police, and other white racists harassed, arrested, and assaulted many of the volunteers.

In June 1964, Klan members abducted and murdered three young civil rights workers: James Earl Chaney, Andrew Goodman, and Michael "Mickey" Schwerner. Their decomposed bodies were found two months later in a cattle pond. While searching for the missing men, authorities found the bodies of eight black males in rivers and swamps. The murders, said one volunteer, were "the end of innocence," after which "things could never be the same."

BLACK POWER Racism in America was not limited to the South. By the mid-sixties, about 70 percent of the nation's African Americans were living in blighted urban areas, and many young blacks in the large cities were losing faith in the strategy of Christian nonviolence promoted by King and others in the South. Inner-city poverty and frustration cried out for its own social-justice movement.

The fragmentation of the civil rights movement was tragically evident on August 11, 1965, when Watts, the largest black ghetto in Los Angeles, exploded in rioting and looting that left thirty-four dead, almost 4,000 in jail, and widespread property damage. Dozens of other large cities experienced similar riots in the summer of 1966. Between 1965 and 1968, nearly 300 racial uprisings shattered the peace of urban America.

The violence revealed the growing civil war within the civil rights movement. As Gil Scot-Heron, a black musician, sang: "We are tired of praying and marching and thinking and learning / Brothers want to start cutting and shooting and stealing and burning." What came to be called "black power" began to compete with the integrationist, nonviolent philosophy espoused by Dr. King and the SCLC.

MALCOLM X The most visible spokesman for the **black power movement** was Malcolm X, born in 1925 in Omaha, Nebraska, as Malcolm Little. His father, a Baptist minister, and his mother, a West Indian, were supporters of Marcus Garvey's crusade for black nationalism in the 1920s, and his childhood home was burned to the ground by white racists. His father was killed when

Malcolm X The black power movement's most influential spokesman.

Malcolm was six, perhaps the victim of white supremacists. After her husband's death, Louise Little suffered a breakdown and was institutionalized for the rest of her life. Young Malcolm was placed in foster care but became an unruly rebel. After being expelled from school in the ninth grade, he drifted from Detroit to New York City to Boston.

By age nineteen, Malcolm, now known as Detroit Red, had become a thief, drug dealer, and pimp. He spent seven years in Massachusetts prisons, where he experienced a conversion and joined a small Chicago-based religious sect, the Nation of Islam (NOI), whose members were called Black Muslims. The organization had little to do with Islam and everything to do with its domineering leader, Elijah Muhammad, and the cultlike devotion he required. Muhammad dismissed whites as "devils" and championed black nationalism, racial pride, self-respect, and self-discipline. By 1953, a year after leaving prison, Malcolm Little was calling himself Malcom X in tribute to his lost African name, and he had become a full-time NOI minister famous for electrifying speeches attacking white racism and black powerlessness.

Malcolm X dismissed King and other mainstream civil rights leaders as "nothing but modern Uncle Toms" who "keep you and me in check, keep us under control, keep us passive and peaceful and nonviolent." His militant speeches inspired thousands of mostly urban blacks to join the Nation of Islam.

More than most black leaders, Malcolm X expressed the emotions and frustrations of the inner-city African American working poor. Yet at the peak of his influence, and just as he was moderating his militant message, he became embroiled in a conflict with Elijah Muhammad that proved fatal. NOI assassins killed Malcolm X in Manhattan on February 21, 1965.

Black militancy did not end with Malcolm X, however. By 1966, "black power" had become a rallying cry for many young militants. When Stokely Carmichael became head of the Student Nonviolent Coordinating Committee (SNCC), he ousted whites from the organization. "When you talk of black power," Carmichael shouted, "you talk of bringing this country to its knees, of building a movement that will smash everything Western civilization has created." Having been beaten by whites and having seen fellow volunteers killed, Carmichael rejected the nonviolent philosophy of the mainstream civil rights movement and urged blacks to defend themselves.

Where Martin Luther King spoke to white America's moral conscience, Carmichael and other firebrands spoke to the seething rage of the young black underclass. Soon Carmichael would move on to the Black Panther party, a group of leather-jacketed black revolutionaries founded in Oakland, California, that promoted incendiary strategies and cultural pride. H. Rap Brown, who succeeded Carmichael as head of SNCC in 1967, urged blacks to "get you some guns" and "kill the honkies [whites]."

THE EFFECT OF BLACK POWER Although widely covered in the media, the black power movement never attracted more than a small minority of African Americans. Still, it forced King and other mainstream black leaders and organizations to shift their focus from the rural South to inner-city ghettos in the North and West. Legal access to restaurants, schools, and other public accommodations, King pointed out, meant little to people mired in chronic poverty. They needed jobs and decent housing.

Panther power Black Panthers issue a black power salute outside a San Francisco Liberation School, where activists raised awareness and appreciation of African American history, a topic ignored by white, mainstream curriculum.

The time had come, King declared while launching his "Poor People's Campaign" in December 1967, for radical new measures "to provide jobs and income for the poor." Yet as he and others stressed, the war in Vietnam was taking funds away from federal programs serving the poor, and black soldiers were dying in disproportionate numbers in Southeast Asia.

The black power movement also motivated African Americans to take greater pride in their racial heritage by pushing for black studies programs in schools and colleges, the celebration of African cultural and artistic traditions, the organizing of inner-city voters to elect black mayors, laws forcing landlords to treat blacks fairly, and the creation of grassroots organizations and community centers in black neighborhoods. It was Malcolm X who insisted that blacks call themselves *African Americans* as a symbol of pride in their roots and as a spur to learn more about their history. As the popular singer James Brown urged, "Say it loud—I'm black and I'm proud."

THE GREAT SOCIETY

Growing federal support for civil rights came from an unlikely source: a drawling white southerner who succeeded John F. Kennedy in the White House. A stunned Lyndon Baines Johnson, the towering Texan known as LBJ, took the presidential oath of office on board the plane that brought Kennedy's body back to Washington from Dallas.

The fifty-five-year-old Johnson, the first southern president since Woodrow Wilson, had excelled as Senate majority leader before becoming vice president. His transition to the presidency was not easy, however. He inherited a political deadlock between the White House and a congressional alliance of Democratic and Republican conservatives that had blocked most of Kennedy's legislative proposals. Johnson had also been kept out of the inner circle of power in the Kennedy White House. The Kennedy brothers despised Johnson and excluded him from key decisions. Robert Kennedy described Johnson as "vicious, an animal in many ways." Johnson, in turn, dismissed "all those Bostons and Harvards" who knew less about the legislative process "than an old maid does about fucking."

Like Kennedy, Johnson was one of the most complex and inexplicable men to occupy the White House. Unlike the wealthy, aristocratic Kennedy, however, Johnson was a rags-to-riches story. With almost superhuman effort and ambition, he had worked his way out of rural Texas poverty during the Great Depression to become one of the Senate's dominant figures.

LBJ's ego and insecurities were as massive as his vanity and ambition; he could not stand being alone; he insisted

The oath of office Less than 90 minutes after Kennedy's death, Johnson took the presidential oath aboard Air Force One between his wife, Lady Bird (left), and Jacqueline Kennedy (right), before flying out of Dallas for Washington, D.C.

on being the center of attention wherever he went. Johnson personalized the presidency; in press conferences, he referred to "my Vietnam policy," "my Security Council," "my Cabinet," "my legislation," and "my boys" fighting in Southeast Asia. George Reedy, the president's press secretary, said that Johnson was a "man of too many paradoxes." Ruthless and often bullying, needy and warmhearted, he was a contradictory whirlwind of workaholic energy and inspiring hopes, a crude idealist and a brutal optimist so thin-skinned that he took all criticism personally. In his view, people were either with him or against him. There was no middle ground.

Few leaders had ever dreamed as big as Lyndon Johnson. His outlook was grandiose. He wanted to be the greatest American president, the one who did the most good for the most people by creating the most new programs and agencies. He promised to "help every child get an education, to help every Negro and every American citizen have an equal opportunity, to help every family get a decent home, and to help bring healing to the sick and dignity to the old."

Those who dismissed Johnson as a traditional southern conservative failed to appreciate his genuine concern for the poor and his embrace of civil rights. "I'm going to be the best friend the Negro ever had," Johnson bragged to a member of the White House staff. His commitment to civil rights was in part motivated by politics, in part by his desire to bring the South into the mainstream of American life, and in part by his life experiences. His first teaching job after college was at an elementary school in Texas serving Mexican-American children. They created in him a lifelong desire to help "those poor little kids. I saw hunger in their eyes and pain in their bodies. Those little brown bodies had so little and needed so much." He grew determined to "fill their souls with ambition and interest and belief in the future."

Politics and Poverty

Johnson managed legislation through Congress better than any president in history. As a woman in Hawaii said, "Johnson is a mover of men. Kennedy could inspire men, but he couldn't move them." LBJ was the consummate wheeler-dealer on Capitol Hill. "It is the politician's task," he asserted, "to pass legislation, not to sit around saying principled things."

In 1964, he set about doing just that, taking advantage of widespread public support to push through Congress Kennedy's stalled measures for tax reductions and civil rights. He later said that he wanted to take Kennedy's incomplete program "and turn it into a martyr's cause."

The Revenue Act of 1964 provided a 20 percent reduction in tax rates. (The top rate was then a whopping 91 percent, compared to 39.6 today.) It was intended to give consumers more money to spend so as to boost economic growth and create new jobs, and it worked. Unemployment fell from 5.2 percent in 1964 to 4.5 percent in 1965 and 3.8 percent in 1966.

THE CIVIL RIGHTS ACT Long thwarted by southern Democrats in Congress, the **Civil Rights Act of 1964** finally became law on July 2. It guaranteed equal treatment under the law for *all* Americans and outlawed discrimination in public places on the basis of race, sex, or national origin. It also prohibited discrimination in the buying, selling, and renting of housing, as well as the hiring and firing of employees.

The civil rights movement set the stage and provided the momentum for the new law, but Johnson pursued its passage with an urgent sense of purpose. He lobbied key legislators one-on-one; one senator who survived the "Johnson treatment," as it came to be called, said that the president would "twist your arm off at the shoulder and beat your head with it" if you did not agree to vote as he wanted.

Soon after becoming president, Johnson hosted Georgia senator Richard Russell, his close friend and an arch-segregationist. Over lunch, the president warned Russell that "you've got to get out of my way. I'm going to run over you" to pass the Civil Rights Act. "You may do that," Russell replied. "But by God, it's going to cost you the South and cost you the election of 1964." Johnson answered: "If that's the price I've got to pay, I'll pay it gladly." Soon thereafter, Johnson told Congress that "we have talked long enough in this country about equal rights. . . . It is time now to write the next chapter, and to write it in the book of law." He added that it would be the best way to honor Kennedy's memory.

Many others helped Johnson convince Congress to pass the Civil Rights Act—Senator Hubert Humphrey, congressional committee chairs (both Republicans and Democrats), labor unions, church leaders, and civil rights organizations. Their collective efforts produced what is arguably the single most important piece of legislation in the twentieth century. The passage of the Civil Rights Act after more than a year of congressional delays marked one of those extraordinary moments when the ideals of democracy, equal opportunity, and human dignity are affirmed by action.

The Civil Rights Act of 1964 dealt a major blow to the deeply entrenched system of racial segregation while giving the federal government new powers to bring lawsuits against organizations or businesses that violated constitutional rights. It also established the Equal Employment Opportunities Commission to ensure that employers treated job applicants equally, regardless of race, gender, or national origin.

On the night after signing the bill, Johnson knew that conservative white southerners would be furious. He correctly predicted that "we have just delivered the South to the Republican party for a long time to come."

A WAR ON POVERTY In addition to fulfilling President Kennedy's legislative priorities that had been stalled in Congress, Lyndon Johnson launched an elaborate legislative program of his own by declaring "unconditional war on poverty in America." Americans had "rediscovered" poverty in 1962 when social critic Michael Harrington published a powerful exposé, *The Other America,* in which he revealed that more than 40 million people were mired in an invisible "culture of poverty." Poverty led to poor housing conditions, which in turn led to such problems as poor health, poor attendance at school or work, alcohol and drug abuse, unwanted pregnancies, and single-parent families. Harrington added that poverty was much more extensive than people realized because much of it was hidden from view in isolated rural areas or inner-city slums. He urged the United States to launch a "comprehensive assault on poverty."

President Kennedy had read Harrington's book and asked his advisers in the fall of 1963, just before his assassination, to investigate the problem and suggest solutions. Upon becoming president, Johnson announced that he wanted an anti-poverty legislative package "that would hit the nation with real impact." Money for the program would come from the tax revenues generated by corporate profits made possible by the tax reduction of 1964, which had led to one of the longest sustained economic booms in history. Johnson knew that the "war" on poverty would be long and costly. He said he did not expect to "wipe out poverty" in "my lifetime. But we can minimize it, moderate it, and in time eliminate it."

The **Economic Opportunity Act of 1964** was the primary weapon in the "War on Poverty." It created an Office of Economic Opportunity (OEO) to administer eleven new community-based programs, many of which still exist. They included a Job Corps training program for inner-city youths ages sixteen to twenty-one; a Head Start educational program for disadvantaged preschoolers; a Legal Services Corporation to provide legal assistance for low-income Americans; financial-aid programs for low-income college students; grants to small farmers and rural businesses; loans to businesses that hired the chronically unemployed; the Volunteers in Service to America program (VISTA) to combat inner-city poverty; and the Community Action Program, which would allow the poor "maximum feasible participation" in organizing and directing their own neighborhood programs. In 1964, Congress also approved the Food Stamp Act, a program to help poor people afford to buy groceries.

THE ELECTION OF 1964 Johnson's successes aroused a conservative Republican counterattack. Arizona senator Barry Goldwater, a wealthy department-store owner, emerged as the blunt-talking leader of the growing right wing of the Republican party. He was one of only six Republican senators to vote against the Civil Rights Act of 1964 and warned that the bill would lead to a "federal police state."

In his best-selling book *The Conscience of a Conservative* (1960), Goldwater had called for ending the income tax and drastically reducing federal entitlement programs such as Social Security. Conservatives controlled the Republican Convention when it gathered in San Francisco in the early summer of 1964, and they ensured Goldwater's nomination. "I would remind you," Goldwater told the delegates, "that extremism in the defense of liberty is no vice." He later explained that his objective was like that of Calvin Coolidge in the 1920s: "to reduce the size of government. Not to pass laws, but repeal them."

As a candidate, Goldwater frightened many voters when he urged whole-sale bombing of North Vietnam and even suggested using atomic weapons. He criticized Johnson's war on poverty as a waste of money, told students that the federal government should not provide any assistance for education, and opposed the nuclear test ban treaty. To Republican campaign buttons that claimed, "In your heart, you know he's right," Democrats responded, "In your guts, you know he's nuts."

Johnson, by comparison, portrayed himself as a responsible centrist. He chose as his running mate Hubert H. Humphrey of Minnesota, a prominent liberal senator who had long promoted civil rights. In contrast to Goldwater's aggressive rhetoric, Johnson pledged that he was "not about to send American boys nine or ten thousand miles from home to do what Asian boys ought to be doing for themselves."

The election was not close. Johnson won 61 percent of the popular vote and dominated the electoral vote by 486 to 52. Goldwater captured only Arizona and five states in the Lower South. In the Senate, the Democrats increased their majority by two (68 to 32) and in the House by thirty-seven (295 to 140).

Goldwater's success in the Lower South, however, accelerated the region's shift to the Republican party, and his candidacy proved to be a turning point in the development of the national conservative movement by inspiring a gen-eration of young activists and the formation of conservative organizations that would transform the dynamics of American politics during the 1970s and 1980s. Their success would culminate in the presidency of Ronald Reagan, the Hollywood actor who co-chaired the California for Goldwater campaign in 1964.

THE GREAT SOCIETY

Lyndon Johnson misread his lopsided victory in 1964 as a mandate for massive changes. He knew, however, that his popularity could quickly fade. "Every day I'm in office," he told his aides, "I'm going to lose votes. I'm going to alienate somebody. . . . We've got to get this legislation fast. You've got to get it during my honeymoon."

As Johnson's war on poverty gathered momentum, his already-outsized ambitions grew even larger. In May 1964, he announced his intention to

War on Poverty In 1964, President Johnson visited Tom Fletcher, a father of eight children living in a tar-paper shack in rural Kentucky. Fletcher became a "poster father" for the War on Poverty, though, as it turned out, his life benefited little from its programs.

develop an array of programs intended to create a "**Great Society**" that would end poverty and racial injustice and provide "abundance and liberty for all."

It soon became clear that Johnson viewed the federal government as the magical lever for raising the quality of life for all Americans—rich and poor. He would surpass Franklin Roosevelt's New Deal in expanding the goals and scope of the federal government to ensure that Americans were a people of plenty.

HEALTH INSURANCE, HOUSING, AND HIGHER EDU-CATION Johnson's first priorities among his "Great Society" programs were federal health insurance and aid for young people to pursue higher education—"liberal" proposals that had first been suggested by President Truman in 1945. For twenty years, the steadfast opposition of the physicians making up the American Medical Association (AMA) had stalled a comprehensive medical-insurance program. Now that Johnson and the Democrats had the votes to pass the measure, however, the AMA joined Republicans in supporting a bill serving those over age sixty-five.

The act that finally emerged created not just a **Medicare** health insurance program for the elderly but also a **Medicaid** program of federal grants to states to help cover medical expenses for the poor of all ages. Johnson signed the bill on July 30, 1965, in Independence, Missouri, with eighty-one-year-old Harry Truman looking on.

The Higher Education Act of 1965 increased federal grants to universities, created scholarships for low-income students, provided low-interest loans for students, and established a National Teachers Corps. "Every child," Johnson asserted, "must be encouraged to get as much education as he has the ability to take."

The momentum generated by the Higher Education and Medicare acts helped carry 435 more Great Society bills through Congress. Among them was the Appalachian Regional Development Act of 1966, which allocated $1 billion for programs in impoverished mountain areas. The Housing and Urban Development Act of 1965 provided $3 billion for urban renewal projects in inner-city ghettoes. Funds to help low-income families pay their rent followed in 1966, and the same year a new Department of Housing and Urban Development appeared, headed by Robert C. Weaver, the first African American cabinet member.

In implementing the many different Great Society programs, Lyndon Johnson had, in the words of one Washington reporter, "brought to harvest a generation's backlog of ideas and social legislation." No president, reported *Time* magazine, was "more passionately, earnestly, and all-encompassingly dedicated to and consumed by his work."

THE IMMIGRATION ACT Little noticed in the stream of Great Society legislation was the Immigration and Nationality Services Act of 1965, which Johnson signed in a ceremony on Liberty Island in New York Harbor. It abolished the discriminatory annual quotas based upon an immigrant's national origin and treated all nationalities and races equally. In place of quotas, it created hemispheric ceilings on visas issued: 170,000 for persons from outside the Western Hemisphere, 120,000 for persons from within. It also stipulated that no more than 20,000 people could come from any one country each year.

VOTING RIGHTS LEGISLATION Building upon the successes of "Freedom Summer," Martin Luther King Jr. organized an effort in early 1965 to register the 3 million unregistered African American voters in the South. On February 6, the White House announced that it would urge Congress to enact a voting rights bill.

To keep the pressure on the president and Congress, activists converged on Selma, Alabama, where only 250 of the 15,000 blacks of voting age were registered voters. King told his staff on February 10 that to get the voting rights bill passed, "we need to make a dramatic" statement. That drama occurred three weeks later.

On Sunday, March 7, some 600 black and white civil rights protesters assembled near the Edmund Pettus Bridge to begin a fifty-four-mile march to the state capitol in Montgomery. Before reaching the bridge, however, the marchers were assaulted by 500 state troopers and local police using billy clubs, tear gas, and bullwhips. In what came to be called "Bloody Sunday," the violence was televised for all to see. Fifty injured marchers were hospitalized. Dr. King, torn between congressional appeals to call off the march and the demands of militants that it continue, announced that a second march would be held. A federal judge agreed to allow the marchers to continue once President Johnson agreed to provide soldiers and federal marshals for their protection.

By March 25, when the demonstrators reached Montgomery, some 25,000 people were with them, and King delivered a rousing address in which he said, "the battle is in our hands. And we can answer with creative nonviolence the call to higher ground to which the new directions of our struggle summons us."

Several days earlier, on March 15, Johnson had urged Congress to "overcome the crippling legacy of bigotry and injustice" by making the cause of civil rights "our cause too." He concluded by slowly speaking the words of the movement's hymn: "And we *shall* overcome."

The resulting **Voting Rights Act of 1965** was one of the most momentous legislative accomplishments of the twentieth century. It ensured *all* citizens the right to vote. It authorized the attorney general to send federal officials to register voters in areas that had long experienced racial discrimination. In states or counties where fewer than half the adults had voted in 1964, the act banned the various ways, like literacy tests, that local officials used to keep blacks and Hispanics from voting.

By the end of the year, some 250,000 African Americans were newly registered to vote in several southern states. By 1968, an estimated 53 percent of blacks in Alabama were registered to vote, compared to 14 percent in 1960. In this respect, the Voting Rights Act was even more important than the Civil Rights Act because it empowered black voters in the South, thereby transforming the white-dominated politics in the region and making possible the election of black public officials. Yet by enabling southern blacks—most of whom preferred Democratic candidates—to vote, it also helped turn the once-solidly Democratic South into a Republican stronghold, as many white voters switched parties.

THE GREAT SOCIETY IN PRACTICE Lyndon B. Johnson sought to give Americans a sense of forward movement in troubled times and show them that he could create a "great society" whereby people would be "more concerned with the quality of their goals than the quantity of their goods."

Franklin Roosevelt passed fifteen major bills in his First Hundred Days, Johnson told an aide in 1966, whereas he had "passed two hundred in the last two years." The scope of Johnson's Great Society programs exceeded Roosevelt's New Deal in part because of the nation's booming prosperity during the mid-1960s. "This country," Johnson proclaimed, "is rich enough to do anything it has the guts to do and the vision to do and the will to do." That proved *not* to be the case, however. As *Time* magazine reported, "No matter how much Lyndon gets, he asks for more." Yet soon there was no more money to spend. In 1966, Johnson warned Congress that if taxes were not raised, the economy would suffer a "ruinous spiral of inflation" and "brutally higher interest rates."

The Great Society and war on poverty never lived up to Johnson's grandiose goals, in part because the Vietnam War soon took priority and siphoned away funding, and in part because neither Johnson nor his congressional supporters understood the stubborn complexity of chronic poverty. In many respects, the Great Society generated its own downfall by inspiring a conservative Republican backlash that would gain political control during the eighties. In the congressional elections of 1966, only 38 of the 71 Democrats elected to the House in 1964 won reelection. The political tide was running against Johnson.

The Great Society programs did, however, include several triumphs. Infant mortality has dropped, college completion rates have soared, malnutrition has virtually disappeared, and far fewer elderly Americans live below the poverty line and without access to health care. The federal guarantee of civil rights and voting rights remains in place. Medicare and Medicaid have become two of the most appreciated government programs. Consumers now have a federal agency protecting them. Head Start programs providing preschool enrichment activities for poor students have produced long-term benefits. The federal food stamp program has improved the nutrition and health of children living in poverty. Finally, scholarships for low-income college students have been immensely valuable providing access to higher education.

Several of Johnson's most ambitious programs, however, were ill-conceived, others were vastly underfunded, and many were mismanaged and even corrupt. Some of the problems they were meant to address actually worsened. Medicare, for example, removed incentives for hospitals to control costs, so medical bills skyrocketed—for everyone. In addition, food stamp fraud occurred as people took selfish advantage of a program intended to ensure healthy nutrition.

Overall, Great Society programs helped reduce the population living in poverty from 19 percent in 1964 to 10 percent in 1973, but it did so largely by providing federal welfare payments, not by finding people decent jobs. In 1966, middle-class resentment over the cost and excesses of the Great Society programs generated a conservative backlash that fueled the Republican resurgence in Congress. By then, however, the Great Society had transformed public expectations of the power and role of the federal government.

The Tragedy of Vietnam

In foreign affairs, Lyndon Johnson was, like Woodrow Wilson, a novice. And, again like Wilson, his presidency would become a victim of his crusading idealism. As racial violence erupted in America's cities, the war in Vietnam reached new levels of intensity and destruction. With weapons and supplies from China and the Soviet Union, North Vietnam provided massive support to the Viet Cong (VC), the guerrillas fighting in South Vietnam to overthrow the U.S.-backed government and unify the divided nation under Communist control.

Johnson inherited a long-standing U.S. commitment to prevent a Communist takeover in Vietnam. Beginning with Harry S. Truman, U.S. presidents had done just enough to avoid being charged with having "lost" Vietnam. Johnson initially sought to do the same, fearing that any other course of action would jeopardize his Great Society programs in Congress. His path, however, took the United States into a deeper military commitment.

In November 1963, when President Kennedy was assassinated, there were 16,000 U.S. military "advisers" in South Vietnam. Early in his presidency, Johnson doubted that Vietnam was worth a more extensive military involvement. In May 1964, he told his national security adviser, McGeorge Bundy, that he had spent a sleepless night worrying about Vietnam: "It looks to me like we are getting into another Korea. . . . I don't think it's worth fighting for.

And I don't think we can get out. It's just the biggest damned mess that I ever saw."

Yet Johnson's fear of appearing weak abroad outweighed his misgivings. By the end of 1965, there were 184,000 U.S. troops in Vietnam; in 1966, there were 385,000; and by 1969, at the height of the war effort, 542,000.

ESCALATION IN VIETNAM

The official justification for the military *escalation*—a Defense Department term favored in the Vietnam era—was the **Tonkin Gulf Resolution**, passed by the Senate on August 7, 1964. On that day, President Johnson, having been fed false information by the secretary of defense, reported that on August 2 and 4, North Vietnamese torpedo boats had attacked two American warships in the Gulf of Tonkin, off the

Hidden A Vietnamese mother hides her son and herself in the bushes near My Lai in 1965 after U.S. Marines murdered Vietnamese villagers.

coast of North Vietnam. As it turned out, the U.S. warships had actually fired first in support of South Vietnamese attacks against two North Vietnamese islands—attacks planned by American advisers.

The Tonkin Gulf Resolution empowered the president to "take all necessary measures to repel any armed attack against the forces of the United States and to prevent further aggression." Only two senators voted against the Tonkin Gulf Resolution, which Johnson interpreted as equivalent to a congressional declaration of war.

In early 1965, Johnson made the crucial decisions that committed America to full-scale war in Vietnam. On February 5, 1965, Viet Cong (VC) guerrillas attacked a U.S. base near Pleiku, in South Vietnam, killing and wounding more than 100 Americans. More attacks that week led Johnson to approve Operation Rolling Thunder, the first sustained U.S. bombing of North Vietnam. Thereafter, there were essentially two fronts in the war: one, in North Vietnam, where U.S. warplanes continued a massive bombing campaign, and the other, in South Vietnam, where nearly all the ground combat occurred.

In March 1965, the U.S. commander, General William C. Westmoreland, greeted the first American combat troops in Vietnam. Soon, U.S. forces launched "search and destroy" operations against VC guerrillas throughout South Vietnam. But the Viet Cong, made up of both men and women, wore no uniforms and dissolved by day into the villages, hiding among civilians. Their elusiveness exasperated American soldiers, most of whom were not trained for such unconventional warfare in Vietnam's dense jungles and intense heat and humidity. The escalating war brought rising U.S. casualties (the number of killed, wounded, and missing), which were announced each week on the television news. Criticism of the war grew, but LBJ stood firm. "We will not be defeated," he told the nation. "We will not grow tired. We will not withdraw."

THE CONTEXT FOR POLICY President Johnson's decision to "Americanize" the war flowed directly from the assumptions that had long guided U.S. foreign policy during the Cold War. The commitment to "contain" the spread of communism, initiated by Harry Truman and continued by Dwight Eisenhower and John Kennedy, guided Johnson as well. "Why are we in Vietnam?" the president asked during a speech in 1965. "We are there because we have a promise to keep. . . . To leave Vietnam to its fate would shake the confidence of all these people in the value of American commitment."

At the same time, Johnson and his advisers believed that military efforts in Vietnam must not reach levels that would cause the Chinese or Soviets to become involved—which meant, in effect, that a military victory was never possible. The United States was not fighting to "win" the war but to prevent the North Vietnamese and Viet Cong from winning and, eventually, force them to sign a negotiated settlement. This meant that the United States would have to maintain a military presence as long as the enemy retained the will to fight.

As the war ground on, opposition at home grew fierce. In 1965, college campuses began hosting "teach-ins" critical of the war effort. The following year, Senator J. William Fulbright of Arkansas, chairman of the Senate Foreign Relations Committee, began congressional investigations into American policy in Vietnam. George F. Kennan, the former State Department diplomat who had inspired the "containment" policy, told the committee that the containment doctrine was appropriate for Europe but not for Southeast Asia, which was not vital to American security. Such opposition to the war effort brought out the worst in Johnson. He labeled his political critics and

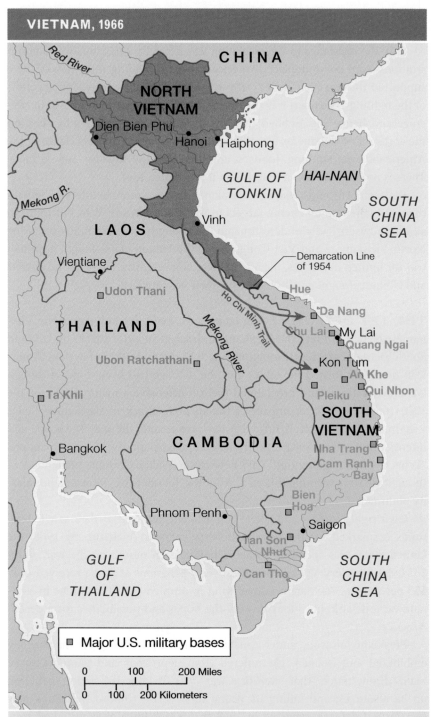

VIETNAM, 1966

Red River

CHINA

NORTH VIETNAM

Dien Bien Phu

Hanoi • Haiphong

GULF OF TONKIN

HAI-NAN

SOUTH CHINA SEA

Mekong R.

• Vinh

LAOS

Vientiane

Demarcation Line of 1954

□ Udon Thani

Hue □

THAILAND

Ho Chi Minh Trail

□ Da Nang

Mekong River

Chu Lai □ • My Lai
□ Quang Ngai

Ubon Ratchathani □

Kon Tum •

□ Ta Khli

An Khe □

□ Qui Nhon

Pleiku •

SOUTH VIETNAM

• Bangkok

CAMBODIA

Nha Trang □ □

Cam Ranh Bay

Bien Hoa □

Phnom Penh •

• Saigon

Tan Son Nhut □

GULF OF THAILAND

Can Tho □

SOUTH CHINA SEA

□ Major U.S. military bases

| 0 | 100 | 200 Miles |
| 0 | 100 | 200 Kilometers |

- Why did the United States intervene militarily in South Vietnam?
- What was the Ho Chi Minh Trail?
- What was the Tet Offensive?

antiwar protesters "Communists" and used government agencies to punish them.

Still, the resistance to the escalating war grew. By 1967, anti-war demonstrations were commonplace. Americans began dividing into "hawks" who supported the war and "doves" who opposed it. Nightly television accounts of the fighting—Vietnam was the first war to receive extended television coverage and hence was dubbed the "living-room war"—called into question the accuracy of statements by military and government officials claiming the Americans were winning. Johnson admitted that the situation was "a mess. There is no question about that. I wish it was better, too."

Between 1965 and 1968, U.S. warplanes dropped more bombs on Vietnam than had fallen on all enemy targets in the Second World War. But Johnson and his advisers badly underestimated the strength and determination of the North Vietnamese and Viet Cong. While the United States fought a limited war for limited objectives, the Vietnamese Communists, aided by the Soviets and Chinese, fought an all-out war for their very survival.

THE TET OFFENSIVE On January 31, 1968, the first day of the Vietnamese New Year (Tet), the Viet Cong unleashed surprise attacks on U.S. and South Vietnamese forces throughout South Vietnam. Within a few days, American firepower turned the tables, but the damage had been done. Although General Westmoreland proclaimed the **Tet offensive** a major defeat for the Viet Cong, the *political* impact of the surprise attack in the United States was dramatic; it decisively turned Americans against the war. The scope and intensity of the Tet offensive contradicted upbeat claims by U.S. commanders. "What the hell is going on?" CBS newscaster Walter Cronkite demanded. "I thought we were winning this war." After the Tet offensive, Johnson's popularity plummeted.

Civil rights leaders and social activists felt betrayed as they saw federal funds earmarked for the war on poverty spent in Vietnam. By 1968, the United States was spending some $2 billion each month on the war, about $322,000 for every VC killed; anti-poverty programs at home received only $53 per person. As Martin Luther King Jr. pointed out, "the bombs in Vietnam explode at home—they destroy the hopes and possibilities for a decent America."

President Johnson, under constant assault by critics, grew increasingly embittered and isolated. He suffered from depression and paranoia as he realized how much "that bitch of a war" was dividing the nation, gobbling up its resources, and killing its young men. Clark Clifford, Johnson's new secretary of defense, reported in 1968 that a task force of experts had concluded that the United States could not "win" the war. It was not what Johnson wanted to hear.

Robert F. Kennedy, now a New York senator, began exploring a run for the presidency to challenge Johnson's Vietnam policy. Senator Eugene McCarthy of Minnesota had already announced his own campaign as an anti-war candidate. In New Hampshire's Democratic primary in March 1968, McCarthy won a stunning 42 percent of the vote to Johnson's 48 percent. Johnson now seemed mortally wounded, and the results in New Hampshire convinced Kennedy to enter the race.

On March 31, 1968, a weary Johnson appeared on national television to announce a limited halt to the bombing of North Vietnam to enable a negotiated cease-fire agreement with the Communists. Then, he made an astounding announcement: "I shall not seek, and I will not accept, the nomination of my party for another term as your President." As his daughter explained, the "agony of Vietnam" had engulfed her father.

Johnson had become a tragic victim of his grandiose ambitions: by promising far more than he could accomplish, he raised false hopes, stoked violent resentments, and fractured society. Although U.S. troops would remain in Vietnam for five more years, the quest for military victory ended with Johnson's presidency.

America tried to fight a "limited war" in Vietnam. The problem with the strategy was that the Vietnamese Communists fought an absolute war in defense of their country. Among other things, the war revealed that the resources of the United States, including its military power, were limited; the nation could not have its way around the world.

Now there were three candidates for the Democratic nomination: McCarthy, Kennedy, and Vice President Hubert Humphrey. Many anti-war Democrats expected McCarthy to drop out in favor of Kennedy, but the Minnesota senator, buoyed by his success and convinced of his moral superiority, refused to leave the race.

Whose war? President Johnson lowers his head in disappointment as he listens to a commander's report from Vietnam in 1968.

THE TURMOIL OF THE SIXTIES

By the late 1960s, traditional notions of authority were under attack as an angry spirit of rebelliousness expanded into a powerful cultural movement. The spirit of resistance was especially evident among disaffected youth who called into question not only the Vietnam War and the credibility of the Johnson administration but virtually every aspect of mainstream life, including the traditional family structure, the middle-class work ethic, universities, religion, and the nonviolent integrationist philosophy underpinning the civil rights movement. Many alienated young Americans, often lumped together as "hippies," felt that they were part of "the Revolution," a magical force that would overthrow a corrupt and outdated way of life.

1968: A TRAUMATIC YEAR All of the turbulent elements affecting American life came to a head in 1968, the most traumatic year in a traumatic decade. As *Time* magazine reported, "Nineteen sixty-eight was a knife blade that severed past from future." On April 4, a white racist named James Earl Ray shot and killed Martin Luther King Jr. as the black leader stood outside the Lorraine Motel in Memphis, Tennessee.

King's murder ignited a wave of violence. Riots occurred in more than 100 cities. Forty-six people died, all but five of them black. Some 20,000 army troops and 34,000 national guardsmen were mobilized across the country, and 21,000 people were arrested.

The night that King died, Robert Kennedy was in Indianapolis, Indiana. Upon hearing the news, he stood on a flatbed truck to speak to a grieving crowd of African Americans. "Those of you who are black can be filled with hatred, with bitterness and a desire for revenge," he said. "We can move toward further polarization. Or we can make an effort, as Dr. King did, to understand, to reconcile ourselves and to love."

Love was hard to find in 1968. Two months after King's death, after midnight on June 6, 1968, Robert Kennedy appeared at the Ambassador Hotel in Los Angeles to celebrate his victory over Eugene McCarthy in the California presidential primary. Kennedy closed his remarks by pledging that "we can end the divisions within the United States, end the violence."

After the applause subsided, Kennedy walked through the hotel kitchen on his way to the press room for interviews. Along the way, a Jordanian Arab named Sirhan Sirhan, resentful of the senator's strong support of Israel, shot Kennedy in the head. He died the next day. Only forty-two years old, Kennedy was buried beside his brother John in Arlington National Cemetery outside of Washington, D.C.

The assassinations of the Kennedys, Martin Luther King, and Malcolm X came to frame the sixties. With their deaths, a wealth of idealism died too—the idealism that Bobby Kennedy had hoped would put a fragmented America back together again. A growing number of young people felt orphaned from the political system. Having lost the leading voices for real change, many of them lost hope in democracy and turned to radicalism and violence—or dropped out of society.

CHICAGO AND MIAMI In August 1968, the nation's social unrest came to a head at the **Chicago Democratic National Convention**, where delegates gathered inside a convention hall to nominate Johnson's faithful vice president, Hubert H. Humphrey, as the party's candidate for president.

Outside, almost 20,000 police officers and national guard soldiers confronted thousands of passionate anti-war protesters who taunted the police with obscenities. Richard J. Daley, Chicago's gruff Democratic mayor, warned that he would not tolerate disruptions. Nonetheless, riots broke out and were televised nationwide. It was war in the streets. As police used tear gas and clubs to pummel the demonstrators, others chanted, "The whole world is watching." As the *New York Times* reported, "Those were our children in the streets, and the Chicago police beat them up." Nationally, the Democratic party began to fragment as a result of the chaos in Chicago.

Three weeks earlier, the Republicans had gathered in Miami Beach to nominate Richard Nixon. In 1962, after losing the California governor's race, Nixon had vowed never again to run for public office. By 1968, however, he had changed his mind and become a self-appointed spokesman for the values of "middle America." He and the Republicans promised they would bring "law and order" to the nation's streets. Nixon appealed to what he called the "**silent majority**," those who viewed the "rabble rousing" street protesters with contempt. In accepting the nomination, Nixon promised to listen to "the voice of the great majority of Americans, the forgotten Americans, the non-shouters, the non-demonstrators, that are not racists or sick, that are not guilty of the crime that plagues the land."

Former Alabama governor George Wallace, an outspoken segregationist, dismissed both Democrats and Republicans as too liberal and ran on the American Independent party ticket, a party he formed to defend racial segregation. Wallace promised to get tough on "scummy anarchists" and

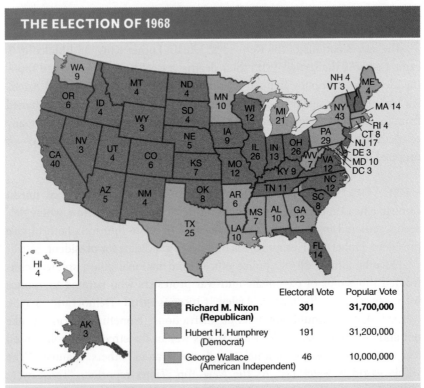

THE ELECTION OF 1968

	Electoral Vote	Popular Vote
Richard M. Nixon (Republican)	**301**	**31,700,000**
Hubert H. Humphrey (Democrat)	191	31,200,000
George Wallace (American Independent)	46	10,000,000

- How did the riots at the Chicago Democratic National Convention affect the 1968 presidential campaign?
- What does the electoral map reveal about the support for each of the three major candidates?
- How was Richard Nixon able to win enough electoral votes in such a close, three-way presidential race?
- What was George Wallace's appeal to 10 million voters?

bring stability to the nation. He appealed even more forcefully than Nixon to voters' concerns about anti-war protesters, the mushrooming federal welfare system, the growth of the federal government, forced racial integration, and rioting in urban ghettos. Wallace hoped to deny Humphrey and Nixon an electoral majority and thereby throw the choice into the House of Representatives.

NIXON TRIUMPHANT George Wallace's hopes were dashed on Election Day, however, as Richard Nixon and his acid-tongued running mate, Governor Spiro Agnew of Maryland, won a narrow victory. Nixon claimed 302 electoral votes to 191 for Hubert Humphrey. Wallace's 46 electoral votes all came from the Lower South. So at the end of the century's most turbulent year, a divided society looked to Richard Nixon to fulfill his promises to bring "peace with honor" in Vietnam and to "bring us together" as a nation.

CHAPTER REVIEW

SUMMARY

- **Kennedy's New Frontier**   President John F. Kennedy promised a *"New Frontier"* in 1961, but many of his domestic policies stalled in Congress. The *Bay of Pigs* fiasco led the Soviet premier, Nikita Khrushchev, to test American resolve by erecting the *Berlin Wall* and installing nuclear-armed missiles in Cuba, which provoked the *Cuban missile crisis*. Determined to stand up to the Soviets, in October 1962 Kennedy ordered a naval "quarantine" of Cuba that led Khrushchev to withdraw the missiles. During his presidency, Kennedy deepened America's commitment in Vietnam.

- **Civil Rights' Achievements**   At the beginning of the decade, growing numbers of African Americans and whites staged acts of *nonviolent civil disobedience* to protest discrimination in the South. In 1960, activists formed the *Student Nonviolent Coordinating Committee* (*SNCC*) to intensify efforts to dismantle desegregation. In 1961, courageous *Freedom Riders* attempted to integrate bus and train stations in the South. The high point of the early phase of the civil rights movement was the 1963 *March on Washington* for Jobs and Freedom, at which Martin Luther King Jr. delivered his famous "I Have a Dream" speech. Later on, the *black power movement* emerged and emphasized militancy, black nationalism, separatism, and, often, violence.

- **Johnson's Great Society**   Lyndon Johnson began his presidency committed to social reform, especially civil rights. He forced the *Civil Rights Act of 1964* through Congress and then declared "war" on poverty by persuading Congress to pass the *Economic Opportunity Act*. After his resounding victory in the 1964 presidential election, he pushed his vision for a *Great Society*. Hundreds of initiatives expanded federal social welfare programs, most noticeably the *Voting Rights Act of 1965*, *Medicare*, and *Medicaid*.

- **1968 Presidential Election**   Frustrated by his failures in Vietnam and aware that he had lost public support, Johnson chose not to seek reelection in 1968. Anti-war Democrats rallied around Senators Eugene McCarthy and Robert Kennedy. In April, Martin Luther King Jr. was assassinated, setting off violent riots in urban ghettos across the country. Then Robert Kennedy was assassinated in June. Ultimately, the Democrats selected Johnson's loyal vice president, Hubert Humphrey, as their nominee, provoking angry protests by anti-war demonstrators at the *1968 Chicago Democratic National Convention*. As they had in 1960, the Republicans nominated Richard Nixon, who claimed to represent the *"silent majority."* In the end, Nixon narrowly bested Humphrey, while Wallace made one of the best showings ever by a third-party candidate.

CHRONOLOGY

February 1960	Students in Greensboro, North Carolina, stage sit-ins
April 1960	Student Nonviolent Coordinating Committee (SNCC) formed
November 1960	John F. Kennedy elected president
April 1961	Bay of Pigs invasion fails
May 1961	Freedom Rides begin
August 1961	Soviets erect the Berlin Wall
October 1962	Cuban missile crisis
August 1963	March on Washington for Jobs and Freedom
November 1963	John F. Kennedy is assassinated
June 1964	Congress passes the Civil Rights Act
August 1964	Congress passes the Tonkin Gulf Resolution
November 1964	Lyndon B. Johnson is elected to a full presidential term
February 1965	Malcolm X is assassinated
July 1965	Congress creates Medicare and Medicaid programs
August 1965	Congress passes the Voting Rights Act
January 1968	Viet Cong stage the Tet offensive
April 1968	Martin Luther King Jr. is assassinated
June 1968	Robert Kennedy is assassinated
November 1968	Richard Nixon is elected president

KEY TERMS

 INQUIZITIVE

Go to InQuizitive to see what you've learned—and learn what you've missed—with personalized feedback along the way.

30 Rebellion and Reaction

1960s and 1970s

Rebels with a Cause Established in 1967, the Vietnam Veterans Against the War (VVAW) grew quickly during the sixties and early seventies. Here, a former Marine throws his service uniform jacket and medals onto the Capitol steps on April 23, 1971, as part of a five-day protest against the U.S. invasion of Laos.

A s Richard M. Nixon entered the White House in early 1969, he took charge of a nation whose social fabric was in tatters. The traumatic events of 1968 had been like a knife cutting the past away from the future, revealing how deeply divided American society had become and how difficult a task Nixon faced in carrying out his campaign pledge to restore social harmony.

Ironically, many of the same forces that had contributed to the complacent prosperity of the crew-cut fifties—the baby boom, the cold war, and the growing consumer culture—helped generate the social upheaval of the sixties and early seventies. The civil rights movement promoting equality for African Americans inspired efforts to ensure equal treatment for other minorities, including women, gays, Native Americans, and Hispanics. It was one of the most turbulent and significant periods in American history.

Despite Nixon's promise to restore the public's faith in the integrity of its leaders, he ended up aggravating the growing cynicism about the motives and methods of government officials. During 1973 and 1974, the Watergate scandal resulted in the greatest constitutional crisis since the impeachment of President Andrew Johnson in 1868, and it ended with the first resignation of a U.S. president.

focus questions

1. What were the origins of the youth revolt? How did it manifest in the New Left and the counterculture?

2. How did the youth revolt and the early civil rights movement influence other protest movements? How did new protest movements affect social attitudes and public policy?

3. How did the political environment of the late sixties shape Richard Nixon's election strategy and domestic policy?

4. How and why did Richard Nixon and Henry Kissinger change military and political strategies to end America's involvement in the Vietnam War?

5. What was the international strategy brought about by Richard Nixon's and Henry Kissinger's diplomacy and foreign policy during the 1970s?

6. How did the Watergate scandal unfold? What was its political significance?

"Forever Young": The Youth Revolt

The Greensboro sit-ins in 1960 not only launched a decade of civil rights activism but also signaled an end to the carefree complacency that had characterized the fifties. Rennie Davis, a sophomore at Ohio's Oberlin College in 1960, remembered that the Greensboro student activists inspired him and many others to work for social reform and political change: "Here were four students from Greensboro who were suddenly all over *Life* magazine. There was a feeling that they were us and we were them, and a recognition that they were expressing something we were feeling as well."

The sit-ins, marches, protests, ideals, and sacrifices associated with the civil rights movement inspired other minority groups—women, Native Americans, Hispanics, gays, and the disabled—to demand justice, freedom, and equality. Many idealistic young people decided that they could no longer turn a blind eye to the growing evidence of injustice and inequality staining the American dream.

A full-fledged youth revolt erupted during the mid-sixties. "Your sons and your daughters are beyond your command," sang Bob Dylan in "The Times They Are a-Changin'." As criticism of U.S. military involvement in Vietnam mounted, disillusioned young people flowed into two distinct yet frequently overlapping movements: the New Left and the counterculture.

THE NEW LEFT The political arm of the youth revolt originated when Tom Hayden and Alan Haber, two University of Michigan students, formed Students for a Democratic Society (SDS), a campus-based organization influenced by the tactics and successes of the civil rights movement. In 1962, Hayden and Haber called a meeting of sixty young men and women activists at Port Huron, Michigan. Their goal was to remake the United States into a more democratic society. Several of the participants were the children of former leftists or Communists; even more were Jewish.

Hayden drafted an impassioned document known as the Port Huron Statement. It began: "We are the people of this generation, bred in at least moderate comfort, housed in universities, looking uncomfortably to the world we inherit." Only by giving power to "the people," the manifesto insisted, could America restore its founding principles. Hayden called for political reforms, racial equality, and workers' rights. Inspired by the example of African American civil rights activists, Hayden declared that college students should engage in "participatory democracy" by snatching "control of the educational process from the administrative bureaucracy."

Hayden and others adopted the term **New Left** to distinguish their efforts at grassroots democracy from those of the "Old Left" of the thirties, which had embraced an orthodox Marxism. SDS grew quickly, forming chapters on more than 1,000 campuses.

In the fall of 1964, students at the University of California at Berkeley took Hayden's New Left program to heart. Several had spent the summer working with the Student Nonviolent Coordinating Committee's (SNCC) voter-registration project in Mississippi, where three volunteers had been killed and many others arrested or harassed. They were eager to bring changes to campus life. When the university's chancellor announced that political demonstrations would no longer be allowed on campus, thousands of students staged a sit-in. After a tense thirty-two-hour standoff, the administration relented. Student groups then formed the free-speech movement (FSM).

Led by Mario Savio, who had participated in Freedom Summer in Mississippi, the FSM became the first major student revolt of the sixties. The FSM initially protested on behalf of students' rights, but it quickly mounted more general criticisms of the university and what Savio called the "depersonalized, unresponsive bureaucracy" smothering American life. In 1964, Savio led hundreds of students into Sproul Hall, UC Berkeley's administration building, and organized another sit-in. At 4 A.M., 600 state police arrested the protesters. But their example lived on. Some 7,000 students filled Sproul Plaza that morning, circulating leaflets and joining folk singer Joan Baez in singing "We Shall Overcome." Finally, the university's president gave in and revoked the ban on political demonstrations. The FSM succeeded, Savio explained, because "it was so obvious to everybody that it was right."

ANTI-WAR PROTESTS The goals and tactics of FSM and SDS soon spread across the country. By 1965, however, the growing U.S. involvement in Vietnam had changed the rebellious students' agenda. Millions of young men suddenly faced the grim prospect of being drafted to fight in the increasingly unpopular conflict.

The Vietnam War was primarily a poor man's fight. Most college students were able to postpone military service until they received their degree or reached the age of twenty-four; in 1965–1966, college students made up only 2 percent of military inductees. African Americans and Hispanics were twice as likely to be drafted as whites.

As the war dragged on, Americans divided into "hawks" and "doves," those who supported the war and those who opposed it. Some 200,000 young men ignored their draft notices, and some 4,000 served prison sentences for doing

All that rises must converge This protester's sign at a Washington, D.C., demonstration bridged the civil rights and anti-war movements, which pursued many of the same racial and political goals.

so. Another 56,000 qualified for conscientious objector status. Others ceremoniously burned their draft cards in front of television cameras while shouting "Hell No, We Won't Go!" Still others fled to Canada or Sweden to avoid military service. The most popular means of escaping the draft was to find a way to flunk the physical examination. Whatever the method, many college students succeeded in avoiding military service.

RISING VIOLENCE Throughout 1967 and 1968, the anti-war movement grew more violent as inner-city ghettos in Cleveland, Detroit, Newark, and other large cities were exploding in flames fanned by racial injustice. Frustration over deeply entrenched patterns of discrimination in employment and housing, as well as staggering rates of joblessness among inner-city African American youths, ignited the rage. "There was a sense everywhere, in 1968," journalist Garry Wills wrote, "that things were giving way. That man had not only lost control of his history, but might never regain it."

During the eventful spring of 1968—when Lyndon Johnson announced that he would not run for reelection and Martin Luther King Jr. and Robert F. Kennedy were assassinated—campus unrest boiled over. The turmoil reached a climax at Columbia University, where SDS student radicals and black militants occupied the president's office and classroom buildings. After a failed attempt by professors to negotiate an end to the takeover, the university's president cancelled classes and called in the New York City police. More than 100 students were injured, 700 were arrested, and the leaders of the uprising were expelled.

The events at Columbia inspired similar clashes at Harvard, Cornell, and San Francisco State, among dozens of other universities. Student radicals adopted a tough, macho style, dismissing traditional approaches to reform and protest as "wimpy" and rooted in "white skin privilege."

Most Americans viewed the student radicals with fear and loathing. Vice President Spiro Agnew dismissed them as "impudent snobs who characterize themselves as intellectuals." Richard Nixon declared that the campus unrest represented "the first major skirmish in a revolutionary struggle to seize the universities."

THE COUNTERCULTURE Looking back over the 1960s, Tom Hayden, the founder of SDS, recalled that most rebellious young Americans "were not narrowly political. Most were not interested in attaining [elected] office but in changing lifestyles. They were not so interested in being opinion makers as in changing the climate of opinion." Hayden acknowledged that the shocking events of 1968 led disaffected young rebels—so-called hippies—to embrace the **counterculture**, an unorganized rebellion against mainstream institutions, values, and behavior that focused more on cultural change than political activism.

Hippies rejected the pursuit of wealth and careers and embraced plain living, authenticity, friendship, peace, and, especially, *freedom*. In a 1967 cover story, the editors of *Time* magazine suggested that "in their independence of material possessions and their emphasis on peacefulness and honesty, hippies lead considerably more virtuous lives than the great majority of their fellow citizens. . . . In the end, it may be that the hippies have not so much dropped out of American society as given it something to think about."

Both the counterculture and the New Left fiercely rejected the status quo, but most hippies preferred to "drop out" of mainstream society rather than try to change the political system. Their preferred slogan was "Make Love, Not War." Like the Beats of the fifties, hippies created their own subculture that promoted personal freedom from virtually all traditional constraints. They were at once defiant, innocent, egalitarian, optimistic, and indulgent as they rejected the authority of the nation's core institutions: the family, government, political parties, corporations, the military, and colleges and universities. The "idea was to liberate yourself from the confining conventions of life and to celebrate the irrational side of your nature, kind of let yourself go," explained a student at the University of Chicago. "Do Your Own Thing" became the unofficial motto of the counterculture.

The counterculture lifestyle included an array of popular ideals and activities: peace, love, harmony, rock music, mystical religions, mind-altering drugs, casual sex, and communal living. Hippie fashion featured defiantly

Flower power Hippies let loose at a 1967 love-in, one of many such gatherings that celebrated peace, free love, and nontheological spirituality, often as a gesture of protest.

long hair for both women and men and clothing that was striking, unusual, or, God forbid, comfortable: flowing cotton dresses, granny gowns, ragged bell-bottom blue jeans, tie-dyed T-shirts, love beads, Tibetan bells, peace symbols, black boots, or sandals. Young men grew beards, and women stopped wearing makeup.

"EIGHT MILES HIGH" Illegal drugs—marijuana, amphetamines, cocaine, peyote, hashish, heroin, and LSD, the "Acid Test"—were common within the counterculture. Said Todd Gitlin, a former SDS president, "More and more, to get access to youth culture" in the late 1960s, "you had to get high." The Byrds sang about getting "Eight Miles High," and Bob Dylan proclaimed that "everybody must get stoned!"

In fact, getting stoned was one of the favorite activities of the millions who participated in the 1967 "Summer of Love," a series of events protesting the Vietnam War and celebrating the youth revolt. The initial event was actually held April 15, when a peace march in New York City attracted 300,000 participants, the most ever assembled for a single event up to that time.

Perhaps the most publicized activity of the "Summer of Love" occurred in San Francisco, where more than 100,000 hippies ("flower children") converged. The loosely organized "Council for the Summer of Love" intended the gathering to be the first step in a grassroots revolution opposing the war by celebrating alternative lifestyles—listening to rock music, experimenting with mind-altering drugs, wearing "psychedelic" clothing, and indulging in casual sex.

COMMUNES For some, the counterculture involved experimenting with alternative living arrangements, especially "intentional communities" or "communes." Communal living in urban areas such as San Francisco's Haight-Ashbury district, New York's Greenwich Village, Chicago's Uptown, and Atlanta's 14th Street neighborhood were popular for a time, as were rural communes. Thousands of hippie romantics flocked to the countryside, eager to liberate themselves from parental and institutional restraints, live in harmony with nature, and coexist in love and openness.

The participants in the back-to-the-land movement, as it became known, were seeking to deepen their sense of self and forge authentic community ties. "Out here," one of the rural communalists reflected, "we've got the earth and ourselves and God above. . . . We came for simplicity and to rediscover God."

Yet all but a handful of the back-to-the-land experiments collapsed within a few months or years. Almost none of those attracted by rural life actually knew how to farm, and many were not willing to do the hard work that living off the land required. "The hippies will not change America," a journalist predicted, "because change means pain, and the hippie subculture is rooted in the pleasure principle." *Newsweek* magazine reported "Trouble in Hippieland" in 1968, noting that most of the flower children were "seriously disturbed youngsters" incapable of sustaining an alternative to mainstream life. In a candid reflection, a young hippie confessed that "we are so stupid, so unable to cope with anything practical."

WOODSTOCK The sixties counterculture thrived on music—initially folk "protest" songs and later psychedelic rock music. During the early sixties, Pete Seeger, Joan Baez, Peter, Paul, and Mary, and Bob Dylan, among others, produced powerful songs intended to spur social reform. In Dylan's "The Times They Are a-Changin'," first sung in 1963, he warns: "There's a battle outside and it's ragin' / It'll soon shake your windows and rattle your walls / For the times, they are a-changin'." Within a few years, however, the hippies' favorite performers were those under the influence of mind-altering drugs, especially the San Francisco–based "acid rock" bands: Jefferson Airplane, Big Brother and the Holding Company, and the Grateful Dead.

Huge outdoor concerts were wildly popular. The largest was the sprawling Woodstock Music and Art Fair ("Aquarian Exposition"). In mid-August 1969, more than 400,000 mostly young people converged on a 600-acre farm near the tiny rural town of Bethel, New York, for what was called the world's "largest happening," three days "of peace and music."

Woodstock's carefree "spirit of love" was short-lived, however. Just four months later, when other concert promoters tried to replicate the "Woodstock Nation" experience at the Altamont Speedway Free Festival near San Francisco, the counterculture fell victim to the criminal culture.

The Rolling Stones hired the Hells Angels motorcycle gang to provide "security" for their show. During the band's performance of "Under My Thumb," a drunken Hells Angel stabbed to death an eighteen-year-old African American man wielding a gun in front of the stage. Three other spectators were accidentally killed. Much of the vitality and innocence of the counterculture died with them. After 1969, the hippie phenomenon began to fade as the spirit of liberation ran up against the hard realities of growing poverty, drug addiction, crime, and mental and physical illness among the "flower children."

SOCIAL ACTIVISM SPREADS

The same liberationist ideals that prompted young people to revolt against mainstream values and to protest against the Vietnam War also led many of them to embrace other causes. The success of the civil rights movement inspired other groups—women; Mexican Americans and Native Americans; gays; the elderly; and the physically and mentally disabled—to demand equal opportunities and equal rights. Still others joined the emerging environmental movement or groups working on behalf of consumers.

THE NEW FEMINISM

The women's movement in the late nineteenth and early twentieth centuries had focused on gaining the right to vote. The feminist movement of the sixties and seventies aimed to challenge the conventional ideal of female domesticity and ensure that women were treated equally in the workplace.

Most women in the early sixties, however, did not view gender equality as possible or even desirable. In 1962, more than two-thirds of women surveyed agreed that the most important family decisions "should be made by the man of the house." Although the Equal Pay Act of 1963 had made it illegal to pay women less than men for doing the same job, discrimination and harassment continued in the workplace and throughout society. Women, who were 51 percent of the nation's population and held 37 percent of the jobs, were paid 42 percent less than men.

Betty Friedan, a forty-two-year-old journalist and mother of three from Peoria, Illinois, emerged as the leader of the **women's movement**. Her influential book *The Feminine Mystique* (1963) helped launch the new phase of female protest. Friedan claimed that "something was very wrong with the way American women are trying to live their lives today." Her generation of white, college-educated women (she did not discuss working-class or African American women) had actually lost ground after the Second World War,

Betty Friedan Author of *The Feminine Mystique* and the first president of NOW.

when many left wartime employment and settled in suburbia as full-time wives and mothers, only to suffer from the "happy homemaker" syndrome which undermined their intellectual capacity and public aspirations. College-educated women, she observed, "seemed suddenly incapable of any ambition, any vision, any passion, except the pursuit of a wedding ring."

Friedan blamed a massive propaganda campaign by advertisers and women's magazines for brainwashing women to embrace the "feminine mystique" of blissful domesticity in which fulfillment came only with marriage and motherhood. Women, Friedan claimed, "were being duped into believing homemaking was their natural destiny."

The Feminine Mystique, an immediate best seller, forever changed American society by defining "the problem that has no name." Friedan's analysis of the "feminine mystique" inspired many well-educated, unfulfilled middle- and upper-class white women who felt trapped by a suffocating suburban ideal of household drudgery.

Moreover, Friedan discovered that there were far more women working outside the home than she had assumed. Many of them were frustrated by the demands of holding "two full-time jobs instead of just one—underpaid clerical worker and unpaid housekeeper." Perhaps most important, Friedan helped empower women to achieve their "full human capacities"—in the home, in schools, in offices, on college campuses, and in politics.

In 1966, Friedan and other activists founded the National Organization for Women (NOW). They chose the acronym NOW because it was part of a popular civil rights chant: "What do you want?" protesters yelled. "FREEDOM!" "When do you want it?" "NOW!"

NOW sought to end gender discrimination in the workplace and spearheaded efforts to legalize abortion and obtain federal and state support for child-care centers. Change came slowly, however. By 1970, there was still only one woman in the U.S. Senate, ten in the House of Representatives, and none on the Supreme Court or in the president's cabinet.

In the early seventies, members of Congress, the Supreme Court, and NOW advanced the cause of gender equality. Title IX of the Educational Amendments of 1972 barred discrimination on the basis of sex in any "education program or activity receiving federal financial assistance." Most notably applied to athletics, Title IX has enabled female participation in high school sports to increase nearly tenfold and almost double at the college level.

Congress also overwhelmingly approved an equal-rights amendment (ERA) to the U.S. Constitution, which, if ratified by the states, would have required equal treatment for women throughout society and politics. By mid-1973, twenty-eight states had approved the amendment, ten short of the thirty-eight needed for approval.

In 1973, the Supreme Court, in its ***Roe v. Wade*** decision, made history by striking down state laws forbidding abortions during the first three months of pregnancy. The Court ruled that women have a fundamental "right to choose" whether to bear a child or not, since pregnancy necessarily affects a woman's health and well-being. The *Roe v. Wade* decision and the ensuing success of NOW's efforts to liberalize local and state abortion laws generated a powerful conservative backlash, especially among Roman Catholics and evangelical Protestants, who mounted a potent "right-to-life" crusade that helped fuel the conservative political resurgence in the seventies and thereafter.

RADICAL FEMINISM During the late sixties, a new wave of younger and more radical feminists emerged. They sought "women's liberation" from all forms of "sexism" (also called "male chauvinism" or "male oppression").

The new feminists, often called "women's libbers," were more militant than those who had established NOW. Many were veterans of the civil rights movement and the anti-war crusade who had come to realize that male revolutionaries could be sexists, too. The women began meeting in small groups to discuss their opposition to the war and racism, only to discover at such "consciousness-raising" sessions that what bound them together was their shared grievances as women in a "man's world."

To gain true liberation, many of them decided, required exercising "sexual politics" whereby women would organize into a political movement based on their common problems and goals. Writer Robin Morgan captured this newly politicized feminism in the slogan, "The personal is political," a radical notion that Betty Friedan rejected. When lesbians demanded a public role in the women's movement, Friedan deplored the "lavender menace" of lesbianism as a divisive distraction that would only enrage their opponents. By 1973, however, NOW had endorsed gay rights.

What women want The Women's Strike for Equality brought tens of thousands of women together on August 26, 1970, to march for gender equality and celebrate the 50th anniversary of the Nineteenth Amendment.

Friedan could not dampen or deflect the younger generation of women activists, just as Martin Luther King Jr. had failed to control the Black Power movement. The goal of the women's liberation movement, said Susan Brownmiller, was to "go beyond a simple concept of equality. NOW's emphasis on legislative change left the radicals cold." For women to be truly equal, Brownmiller and others believed, required transforming *every* aspect of society: child rearing, entertainment, domestic duties, business, and the arts. Feminists demanded that their "hidden history," the story of women's rights advocates over the centuries, be taught in schools and colleges. They also took direct action, such as picketing the 1968 Miss America Pageant, burning copies of *Playboy* and other men's magazines, and tossing their bras and high-heeled shoes into "freedom cans."

FRACTURED FEMINISM By the end of the seventies, sharp disputes between moderate and radical feminists had fractured the women's movement in ways similar to the fragmentation experienced by civil rights organizations a decade earlier. The movement's failure to broaden its appeal much beyond the confines of the white middle class also caused reform efforts to stall.

Ratification of the Equal Rights Amendment, which had once seemed a straightforward assertion of equal opportunity ("Equality of rights under the law shall not be denied or abridged by the United States or by any State on account of sex"), was stymied in several state legislatures by conservative groups. By 1982, it had died, three states short of ratification.

Yet the successes of the women's movement endured. The women fighting for equal rights focused on several basic issues: gender discrimination in the workplace; equal pay for equal work; an equal chance at jobs traditionally reserved for men; the availability of high-quality, government-subsidized child-care centers; and easier access to birth-control devices, prenatal care, and abortion. Feminists also helped win improvements in divorce laws.

Feminists called attention to issues long hidden or ignored. In 1970, for example, 36 percent of the nation's "poor" families were headed by women, as were most urban families dependent on federal welfare services. Nearly 3 million poor children needed access to day-care centers, but there were places for only 530,000.

The feminist movement helped women achieve mass entry into the labor market and enjoy steady improvements toward equal pay and treatment. In 1960, some 38 percent of women were working outside the home; by 1980, some 52 percent were doing so.

Their growing presence in the labor force brought women a greater share of economic and political influence. By 1976, more than half of married women, and nine of ten female college graduates, were employed outside the home, a development that one economist called "the single most outstanding phenomenon of this century." Women also enrolled in graduate and professional schools in record numbers. During the 1970s, women began winning elected offices at the local, state, and national levels.

THE SEXUAL REVOLUTION AND THE PILL The feminist movement coincided with the so-called sexual revolution. Americans became more tolerant of premarital sex, and women became more sexually active. Between 1960 and 1975, the number of college women engaging in sexual intercourse doubled, to 50 percent. Enabling this change, in large part, was a scientific breakthrough: the birth-control pill, approved for public use by the Food and Drug Administration in 1960.

Widespread access to the pill gave women a greater sense of sexual freedom and led to more-open discussion of birth control, reproduction, and sexuality in general. By 1990, the world would have 400 million fewer people as a result of the pill.

Although the birth-control pill contributed to a rise in sexually transmitted diseases, many women viewed it as an inexpensive, nonintrusive way to gain better control over their bodies and their futures. "It was a savior," recalled Eleanor Smeal, president of the Feminist Majority Foundation.

HISPANIC RIGHTS

The activism of student revolts, the civil rights movement, and the crusade for women's rights soon spread to various ethnic minority groups. The word *Hispanic*, referring to people who trace their ancestry to Spanish-speaking Latin America or Spain, came into increasing use after 1945 in conjunction with growing efforts to promote economic and social justice. (Although frequently used as a synonym for Hispanic, the term *Latino* technically refers only to people of Latin American descent.)

Labor shortages during the Second World War had led defense industries to offer Hispanic Americans their first significant access to skilled-labor jobs. And as with African Americans, service in the military helped to heighten an American identity among Hispanic Americans and increase their desire for equal rights and social opportunities.

Social equality, however, remained elusive. After the Second World War, Hispanic Americans still faced widespread discrimination in hiring, housing, and education, and in 1960, the median income of a Mexican American family was only 62 percent of the national average. Hispanic American activists denounced segregation, called for improved public schools, and struggled to increase Hispanic political influence, economic opportunities, and visibility in the curricula of schools and colleges.

Hispanic civil rights leaders also faced an awkward dilemma: What should they do about the continuing stream of undocumented Mexican immigrants flowing across the border into the United States? Many Mexican Americans argued that their hopes for economic advancement and social equality were threatened by the influx of Mexican laborers willing to accept low-paying jobs. Mexican American leaders thus helped end the *bracero* program in 1964 (which trucked in contract day-laborers from Mexico during harvest season).

THE UNITED FARM WORKERS In the early sixties, Mexican American workers formed their own civil rights organization, the **United Farm Workers (UFW)**. Its founder was the charismatic Cesar Chavez. Born in 1927 in Yuma, Arizona, the son of Mexican immigrants, Chavez served in the

U.S. Navy during the Second World War, and afterward worked as a migrant laborer and community organizer focused on registering Latinos to vote.

Then, along with Dolores Huerta, he created the UFW, a union for migrant lettuce workers and grape pickers, many of them undocumented immigrants who could be deported at any time. Up and down California, Chavez led nonviolent protest marches that had the energy of religious pilgrimages. He staged hunger strikes and managed nationwide boycotts.

The United Farm Workers gained national attention in September 1965 when the union organized a strike (*la huelga*) against the corporate grape growers in California's San Joaquin Valley. As Huerta explained, "We have to get farmworkers the same type of benefits, the same type of wages, and the respect that they deserve because they do the most sacred work of all. They feed our nation every day."

The chief strength of the Hispanic rights movement lay less in the tactics of sit-ins and protest marches than in the rapid growth of the Hispanic American population. In 1970, Hispanics in the United States numbered 9 million (4.8 percent of the total population); by 2000, their numbers had increased to 35 million (12.5 percent); and in 2015, they numbered 55 million, mak-

Cesar Chavez The usually energetic Chavez is visibly weakened from what would be a twenty-five-day hunger strike in support of the United Farm Workers Union in March 1968. Robert F. Kennedy, a great admirer of Chavez, is seated to his right.

ing them the nation's largest minority group (17 percent). The voting power of Hispanics and their concentration in states with key electoral votes have helped give them significant political clout.

NATIVE AMERICAN RIGHTS

American Indians—many of whom had begun calling themselves *Native Americans*—also emerged as a political force in the late sixties. Two conditions combined to make Indian rights a priority. First, many whites felt guilty for the destructive actions of their ancestors toward a people who had, after all, been here first. Second, Native Americans faced desperate times: Indian unemployment was ten times the national rate, life expectancy was twenty years lower than the national average, and the suicide rate was a hundred times higher than the rate for whites.

Although President Lyndon Johnson attempted to funnel federal anti-poverty-program funds to reservations, militants within the Indian community grew impatient with the pace of change. Those promoting "**Red Power**" organized protests and demonstrations against local, state, and federal agencies.

In 1968, two Chippewas (or Ojibwas) living in Minneapolis, George Mitchell and Dennis Banks, founded the American Indian Movement (AIM). In October 1972, AIM organized the Trail of Broken Treaties caravan, which traveled by bus and car from the West Coast to Washington, D.C., drawing attention to the federal government's broken promises. When Nixon administration officials refused to meet with them, the protesters occupied the federal Bureau of Indian Affairs. The sit-in ended when government negotiators agreed to renew discussions of Native American grievances about the government programs intended to improve their quality of life.

In 1973, AIM led 200 Sioux in the occupation of the tiny South Dakota village of Wounded Knee, where the U.S. Seventh Cavalry had massacred a Sioux village in 1890. Outraged by the light sentences given a group of local whites who had killed a Sioux in 1972, the organizers sought to draw attention to the plight of the Indians. After the militants took eleven hostages, federal marshals and FBI agents surrounded the encampment.

When AIM leaders tried to bring in food and supplies, a shoot-out erupted, with one Indian killed and another wounded. The confrontation ended with a government promise to reexamine Indian treaty rights.

Indian protesters subsequently discovered a more effective tactic: they went into federal courts armed with copies of old treaties and demanded that the documents become the basis for financial restitution for the lands taken from them. In Alaska, Maine, South Carolina, and Massachusetts, they won substantial settlements that officially recognized their tribal rights and awarded monetary compensation at levels that upgraded the standard of living on several reservations.

GAY RIGHTS

The liberationist impulses of the sixties also encouraged homosexuals to assert their right to equal treatment. Throughout the sixties, gay men and lesbians were treated with disgust, cruelty, and violence. On Saturday night, June 28, 1969, New York City vice police raided the Stonewall Inn, a popular gay bar in Greenwich Village. Instead of dispersing, the patrons fought back, and the struggle spilled into the streets. Hundreds of other gays and their supporters joined the fracas.

The **Stonewall riots** lasted throughout the weekend, during which the Stonewall Inn burned down. When the turmoil ended, gays had forged a sense of solidarity embodied in two new organizations, the Gay Liberation Front and the Gay Activists' Alliance, both of which focused on ending discrimination and harassment against gays and transgender people.

Gay Pride in the Seventies Gay rights activists march in the Fifth Annual Gay Pride Day demonstration, commemorating the fifth anniversary of the Stonewall riots which jumpstarted the modern gay rights movement in the United States.

As news of the Stonewall rebellion spread, the gay rights movement grew. By 1973, almost 800 gay organizations had been formed across the country. That year, the American Psychiatric Association removed homosexuality from its official manual of "mental illnesses." Colleges and universities began offering courses and majors in "Gay Studies" (also called Queer Studies), and groups began pushing for official government recognition of same-sex marriages. As with the civil rights and women's movements, however, the campaign for gay rights soon suffered from internal divisions and a conservative counterattack.

Nixon and the Revival of Conservatism

The turmoil of the sixties spawned a cultural backlash among what Richard Nixon called the "great silent majority" of middle-class Americans that propelled him to a narrow election victory in 1968. He had been elected president as the representative of middle America—voters fed up with liberal politics, hippies, radical feminism, and **affirmative-action** programs giving preferential treatment to minorities and women to atone for past injustices.

THE CONSERVATIVE BACKLASH Alabama's Democratic governor, George Wallace, led the conservative counterattack. He was a fierce champion of states' rights and the voice of the white backlash against civil rights and cultural rebellion. "Liberals, intellectuals, and long hairs," he shouted, "have run the country for too long." Wallace repeatedly lashed out at "welfare queens," unmarried women he claimed "were breeding children as a cash crop" to receive federal child-support checks. Wallace became the voice for many working-class whites fed up with political liberalism and social radicalism.

RICHARD NIXON Richard Nixon appealed to the working- and middle-class whites who feared that America was being corrupted by permissiveness, anarchy, and the tyranny of the rebellious minority. He explicitly appealed to voters "who did not break the law, people who pay their taxes and go to work, people who send their children to school, who go to their churches, people who are not haters, people who love this country." Above all, he promised to restore "law and order."

In 1952, Senator Robert A. Taft of Ohio, known as "Mr. Republican," had characterized young Senator Nixon as a "little man in a big hurry" with "a mean and vindictive streak." A grocer's son from Whittier, California, Nixon was a humorless man of fierce ambition and extraordinary perseverance. Raised in a family that struggled with poverty, he had to claw and struggle to the top, and he nursed a deep resentment of people who had an easier time of it (the "moneyed class").

Nixon was smart, shrewd, cunning, and doggedly determined to succeed in politics. He was also famously hard to get to know. Republican senator Barry Goldwater described Nixon as "the most complete loner I've ever known." Throughout his career, Nixon displayed violent mood swings punctuated by raging temper tantrums, profanity, and anti-Semitic outbursts. He was driven as much by anger and resentment as by civic duty. Critics nicknamed him "Tricky Dick" because he was a good liar. In his speech accepting the Republican nomination in 1968, Nixon pledged "to find the truth, to speak the truth, and live with the truth." In fact, however, he often did the opposite. One of his presidential aides admitted that "we did often lie, mislead, deceive, try to use [the media], and to con them."

NIXON'S APPOINTMENTS In his first term, Nixon selected for his cabinet and staff only white men who would blindly carry out his orders. John Mitchell, the gruff attorney general who had been a senior partner in Nixon's New York law firm, was his closest confidant. H. R. (Bob) Haldeman, a former advertising executive, served as chief of staff. As Haldeman explained, "Every President needs a son of a bitch, and I'm Nixon's." John Ehrlichman, a Seattle attorney and college schoolmate of Haldeman, was chief domestic-policy adviser. John W. Dean III, an associate deputy in the office of the U.S. Attorney General, became the White House legal counsel.

Nixon tapped as secretary of state his old friend William Rogers, who had served as attorney general under Dwight D. Eisenhower. Nixon, however, had no intention of making Rogers the nation's chief diplomat. Instead, the president virtually ignored Rogers while forging an unlikely partnership with Dr. Henry Kissinger, a brilliant German-born Harvard political scientist who had become the nation's leading foreign-policy expert. Kissinger's thick accent, owlish appearance, and outsized ego had helped to make him an international celebrity, courted by presidents of both parties. In 1969, Nixon named Kissinger his National Security Adviser, and in 1973 Kissinger became secretary of state.

THE SOUTHERN STRATEGY A major reason for Nixon's election victories in 1968 and 1972 was his shrewd southern strategy, designed to win over white southern Democrats upset by the civil rights revolution. Of all the nation's regions, the South had long been the most conservative. The majority of white southern voters were religious and patriotic, fervently anti-Communist and anti-union, and skeptical of social-welfare programs.

For a century, whites in the "Solid South" had steadfastly voted for Democrats. This trend reflected lingering resentments, dating to the Civil War and Reconstruction, against Abraham Lincoln and his Republican successors for imposing northern ways of life on the South, including racial integration. During the late sixties and seventies, however, a surging economy and a spurt of population growth transformed the South.

Between 1970 and 1990, the South's population grew by 40 percent, more than twice the national average. The region's warm climate, low cost of living, absence of labor unions, low taxes, and government incentives for economic development convinced waves of businesses to relocate there. During the seventies, job growth in the South was seven times greater than in New York and Pennsylvania.

Southern "redneck" culture suddenly became all the rage, as the nation embraced stock car racing, cowboy boots, pickup trucks, barbecue, and country music. As George Wallace had claimed while campaigning for president in 1968, "For 100 years, both parties have looked down their noses and called us rednecks down here in this part of the country. I'm sick and tired of it, and on November 5, they're goin' to find out there are a lot of rednecks in this country." Rapid population growth—and the continuing spread of air-conditioning—brought the sunbelt states of the South, the Southwest, and California more congressional seats and more electoral votes. Every president elected between 1964 and 2008 had roots in the sunbelt.

Nixon's favorite singer, country star Merle Haggard, crooned in his smash hit, "Okie from Muskogee": "We don't smoke marijuana in Muskogee / We don't take our trips on LSD / We don't burn our draft cards down on Main Street / We like livin' right and bein' free." Haggard's conservative working-class fans bristled at anti-war protesters, hippies, rising taxes, social-welfare programs, and civil rights activism. The alienation of many blue-collar whites from the Democratic party, the demographic changes transforming sunbelt states, and the white backlash against court-ordered integration created an opportunity to gain southern white votes that the Republican party eagerly exploited.

In the 1968 presidential campaign, Nixon's southern strategy won over traditionally Democratic white voters. He shrewdly "played the race card," assuring white conservatives that he would appoint justices to the Supreme Court who would undermine federal enforcement of civil rights laws, such as mandatory school busing to achieve racial integration and affirmative-action programs that gave minorities priority in hiring decisions and the awarding of government contracts. Nixon also appealed to the economic concerns of middle-class southern whites by promising lower tax rates and less government regulation.

In the 1972 election, Nixon carried every southern state by whopping majorities. The Republican takeover of the once "solid" Democratic South was the greatest realignment in American politics since Franklin D. Roosevelt's election in 1932.

NIXON'S DOMESTIC AGENDA As president, Richard Nixon shared with his predecessors John Kennedy and Lyndon Johnson an urge to increase presidential power. They believed that the presidency had become the central source of governmental action, that foreign policy should be managed from the White House rather than the State Department, and that the president had the authority to wage war without a congressional declaration of war.

Nixon was less a rigid conservative ideologue than a crafty politician. Forced to deal with a Congress controlled by Democrats, he chose his battles carefully and showed surprising flexibility, leading journalist Tom Wicker to describe him as "at once liberal and conservative, generous and begrudging, cynical and idealistic, choleric and calm, resentful and forgiving."

Nixon's focus during his first term was developing policies and programs that would help him be reelected. To please Republicans and recruit conservative Democrats, he touted his New Federalism, whereby he sent federal monies to state and local governments to spend as they saw fit. He also disbanded the core agency of Lyndon Johnson's war on poverty—the Office of Economic Opportunity—and cut funding to several Great Society programs.

At the same time, the Democrats in Congress passed significant legislation that Nixon signed: the right of eighteen-year-olds to vote in national elections (1970) and in all elections under the Twenty-Sixth Amendment (1971); increases in Social Security benefits and food-stamp funding; the Occupational Safety and Health Act (1970) to ensure safer workplace environments; and the Federal Election Campaign Act (1971), which modified the rules governing corporate financial donations to political campaigns.

NIXON AND CIVIL RIGHTS During his first term, President Nixon followed through on campaign pledges to blunt the momentum of the civil rights movement. He appointed no African Americans to his cabinet and refused to meet with the all-Democratic Congressional Black Caucus. "We've had enough social programs: forced integration, education, housing," he told his chief of staff. "People don't want more [people] on welfare. They don't want to help the working poor, and our mood needs to be harder on this, not softer."

Nixon also launched a concerted effort to block congressional renewal of the Voting Rights Act of 1965 and to delay implementation of federal court orders requiring the racial desegregation of school districts in Mississippi. Sixty-five lawyers in the Justice Department signed a letter protesting Nixon's stance. The Democratic-controlled Congress then extended the Voting Rights Act over Nixon's veto.

The Supreme Court also thwarted Nixon's efforts to slow desegregation. In its first decision under the new chief justice, Warren Burger—a Nixon appointee—the Court ordered the racial integration of the Mississippi public schools in *Alexander v. Holmes County Board of Education* (1969). During Nixon's first term, more schools were desegregated under court orders than in all the Kennedy–Johnson years combined.

Off to school Because of violent protests by whites against forced desegregation, school buses in South Boston are escorted by police in October 1974.

Nixon's efforts to block desegregation in urban areas also failed. The Burger Court ruled unanimously in *Swann v. Charlotte-Mecklenburg Board of Education* (1971) that school systems must bus students out of their neighborhoods if necessary to achieve racially integrated schools. Protests over busing erupted in the North, the Midwest, and the Southwest, as white families denounced the destruction of "the neighborhood school." Angry white parents in Pontiac, Michigan, were so determined to stop mandatory busing that they firebombed empty school buses.

NIXON AND ENVIRONMENTAL PROTECTION Dramatic increases in the price of oil and gasoline during the seventies fueled a major energy crisis in the United States. Natural resources grew limited—and increasingly precious. Nixon recognized that the public mood had shifted in favor of greater federal environmental protections, especially after two widely publicized environmental events in 1969.

The first was a massive oil spill off the coast of Santa Barbara, California, when an enormous slick of crude oil contaminated 200 miles of California beaches, killing thousands of sea birds and marine animals. Six months later, on June 22, 1969, the Cuyahoga River, an eighty-mile-long stream that slices through Cleveland, Ohio, spontaneously caught fire. Fouled with oil and grease, bubbling with subsurface gases, and littered with debris, the river burned for five days, its flames leaping fifty feet into the air. As with the Santa Barbara oil spill, the images of the burning river helped raise environmental awareness. A 1969 survey of college campuses by the *New York Times* revealed that many young people were transferring their attention and idealism from the anti-war movement to the environmental movement.

Nixon knew that if he vetoed legislative efforts to improve environmental quality, the Democratic majorities in Congress would overrule him, so he chose not to stand in the way. In late 1969, he signed the amended Endangered Species Preservation Act and the National Environmental Policy Act. The latter became effective on January 1, 1970, the year that environmental groups established an annual Earth Day celebration.

In 1970, Nixon by executive order created two new federal environmental agencies, the **Environmental Protection Agency (EPA)** and the National Oceanic and Atmospheric Administration (NOAA). The same year, he signed the Clean Air Act. Two years later, he vetoed a new clean water act, only to see Congress override his effort. He also undermined many of the new environmental laws by refusing to spend money appropriated by Congress to fund them.

"**STAGFLATION**" The major domestic development during the Nixon administration was a floundering economy. The accumulated expense of the Vietnam War and the Great Society programs helped quadruple the annual inflation rate from 3 percent in 1967 to 12 percent in 1974. Meanwhile, unemployment, at 3.3 percent when Nixon took office, nearly doubled to 6 percent by the end of 1970. Economists coined the term "**stagflation**" to describe the simultaneous problems of stalled economic growth (stagnation), rising inflation, and high unemployment. Consumer prices usually rose with a rapidly growing economy and rising employment. Now it was just the reverse, and there were no easy ways to fight the unusual combination of recession and inflation.

During the seventies, stagflation worsened because oil and gasoline became scarcer and costlier when the Organization of Petroleum Exporting Countries

(OPEC) decided to use its huge oil supplies as a political and economic weapon. In 1973, the United States sent massive aid to Israel after a devastating Syrian-Egyptian attack launched on Yom Kippur, the holiest day on the Jewish calendar. OPEC responded by announcing that it would not sell oil to nations supporting Israel and that it was raising its oil prices by 400 percent.

The Arab oil embargo caused gasoline shortages and skyrocketing prices. American motorists suddenly faced mile-long lines at gas stations, and factories cut production because of spiking fuel costs.

Another condition leading to stagflation was the flood of new workers—mainly baby boomers and women. From 1965 to 1980, the workforce grew by almost 30 million, a number

Oil crisis, 1973 The scarcity of imported Arab oil forced the rationing of gasoline. Gas stations, such as this one in Colorado, closed on Sundays to conserve supplies.

greater than the total labor force of France or West Germany. The number of new jobs could not keep up with the growth of the workforce, leaving many unemployed.

The Nixon administration responded erratically and ineffectively to stagflation. First, the president sought to reduce the federal deficit by raising taxes and cutting the budget. When the Democratic Congress refused to cooperate, he encouraged the Federal Reserve Board to reduce the nation's money supply by raising interest rates. The stock market immediately nose-dived, and the economy plunged into the "Nixon recession."

"PEACE WITH HONOR": ENDING THE VIETNAM WAR

By the time Richard Nixon entered the White House in January 1969, he and Henry Kissinger had developed a comprehensive vision of a new world order. The result was a dramatic transformation of U.S. foreign policy. Since 1945, the United States had lost its monopoly on nuclear weapons, its overwhelming economic dominance, and much of its geopolitical influence. The rapid rise of competing power centers in Europe, China, and Japan further complicated the cold war as well as international relations in general.

Nixon and Kissinger envisioned defusing the cold war by pursuing peaceful coexistence with the Soviets and Chinese. After a "period of confrontation," Nixon explained in his 1969 inaugural address, "we are entering an era of negotiation." Preoccupied with secrecy, Nixon and Kissinger bypassed the State Department and Congress in their efforts to take advantage of shifting world events.

Their immediate task was ending the war in Vietnam. Until all troops had returned home, the nation would find it difficult to achieve the social harmony that Nixon had promised. Privately, he had decided "there's no way to win the war," so he sought what he called "peace with honor." That is, the United States needed to withdraw in a way that upheld the credibility of its military alliances around the world. Peace, however, was long in coming, not very honorable, and shockingly brief.

GRADUAL WITHDRAWAL The Vietnam policy implemented by President Nixon and Henry Kissinger moved along three fronts. First, U.S. negotiators in Paris demanded the withdrawal of Viet Cong forces from South Vietnam and the preservation of the U.S.-backed government of President Nguyen Van Thieu. The North Vietnamese and Viet Cong negotiators, for their part, insisted on retaining a Communist military presence in the south and reunifying the Vietnamese people under a government dominated by the Communists. Hidden from public awareness and from America's South Vietnamese allies were secret meetings between Kissinger and the North Vietnamese.

On the second front, Nixon sought to defuse the anti-war movement by reducing the number of U.S. troops in Vietnam, justifying the reduction as the natural result of "**Vietnamization**"—the equipping and training of South Vietnamese soldiers and pilots to assume the burden of combat. The president began withdrawing troops while expanding the American bombing of North Vietnam to buy time for the transition. From a peak of 560,000 troops in January 1969, only 50,000 remained in Vietnam by 1973.

In 1969, Nixon also established a draft lottery whereby the birthdates of nineteen-year-old men were randomly selected and assigned a number between 1 and 366. Those with low lottery numbers would be the first drafted into military service. The lottery system eliminated many inequities and clarified the likelihood of being drafted. Four years later, in 1973, the president did away with the draft altogether by creating an all-volunteer military.

These initiatives, coupled with the troop withdrawals, defused the antiwar movement. Opinion polls showed strong support for Nixon's war policies. "We've got those liberal bastards on the run now," the president gloated, "and we're going to keep them on the run."

On the third front, Nixon and Kissinger greatly expanded the bombing of North Vietnam in hopes of pressuring the Communist leaders to end the war. Kissinger felt that "a fourth-rate power" like North Vietnam must have a "breaking point." Nixon agreed, suggesting that they let the North Vietnamese leaders know that he was so "obsessed about Communism" that he might use the "nuclear button" if necessary.

In March 1969, the United States began a fourteen-month-long bombing campaign aimed at Communist forces using neighboring Cambodia as a base for raids into South Vietnam. The total tonnage of bombs dropped was four times that dropped on Japan during the Second World War. Still, Hanoi's leaders did not flinch.

Then, on April 30, 1970, Nixon announced an "incursion" into "neutral" Cambodia to "clean out" hidden Communist military bases. Privately, Nixon told Kissinger, who strongly endorsed the decision, "If this doesn't work, it'll be your ass, Henry." Nixon knew that sending troops into Cambodia would reignite the anti-war movement. Secretary of State William Rogers predicted that "this will make the [anti-war] students puke."

DIVISIONS AT HOME Strident public opposition to the war and Nixon's slow withdrawal of combat forces had a devastating effect on the military's morale and reputation. "No one wants to be the last grunt to die in this lousy war," said one soldier. Between 1969 and 1971, there were 730 reported fragging incidents (efforts by troops to kill or injure their own officers). Drug abuse became a major problem; in 1971, four times as many troops were hospitalized for drug overdoses as for combat-related wounds.

Revelations of atrocities committed by U.S. soldiers caused even the staunchest supporters of the war to wince. Late in 1969, the story of the My Lai Massacre plunged the country into two years of exposure to the tale of William L. "Rusty" Calley, a twenty-six-year-old army lieutenant who ordered the murder of 347 Vietnamese civilians in the village of My Lai in 1968. One soldier described it as "point-blank murder, and I was standing there watching it." As newsmagazines published gruesome photos of the massacre, Americans debated the issues it raised. A father in northern California grumbled that Calley "would have been a hero" in the Second World War. His son shot back: "Yeah, if you were a Nazi." Twenty-five army officers were charged with complicity in the massacre and subsequent cover-up, but only Calley was convicted. Nixon later granted him parole.

Just as Nixon had expected, the escalation of the air war in Vietnam and the extension of the war into Cambodia triggered widespread anti-war demonstrations. The president, however, was unmoved. "As far as this kind of activity is concerned," he gruffly explained, "we expect it; however, under no circumstances will I be affected whatever by it."

In the spring of 1970, news of the secret Cambodian "incursion" by U.S. forces set off explosive demonstrations on college campuses. At Kent State University, the Ohio National Guard was called in to control rioting on May 4. As radicals hurled insults and rocks at the soldiers, the poorly trained guardsmen panicked and opened fire. Thirteen students were hit, and four of them, all bystanders, were killed. The killings at Kent State added new fury to the anti-war and anti-Nixon movements. That spring, demonstrations occurred on more than 350 campuses.

A presidential commission charged with investigating the Kent State shootings concluded that they were "unnecessary and unwarranted." Not all agreed. A resident of Kent told a reporter that "anyone who appears on the streets of a city like Kent with long hair, dirty clothes, or barefooted deserves to be shot. . . . It would have been better if the Guard had shot the whole lot of them." Singer Neil Young had a different view. Shortly after the killings, he composed a song called "Ohio":

> Tin soldiers and Nixon's coming.
> We're finally on our own.
> This summer I hear the drumming.
> Four dead in Ohio.

The Ohio governor banned radio stations from playing the song, which only made it more popular.

Eleven days after the Kent State tragedy, on May 15, Mississippi highway patrolmen riddled a dormitory at Jackson State College with bullets, killing two students who were protesting the war. In New York City, anti-war demonstrators who gathered to protest the student deaths and the invasion of Cambodia were attacked by conservative "hard-hat" construction workers shouting "America, Love It or Leave It," who forced the protesters to disperse, and then marched on City Hall to raise the U.S. flag, which had been lowered to half-staff in mourning for the Kent State victims. "Thank God for the hard hats," Nixon exclaimed.

The following year, in June 1971, the *New York Times* began publishing excerpts from *The History of the U.S. Decision-Making Process of Vietnam*

Shooting at Kent State Mary Ann Vecchio, a teenage runaway participating in the anti-war demonstration, decries the murder of a Kent State student after the National Guard fired into the crowd.

Policy, a secret Defense Department study commissioned by Robert McNamara before his resignation as secretary of defense in 1968.

The so-called Pentagon Papers, leaked to the press by Daniel Ellsberg, a former Defense Department official, confirmed what many critics of the war had long suspected: Congress and the public had not received the full or accurate story about the Gulf of Tonkin incident of 1964, and contingency plans for U.S. entry into the war were being drawn up even as President Johnson was promising that combat troops would never be sent to Vietnam.

Although the Pentagon Papers dealt with events only up to 1965, the Nixon administration blocked their publication, arguing that their release would endanger national security and prolong the war. By a vote of 6 to 3, the Supreme Court ruled against the government. Newspapers throughout the country began publishing the documents the next day.

WAR WITHOUT END In the summer of 1972, Henry Kissinger renewed private meetings with the North Vietnamese negotiators in Paris. He now dropped his insistence upon the removal of all North Vietnamese troops from South Vietnam before the withdrawal of the remaining U.S. troops.

On October 26, only a week before the U.S. presidential election, Kissinger announced that "Peace is at hand."

As it turned out, however, this was a cynical ploy to win votes. Several days earlier, the Thieu regime in South Vietnam had rejected the Kissinger plan for a cease-fire, fearful that allowing North Vietnamese troops to remain in the south would virtually guarantee a Communist victory. The peace talks broke off on December 16, and two days later the newly reelected Nixon ordered massive bombings of Hanoi and Haiphong, the two largest cities in North Vietnam. The so-called Christmas bombings and the simultaneous U.S. mining of North Vietnamese harbors aroused worldwide protest.

Yet the talks in Paris soon resumed, and on January 27, 1973, the United States, North and South Vietnam, and the Viet Cong signed an "agreement on ending the war and restoring peace in Vietnam," known as the Paris Peace Accords.

In fact, it was a carefully disguised surrender that enabled the United States to end its combat role. While Nixon and Kissinger claimed that the bombings had brought North Vietnam to its senses, in truth the North Vietnamese never altered their basic stance; they kept 150,000 troops in South Vietnam and remained committed to the reunification of Vietnam under one government. What had changed was the willingness of the South Vietnamese, who were never allowed to participate in the negotiations, to accept the agreement on the basis of Nixon's promise that the United States would respond "with full force" to any Communist violation of the agreement.

By the time the Paris Peace Accords were signed in 1973, another 20,000 Americans had died since Nixon had taken office in 1969, the morale of the U.S. military had been shattered, and millions of Southeast Asians had been killed or wounded. Fighting soon broke out again in both Vietnam and Cambodia. In the end, Nixon and Kissinger's diplomatic efforts gained nothing the president could not have accomplished in 1969 by ending the war on similar terms.

THE COLLAPSE OF SOUTH VIETNAM On March 29, 1973, the last U.S. combat troops left Vietnam. The same day, almost 600 American prisoners of war, most of them downed pilots, were released from Hanoi. Within months, however, the cease-fire collapsed, the war between North and South resumed, and Communist forces gained the upper hand. In Cambodia (renamed the Khmer Republic after a 1970 military coup) and Laos, where fighting had been sporadic, a Communist victory also seemed inevitable.

In 1975, the North Vietnamese launched a full-scale invasion of South Vietnam, sending the South Vietnamese army and civilians into headlong panic. President Thieu desperately appealed to Washington for the U.S. assistance promised in the Paris Peace Accords. But Congress, weary of spending dollars and lives in Vietnam, refused. On April 21, Thieu resigned and flew to Taiwan.

In the end, "peace with honor" was simply a nice way of saying the Americans had lost their war in Vietnam. It was also hard to see the "honor" in the way the war ended. The negotiated settlement had given the United States just enough time to remove itself before the collapse of the South Vietnamese government. On April 30, 1975, Americans watched on television as North Vietnamese tanks rolled into Saigon, soon to be renamed Ho Chi Minh City, and military helicopters lifted desperate U.S. embassy and South Vietnamese officials and their families to warships waiting offshore.

The longest, most controversial, and least successful war in American history to that point was finally over. It left a bitter legacy. During the period of U.S. involvement, the combined death count for combatants and civilians reached nearly 2 million. North Vietnam absorbed incredible losses— some 600,000 soldiers and countless civilians. South Vietnam lost 240,000 soldiers, and more than 500,000 Vietnamese became refugees in the United States. More than 58,000 Americans died in Vietnam; another 300,000 were wounded, 2,500 were declared missing, and almost 100,000 returned missing one or more limbs. The United States spent more than $699 billion on the war.

The Vietnam War was the defining life event for the baby boomers, the generation that provided most of the U.S. troops as well as most of the antiwar protesters. The controversial war divided them in ways that would be felt for years. The "loss" of the war, combined with news of atrocities committed by American soldiers, eroded respect for the military so thoroughly that many young people came to regard military service as corrupting and dishonorable.

Vietnam combat veterans (average age nineteen, compared to twenty-six among servicemen in the Second World War) had "lost" a war in which their country had lost interest. When they returned, many found that even their families were unwilling to talk about what the soldiers had experienced, or were embarrassed about their involvement in the war. "I went over there thinking I was doing something right and came back a bum," said Larry Langowski from Illinois. "I came back decked with medals on my uniform, and I got spit on by a hippie girl."

The Vietnam War, initially described as a crusade for democratic ideals, revealed that democracy was not easily transferable to regions of the world that lacked any historical experience with democratic government. Fought to contain the spread of communism, the war instead fragmented the national

Leave with honor Hundreds of thousands of terrified South Vietnamese tried to flee the Communist forces with evacuating Americans. Here, a U.S. official punches a Vietnamese man trying to join his family in an overflowing airplane at Nha Trang.

consensus that had governed foreign affairs since 1947, when President Truman developed policies to "contain" communism around the world.

THE NIXON DOCTRINE AND A THAWING COLD WAR

Despite the frustrations associated with his efforts to end the Vietnam War, Richard Nixon, like John F. Kennedy, greatly preferred foreign policy over domestic policy (which he compared to building "sewer projects"), and his greatest successes were in international relations. Nixon was an expert in foreign affairs and had traveled abroad frequently as Dwight Eisenhower's vice president during the 1950s.

As president, Nixon benefited greatly from the expertise and strategic vision of Henry Kissinger. Their grand design for U.S. foreign policy after the Vietnam War centered on developing friendly relations with the Soviet

Union and Communist China. Nixon envisioned a post–cold war world, "an era of negotiation rather than confrontation." He and Kissinger pressed for a return to an Eisenhower-era approach that entailed reducing large-scale military interventions around the world and using the Central Intelligence Agency (CIA) to pursue America's strategic interests covertly.

THE CIA IN CHILE Ever since Fidel Castro and his supporters gained control of Cuba in 1959, American presidents had been determined to prevent any more Communist insurgencies in the Western Hemisphere. In 1970, Salvador Allende, a Marxist, Socialist party leader, and friend of Castro, was a leading presidential candidate in Chile, on the southwest coast of South America. President Nixon and Henry Kissinger knew that, if elected, Allende planned to "nationalize" Chilean industries, including those owned by U.S. corporations. They did not want "another Castro" in Latin America.

In September 1970, Nixon urged the CIA to do anything to prevent an Allende presidency. Although CIA agents provided campaign funds to his opponents, Allende was elected on October 24, 1970. The CIA then encouraged Chilean military leaders to oust him. In September 1973, the army took control, Allende either committed suicide or was murdered, and General Augusto Pinochet, a ruthless military dictator supposedly friendly to the United States, declared himself head of the government.

In consolidating control over Chile, Pinochet executed thousands. It was yet another example of the United States being so obsessed by anti-communism and protecting American business interests that it was willing to interfere in the democratic process of other nations.

THE NIXON DOCTRINE In July 1969, while announcing the first troop withdrawals from Vietnam, President Nixon unveiled what came to be called the Nixon Doctrine, a new approach to America's handling of international crises. Unlike John F. Kennedy, who had declared that the United States would "pay any price, bear any burden" to win the cold war, Nixon explained that "America cannot—and will not—conceive *all* the plans, design *all* the programs, execute *all* the decisions, and undertake *all* the defense of the free nations of the world." Those nations experiencing Communist insurgencies must in the future assume primary responsibility for their own defense. The United States would provide weapons and money but not soldiers.

At the same time, Nixon announced that the United States would pursue partnerships with Communist countries in areas of mutual interest. That Nixon, a Republican with a history of rabid anti-communism, would pursue such a policy of **détente** (a French word meaning "easing of relations") with

America's Communist archenemies shocked many and demonstrated yet again his pragmatic flexibility.

THE PEOPLE'S REPUBLIC OF CHINA Richard Nixon had a genius for surprise. In 1971, without informing Secretary of State William Rogers, Nixon sent Henry Kissinger on a secret trip to Beijing to explore the possibility of U.S. recognition of Communist China. Since 1949, when Mao Zedong's revolutionary movement established control, the United States had refused to recognize the People's Republic of China, preferring to regard Chiang Kai-shek's exiled regime on Taiwan as the legitimate Chinese government. But now, the time seemed ripe for a bold renewal of ties. Both the United States and Communist China were exhausted from intense domestic strife (anti-war protests in America, the Cultural Revolution in China), and both were eager to resist Soviet expansionism.

Nixon's bombshell announcement on July 15, 1971, that Kissinger had just returned from Beijing and that the president himself would be going to China the following year sent shock waves around the world. Nixon became the first U.S. president to use the term *People's Republic of China*, an important symbolic step in normalizing relations. The Nationalist Chinese on Taiwan felt betrayed, and the Japanese, historic enemies of China, were furious. In October 1971, the United Nations voted to admit the People's Republic of China and expel Taiwan.

On February 21, 1972, during the "week that changed the world," Americans turned on their televisions and saw President Nixon shake hands and drink toasts with Prime Minister Zhou Enlai and Communist party Chairman Mao Zedong. In one simple but astonishing stroke, Nixon and Kissinger had ended two decades of diplomatic isolation of the People's Republic of China.

During the president's week-long visit, the two nations agreed to scientific and cultural exchanges, steps

Nixon goes to China President Nixon and Chinese premier Zhou Enlai toast each other at the lavish farewell banquet in Shanghai celebrating the historic visit.

toward resuming trade, and the eventual reunification of Taiwan with the mainland. A year after Nixon's visit, "liaison offices" that served as unofficial embassies were established in Washington and Beijing. In 1979, diplomatic recognition was formalized.

As a conservative anti-Communist, Nixon had accomplished a diplomatic feat that his Democratic predecessors could not have attempted for fear of being branded "soft" on communism. Nixon and Kissinger's bold move had the added benefit of giving them leverage with the Soviet Union, which was understandably nervous about a U.S.-Chinese alliance.

EMBRACING THE SOVIET UNION In truth, China welcomed the breakthrough in relations because of tensions with the Soviet Union, with which it shared a long but contested border. By 1972, the Chinese leadership had become more fearful of the Soviet Union than the United States.

The Soviets, troubled by the agreements between China and the United States, were also eager to ease tensions with the Americans. Once again, President Nixon surprised the world by announcing that he would visit Moscow in 1972 for discussions with Leonid Brezhnev, the Soviet premier. The high drama of the China visit was repeated in Moscow, with toasts and elegant dinners attended by world leaders who had previously regarded each other as incarnations of evil.

What became known as détente with the Soviets offered the promise of less intense competition between the superpowers. Nixon and Brezhnev signed the pathbreaking **Strategic Arms Limitation Treaty (SALT I)**, which negotiators had been working on since 1969. The SALT agreement did not end the nuclear arms race, but it did limit the number of missiles with nuclear warheads and prohibited the construction of missile-defense systems. The Moscow summit also produced new trade agreements, including an arrangement whereby the United States sold almost a quarter of its wheat crop to the Soviets at a favorable price. (Critics called it the Great Grain Robbery.)

The summit resulted in the dramatic easing of tensions between the two superpowers. As Nixon told Congress upon his return, "never before have two adversaries, so deeply divided by conflicting ideologies and political rivalries, been able to limit the armaments upon which their survival depends."

For Nixon and Kissinger, the agreements with China and the Soviet Union represented monumental changes in the global order. Over time, détente with the Soviet Union would help end the cold war altogether by lowering Soviet hostility to Western influences, which in turn slowly eroded Communist rule from the inside.

SHUTTLE DIPLOMACY The Nixon–Kissinger initiatives in the Middle East were less dramatic and less conclusive than those in China and the Soviet Union, but they did show that the United States at last recognized the legitimacy of Arab interests in the region and its own dependence upon Middle Eastern oil. In the Six-Day War of 1967, Israeli forces had routed the armies of Egypt, Syria, and Jordan, and seized territory from all three nations. Moreover, the number of Palestinian refugees, many of them homeless since the creation of Israel in 1948, increased after the Israeli victory.

The Middle East remained a tinderbox of tensions. On October 6, 1973, the Jewish holy day of Yom Kippur, Syria and Egypt, backed by Saudi Arabia and armed with Soviet weapons, attacked Israel, igniting what became the Yom Kippur War. It created the most dangerous confrontation between the United States and the Soviet Union since the Cuban missile crisis.

When the Israeli army, with weapons supplied by the United States, launched a fierce counterattack that appeared likely to overwhelm Egypt, the Soviets threatened to intervene militarily. Nixon, whose presidency was at risk because of the ongoing Watergate investigations, was bedridden because he was drunk, according to Henry Kissinger and other aides, so Kissinger, as secretary of state, presided over a National Security Council meeting that placed America's military forces on full alert.

On October 20, Kissinger flew to Moscow to meet with Soviet premier Brezhnev. Kissinger skillfully negotiated a cease-fire agreement and exerted pressure on the Israelis to prevent them from taking additional Arab territory. In an attempt to broker a lasting settlement, Kissinger made numerous flights among the capitals of the Middle East. His "shuttle diplomacy" won acclaim from all sides, though he failed to find a comprehensive formula for peace. He did, however, lay the groundwork for an important treaty between Israel and Egypt in 1977.

WATERGATE

Nixon's foreign policy achievements allowed him to stage the presidential campaign of 1972 as a triumphal procession. Early on, the main threat to his reelection came from George Wallace, who had the potential as a third-party candidate to deprive the Republicans of conservative white southern votes and thereby throw the election to the Democrats. That threat ended, however, on May 15, 1972, when Wallace was shot in an assassination attempt. Although he survived, he was left paralyzed below the waist and had to withdraw from the campaign.

Meanwhile, the Democrats nominated Senator George McGovern of South Dakota, an anti-war liberal. A poor campaigner who was viewed by many Americans as a left-wing extremist, he never had a chance. Nixon won the greatest victory of any Republican presidential candidate in history, capturing 520 electoral votes to only 17 for McGovern. The popular vote was equally decisive: 46 million to 28 million, a proportion of the total vote (60.8 percent) that was second only to Lyndon Johnson's victory over Barry Goldwater in 1964.

For all of his abilities and accomplishments, however, Nixon was chronically insecure. He nursed grudges and took politics personally, and he could be ruthless in attacking his opponents. As president, he began keeping a secret "enemies list" and launched numerous efforts to embarrass and punish those on the list. Little did he know that such behavior would bring him crashing down.

"DIRTY TRICKS" By the spring of 1972, senior Nixon aide John Ehrlichman was overseeing a secret team of agents who performed various acts of sabotage against Democrats, such as falsely accusing Democratic senators Hubert H. Humphrey and Henry Jackson of sexual improprieties, forging press releases, setting off stink bombs at Democratic campaign events, and planting spies on George McGovern's campaign plane. Charles "Chuck" Colson, one of the most active "dirty tricksters," admitted that "we did a hell of a lot of things and never got caught."

During the campaign, McGovern had complained about the "dirty tricks" orchestrated by members of the Nixon administration. Nixon, it turned out, had ordered illegal wiretaps on his opponents (as well as on his own aides), tried to coerce the Internal Revenue Service to intimidate Democrats, and told his chief of staff, Bob Haldeman, to break into the safe at the Brookings Institution, a Washington research center with Democratic ties.

McGovern was especially disturbed by an incident on June 17, 1972, when five men were caught breaking into the Democratic National Committee headquarters in the exclusive **Watergate** apartment and office complex in Washington, D.C. The burglars were former CIA agents, and one, James W. McCord, worked for Nixon's campaign. At the time, McGovern's complaints seemed like sour grapes from a candidate running far behind in the polls.

Nixon denied any involvement in this "very bizarre incident." Privately, however, he and his senior aides began feverish efforts to cover up the Watergate affair. The president told Alexander Haig, his chief of staff, that "we will cover up until hell freezes over." They secretly provided $400,000 to the jailed burglars to buy their silence and tried to keep the FBI out of the investigation. They also discussed using the CIA to derail the Justice Department's investigation.

UNCOVERING THE COVER-UP During the trial of the accused Watergate burglars in January 1973, relentless questioning by federal judge John J. Sirica led one of the accused to tell the full story of the Nixon administration's involvement. James W. McCord, security chief of the Committee to Re-Elect the President (CREEP), was the first in what would become a long line of informers to reveal the systematic efforts of Nixon and his aides to create an "imperial presidency." By the time of the Watergate break-in, money to finance "dirty tricks" was being illegally collected through CREEP and controlled by the White House staff.

The trail of evidence pursued first by Sirica, then by a grand jury, and then by a Senate committee headed by Democrat Samuel J. Ervin Jr. of North Carolina, led directly to what White House legal counsel John Dean called a "cancer close to the Presidency." Nixon was personally involved in the cover-up, using his power to discredit and block the investigation. He ordered the CIA to keep the FBI off the case and even coached his aides how to lie under oath. Most alarming, as it turned out, the Watergate burglary was merely part of a larger pattern of corruption and criminality sanctioned by the Nixon White House.

The cover-up unraveled further later that year when L. Patrick Gray, acting director of the FBI, resigned after confessing that he had destroyed several incriminating documents. On April 30, 1973, Ehrlichman and Haldeman resigned (they would later serve time in prison), as did Attorney General Richard Kleindienst. A few days later, Nixon nervously assured the public in a television address, "I am not a crook." Then Dean, whom Nixon had dismissed because of his cooperation with prosecutors, shocked the nation by testifying before the Ervin committee that there had been a cover-up approved by the president.

Nixon thereafter became preoccupied with legal self-defense and political survival. He refused to provide Ervin's committee with documents it requested, citing "executive privilege" to protect national security. In another shocking disclosure, a White House aide told the committee that Nixon had installed a secret taping system in the White House, and that many of the conversations about the Watergate burglary and cover-up had been recorded.

The bombshell news set off a legal battle for the "Nixon tapes." Harvard law professor Archibald Cox, whom Nixon's new attorney general, Elliot Richardson, had appointed as special prosecutor to investigate the Watergate case, took the president to court in October 1973 to obtain the tapes. Nixon refused to release the recordings and ordered Cox fired.

On October 20, in what became known as the "Saturday Night Massacre," Richardson and Deputy Attorney General William Ruckelshaus resigned rather than fire Cox. (Solicitor General Robert Bork finally fired him.) Cox's dismissal produced a firestorm of public indignation. Numerous newspaper and magazine editorials, as well as a growing chorus of legislators, called for the president to be impeached for obstructing justice. A Gallup poll revealed that Nixon's approval rating had plunged to 17 percent, the lowest level any president had ever received.

The new special prosecutor, Leon Jaworski, also took the president to court. In March 1974, the Watergate grand jury indicted Ehrlichman, Haldeman, and former attorney general John Mitchell for obstruction of justice and named Nixon an "unindicted co-conspirator."

On April 30, Nixon, still refusing to turn over the actual tapes, released 1,254 pages of transcribed recordings that he had edited himself, often substituting the phrase "expletive deleted" for his vulgar language and anti-Semitic rants. The transcripts revealed a president whose Oval Office conversations were so petty, self-serving, bigoted, and profane that they degraded the stature of the office and fueled growing demands for Nixon to resign.

By the summer of 1974, Nixon was in full retreat. He became alternately combative, melancholy, and petty. Henry Kissinger found him increasingly unstable and drinking heavily. Nixon's efforts to orchestrate the cover-up obsessed, unbalanced, and unhinged him. After meeting with the president, Senator Barry Goldwater reported that Nixon "jabbered incessantly, often incoherently." He seemed "to be cracking."

Americans watched the Ervin committee hearings as if they were episodes in a soap opera. On July 24, 1974, the Supreme Court ruled unanimously, in *United States v. Richard M. Nixon*, that the president must surrender *all* of the tape recordings. A few days later, the House Judiciary Committee voted to recommend three articles of impeachment: obstruction of justice through the payment of "hush money" to witnesses and the withholding of evidence; abuse of power through the use of federal agencies to deprive citizens of their constitutional rights; and defiance of Congress by withholding the tapes.

Before the House of Representatives could vote on impeachment, Nixon grudgingly handed over the complete set of White House tapes. The drama continued, however, when investigators learned that sections of certain key recordings were missing, including eighteen minutes of a conversation in June 1972 during which Nixon first mentioned the Watergate burglary.

The president's loyal secretary took the blame for the erasure, claiming that she had accidentally pushed the wrong button, but technical experts later concluded that the missing segments had been intentionally deleted. The other recordings,

V for "Victory" Before boarding the White House helicopter following his resignation, Nixon flashes a bright smile and his trademark V-for-Victory sign to the world on August 9, 1974.

however, provided more than enough evidence of Nixon's involvement in the cover-up. At one point, he had yelled at aides who were asking what they and others should say to Watergate investigators: "I don't give a shit what happens. I want you all to stonewall it, let them plead the Fifth Amendment, cover up or anything else."

The recordings led Republican leaders to urge Nixon to quit rather than face an impeachment trial in the Senate. On August 9, 1974, the embattled president resigned from office, the only president to do so. In 1969, he had begun his presidency hoping to heal America, to "bring people together." Now he left the White House for a self-imposed exile at his home in San Clemente, California, having deeply wounded the nation.

Nixon was one of the strangest, most complicated, and most interesting political figures in American history. He never understood why the Watergate affair could have ended his presidency; in his view, his only mistake was getting caught. Nixon claimed that a president's actions could not be "illegal." He was wrong. The Watergate affair's clearest lesson was that not even a president is above the law. But the fact that the system worked by calling a president to justice did not prevent many Americans from losing faith in the credibility of elected officials. The *New York Times* reported that people across the country "think and feel differently from what they once did" as a result of the Watergate crisis. "They ask questions, they reject assumptions, they doubt what they are told."

WATERGATE AND THE PRESIDENCY If there was a silver lining in the dark cloud of Watergate, it was the vigor and resilience of the institutions that had brought a rogue president to justice—the press, Congress, the courts, and public opinion.

In the aftermath of the scandal, Congress passed several pieces of legislation designed to curb executive power. Nervous about possible efforts to renew military assistance to South Vietnam, the Democratic Congress passed the

War Powers Act (1973), which requires a president to inform Congress within forty-eight hours if U.S. troops are deployed in combat abroad and to withdraw troops after sixty days unless Congress specifically approves their stay.

To correct abuses in the use of campaign funds, Congress enacted legislation in 1974 that set new ceilings on political contributions and expenditures. And in reaction to the Nixon claim of "executive privilege" as a means of withholding evidence, Congress strengthened the 1966 Freedom of Information Act to require prompt responses to requests for information from government files and to place on government agencies the burden of proof for classifying information as secret.

AN UNELECTED PRESIDENT During Richard Nixon's last year in office, the Watergate crisis so dominated national politics that major domestic and foreign problems received little attention. Vice President Spiro Agnew had himself been forced to resign in October 1973 for accepting bribes from contractors before and during his term in office. The vice president at the time of Nixon's resignation was Gerald Ford, a congenial former House minority leader from Michigan whom Nixon had appointed to succeed Agnew under the provisions of the Twenty-Fifth Amendment. On August 9, 1974, Ford was sworn in as the nation's first politically appointed chief executive, the only person in history to serve as both vice president and president without having been elected to those offices.

Restoring public confidence in elected leaders was not easy. Only a month after taking office, Ford reopened the wounds of Watergate by issuing Nixon a "full, free, and absolute pardon." Many Americans were not in a forgiving mood, and Ford's pardon unleashed a storm of controversy. He was grilled by a House subcommittee wanting to know whether Nixon had made a secret deal for the pardon. Ford vigorously denied the charge, but the pardon hobbled his presidency. His approval rating plummeted from 71 percent to 49 percent in one day, the steepest drop ever recorded. Even his press secretary resigned in protest.

THE FORD YEARS As president, Gerald Ford soon adopted the posture he had developed as the minority leader in the House of Representatives: naysaying head of the opposition who believed that the federal government exercised too much power. In his first fifteen months as president, he vetoed thirty-nine bills passed by Congress, outstripping Herbert Hoover's all-time veto record in less than half the time.

By far the most important development during Ford's brief presidency was the struggling economy. During the fall of 1974, the nation had entered

Gerald Ford The 38th president listens apprehensively to news of rising rates of unemployment and inflation in 1974.

its deepest recession since the Great Depression. Unemployment jumped to 9 percent in 1975, the annual rate of inflation reached double digits, and the federal budget deficit soon hit a record. Ford announced that inflation had become "Public Enemy No. 1," but instead of taking bold action, he launched a timid public relations campaign featuring lapel buttons that simply read WIN, symbolizing the administration's determination to "Whip Inflation Now."

The WIN buttons became a national joke and a symbol of Ford's ineffectiveness. He later admitted that they were a failed "gimmick." Ford initially supported increasing taxes to fight inflation, then reversed himself. By 1975, when he delivered his State of the Union address, he lamely conceded that "the state of the union is not good." In March 1975, Ford signed a tax reduction bill that failed to stimulate economic growth. The federal budget deficit grew from $53 billion in 1975 to $74 billion in 1976.

In foreign policy, Ford retained Henry Kissinger as secretary of state (while stripping him of his dual role as national security adviser) and pursued Nixon's goals of stability in the Middle East, friendly relations with China, and détente with the Soviet Union. Kissinger's tireless Middle East diplomacy produced an important agreement: Israel promised to return to Egypt most of the Sinai territory captured in the 1967 war, and the two nations agreed to rely on negotiations rather than force to settle future disagreements.

These limited but significant achievements should have enhanced Ford's image, but they were drowned in the criticism over the collapse of the South Vietnamese government in the face of the North Vietnamese invasion.

THE ELECTION OF 1976 Both political parties were in disarray as they prepared for the 1976 presidential election. At the Republican convention, Gerald Ford had to fend off a powerful challenge from the darling of the party's growing conservative wing, Ronald Reagan, a former two-term California governor and Hollywood actor.

The Democrats chose James Earl Carter Jr., who had served one term as governor of Georgia. A former naval officer and engineer turned peanut farmer, Carter was one of several Democratic southern governors who sought to move their party away from its traditional "tax and spend" liberalism.

Carter capitalized on post-Watergate cynicism by promising that he would "never tell a lie to the American people." He also trumpeted his status as a political "outsider" whose inexperience in Washington politics would be an asset. Carter was certainly different from conventional candidates. Reporters covering the campaign marveled at a Southern Baptist candidate who was a "born again" Christian.

To the surprise of many, Carter revived the New Deal voting alliance of southern whites, blacks, urban labor unionists, and ethnic groups like Jews and Hispanics to eke out a narrow win, receiving 41 million votes to Ford's 39 million. A heavy turnout of African Americans in the South enabled Carter to sweep every state in the region except Virginia. He also benefited from the appeal of Walter F. Mondale, his liberal running mate and a favorite among blue-collar workers and the urban poor.

The most significant story of the election, however, was the low voter turnout. Almost half of eligible voters, apparently alienated by Watergate, the stagnant economy, and the two lackluster candidates, chose to sit out the election. It was not a good omen for the incoming Democratic president.

CHAPTER REVIEW

SUMMARY

- **Youth Revolt**   Civil rights activism inspired a heightened interest in social causes during the sixties, especially among the young. Students for a Democratic Society (SDS) embodied the *New Left* ideology, and their ideas and tactics spread to many other campuses. By 1970, a distinctive *counterculture* had emerged among disaffected youth, and attracted young people ("hippies") alienated by mainstream American values and institutions.

- **The Inspirational Effects of the Civil Rights Movement**   The energy, ideals, tactics, and courage of the civil rights movement inspired many other social reform movements during the sixties and seventies, including the *women's movement*, the *Red Power* movement among Native Americans, and the *United Farm Workers* (*UFW*). The *Stonewall riots* in New York City in 1969 marked a militant new era for gay rights.

- **Reaction and Domestic Agenda**   Richard Nixon's "southern strategy" drew conservative southern white Democrats into the Republican party. As president, he sought to slow the momentum of the civil rights movement, including *affirmative action* programs giving special treatment to minorities, and vetoed the extension of the Voting Rights Act of 1968, but Congress overrode his veto. Nixon did grudgingly support new federal environmental policies such as the creation of the *Environmental Protection Agency* (*EPA*).

- **End of the Vietnam War**   In 1968, Nixon campaigned for the presidency pledging to secure "peace with honor" in Vietnam, but years would pass before the war ended. Nixon implemented what was called the *Vietnamization* of the war, which involved increasing economic and military aid to the South Vietnamese, reducing U.S. ground forces, and escalating the bombing of North Vietnam (and Cambodia), while attempting to negotiate a cease-fire agreement. The publication of the Pentagon Papers in 1971 and the intense bombing of North Vietnam in December 1972 aroused more protests, but a month after the bombings began, North and South Vietnam agreed to a cease-fire called the Paris Peace Accords.

- **Détente**   Nixon's greatest accomplishments were in foreign policy. He opened diplomatic relations with Communist China and pursued *détente* with the Soviet Union. He and Henry Kissinger also helped ease tensions in the Middle East.

- **Watergate**   During the 1972 presidential campaign, burglars were caught breaking into the Democratic party's national campaign headquarters at the *Watergate* complex in Washington, D.C. Nixon tried to block congressional investigations, which eventually led to calls for his impeachment for obstruction of justice. Nixon resigned in 1974 to avoid being impeached. He was succeeded by Vice President Gerald Ford, whose presidency was undermined by economic struggles, international incidents, and his controversial decision to pardon Nixon.

CHRONOLOGY

1960	Students for a Democratic Society (SDS) founded
1962	United Farm Workers (UFW) established
1965	Vietnam War expands
1966	National Organization for Women (NOW) founded
1967	Six-Day War in Middle East
1968	Richard M. Nixon elected president
June 1969	Stonewall riots in New York City
August 1969	Woodstock music festival attracts 400,000 people
1970	EPA created and Clean Air Bill passed
	Shooting of students at Kent State University
1971	Ratification of the Twenty-Sixth Amendment
	Nixon ends draft, begins withdrawing troops from Vietnam
1972	Nixon wins reelection and visits Communist China
	Nixon visits USSR and signs SALT I treaty
1972–1974	Watergate scandal unfolds
January 1973	The United States, North and South Vietnam, and the Viet Cong agree to a cease-fire
1973	Supreme Court overturns anti-abortion laws in *Roe v. Wade*
1974	Gerald Ford becomes president after Nixon's resignation
April 1975	Saigon falls to the North Vietnamese

KEY TERMS

New Left p. 1123

counterculture p. 1125

women's movement p. 1129

Roe v. Wade p. 1130

United Farm Workers (UFW) p. 1133

Red Power p. 1135

Stonewall riots p. 1136

affirmative action p. 1137

Environmental Protection Agency (EPA) p. 1142

stagflation p. 1142

Vietnamization p. 1144

détente p. 1151

Strategic Arms Limitation Treaty (SALT I) p. 1153

Watergate (1972–1974) p. 1155

War Powers Act (1973) p. 1159

 INQUIZITIVE

Go to InQuizitive to see what you've learned—and learn what you've missed—with personalized feedback along the way.

31 Conservative Revival

1977–1990

Feels good to be Right This proud Republican and Reagan supporter lets his cowboy hat adorned with campaign buttons speak for him at the 1980 Republican National Convention. Held in Detroit, Michigan, the convention nominated former California governor Ronald Reagan, who promised to "make America great again."

During the seventies, the United States lost much of its self-confidence. The Vietnam War, the Watergate scandal, and the spike in world oil prices, interest rates, and consumer prices revealed the limits of American power, prosperity, and virtue. For a nation accustomed to economic growth and spreading prosperity, the frustrating persistence of stagflation and gasoline shortages undermined national optimism. In July 1976, as the United States celebrated the bicentennial of its independence, many people were downsizing their expectations of the American Dream.

Jimmy Carter, the first president from the Lower South, took office in 1977 promising a government that would be "competent" as well as "decent, open, fair, and compassionate." But after four years as president, Carter had little to show for his efforts. The economy remained sluggish, consumer prices continued to increase at historic levels, and failed efforts to free Americans held hostage in Iran prompted critics, including Democrats, to denounce the administration as indecisive and inept. In the end, Carter's inability to mobilize national support for an ill-fated energy program and his call for "a time of national austerity" revealed both his ineffective legislative skills and his misreading of the public mood.

The Republicans capitalized by electing Ronald Reagan president in 1980. Where Carter had denounced the evils of unregulated capitalism, Reagan

focus questions

1. Why did Jimmy Carter have such limited success as America's thirty-ninth president?

2. What were the factors that led to the election of Ronald Reagan, the rise of the conservative movement, and the resurgence of the Republican party?

3. What is "Reaganomics"? What were its effects on American society and economy?

4. How did Reagan's Soviet strategy help end the cold war?

5. What were the social and economic issues and innovations that emerged during the 1980s?

6. What was the impact of the end of the cold war and the efforts of President George H. W. Bush to create a post–cold war foreign policy?

promised to unleash the capitalist spirit, restore national pride, and regain international respect. He did all of that and more. During his two terms as president, he inspired a conservative resurgence in politics, helped restore prosperity and raise the nation's morale, and accelerated the forces that would cause the collapse of the Soviet Union and the end of the cold war.

The Carter Presidency

James (Jimmy) Earl Carter Jr. won the 1976 election because he convinced voters that he was a common man of pure motives who would restore integrity and honesty to the presidency in the aftermath of the Watergate scandal. He represented a new generation of "moderate" southern Democrats who were committed to restraining "big-government" spending. In his inaugural address, Carter stressed America's limitations rather than its power: "We have learned that 'more' is not necessarily 'better,' that even our great nation has its recognized limits, and that we can neither answer all questions nor solve all problems." That may have been true, but it was not what many Americans wanted to hear.

The Carters After his inauguration in 1977, President Jimmy Carter forgoes the traditional limousine and walks down Pennsylvania Avenue with his wife, Rosalynn.

Jimmy Who?

Like Gerald Ford before him, Jimmy Carter was honest and forthright. But his public modesty masked a complex and at times contradictory personality. No modern president was as openly committed to his Christian faith as Carter. At the same time, few presidents were as tough on others as Carter.

The former governor of Georgia who came out of nowhere to win the presidential campaign ("Jimmy Who?") was both blessed and cursed by a surplus of self-confidence. All his life, he had displayed a fierce determination to succeed. He expected those around him to show the same tenacity.

As he entered the White House in early 1977, the former naval officer, nuclear engineer, efficiency expert, and business executive stressed that he wanted to be a "strong, aggressive president" who would reshape the federal government by eliminating waste and providing expert management.

Carter faced difficult economic problems and formidable international challenges. He was expected to cure the stubborn recession and reduce inflation at a time when industrial economies around the world were struggling. Carter was also expected to restore U.S. stature abroad and lift the national spirit in the wake of the Watergate scandal. Meeting such expectations would be miraculous, but Carter displayed a sunburst smile, flinty willpower, and an "almost arrogant self-confidence," as *Time* magazine described it. As it turned out, however, he was no miracle worker.

EARLY SUCCESS During the first two years of his presidency, Carter enjoyed several successes, both symbolic and real. He reduced the size of the White House staff by a third and told cabinet officers to give up their government cars. His administration included more African Americans and women than any before. He fulfilled a controversial campaign pledge by offering amnesty (forgiveness) to the thousands of young men who had fled the country rather than serve in Vietnam. He reorganized the executive branch and reduced government red tape.

Carter also pushed through the Democratic-controlled Congress several significant environmental initiatives, including stricter controls over the stripmining of coal, the creation of a $1.6 billion "Superfund" to clean up toxic chemical waste sites, and a bill protecting more than 100 million acres of Alaskan land from development. At the end of his first 100 days in office, Carter enjoyed a 75 percent public approval rating.

CARTER'S LIMITATIONS But President Carter's successes were short-lived. More than most presidents, he faced difficulties beyond his control, including ongoing inflation and a global energy crisis. Carter, however, contributed to the perception that he was not up to the challenges. He was less an inspiring leader than an efficiency-minded bureaucrat, a compulsive micromanager who failed to establish a compelling vision for the nation's future. Carter tried to do too much too fast, deciding disastrously that he needed no chief of staff to help manage his schedule and implement his decisions. His senior aides were often more a burden than a blessing. The "outsider" president saw little need to consult with Democratic leaders in Congress, which helps explain why many of his legislative requests were voted down.

Ultimately, Carter's mismanagement of the economy crippled his presidency. He first tried to attack unemployment, authorizing some $14 billion in federal spending to trigger job growth while cutting taxes by $34 billion. His actions helped generate new jobs but also caused a spike in inflation. Annual inflation (increases in consumer prices) jumped from 5 percent when he took office to as much as 13 percent during 1980. The result was a deepening recession and rising unemployment.

What made Carter's efforts to restore prosperity more challenging was the worsening global "energy crisis." Since the Arab oil embargo in 1973, the price of imported oil had doubled, while U.S. dependence on foreign oil had grown from 35 percent to 50 percent of its annual needs. In April 1977, Carter presented Congress with a comprehensive energy proposal designed to cut oil consumption. But legislators defeated most of the bill's significant measures.

In 1979, the energy crisis grew more troublesome when Islamic fundamentalists took over the government in oil-rich Iran and shut off the supply of Iranian oil to the United States, creating shortages of gasoline and much higher prices. Warning that the "growing scarcity in energy" would paralyze the U.S. economy, Carter asked Congress for a new and much more comprehensive energy bill. But legislators again turned down its most important energy conservation provisions intended to reduce dependence on foreign oil.

A "CRISIS OF CONFIDENCE"   By July 1979, Carter had grown so discouraged that he took an unusual step: for two weeks he holed up at Camp David, the presidential retreat in the Maryland mountains. There he met privately with leaders from all walks of life—business, labor, education, religion, even psychiatry. Then, on July 15, he returned to the White House and delivered a televised speech in which he admitted that the people had lost confidence in his leadership.

Carter then made a crucial mistake when he blamed Americans for the nation's problems. "All the legislation in the world can't fix what's wrong with America," he said, sounding more like an angry preacher than an uplifting president. People had become preoccupied with "owning and consuming things" at the expense of "hard work, strong families, close-knit communities, and our faith in God." The nation was at a crossroads, he concluded. Americans could choose continued self-indulgence and political stalemate, or they could revive traditional values such as thrift, mutual aid, simple living, and spirituality. "We can take the first step down that path as we begin to solve our energy problem. Energy will be the immediate test of our ability to unite this nation."

Americans were not inspired by the president's "sad and worried" speech. An Arizona newspaper expressed the feelings of many when it said that "the nation did not tune in Carter to hear a sermon. It wanted answers. It did not get them." Carter's new energy proposals got nowhere in Congress, and by the end of the summer, his negative ratings were the highest in history. "Our greatest single failure," said Hamilton Jordan, Carter's chief of staff, "is that we have not communicated effectively a description of the country's problems or a pertinent solution to those problems."

CARTER'S FOREIGN POLICY

Carter's greatest success was facilitating a 1978 peace agreement between Prime Minister Menachem Begin of Israel and President Anwar Sadat of Egypt. When negotiations between the enemies stalled, Carter invited Begin and Sadat to Camp David. For twelve days in September, the three leaders engaged in non-stop discussions.

Carter played a crucial role in convincing Sadat and Begin to compromise on key issues. Their efforts resulted in two landmark treaties, thereafter called the **Camp David Accords**. The first provided the framework for an eventual peace treaty. The Israelis pledged to end their military occupation of the Sinai region of Egypt, and the Egyptians promised to restore Israeli access to the Suez Canal. The second treaty called for a comprehensive settlement of the Arab-Israeli tensions based on Israel's willingness to allow the Palestinians living in the Israeli-controlled West Bank and Gaza Strip to govern themselves.

Sadat's willingness to recognize the legitimacy of the Israeli nation and sign the two treaties sparked waves of violent protests across the Arab world. The Arab League expelled Egypt and announced an economic boycott, and the Israelis later backtracked on aspects of the agreements. Sadat, however, paid the highest price. Most Arab nations condemned him as a traitor, and Islamic extremists assassinated him in 1981. Still, Carter's high-level diplomacy made an all-out war between Israel and the Arab world less likely.

Carter was also caught in a political crossfire when he vowed that "the soul of our foreign policy" should be an absolute "commitment to human rights" abroad, drawing a direct contrast between his international "idealism" and the geopolitical "realism" practiced by Richard Nixon and Henry Kissinger. Carter created an Office of Human Rights within the State Department and selectively cut off financial assistance to some repressive governments.

Critics noted that the United States had its own human rights issues, including the plight of Native Americans and African Americans, and that Carter ignored abuses occurring among key allies, such as the shah of Iran.

Others asserted that Carter's definition of human rights was so vague and sweeping that few nations could satisfy it. Critics on the right argued that he was sacrificing America's global interests to promote an impossible standard of international moral purity, while critics on the left highlighted his seeming hypocrisy in pursuing human rights in a few nations but not everywhere.

In 1979, Carter faced another crisis when the Soviet army invaded Afghanistan, where a faltering Communist government was being challenged by Islamist *jihadis* ("holy warriors") and ethnic warlords. Carter responded with a series of steps: he refused to sign a Strategic Arms Limitation Talks treaty with the Soviets (SALT II), suspended grain shipments to the Soviet Union, began supplying Afghan "freedom fighters" with weapons smuggled through Pakistan, requested large increases in military spending, required all nineteen-year-old men to register for the military draft, and called for an international boycott of the 1980 Olympic Games, which were to be held that summer in Moscow.

The Soviet invasion of Afghanistan also prompted Carter to announce what came to be called the Carter Doctrine, in which he threatened to use military force to prevent any nation from gaining control of the Persian Gulf waterways, through which most of the oil from the Middle East made its way to foreign ports.

CRISIS IN IRAN   Then came the **Iranian hostage crisis**, a series of dramatic events that illustrated the inability of the United States to control world affairs. In January 1979, Islamic revolutionaries had ousted the pro-American government led by the shah of Iran, Mohammad Reza Pahlavi, who owed his rule to a CIA intervention in 1953 that overthrew the elected Iranian government.

The rebel leaders executed hundreds of the shah's former officials. Thousands more Iranians were imprisoned, tortured, or executed for refusing to abide by strict Islamic social codes. The turmoil led to a sharp drop in oil production, driving gasoline prices up worldwide. By the spring of 1979, Americans were again waiting in long lines to pay record prices for limited amounts of gas.

In October, the Carter administration allowed the deposed shah to receive medical treatment for cancer at an American hospital. This "humanitarian" decision enraged Iranian revolutionaries, millions of whom took to the streets to demand that the United States return the shah to Iran. On November 4, 1979, a frenzied mob stormed the U.S. embassy in Tehran and seized sixty-six diplomats and staff, including fifty-two American citizens. Iranian leader Ayatollah Ruhollah Khomeini endorsed the mob action and demanded the return of the hated shah (along with all his wealth) in exchange for the release of the

A king's ransom An Iranian militant holds a group of U.S. embassy staff members hostage in Tehran, Iran, in 1979.

hostages. Nightly television coverage of the taunting Iranian rebels generated among viewers a near obsession with the fate of the hostages.

Angry Americans, including many in Congress, demanded a military response to the kidnappings. Carter, however, believed his options were limited; he wanted to keep the hostages alive. He appealed to the United Nations, but Khomeini scoffed at UN efforts to free the hostages. Carter then froze all Iranian financial assets in America and asked Europe to join the United States in a trade embargo of Iran, including its oil. The trade restrictions were only partially effective because America's allies were not willing to lose access to Iranian oil.

As the crisis continued and gasoline prices rose to record levels, Carter authorized a risky rescue attempt by U.S. commandos on April 24, 1980. (His decision caused his secretary of state, Cyrus Vance, to resign in protest.) The raid had to be cancelled when three of the eight helicopters developed mechanical problems; it ended with eight U.S. deaths when a helicopter collided with a transport plane in the Iranian desert.

For fourteen months, the Iranian hostage crisis paralyzed Carter's ability to lead the nation. For many, the prolonged standoff became a symbol of his failed presidency. "For the first time in its history," *Business Week* magazine's editors observed, "the United States is no longer growing in power and influence among the nations of the world." The crisis finally ended after 444 days, on January 20, 1981, when Carter, just hours before leaving office, released several billion dollars of Iranian assets to ransom the hostages.

THE RISE OF RONALD REAGAN

No sooner had Carter been elected in 1976 than conservative Republicans (the "New Right") began working to ensure that he would not win a second term. Their plans centered on the popularity of tall, square-shouldered, plain-speaking Ronald Reagan, the Hollywood actor, two-term California governor, and prominent political commentator. Reagan was not a deep thinker, but he was a superb reader of the public mood, an outspoken patriot, and a committed champion of conservative principles.

THE ACTOR TURNED PRESIDENT

Born in the town of Tampico, Illinois, in 1911, the son of an often-drunk, Irish Catholic shoe salesman and a devout, Bible-quoting mother who preached a prairie Protestantism centered on individual freedom, Ronald Reagan grew up in a household short of money and frequently on the move. A football scholarship enabled him to attend tiny Eureka College during the Great Depression; he washed dishes in the dining hall to pay for his meals. After graduation, Reagan worked as a radio sportscaster before starting a movie career in Hollywood. He served three years in the army during the Second World War, making training films. At that time, as he recalled, he was a Democrat, "a New Dealer to the core" who voted "blindly" for Franklin D. Roosevelt four times.

After the war, Reagan became president of the acting profession's union, the Screen Actors Guild (SAG), where he honed his negotiating skills and fended off Communist efforts to infiltrate the union. Reagan supported Democrat Harry S. Truman in the 1948 presidential election, but during the fifties he decided that federal taxes were too high. In 1960, he campaigned as a Democrat for Richard Nixon, and two years later he joined the Republican party. Reagan achieved political stardom in 1964 when he delivered a rousing speech on national television on behalf of Barry Goldwater's presidential candidacy. Wealthy admirers convinced him to run for governor of California in 1966, and he won by a landslide.

As the Republican presidential nominee in 1980, Reagan set about drawing a vivid contrast between his optimistic vision of America's future and Jimmy

Carter's bleak outlook. Reagan insisted that there was "nothing wrong with the American people" and that there were "simple answers" to the complex problems facing the country, although they were not *easy* answers. He pledged to slash social-welfare programs, increase military spending to "win" the cold war, dismantle the "bloated" federal bureaucracy, restore states' rights, reduce taxes and government regulation of businesses ("get the government off our backs and release the energies of free enterprise"), and appoint conservative judges to the federal courts. He also promised to affirm old-time religious values by banning abortions and reinstituting prayer in public schools. (He ended up achieving neither.)

Reagan's popularity resulted in part from his skill as a speaker (journalists dubbed him the "Great Communicator") and his steadfast commitment to

Ronald Reagan The "Great Communicator" flashes his charming, trademark smile.

a few basic principles and simple themes. Blessed with a reassuring baritone voice and a wealth of entertaining stories, he charmed audiences while rejecting Carter's assumption that Americans needed "to start getting along with less, to accept a decline in our standard of living." He instead promised boundless economic expansion.

THE RISE OF THE "NEW RIGHT"

By 1980, social developments had made Ronald Reagan's anti-liberal stance a major asset. An increase in the number of senior citizens, a group that tends to be more politically and socially conservative, and the steady migration of people—especially older Americans—to the conservative sunbelt states were shifting the political balance of power. Fully 90 percent of the nation's population growth during the eighties occurred in southern or western sunbelt states, while the Northeast and industrial states of the Midwest—Ohio, Michigan, and Illinois (called the "rust belt")—experienced economic decline and population losses.

A related development was a growing grassroots tax revolt. As consumer prices and home values rose, so did property taxes. In California, Reagan's home state, skyrocketing property taxes threatened to force many working-class people from their homes. This led to efforts to cut back on the size and cost of government to enable reductions in property taxes. In June 1978, tax rebels, with Reagan's support, succeeded in putting an initiative known as Proposition 13 on the state ballot. An overwhelming majority of voters approved the measure, which slashed property taxes by 57 percent and amended the state constitution to make it more difficult to raise taxes. The "Prop 13" tax revolt soon spread across the nation, leading the *New York Times* to call it a "modern Boston Tea Party."

THE RELIGIOUS RIGHT   The California tax revolt fed into a national conservative resurgence led by the "religious Right." Religious conservatives pushing a faith-based political agenda formed the strongest grassroots movement of the late twentieth century. By the eighties, Catholic conservatives and Protestant evangelicals owned television and radio stations, operated their own schools and universities, and organized "mega churches" from which such "televangelists" as the Reverend Jerry Falwell launched a cultural crusade against the "demonic" forces of liberalism at home and communism abroad.

In 1979, Falwell formed a group he called the **Moral Majority** (later renamed the Liberty Alliance) to campaign for the major political and social goals of the religious Right: the economy should operate without "interference" by the government, which should be reduced in size; the Supreme Court decision in *Roe v. Wade* (1973) legalizing abortion should be reversed; Darwinian evolution should be replaced in school textbooks by the biblical story of creation; prayer should return to public schools; women should submit to their husbands; and, communism should be opposed as a form of pagan totalitarianism.

That Ronald Reagan became the hero of the religious Right was a tribute to his political skills, for he rarely attended church and had no strong religious affiliations. President Carter, though famous as a born-again Baptist Sunday School teacher, lost the support of religious conservatives because he was not willing to ban abortions or restore prayers in public schools. His push for state ratification of the equal-rights constitutional amendment (ERA) also cost him the support of anti-feminist conservatives.

ANTI-FEMINIST BACKLASH   By the late seventies, a well-organized and well-financed backlash against the feminist movement reinforced the rise of the "New Right." Activists like Republican Phyllis Schlafly, a conservative

Catholic attorney from Illinois, campaigned successfully to keep the ERA from being ratified by the required thirty-eight states. Schlafly's STOP (Stop Taking Our Privileges) ERA organization warned that the ERA would allow husbands to abandon their wives, force women into military service, and give gay "perverts" the right to marry. She and others stressed that the gender equality promised by the proposed amendment violated biblical teachings about women's "God-given" roles as nurturers and helpmates. By the late seventies, the effort to gain ratification of the ERA had failed, largely because no states in the conservative South and West had ratified it.

Look on the Right side The rise of the religious right saw protests against Supreme Court rulings that reinforced the separation of church and state. Here, in a 1984 rally organized by the Moral Majority, students chant "Kids want to pray!" in support of an amendment to reinstate prayer in public schools. (The effort failed.)

Many of Schlafly's supporters also participated in the growing anti-abortion, or "pro-life," movement. The National Right to Life Committee, supported by the National Conference of Catholic Bishops, denounced abortion as murder, and the emotional intensity of the issue made it a powerful political force. Reagan highlighted his support for traditional "family values," gender roles, and the "rights" of the unborn, which helped persuade many northern Democrats—mostly working-class Catholics—to support him.

FINANCING CONSERVATISM The business community as well had become a source of revitalized conservative activism. In 1972, the leaders of the nation's largest corporations formed the Business Roundtable to promote their interests in Congress. Within a few years, many of them had created political action committees (PACs) to distribute money to pro-business political candidates. Corporate donations also helped fund conservative "think tanks," such as the American Enterprise Institute, the Cato Institute, and the Heritage Foundation. By 1980, the conservative insurgency had become a powerful political force with substantial financial resources, carefully crafted ideas, and grassroots energy.

THE ELECTION OF 1980 Ronald Reagan's supporters during the 1980 campaign loved his simple solutions, upbeat personality, and folksy humor, and they responded passionately to his recurring question: "Are you better off than you were four years ago?" Their answer was a resounding "No!" On Election Day, Reagan swept to a lopsided victory, with 489 electoral votes to 49 for Jimmy Carter, who carried only six states. The popular vote was 44 million (51 percent) for Reagan to Carter's 35 million (41 percent), with 7 percent going to John Anderson, a moderate Republican who ran as an independent. Reagan's resounding victory signaled a major realignment of voters in which many so-called Reagan Democrats—conservative white southern Protestants and blue-collar northern Catholics—crossed over to the Republican party. The Reagan era had begun.

THE REAGAN REVOLUTION

Democrats who dismissed sixty-nine-year-old Ronald Reagan, the oldest man to assume the presidency, as a third-rate actor and mental lightweight underrated his many virtues. Few people in public life had Reagan's stage presence—or confidence. He may have been a mediocre actor, but no one played the part of president better. His remarkable ability to make Americans believe again in the greatness of their country won him two presidential elections, in 1980 and 1984, and ensured the victory of his anointed successor, Vice President George H. W. Bush, in 1988. Just how revolutionary the "Reagan era" was remains a subject of debate, but it cannot be denied that Reagan's actions and beliefs set the tone for the decade's political and economic life.

REAGAN'S FIRST TERM

"Fellow conservatives," President Reagan said in a speech in 1981, "our moment has arrived." He and others were determined to "get America moving again." In his inaugural address, he promised to help Americans "renew our faith and hope" in their nation as a "shining city on a hill" for the rest of the world to emulate.

Reagan helped restore the prestige of the presidency through the force of his personality and the appeal of his ideas and ideals. He succeeded for three main reasons. First, he focused on a few priorities (slowing the rate of inflation, lowering tax rates, reducing the scope of the federal government, increasing military spending, and conducting an anti-Soviet foreign policy), and he pursued those goals with what an aide called a "warmly ruthless" intensity.

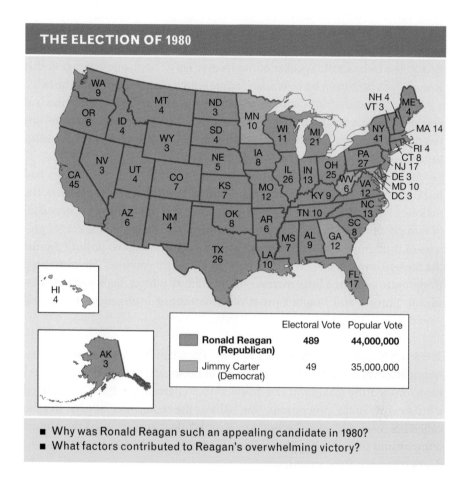

THE ELECTION OF 1980

		Electoral Vote	Popular Vote
	Ronald Reagan (Republican)	489	44,000,000
	Jimmy Carter (Democrat)	49	35,000,000

- Why was Ronald Reagan such an appealing candidate in 1980?
- What factors contributed to Reagan's overwhelming victory?

Second, Reagan, unlike Carter, was skilled at negotiating with congressional leaders and foreign heads of states. He also recognized that politics is a profession built on compromises. Because the Democrats controlled Congress, Reagan was forced to convince the public to pressure their legislators to support his initiatives.

Third, Reagan's infectious optimism gave people a sense of renewed confidence. Voters wanted to believe his insistent claim that America could do no wrong. An uncommon politician, he avoided both the arrogance and self-importance that often accompany the highest office.

Public affection for Reagan spiked just two months into his presidency when an assassination attempt left him with a punctured lung and a bullet lodged near his heart. The witty Reagan told doctors as they prepared for surgery: "Please tell me you're Republicans." His gritty response to his injuries created an outpouring of support that gave added momentum to his presidency. The Democratic Speaker of the House, Tip O'Neill, told colleagues that Reagan "has become a hero. We can't argue with a man as popular as he is."

Reagan inherited an economy in shambles: the annual rate of inflation had reached 13 percent, and unemployment hovered at 7.5 percent. None of this fazed him, however. His philosophy was simple: "Government is not the solution to our problem. Government *is* the problem."

At the same time, the cold war was heating up again. The Soviet Union had just invaded Afghanistan and had placed missiles with nuclear weapons in the nations of central and Eastern Europe under its control, which threatened all of Europe. But Reagan refused to be intimidated. He discarded the earlier policies of containment and détente in favor of a confrontational posture against the Soviet Union which he summarized as "We win, you lose." He convinced Congress to support a huge increase in the military budget, deployed U.S. missiles in Europe, and sought to root out Communist insurgencies in Central America.

REAGANOMICS On August 1, 1981, President Reagan signed the Economic Recovery Tax Act (ERTA), which cut personal income taxes by 25 percent, lowered the maximum rate from 70 to 50 percent for 1982, and offered a broad array of tax concessions. The bill was the centerpiece of what Reagan called his "common sense" economic plan. While theorists called the philosophy behind the plan "supply-side economics," journalists dubbed the president's proposals **Reaganomics**.

Simply put, Reaganomics argued that the stagflation of the seventies had resulted from excessive taxes, which weakened incentives for individuals and businesses to increase productivity, save money, and reinvest in economic expansion. The Reaganomics solution was to slash tax rates, especially on the wealthy, in the belief that they would spend their tax savings on business expansion and consumer goods (the "supply side" of the economy). Such spending, advocates believed, would provide "trickle down" benefits to the masses. By generating economic growth, Reaganomics promised to produce enough new tax revenues from rising corporate profits and personal incomes to pay for the tax cuts. In the short term, however, ERTA did not work as planned. The federal budget deficit grew, and by November 1981, the economy was officially in recession.

MANAGING THE BUDGET To offset the loss of government tax revenues, David Stockman, President Reagan's budget director, proposed sharp

A miss for Reaganomics A throng of more than 5,000 senior citizens staged a demonstration in downtown Detroit against Reagan's decision to make cuts in Social Security and other federal programs supporting the elderly in 1982.

reductions in federal spending, including Social Security and Medicare, the two most expensive—and most popular—federal programs. Liberal Democrats howled at Stockman's proposal, and Reagan responded that he was committed to maintaining the "safety net" of government services for the "truly needy." According to Stockman, Reagan was "too kind, gentle, and sentimental" to make the drastic cuts needed to balance the budget.

The Reagan administration also continued huge federal subsidies to corporations and agribusinesses—what critics called "welfare for the rich." In the end, Reagan never dismantled the major New Deal programs that he had savagely criticized. Conservative political columnist George Will explained Reagan's failure to make substantial cuts in federal spending by noting that "Americans are conservative. What they want to conserve is the New Deal."

Within a year, Stockman realized that the cuts in domestic spending approved by Reagan had fallen far short of what would be needed to balance the budget in four years, as the president had promised. Massive increases in military spending greatly complicated the situation. In essence, Reagan gave the Defense Department a blank check. Over the next five years, the administration would spend some $1.2 *trillion* on military expenses. Something had to give.

In the summer of 1981, Stockman warned that "we're heading for a crash landing on the budget. We're facing potential deficit numbers so big that they could wreck the president's entire economic program." The fast-growing federal deficit, which had helped trigger the worst economic recession since the 1930s, was Reagan's greatest failure, as he himself admitted. During 1982, an estimated 10 million Americans were unable to find jobs. Stockman and other aides finally convinced the president that the government needed "revenue enhancements" (tax increases). With Reagan's support, Congress passed a tax bill in 1982 that would raise almost $100 billion, but the economic slump persisted for a time. In the 1982 congressional midterm elections, Democrats picked up twenty-six seats in the House of Representatives.

But Reagan's determination to "stay the course" with his economic program began to pay off. By the summer of 1983, a major economic recovery was under way, in part because of increased government spending and lower interest rates and in part because of lower tax rates. Inflation subsided, as did unemployment. Reaganomics was not helping to balance the budget, however. In fact, the federal deficits had grown larger—so much so that the president had in fact run up an accumulated debt larger than that of all his predecessors combined. Reagan was willing to tolerate the deficits in part because he believed that they would force more responsible spending behavior in Congress, and in part because he was so committed to increased military spending as a way to intimidate the Soviets.

REAGAN'S ANTI-LIBERALISM   During Reagan's presidency, organized labor suffered severe setbacks, even though Reagan himself had been a union leader. In 1981, he fired members of the Professional Air Traffic Controllers Organization who had participated in an illegal strike intended to shut down air travel (air traffic controllers were deemed essential to public safety and therefore were prohibited from striking). Reagan's actions broke the political power of the American Federation of Labor–Congress of Industrial Organizations (AFL-CIO), the national confederation of labor unions that traditionally supported Democratic candidates. His criticism of unions reflected a general trend in public opinion. Although record numbers of jobs were created during the eighties, union membership steadily dropped. By 1987, unions represented only 17 percent of the nation's full-time workers, down from 24 percent in 1979.

Reagan also went on the offensive against feminism. He opposed the Equal Rights Amendment, legal abortion, and proposals to require equal pay for jobs of comparable worth. He did name Sandra Day O'Connor as the first woman Supreme Court justice, but critics labeled it a token gesture. In addition, he cut funds for civil rights enforcement and the Equal Employment Opportunity Commission, and he opposed renewal of the Voting Rights Act of 1965 before being overruled by Congress.

Sandra Day O'Connor Her Supreme Court confirmation hearing in September 1981 was picketed by conservatives who decried her pro-abortion stance.

THE ELECTION OF 1984 By 1983, prosperity had returned, the stock market was soaring, and President Reagan's "supply-side" economic program was at last working as advertised—except for the growing budget deficit. Like the liberal presidents he often criticized, Reagan was a big spender, especially when it came to military growth. At the same time, his decision to remove price controls on oil and natural gas and his efforts to pressure Saudi Arabia to increase oil production produced a decline in energy prices that helped to stimulate economic growth.

By 1984, reporters had begun to speak of the "Reagan Revolution." The slogan at the Republican National Convention was "America is back and standing tall." The Democrats' presidential nominee, Walter Mondale (Jimmy Carter's vice president), struggled to present a competing vision. Endorsed by the AFL-CIO, the National Organization for Women (NOW), and many prominent African Americans, Mondale was viewed as the candidate of liberal special-interest groups. He set a precedent by choosing as his running mate Geraldine Ferraro, a New York congresswoman, who was quickly placed on the defensive by the need to explain her husband's complicated business dealings.

A bit of frankness in Mondale's acceptance speech ended up hurting his campaign. "Mr. Reagan will raise taxes, and so will I," he told the convention. "He won't tell you. I just did." Reagan responded by vowing never to approve a tax increase (a promise he could not keep) and by chiding Mondale for his stance. Reagan also repeated a theme he had used against Carter: the future, according to Mondale and the Democrats, was "dark and getting darker."

Reagan's vision of America's future, however, was bright. As his campaign ads claimed, "It's morning again in America," and record numbers of Americans were headed to work. In the end, Reagan took 59 percent of the popular vote and lost only Minnesota (Mondale's home state) and the District of Columbia.

REAGAN'S SECOND TERM

Spurred by his overwhelming victory, Ronald Reagan called for "a Second American Revolution of hope and opportunity." He dared Democrats to raise taxes; his veto pen was ready. "Go ahead and make my day," he said, echoing a popular line from a Clint Eastwood movie. Through much of 1985, the president drummed up support for a tax-simplification plan. After vigorous debate, Congress passed a comprehensive Tax Reform Act in 1986. The measure cut the number of federal tax brackets from fourteen to two and reduced rates from the maximum of 50 percent to 15 and 28 percent—the lowest since Calvin Coolidge was president in the twenties.

REAGAN'S HALF-HEARTED REVOLUTION Although Ronald Reagan had promised to "curb the size and influence of the federal establishment," the number of federal employees actually *grew* during his two terms as president. Neither the Social Security system nor Medicare, the two largest federal social programs, were overhauled, and the federal agencies that Reagan had threatened to abolish, such as the Department of Education, not only survived but saw their budgets grow.

The federal deficit almost tripled during Reagan's two terms. He blamed Congress for the problem, "since only Congress can spend money," but in fact the legislators essentially approved the budgets that Reagan submitted to them (and he never submitted a balanced budget). As Dick Cheney, a future Republican vice president, quipped, "Reagan showed that deficits don't matter."

The cost of Social Security, the most expensive "entitlement" program, grew by 27 percent under Reagan, as some 6,000 Americans each day turned 65. Moreover, Reagan failed to fulfill his campaign promises to the religious Right, such as reinstituting daily prayer in public schools and a ban on abortions. But he did follow through on his pledge to reshape the federal court system. He appointed 368 mostly conservative judges, three of them to the U.S. Supreme Court: Sandra Day O'Connor, Antonin Scalia, and Anthony Kennedy.

Martin Anderson, Reagan's domestic policy adviser, stressed that it was "a mistake to think that there ever was a Reagan Revolution, or that Reagan gave it life." It was the grassroots conservative revolution that "caused Reagan—and the same forces will continue to the end of the century." What Reagan did accomplish was to end the prolonged period of "stagflation" and set in motion what economists called "The Great Expansion," an unprecedented, twenty-year burst of productivity and prosperity. True, Reagan's presidency left the nation with a massive debt burden that would eventually cause major problems, but the "Great Communicator" also renewed the nation's strength, self-confidence, and soaring sense of possibilities.

Ronald Reagan was a transformational president. While restoring the stature of the presidency and reviving the economy, he transformed political life by accelerating the nation's shift toward conservatism and by revitalizing the Republican party. He put the Democrats on the defensive and forced conventional New Deal "liberalism" into a panicked retreat. For the next twenty years or so, Reagan's anti-government, anti-tax conservative agenda would dominate the national political landscape.

AN ANTI-SOVIET FOREIGN POLICY

On a flight to Detroit, Michigan, to accept the Republican party's presidential nomination in the summer of 1980, Ronald Reagan was asked why he wanted to be president. He answered: "To end the cold war." As president, Reagan systematically promoted what he called his "peace through strength" strategy. Through a series of bold steps, he would build up U.S. military strength to the point it would overwhelm the Soviet Union, both financially and militarily.

Reagan also launched a "war of ideas" by charging that the Soviet Union was "the focus of evil in the modern world." What came to be called the Reagan Doctrine pledged to combat Soviet adventurism throughout the world, even if it meant partnering with brutal dictatorships. Reagan believed that aggressive CIA-led efforts to stymie Soviet expansionism would eventually cause the unstable Soviet system to implode "on the ash heap of history."

A MASSIVE DEFENSE BUILDUP   Reagan's conduct of foreign policy reflected his belief that trouble in the world stemmed mainly from Moscow, the capital of what he called the "evil empire." Reagan had long believed that Nixon and Ford—following the advice of Henry Kissinger—had been too soft on the Soviets. Kissinger's emphasis on détente, he said, had been a "one-way street" favoring the Soviets. Reagan first wanted to reduce the risk of nuclear war by convincing the Soviets that they could not win such a conflict.

To do so, he and Secretary of Defense Caspar Weinberger embarked upon a major buildup of nuclear and conventional weapons. Under Reagan, defense spending came to represent a fourth of all federal government expenditures. Reagan claimed that the defense allocations had another purpose: to bankrupt the Soviets by forcing them to spend much more on their own military budgets. To critics who complained about the defense spending, Reagan replied, "It will break the Soviets first." It did.

"STAR WARS" In 1983, Reagan escalated the nuclear arms race by authorizing the Defense Department to develop the controversial **Strategic Defense Initiative (SDI)**, featuring a complex anti-missile defense system that would position satellites with laser weapons in outer space to "intercept and destroy" Soviet missiles in flight. Despite skepticism among the media, scientists, and even government officials that such a defense system (dubbed "Star Wars" by the media) could be built, Congress approved the first stage of funding, which forced the Soviets to launch an expensive research and development effort of their own.

Reagan also borrowed the rhetoric of Harry S. Truman, John Foster Dulles, and John F. Kennedy to express resolve in the face of "Communist aggression anywhere in the world." When the Polish government imposed martial law during the winter of 1981, Reagan forcefully protested and imposed economic sanctions against Poland's Communist government. He also worked behind the scenes to support the Polish protest movement, Solidarity, which sought independence from Soviet control.

THE AMERICAS President Reagan's foremost international concern, however, was Central America, where he detected the most serious Communist threat. The tiny nation of El Salvador, caught up since 1980 in a brutal struggle between Communist-supported revolutionaries and right-wing militants, received U.S. economic and military assistance. Critics argued that U.S. involvement ensured that the revolutionary forces would gain favor by capitalizing on "anti-Yankee" sentiment. Reagan's supporters countered that a victory by the revolutionaries would lead all of Central America into the Communist camp (a new "domino" theory). By 1984, the U.S.-backed government of President José Napoleón Duarte had brought some stability to El Salvador.

More troubling to Reagan was the situation in Nicaragua. The State Department claimed that the Cuban-sponsored Sandinista socialist government, which had seized power in 1979, was sending arms to leftist Salvadoran rebels. In response, the Reagan administration ordered the CIA to train anti-

Communist Nicaraguans, or Contras (short for *contrarevolucionarios*, or counterrevolutionaries), who staged attacks on Sandinista bases from sanctuaries in Honduras. In supporting these "freedom fighters," Reagan sought not only to impede the traffic in arms to Salvadoran rebels but also to replace the Sandinistas with a democratic government. Critics accused the Contras of being mostly right-wing fanatics who killed indiscriminately. They also feared that the United States might eventually commit its own combat forces, leading to a Vietnam-like intervention. Reagan warned that if the Communists prevailed in Central America, "our credibility would collapse, our alliances would crumble, and the safety of our homeland would be jeopardized."

THE IRAN-CONTRA AFFAIR Reports surfaced in late 1986 that the United States had been secretly selling arms to U.S.-hating Iran (which Reagan had called an "outlaw state") in the hope of securing the release of American hostages held in Lebanon by extremist groups sympathetic to Iran. Such action contradicted Reagan's insistence that his administration would never negotiate with terrorists. The disclosures angered America's allies as well as many Americans who vividly remembered the 1979 Iranian takeover of the embassy in Tehran. Over the next several months, revelations emerged of a complicated series of covert activities carried out by administration officials.

At the center of what came to be called the **Iran-Contra affair** was marine lieutenant colonel Oliver North, a National Security Council aide who specialized in counterterrorism. Working from the basement of the White House, North had been secretly selling military supplies to Iran and using the proceeds to support the Contra rebels in Nicaragua at a time when Congress had voted to ban such aid.

North's illegal activities, it turned out, had been approved by national security adviser Robert McFarlane; McFarlane's successor, Admiral John Poindexter; and CIA director William Casey. Both Secretary of State George Shultz and Secretary of Defense Caspar Weinberger criticized the arms sales to Iran, but their objections were ignored, and they were thereafter kept in the dark about what was going on—as was Reagan. After information about the secret dealings surfaced, North and

Iran-Contra hearings Admiral John Poindexter listens warily to a question from the Congressional investigation committee on July 21, 1987.

others erased incriminating computer files and destroyed documents. McFarlane attempted suicide before being convicted of withholding information from Congress; Poindexter resigned; and North was fired. Casey, who denied any connection to the clumsy operation, left the CIA and died shortly thereafter from a brain tumor.

Facing a barrage of criticism, Reagan appointed a three-member commission, led by former Republican senator John Tower, to investigate the scandal. The Tower Commission issued a devastating report early in 1987 that placed much of the responsibility for the Iran-Contra affair on Reagan's loose management style. When asked if he had known of Colonel North's illegal actions, the president simply replied: "I don't remember." He was stunned that "for the first time in my life, people didn't believe me." During the spring and summer of 1987, a joint House-Senate committee began holding hearings into the Iran-Contra affair.

The investigations led to six indictments in 1988. North was found guilty of three relatively minor charges but innocent of nine more serious counts, apparently reflecting the jury's reasoning that he acted as an agent of higher-ups. His conviction was later overturned on appeal. Of those involved, only John Poindexter received a jail sentence—six months for obstructing justice and lying to Congress.

A HISTORIC TREATY The most positive achievement at the end of Reagan's second term was a surprising arms-reduction agreement with the Soviet government. Under Mikhail Gorbachev, who came to power in 1985, the Soviets pursued renewed détente so that they could reduce military spending and focus on more pressing problems, especially a notoriously inefficient economy and a losing war in Afghanistan. Gorbachev also instituted what he called *perestroika* (restructuring), an ambitious effort to streamline the clunky Soviet government bureaucracy and make it more efficient. And, third, Gorbachev encouraged *glasnost* (openness), a radical reappraisal of the Soviet system that allowed for open debate and shared information.

In October 1986, Reagan and Gorbachev met in Reykjavik, Iceland, to discuss ways to reduce the threat of nuclear war. At one point, Reagan shocked the Soviets by saying, "It would be fine with me if we eliminated all nuclear weapons." Equally shocking was Gorbachev's reply: "We can do that."

By the end of the meeting, however, the two sides were still far apart, and Gorbachev privately called Reagan a "feebleminded cave man." The main sticking point was Reagan's insistence that the United States would continue to develop its Strategic Defense Initiative (SDI, or "Star Wars"). Reagan's arms control director, Kenneth Adelman, privately admitted that SDI was unworkable, "little more than pie in the colorful sky of Ronald Reagan's imagination."

But it became a dazzling bluff in the standoff with the Soviet Union.

The logjam in the disarmament negotiations suddenly broke in 1987, when Gorbachev announced that he was willing to consider mutual reductions in nuclear weaponry. A member of the Soviet negotiating team acknowledged Reagan's role in the breakthrough. The U.S. president, he explained, "takes you by the arm, walks you to the cliff's edge, and invites you to step forward for the good of humanity."

After nine months of strenuous negotiations, Reagan and Gorbachev met amid much fanfare in Washington, D.C., on December 9, 1987, and signed the **Intermediate-Range Nuclear Forces (INF) Treaty**, an agreement to eliminate intermediate-range (300- to 3,000-mile) missiles. The treaty marked the first time that the two nations had agreed to destroy a whole class of weapons systems and produced the most sweeping cuts in nuclear weaponry in history.

Mikhail Gorbachev Deputy chairman, and later president, of the Soviet Union in 1988.

Gorbachev's successful efforts to liberalize Soviet domestic life and improve East–West relations cheered Americans. In the Middle East, the Soviets urged the Palestine Liberation Organization, founded in 1964 to represent the Palestinian people, to recognize Israel's right to exist and advocated a greater role for the United Nations in the volatile Persian Gulf. Perhaps the most dramatic symbol of the thawing cold war was the phased withdrawal of 115,000 Soviet troops from Afghanistan, which began in 1988.

REAGAN'S GLOBAL LEGACY Ronald Reagan achieved the unthinkable by helping to end the cold war. Although his massive defense buildup almost bankrupted the United States, it forced the Soviet Union to the bargaining table. By negotiating the nuclear disarmament treaty and lighting the fuse of democratic freedom in Soviet-controlled East Germany, Hungary, Poland, and Czechoslovakia, Reagan set in motion events that would cause the collapse of the Soviet Union.

In June 1987, Reagan visited the Berlin Wall in East Germany and, in a dramatic speech, called upon the Soviet Union to allow greater freedom within the countries under its control. "General Secretary Gorbachev, if you seek peace, if you seek prosperity for the Soviet Union and Eastern Europe, if you seek liberalization: Come here to this gate! Mr. Gorbachev, open this gate! Mr. Gorbachev, tear down this wall!" It was great theater and good politics.

THE CHANGING ECONOMIC AND SOCIAL LANDSCAPE

During the eighties, the U.S. economy went through a wrenching transformation in adapting to an increasingly interconnected global marketplace. The nations that had been devastated by the Second World War—France, Germany, the Soviet Union, Japan, and China—had now developed formidable economies with higher levels of productivity than the United States. More and more American companies shifted their production overseas, accelerating the transition of the economy from its once-dominant industrial base to a more services-oriented approach. Driving all of these changes were the impact of the computer revolution and the development of the Internet.

THE COMPUTER REVOLUTION The idea of a programmable machine that would rapidly perform mental tasks had been around since the eighteenth century, but it took the Second World War to marshal the intellectual and financial resources needed to create such a "computer." In 1946, a team of engineers at the University of Pennsylvania developed ENIAC (electronic numerical integrator and computer), the first all-purpose, all-electronic digital computer.

The next major breakthrough was the invention in 1971 of the **microprocessor**—virtually a tiny computer on a silicon chip. Functions once performed by huge computers that filled entire rooms could now be performed by a microchip the size of a postage stamp. The microchip made possible the personal computer. In 1975, an engineer named Ed Roberts developed the Altair 8800, the prototype of the personal computer. Its potential excited a Harvard University sophomore named Bill Gates, who improved the software of the Altair 8800, dropped out of college, and formed a company called Microsoft.

By 1977, Gates and others had helped transform the personal computer into a mass consumer product. The development of the Internet, electronic mail (e-mail), and cell-phone technology during the eighties and nineties allowed for instantaneous communication, thereby accelerating the globalization of the economy and dramatically increasing productivity in the workplace.

DEBT AND THE STOCK MARKET PLUNGE   In the late seventies, Jimmy Carter had urged Americans to lead simpler lives, cut back on conspicuous consumption, reduce energy use, and invest more time in faith and family. During the eighties, Ronald Reagan promoted very different behavior: he reduced tax rates so people would have more money to spend. Americans preferred Reagan's emphasis on prosperity rather than Carter's focus on propriety, for it endorsed entrepreneurship as well as an increasingly consumption-oriented and hedonistic leisure culture.

But Reagan succeeded too well in shifting the public mood back to the "more is more," "bigger is better" tradition of heedless consumerism. During the "age of Reagan," marketers and advertisers celebrated instant gratification at the expense of the future. Michelob beer commercials began assuring Americans that "you can have it all," and many consumers went on a self-indulgent spending spree. The more they bought the more they wanted. In 1984, Hollywood producers launched a new TV show called *Lifestyles of the Rich and Famous* that exemplified the decade's runaway materialism. As the stock market soared, the number of multi-millionaires working on Wall Street and in the financial industry nationwide mushroomed. The money fever was contagious. Compulsive shoppers donned T-shirts proclaiming: "Born to Shop." By 1988, 110 million Americans had an average of seven credit cards each.

Money—lots of it—came to define the American Dream. In the hit movie *Wall Street* (1987), the high-flying land developer and corporate raider Gordon Gekko, played by actor Michael Douglas, announced that "greed . . . is good. Greed is right." During the eighties, many Americans caught up in the materialism of the times began spending more money than they earned. All kinds of debt—personal, corporate, and government—increased dramatically. Americans in the sixties had saved on average 10 percent of their income; in 1987 the figure was less than 4 percent. The federal debt more than tripled, from $908 billion in 1980 to $2.9 trillion at the end of the 1989 fiscal year.

Then, on October 19, 1987, the bill collector suddenly arrived at the nation's doorstep. On that "Black Monday," the stock market experienced a tidal wave of selling reminiscent of the 1929 crash. The Dow Jones industrial average plummeted an astounding 22.6 percent. The market plunge nearly doubled the record 12.8 percent fall on October 28, 1929. Wall Street's selling frenzy reverberated throughout the capitalist world, sending stock prices plummeting in Tokyo, London, Paris, and Toronto.

In the aftermath of the calamitous selling spree on Black Monday, fears of an impending recession led business leaders and economists to attack President Reagan for allowing such huge budget deficits. Within a few weeks, Reagan had agreed to work with Congress to develop a deficit-reduction package and for the first time indicated a willingness to include increased taxes in such a package. But the eventual compromise plan was so modest that it did little to restore investor confidence. As one Republican senator lamented, "There is a total lack of courage among those of us in the Congress to do what we all know has to be done."

THE POOR The eighties were years of vivid contrast. Despite unprecedented prosperity, homelessness became the most acute social issue. A variety of causes had led to a shortage of low-cost housing. The government had given up on building public housing, urban-renewal programs had demolished blighted areas but provided no housing for those who were displaced, and owners had abandoned unprofitable buildings in poor neighborhoods or converted them into expensive condominiums, a process called gentrification. In addition, after new medications allowed for the release of some mentally ill patients from institutions, many of them ended up on the streets because the promised mental-health services failed to materialize. Drug and alcohol abuse were rampant among the homeless, mostly unemployed single adults. A quarter of them had spent time in mental institutions; some 40 percent had spent time in jail; a third were delusional.

Act Up! Members of the influential AIDS activist group Act Up! protest a New Orleans convention center where President Reagan was scheduled to speak in 1988. The protester in the front holds a sign which reads "He Kills Me."

THE AIDS EPIDEMIC Still another group of outcasts included those suffering from a newly identified disease called AIDS (acquired immunodeficiency syndrome). At the beginning of the eighties, public health officials had reported that gay men and intravenous drug users were especially at risk for developing AIDS. People contracted the human immunodeficiency virus (HIV), which causes AIDS, by coming into contact with the blood or body fluids of an infected person. Those infected with the virus showed signs of extreme fatigue, developed a strange combination of infections, and soon died.

The Reagan administration showed little interest in AIDS in part because it was initially viewed as a "gay" disease. Patrick Buchanan, who served as Reagan's director of communications, said that homosexuals had "declared war on nature, and now nature is extracting an awful retribution." Buchanan and others convinced Reagan not to engage the **HIV/AIDS** issue. By 2000, AIDS had claimed almost 300,000 American lives. Nearly 1 million Americans were carrying the deadly virus, and it had become the leading cause of death among men ages twenty-five to forty-four.

THE PRESIDENCY OF GEORGE H. W. BUSH

During 1988, Ronald Reagan's final year in office, his influence waned. His claim that "government is the problem, not the solution" was losing its appeal, and people were ready for a new approach to governing. Kevin Phillips, a Republican strategist, explained that during the 1986 congressional elections, voters chose candidates who promised to "make the government work" for the public good. Even conservatives had come to realize that "Hey, we need something from government after all."

Reagan's two-term vice president, George H. W. Bush, won the Republican presidential nomination in 1988 because he pledged to insist on ethical government, be a more "hands on" president than Reagan, and promote "a more compassionate conservatism."

Born into a prominent New England family, the son of a U.S. senator, George H. W. Bush had, at the age of eighteen, enlisted in the U.S. Navy at the start of the Second World War, becoming America's youngest combat pilot. After his distinguished military service, Bush graduated from Yale University and became a wealthy oil executive in Texas before entering government service. He served first as a member of the U.S. House of Representatives, then as U.S. ambassador to the United Nations, chair of the Republican National Committee, a diplomat in China, and director of the CIA before becoming Reagan's loyal vice president, patiently waiting his turn.

In all of those roles, Bush had displayed intelligence, integrity, and courage. But he lacked Reagan's charm and eloquence. One Democrat described

Bush as a man born "with a silver foot in his mouth." A centrist Republican who had never embraced right-wing conservatism, Bush promised to use the White House to fight bigotry, illiteracy, and homelessness. "I want a kinder, gentler nation," Bush said in accepting the Republican nomination. But his most memorable line in his acceptance speech was a defiant statement ruling out any tax increases: "The Congress will push me to raise taxes, and I'll say no, and they'll push, and I'll say no, and they'll push again. And I'll say to them: Read my lips. No new taxes."

In the end, Bush won a decisive victory over the Democratic nominee, Massachusetts governor Michael Dukakis. Dukakis carried only ten states plus the District of Columbia. Bush won with a margin of about 54 percent to 46 percent in the popular vote and 426 to 111 in the electoral college, but the Democrats retained control of the House and Senate.

THE ELECTION OF 1988

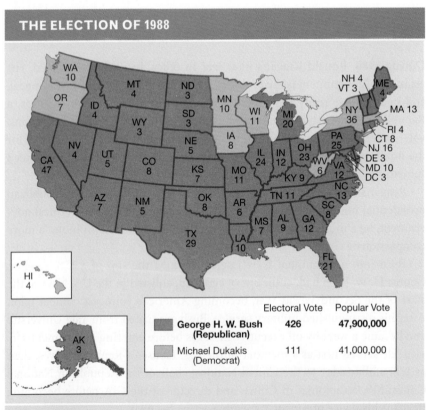

	Electoral Vote	Popular Vote
George H. W. Bush (Republican)	**426**	**47,900,000**
Michael Dukakis (Democrat)	111	41,000,000

- How did George H. W. Bush overtake Michael Dukakis in the campaign?
- What were the differences between the goals of Bush and Reagan?

Bush sought to consolidate the initiatives that Reagan had put in place rather than launch his own array of programs and policies. "We don't need to remake society," he announced. As an example of his compassionate conservatism, Bush supported the Democratic-proposed Americans with Disabilities Act (1990), which strengthened the civil rights of the physically or mentally disabled in areas such as employment, public transportation, and housing. The act also required organizations (for-profit, non-profit, and governmental) to ensure that people with disabilities could access facilities by providing amenities such as mechanized doors, wheelchair ramps, and elevators.

THE FEDERAL DEBT AND RECESSION The biggest problem facing the Bush administration was the huge national debt, which stood at $2.6 trillion in 1989, nearly three times its 1980 level. Bush's pledge not to increase taxes (mainly meaning income taxes) made it more difficult to reduce the deficit or trim the debt. Likewise, Bush was not willing to make substantial cutbacks in spending on defense or social-welfare programs like Social Security, Medicare, and food stamps. As a result, by 1990 the country faced "a fiscal mess."

During the summer of 1990, Bush agreed with congressional Democrats that the size of the deficit required "tax revenue increases," which he had sworn to avoid. His decision set off a revolt among conservative Republicans from which he never recovered. Increasing the top tax rate from 28 to 31 percent raised federal revenue but eroded Bush's political support, in part because the tax increases coincided with a prolonged economic recession. The economy barely grew at all during the first three years of the Bush administration—the worst record since the end of the Second World War.

THE DEMOCRACY MOVEMENT ABROAD In the Soviet Union, amazing changes were under way. With his nation's economy failing, Mikhail Gorbachev accelerated the implementation of his policies designed to democratize Soviet life. And his foreign policy sought harmony and trade with the West, staking the Soviet Union's future on cooperation and trade with its cold war enemies.

Early in 1989, Soviet troops left Afghanistan after nine years. Gorbachev then renounced the right of the Soviet Union to intervene in the internal affairs of other Communist countries. Soon thereafter, the Communist regimes in Eastern Europe fell with surprisingly little bloodshed, first in Poland and Hungary, then in Czechoslovakia and Bulgaria. In Romania, the year of peaceful revolution ended when the people joined the army in a bloody uprising against Nicolae Ceaușescu, the country's brutal dictator. He and his wife were captured and tried, then executed on Christmas Day.

A hammer to the Soviet Empire

A West German demonstrator pounds away at the Berlin Wall on November 11, 1989, while East German border guards look on. Two days later, all the crossings between East and West Germany were opened.

THE DESTRUCTION OF THE BERLIN WALL The most spectacular event in the collapse of the Soviet Empire came on November 9, 1989, when Germans tore down the Berlin Wall, the chief symbol of the cold war. With the borders to West Germany now fully open, the Communist government of East Germany collapsed. On October 3, 1990, the five states of East Germany were united with West Germany.

The reform impulse that Gorbachev helped unleash in the Eastern-bloc countries sped out of control within the Soviet Union itself, however. Gorbachev had proven unusually adept at political restructuring and building a new presidential system that gave him, if anything, increased powers. His skills, however, could not salvage an antiquated economy that resisted change.

COMMUNIST COUP FAILS Gorbachev's popularity shrank in the Soviet Union as it grew abroad. Communist hard-liners saw in his reforms the unraveling of their bureaucratic and political empire. On August 18, 1991, a group of political and military leaders accosted Gorbachev at his vacation retreat in Crimea and demanded that he proclaim a state of emergency and transfer his powers to them. He replied, "Go to hell," whereupon he was placed under house arrest.

The coup, however, was poorly planned and clumsily implemented. The plotters failed to arrest popular leaders such as Boris Yeltsin, the president of the Russian Republic. They also neglected to close the airports or cut off telephone and television communications, and they were opposed by key elements of the military and KGB (the Soviet secret police).

On August 20, President Bush responded favorably to Yeltsin's request for support and persuaded other leaders to join him in refusing to recognize the new Soviet government. The next day, word began to seep out that the plotters had given up and were fleeing. Several committed suicide, and a newly released Gorbachev ordered the others arrested. Although Gorbachev reclaimed the title of president, he was forced to resign as head of the Communist party and admit that he had made a grave mistake in appointing the men who had turned against him. Yeltsin emerged as the most popular political figure in the country.

What had begun as a reactionary coup turned into a powerful accelerant for astonishing changes in the Soviet Union, or the "Soviet Disunion," as one journalist termed it. Most of the fifteen republics proclaimed their independence from Russia, with the Baltic states of Latvia, Lithuania, and Estonia regaining the status of independent nations. The Communist party was dismantled, prompting celebrating crowds to topple statues of Lenin and other Communist heroes.

PANAMA The end of the cold war did not spell the end of international tensions, however. Since the collapse of the Soviet Union, the world has experienced numerous wars, violent turbulence, and fractious fundamentalisms of all sorts—religious, ethnic, and imperial. Before the close of 1989, U.S. troops were engaged in battle in Panama, where a petty tyrant provoked the first of America's military engagements under President Bush. In 1983, General Manuel Noriega had become leader of the Panamanian Defense Forces, which made him head of the government in fact if not in title.

In 1988, federal grand juries in Florida indicted Noriega and fifteen others on charges of drug trafficking. The next year, the Panamanian president tried to fire Noriega, but the National Assembly ousted the president instead and named Noriega "maximum leader." The legislators then declared Panama "in a state of war" with the United States. On December 16, 1989, a U.S. marine in Panama was killed. Bush thereupon ordered an invasion to capture Noriega and install a government to be headed by Guillermo Endara, who had won the presidency in an election that was nullified by Noriega.

In the early morning of December 20, U.S. troops struck at strategic targets. Noriega surrendered within hours. Twenty-three U.S. servicemen were killed; estimates of Panamanian casualties were as high as 4,000, including civilians. In April 1992, Noriega was convicted in the United States on eight counts of racketeering and drug distribution.

THE GULF WAR Months later, Saddam Hussein, dictator of Iraq, focused U.S. attention back upon the Middle East when his army suddenly invaded its tiny neighbor, Kuwait, on August 2, 1990. Kuwait had increased its production of oil, contrary to agreements with the Organization of the

Petroleum Exporting Countries (OPEC). The resulting drop in global oil prices offended the Iraqi regime, which was deeply in debt and heavily dependent upon oil revenues.

President Bush condemned Iraq's "naked aggression" and dispatched warplanes and troops to Saudi Arabia on a "wholly defensive" mission: to protect Saudi Arabia. British forces soon joined in, as did Arab units from Egypt, Morocco, Syria, Oman, the United Arab Emirates, and Qatar. Iraq refused to yield, and on January 12, 1991, Congress authorized the use of U.S. armed forces. Four days later, more than thirty nations, including ten Islamic countries, launched **Operation Desert Storm**. During the next six weeks, Iraqi soldiers surrendered by the thousands, and on February 28, Bush called for a cease-fire. The Iraqis accepted. There were 137 American fatalities. The lowest estimate of Iraqi deaths, civilian and military, was 100,000. But although coalition forces occupied about a fifth of Iraq, Hussein's tyrannical regime remained intact.

What came to be called the First Gulf War was thus a triumph without victory. Hussein had been defeated, but he was allowed to escape to foster greater mischief. The consequences of the brief but intense war would be played out

Operation Desert Storm Allied soldiers patrol the southern Iraqi town of Salman on February 27, 1991. On the side of a building is a propaganda mural of dictator Saddam Hussein in military uniform.

in the future, as Arabs humiliated by the American triumph began plotting revenge that would spiral into a new war of terrorism.

BUSH'S "NEW WORLD ORDER" For months after the First Gulf War, George Bush seemed unbeatable; his public approval rating soared to 91 percent. But the aftermath of Desert Storm was mixed, with Saddam Hussein's iron grip on Iraq still intact. The Soviet Union, meanwhile, stumbled to its surprising end. On December 25, 1991, the Soviet flag over the Kremlin was replaced by the flag of the Russian Federation. The cold war had ended with the dismemberment of the Soviet Union and its fifteen republics.

"Containment" of the Soviet Union, the bedrock of U.S. foreign policy for more than four decades, had suddenly become irrelevant. For all of its potential horrors, the cold war had brought stability; the two superpowers, the United States and the Soviet Union, had restrained themselves from an all-out war using nuclear weapons. Now the world would witness a growing number of unresolved crises and unstable regimes, some of which had access to weapons of mass destruction—nuclear as well as chemical and biological weapons.

Bush struggled to understand the fluid new international scene. He spoke of a "new world order" but never defined it, admitting he had trouble with "the vision thing." He faced a challenge in the Republican primary from Patrick Buchanan, the conservative commentator and former White House aide, who adopted the slogan "America First" and called on Bush to "bring home the boys."

The excitement over the victory in the Gulf War also gave way to anxiety over the depressed economy. In addressing the recession, Bush tried a clumsy balancing act, on the one hand acknowledging that "people are hurting" while on the other telling Americans that "this is a good time to buy a car." By 1991, the public approval rating of his economic policy had plummeted to 18 percent.

THE ELECTION OF 1992 At the 1992 Republican National Convention, Patrick Buchanan, who had won about a third of the votes in the party's primaries, blasted Bush for breaking his pledge not to raise taxes and for becoming the "biggest spender in American history." As the 1992 election unfolded, however, Bush's real problem proved to be his failed effort to improve the economy. A popular bumper sticker reflected the growing public frustration: "Saddam Hussein still has his job. What about you?"

In contrast, the Democrats at their convention presented an image of moderate forces in control. For several years, the Democratic Leadership Council, led by Arkansas governor William Jefferson Clinton, had been pushing the party from the liberal left to the center. The 1992 campaign also featured a third-party candidate, Texan H. Ross Perot, a puckish billionaire who found a large audience for his criticism of Reaganomics as "voodoo economics" (a phrase originally used by Bush in the 1980 Republican primary before he was named the vice-presidential candidate).

Born in 1946 in Hope, Arkansas, Bill Clinton never knew his biological father, a traveling salesman who died before his son was born. As a teen, Clinton yearned to be a political leader on a national scale. He attended Georgetown University in Washington, D.C., won a Rhodes Scholarship to Oxford University, and earned a law degree from Yale University, where he met his future wife, Hillary Rodham. Clinton returned to Arkansas and won election as the state's attorney general. By 1979, at age thirty-two, he was the youngest governor in the country. He served three more terms as Arkansas governor and emerged as a dynamic national leader of the **"New Democrats"** committed to winning back the middle-class whites ("Reagan Democrats") who had voted Republican during the 1980s.

In seeking the Democratic nomination, Clinton promised to cut the defense budget, provide tax relief for the middle class, and create a massive economic aid package to help the former republics of the Soviet Union forge democratic societies. Witty, intelligent, and charismatic, with an in-depth knowledge of public policy, Clinton projected energy, youth, and optimism, reminding many of John F. Kennedy, his boyhood hero.

But beneath Clinton's charisma and expertise were several flaws. The *New York Times* explained that Clinton was "emotionally needy, indecisive, and undisciplined." He had also earned a well-deserved reputation for half-truths, exaggerations, and talking out of both sides of his mouth. Clinton used opinion polls to shape his stances on issues, pandered to special-interest groups, and flip-flopped on controversial subjects, leading critics to label him "Slick Willie." Even more enticing to the media were charges that Clinton was a chronic adulterer and that he had manipulated the Reserve Officers' Training Corps (ROTC) program during the Vietnam War to avoid military service. Clinton's evasive denials could not dispel a lingering mistrust of his character.

After a series of bruising primaries, Clinton won the Democratic presidential nomination and promised to restore the "hopes of the forgotten middle class." He chose Senator Albert "Al" Gore Jr. of Tennessee as his running mate. Gore described himself as a "raging moderate." Flushed with their convention victory and sporting a ten-point lead over Bush in the polls, the Clinton-Gore team hammered the president on economic issues. Clinton pledged that, if elected, he would cut the federal budget deficit in half in four years while reducing taxes on middle-class Americans.

Such promises helped Clinton win with 370 electoral votes and about 43 percent of the vote. Bush received 168 electoral votes and 39 percent of the vote. Perot garnered 19 percent of the popular vote, more than any third-party candidate since Theodore Roosevelt in 1912. As 1992 came to an end, Bill Clinton, the "New Democrat," prepared to lead the United States through the last decade of the twentieth century. "The urgent question of our time," he said, "is whether we can make change our friend and not our enemy." Clinton would embrace unexpected changes while ushering America into the twenty-first century.

CHAPTER REVIEW

SUMMARY

- **The Carter Presidency**   While Jimmy Carter had some notable achievements, such as the *Camp David Accords*, his administration suffered from legislative inexperience, a deepening economic recession, soaring inflation, and the *Iranian hostage crisis*. His sermonizing about the need for Americans to lead simpler lives compounded the public's loss of faith in his presidency.

- **The Rise of Conservatism**   Ronald Reagan's charm, coupled with disillusionment over Carter's presidency, won Reagan the election in 1980. The Republican insurgency was dominated by Christian conservatives like those who made up the *Moral Majority*. The migration of older Americans and others to conservative southern and western states increased the voting power of the so-called sunbelt, where voters were socially conservative and favored lower taxes and a smaller, less intrusive federal government.

- **Reaganomics**   Reagan introduced a "supply-side" economic philosophy, commonly called *Reaganomics*, that championed tax cuts for the rich, reductions in government regulations, cuts to social-welfare programs, and increased defense spending. Reagan was unable to cut domestic spending, however, and the tax cuts failed to pay for themselves as promised. The result was a dramatic increase in the national debt.

- **The End of the Cold War**   Reagan's military buildup, including preliminary development of a space-based antiballistic-missile system called the *Strategic Defense Initiative (SDI)*, helped force the Soviets to the negotiating table to conclude the *Intermediate-Range Nuclear Forces (INF) Treaty*—the beginning of the end of the cold war. But Reagan's foreign-policy efforts were badly tarnished by the *Iran-Contra affair*, in which members of his administration sold American-made armaments to Iran in exchange for Iranian influence to secure the release of American hostages held in Lebanon (despite the president's public claims that he would never deal with terrorists).

- **America in the 1980s**   Americans in the eighties not only experienced unprecedented prosperity but also rising poverty and homelessness. Conservatives condemned (and dismissed) *HIV/AIDS* as a "gay" disease. The development of the *microprocessor* paved the way for the computer revolution, which dramatically increased productivity and communications while generating whole new industries. Consumerism flourished all too well during the eighties, the result of which was massive public and private debt.

- **A New World Order**   Toward the end of the 1980s, democratic political movements emerged in Eastern Europe. In the Soviet Union, Mikhail Gorbachev's steps to restructure the economy (*perestroika*) and promote more open policies (*glas-*

nost) led to further reform and the collapse of the Soviet Empire. But new trouble spots quickly emerged. Iraq, led by Saddam Hussein, invaded neighboring Kuwait in 1990. When Iraq did not withdraw, American-led allied forces launched *Operation Desert Storm*, and the Iraqis surrendered within six weeks.

CHRONOLOGY

1978	President Carter helps negotiate the Camp David Accords between Egypt and Israel
	Tax revolt in California leads to the passage of Proposition 13
November 1979	Islamist militants storm the U.S. embassy in Tehran and take fifty-two Americans hostage
1980	Ronald Reagan elected president
1981	President Reagan enacts major tax cuts
1983	President Reagan authorizes development of the Strategic Defense Initiative (SDI)
1987	Reagan delivers his famous Berlin Wall speech
1988	George H. W. Bush is elected president
November 1989	Berlin Wall is torn down
December 1989	U.S. troops invade Panama and capture Manuel Noriega
1991	Iraq forced from Kuwait in the First Gulf War
	Breakup of the USSR
1992	Bill Clinton is elected president

KEY TERMS

Camp David Accords p. 1169

Iranian hostage crisis p. 1170

Moral Majority p. 1174

Reaganomics p. 1178

Strategic Defense Initiative (SDI) p. 1184

Iran-Contra affair p. 1185

perestroika p. 1186

glasnost p. 1186

Intermediate-Range Nuclear Forces (INF) Treaty p. 1187

microprocessor p. 1188

HIV/AIDS p. 1191

Operation Desert Storm p. 1196

"New Democrats" p. 1198

 INQUIZITIVE

Go to InQuizitive to see what you've learned—and learn what you've missed—with personalized feedback along the way.

32 Twenty-First-Century America

1993–Present

Youth speaks The Occupy Wall Street movement was born when thousands of protesters, many of them unemployed young adults, "occupied" Wall Street, the famous financial district in downtown Manhattan, to protest the "tyrannical" power of corporate America. The grassroots movement soon spread across the nation, then the world. Here, members of the movement stage a protest outside the New York Stock Exchange in September 2011.

The United States entered the final decade of the twentieth century triumphant. American persistence in fighting and financing the cold war had contributed to the collapse of the Soviet Union and the birth of democracy and capitalism in Eastern Europe. By the end of the century, the United States was the world's only superpower.

Yet no sooner did the century come to an end than America's sense of physical security and material comfort was shattered by terrorist attacks in 2001 on New York City and Washington, D.C. The attacks killed thousands, plunged the economy into recession, and raised profound questions about national security.

In leading the fight against global terrorism, the United States became embroiled in long, costly, and controversial wars in Iraq and Afghanistan. Opposition to the wars would provide much of the momentum for Democrat Barack Obama to win election in 2008 as the nation's first African American president. Obama entered the White House at the same time that the United States and Europe were experiencing the Great Recession, a prolonged economic downturn that threatened the global banking system, caused widespread unemployment, and ignited social unrest and political tensions at home and abroad.

focus questions

1. What were the major population trends (demographics) in the United States during the twenty-first century? How did they impact the nation's politics?

2. What were the accomplishments and the setbacks of Bill Clinton's presidency?

3. What was the impact of global terrorism on the United States during the presidency of George W. Bush? How effective was his "war on terror?"

4. What were the issues and developments during Bush's second term that helped lead to Barack Obama's historic victory in the 2008 presidential election?

5. What were President Obama's priorities at home and abroad? How effective were his efforts to pursue them?

America's Changing Population

As the twenty-first century dawned, the United States began experiencing dramatic social changes. In 2015, the country's population surpassed 322 million, more than 80 percent of whom lived in cities or suburbs. Even more important, the nation's racial and ethnic composition was changing rapidly. In 1980, the population was 80 percent white. By 2015, that percentage had fallen below 63 percent.

In 2005, Hispanics became the nation's largest minority group. In 1980, Hispanics were 6 percent; in 2015, that number had tripled to 18 percent and was growing rapidly. More than 56 million Americans were Hispanic in origin, and a third of them were under the age of eighteen.

African Americans were at 13 percent, Asians about 8 percent, and Native Americans 1 percent. The rate of increase among those four groups was twice what it had been during the 1980s. Yet the fastest-growing group in the nation were the nearly 10 million who described themselves as "multiracial," representing more than 3 percent of the entire population.

The primary cause of this dramatic change in the nation's ethnic mix was a surge of immigration. In 2015, the United States had more foreign-born residents than ever before—more than 45 million, 11 million of whom were undocumented immigrants (formerly classified as "illegal aliens"). In the first decade of the twenty-first century, the United States became home to more than twice as many immigrants as *all* other countries combined. For the first time, the majority of immigrants came not from Europe but from other parts of the world: Asia, Latin America, and Africa. Mexicans made up the largest share of Hispanics, followed by Puerto Ricans and Cubans. Asian Americans increased their numbers at a faster rate than any other ethnic group, largely because of a surge in Chinese immigrants.

The nation's changing ethnic composition has had an increasingly significant impact on social life. In 1980, Hispanic Americans lived mainly in five states: California, Arizona, New Mexico, Texas, and Florida. By 2014, *every* state had a rapidly growing Hispanic population. Demographers projected that by 2044, whites would become a minority in the United States.

Immigration also is having potent political effects, as almost one 1 million Hispanics reach voting age each year. Hispanics are usually Catholic and tend to vote Democratic. In 1980, there were six Hispanic Americans serving in the U.S. Congress. By 2010, there were more than five times as many. In 1992, Hispanics constituted only 2 percent of American voters; by 2014, they were 10 percent.

Only 23 percent of baby boomers born during and after the Second World War consider the surge in American diversity a "change for the better." They worry that Hispanics will always be a race apart from mainstream American culture, a permanent underclass of people tied closely to their ancestral homelands. Yet such concerns are countered by growing evidence that Hispanics are integrating themselves into American society and embracing its ideals. High-school graduation and college enrollment rates among Hispanics are rising, teen pregnancy is falling, and more and more are learning English. In recent years, more than a quarter of Hispanic marriages have involved a non-Hispanic partner. Far from being a disaster, the growing Hispanic population is providing the nation with a surge of youthful energy and vitality—and demonstrating such traditional American attributes as self-reliance, rugged individualism, thrift, close family ties, strong religious beliefs, disproportionate participation in the military, and an ethic of hard work.

Over the quota, under the radar Large numbers of Chinese risked their lives to gain entry to the United States during the late twentieth century. A freighter carrying undocumented immigrants ran aground near Rockaway Beach, New York, in June 1993, forcing its undocumented passengers to swim ashore.

THE CLINTON PRESIDENCY

Bill Clinton arrived at the White House in 1993 with an almost legendary combination of strengths and weaknesses. At forty-six years old, he was the third youngest president in history, only slightly older than John Kennedy and Theodore Roosevelt. Like Ronald Reagan, Clinton charmed people, and his speeches inspired them. He was shrewdly smart, full of energy, resilient, persistent, and a self-described "policy wonk" who loved debating the fine points of new legislative ideas. Clinton resembled Jimmy Carter in his determination to be a "centrist" Democrat who reached out to working- and middle-class voters who no longer trusted liberals "to take their tax money and spend it with discipline."

But Clinton's inexperience in international affairs and congressional maneuvering led to several missteps in his first year as president. Like

George H. W. Bush before him, he reneged on several campaign promises. In a bruising battle with Congress, he was forced to abandon his proposed middle-class tax cut to keep another campaign promise to reduce the federal deficit. Then he dropped his promise to allow gays to serve openly in the armed forces after military commanders expressed strong opposition. He later announced an ambiguous policy that came to be known as "don't ask, don't tell" (DADT), which allowed gays, lesbians, and bisexuals to serve in the military but only if they kept their sexual orientation secret.

"I got the worst of both worlds," Clinton later confessed. "I lost the fight, and the gay community was highly critical of me for the compromise." In his first two weeks in office, his approval rating dropped 20 percent. Throughout his presidency, however, he displayed a remarkable ability to manage crises and rebound from adversity.

THE ECONOMY As a candidate, Bill Clinton had pledged to reduce the federal deficit without damaging the economy or hurting the nation's most vulnerable people. To this end, he proposed $241 billion in higher taxes for corporations and for the wealthiest individuals (the top income tax rate rising from 33 to 39.6 percent) over four years, and $255 billion in spending cuts over the same period. The hotly contested bill passed the Democratic-controlled Congress by the slimmest of margins: 218 to 216 in the House and 51 to 50 in the Senate, with Vice President Al Gore providing the tie-breaking vote. In the end, the deficit-reduction effort worked as planned. It led to lower interest rates, which, along with low energy prices, helped spur dramatic economic growth.

Equally difficult was gaining congressional approval of the **North American Free Trade Agreement (NAFTA)**, which the Bush administration had negotiated with Canada and Mexico. Clinton urged approval of NAFTA, which would make North America the largest free-trade zone in the world. Opponents favored tariffs to discourage the importation of cheaper foreign products, especially from Mexico. Yet Clinton prevailed with solid Republican support while losing a sizable minority of Democrats, mostly labor unionists and southerners, who feared that textile mills would lose business (and millions of jobs) to "cheap labor" countries—as they did.

HEALTH CARE REFORM Clinton's primary public-policy initiative was an ambitious plan to overhaul the nation's health care system. Public support for government-administered health insurance had spread as annual medical costs skyrocketed and some 37 million Americans, most of them poor or unemployed, went without it.

The Clinton administration argued that providing medical insurance to everyone, regardless of income, would reduce the costs of health care to the nation as a whole, but critics questioned the savings as well as the ability of the federal government to manage such a huge program. The plan, known as the Health Security Act, called for large corporations to pay for most of the medical insurance expenses of their employees and required small businesses to form "health alliances" so that they, too, could provide subsidized health insurance to their workers.

By the summer of 1994, Clinton's 1,364-page health insurance plan, developed by a task force headed by the First Lady, Hillary Rodham Clinton, was doomed, in part because the president opposed any changes and in part because the report was impossibly complicated. Strenuously opposed by Republicans and health care interest groups, especially the pharmaceutical and insurance industries, Clinton's prized bill was voted down by Congress in August 1994.

LANDSLIDE REPUBLICAN VICTORY The health care bill disaster influenced the 1994 midterm elections. In the most stunning congressional victory of the twentieth century, the Republicans captured both houses of Congress and won 32 governorships, including the largest states of California, New York, and Texas.

The Republican victory was led by a combative Georgia conservative named Newton ("Newt") Leroy Gingrich. In early 1995, he became the first Republican Speaker of the House in forty-two years. Gingrich, a former history professor with a lust for controversy and an unruly ego, was a superb tactician who had helped mobilize religious and social conservatives associated with the Christian Coalition.

The Christian Coalition, organized by television evangelist Pat Robertson in 1989 to replace Jerry Falwell's Moral Majority (which had disbanded that year), was pro–school prayer, anti-abortion, anti-feminist, and anti–gay rights. In addition to celebrating "traditional family values," it urged politicians to "radically downsize" government. In many respects, the religious Right took control of the political and social landscape in the nineties.

In 1994, Gingrich and his fellow Republicans rallied conservative voters

Newt Gingrich Joined by 160 of his fellow House Republicans, Gingrich promotes the Contract with America in April 1995.

by promising a **Contract with America**, a pledge to dismantle the "corrupt liberal welfare state" created by Democrats. The ten-point, anti-big-government "contract" promised a smaller federal government by reducing the regulation of businesses, environmental protections, requiring term limits for members of Congress, slashing social-welfare programs, and passing a constitutional amendment requiring a balanced annual federal budget. As Texan Tom DeLay, a leading House Republican, explained, "You've got to understand, we are ideologues. We have an agenda. We have a philosophy." Yet the much-trumpeted Contract with America quickly fizzled. The conservatives pushed too hard and too fast, realizing too late that their slim majority in Congress could not launch a revolution. They were able to pass only four minor elements of their "contract."

Gingrich's heavy-handed methods contributed to the disintegration of the Contract with America. Republican senator Bob Dole said Gingrich was "a one-man band who rarely took advice." He was too ambitious, too abrasive, too divisive. When Clinton refused to go along with Republican demands for a balanced-budget pledge, Gingrich twice shut down the federal government during the fall of 1995. The tactic backfired. By 1996, Gingrich had higher negative ratings in public surveys than the president.

THE SUPREME COURT AND RACE The conservative mood also revealed itself in Supreme Court rulings that undermined affirmative-action programs, which gave African American students special consideration in college admissions and financial aid awards. Between 1970 and 1977, African American enrollment in colleges and universities doubled, even as white students and their parents complained about "reverse discrimination."

In 1996, two major rulings affected affirmative action in college admissions. In *Hopwood v. Texas*, a federal court ruled that race could not be used as a consideration for admission. Later that year, California voters passed Proposition 209 (also known as the California Civil Rights Initiative or CCRI), which ruled out preferential treatment ("affirmative action") in government hiring, government contracting, and public schools based on race, sex, ethnicity, or national origin. Similar complaints were directed against affirmative-action programs that awarded government contracts to minority-owned businesses. In 1995, the Court in *Adarand Constructors v. Peña* declared that affirmative-action programs had to be "narrowly tailored" to serve a "compelling national interest." The implication of such vague language was clear: the Court had come to share the growing public suspicion of the value and legitimacy of programs designed to benefit a particular race, gender, or ethnic group.

LEGISLATIVE BREAKTHROUGH After the surprising 1994 Republican takeover of Congress, Bill Clinton shrewdly resolved to save his presidency by reinforcing his claim that he was a "centrist." He co-opted much of the energy of the conservative movement by announcing that "the era of big government is over" and by reforming the federal system of welfare payments to the poor, created during the 1930s under the New Deal.

Late in the summer of 1996, the Republican Congress passed a comprehensive welfare-reform measure that Clinton signed after some revisions. The **Personal Responsibility and Work Opportunity Act of 1996 (PRWOA)** illustrated Clinton's efforts to move the Democratic party away from the liberalism it had promoted since the 1930s. PRWOA abolished the Aid to Families with Dependent Children (AFDC) program, which provided poor families with almost $8,000 a year, and replaced it with the Temporary Assistance for Needy Families program, which limited the duration of welfare payments to two years in an effort to encourage unemployed people to get self-supporting jobs.

Liberal Democrats bitterly criticized Clinton's "welfare reform" deal. Yet the new approach to supporting the poor was a statistical success. Both the number of welfare recipients and poverty rates declined during the late nineties, leading the editors of the left-leaning *New Republic* to report that the PRWOA had "worked much as its designers had hoped."

THE 1996 CAMPAIGN The Republican takeover of Congress in 1994 gave the party hope that they could prevent President Clinton's reelection. After clinching the Republican presidential nomination in 1996, Senate majority leader Bob Dole resigned his seat to devote his attention to the campaign. Clinton, however, maintained a large lead in the polls. With an improving economy and no major foreign-policy crises, cultural and personal issues surged into prominence.

Concern about Dole's age (seventy-three) and his gruff public personality, as well as tensions between economic conservatives and social conservatives over volatile issues such as abortion and gun control, hampered Dole's efforts to generate widespread support, especially among independent voters. Clinton was able to frame the election as a stark choice between Dole's desire to build a bridge to the past and Clinton's promise to build a bridge to the future.

On November 5, 1996, Clinton won a second term with an electoral vote victory of 379 to 159 and 49 percent of the popular vote. Dole received 41 percent of the popular vote, and third-party candidate Ross Perot got 8 percent.

THE "NEW ECONOMY"   Bill Clinton's presidency benefited from a prolonged period of unprecedented economic prosperity. During his last three years in office (1998–2000), the federal government generated unheard-of budget *surpluses*. What came to be called the "new economy" featured high-flying electronics, computer, software, telecommunications (cellular phones, cable TV, etc.), and e-commerce Internet firms called "dot-com" companies.

These dynamic "tech" enterprises helped the economy set records in every area: low inflation, low unemployment, corporate profits, and personal fortunes. The stock-market value of U.S. companies nearly tripled, and people began to claim that the new economy defied the boom-and-bust cycles of the previous hundred years. Alan Greenspan, the Federal Reserve Board chairman, suggested that "we have moved beyond history" into an economy that seemed only to grow. He would be proven wrong.

GLOBALIZATION   Another major feature of the new economy was **globalization**. The end of the cold war and the disintegration of the Soviet Union opened many new opportunities for U.S. companies in international trade. In addition, new globe-spanning communication technologies and massive new container-carrying ships and cargo jets shortened time and distance, enabling United States–based multinational companies to conduct more business abroad.

Bill Clinton accelerated the process of globalization. "The global economy," he said, "is giving more of our own people, and billions around the world, the chance to work and live and raise their families with dignity." He especially welcomed the World Wide Web, which opened the Internet to everyone, and, by doing so, greatly accelerated U.S. dominance of the international economy.

By 2000, more than a third of the production of U.S. multinational companies was occurring abroad, compared with only 9 percent in 1980. In 1970, there were 7,000 American multinational companies; by 2000, the number had soared to 63,000. Many U.S. multinational companies pursued controversial "outsourcing" strategies by which they moved their production "offshore" to nations such as Mexico and China to take advantage of lower labor costs and fewer workplace and environmental regulations. At the same time, many European and Asian companies, especially automobile manufacturers, built large plants in the United States to reduce the shipping expenses required to get their products to American markets. The U.S. economy had become internationalized to such an extent that global concerns exercised an ever-increasing influence on domestic and foreign policies.

FOREIGN POLICY IN THE NINETIES

Unlike George H. W. Bush, Bill Clinton had little interest in global politics. Untrained and inexperienced in international relations, he had to focus on creating opportunities around the world for U.S. business expansion. Yet, as international analyst Leslie Gelb cautioned the new president, "A foreign economic policy is not a foreign policy, and it is not a national security strategy." Events soon forced Clinton to intervene to help nations in crisis.

THE MIDDLE EAST   President Clinton continued George H. W. Bush's policy of orchestrating patient negotiations between the Arabs and the Israelis. A new development was the inclusion of the Palestinian Liberation Organization (PLO). In 1993, secret talks between Israeli and Palestinian representatives resulted in a draft agreement between Israel and the PLO that provided for the restoration of Palestinian self-rule in the occupied Gaza Strip and in Jericho, on the West Bank, in a "land for peace" exchange as outlined in United Nations Security Council resolutions. A formal signing occurred at the White House on September 13, 1993. With Clinton presiding, Israeli prime minister Yitzhak Rabin and PLO leader Yasir Arafat exchanged handshakes, and their foreign ministers signed the agreement.

Clinton and the Middle East President Clinton presides as Israeli prime minister Yitzhak Rabin (left) and PLO leader Yasir Arafat (right) agree to a pathbreaking peace accord between Israel and the Palestinians, September 1993.

The Middle East peace process suffered a terrible blow in early November 1995, however, when Rabin was assassinated by an Israeli zealot who resented the efforts to negotiate with the Palestinians. Some observers feared that the assassin had killed the peace process as well when, seven months later, conservative hard-liner Benjamin Netanyahu narrowly defeated the United States–backed Shimon Peres in the Israeli national elections. Yet in October 1998, Clinton brought Arafat, Netanyahu, and King Hussein of Jordan together at a conference in Maryland, where they reached an agreement. Under the Wye River Accords, Israel agreed to surrender land in return for security guarantees by the Palestinians.

THE BALKANS   Clinton also felt compelled to address turmoil in the Eastern European nations now free from Soviet domination. In 1991, Yugoslavia had disintegrated into ethnic warfare as four of its six multiethnic republics declared their independence. Serb minorities, backed by the new Republic of Serbia, stirred up civil wars in neighboring Croatia and Bosnia. In Bosnia, the conflict involved systematic efforts to eliminate Muslims. Clinton decided that the situation was "intolerable" because the massacres of tens of thousands of people "tore at the very fabric" of human decency. He ordered food and medical supplies sent to besieged Bosnian Muslims and dispatched warplanes to stop the massacres.

In 1995, U.S. negotiators finally persuaded the foreign ministers of Croatia, Bosnia, and Yugoslavia (by then a loose federation of the republics of Serbia and Montenegro) to agree to a comprehensive peace plan. Bosnia would remain a single nation but would be divided into two states: a Muslim-Croat federation controlling 51 percent of the territory, and a Bosnian-Serb republic controlling the rest. Basic human rights would be restored, and free elections would be held. To enforce the agreement, 60,000 NATO peacekeeping troops were dispatched to Bosnia.

McRubble Pro-Milošević residents of Belgrade, Yugoslavia, destroy the storefront of a McDonald's restaurant in 1999 to protest NATO and the United States' airstrikes on their homeland.

In 1998, the Balkan tinderbox flared up again, this time in the Yugoslav province of Kosovo, which had long been considered sacred ground by Christian Serbs, although 90 percent of the 2 million Kosovars were in fact

Albanian Muslims. In 1998, Yugoslav president Slobodan Milošević began a program of "**ethnic cleansing**" whereby Yugoslav forces burned Albanian villages, murdered men, raped women, and displaced hundreds of thousands of Muslim Kosovars.

On March 24, 1999, NATO, relying heavily upon U.S. military resources and leadership, launched air strikes against Yugoslavian military targets. After seventy-two days of bombardment, Milošević sued for peace on NATO's terms, in part because his Russian allies had finally abandoned him. An agreement was reached on June 3, 1999, and Clinton pledged extensive U.S. aid to help the Yugoslavs rebuild.

THE SCANDAL MACHINE

For a time, Clinton's preoccupation with foreign crises helped deflect attention from a growing number of investigations into his personal conduct. During his first term, he was dogged by old charges about investments he and his wife had made in Whitewater, a planned resort development in Arkansas. The project turned out to be a fraud and a failure, and the Clintons were accused of conspiring with the developer. In 1994, Kenneth Starr, a former judge and a conservative Republican, was appointed to investigate the Whitewater case.

Starr did not uncover any evidence that the Clintons were directly involved in the Whitewater fraud, but in the course of another investigation he happened upon evidence of a White House sex scandal. For years, rumors had circulated about the president's dalliances with women. James Carville, Clinton's political consultant, once asked Clinton about his sexual risk-taking. "Well," Clinton replied, "they haven't caught me." He spoke too soon.

MONICAGATE   Between 1995 and 1997, Clinton had engaged in a sexual affair with a twenty-two-year-old White House intern, Monica Lewinsky. More disturbing, he had pressed her to lie about their relationship, even under oath. Clinton initially denied the charges, telling the nation in late January 1998 that "I did not have sexual relations with that woman, Miss Lewinsky." Yet the scandal would not disappear.

For the next thirteen months, the media circus surrounding the "Monicagate" or "Zippergate" affair captured public attention. (After the Watergate affair in 1973–1974, journalists have loved to attach the suffix "-gate" to scandals.) Other women stepped forward to claim that Clinton had engaged in improper relations with them over the years, charges that the president denied.

The First Lady, Hillary Clinton, grimly stood by her husband, declaring that the rumors were the result of a "vast right-wing conspiracy" to bring him down. With the economy booming, Clinton's public approval ratings actually rose during 1998. In August, however, Lewinsky agreed to provide a federal grand jury with a detailed account of her relationship with the president.

Soon thereafter, Clinton became the first president to testify before a grand jury. On August 17, the self-pitying, defiant president admitted having had "inappropriate, intimate physical contact" with Lewinsky but insisted that he had done nothing illegal. Public reaction was mixed. A majority expressed sympathy for the president because of his public humiliation and because the Lewinsky affair was a private act of consensual sex. Others, however, were eager to see the president impeached.

THE IMPEACHMENT OF CLINTON   On September 9, 1998, Kenneth Starr, the special prosecutor, submitted to Congress thirty-six boxes of documents that included a disturbingly graphic account of the president's White House encounters with Lewinsky. The report claimed that there was "substantial and creditable" evidence of presidential wrongdoing (perjury, obstructing justice, and abusing his presidential powers). The Starr report prompted the Republican-dominated House of Representatives on October 8 to begin a wide-ranging impeachment inquiry.

On December 19, 1998, William Jefferson Clinton was impeached (charged with "high crimes and misdemeanors") by the House of Representatives. The House officially approved two articles of impeachment, charging Clinton with lying under oath to a federal grand jury and obstructing justice.

House Speaker Newt Gingrich, who had been censured (officially condemned) by his Republican colleagues in 1997 for several "serious violations" of House rules, led the effort to impeach the president, even though he himself was, at the time, secretly engaged in a six-year-long affair with a congressional staff member. (Gingrich resigned as Speaker in November 1998.) Journalists began calling Clinton's Senate trial the "soap opera" impeachment after Gingrich's successor as Speaker, Robert Livingston of Louisiana, suddenly resigned from Congress in late December after admitting that he, too, had engaged in adulterous affairs.

The impeachment trial began on January 7, 1999. Five weeks later, on February 12, a majority of senators, by a 55–45 vote, decided that Clinton's adultery and lies were not the "high crimes and misdemeanors" required to remove a president from office. The president was acquitted—much to the regret of many Republicans. The situation called to mind an old Texas saying: "We tried to hang him, but the rope broke." Though the impeachment effort failed, Clinton's final eighteen months in office were stained and distracted by the scandal.

ASSESSING THE CLINTON PRESIDENCY Bill Clinton presided over an unprecedented period of prosperity (115 consecutive months of economic growth and the lowest unemployment rate in 30 years), generated unheard-of federal budget surpluses, and passed a welfare-reform measure with support from both parties. In the process, he re-centered and revitalized the Democratic party along "moderate" lines. Clinton also helped bring peace and stability to the Balkans, one of the most violent regions of Europe.

At times, however, his boundless self-confidence led to arrogant recklessness. He debased the presidency with his sexual escapades, and his effort to bring health insurance to the uninsured was a clumsy failure. Clinton was less a great statesman than a great escape artist. In 2000, his last year in office, he enjoyed a public approval rating of 65 percent, the highest end-of-term rating since President Dwight D. Eisenhower. Yet his popularity was not enough to ensure the election of his vice president, Al Gore, as his successor.

A Chaotic Start to a New Century

Wild celebrations around the world ushered in the year 2000, but the joyous mood did not last. Powerful new forces were emerging, the most dangerous of which were global networks of menacing terrorists eager to disrupt and destroy American values and institutions.

A Disputed Election

The presidential election of 2000 proved to be one of the closest and most controversial in history. The two major-party candidates, Vice President Albert Gore Jr., the Democrat, and Texas governor George W. Bush, son of the former Republican president, offered contrasting views on the role of the federal government, tax cuts, environmental policies, and the best way to preserve Social Security and Medicare.

Gore, a Tennessee native and Harvard graduate whose father had been a prominent senator, favored an active federal government that would do much more to protect the environment. Bush campaigned on a theme of "compassionate conservatism," promised to restore "honor and dignity" to the White House, and proposed to transfer power from the federal government to the states. A "born-again" evangelical Christian with degrees from Yale University and Harvard Business School, Bush also urged tax cuts and a more "humble" foreign policy that would end U.S. efforts to install democratic governments in undemocratic societies ("nation building").

THE ELECTION OF 2000

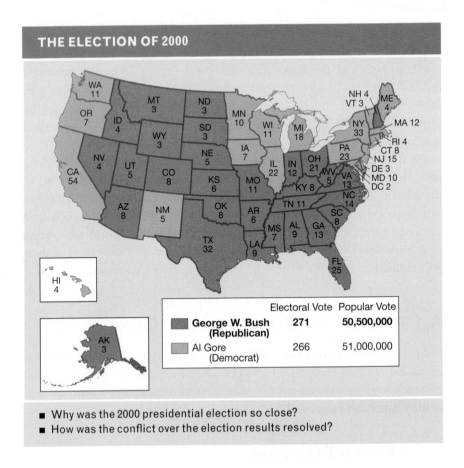

		Electoral Vote	Popular Vote
■	**George W. Bush** **(Republican)**	**271**	**50,500,000**
■	Al Gore (Democrat)	266	51,000,000

- Why was the 2000 presidential election so close?
- How was the conflict over the election results resolved?

The November election created high drama. The television networks initially reported that Gore had narrowly won the state of Florida and its decisive twenty-five electoral votes. Later in the evening, however, they reversed themselves, saying that Florida was too close to call. In the chaotic early-morning hours, the networks declared that Bush had been elected president. The final tally showed Bush with a razor-thin lead, but Florida law required a recount. For the first time in 125 years, the results of a presidential election remained in doubt for weeks after the voting.

As a painstaking hand recount proceeded, supporters of Bush and Gore sparred in the courts. Each side accused the other of trying to steal the election. The political drama lasted for five weeks, until, on December 12, a bitterly divided U.S. Supreme Court decided, with a 5–4 majority ruling, that the recount was to be halted. Bush was declared the winner in Florida by 537 votes. Gore had amassed a 540,000-vote lead nationwide, but losing

Florida meant he lost in the electoral college by two votes. Although Gore "strongly disagreed" with the Supreme Court's decision, he asked voters to rally around President-elect Bush and move forward. "Partisan rancor," he urged, "must be put aside."

The ferocious sparring between the two national parties was not put aside, however, in part because Bush chose as key advisers men known for their brusqueness and strong ideological convictions. One of them, Richard "Dick" Cheney, a former Wyoming congressman and influential member of the Nixon, Ford, and Bush administrations, quickly became the most powerful vice president in history. Cheney used his experience with the government bureaucracy to fill the administration with like-minded associates who helped him control the flow of information to the president. He became a domineering influence on the inexperienced Bush.

The recount In yet another recount on November 24, 2000, Judge Robert Rosenberg examines a ballot with a magnifying glass. That Florida's voting machines were so unreliable introduced doubt about the legitimacy of the close results.

A CHANGE OF DIRECTION

George W. Bush had promised to cut taxes for the wealthy, increase military spending, oppose strict environmental regulations, and "privatize" Social Security by investing workers' retirement pension funds in the stock market.

First, however, he had to deal with a sputtering economy. By March 2001, the economy was in recession for the first time in more than a decade. Bush decided that cutting taxes was the best way to boost economic growth. On June 7, 2001, he signed the Economic Growth and Tax Relief Act, which cut $1.35 trillion in taxes.

Instead of paying for themselves in renewed economic growth, however, the Bush tax cuts led to a sharp drop in federal revenue, producing in turn a fast-growing budget deficit as the Clinton surpluses were quickly used up. Huge increases in the costs of Medicare and Medicaid resulting from the aging of the baby boom generation contributed to the soaring deficits, as did military expenditures caused by an unexpected war.

Bush was also distracted by global crises. Islamic militants around the world bitterly resented what they viewed as the "imperial" globalization of U.S. culture and power. With increasing frequency, they used terrorism, including suicide bombings, to gain notoriety, exact vengeance, and generate fear and insecurity.

Throughout the nineties, the United States had fought a losing struggle against global terrorist groups, in part because terrorism thrives in nations with weak governments overwhelmed by rapid population growth, scarce resources, widespread poverty, and huge numbers of unemployed young men—symptoms many nations were suffering. The ineffectiveness of U.S. intelligence agencies in tracking the movements and intentions of militant extremists became tragically evident in the late summer of 2001.

9/11—A NEW DAY OF INFAMY At 8:45 A.M. on September 11, 2001, an airliner that had been hijacked by Islamist terrorists slammed into the north tower of the World Trade Center in New York City. Eighteen minutes later, a second hijacked jumbo jet crashed into the south tower. The twin towers, 110 stories tall and filled with 50,000 workers, burned fiercely, the infernos forcing hundreds of desperate people to jump to their deaths as thousands more on the floors below the points of impact struggled to evacuate. The steel structures quickly collapsed from the intense heat, destroying surrounding buildings and killing nearly 3,000 people, including more than 400 firefighters, police officers, and emergency responders. The southern end of Manhattan—"ground zero"—became a hellish scene of twisted steel, suffocating smoke, wailing sirens, and panicked people.

While the catastrophic drama in New York City was unfolding, a third hijacked plane crashed into the Pentagon in Washington, D.C. A fourth airliner, probably headed for the White House, missed its mark when the passengers—who had heard reports of the earlier hijackings via their cell phones—assaulted the hijackers to prevent the plane from being used as a weapon. During the struggle, the plane went out of control and plummeted into the ground near Shanksville, Pennsylvania, killing all aboard.

Within hours of the hijackings, the nineteen dead terrorists were identified as members of al Qaeda (Arabic for "the Base"), a well-financed network of Islamic extremists led by a wealthy Saudi renegade, Osama bin Laden. Years before, bin Laden had declared *jihad* (holy war) on the United States, Israel, and the Saudi monarchy in his effort to create a single Islamist *caliphate* (global empire). He used remote bases in Sudan and war-torn Afghanistan as training

September 11th Smoke pours out of the north tower of the World Trade Center as the south tower bursts into flames after being struck by a second hijacked airplane. Both iconic buildings would collapse within an hour.

centers for jihadist fighters. Collaborating with bin Laden's terrorist network was Afghanistan's ruling Taliban, a coalition of ultraconservative Islamists who provided bin Laden a safe haven.

The "War on Terror"

The 9/11 assault on the United States, like the Japanese attack on Pearl Harbor on December 7, 1941, changed the course of modern life. People were initially paralyzed by grief, fear, and anger. The U.S. economy, already in decline, went into free fall. President Bush was thrust into the role of commander in chief of a nation eager for vengeance.

Bush said that he was going to launch a global **war on terror** "to answer these attacks and rid the world of evil." He warned other nations that "either you are with us or you are with the terrorists." A wave of patriotic fervor rolled across the nation. People formed long lines to donate blood, and many signed up for military service.

Bush demanded that Afghanistan's Taliban government surrender the al Qaeda terrorists or risk military attack. The Taliban refused, and on October 7, 2001, the United States and its allies launched Operation Enduring Freedom. After American and British cruise missiles and bombers destroyed Afghan military installations and al Qaeda training camps, ground troops from the United States and some of its NATO allies routed Taliban forces. On December 9, the Taliban regime collapsed. The war in Afghanistan then transitioned into a high-stakes manhunt for the elusive Osama bin Laden, who had escaped into the mountains of Pakistan.

FIGHTING TERROR AT HOME While the military campaign continued in Afghanistan, officials in Washington worried that terrorists might attack the United States with biological, chemical, or even nuclear weapons. To address the threat and to help restore public confidence, President Bush established the Office of Homeland Security. Another new federal agency, the Transportation Security Administration, assumed responsibility for screening airline passengers for weapons and bombs.

At the same time, Bush and a supportive Congress created the **USA Patriot Act**, which gave government agencies the right to eavesdrop on confidential conversations between prison inmates and their lawyers and permitted suspected terrorists to be tried in secret military courts. Civil liberties groups voiced grave concerns that the measures jeopardized constitutional rights and protections, but most people supported these extraordinary steps.

What the public did not know was that Vice President Dick Cheney, Secretary of Defense Donald Rumsfeld, and others had convinced the president to authorize the use of torture ("enhanced interrogation techniques") in the CIA's and FBI's treatment of captured terrorist suspects. Such tactics violated international law and compromised the human rights ideals that had always been America's greatest strength.

War fever President George W. Bush addresses members of the Special Forces in July 2002 as part of an appeal to Congress to increase defense spending after the September 11 terrorist attacks.

THE BUSH DOCTRINE In the fall of 2002, President Bush unveiled a dramatic new national security policy. The **Bush Doctrine** said that the growing menace posed by "shadowy networks" of terrorist groups and unstable rogue nations with **"weapons of mass**

destruction" **(WMDs)** required the United States at times to use preemptive military action. "If we wait for threats to fully materialize," or wait for allies to join America, he explained, "we will have waited too long. In the world we have entered, the only path to safety is the path of action. And this nation will *act*."

The dangerously sweeping Bush Doctrine promised to "extend the benefits of freedom across the globe . . . for all peoples everywhere," without reference to the potential human and financial cost of such an open-ended commitment.

THE SECOND IRAQ WAR   During 2002 and 2003, Iraq emerged as the focus of the Bush administration's policy of "preemptive" military action. Three of the president's most influential advisers, Vice President Cheney, Secretary of Defense Rumsfeld, and Deputy Defense Secretary Paul Wolfowitz, convinced him that the dictatorial regime of Saddam Hussein and his loyal Sunni faction of Muslims, who lorded over the nation's Shiite majority and the ethnic Kurds in the north, represented a "grave and gathering danger" because of its supposed possession of biological and chemical weapons of mass destruction.

On March 17, 2003, Bush issued Hussein an ultimatum: he and his sons must leave Iraq within forty-eight hours or face a United States–led invasion. Hussein refused. Two days later, on March 19, American and British forces attacked. France and Germany refused to participate in what they viewed as unnecessary American aggression.

"Operation Iraqi Freedom," according to Bush and his advisers, would quickly topple Hussein with overwhelming military force and then usher in a new era of democracy in Iraq. It began with a massive bombing campaign, followed by a fast-moving invasion from bases in Kuwait. Some 250,000 American soldiers, sailors, and marines were joined by 50,000 British troops. On April 9, after three weeks of intense fighting amid sweltering heat and blinding sandstorms, U.S. forces captured Baghdad, the capital of Iraq. Saddam Hussein's regime and his inept, demoralized army collapsed a week later.

The six-week war came at a cost of fewer than 200 combat deaths among the 300,000 allied troops. More than 2,000 Iraqi soldiers were killed; civilian casualties numbered in the tens of thousands. President Bush staged a celebration on a U.S. aircraft carrier at which he announced victory under a massive banner proclaiming "MISSION ACCOMPLISHED." But he spoke too soon; the initial military triumph carried with it the seeds of deception and disaster, for no weapons of mass destruction were to be found in Iraq. Bush later said that the absence of WMDs in Iraq left him with a "sickening feeling," for he knew that his primary justification for the war had evaporated.

REBUILDING IRAQ It proved far easier to win the brief war than to rebuild Iraq in America's image. Unprepared U.S. officials faced the daunting task of installing a democratic government in a nation fractured by religious feuds and ethnic tensions made worse by the breakdown in law and order caused by the allied invasion. The successful invasion triggered a vicious civil war in Iraq and the disintegration of law and order. Looting and violence engulfed the war-torn country, large parts of which fell under the control of warlords and criminal gangs. In the process, the entire Middle East, already volatile, was further destabilized.

Within weeks, vengeful Islamic radicals streamed into the crippled nation to wage a merciless campaign of terror, sabotage, and suicide bombings against the U.S. forces. Bush's macho reaction to the insurgency—"Bring 'em on!"—revealed how uninformed he was about the fast-deteriorating situation. The leader of the new Iraqi government, Prime Minister Nourial-Maliki, quickly imposed his own authoritarian, Shiite-dominated regime which discriminated against the Sunnis, the Kurds, and other ethnic and religious minorities.

Defense Secretary Rumsfeld greatly underestimated the difficulty and expense of occupying, pacifying, and reconstructing postwar Iraq. By the fall of 2003, Bush admitted that substantial numbers of American troops (around 150,000) would have to remain in Iraq much longer than anticipated. He also said that rebuilding Iraq would take years and cost almost a *trillion* dollars. Investigative reporter James Fallows concluded that the U.S. "occupation in Iraq is a debacle not because the government did no planning but because a vast amount of expert planning was willfully ignored by the people in charge."

Victory on the battlefields of Iraq did not bring victory in the "war on terrorism." Militant Islamist groups remained a global threat. Americans grew more and more dismayed as the number of casualties and the expense of the military occupation in Iraq soared. The nation became more alienated when journalists revealed graphic pictures of U.S. soldiers abusing and torturing Arab detainees in the Abu Ghraib prison near Baghdad. "When you lose the moral high ground," an army general sadly observed, "you lose it all."

President Bush urged Americans to "stay the course," insisting that a democratic Iraq would bring stability to the Middle East and thereby blunt the momentum of Islamic terrorism. Yet even though Saddam Hussein was captured in December 2003 and later hanged, Iraq seemed less secure than ever.

By the beginning of 2004, an estimated 1,000 Americans had died in the conflict, and more than 10,000 had been wounded. The ethnic and religious tensions only worsened as violent Sunni jihadists allied with al Qaeda to undermine the new Iraqi government and assault U.S. forces.

The U.S. effort in Iraq was the wrong war in the wrong place fought in the wrong way. It forced Bush to spend government funds at a rate faster than any president since Lyndon Johnson, and it distracted attention from the revival of the Taliban and other terrorist groups in Afghanistan. "We thank God for appeasing us with the [U.S.] dilemmas in Iraq and Afghanistan," snickered bin Laden's deputy, Ayman al-Zawahiri.

Freedom for whom? The American torture of Iraqis in Abu Ghraib prison only exacerbated the anger and humiliation that Iraqis experienced since the First Gulf War. In response to America's incessant promises of peace and autonomy, a Baghdad mural fires back: "That Freedom for B[u]sh."

THE ELECTION OF 2004 Growing public concern about Iraq complicated George W. Bush's campaign for a second presidential term in 2004. The Democratic nominee, Senator John Kerry of Massachusetts, condemned Bush for misleading the nation about weapons of mass destruction and for his slipshod handling of the reconstruction of postwar Iraq. Kerry also highlighted the Bush administration's record budget deficits. Bush countered that the tortuous efforts to create a democratic government in Iraq would enhance America's long-term security.

On Election Day, November 2, 2004, exit polls suggested a Kerry victory, but in the end the election hinged on the crucial swing state of Ohio. No Republican had ever lost Ohio and won the presidency. Despite early returns indicating a Kerry victory in Ohio, late returns tipped the balance toward Bush, even as rumors of electoral "irregularities" began to circulate. Nevertheless, Kerry conceded the election. "The outcome," he stressed, "should be decided by voters, not a protracted legal battle."

By narrowly winning Ohio, Bush captured 286 electoral votes to Kerry's 251. Yet in some respects, the election was not so close. Bush received 3.5 million more votes nationwide than Kerry, and Republicans increased their majorities in both houses of Congress. A reelected Bush pledged to bring democracy

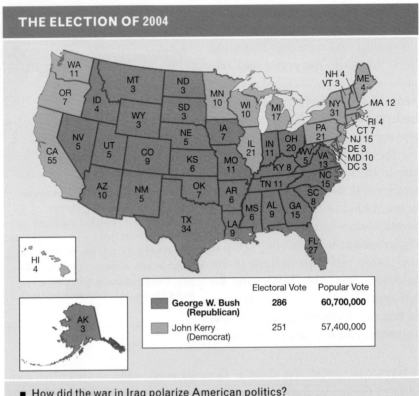

THE ELECTION OF 2004

	Electoral Vote	Popular Vote
George W. Bush (Republican)	286	60,700,000
John Kerry (Democrat)	251	57,400,000

- How did the war in Iraq polarize American politics?
- In what ways did the election of 2004 give Republicans a mandate for change?

and stability to Iraq, trim the federal deficit, pass a major energy bill, create more jobs, and "privatize" Social Security funds by investing them in the stock market. "I earned capital in the campaign, political capital, and now I intend to spend it," he told reporters.

SECOND-TERM BLUES

George Bush's second term was beset by thorny political problems, a sluggish economy, and continuing turmoil in Iraq. In 2005, he pushed through Congress an energy bill and a Central American Free Trade Act. But his effort to privatize Social Security retirement accounts by enabling individuals to invest their accumulated pension dollars themselves went nowhere, and soaring budget deficits made many fiscal conservatives feel betrayed by the supposedly "conservative" Bush. The editors of the *Economist*, an influential conservative newsmagazine, declared that Bush had become "the least popular re-elected president since Richard Nixon."

HURRICANE KATRINA In 2005, President Bush's eroding public support suffered another blow. In late August, a killer hurricane named Katrina slammed into the Gulf coast, devastating large areas of Alabama, Mississippi, and Louisiana. Katrina left more than 1,000 dead and millions homeless and hopeless, especially in New Orleans. Local officials and the Federal Emergency Management Agency (FEMA) were caught unprepared as the catastrophe unfolded, and confusion and incompetence abounded. In the face of blistering criticism, Bush accepted responsibility for the balky federal response and accepted the resignation of the FEMA director. Rebuilding the Gulf coast would take a long time and a lot of money.

The backlash over the federal response to Katrina contributed to a devastating defeat for Republicans in the November 2006 congressional elections. The Democrats capitalized on widespread public disapproval of the Bush administration to win control of the House of Representatives, the Senate, and a majority of governorships and state legislatures. Former Texas Republican congressman Dick Armey said that "the Republican Revolution of 1994 offi-

The aftermath of Hurricane Katrina Two men use boards to paddle through high water in flood-devastated New Orleans.

cially ended" with the 2006 election. The transformational election also included a significant milestone: Californian Nancy Pelosi, the leader of the Democrats in the House of Representatives, became the highest-ranking woman in the history of the U.S. Congress upon her election as House Speaker in January 2007.

THE "SURGE" IN IRAQ   George W. Bush bore the brunt of public indignation over the bungled federal response to the Katrina disaster and the costs and casualties of the war in Iraq. The Iraq Study Group, a bipartisan task force appointed by the president, issued a report recommending the withdrawal of combat forces from a "grave and deteriorating Iraq" by the spring of 2008.

Bush disagreed with those who urged a phased withdrawal. On January 10, 2007, he announced that he was sending a "surge" of 20,000 (eventually 30,000) more troops to Iraq, bringing the total to almost 170,000. From a military perspective, the "surge" succeeded. By the fall of 2008, violence in Iraq had declined dramatically, and the Iraqi government had grown in stature and confidence. The U.S. general who masterminded the increase in troops admitted that the gains were "fragile and reversible," however, and as the number of U.S. combat deaths in Iraq passed 4,000, Bush acknowledged that the conflict was "longer and harder and more costly than we anticipated." By 2008, more than 60 percent of Americans said that the war had been a mistake.

ECONOMIC SHOCK   After the intense but brief 2001 recession, the boom/bust capitalist economy had begun another period of prolonged expansion. Between 1997 and 2006, home prices in the United States, especially in the fast-growing sunbelt states, rose 85 percent, leading to a frenzy of irresponsible mortgage lending—and a debt-financed consumer spending spree. Tens of millions of people bought houses they could not afford, refinanced their mortgages, or tapped home-equity loans to make discretionary purchases. The irrational confidence in soaring housing prices also led government regulatory agencies and mortgage lenders to ease credit restrictions so that unqualified people could buy homes without making any down payments.

The housing bubble burst in 2007, when home values and sales began a sharp decline. The loss of trillions of dollars in home values set off a seismic shock across the economy, as record numbers of borrowers defaulted on their mortgage payments. Foreclosures and bankruptcies soared, and banks lost billions, first on the shaky mortgages, then on most other categories of overleveraged debt: credit cards, car loans, student loans, and commercial mortgage-backed securities.

The sudden contraction of corporate spending and consumer purchases pushed the economy into a deep recession in 2008. Some of the nation's largest banks, investment firms, and insurance companies went belly up. The price of food and gasoline spiked, and unemployment soared. What had begun as a sharp decline in home prices became a global economic meltdown.

The crisis demanded decisive action. On October 3, 2008, President Bush signed into law the Troubled Asset Relief Program (TARP), which called for the Treasury Department to spend $700 billion to keep big banks and other large financial institutions afloat. Yet the passage of the bill did little to restore confidence in the economy as a whole. In early October, stock markets around the world began to crash with the onset of what came to be called the **Great Recession**, which technically lasted from December 2007 to January 2009 and forced almost 9 million people out of work. Its effects would linger, however, and the economic recovery that began in June 2009 would be the weakest since the end of the Second World War.

The Great Recession had powerful political effects. Bush, who as governor of Texas had described himself as "a uniter, not a divider," became one of the least popular and most divisive presidents in American history. Just 29 percent of voters "approved" of his leadership, and more than 80 percent said that the nation was headed in the "wrong direction."

A Historic New Presidency

George Bush's unpopularity excited Democrats about regaining the White House in 2008. The early front-runner for the nomination was New York senator Hillary Rodham Clinton, the spouse of ex-president Bill Clinton. Like her husband, she displayed an impressive command of policy issues and mobilized a well-funded campaign team. And, as the first woman with a serious chance of gaining the presidency, she had widespread support among voters eager for female leadership.

In the end, however, an overconfident Clinton was upset in the Democratic primaries and caucuses by Barack Obama of Illinois, a little-known first-term senator. Young, handsome, and intelligent, a vibrant mixture of idealism and pragmatism, coolness and passion, Obama was an inspiring speaker

The Clinton campaign Democratic presidential candidate Senator Hillary Rodham Clinton speaks at a rally in Fort Worth, Texas.

Barack Obama The president-elect and his family wave to supporters in Chicago's Grant Park.

who attracted huge crowds by promising a "politics of hope." He mounted an innovative Internet-based campaign directed at grassroots voters, donors, and volunteers. In early June 2008, he gained enough delegates to secure the nomination, with Senator Joseph Biden of Delaware as his running mate.

Obama was the first African American presidential nominee of either party, the gifted biracial son of a white mother from Kansas and a black father from Kenya who left the household and returned to Africa when Barack was a toddler. Obama eventually graduated from Columbia University before earning a law degree from Harvard. The forty-seven-year-old senator presented himself as a deal maker who could inspire, unite, and forge bipartisan collaborations. He and his strategists were able to turn his vitality and political inexperience into strengths at a time when voter disgust with politics was widespread. By contrast, his Republican opponent, seventy-two-year-old Arizona senator John McCain, was the oldest presidential candidate in history.

On November 4, 2008, Barack Obama made history by becoming the first person of color to be elected president. He won the popular vote by 53 percent to 46 percent, and the electoral college 365 to 173. Obama also helped the Democrats win solid majorities in both houses of Congress.

Within days of his victory, Obama adopted a bipartisan approach in selecting his new cabinet members. He appointed Hillary Clinton secretary of state, retained Republican Robert Gates as secretary of defense, selected retired general James Jones, who had campaigned for McCain, as his national security adviser, and appointed Eric Holder as the nation's first African American attorney general. But picking a bipartisan cabinet proved easier than forging a bipartisan presidency.

OBAMA'S FIRST TERM President Obama and his administration inherited two unpopular wars and the worst economic situation in eighty years. His most pressing challenge was to keep the Great Recession from becoming a prolonged depression. Unemployment in early 2009 had passed

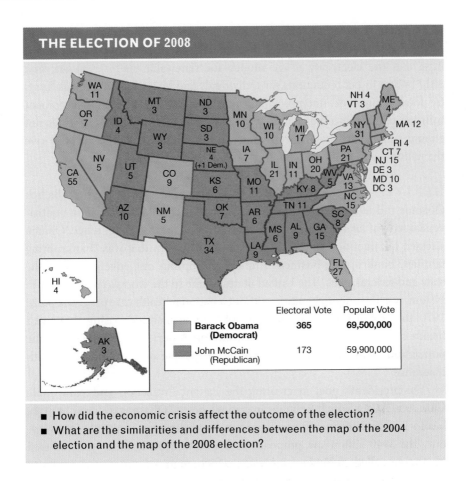

THE ELECTION OF 2008

	Electoral Vote	Popular Vote
Barack Obama (Democrat)	365	69,500,000
John McCain (Republican)	173	59,900,000

■ How did the economic crisis affect the outcome of the election?
■ What are the similarities and differences between the map of the 2004 election and the map of the 2008 election?

8 percent and was still rising. The financial sector remained paralyzed, and public confidence had plummeted.

To enable banks to start lending again, the new administration continued the TARP program that provided massive government bailouts to the largest banks and financial institutions. The bailouts were attacked by both the Left and the Right as deeply unfair to most struggling Americans. Treasury secretary Timothy Geithner later explained, "We had to do whatever we could to help people feel their money was safe in the [banking] system, even if it made us unpopular." Had they not saved the big banks, Obama and Geithner argued, the economy would have crashed.

Preserving the banking system did not create many jobs, however. To do so, in mid-February 2009, Congress passed, and Obama signed, an $832 billion economic-stimulus bill called the American Recovery and Reinvestment

Act. The bill included cash distributions to states for construction projects to renew the nation's infrastructure (roads, bridges, levees, government buildings, and the electricity grid), money for renewable-energy systems, and $212 billion in tax reductions for individuals and businesses, as well as funds for food stamps and unemployment benefits. It was the largest government infusion of cash into the economy in history. In the end, however, it was not enough to generate a robust economic recovery, but Obama's actions did save the nation—and the world economy—from a financial meltdown.

HEALTH CARE REFORM The economic crisis merited Barack Obama's full attention, but he chose as his top legislative priority a controversial federal health insurance program. From his first day in office, Obama stressed his intention to reform a health care system that was "bankrupting families, bankrupting businesses, and bankrupting our government at the state and federal level." The United States, home to the world's costliest health system, was the only rich nation without a national health care program. Since 1970, the proportion of uninsured people had been steadily rising along with health care costs. In 2010, roughly 50 million Americans (16 percent of the population), most of them poor, young, or people of color, had no health insurance.

The president's goal in creating the Patient Protection and **Affordable Care Act (ACA)**, which Republican critics labeled "**Obamacare**," was to make health insurance more affordable and make health care accessible for everyone. The $940 billion law, proposed in 2009 and debated for a year, centered on the so-called *individual mandate*, which required uninsured adults to purchase an approved *private* insurance policy made available through state-run exchanges (websites where people could shop for insurance) or pay a tax penalty. Lower-income Americans could receive federal subsidies to help pay for their coverage, and insurance companies could no longer deny coverage to people with preexisting illnesses. Employers who did not offer health insurance would have to pay higher taxes, and drug companies and manufacturers of medical devices would have to pay annual government fees. Everyone, but especially the wealthy, would pay higher Medicare payroll taxes to help fund the changes.

The individual mandate was designed to ensure that all Americans had health insurance so as to reduce the skyrocketing costs of hospitals providing "charity care" for the uninsured. The ACA did not change the American tradition of employment-based health insurance provided by private companies. But the idea of *forcing* people to buy health insurance flew in the face of such ideals as individual freedom and personal responsibility. Critics questioned not only the individual mandate but the administration's projections that the program would reduce federal expenditures over the long haul.

Republicans mobilized to defeat the ACA. "If we're able to stop Obama on this it will be his Waterloo. It will break him," predicted South Carolina senator Jim DeMint. Despite heated opposition, however, the ACA passed with narrow party-line majorities in both houses of Congress. Obama signed it into law on March 23, 2010. Its complex provisions, to be implemented over a four-year period, would bring health insurance to 32 million people, half of whom would be covered by expanded Medicaid and the other half by the individual mandate. In its scope and goals, the ACA was a landmark in the history of health and social welfare—as well as the expansion of the federal government.

OBAMACARE AND THE COURTS No sooner had President Obama pushed his health care plan through Congress than Republicans began challenging its constitutionality. On June 28, 2012, in the case of *National Federation of Independent Business v. Sebelius,* the Supreme Court surprised observers by ruling 5–4 that most of the new law was constitutional. Even more surprising was that the chief justice, John G. Roberts, a philosophical conservative who had never before voted with the four "liberal" justices on the Court, cast the deciding vote. Roberts upheld the ACA's individual mandate that required people to buy private health insurance or pay a tax, arguing that it was within Congress's power to impose taxes as outlined in Article 1 of the Constitution. Many conservatives, including the four dissenting justices, felt betrayed. The verdict led the *New York Times* to predict that the ruling "may secure Obama's place in history."

Foreign Affairs

President Obama had more success in dealing with foreign affairs than in reviving the American economy. What journalists came to call the Obama Doctrine was very much like the Nixon Doctrine (1970), stressing that the United States could not continue to be the world's principal policeman. Yet the fate of America's economy and security was entangled more than ever with the fate of an unstable and often violent world.

THE OBAMA DOCTRINE The loosely defined Obama Doctrine grew out of efforts to end the expensive wars in Iraq and Afghanistan. In essence, the president wanted to replace confrontation and military intervention with a stance of cooperation and negotiation. The president told administration officials that his doctrine could be summed up in the phrase, "Don't do stupid stuff." On February 27, 2009, Obama announced that all 142,000 U.S. troops would be withdrawn from Iraq by the end of 2011, as the Iraqi government and the Bush administration had agreed in 2008. True to his word, the last U.S. combat troops left Iraq in December 2011.

Their departure marked the end of a bitterly divisive war that had raged for nearly nine years, killed more than 110,000 Iraqis, and left the nation shattered and unstable, despite Obama's claim that the departing U.S. forces were "leaving behind a sovereign, stable, and self-reliant Iraq with a representative government."

The war had cost more than 4,500 American lives, 30,000 wounded (many grievously so), and $2 trillion. Perhaps the greatest embarrassment was that the Iraqi government the United States left behind was inept and not even friendly to American interests. The long and chaotic war was an expensive mistake and a prolonged distraction for the government, the military, and the nation. As it turned out, there were no weapons of mass destruction, nor was there a direct link between the al Qaeda terrorists and Saddam Hussein. Al Qaeda, in fact, did not arrive in Iraq until *after* the American invasion. "The first Iraq war, in which I led a tank platoon, was necessary," said John Nagel, a retired army officer. "This one was not."

American efforts at nation building had failed. In June 2014, a journalist said that "it was time to admit that we cannot force a pluralistic society" on a dysfunctional Iraq torn by sectarian and ethnic violence into three rival regional states: one Shiite, one Sunni ("governed" by jihadists), and one Kurdish. Even Leon Panetta, who served as CIA director and secretary of defense under Obama, scolded the president for being so eager to withdraw U.S. forces that he failed to create the circumstances "that would preserve our influence and interests" in Iraq. Obama's hopes that the United States could get out of fighting wars in the Middle East and that the Iraqis could sustain a stable and secure government in the face of terrorist incursions and sectarian fighting proved to be fantasies. Iraq's woeful self-government and the fractious nation's constant sectarian strife and disorder required continued infusions of U.S. military assistance, daily bombing raids, and massive economic aid.

"SURGE" IN AFGHANISTAN   At the same time that President Obama was ending U.S. military involvement in Iraq, he dispatched 21,000 additional troops to Afghanistan in what was called a "surge." While doing so, however, he narrowed the focus of the U.S. mission to suppressing terrorists rather than transforming strife-torn Afghanistan into a stable capitalist democracy.

The surge worked. By the summer of 2011, Obama announced that the "tide of war was receding" and that the United States had largely achieved its goals in Afghanistan, setting in motion a substantial withdrawal of forces that lasted until 2014. Obama stressed that the Afghans must determine their country's future stability. "We will not try to make Afghanistan a perfect place," he said. "We will not police its streets or patrol its mountains indefinitely. That is the responsibility of the Afghan government." In the thirteen years since its 2001 invasion of Afghanistan, America had spent more than a trillion dollars there and lost 2,300 servicemen.

THE DEATH OF OSAMA BIN LADEN The crowning achievement of President Obama's anti-terrorism efforts was the discovery, at long last, of Osama bin Laden's hideout. Ever since the attacks of 9/11, bin Laden had eluded an intensive manhunt. In August 2010, however, U.S. intelligence analysts discovered his sanctuary in a walled residential compound outside of Abbottabad, Pakistan. On May 1, 2011, Obama authorized a daring night raid by a U.S. Navy SEAL team transported by helicopters from Afghanistan. After a brief firefight, the SEALs killed bin Laden. His death was a watershed moment, but it did not spell the end of Islamist terrorism.

THE "ARAB AWAKENING" In late 2010 and early 2011, spontaneous democratic uprisings erupted throughout much of the Arab world as long-oppressed peoples rose up against authoritarian regimes. Corrupt tyrants were forced out of power by a new generation of young activists inspired by democratic ideals and connected by social media on the Internet. What was soon dubbed "the Arab Awakening" sent waves of youthful unrest across Tunisia, Algeria, Bahrain, Jordan, Morocco, Egypt, Oman, Yemen, Libya, Saudi Arabia, and Syria during what came to be called the Arab Spring of 2011. Dictators were toppled while democracy was embraced as the remarkable uprisings heralded a new era in the history of the Middle East. Yet the heroic days of revolutionary idealism soon gave way to the harsh

Arab Awakening Thousands of protesters converge in Cairo's Tahrir Square to call for an end to Mubarak's rule.

reality that the rebels were so busy fighting among each other that they could not forge unified political alternatives. Building new democratic governments proved much harder than expected. The grassroots revolutionary movements in most Arab nations stumbled and stalled by 2014. Egypt reverted to an authoritarianism even harsher than that in place before the Arab Spring. Libya lapsed into chaos and Yemen exploded in civil war.

THE CUBAN THAW At the end of 2014, President Obama surprised the world by announcing that the United States and Cuba were going to restore normal relations after more than fifty years of bitter hostility. As a first step, Obama relaxed restrictions on American tourists visiting Cuba. Six months later, in mid-2015, the two nations took a much more substantial step toward normalization when they reestablished embassies in each other's capital cities. The bold move was controversial, however. The powerful Cuban community in south Florida fiercely criticized Obama's decision, and Congressional Republicans threatened to block the appointment of a U.S. ambassador to Cuba because of its communist government. But the president persisted in his efforts, insisting that isolating Cuba had not worked. "Americans and Cubans alike are ready to move forward," he said in July 2015. "I believe it's time for Congress to do the same."

POLARIZED POLITICS

Barack Obama had campaigned in 2008 on the promise of bringing dramatic change to the federal government in a way that would reduce the partisan warfare between the two national parties. By the end of his first year in office, however, a Gallup poll found that he had become the most polarizing president in modern history. In part, the widening partisan divide resulted from Obama's aloof presidential style. Like Jimmy Carter, he does not like to lobby and horse-trade his way to legislative approval. Even Democrats criticized his growing "aloofness" from the messy business of working with legislators. Yet the standoff with Congress was not solely his fault. His Republican opponents had no interest in negotiating with him, and American political culture had become so polarized that it resembled two separate nations. Each party had its own cable-news station and rabidly partisan commentators, its own newspapers, its own think tanks, and its own billionaire donors. Governing, Obama quickly discovered, is far more difficult than campaigning.

THE TEA PARTY No sooner was Barack Obama sworn in than anti-government conservatives mobilized against him and the "tax-and-spend" liberalism he represented in their eyes. In January 2009, a New York stock trader named Graham Makohoniuk sent an e-mail message urging people to send tea bags to their congressional representatives to symbolize the Boston Tea Party of 1773, when American colonists protested against British tax policies.

Within a year or so, the tax revolt had become a national **Tea Party** movement, with groups in all fifty states. The Tea Party is not so much a cohesive political organization as it is a mood, an attitude, and an ideology, a diverse collection of self-described "disaffected," "angry," and "very conservative" activists, mostly white, male, married, middle-class Republicans over forty-five.

To the anti-tax rebels, the federal bailouts ordered by Presidents Bush and Obama in the wake of the 2008 economic meltdown were a form of "crony capitalism" whereby the "elite" rewarded the big companies that had funded their campaigns. Tea Party members demanded a radically smaller federal government (although most of them supported Social Security and Medicare, the two most expensive federal social programs). Democrats, including Obama, initially dismissed the Tea Party as a fringe group, but the 2010 election results proved them wrong.

Democratic House and Senate candidates (as well as moderate Republicans), including many long-serving leaders, were defeated in droves when conservative Republicans, many of them aligned with the Tea Party, gained sixty-three seats to recapture control of the House of Representatives. They won a near majority in the Senate as well. It was the most lopsided midterm election since 1938. Thereafter, the bickering between both parties prevented meaningful action on the languishing economy, chronic joblessness, and the runaway federal budget deficit. Neither party wanted to negotiate or compromise.

OCCUPY WALL STREET The emergence of the Tea Party was mirrored on the left by the Occupy Wall Street (OWS) movement, mobilized in the fall of 2011 when a call went out over the Internet to "Occupy Wall Street. Bring tent." Dozens, then hundreds, then thousands of people, many of them unemployed young adults, converged on Zuccotti Park in lower Manhattan. They formed tent villages and gathered to "occupy" Wall Street, protesting the "tyrannical" power of major banks and investment companies.

The protesters described themselves as the voice of the 99 percent of Americans who were being victimized by the 1 percent—the wealthiest and most politically connected Americans. Unlike the Tea Party, however, OWS did not have staying power. Within a year, its energies and visibility had waned, in part because of mass arrests, in part because it was an intentionally "leaderless" movement more interested in saying what it was *against* than explaining what it was *for*.

Bold Decisions

For all of the political sniping, however, attitudes toward "hot-button" cultural values were slowly changing. In December 2010, Congress repealed the "don't ask, don't tell" (DADT) military policy that, since 1993, had resulted in some 9,500 gay men and women being discharged from the armed forces. A year later, a report by army officers concluded that the repeal "had no overall negative impact on military readiness or its component dimensions, including cohesion, recruitment, retention, assaults, harassment, or morale."

GAY MARRIAGE In May 2012, President Obama became the first sitting president to support the right of gay and lesbian couples to marry. That his statement came a day after the North Carolina legislature voted to ban all rights for gay couples illustrated how incendiary the issue was. While asserting that it was the "right" thing to do, Obama knew that endorsing **same-sex marriage** had powerful political implications. The gay community would play an energetic role in the 2012 presidential election, and the youth vote—the under-thirty electorate who most supported gay marriage—would be crucial. No sooner had Obama made his announcement than polls showed that American voters for the first time were evenly split on the charged issue, with Democrats and independent voters providing the bulk of support for same-sex marriage.

THE DREAM ACT In June 2012, Obama again made waves by issuing an executive order (soon labeled the DREAM Act) that allowed 1.5 million undocumented immigrants who had been brought to the United States as children to remain as citizens. His unanticipated decision thrilled Hispanic supporters who had lost heart over his failure to convince Congress to support more-comprehensive immigration reform. Congressional Republicans steadfastly opposed giving the estimated 12 million undocumented immigrants, 80 percent of whom were Latinos, a "pathway to citizenship" without first ensuring that the border with Mexico was secured.

The DREAM Act, however, had unexpected consequences. It excited masses of Central Americans willing to endure enormous risks to live in America. Panicked parents in El Salvador, Guatemala, and Honduras, worried about widespread drug-related gang violence, started sending their children through Mexico to the United States in hopes of connecting with relatives and being granted citizenship. During 2014, some 57,000 young migrants were caught along the nearly 2,000-mile-long border with Mexico, and communities across the nation rushed to find families to "sponsor" the unaccompanied children.

At the same time, the Obama administration was deporting record numbers of undocumented immigrants (more than 2 million by the end of 2014),

Refugees from gangland Braving hundreds of miles on foot, children from Honduras and El Salvador are sent off by their parents for a better life in the United States, away from the drug-dealing violence of Central America. Here, border guards stop a group of child refugees in Granjeno, Texas.

some of whom had been working in the nation for decades, in what was called the "great expulsion." Obama, called the "Deporter in Chief" by critics, claimed that he was only following the laws written by anti-immigration Republicans. Others suggested that the harsh deportation policy was part of Obama's "grand strategy" to force Congress to pass a comprehensive immigration reform bill. Either way, the immigrants were caught in the middle.

THE SUPREME COURT IN THE TWENTY-FIRST CENTURY
The Supreme Court surprised observers in 2013 by overturning the Defense of Marriage Act (DOMA) of 1996, which had denied gay and lesbian couples who married in states allowing such unions the right to federal benefits. In *United States v. Windsor* (2013), the Court voted 5–4 that the federal government could not withhold spousal benefits from same-sex couples who had been legally married. While restoring federal benefits, the Court did not rule that same-sex marriage was a *right* guaranteed under the Constitution. The issue would have to be resolved by a future U.S. Supreme Court decision, scheduled for the summer of 2015. In the meantime, each state could decide whether to allow such marriages. During 2014, however, federal courts repeatedly overturned state laws banning same-sex marriages, arguing that the right to marry *was* guaranteed by the Constitution.

While the Court disappointed social conservatives with its *Windsor* decision, its five conservative justices continued to make rulings intended to restrict the powers of the federal government. In June 2013, in *Shelby County v. Holder* (2013), the Court gutted key provisions of the 1965 Voting Rights Act (VRA), which had outlawed discrimination directed toward voters "on account of race or color." The majority opinion declared that in five of the six southern states originally covered by the VRA, black voter turnout now exceeded white turnout.

To the judges, this seemed to prove that there was no evidence of continuing racial discrimination. Today's laws "must be justified by current needs," Chief Justice John Roberts wrote. Soon after the Court's ruling, counties and states in the South pushed through new laws that had the effect of making it more difficult for minorities and poor people to vote by reducing voting hours or requiring that driver's licenses be shown on voting days.

THE 2012 ELECTION As the November 2012 presidential election approached, one thing was certain: it would be the most expensive election ever, in part because the Supreme Court ruled in *Citizens United v. Federal Elections Committee* (2010) that corporations could spend as much as they wanted in support of candidates.

After a divisive battle in the primaries, Mitt Romney, a former corporate executive and Massachusetts governor, won the Republican nomination. The main question for Romney was whether the still-powerful religious Right would allow him to sidestep tough social issues; the question for President Obama was whether he could sidestep his failure to restore prosperity.

Two factors injured Romney's candidacy toward the end of the most expensive campaign in history ($6 billion). The first was his decision to please right-wing voters by opposing immigration reforms that might allow undocumented immigrants a pathway to citizenship. The second was the disclosure that he had privately told a group of wealthy contributors that he "did not care" about the 47 percent of Americans who failed "to take personal responsibility and care for their lives." It was not his job "to worry about" those who did not pay federal income taxes because they were dependent on federal government programs. The Obama campaign seized on the impolitic statement and demonized the wealthy Romney as an uncaring elitist. On Election Day, Obama won with 66 million votes to Romney's 61 million, and 332 electoral votes to 206.

Nearly 60 percent of white voters chose Romney. But the nation's fastest growing groups—Hispanics, Asian Americans, and African Americans—voted overwhelmingly for Obama, as did college-educated women. David Frum, a prominent Republican speechwriter and columnist, confessed that his party was becoming "increasingly isolated and estranged from modern America."

Obama began his second term on an assertive note. In January 2013, the Defense Department lifted its ban on women serving in combat. The following month, Obama announced that more U.S. troops would be withdrawn from Afghanistan over the next year, leaving 34,000 by early 2014. It had become America's longest war.

OBAMACARE ON THE DEFENSIVE President Obama's proudest achievement, the Affordable Care Act, was so massive in its scope and complicated in its implementation that it took four years before it was ready to "roll out." In the fall of 2013, the federal online health insurance "exchange," where people without insurance could sign up, opened with great fanfare. Obama assured Americans that using the online registration system would be "real simple." It was not. On October 1, millions tried to sign up; only *six* succeeded. As it turned out, the website had never been properly tested, and it was hobbled with technical glitches. It also became evident that Obama had misled the nation about key elements of the plan. In campaigning for its passage in 2010, he had repeatedly told voters that if they liked their current health insurance plan, they could, under Obamacare, "keep that insurance. Period. End of story." As it turned out, however, many had their policies canceled by insurers.

Congressional Republicans, as well as many Democrats, condemned the president for his misleading statements and inept management of his signature program. During the winter of 2013–2014, the Republican-led House of Representatives repeatedly tried—and failed—to overturn the ACA, at one point passing a budget that would have stripped the program of funding. When the president refused to sign the bill, the federal government (some 800,000 employees) shut down after the existing budget expired on September 30. For sixteen days, every nonessential federal agency was closed, costing the government $2 billion.

The Republicans' shutdown strategy failed, however, as it had in 1995, when citizen outrage was directed not at President Clinton, but at Republican legislators. In response to widespread criticism and the threat of global economic repercussions, House Republicans on October 16 passed a revised, Senate-approved budget that removed the anti-ACA provision. Democrats had little time to celebrate, however. By November 2013, some 57 percent of voters said they opposed Obamacare, in part because the program benefited only a quarter of the population—the uninsured and the underinsured.

Eventually, the ACA website was fixed, and by August 2014, more than 9 million people, well above the original target number, had signed up for health insurance. "The Affordable Care Act is here to stay," Obama said. But even though the sign-up system was fixed, public perception of the government's ability to manage the program never recovered.

New Global Challenges in an Age of Insecurity

In 2013, the United States held its first high-level talks with Iran since 1979, when Iranian militants took U.S. embassy employees in Tehran hostage. On November 23, Secretary of State John Kerry reached a multinational agreement with Iran to scale back its nuclear development program for six months as a first step toward a more comprehensive agreement not to develop nuclear weapons.

At the same time, an increasingly bloody civil war in Syria that had claimed 150,000 lives was beginning to have major international repercussions. In 2013, U.S. intelligence analysts confirmed that the Syrian government, ruled with an iron fist by Bashar al-Assad, on August 21 had used chemical weapons to kill 1,400 people, many of them children.

President Obama had repeatedly warned that such use of weapons of mass destruction was a "red line" that would trigger international military intervention. In late August, he (and the French government) hesitantly began preparing for a military strike, although Congress and most Americans opposed such action. It appeared that Obama had gotten cold feet about a military intervention. His former secretary of defense, Leon Panetta, argued that Obama's failure to follow through on his threat "was a blow to American credibility. When the president as commander in chief draws a red line, it is critical that he act if the line is crossed."

On September 9, Secretary of State Kerry defused the crisis by signing an agreement with Russia to dispose of Syria's chemical weapons. By the end of October, all the chemical weapon stockpiles had been destroyed or dismantled, but the civil war raged on.

UKRAINE As the Syrian civil war continued, a civil uprising occurred in Ukraine, the former Soviet republic of 46 million people that had gained its independence in 1991. For nearly a quarter of a century, Russian president Vladimir Putin had viewed the disintegration of the Soviet Union as the "greatest geopolitical catastrophe of the century." To restore Russian influence and divide NATO and the European Union, he had exerted economic and political pressure on the republics of the former Soviet Union.

On February 27, Putin sent troops into the Crimea, a part of Ukraine along the Black Sea long claimed by Russia. A week later, the Crimean parliament voted to become part of the Russian Federation. Putin, claiming that Crimea had "always been an inseparable part of Russia," quickly made the illegal annexation official by positioning Russian troops there, while denying their presence.

In response, the United States and the European Union hurriedly organized diplomatic efforts to "de-escalate the crisis." They refused to recognize

Civil war in Ukraine A protester in the Ukrainian capital of Kiev throws a Molotov cocktail during violent clashes with police on January 22, 2014. A month later, Russian President Vladimir Putin would use the unrest as an excuse to seize control of the Crimean region.

the legitimacy of the annexation of Crimea and announced economic sanctions against Russia while pledging financial assistance to Ukraine. "If Russia continues to interfere in Ukraine, we stand ready to impose further sanctions," Obama said. By a vote of 100–11, the United Nations General Assembly also opposed the annexation.

In April 2014, heavily armed pro-Russian separatists, as many as a third of whom were Russian soldiers and agents, seized control of several cities in eastern Ukraine. They declared a "people's republic" and called for secession.

Pressure mounted to impose even more sanctions when a Malaysian passenger jet flying across eastern Ukraine was shot down by a Russian-made rocket in July 2014, killing all 298 on board. The United States and its allies slammed Russia with more economic sanctions, but the coldly calculating Putin showed no sign of backing away. In fact, his popularity in Russia had soared, leaving the United States once again in the position of containing Russia's expansionist ambitions.

THE BURDENS OF LEADERSHIP Rarely are presidents more popular than on their first day in office. To govern is to make decisions, and decisions in democratic nations inevitably produce disappointments, disagreements, and criticism. During his presidency, Barack Obama has discovered how hard it is to lead the world's economic and military superpower in the post–cold war era. He has struggled to stabilize a cluster of unstable nations—Iraq, Afghanistan, Libya, Ukraine, and Syria—that craved U.S. resources but resented American meddling.

Overall, Obama adopted a posture of restraint in world affairs. He was determined to "avoid stupid errors," wind down the wars in Iraq and Afghanistan, stay aloof from the Arab Awakening, and reduce the use of U.S. military power abroad so as to concentrate on issues at home.

Yet he and others were naive to think that the United States could avoid the burdens of being the only superpower in a post-cold war world of growing anarchy and violence. There is no diplomatic solution to be found for groups seeking the total destruction of the American and European democracies.

ISLAMISTS ON THE MOVE Unexpected events overseas during the summer of 2014 gave Obama the opportunity to take decisive action. In June, the volatile Middle East took a sudden turn for the worse when Sunni jihadists who had been fighting in Syria invaded northern Iraq and announced the creation of their own nation (caliphate), called the Islamic State (ISIS). With lightning speed, the Islamic State emerged as the largest, best-financed, most heavily-armed, and most brutal of the many jihadist terrorist groups, financing its far-flung operations and 40,000 fanatical fighters by selling captured oil and ransoming hostages.

ISIS was both the culmination of decades of Arab Islamist rage against Europe and the United States and the collapse of effective government and security in Syria and Iraq. Once American forces left Iraq and Sunnis grew frustrated with the Shia-dominated government, ISIS swept in, setting off a panic that helped topple the government. In the areas it captured, ISIS established its own tyrannical form of government based on what it called the "management of savagery."

In the face of the ISIS advance, many Iraqi government soldiers that the United States had spent billions of dollars training and equipping fled, leaving their valuable weapons and vehicles. Sadistic ISIS fighters seized huge tracts of territory in Syria and Iraq while enslaving, terrorizing, raping, massacring, crucifying, or beheading thousands of men, women, and children who in some way fell short of their ruthless version of the Sunni faith. In August 2014, after ISIS terrorists gruesomely beheaded two captured Americans, President Obama ordered "systematic" airstrikes, first in Iraq and later in Syria, to prevent genocide as ISIS fighters assaulted Christians, Yazidis, and Kurds in the region. Those airstrikes continue.

Obama pulled off a diplomatic coup by building a broad coalition of Arab and European partners, but U.S. warplanes bore the brunt of the action. Obama assured Americans that he would not "get dragged into another ground war," but the latest military intervention remained a bitter setback for a president committed to ending U.S. wars in the Middle East.

Obama characterized the effort to stop the vicious ISIS attacks as "American leadership at its best." Preventing genocide and deterring terrorists is not simply a burden of great power, he decided; it is a responsibility in an era burdened by constant warfare.

THE AGE OF GRIDLOCK

American politics has always been chaotic and combative; its raucous energy is one of its great strengths. During Barack Obama's two-term presidency, however, the emergence of the Tea Party and Occupy Wall Street symbolized how savage political combat had become. *Compromise* and *moderation* had become dirty words. The scorched-earth tactics of Republicans in Congress were designed to protect the political status quo. "We're the party of 'Hell, no!'" cried Sarah Palin, the former Republican governor of Alaska who had run for vice president alongside John McCain in 2008 before becoming the darling of the Tea Party.

Intense partisanship dominated the 2014 congressional elections, when Republicans gained nine Senate seats, giving them control of the Senate for the first time since 2006. They also strengthened their hold on the House, added governorships, and tightened their control of state legislatures. Republicans campaigned on a single theme: the "failure" of President Obama and the "disaster" of Obamacare. Kentucky senator Rand Paul vowed that he and his colleagues would send "the president bill after bill until he wearies of it," including renewed efforts to repeal Obamacare.

Political moderates became a dying breed. By late 2014, the percentage of voters who described themselves as liberals or conservatives had doubled since 1994, and more than twice as many Democratic and Republican voters as in 1994 had a "very unfavorable" view of the other party. Congress included mostly Republicans on the far right, Democrats on the far left, and hardly anyone in the middle. "That alignment," said Gerald Seib of the *Wall Street Journal*, created a Congress "that does less, and does it less well, than any time in memory."

By 2014, six years after taking office on the promise of "hope and change," President Obama had discovered how difficult it is to preside over a polarized nation, much less bring it together. "You know I love this job," Obama told an adviser early in his presidency. "I love diving into problems. But dealing with some of the people you have to deal with . . . wears you out."

In the final months of his presidency, Obama's greying hair and waning energy revealed a weariness that mirrored his public approval ratings, which were well below 50 percent. James Bennet, editor of the *Atlantic Monthly*, pointed out that every modern two-term president had experienced plummeting support. "If we weren't sick of the guy to start with, we certainly are by now. What once seemed like roguish charm, or bracing surety, or nuanced intelligence, has curdled into self-indulgence, or arrogance, or passivity."

Voters hoping for a more energetic and engaged Obama after his reelection were disappointed by what seemed to be his slow withdrawal from leadership. He seemed disheartened by the troubling "gap between the magnitude of our challenges and the smallness of our politics." Critics savaged him for playing golf more often than any president since Eisenhower. Even prominent Democrats joined in the attacks. A successful presidency, former secretary of state Hillary Clinton said, needed "organizing principles, and 'Don't do stupid stuff' is not an organizing principle."

Obama repeatedly blamed Republicans for stalemating his second term, but the president was not blameless. Cabinet member Leon Panetta stressed that Obama's "most conspicuous weakness" was "a frustrating reticence to engage his opponents and rally support for his cause." While acknowledging that the president was "supremely intelligent," Panetta added that Obama "avoids the battle, complains, and misses opportunities."

Obama was a talented man drawn to political power but frustrated by horse-trading politics, a leader eager to have power but increasingly reluctant to exercise it. To many Americans, his naturally cautious and careful approach to foreign policy came across as indecisive and weak, and his coolness smacked of aloofness. "George W. Bush was a leader who didn't like to think," said Ian Bremmer, an international consultant. "Barack Obama is a thinker who doesn't like to lead."

RENEWED ENERGY   Yet during the summer of 2015, in the sunset of his presidency, Obama regained his energy and momentum. While restoring normal relations with Cuba, he benefited from two surprising U.S. Supreme Court rulings in late June. For years, Republicans had waged all-out war on the Affordable Care Act ("Obamacare"). Unable to halt the implementation of the new program in Congress, the critics turned to the courts to challenge the "flawed" new health care law. In a surprising 6-3 decision in a case called *King v. Burwell*, the Supreme Court saved the controversial health care law that will define Obama's presidency for generations to come. Chief Justice Roberts explained in the majority opinion that some of the sloppy language in the original Congressional legislation should not be used to destroy the new program. "Congress passed the Affordable Care Act to improve health insurance markets, not to destroy them,"

Roberts stressed. "If at all possible, we must interpret the Act in a way that is consistent with the former, and avoids the latter." President Obama was overjoyed by the much-anticipated ruling. "Five years ago, after nearly a century of talk, decades of trying, a year of bipartisan debate, we finally declared that in America, health care is not a privilege for a few but a right for all," Obama said from the White House. "The Affordable Care Act is here to stay."

Then, just a day later, the U.S. Supreme Court issued another bombshell ruling when it announced a 5-4 decision in the *Obergefell v. Hodges* case, which banned states from preventing same-sex marriages. The landmark decision that same-sex couples had a constitutional right to marry infuriated the Religious Right. Rick Scarborough, a Baptist minister in Texas, vowed that he and others would "denounce this practice in our [religious] services, we will not teach it in our schools, we will refuse to officiate at this type of wedding, and we will not accept any encroachments on our First Amendment rights."

Yet the Supreme Court's affirmation of same-sex marriage reflected the profound change in public attitudes toward homosexual rights during the early twenty-first century. In 2008, presidential candidate Barack Obama had felt the need to disavow support for marriage equality. By 2012, he had reversed himself by embracing the right of same-sex marriage. His change of mind reflected a resurgent social transformation in American life. Cultural diversity, like Obamacare, was here to stay. Obama, for example, the nation's first African American president, had appointed two women to the U.S. Supreme Court, including the first Latina justice. He also ended the ban on open homosexuality in the military.

The unexpected momentum of the Court decisions in June 2015 bolstered Obama's efforts in another controversial arena: foreign policy. In his 2009 inaugural address, he had vowed to international enemies that "we will extend a hand if you are willing to unclench your fist." That effort finally paid off in 2015, not only with the normalizing of relations with Cuba but also when the United States and five other major world powers announced a draft treaty with Iran intended to thwart its efforts to develop a nuclear weapon. In exchange for ending the international trade embargo against Iran, the agreement called for the Iranians to dismantle much of their nuclear program and allow for international inspectors to confirm their actions. Obama warned Congressional critics that voting against such a treaty would mean "a greater chance of war in the Middle East."

A Fading American Dream?

When Barack Obama won the Democratic nomination for president in 2008, he and his supporters touted him as an uplifting example of the American Dream, a biracial man who had defied the odds and achieved great success.

His inspiring story echoed one of the most powerful themes in the nation's history: America as a mythic land of unique opportunities for people from around the world.

The ideal of equal opportunity has always been the engine of American distinctiveness. By the early twenty-first century, though, that ideal seemed increasingly out of reach to millions. The most striking change in modern life since the 1970s was the *widening* inequality of income and wealth. Modern America had become a tale of two very different societies in which "the rich get richer and the poor get poorer," to quote a famous song.

As Nobel Prize–winning economist Joseph Stiglitz said in 2012, "the United States has less equality of opportunity than almost any other advanced industrial country." The American dream of the poor having an equal chance to succeed, he said, was now more of a myth. Most of the economic benefits generated by the slow economic recovery under Obama were enjoyed by salaried executives and stockholders rather than the working and middle classes. Although unemployment dropped below 6 percent in 2015, wages had barely risen since 2007.

Between the end of the Second World War in 1945 and 1973, income inequality had narrowed as average wages rose and a growing majority of people achieved a middle-class standard of living. At the same time, governments, both state and federal, had expanded social-welfare programs for the most disadvantaged Americans. In 1979, the richest 1 percent, mostly people engaged in global investment, banking, and business, controlled 9 percent of the nation's total income. By 2014, they controlled more than 20 percent.

The 46 million Americans living *below* the official poverty line in 2014 ($11,702 annual income for an individual, $23,850 for a family of four) were the most in history. One of every five children lived in poverty. At the other extreme, corporate executives were reaping an ever-higher percentage of national wealth. In 1993, the disparity in pay between corporate leaders and the average U.S. worker was 195 to 1; in 2012, it was 360 to 1. "Increasingly," journalist Hedrick Smith reported in 2012, America is becoming a society in which "privilege sustains privilege; poverty begets poverty," resulting in the "slow, poisonous polarization and disintegration of our great democracy."

Whatever its causes, what came to be called the "great divide" between the "1 percent" and the "99 percent" had profound social and political consequences, as well as moral dimensions. A nation founded on the idea that "All men are created equal" had become richer but less equal and less socially mobile than other advanced industrial nations. The true test of a capitalist democracy is not how wealthy the richest citizens are, but the quality of life of the average citizen.

The unresolved tension created by such inequality emerged as the foremost social issue of the twenty-first century. In an August 2014 national poll,

64 percent of Americans no longer believed that the nation offered everyone an equal chance to succeed, fewer than 10 percent trusted Congress, and 76 percent were not confident that the quality of life of their children's generation would be "better than it has been for us." Billionaire investor Bill Gross worried in 2014 that the new high-tech global economy was "producing one world for the rich and an entirely different world for the working class. It can't go on like this, either from the standpoint of the health of the capitalist system itself or the health of individuals and the family."

As the 2016 presidential campaign began in earnest, income inequality emerged as a major issue. Democratic frontrunner Hillary Clinton claimed she was reaching out to "everyday Americans" by calling for higher wages while criticizing the "bloated" salaries of corporate executives. Florida senator Marco Rubio urged his fellow Republicans to make their party "the champion of the working class."

Raising the minimum wage
Demonstrators rally in Albany, New York, for an increase to the minimum wage, a movement that gained national traction in 2014 and reflected the growing attention paid to wealth disparity in the country.

The United States has so far survived its growing economic inequalities and social strife without serious upheavals. For all its diversity and divisions, the nation remains united under a common government and political system, something that few societies can claim. For centuries, Americans have also displayed a distinctively self-critical temperament, especially noticeable to foreign visitors. In the early nineteenth century, English writer Charles Dickens said that the American "always is depressed, and always is stagnated, and always is at an alarming crisis, and never was otherwise."

Perhaps that is why the nation always overcomes its greatest crises; Americans eventually summon the will and creativity to address their urgent problems. The nation has a remarkable genius for self-renewal and a confident ability to maneuver through the most difficult threats and challenges. It needs such innovative resilience today, for unless the entwined ideals of equal opportunity and fair reward are addressed, Americans may lose what has always united them and informed their sense of purpose: the widely shared hope, even expectation, of a better future for all based on hard work, ingenuity, and sacrifice.

CHAPTER REVIEW

SUMMARY

- **Changing Demographics**   From 1980 to 2010, the population of the United States grew by 25 percent, to 306 million. The nation was quickly becoming even more racially and ethnically diverse, and a wave of immigration from Latin America allowed Hispanics to surpass African Americans as the nation's largest minority. By 2012, the U.S. population included more foreign-born and first-generation residents than ever before.

- **Divided Government**   Just two years after the election of "New Democrat" Bill Clinton in 1992, Republican Speaker of the House Newt Gingrich crafted his *Contract with America* and achieved a Republican landslide in the midterm elections of 1994. Despite the bipartisan success of the 1993 *North American Free Trade Act (NAFTA)* and the *Personal Responsibility and Work Opportunity Act of 1996*—and a prosperous, high-tech "new economy" thriving on the *globalization* of commerce that helped balance the federal budget—Clinton's private life produced a sex scandal that resulted in impeachment proceedings against him. Clinton was ultimately acquitted and went on to intervene in the Balkans to stop *ethnic cleansing* and to broker the land-for-peace Wye River Accords in the Middle East.

- **Global Terrorism**   The 9/11 attacks led President George W. Bush to declare a *war on terror* that commenced with the U.S. invasion of Afghanistan to capture Osama bin Laden and oust the Islamist Taliban government. Through the *USA Patriot Act*, Congress authorized the federal government to monitor Americans for possible terrorist activities at home. The *Bush Doctrine* declared America's right to initiate preemptive military strikes against terrorists or rogue nations possessing *weapons of mass destruction (WMDs)*. In 2003, Bush invoked this doctrine against Saddam Hussein, the leader of Iraq. The ensuing second Iraq War removed Hussein from power but turned up no WMDs.

- **A Historic Election**   The 2008 presidential primary campaigns featured Democratic senators Hillary Rodham Clinton, the first formidable female candidate, and Barack Obama, the first truly contending African American candidate, as well as Republican senator John McCain, the oldest candidate in history. Obama won his party's nomination and went on to take the election, becoming the nation's first African American president. His victory resulted in large part from public dismay about the start of the *Great Recession*, as well as voters' weariness with President Bush.

- **Obama's Priorities**   Obama's first priority was to shore up the failing economy, which he attempted through controversial Wall Street "bailouts" and a huge "economic stimulus" package. Yet the recovery remained slow and unequal, widening the economic divide and spawning the short-lived Occupy Wall Street movement. The *Affordable Care Act* ("*Obamacare*") incited increasingly bitter opposition from the conservative *Tea Party*. Obama was more successful in winning public support to reduce American military deployment abroad, removing all combat troops from

Iraq in 2011 and downsizing their presence in Afghanistan. Obama also intervened in the nation's culture wars, endorsing *same-sex marriage* and a path to citizenship for undocumented residents.

CHRONOLOGY

1992	Bill Clinton elected president
1993	Congress passes NAFTA
1995	The Contract with America
1996	Congress passes PRWOA
1998	President Clinton impeached and acquitted
2000	George W. Bush elected after controversial recount
September 11, 2001	Terrorists attack New York City
October 2001	Operation Enduring Freedom begins in Afghanistan
March 2003	Iraq War begins with Operation Iraqi Freedom
August 2005	Hurricane Katrina devastates Gulf coast
2008	Global financial markets collapse; Great Recession begins
2009	Barack Obama becomes the nation's first black president
2010	Congress passes the Affordable Care Act ("Obamacare")
August 2011	Al Qaeda leader Osama bin Laden killed
2013	U.S. Supreme Court overturns the Defense of Marriage Act (DOMA) in *United States v. Windsor*
2015	U.S. Supreme Court upholds the Affordable Care Act and decides that same-sex couples have a constitutional right to marry

KEY TERMS

North American Free Trade Agreement (NAFTA) p. 1206

Contract with America p. 1208

Personal Responsibility and Work Opportunity Act of 1996 (PRWOA) p. 1209

globalization p. 1210

ethnic cleansing p. 1213

war on terror p. 1219

USA Patriot Act p. 1220

Bush Doctrine p. 1220

weapons of mass destruction (WMDs) p. 1220

Great Recession p. 1227

Affordable Care Act (ACA—also called Obamacare) p. 1230

Tea Party p. 1235

same-sex marriage p. 1236

 INQUIZITIVE

Go to InQuizitive to see what you've learned—and learn what you've missed—with personalized feedback along the way.

GLOSSARY

1968 Chicago Democratic National Convention The meeting of Democratic delegates in Chicago to nominate a candidate for the 1968 presidential elections, which were marred by violent anti-war protests.

36°30' According to the Missouri Compromise, any part of the Louisiana Purchase north of this line (Missouri's southern border) was to be excluded from slavery.

abolition In the early 1830s, the anti-slavery movement shifted its goal from the gradual end of slavery to the immediate end or abolition of slavery.

abolitionism Movement that called for an immediate end to slavery throughout the United States.

Abigail Adams (1744–1818) As the wife of John Adams, she endured long periods of separation from him while he served in many political roles. During these times apart, she wrote often to her husband; their correspondence has provided a detailed portrait of life during the Revolutionary War.

John Adams (1735–1826) He was a signer of the Declaration of Independence and a delegate to the First and Second Continental Congresses. A member of the Federalist Party, he served as the first vice president of the United States and the second president. As president, he passed the Alien and Sedition Acts and endured a stormy relationship with France, which included the XYZ affair.

John Quincy Adams (1767–1848) As secretary of state, he urged President Monroe to issue the Monroe Doctrine, which incorporated his belief in an expanded use of federal powers. As the sixth president, Adams's nationalism and praise of European leaders caused a split in his party, causing some Republicans to leave and form the Democrat party.

Samuel Adams (1722–1803) A genius of revolutionary agitation, he believed that English Parliament had no right to legislate for the colonies. He organized the Sons of Liberty as well as protests in Boston against the British.

Jane Addams (1860–1935) She founded and ran of one of the best known settlement houses, the Hull House. Active in the peace and suffragist movements, she established child care for working mothers, health clinics, job training, and other social programs.

affirmative action Programs designed to give preferential treatment to women and minorities as compensation for past injustices.

Affordable Care Act (ACA), or Obamacare (2010) Vast health care reform initiative signed into law and championed by President Obama and widely criticized by Republicans that aims to make health insurance more affordable and make health-care accessible to everyone, regardless of income or prior medical conditions.

Agricultural Adjustment Act (1933) Legislation that paid farmers to produce less in order to raise crop prices for all; the act was later declared unconstitutional by the U.S. Supreme Court in the case of *United States v. Butler* (1936).

Emilio Aguinaldo (1869?–1964) He was a leader in Filipino struggle for independence. During the Spanish-American War (the War of 1898), Commodore George Dewey brought Aguinaldo back to the Philippines from exile to help fight the Spanish. However, after the Spanish surrendered to Americans, America annexed the Philippines and Aguinaldo fought against the American military until he was captured in 1901.

Alamo, Battle of the Siege in the Texas War for Independence of 1836, in which the San Antonio mission fell to the Mexicans. Davy Crockett and Jim Bowie were among the courageous defenders.

Albany Plan of Union A failed proposal by the seven northern colonies in anticipation of the French and Indian War, urging the unification of the colonies under one Crown-appointed president.

Alien and Sedition Acts of 1798 Four measures passed during the undeclared war with France that limited the freedoms of speech and press and restricted the liberty of non-citizens.

alliance with France Critical diplomatic, military, and economic alliance between France and the newly independent United States, codified by the Treaty of Amity and Commerce and the Treaty of Alliance (1778).

Allied Powers The nations fighting the Central Powers during the First World War, including France, Great Britain, and Russia; later joined by Italy and, after Russia quit the war in 1917, the United States.

American Anti-Imperialist League Coalition of anti-imperialist groups united in 1899 to protest American territorial expansion, especially in the Philippine Islands; its membership included prominent politicians, industrialists, labor leaders, and social reformers.

American Colonization Society (ACS) Established in 1817, an organization whose mission was to return freed slaves to Africa.

American Federation of Labor (AFL) Founded in 1881 as a national federation of trade unions made up of skilled workers.

American Indian Movement (AIM) Fed up with the poor conditions on Indian reservations and the federal government's unwillingness to help, Native Americans founded the American Indian Movement in 1963. In 1973, AIM led 200 Sioux in the occupation of Wounded Knee. After a ten-week standoff with the federal authorities, the government agreed to reexamine Indian treaty rights and the occupation ended.

American Recovery and Reinvestment Act Hoping to restart the weak economy, President Obama signed this $787 billion economic stimulus bill in February 2009. The bill included cash distributions to states, funds for food stamps, unemployment benefits, construction projects to renew the nation's infrastructure, funds for renewable-energy systems, and tax reductions.

American System Economic plan championed by Henry Clay of Kentucky that called for federal tariffs on imports, a strong national bank, and federally-financed internal improvements—roads, bridges, canals—all intended to strengthen the national economy and end American dependence on Great Britain.

American Tobacco Company Business founded in 1890 by North Carolina's James Buchanan Duke, who combined the major tobacco manufacturers of the time, ultimately controlling 90 percent of the country's cigarette production.

Anaconda Plan Union's primary war strategy calling for a naval blockade of major southern seaports and then dividing the Confederacy by gaining control of the Tennessee, Cumberland, and Mississippi Rivers.

Antietam, Battle of (1862) Turning-point battle near Sharpsburg, Maryland, leaving over 20,000 soldiers dead or wounded, in which Union forces halted a Confederate invasion of the North.

anti-Federalists Opponents of the Constitution as an infringement on individual and states' rights, whose criticism led to the addition of a Bill of Rights to the document. Many anti-Federalists later joined Thomas Jefferson's Democratic-Republican party.

Anti-Masonic party This party grew out of popular hostility toward the Masonic fraternal order and entered the presidential election of 1832 as a third party. It was the first party to run as a third party in a presidential election, as well as the first to hold a nomination convention and announce a party platform.

Appomattox Court House Virginia village where Confederate general Robert E. Lee surrendered to Union general Ulysses S. Grant on April 9, 1865.

Arab Awakening A wave of spontaneous democratic uprisings that spread throughout the Arab world beginning in 2011, in which long-oppressed peoples demanded basic liberties from generations-old authoritarian regimes.

Armory show A divisive and sensational art exhibition in 1913 which introduced European-inspired modernism to American audiences.

Benedict Arnold (1741–1801) A traitorous American commander who planned to sell out the American garrison at West Point to the British, but his plot was discovered before it could be executed and he joined the British army.

Articles of Confederation The first form of government for the United States, ratified by the original thirteen states in 1781; weak in central authority, it was replaced by the U.S. Constitution in 1789.

Atlanta Compromise (1895) A speech by Booker T. Washington that called for the black community to strive for economic prosperity before attempting political and social equality.

Atlantic Charter (1941) Joint statement crafted by Franklin D. Roosevelt and British prime minister Winston Churchill that listed the war goals of the Allied Powers.

Crispus Attucks (1723–1770) During the Boston Massacre, he was supposedly at the head of the crowd of hecklers who baited the British troops. He was killed when the British troops fired on the crowd.

Stephen F. Austin (1793–1836) He established the first colony of Americans in Texas, which eventually attracted 2,000 people.

"Axis" alliance Military alliance formed in 1937 by the three major fascist powers: Germany, Italy, and Japan.

Aztec Empire Mesoamerican people who were conquered by the Spanish under Hernando Cortés, 1519–1528.

baby boom Markedly high birth rate in the years following World War II, leading to the biggest demographic "bubble" in U.S. history.

Bacon's Rebellion Unsuccessful 1676 revolt led by planter Nathaniel Bacon against Virginia governor William Berkeley's administration, which, Bacon charged, had failed to protect settlers from Indian raids.

Bank of the United States (1791) National bank responsible for holding and transferring federal government funds, making business loans, and issuing a national currency.

Bank War Political struggle in the early 1830s between President Jackson and financier Nicholas Biddle over the renewing of the Second Bank's charter.

Barbary pirates North Africans who waged war (1801–1805) on the United States after President Thomas Jefferson refused to pay tribute (a bribe) to protect American ships.

Bay of Pigs Failed CIA operation that, in April 1961, deployed a band of Cuban rebels to overthrow Fidel Castro's Communist regime.

Bear Flag Republic On June 14, 1846, a group of Americans in California captured Sonoma from the Mexican army and declared it the Republic of California, whose flag featured a grizzly bear. In July, the commodore of the U.S. Pacific Fleet landed troops on California's shores and declared it part of the United States.

Beats Group of bohemian, downtown New York writers, artists, and musicians who flouted convention in favor of liberated forms of self-expression.

Berlin airlift (1948) Effort by the United States and Great Britain to deliver massive amounts of food and supplies flown in to West Berlin in response to the Soviet land blockade of the city.

Berlin Wall Twenty-seven-mile-long concrete wall constructed in 1961 by East German authorities to stop the flow of East Germans fleeing to West Berlin.

Bessemer converter Apparatus which blasts air through molten iron to produce steel in very large quantities.

Nicholas Biddle (1786–1844) He was the president of the second Bank of the United States. In response to President Andrew Jackson's attacks on the bank, Biddle curtailed the bank's loans and exchanged its paper currency for gold and silver. In response, state banks began printing paper without restraint and lent it to speculators, causing a binge in speculating and an enormous increase in debt.

Bill of Rights First ten amendments to the U.S. Constitution, adopted in 1791 to guarantee individual rights and to help secure ratification of the Constitution by the states.

Osama bin Laden (1957–2011) The Saudi-born leader of al Qaeda, whose members attacked America on September 11, 2001. Years before the attack, he had declared *jihad* (holy war) on the United States, Israel, and the Saudi monarchy. In Afghanistan, the Taliban leaders gave bin Laden a safe haven in exchange for aid in fighting the Northern Alliance, who were rebels opposed to the Taliban. Following the Taliban's refusal to turn over bin Laden to the United States, America and a multinational coalition invaded Afghanistan and overthrew the Taliban. In May 2011, bin Laden was shot and killed by American special forces during a covert operation in Pakistan.

birth rate Proportion of births per 1,000 of the total population.

black codes Laws passed in southern states to restrict the rights of former slaves; to combat the codes, Congress passed the Civil Rights Act of 1866 and the Fourteenth Amendment and set up military governments in southern states that refused to ratify the amendment.

black power movement Militant form of civil rights protest focused on urban communities in the North and led by Malcolm X that grew as a response to impatience with the nonviolent tactics of Martin Luther King Jr.

James Gillepsie Blaine (1830–1893) As a Republican congressman from Maine, he developed close ties with business leaders, which contributed to him losing the presidential election of 1884. He later opposed President Cleveland's efforts to reduce tariffs, which became a significant issue in the 1888 presidential election. Blaine served as secretary of state under President Benjamin Harrison.

Bleeding Kansas (1856) A series of violent conflicts in the Kansas territory between anti-slavery and pro-slavery factions over the status of slavery.

blitzkrieg (1940) The German "lightning war" strategy characterized by swift, well-organized attacks using infantry, tanks, and warplanes.

Bolsheviks Under the leadership of Vladimir Lenin, this Marxist party led the November 1917 revolution against the newly formed provisional government in Russia. After seizing control, the Bolsheviks negotiated a peace treaty with Germany, the Treaty of Brest-Litovsk, and ended their participation in World War I.

Bonus Expeditionary Force (1932) Protest march on Washington, D.C., by thousands of World War I veterans and their families, calling for immediate payment of their service bonuses certificates; violence ensued when President Herbert Hoover ordered their tent villages cleared.

boomtown Town, often in the West, that developed rapidly due to the sudden influx of wealth and work opportunities; often male-dominated with a substantial immigrant population.

Daniel Boone (1734–1820) He found and expanded a trail into Kentucky, which pioneers used to reach and settle the area.

John Wilkes Booth (1838?–1865) He assassinated President Abraham Lincoln at the Ford's Theater on April 14, 1865. He was pursued to Virginia and killed.

Boston Massacre Violent confrontation between British soldiers and a Boston mob on March 5, 1770, in which five colonists were killed.

Boston Tea Party Demonstration against the Tea Act of 1773 in which the Sons of Liberty, dressed as Indians, dumped hundreds of chests of British-owned tea into Boston Harbor.

bracero program System created in 1942 that permitted seasonal farm workers from Mexico to work in the United States on year-long contracts.

Joseph Brant (1742?–1807) He was the Mohawk leader who led the Iroquois against the Americans in the Revolutionary War.

brinkmanship Secretary of State John Foster Dulles believed that communism could be contained by bringing America to the brink of war with an aggressive communist nation. He believed that the aggressor would back down when confronted with the prospect of receiving a mass retaliation from a country with nuclear weapons.

John Brown (1800–1859) In response to a pro-slavery mob's sacking of a free-state town of Lawrence, Kansas, Brown went to the pro-slavery settlement of Pottawatomie, Kansas, which led to a guerrilla war in the Kansas territory. In 1859, he attempted to raid the federal arsenal at Harpers Ferry, hoping to use the stolen weapons to arm slaves, but he was captured and executed.

***Brown v. Board of Education* (1954)** Landmark Supreme Court case that struck down racial segregation in public schools and declared "separate-but-equal" unconstitutional.

William Jennings Bryan (1860–1925) He delivered the pro-silver "cross of gold" speech at the 1896 Democratic Convention and won his party's nomination for president. Disappointed pro-gold Democrats chose to walk out of the convention and nominate their own candidate, which split the Democratic party and cost them the White House. Bryan's loss also crippled the Populist movement that had endorsed him.

"Bull Moose" Progressive party *See* Progressive party

Bull Run, Battles of (First and Second Manassas) First land engagement of the Civil War took place on July 21, 1861, at Manassas Junction, Virginia, at which surprised Union troops quickly retreated; one year later, on August 29–30, Confederates captured the federal supply depot and forced Union troops back to Washington.

Martin Van Buren (1782–1862) During President Jackson's first term, he served as secretary of state and minister to London. In 1836, Van Buren was elected president, and he inherited a financial crisis. He believed that the government should not continue to keep its deposits in state banks and set up an independent Treasury, which was approved by Congress after several years of political maneuvering.

General John Burgoyne (1722–1792) He was the commander of Britain's northern forces during the Revolutionary War. He and most of his troops surrendered to the Americans at the Battle of Saratoga.

burial mounds A funeral tradition, practiced in the Mississippi and Ohio Valleys by the Adena-Hopewell cultures, of erecting massive mounds of earth over graves, often in the designs of serpents and other animals.

burned-over district Area of western New York strongly influenced by the revivalist fervor of the Second Great Awakening. Disciples of Christ and Mormons are among the many sects that trace their roots to the phenomenon.

Aaron Burr (1756–1836) Even though he was Thomas Jefferson's vice president, he lost favor with Jefferson's supporters who were Republicans. He sought to work with the Federalists and run as their candidate for the governor of New York. Alexander Hamilton opposed Burr's candidacy and his stinging remarks on the subject led to Burr challenging him to duel in which Hamilton was killed.

George H. W. Bush (1924–) He had served as vice president during the Reagan administration and then won the presidential election of 1988. His presidency was marked by raised taxes in the face of the federal deficit, the creation of the Office of National Drug Control Policy, and military activity abroad, including the invasion of Panama and Operation Desert Storm in Kuwait. He lost the 1992 presidential election to Bill Clinton.

George W. Bush (1946–) In the 2000 presidential election, Texas governor George W. Bush won as the Republican nominee against Democratic nominee Vice President Al Gore. After the September 11 terrorist attacks, he launched his "war on terrorism." President Bush adopted the Bush Doctrine, and United States invaded Afghanistan and Iraq with unclear outcomes, leaving the countries divided. In September 2008, the nation's economy nosedived as a credit crunch spiraled into a global economic meltdown. Bush signed into law the bank bailout fund called Troubled Asset Relief Program (TARP), but the economy did not improve.

Bush v. Gore (2000) The close 2000 presidential election came down to Florida's decisive twenty-five electoral votes. The final tally in Florida gave Bush a slight lead, but it was so small that a recount was required by state law. While the votes were being recounted, a legal battle was being waged to stop the recount. Finally, the case, *Bush v. Gore*, was present to the Supreme Court who ruled 5–4 to stop the recount and Bush was declared the winner.

Bush Doctrine National security policy launched in 2002 by which the Bush administration claimed the right to launch preemptive military attacks against perceived enemies, particularly outlaw nations or terrorist organizations believed to possess weapons of mass destruction.

buying (stock) on margin The investment practice of making a small down payment (the "margin") on a stock and borrowing the rest of the money needed for the purchase from a broker who held the stock as security against a down market. If the stock's value declined and the buyer failed to meet a margin call for more funds, the broker could sell the stock to cover his loan.

Cahokia The largest chiefdom and city of the Mississippian Indian culture located in present-day Illinois, and the site of a sophisticated farming settlement that supported up to 15,000 inhabitants.

John C. Calhoun (1782–1850) He served in both the House of Representatives and the Senate for South Carolina before becoming secretary of war under President Monroe and then John Quincy Adams's vice president. Though he started his political career as an advocate of a strong national government, he eventually believed that states' rights, limited central government, and the power of nullification were necessary to preserve the Union.

California gold rush (1849) A massive migration of gold hunters, mostly men, who transformed the economy of California after gold was discovered in the foothills of the Sierra Nevada mountains in the Sacramento River Valley in northern California.

Camp David Accords Peace agreement in 1978 between Prime Minister Menachem Begin of Israel and President Anwar Sadat of Egypt, the first Arab head of state to officially recognize the state of Israel.

"Scarface" Al Capone (1899–1947) He was the most successful gangster of the Prohibition era whose Chicago-based criminal empire included bootlegging, prostitution, and gambling.

Andrew Carnegie (1835–1919) He was a steel magnate who believed that the general public benefited from big business even if these companies employed harsh business practices. This philosophy became deeply ingrained in the conventional wisdom of some Americans. After retiring, he devoted himself to philanthropy in hopes of promoting social welfare and world peace.

Carnegie Steel Company Corporation under the leadership of Andrew Carnegie that came to dominate the American steel industry.

Carolina colonies English proprietary colonies comprised of North and South Carolina, whose semitropical climate made them profitable centers of rice, timber, and tar production.

carpetbaggers Northern emigrants who participated in the Republican governments of the reconstructed South.

Jimmy Carter (1924–) Elected president in 1976, Jimmy Carter was an outsider to Washington. He created the departments of Energy and Education and signed into law several environmental initiatives. In 1978, he successfully brokered a peace agreement between Israel and Egypt called the Camp David Accords. However, his unwillingness to make deals with legislators caused other bills to be either gutted or stalled in Congress. His administration was plagued with a series of crises: a recession and increased inflation, a fuel shortage, the Soviet invasion of Afghanistan, and the overthrow of the Shah of Iran, leading to the Iran Hostage Crisis Carter struggled to get the hostages released and was unable to do so until after he lost the 1980 election to

Ronald Reagan. He was awarded the Nobel Peace Prize in 2002 for his efforts to further peace and democratic elections around the world.

Jacques Cartier (1491–1557) He led the first French effort to colonize North America and explored the Gulf of St. Lawrence and reached as far as present day Montreal on the St. Lawrence River.

Fidel Castro (1926–) In 1959, his Communist regime came to power in Cuba after two years of guerrilla warfare against the dictator Fulgenico Batista. He enacted land redistribution programs and nationalized all foreign-owned property. The latter action as well as his political trials and summary executions damaged relations between Cuba and America. Castro was turned down when he asked for loans from the United States. However, he did receive aid from the Soviet Union.

Carrie Chapman Catt (1859–1947) She was a leader of a new generation of activists in the women's suffrage movement who carried on the work started by Elizabeth Cady Stanton and Susan B. Anthony.

Central Intelligence Agency (CIA) Intelligence-gathering government agency founded in 1947; under President Eisenhower's orders, secretly undermined elected governments deemed susceptible to communism.

Central Powers One of the two sides during the First World War, including Germany, Austria-Hungary, the Ottoman Empire (Turkey), and Bulgaria.

Cesar Chavez (1927–1993) He founded the United Farm Workers (UFW) in 1962 and worked to organize migrant farm workers. In 1965, the UFW joined Filipino farm workers striking against corporate grape farmers in California's San Joaquin Valley. In 1970, the strike and a consumer boycott on grapes compelled the farmers to formally recognize the UFW. As the result of Chavez's efforts, wages and working conditions improved for migrant workers. In 1975, the California state legislature passed a bill that required growers to bargain collectively with representatives of the farm workers.

child labor The practice of sending children to work in mines, mills, and factories, often in unsafe conditions; widespread among poor families in the late nineteenth century.

Chinese Exclusion Act (1882) Federal law that barred Chinese laborers from immigrating to America.

Church of Jesus Christ of Latter-day Saints Founded in 1830 by Joseph Smith, the sect was a product of the intense revivalism of the burned-over district of New York; Smith's successor Brigham Young led 15,000 followers to Utah in 1847 to escape persecution.

Winston Churchill (1874–1965) The British prime minister who led the country during the Second World War. Along with Roosevelt and Stalin, he helped shape the post-war world at the Yalta Conference. He also coined the term "iron curtain," which he used in his famous "The Sinews of Peace" speech.

citizen-soldiers Part-time nonprofessional soldiers, mostly poor farmers or recent immigrants who had been indentured servants, who played an important role in the Revolutionary War.

Civil Rights Act of 1957 First federal civil rights law since Reconstruction; established the Civil Rights Commission and the Civil Rights Division of the Department of Justice.

Civil Rights Act of 1964 Legislation that outlawed discrimination in public accommodations and employment, passed at the urging of President Lyndon B. Johnson.

civil service reform An extended effort led by political reformers to end the patronage system; led to the Pendleton Act (1883), which called for government positions to be awarded based on merit rather than party loyalty.

Henry Clay (1777–1852) In the first half of the nineteenth century, he was the foremost spokesman for the American system. As Speaker of the House in the 1820s, he promoted economic nationalism, "market revolution," and the rapid development of western states and territories. A broker of compromise, he formulated the "second" Missouri Compromise and the Compromise of 1850. In 1824, Clay supported John Quincy Adams, who won the presidency and appointed Clay to secretary of state. Andrew Jackson claimed that Clay had entered into a "corrupt bargain" with Adams for his own selfish gains.

Clayton Anti-Trust Act (1914) Legislation that served to enhance the Sherman Anti-Trust Act (1890) by clarifying what constituted "monopolistic" activities and declaring that labor unions were not to be viewed as "monopolies in restraint of trade."

Bill Clinton (1946–) The governor of Arkansas won the 1992 presidential election against President George H. W. Bush. In his first term, he pushed through Congress a tax increase, an economic stimulus package, the adoption of the North America Free Trade Agreement, welfare reform, a raise in the minimum wage, and improved public access to health insurance. His administration also negotiated the Oslo Accord and the Dayton Accords. After his reelection in 1996, he was involved in two high-profile scandals: his investment in the fraudulent Whitewater Development Corporation (but no evidence was found of him being involved in any wrongdoing) and his sexual affair with a White House intern. His attempt to cover up the affair led to a vote in Congress on whether or not to begin an impeachment inquiry. The House of Representatives voted to impeach Clinton, but the Senate found him not guilty.

Hillary Rodham Clinton (1947–) In the 2008 presidential election, Senator Hillary Clinton, the spouse of former President Bill Clinton, initially was the front-runner for the Democratic nomination, which made her the first woman with a serious chance to win the presidency. However, Senator Barack Obama's Internet-based and grassroots-orientated campaign garnered him enough delegates to win the nomination. After Obama became president, she was appointed secretary of state. Clinton stepped down from her Cabinet position in 2013 and, in 2015, announced her second presidential bid.

clipper ships Tall, slender, mid-nineteenth-century sailing ships that were favored over older merchant ships for their speed, but ultimately gave way to steamships because they lacked cargo space.

Coercive Acts Four parliamentary measures of 1774 that required the colonies to pay for the Boston Tea Party's damages, imposed a military government, disallowed colonial trials of British soldiers, and forced the quartering of troops in private homes.

Columbian Exchange The transfer of biological and social elements, such as plants, animals, people, diseases, and cultural practices, among Europe, the Americas, and Africa in the wake of Christopher Columbus's voyages to the "New World."

Christopher Columbus (1451–1506) The Italian sailor who persuaded King Ferdinand and Queen Isabella of Spain to fund his expedition across the Atlantic to discover a new trade route to Asia. Instead of arriving at China or Japan, he reached the Bahamas in 1492.

Committee of Correspondence Group organized by Samuel Adams in retaliation for the *Gaspée* incident to address American grievances, assert American rights, and form a network of rebellion.

Committee to Re-elect the President (CREEP) During Nixon's presidency, his administration engaged in a number of immoral acts, such as attempting to steal information and falsely accusing political appointments of sexual improprieties. These acts were funded by money illegally collected through CREEP.

Common Sense Popular pamphlet written by Thomas Paine attacking British principles of hereditary rule and monarchical government, and advocating a declaration of American independence.

Compromise of 1850 A package of five bills presented to the Congress by Henry Clay intended to avoid secession or civil war by reducing tensions between North and South over the status of slavery.

Compromise of 1877 Deal made by a special congressional commission on March 2, 1877, to resolve the disputed presidential election of 1876; Republican Rutherford B. Hayes, who had lost the popular vote, was declared the winner in exchange for the withdrawal of federal troops from the South, marking the end of Reconstruction.

Comstock Lode Mine in eastern Nevada acquired by Canadian fur trapper Henry Comstock that between 1860 and 1880 yielded almost $1 billion worth of gold and silver.

Conestoga wagons These large horse-drawn wagons were used to carry people or heavy freight long distances, including from the East to the western frontier settlements.

Congressional Reconstruction A more radical phase of Reconstruction, beginning in 1867, in which Congress, over President Johnson's objections, passed the Military Reconstruction Act that abolished the new Southern state governments in favor of federal military control. In addition, the Act required each state to draft a new constitution that guaranteed voting rights to all adult males regardless of race or economic status.

conquistadores Spanish term for "conquerors," applied to Spanish and Portuguese soldiers who conquered lands held by indigenous peoples in central and southern America as well as the current states of Texas, New Mexico, Arizona, and California.

consumer culture A society in which mass production and consumption of nationally advertised products comes to dictate much of social life and status.

containment U.S. cold war strategy that sought to prevent global Soviet expansion and influence through political, economic, and, if necessary, military pressure as a means of combating the spread of communism.

Continental army Army authorized by the Continental Congress (1775–1784) to fight the British; commanded by General George Washington.

contrabands Slaves who sought refuge in Union military camps or who lived in areas of the Confederacy under Union control.

Contract with America A list of conservatives' promises in response to the supposed liberalism of the Clinton administration, that was drafted by Speaker of the House Newt Gingrich and other congressional Republicans as the GOP platform for the 1994 midterm elections. More a campaign tactic than a practical program, few of its proposed items ever became law.

Contras The Reagan administration ordered the CIA to train and supply guerrilla bands of anti-Communist Nicaraguans called Contras. They were fighting the Sandinista government that had recently come to power in Nicaragua. The State Department believed that the Sandinista government was supplying the leftist Salvadoran rebels with Soviet and Cuban arms. A cease-fire agreement between the Contras and Sandinistas was signed in 1988.

Calvin "Silent Cal" Coolidge (1872–1933) After President Harding's death, his vice president, Calvin Coolidge, assumed the presidency. Coolidge believed that the nation's welfare was tied to the success of big business, and he worked to end government regulation of business and industry as well as reduce taxes. In particular, he focused on the nation's industrial development.

Copperhead Democrats Democrats in northern states who opposed the Civil War and argued for an immediate peace settlement with the Confederates; Republicans labeled them "Copperheads," likening them to venomous snakes.

General Charles Cornwallis (1738–1805) He was in charge of British troops in the South during the Revolutionary War. His surrendering to George Washington at the Battle of Yorktown ended the Revolutionary War.

Corps of Discovery Meriwether Lewis and William Clark led this group of men on an expedition of the newly purchased Louisiana territory, which took them from Missouri to Oregon. As they traveled, they kept detailed journals and drew maps of the previously unexplored territory. Their reports attracted traders and trappers to the region and gave the United States a claim to the Oregon country by right of discovery and exploration.

"corrupt bargain" Scandal in which presidential candidate and Speaker of the House Henry Clay secured John Quincy Adams's victory over Andrew Jackson in the 1824 election, supposedly in exchange for Clay being named secretary of state.

Hernán Cortés (1485–1547) The Spanish conquistador who conquered the Aztec Empire and set the precedent for other plundering conquistadores.

cotton White fibers harvested from cotton plants, spun into yarn, and woven into textiles that made comfortable, easy-to-clean products, especially clothing; the most valuable cash crop driving the economy in the United States and Great Britain during the nineteenth century.

cotton gin Hand-operated machine invented by Eli Whitney in the late eighteenth century that quickly removed seeds from cotton bolls, enabling the mass production of cotton in nineteenth-century America.

Cotton Kingdom Cotton-producing region, relying predominantly on slave labor, that spanned from North Carolina west to Louisiana and reached as far north as southern Illinois.

counterculture "Hippie" youth culture of the 1960s, which rejected the values of the dominant culture in favor of illicit drugs, communes, free sex, and rock music.

"Court-packing" scheme President Franklin D. Roosevelt's failed 1937 attempt to increase the number of U.S. Supreme Court justices from nine to fifteen in order to save his Second New Deal programs from constitutional challenges.

crop-lien system Credit system used by sharecroppers and share tenants who pledged a portion ("share") of their future crop to local merchants or land owners in exchange for farming supplies and food.

"cross of gold" speech In the 1896 election, the Democratic Party split over the issue of whether to use gold or silver to back American currency. Significant to this division was the pro-silver "cross of gold" speech that William Jennings Bryan delivered at the Democratic convention, which was so well received that Bryan won the nomination to be their presidential candidate. Disappointed pro-gold Democrats chose to walk out of the convention and nominate their own candidate.

Cuban missile crisis Thirteen-day U.S.-Soviet standoff in October 1962, sparked by the discovery of Soviet missile sites in Cuba; the crisis was the closest the world has come to nuclear war since 1945.

cult of domesticity A pervasive nineteenth-century ideology that urged women to celebrate their role as manager of the household and nurturer of the children.

George A. Custer (1839–1876) He was a reckless and glory-seeking lieutenant colonel of the U.S. Army who fought the Sioux Indians in the Great Sioux War. In 1876, he and his detachment of soldiers were entirely wiped out in the Battle of Little Bighorn.

Dartmouth College v. Woodward (1819) Supreme Court ruling that enlarged the definition of *contract* to put corporations beyond the reach of the states that chartered them.

Daughters of Liberty Colonial women who protested the British government's tax policies by boycotting British products, such as clothing, and who wove their own fabric, or "homespun."

Dawes Severalty Act (1887) Federal legislation that divided ancestral Native American lands among the heads of each Indian family in an attempt to "Americanize" Indians by forcing them to become farmers working individual plots of land.

Jefferson Davis (1808–1889) He was the president of the Confederacy during the Civil War. When the Confederacy's defeat seemed inevitable in early 1865, he refused to surrender. Union forces captured him in May of that year.

death rate Proportion of deaths per 1,000 of the total population; also called *mortality rate*.

D-day June 6, 1944, when an Allied amphibious assault landed on the Normandy coast and established a foothold in Europe from which Hitler's defenses could not recover.

Eugene V. Debs (1855–1926) He founded the American Railway Union, which he organized against the Pullman Palace Car Company during the Pullman strike. Later he organized the Social Democratic party, which eventually became the Socialist Party of America. In the 1912 presidential election, he ran as the Socialist party's candidate and received more than 900,000 votes.

Declaration of Independence Formal statement, principally drafted by Thomas Jefferson and adopted by the Second Continental Congress on July 4, 1776, that officially announced the thirteen colonies' break with Great Britain.

Declaration of Rights and Sentiments Document based on the Declaration of Independence that called for gender equality, written primarily by Elizabeth Cady Stanton and signed by Seneca Falls Convention delegates in 1848.

Declaratory Act Following the repeal of the Stamp Act in 1766, Parliament passed this act that asserted Parliament's full power to make laws binding the colonies "in all cases whatsoever."

Deists Those who applied Enlightenment thought to religion, emphasizing reason, morality, and natural law rather than scriptural authority or an ever-present God intervening in human life.

détente Period of improving relations between the United States and Communist nations, particularly China and the Soviet Union, during the Nixon administration.

George Dewey (1837–1917) On April 30, 1898, Commodore George Dewey's small U.S. naval squadron defeated the Spanish warships in Manila Bay in the Philippines. This quick victory aroused expansionist fever in the United States.

John Dewey (1859–1952) He is an important philosopher of pragmatism. However, he preferred to use the term *instrumentalism*, because he saw ideas as instruments of action.

Dien Bien Phu Cluster of Vietnamese villages and site of a major Vietnamese victory over the French in the First Indochina War.

Ngo Dinh Diem (1901–1963) Following the Geneva Accords, the French, with the support of America, forced the Vietnamese emperor to accept Dinh Diem as the new premier of South Vietnam. President Eisenhower sent advisers to train Diem's police and army. In return, the United States expected Diem to enact democratic reforms and distribute land to the peasants. Instead, he suppressed his political opponents, did little or no land distribution, and let corruption grow. In 1956, he refused to participate in elections to reunify Vietnam. Eventually, he ousted the emperor and declared himself president.

Distribution Act (1836) Law requiring the distribution of the federal budget surplus to the states, creating chaos among state banks that had become dependent on such federal funds.

Dorothea Lynde Dix (1802–1887) She was an important figure in increasing the public's awareness of the plight of the mentally ill. After a two-year investigation of the treatment of the mentally ill in Massachusetts, she presented her findings and won the support of leading reformers. She eventually convinced twenty states to reform their treatment of the mentally ill.

Dixiecrats Breakaway faction of southern Democrats who defected from the national Democratic party in 1948 to protest the party's increased support for civil rights and to nominate their own segregationist candidates for elective office.

"dollar diplomacy" Practice advocated by President Theodore Roosevelt in which the U.S. government fostered American investments in less-developed nations and then used U.S. military force to protect those investments.

Donner party Forty-seven surviving members of a group of migrants to California were forced to resort to cannibalism to survive a brutal winter trapped in the Sierra Nevadas, 1846–1847; highest death toll of any group traveling the Overland Trail.

dot-coms In the late 1990s, the stock market soared to new heights and defied the predictions of experts that the economy could not sustain such a performance. Much of the economic success was based on dot-com enterprises, which were firms specializing in computers, software, telecommunications, and the Internet. However, many of the companies' stock market values were driven higher and higher by speculation instead of financial success. Eventually the stock market bubble burst.

Stephen A. Douglas (1812–1861) As a senator from Illinois, he authored the Kansas-Nebraska Act. Running for senatorial reelection in 1858, he engaged Abraham Lincoln in a series of public debates about slavery in the territories. Even though Douglas won the election, the debates gave Lincoln a national reputation.

Frederick Douglass (1818–1895) He escaped from slavery and become an eloquent speaker and writer against slavery. In 1845, he published his autobiography entitled *Narrative of the Life of Frederick Douglass* and two years later he founded an abolitionist newspaper for blacks called the *North Star.*

***Dred Scott v. Sandford* (1857)** U.S. Supreme Court ruling that slaves were not U.S. citizens and therefore could not sue for their freedom and that Congress could not prohibit slavery in the western territories.

W. E. B. Du Bois (1868–1963) He criticized Booker T. Washington's views on civil rights as being accommodationist. He advocated "ceaseless agitation" for civil rights and the immediate end to segregation and an enforcement of laws to protect civil rights and equality. He promoted an education for African Americans that would nurture bold leaders who were willing to challenge discrimination in politics.

John Foster Dulles (1888–1959) As President Eisenhower's secretary of state, he institutionalized the policy of containment and introduced the strategy of deterrence. He believed in using brinkmanship to halt the spread of communism. He attempted to employ it in Indochina, which led to the United States' involvement in Vietnam.

Dust Bowl Vast area of the Midwest where windstorms blew away millions of tons of topsoil from parched farmland after a long drought in the 1930s, causing great social distress and a massive migration of farm families.

Eastern Woodlands peoples Various Native American peoples, particularly the Algonquian, Iroquoian, and Muskogean regional groups, who once dominated the Atlantic seaboard from Maine to Louisiana.

Peggy Eaton (1796–1879) The wife of John Eaton, President Jackson's secretary of war, was the daughter of a tavern owner with an unsavory past. Supposedly her first husband had committed suicide after learning that she was having an affair with John Eaton. The wives of members of Jackson's cabinet snubbed her because of her lowly origins and past, resulting in a scandal known as the Eaton Affair.

Economic Opportunity Act (1964) Key legislation in President Johnson's "War on Poverty" which created the Office of Economic Opportunity and programs like Head Start and work-study.

Jonathan Edwards (1703–1758) New England Congregationalist minister, who began a religious revival in his Northampton church and was an important figure in the Great Awakening.

General Dwight D. Eisenhower (1890–1969) During the Second World War, he commanded the Allied Forces landing in Africa and was the supreme Allied commander as well as planner for Operation Overlord. In 1952, he was elected president on his popularity as a war hero and his promises to clean up Washington. His administration sought to cut the nation's domestic programs and budget, ended the fighting in Korea, and institutionalized the policies of containment and deterrence. He established the Eisenhower doctrine, which promised to aid any nation against aggression by a communist nation.

election of 1800 Presidential election between Thomas Jefferson and John Adams; resulted in the first Democratic-Republican victory after the Federalist administrations of George Washington and John Adams.

election of 1828 Highly contentious presidential election between Andrew Jackson and incumbent President John Quincy Adams; Jackson effectively campaigned as a war hero and champion of the "common man" to become the seventh president of the United States.

election of 1864 Abraham Lincoln's successful reelection campaign, capitalizing on Union military successes in Georgia, to defeat Democratic opponent, former general George B. McClellan, who ran on a peace platform.

election of 1912 The presidential election of 1912 featured four candidates: Wilson, Taft, Roosevelt, and Debs. Each candidate believed in the basic assumptions of progressive politics, but each had a different view on how progressive ideals should be implemented through policy. In the end, Taft and Roosevelt split the Republican party votes and Wilson emerged as the winner.

Queen Elizabeth I of England (1533–1603) The protestant daughter of Henry VIII, she was Queen of England from 1558–1603 and played a major role in the Protestant

Reformation. During her long reign, the doctrines and services of the Church of England were defined and the Spanish Armada was defeated.

Ellis Island Reception center in New York Harbor through which most European immigrants to America were processed from 1892 to 1954.

Emancipation Proclamation (1863) Military order issued by President Abraham Lincoln that freed slaves in areas still controlled by the Confederacy.

Embargo Act (1807) A law promoted by President Thomas Jefferson prohibiting American ships from leaving for foreign ports, in order to safeguard them from British and French attacks. This ban on American exports proved disastrous to the U.S. economy.

Ralph Waldo Emerson (1803–1882) As a leader of the transcendentalist movement, he wrote poems, essays, and speeches that discussed the sacredness of nature, optimism, self-reliance, and the unlimited potential of the individual. He wanted to transcend the limitations of inherited conventions and rationalism to reach the inner recesses of the self.

encomienda A land-grant system under which Spanish army officers (*conquistadores*) were awarded large parcels of land taken from Native Americans.

Enlightenment A revolution in thought begun in Europe in the seventeenth century that emphasized reason and science over the authority and myths of traditional religion.

Environmental Protection Agency (EPA) Federal environmental agency created in 1970 by Nixon to appease the demands of congressional Democrats for a federal environmental watchdog agency.

Erie Canal Most important and profitable of the many barge canals built in the early nineteenth century. It spanned 364 miles across New York state from west to east, connecting the Great Lakes to the Hudson River, and conveying so much cargo that it made New York City the nation's largest port.

ethnic cleansing The systematic removal of an ethnic group from a territory through violence or intimidation in order to create a homogenous society; the term was popularized by the Yugoslav policy brutally targeting Albanian Muslims in Kosovo.

Exodusters African Americans who migrated west from the South in search of a haven from racism and poverty after the collapse of Radical Republican rule.

Fair Deal (1949) President Truman's proposals to build upon the New Deal with national health insurance, the repeal of the Taft-Hartley Labor Act, new civil rights legislation, and other initiatives; most were rejected by the Republican-controlled Congress.

"falling domino" theory Theory that if one country fell to communism, its neighboring countries would follow suit.

Farmers' Alliances Like the Granger Movement, these organizations sought to address the issues of small farming communities; however Alliances emphasized more political action and called for the creation of a third party to advocate their concerns.

fascism A radical form of totalitarian government that emerged in Italy and Germany in the 1920s in which a dictator uses propaganda and brute force to seize control of all aspects of national life.

Federal-Aid Highway Act (1956) Largest federal project in U.S. history that created a national network of interstate highways and was the largest federal project in history.

Federal Deposit Insurance Corporation (FDIC) (1933) Independent government agency, established to prevent bank panics, that guarantees the safety of deposits in citizens' savings accounts.

Federal Reserve Act (1913) Legislation passed by Congress to create a new national banking system in order to regulate the nation's currency supply and ensure the stability and integrity of member banks who made up the Federal Reserve System across the nation.

Federal Trade Commission (FTC) (1914) Independent agency created by the Wilson administration that replaced the Bureau of Corporations as an even more powerful tool to combat unfair trade practices and monopolies.

Federal Writers' Project During the Great Depression, this project provided writers, such as Ralph Ellison, Richard Wright, and Saul Bellow, with work, which gave them a chance to develop as artists and be employed.

federalism Concept of dividing governmental authority between the national government and the states.

The Federalist Papers Collection of eighty-five essays, published widely in newspapers in 1787 and 1788, written by Alexander Hamilton, James Madison, and John Jay in support of adopting the proposed U.S. Constitution.

Federalists Proponents of a centralized federal system and the ratification of the Constitution. Most Federalists were relatively young, educated men who supported a broad interpretation of the Constitution whenever national interest dictated such flexibility. Notable Federalists included Alexander Hamilton and John Jay.

Geraldine Ferraro (1935–) In the 1984 presidential election, Democratic nominee Walter Mondale chose her as his running mate. As a member of the U.S. House of Representatives from New York, she was the first woman to be a vice-presidential nominee for a major political party. However, she was placed on the defensive because of her husband's complicated business dealings.

field hands Slaves who toiled in the cotton or cane fields in organized work gangs.

Fifteenth Amendment (1870) This amendment forbids states to deny any person the right to vote on grounds of "race, color or pervious condition of servitude." Former Confederate states were required to ratify this amendment before they could be readmitted to the Union.

"final solution" The Nazi party's systematic murder of some 6 million Jews along with more than a million other people including, but not limited to, gypsies, homosexuals, and handicap individuals.

First New Deal (1933–1935) Franklin D. Roosevelt's ambitious first-term cluster of economic and social programs designed to combat the Great Depression with a "new deal for the

American people;" the phrase became a catchword for his ambitious plan of economic programs.

First Red Scare (1919–1920) Outbreak of anti-Communist hysteria that included the arrest without warrants of thousands of suspected radicals, most of whom (mostly Russian immigrants) were deported.

flappers Young women of the 1920s whose rebellion against prewar standards of femininity included wearing shorter dresses, bobbing their hair, dancing to jazz music, driving cars, smoking cigarettes, and indulging in illegal drinking and gambling.

Food Administration After America's entry into World War I, the economy of the home front needed to be reorganized to provide the most efficient means of conducting the war. The Food Administration was a part of this effort. Under the leadership of Herbert Hoover, the organization sought to increase agricultural production while reducing civilian consumption of foodstuffs.

Force Bill (1833) Legislation, sparked by the nullification crisis in South Carolina, that authorized the president's use of the army to compel states to comply with federal law.

Gerald Ford (1913–2006) He was appointed to the vice presidency under President Nixon after the resignation of Spiro Agnew, and assumed the presidency after President Nixon's resignation. He resisted congressional pressure to both reduce taxes and increase federal spending, which sent the American economy into the deepest recession since the Great Depression. Ford retained Kissinger as his secretary of state and continued Nixon's foreign policy goals. He was heavily criticized following the collapse of South Vietnam.

Fort Laramie Treaty (1851) Restricted the Plains Indians from using the Overland Trail and permitted the building of government forts.

Fort Necessity After attacking a group of French soldiers, George Washington constructed and took shelter in this fort from vengeful French troops. Washington eventually surrendered to them after a day-long battle. This conflict was a significant event in igniting the French and Indian War.

Fort Sumter First battle of the Civil War, in which the federal fort in Charleston (South Carolina) Harbor was captured by the Confederates on April 14, 1861, after two days of shelling.

"forty-niners" Speculators who went to northern California following the discovery of gold in 1848; the first of several years of large-scale migration was 1849.

Fourteen Points (1918) President Woodrow Wilson's proposed plan for the peace agreement after the First World War that included the creation of a "league of nations" intended to keep the peace.

Fourteenth Amendment (1866) Guaranteed rights of citizenship to former slaves, in words similar to those of the Civil Rights Act of 1866.

Franciscan missions In 1769, Franciscan missionaries accompanied Spanish soldiers to California and over the next fifty years established a chain of missions from San Diego to San Francisco. At these missions, friars sought to convert Indians to Catholicism and make them members of the Spanish empire. The friars stripped the Indians of their native heritage and used soldiers to enforce their will.

Benjamin Franklin (1706–1790) A Boston-born American who epitomized the Enlightenment for many Americans and Europeans, Franklin's wide range of interests led him to become a publisher, inventor, and statesman. As the latter, he contributed to the writing of the Declaration of Independence, served as the minister to France during the Revolutionary War, and was a delegate to the Constitutional Convention.

Free-Soil party A political coalition created in 1848 that opposed the expansion of slavery into the new western territories.

Freedmen's Bureau Reconstruction agency established in 1865 to protect the legal rights of former slaves and to assist with their education, jobs, health care, and landowning.

Freedom Riders Activists who, beginning in 1961, traveled by bus through the South to test federal court rulings that banned segregation on buses and trains.

John C. Frémont, or "the Pathfinder" (1813–1890) He was an explorer and surveyor who helped inspire Americans living in California to rebel against the Mexican government and declare independence.

French and Indian War (Seven Years' War) The last—and most important—of four colonial wars fought between England and France for control of North America east of the Mississippi River.

French Revolution Revolutionary movement beginning in 1789 that overthrew the monarchy and transformed France into an unstable republic before Napoleon Bonaparte assumed power in 1799.

Sigmund Freud (1865–1939) He was the founder of psychoanalysis, which suggested that human behavior was motivated by unconscious and irrational forces. By the 1920s, his ideas were being discussed more openly in America.

frontier revivals Religious revival movement within the Second Great Awakening, that took place in frontier churches in western territories and states in the early nineteenth century.

Fugitive Slave Act (1850) Part of the Compromise of 1850, a provision that authorized federal officials to help capture and then return escaped slaves to their owners without trials.

fundamentalism Anti-modernist Protestant movement started in the early twentieth century that proclaimed the literal truth of the Bible; the name came from *The Fundamentals*, published by conservative leaders.

William Lloyd Garrison (1805–1879) In 1831, he started the anti-slavery newspaper *Liberator* and helped start the New England Anti-Slavery Society. Two years later, he assisted Arthur and Lewis Tappan in the founding of the American Anti-Slavery Society. He and his followers believed that America had been thoroughly corrupted and needed a wide range of reforms, embracing abolition, temperance, pacifism, and women's rights.

Marcus Garvey (1887–1940) He was the leading spokesman for Negro Nationalism, which exalted blackness, black cultural expression, and black exclusiveness. He called upon African Americans to liberate themselves from the surrounding white culture and create their own businesses, cultural centers, and newspapers. He was also the founder of the Universal Negro Improvement Association.

Citizen Genet (1763–1834) As the ambassador to the United States from the new French Republic, he engaged American privateers to attack British ships and conspired with frontiersmen and land speculators to organize an attack on Spanish Florida and Louisiana. His actions and the French radicals' excessive actions against their enemies in the new French Republic caused the French Revolution to lose support among Americans.

Geneva Accords In 1954, the Geneva Accords were signed, which ended French colonial rule in Indochina. The agreement created the independent nations of Laos and Cambodia and divided Vietnam along the 17th parallel until an election in 1956 would reunify the country.

Gettysburg, Battle of (1863) A monumental three-day battle in southern Pennsylvania, widely considered a turning point in the war, in which Union forces successfully countered a second Confederate invasion of the North.

Ghost Dance movement A spiritual and political movement among Native Americans whose followers performed a ceremonial "ghost dance" intended to connect the living with the dead and make the Indians bulletproof in battles intended to restore their homelands.

GI Bill of Rights (1944) Provided unemployment, education, and financial benefits for World War II veterans to ease their transition back to the civilian world.

***Gibbons v. Ogden* (1824)** Supreme Court case that gave the federal government the power to regulate interstate commerce.

Newt Gingrich (1943–) He led the Republican insurgency in Congress in the mid-1990s through mobilizing religious and social conservatives. Along with other Republican congressmen, he created the Contract with America, which was a ten-point anti–big government program. However, the program fizzled out after many of its bills were not passed by Congress.

Gilded Age (1860–1896) An era of dramatic industrial and urban growth characterized by widespread political corruption and loose government oversight over corporations.

The Gilded Age Mark Twain and Charles Dudley Warner's 1873 novel, the title of which became the popular name for the period from the end of the Civil War to the turn of the century.

glasnost Russian term for "openness"; applied to the loosening of censorship in the Soviet Union under Mikhail Gorbachev.

globalization An important, and controversial, transformation of the world economy whereby the Internet helped revolutionize global commerce by creating an international marketplace for goods and services. Led by the growing number of multinational companies and the Americanization of many foreign consumer cultures, with companies like McDonald's and Starbucks appearing in all of the major cities of the world.

Glorious Revolution Successful 1688 coup, instigated by a group of English aristocrats, which overthrew King James II and instated William of Orange and Mary, his English wife, to the British throne.

Barry Goldwater (1909–1998) He was a leader of the Republican right whose book, *The Conscience of a Conservative*, was highly influential to that segment of the party. He proposed eliminating the income tax and overhauling Social Security. In 1964, he ran as the Republican presidential candidate and lost to President Johnson. He campaigned against Johnson's war on poverty, the tradition of New Deal, the nuclear test ban and the Civil Rights Act of 1964. He advocated the wholesale bombing of North Vietnam.

Samuel Gompers (1850–1924) He served as the president of the American Federation of Labor from its inception until his death. He focused on achieving concrete economic gains such as higher wages, shorter hours, and better working conditions.

"good neighbor" policy Proclaimed by President Franklin D. Roosevelt in his first inaugural address in 1933, it sought improved diplomatic relations between the United States and its Latin American neighbors.

Mikhail Gorbachev (1931–) In the late 1980s, Soviet leader Mikhail Gorbachev attempted to reform the Soviet Union through his programs of *perestroika* and *glasnost* and pursued a renewal of détente with America, signing new arms-control agreements with President Reagan. Gorbachev allowed the velvet revolutions of Eastern Europe to occur without outside interference. Eventually the political, social, and economic upheaval he had unleashed would lead to the breakup of the Soviet Union.

Albert Gore Jr. (1948–) He served as a senator of Tennessee and then as President Clinton's vice president. In the 2000 presidential election, he was the Democratic candidate against Governor George W. Bush. The close election came down to Florida's electoral votes. While the votes were being recounted as required by state law, a legal battle was being waged to stop the recount. Finally, the case, *Bush v. Gore*, was presented to the Supreme Court who ruled 5–4 to stop the recount, and Bush was declared the winner.

Jay Gould (1836–1892) As one of the biggest railroad robber barons, he was infamous for buying rundown railroads, making cosmetic improvements, and then reselling them for a profit. He used corporate funds for personal investments and to bribe politicians and judges.

gradualism This strategy for ending slavery involved promoting the banning of slavery in the new western territories and encouraging the release of slaves from slavery. Supporters of this method believed that it would bring about the gradual end of slavery.

Granger Movement Began by offering social and educational activities for isolated farmers and their families and later started to promote "cooperatives" where farmers could join together to buy, store, and sell their crops to avoid the high fees charged by brokers and other middlemen.

Ulysses S. Grant (1822–1885) After distinguishing himself in the western theater of the Civil War, he was appointed general-in-chief of the Union army in 1864. Afterward, he defeated General Robert E. Lee through a policy of aggressive attrition. Lee surrendered to Grant on April 9, 1865 at the Appomattox Court House. His presidential tenure suffered from scandals and fiscal problems, including the debate on whether or not greenbacks, that is, paper money, should be removed from circulation.

Great Awakening Fervent religious revival movement that swept the thirteen colonies from the 1720s through the 1740s.

Great Compromise (Connecticut Compromise) Mediated the differences between the New Jersey and Virginia delegations to the Constitutional Convention by providing for a bicameral legislature, the upper house of which would have equal representation and the lower house of which would be apportioned by population.

Great Depression (1929–1941) Worst economic downturn in American history; it was spurred by the stock market crash in the fall of 1929 and lasted until the Second World War.

Great Migration Mass exodus of African Americans from the rural South to the Northeast and Midwest during and after the First World War.

Great Railroad Strike (1877) A series of demonstrations, some violent, held nationwide in support of striking railroad workers in Martinsburg, West Virginia, who refused to work due to wage cuts.

Great Recession Massive, prolonged economic downturn sparked by the collapse of the housing market and the financial institutions holding unpaid mortgages; it lasted from December 2007 to January 2009 and resulted in 9 million Americans losing their jobs.

Great Sioux War Conflict between Sioux and Cheyenne Indians and federal troops over lands in the Dakotas in the mid-1870s.

Great Society Term coined by President Lyndon B. Johnson in his 1965 State of the Union address, in which he proposed legislation to address problems of voting rights, poverty, diseases, education, immigration, and the environment.

Horace Greeley (1811–1872) In reaction to Radical Reconstruction and corruption in President Ulysses S. Grant's administration, a group of Republicans broke from the party to form the Liberal Republicans. In 1872, the Liberal Republicans chose as their presidential candidate Horace Greeley, who ran on a platform of favoring civil service reform and condemning the Republican's Reconstruction policy.

Greenback party Formed in 1876 in reaction to economic depression, the party favored issuance of unsecured paper money to help farmers repay debts; the movement for free coinage of silver took the place of the greenback movement by the 1880s.

greenbacks Paper money issued during the Civil War. After the war ended, a debate emerged on whether or not to remove the paper currency from circulation and revert back to hard-money currency (gold coins). Opponents of hard money feared that eliminating the greenbacks would shrink the money supply, which would lower crop prices and make it more difficult to repay long-term debts. President Ulysses S. Grant, as well as hard-money currency advocates, believed that gold coins were morally preferable to paper currency.

General Nathanael Greene (1742–1786) He was appointed by Congress to command the American army fighting in the South during the Revolutionary War. Using his patience and his skills of managing men, saving supplies, and avoiding needless risks, he waged a successful war of attrition against the British.

Sarah Grimké (1792–1873) and **Angelina Grimké (1805–1879)** These two sisters gave anti-slavery speeches to crowds of mixed gender that caused some people to condemn them for engaging in unfeminine activities. In 1840, William Lloyd Garrison convinced the Anti-Slavery Society to allow women equal participation in the organization.

Alexander Hamilton (1755–1804) His belief in a strong federal government led him to become a leader of the Federalists. As the first secretary of the Treasury, he laid the foundation for American capitalism through his creation of a federal budget, funded debt, a federal tax system, a national bank, a customs service, and a coast guard. His "Reports on Public Credit" and "Reports on Manufactures" outlined his vision for economic development and government finances. He died in a duel against Aaron Burr.

Alexander Hamilton's economic reforms Various measures designed to strengthen the nation's economy and generate federal revenue through the promotion of new industries, the adoption of new tax policies, the payment of war debts, and the establishment of a national bank.

Warren G. Harding (1865–1923) In the 1920 presidential election, he was the Republican nominee who promised Americans a "return to normalcy." Once in office, Harding's administration dismantled many of the social and economic components of progressivism and pursued a pro-business agenda. Harding appointed four pro-business Supreme Court Justices, cut taxes, increased tariffs, and promoted a lenient attitude toward regulation of corporations. However, he did speak out against racism and ended the exclusion of African Americans from federal positions.

Harlem Renaissance The nation's first self-conscious black literary and artistic movement; it was centered in New York City's Harlem district, which had a largely black population in the wake of the Great Migration from the South.

Hartford Convention A series of secret meetings in December 1814 and January 1815 at which New England Federalists protested American involvement in the War of 1812 and discussed several constitutional amendments, including limiting each president to one term, designed to weaken the dominant Republican Party.

Haymarket Riot (1886) Violent uprising in Haymarket Square, Chicago, where police clashed with labor demonstrators in the aftermath of a bombing.

headright A land-grant policy that promised fifty acres to any colonist who could afford passage to Virginia, as well as fifty more for any accompanying servants. The headright policy was eventually expanded to include any colonists—and was also adopted in other colonies.

Patrick Henry (1736–1799) He inspired the Virginia Resolves, which declared that Englishmen could only be taxed by their elected representatives. In March of 1775, he met with other colonial leaders to discuss the goals of the upcoming Continental Congress and famously declared "Give me liberty or give me death." During the ratification process of the U.S. Constitution, he became one of the leaders of the anti-federalists.

Hessians German mercenary soldiers who were paid by the royal government to fight alongside the British army.

Hiroshima Japanese port city that was the first target of the newly developed atomic bomb on August 6, 1945. Most of the city was destroyed.

Alger Hiss (1904–1996) During the second Red Scare, he served in several government departments and was accused of being a spy for the Soviet Union. He was convicted of lying about espionage. The case was politically damaging to the Truman administration because the president called the charges against Hiss a "red herring."

Adolf Hitler, or "*Führer*" **(1889–1945)** The leader of the Nazis who advocated a violent anti-Semitic, anti-Marxist, pan-German ideology. He started World War II in Europe and orchestrated the systematic murder of some 6 million Jews along with more than a million others.

HIV/AIDS Human immunodeficiency virus (HIV) transmitted via the bodily fluids of infected persons to cause acquired immunodeficiency syndrome (AIDS), an often-fatal disease of the immune system when it appeared in the 1980s.

holding company A corporation established to own and manage other companies' stock rather than to produce goods and services itself.

Holocaust Systematic racist attempt by the Nazis to exterminate the Jews of Europe, resulting in the murder of over 6 million Jews and more than a million other "undesirables."

Homestead Act (1862) Legislation granting "homesteads" of 160 acres of government-owned land to settlers who agreed to work the land for at least five years.

Homestead Steel strike (1892) Labor conflict at the Homestead steel mill near Pittsburgh, Pennsylvania, culminating in a battle between strikers and private security agents hired by the factory's management.

Herbert Hoover (1874–1964) Prior to becoming president, Hoover served as the secretary of commerce in both the Harding and Coolidge administrations. As president during the Great Depression, he believed that the nation's business structure was sound and sought to revive the economy through boosting the nation's confidence. He also tried to restart the economy with government constructions projects, lower taxes, and new federal loan programs, but nothing worked.

horizontal integration The process by which a corporation acquires or merges with its competitors.

horse A tall, four-legged mammal (*Equus caballus*), domesticated and bred since prehistoric times for carrying riders and pulling heavy loads. The Spanish introduced horses to the Americas, eventually transforming many Native American cultures.

House Committee on Un-American Activities (HUAC) Committee of the U.S. House of Representatives formed in 1938; it was originally tasked with investigating Nazi subversion during the Second World War and later shifted its focus to rooting out Communists in the government and the motion-picture industry.

Sam Houston (1793–1863) During Texas's fight for independence from Mexico, Sam Houston was the commander in chief of the Texas forces, and he led the attack that captured General Antonio López de Santa Anna. After Texas gained its independence, he was named its first president.

Jacob Riis' *How the Other Half Lives* Jacob Riis was an early muckraking journalist who exposed the slum conditions in New York City in his book *How the Other Half Lives*.

General William Howe (1729–1814) As the commander of the British army in the Revolutionary War, he seized New York City from Washington's army, but failed to capture it. He missed several more opportunities to quickly end the rebellion, and he resigned his command after the British defeat at Saratoga.

Saddam Hussein (1937–2006) The former dictator of Iraq who became the head of state in 1979. In 1980, he invaded Iran and started the eight-year-long Iran-Iraq War. In 1990, he invaded Kuwait, which caused the Gulf War of 1991. In 2003, he was overthrown and captured when the United States invaded. He was sentenced to death by hanging in 2006.

Anne Hutchinson (1591–1643) The articulate, strong-willed, and intelligent wife of a prominent Boston merchant, who espoused her belief in direct divine revelation. She quarreled with Puritan leaders over her beliefs, and they banished her from the colony.

Immigration Act of 1924 Federal legislation intended to favor northern and western European immigrants over those from southern and eastern Europe by restricting the number of immigrants from any one European country to 2 percent of the total number of immigrants per year, with an overall limit of slightly over 150,000 new arrivals per year.

Immigration and Nationality Services Act of 1965 Legislation that abolished discriminatory quotas based upon immigrants' national origin and treated all nationalities and races equally.

imperialism The use of diplomatic or military force to extend a nation's power and enhance its economic interests, often by acquiring territory or colonies and justifying such behavior with assumptions of racial superiority.

impressment The British navy used press-gangs to kidnap men in British and colonial ports who were then forced to serve in the British navy.

indentured servants Settlers who consented to a defined period of labor (often four to seven years) in exchange for having their passage to the New World paid by their "master."

Independent Treasury Act (1840) System created by President Martin Van Buren and approved by Congress in 1840 whereby the federal government moved its funds from favored state banks to the U.S. Treasury, whose financial transactions could only be in gold or silver coins of paper currency backed by gold or silver.

"Indian New Deal" This phrase refers to the reforms implemented for Native Americans during the New Deal era. John Collier, the commissioner of the Bureau of Indian Affairs (BIA), increased the access Native Americans had to relief programs and employed more Native Americans at the BIA. He worked to pass the Indian Reorganization Act. However, the version of the act passed by Congress was a much-diluted version of Collier's original proposal and did not greatly improve the lives of Native Americans.

Indian Removal Act (1830) Law permitting the forced relocation of Indians to federal lands west of the Mississippi River in exchange for the land they occupied in the East and South.

Indian wars Bloody conflicts between U.S. soldiers and Native Americans that raged in the West from the early 1860s to the late 1870s, sparked by American settlers moving into ancestral Indian lands.

Indochina This area of Southeast Asian consists of Laos, Cambodia, and Vietnam and was once controlled by France as a colony. After the Viet Minh defeated the French, the Geneva Accords were signed, which ended French colonial rule. The agreement created the independent nations of Laos and Cambodia and divided Vietnam along the 17th parallel until an election would reunify the country. Fearing a communist takeover, the U.S. government began intervening in the region during the Truman administration, which led to President Johnson's full-scale military involvement in Vietnam.

industrial war A new concept of war enabled by industrialization that developed from the early 1800s through the Atomic Age. New technologies, including automatic weaponry, forms of transportation like the railroad and airplane, and communication technologies such as the telegraph and telephone, enabled nations to equip large, mass-conscripted armies with chemical and automatic weapons to decimate opposing armies in a "total war."

industrialization Major shift in the nineteenth century from hand-made manufacturing to mass production in mills and factories using water-, coal-, and steam-powered machinery.

infectious diseases Also called contagious diseases, illnesses that can pass from one person to another by way of invasive biological organisms able to reproduce in the bodily tissues of their hosts. Europeans unwittingly brought many such diseases to the Americas, devastating the Native American peoples.

Alfred Thayer Mahan's *The Influence of Sea Power upon History, 1660–1783* (1890) Historical work in which Rear Admiral Alfred Thayer Mahan argues that a nation's greatness and prosperity comes from the power of its navy; the book helped bolster imperialist sentiment in the United States in the late nineteenth century.

Intermediate-Range Nuclear Forces (INF) Treaty (1987) Agreement signed by U.S. president Ronald Reagan and Soviet premier Mikhail Gorbachev to eliminate the deployment of intermediate-range missiles with nuclear warheads.

internal improvements Construction of roads, bridges, canals, harbors, and other infrastructure projects intended to facilitate the flow of goods and people.

Interstate Commerce Commission (ICC) An independent federal agency established in 1887 to oversee businesses engaged in interstate trade, especially railroads, but whose regulatory power was limited when tested in the courts.

interstate highway system In the late 1950s, construction began on a national network of interstate superhighways for the purpose of commerce and defense. The interstate highways would enable the rapid movement of military convoys and the evacuation of cities after a nuclear attack.

Iran-Contra affair Reagan administration scandal in 1987 over the secret, unlawful U.S. sale of arms to Iran in partial exchange for the release of hostages in Lebanon; the arms money in turn was used illegally to aid Nicaraguan right-wing insurgents, the Contras.

Iranian hostage crisis Storming of the U.S. embassy in Tehran in 1979 by Iranian revolutionaries, who held fifty-two Americans hostage for 444 days, despite President Carter's appeals for their release as well as a botched rescue attempt.

Irish Potato Famine In 1845, an epidemic of potato rot brought a famine to rural Ireland that killed over 1 million peasants and instigated a huge increase in the number of Irish immigrating to America. By 1850, the Irish made up 43 percent of the foreign-born population in the United States; in the 1850s, they made up over half the population of New York City and Boston.

iron curtain Term coined by Winston Churchill to describe the cold war divide between western Europe and the Soviet Union's Eastern European satellites.

Iroquois League An alliance of the Iroquois tribes, originally formed sometime between 1450 and 1600, that used their combined strength to pressure Europeans to work with them in the fur trade and to wage war across what is today eastern North America.

Andrew Jackson (1767–1837) As a major general in the Tennessee militia, he had a number of military successes. As president, he worked to enable the "common man" to play a greater role in the political arena. He vetoed the rechartering of the Second National Bank and reduced federal spending. When South Carolina nullified the Tariffs of 1828 and 1832, Jackson requested that Congress pass a "force bill" that would authorize him to use the army to compel the state to comply with the tariffs. He forced eastern Indians to move west of the Mississippi River so their lands could be used by white settlers. Groups of those who opposed Jackson came together to form a new political party called the Whigs.

Thomas "Stonewall" Jackson (1824–1863) He was a Confederate general who was known for his fearlessness in leading rapid marches, bold flanking movements, and furious assaults. He earned his nickname at the Battle of the First Bull Run for standing courageously against Union fire. During the battle of Chancellorsville, his own men accidently mortally wounded him.

William James (1842–1910) He was the founder of Pragmatism and one of the fathers of modern psychology. He believed that ideas gained their validity not from their inherent truth, but from their social consequences and practical application.

Jay's Treaty (1794) Agreement between Britain and the United States, negotiated by Chief Justice John Jay, that settled disputes over trade, prewar debts owed to British merchants, British-occupied forts in American territory, and the seizure of American ships and cargo.

"Jazz Age" Term coined by writer F. Scott Fitzgerald to characterize the spirit of rebellion and spontaneity among young Americans in the 1920s, a spirit epitomized by the hugely popular jazz music of the era.

Thomas Jefferson (1743–1826) He was a plantation owner, author, the drafter of the Declaration Independence, ambassador to France, leader of the Republican party, secretary of state, and the third president of the United States. As president, he purchased the Louisiana territory from France, withheld appointments made by President Adams leading to *Marbury v. Madison*, outlawed foreign slave trade, and was committed to a "wise and frugal" government.

Jeffersonian Republicans Political party founded by Thomas Jefferson in opposition to the Federalist Party led by Alexander Hamilton and John Adams; also known as the Democratic-Republican Party.

Jesuits A religious order founded in 1540 by Ignatius Loyola. They sought to counter the spread of Protestantism during the Protestant Reformation and spread the Catholic faith through work as missionaries. Roughly 3,500 served in New Spain and New France.

"Jim Crow" laws In the New South, these laws mandated the separation of races in various public places that served as a way for the ruling whites to impose their will on all areas of black life.

Andrew Johnson (1808–1875) He was elevated to the presidency after Abraham Lincoln's assassination. In order to restore the Union after the Civil War, he issued an amnesty proclamation and required former Confederate states to ratify the Thirteenth Amendment. After disagreements over the power to restore states' rights, the Radical Republicans attempted to impeach Johnson but fell short on the required number of votes needed to remove him from office.

Lyndon B. Johnson (1908–1973) Former member of the House of Representatives and the former Majority Leader of the Senate, Vice President Lyndon B. Johnson assumed the presidency after President Kennedy's assassination. During his presidency, he passed the Civil Rights Act of 1964, declared a "war on poverty" promoting his own social program called the Great Society, and signed the Immigration and Nationality Service Act of 1965. Johnson greatly increased America's role in Vietnam.

Johnson's Restoration Plan President Andrew Johnson's post–Civil War plan to readmit Confederate states into the Union; requirements included the appointment of a Unionist as a provisional governor in each southern state, ratification of the Thirteenth Amendment, and the extension of voting rights to "educated" blacks.

joint-stock companies Businesses owned by investors, who purchase shares of companies' stocks and share all the profits and losses.

Kansas-Nebraska Act (1854) Controversial legislation that created two new territories taken from Native Americans, Kansas and Nebraska, where residents would vote to decide whether slavery would be allowed (popular sovereignty).

Florence Kelley (1859–1932) As the head of the National Consumer's League, she led the crusade to promote state laws to regulate the number of working hours imposed on women who were wives and mothers.

George F. Kennan (1904–2005) While working as an American diplomat, he devised the strategy of containment, which called for the halting of Soviet expansion. It became America's choice strategy throughout the cold war.

John F. Kennedy (1917–1963) He was elected president in 1960. Despite the difficulties he had in getting his legislation through Congress, he established the Alliance for Progress programs to help Latin America, the Peace Corps, the Trade Expansion Act of 1962, and funding for urban renewal projects and the space program. His foreign political involvement included the failed Bay of Pigs invasion and the missile crisis in Cuba, as well as support of local governments in Indochina. In 1963, he was assassinated by Lee Harvey Oswald in Dallas, Texas.

Kent State During the spring of 1970, students on college campuses across the country protested the expansion of the Vietnam War into Cambodia. At Kent State University, the National Guard attempted to quell the rioting students. The guardsmen panicked and shot at rock-throwing demonstrators. Four student bystanders were killed.

Kentucky and Virginia Resolutions (1798–1799) Passed in response to the Alien and Sedition Acts, the resolutions advanced the state-compact theory that held states could nullify an act of Congress if they deemed it unconstitutional.

Francis Scott Key (1779–1843) During the War of 1812, he watched British forces bombard Fort McHenry, but fail to take it. Seeing the American flag still flying over the fort at dawn inspired him to write "The Star-Spangled Banner," which became the American national anthem.

Martin Luther King Jr. (1929–1968) A central leader of the civil rights movement, he urged people to use nonviolent civil disobedience to demand their rights and bring about change. He successfully led the Montgomery Bus Boycott. While in jail for his role in the demonstrations, he wrote his famous "Letter from Birmingham City Jail," in which he defended his strategy of nonviolent protest. In 1963, he delivered his famous "I Have a Dream" speech from the steps of the Lincoln Memorial as a part of the March on Washington. A year later, he was awarded the Nobel Peace Prize. In 1968, he was assassinated.

King Philip's War A bloody, three-year war in New England (1675–1678), resulting from the escalation of tensions between Indians and English settlers; the defeat of the Indians led to broadened freedoms for the settlers and their dispossessing the region's Indians of most of their land.

King William's War (War of the League of Augsburg) First (1689–1697) of four colonial wars between England and France.

Henry Kissinger (1923–) He served as the secretary of state and national security adviser in the Nixon administration. He negotiated with North Vietnam for an end to the Vietnam War, but the cease-fire did not last; South Vietnam fell to North Vietnam. He helped organize Nixon's historic trips to China and the Soviet Union. In the Middle East, he negotiated a cease-fire between Israel and its neighbors following the Yom

Kippur War and solidified Israel's promise to return to Egypt most of the land it had taken during the 1967 war.

Knights of Labor A national labor organization with a broad reform platform; reached peak membership in the 1880s.

Know-Nothings Nativist, anti-Catholic third party organized in 1854 in reaction to large-scale German and Irish immigration.

Ku Klux Klan (KKK) Organized in Pulaski, Tennessee, in 1866 to terrorize former slaves who voted and held political offices during Reconstruction; a revived organization in the 1910s and 1920s stressed white, Anglo-Saxon, fundamentalist Protestant supremacy; the Klan revived a third time to fight the civil rights movement of the 1950s and 1960s in the South.

Marquis de Lafayette (1757–1834) A wealthy French idealist excited by the American cause, he offered to serve in Washington's army for free in exchange for being named a major general. He overcame Washington's initial skepticism to become one of his most trusted aides.

laissez-faire **("leave things alone")** An economic doctrine holding that businesses and individuals should be able to pursue their economic interests without government interference.

Land Ordinance of 1785 Directed surveying of the Northwest Territory into townships of thirty-six sections (square miles) each, the sale of the sixteenth section of which was to be used to finance public education.

Bartolomé de Las Casas (1484–1566) A Catholic missionary who renounced the Spanish practice of coercively converting Indians and advocated their better treatment. In 1552, he wrote *A Brief Relation of the Destruction of the Indies*, which described the Spanish's cruel treatment of the Indians.

League of Nations Organization of nations formed in the aftermath of the First World War to mediate disputes and maintain international peace; despite President Wilson's intense lobbying for the League of Nations, Congress did not ratify the treaty and the United States failed to join.

Mary Elizabeth Lease (1850–1933) She was a leader of the farm protest movement who advocated violence if change could not be obtained at the ballot box. She believed that the urban-industrial East was the enemy of the working class.

Robert E. Lee (1807–1870) Even though he had served in the U.S. Army for thirty years, he chose to fight on the side of the Confederacy. Lee was excellent at using his field commanders and his soldiers respected him. However, General Ulysses S. Grant eventually wore down his army, and Lee surrendered to Grant at the Appomattox Court House on April 9, 1865.

Lend-Lease Act (1941) Legislation that allowed the president to lend or lease military equipment to any country whose own defense was deemed vital to the defense of the United States.

Levittown First low-cost, mass-produced development of suburban tract housing built by William Levitt on Long Island, New York, in 1947.

Lewis and Clark expedition (1804) Led by Meriwether Lewis and William Clark, a mission to the Pacific coast commissioned for the purposes of scientific and geographical exploration.

Lexington and Concord, Battle of The first shots fired in the Revolutionary War, on April 19, 1775, near Boston; approximately 100 Minutemen and 250 British soldiers were killed.

Liberator William Lloyd Garrison started this anti-slavery newspaper in 1831 in which he renounced gradualism and called for abolition.

Queen Liliuokalani (1838–1917) In 1891, she ascended to the throne of the Hawaiian royal family and tried to eliminate white control of the Hawaiian government. Two years later, Hawaii's white population revolted and seized power with the support of American marines.

Abraham Lincoln (1809–1865) Shortly after he was elected president in 1860, southern states began seceding from the Union, and in April 1861, he declared war on the seceding states. On January 1, 1863, Lincoln signed the Emancipation Proclamation. At the end of the war, he favored a reconstruction strategy for the former Confederate states that did not radically alter southern social and economic life. He was assassinated by John Wilkes Booth at Ford's Theater on April 14, 1865.

Lincoln-Douglas debates (1858) In the Illinois race between Republican Abraham Lincoln and Democrat Stephen A. Douglas for a seat in the U.S. Senate, a series of seven dramatic debates focusing on the issue of slavery in the territories.

John Locke (1632–1704) An English philosopher whose ideas were influential during the Enlightenment. He argued in his *Essay on Human Understanding* (1690) that humanity is largely the product of the environment, the mind being a blank tablet, *tabula rasa*, on which experience is written.

Henry Cabot Lodge (1850–1924) He was the chairman of the Senate Foreign Relations Committee who favored limiting America's involvement in the League of Nations' covenant and sought to amend the Treaty of Versailles.

de Lôme letter Private correspondence written in 1898 by the Spanish ambassador to the U.S., Depuy de Lôme, that described President McKinley as "weak"; the letter was stolen by Cuban revolutionaries and published in the *New York Journal*, deepening American resentment of Spain and moving the two countries closer to war in Cuba.

Lone Star Republic After winning independence from Mexico, Texas became its own nation and was called the Lone Star Republic. In 1836, Texans drafted themselves a constitution, legalized slavery, banned free blacks, named Sam Houston president, and voted for the annexation to the United States. However, quarrels over adding a slave state and fears of instigating a war with Mexico delayed Texas's entrance into the Union until December 29, 1845.

Huey P. Long (1893–1935) He began his political career in Louisiana where he developed a reputation for being an unscrupulous reformer. As a U.S. senator, he became a critic of President Roosevelt's New Deal Plan and offered his alternative: the Share-the-Wealth program. He was assassinated in 1935.

Lost Generation Label given to modernist writers and authors, such as F. Scott Fitzgerland and Ernest Hemingway, who had lost faith in the values and institutions of Western civilization in the aftermath of the Great War.

Louisiana Purchase (1803) President Thomas Jefferson's purchase of the Louisiana Territory from France for $15 million, doubling the size of U.S. territory.

Lowell girls Young female factory workers at the textile mills in Lowell, Massachusetts, which in the early 1820s provided its employees with prepared meals, dormitories, moral discipline, and educational opportunities.

Lowell system Model New England factory communities that during the first half of the nineteenth century provided employees, mostly young women, with meals, a boardinghouse, and moral discipline, as well as educational and cultural opportunities.

Loyalists Colonists who remained loyal to Great Britain before and during the Revolutionary War.

Lusitania British ocean liner torpedoed and sunk by a German U-boat; the deaths of nearly 1,200 of its civilian passengers, including many Americans, caused international outrage.

Martin Luther (1483–1546) A German monk who founded the Lutheran church. He protested abuses in the Catholic Church by posting his Ninety-five Theses, which began the Protestant Reformation.

General Douglas MacArthur (1880–1964) During World War II, he and Admiral Chester Nimitz dislodged the Japanese military from the Pacific Islands they had occupied. Following the war, he was in charge of the occupation of Japan. After North Korea invaded South Korea, Truman sent the U.S. military to defend South Korea under the command of MacArthur. Later in the war, Truman expressed his willingness to negotiate the restoration of prewar boundaries, which MacArthur attempted to undermine. Truman fired MacArthur for his open insubordination.

James Madison (1751–1836) He participated in the Constitutional Convention during which he proposed the Virginia Plan. He believed in a strong federal government and was a leader of the Federalists. However, he also presented to Congress the Bill of Rights and drafted the Virginia Resolutions. As secretary of state, he withheld a commission for William Marbury, which led to the landmark *Marbury v. Madison* decision. During his presidency, he declared war on Britain in response to violations of American shipping rights, which started the War of 1812.

maize (corn) The primary grain crop in Mesoamerica yielding small kernels often ground into cornmeal. Easy to grow in a broad range of conditions, it enabled a global population explosion after being brought to Europe, Africa, and Asia.

Malcolm X (1925–1964) The most articulate spokesman for black power. Originally the chief disciple of Elijah Muhammad, the black Muslim leader in the United States, Malcolm X broke away and founded his own organization committed to establishing relations between African Americans and the nonwhite peoples of the world. Near the end of his life, he began to preach a biracial message of social change. In 1964, he was assassinated by members of a rival group of black Muslims.

manifest destiny The widespread belief that America was "destined" by God to expand westward across the continent into lands claimed by Native Americans as well as European nations.

Horace Mann (1796–1859) He believed the public school system was the best way to achieve social stability and equal opportunity. As a reformer of education, he sponsored a state board of education, the first state-supported "normal" school for training teachers, a state association for teachers, and the minimum school year of six months. He led the drive for a statewide school system.

Marbury v. Madison **(1803)** First Supreme Court decision to declare a federal law—the Judiciary Act of 1801—unconstitutional.

March on Washington Civil rights demonstration on August 28, 1963, on the National Mall, where Martin Luther King Jr. gave his famous "I Have a Dream" speech.

"March to the Sea" The Union army's devastating march through Georgia from Atlanta to Savannah, led by General William T. Sherman, intended to demoralize civilians and destroy the resources the Confederate army needed to fight.

market-based economy Large-scale manufacturing and commercial agriculture that emerged in America during the first half of the nineteenth century, displacing much of the premarket subsistence and barter-based economy and producing boom-and-bust cycles while raising the American standard of living.

George C. Marshall (1880–1959) As the chairman of the Joint Chiefs of Staff, he orchestrated the Allied victories over Germany and Japan in the Second World War. In 1947, he became President Truman's secretary of state and proposed the massive reconstruction program for western Europe called the Marshall Plan.

Chief Justice John Marshall (1755–1835) During his long tenure as chief justice of the Supreme Court (1801–1835), he established the foundations for American jurisprudence, the authority of the Supreme Court, and the constitutional supremacy of the national government over states.

Marshall Plan (1948) Secretary of State George C. Marshall's post–World War II program providing massive U.S. financial and technical assistance to war-torn European countries.

Massachusetts Bay Colony English colony founded by English Puritans in 1630 as a haven for persecuted Congregationalists.

massive resistance White rallying cry disrupting federal efforts to enforce racial integration in the South.

massive retaliation Strategy that used the threat of nuclear warfare as a means of combating the global spread of communism.

Mayflower Compact A formal agreement signed by the Separatist colonists aboard the *Mayflower* in 1620 to abide by laws made by leaders of their own choosing.

Senator Joseph R. McCarthy (1908–1957) In 1950, this senator became the shrewdest and most ruthless exploiter of America's anxiety of communism. He claimed that the U.S. government was full of Communists and led a witch hunt to find them, but he was never able to uncover a single communist agent.

McCarthyism Anti-Communist hysteria led by Senator Joseph McCarthy's "witch hunts" attacking the loyalty of politicians, federal employees, and public figures, despite a lack of evidence.

George B. McClellan (1826–1885) In 1861, President Abraham Lincoln appointed him head of the Army of the Potomac and, later, general-in-chief of the U.S. Army. He built his army into a well-trained and powerful force. After failing to achieve a decisive victory against the Confederacy, he was removed from command in 1862.

Cyrus Hall McCormick (1809–1884) In 1831, he invented a mechanical reaper to harvest wheat, which transformed the scale of agriculture. By hand, a farmer could only harvest half an acre a day, while the McCormick reaper allowed two people to harvest twelve acres of wheat a day.

McCormick reapers Mechanical reapers invented by Cyrus Hall McCormick in 1831 that dramatically increased the production of wheat.

***McCulloch v. Maryland* (1819)** A decision by the Marshall-led Supreme Court that ruled unanimously that Congress had the authority to charter the Bank of the United States and that states did not have the right to tax the national bank.

William McKinley (1843–1901) As a congressman, he was responsible for the McKinley Tariff of 1890, which raised the duties on manufactured products to their highest level ever. Voters disliked the tariff and McKinley, as well as other Republicans, lost his seat in Congress the next election. However, he won the presidential election of 1896 and raised the tariffs again. In 1898, he annexed Hawaii and declared war on Spain. The war concluded with the Treaty of Paris, which gave America control over Puerto Rico, Guam, and the Philippines. Soon America was fighting Filipinos, who were seeking independence for their country. In 1901, McKinley was assassinated.

Robert McNamara (1916–2009) He was the secretary of defense for both President Kennedy and President Johnson and a supporter of America's involvement in Vietnam.

Medicare and **Medicaid** Health care programs designed to aid the elderly and disadvantaged, respectively, as part of President Johnson's Great Society initiative.

Andrew W. Mellon (1855–1937) As President Harding's secretary of the Treasury, he sought to generate economic growth by reducing government spending and lowering taxes. However, he insisted that the tax reductions mainly go to the rich because he believed the wealthy would reinvest their money. In order to bring greater efficiency and nonpartisanship to the government's budget process, he persuaded Congress to created a new Bureau of the Budget and a General Accounting Office.

mercantilism Policy of Great Britain and other imperial powers of regulating the economies of colonies to benefit the mother country.

James Meredith (1933–) In 1962, the governor of Mississippi defied a Supreme Court ruling and refused to allow James Meredith, an African American, to enroll at the University of Mississippi. Federal marshals were sent to enforce the law, which led to clashes between a white mob and the marshals. Federal troops intervened and two people were killed and many others were injured. A few days later, Meredith was able to register at the university.

Metacomet (?–1676) or **King Philip** The chief of the Wampanoages, whom the colonists called King Philip. He resented English efforts to convert Indians to Christianity and waged a war against the English colonists, one in which he was killed.

Mexica Otherwise known as "Aztecs," a Mesoamerican people of northern Mexico who founded the vast Aztec Empire in the fourteenth century, later conquered by the Spanish under Hernán Cortés in 1521.

microprocessor An electronic circuit printed on a small silicon chip; a major technological breakthrough in 1971, it paved the way for the development of the personal computer.

Middle Passage The hellish and often deadly middle leg of the transatlantic "Triangular Trade" in which European ships carried manufactured goods to Africa, then transported enslaved Africans to the Americas and the Caribbean, and finally conveyed American agricultural products back to Europe; from the late sixteenth to the early nineteenth centuries, some 12 million Africans were transported via the Middle Passage, unknown millions more dying en route.

Midway, Battle of A 1942 battle that proved to be a turning point in the Pacific front during World War II; it was the Japanese navy's first major defeat in 350 years.

militant nonviolence After the success of the Montgomery bus boycott, people were inspired by Martin Luther King Jr.'s use of this nonviolent form of protest. Throughout the civil rights movement, demonstrators used this method of protest to challenge racial segregation in the South.

Militia Act (1862) Congressional measure that permitted freed slaves to serve as laborers or soldiers in the United States Army.

Ho Chi Minh (1890–1969) He was the Vietnamese communist resistance leader who drove France and the United States out of Vietnam. After the Geneva Accords divided the region into four countries, he controlled North Vietnam, and ultimately became the leader of all of Vietnam at the conclusion of the Vietnam War.

minstrelsy A form of entertainment that was popular from the 1830s to the 1870s. The performances featured white performers who were made up as African Americans, or blackface. They performed banjo and fiddle music, "shuffle" dances, and lowbrow humor that reinforced racial stereotypes.

Minutemen Special units organized by the militia to be ready for quick mobilization.

***Miranda v. Arizona* (1966)** U.S. Supreme Court decision required police to advise persons in custody of their rights to legal counsel and against self-incrimination.

Mississippi Plan Series of state constitutional amendments in 1890 which sought to severely disenfranchise black voters and was quickly adopted by other southern states.

Missouri Compromise (1820) Legislative decision to admit Missouri as a slave state and abolish slavery in the area west of the Mississippi River and north of the parallel 36°30'.

Model T Henry Ford developed this model of car so that it was affordable for everyone. Its success led to an increase in the production of automobiles, which stimulated other related industries such steel, oil, and rubber. The mass use of automobiles increased the speed goods could be transported, encouraged urban sprawl, and sparked real estate booms in California and Florida.

moderate Republicanism Promise to curb federal government and restore state and local government authority, spearheaded by President Eisenhower.

modernism An early-twentieth-century intellectual and artistic movement that rejected traditional notions of reality and adopted radical new forms of artistic expression.

"money question" Late-nineteenth-century national debate over the nature of U.S. currency; supporters of a fixed gold standard were generally money lenders, and thus preferred to keep the value of money high, while supporters of silver (and gold) coinage were debtors, they owed money, so they wanted to keep the value of money low by increasing the currency supply (inflation).

monopoly A corporation so large that it effectively controls the entire market for its products or services.

James Monroe (1758–1831) He served as secretary of state and war under President Madison and was elected president. As the latter, he signed the Transcontinental Treaty with Spain, which gave Florida to the United States and expanded the Louisiana territory's western border to the Pacific coast. In 1823, he established the Monroe Doctrine. This foreign policy proclaimed that the American continents were no longer open to colonization and America would be neutral in European affairs.

Monroe Doctrine (1823) U.S. foreign policy that barred further colonization in the Western Hemisphere by European powers and pledged that there would be no American interference with any existing European colonies.

Montgomery bus boycott Boycott of bus system in Montgomery, Alabama, organized by civil rights activists after the arrest of Rosa Parks.

Moral Majority Televangelist Jerry Falwell's political lobbying organization, the name of which became synonymous with the religious right; conservative evangelical Protestants who helped ensure President Ronald Reagan's 1980 victory.

J. Pierpont Morgan (1837–1913) As a powerful investment banker, he would acquire, reorganize, and consolidate companies into giant trusts. His biggest achievement was the consolidation of the steel industry into the United States Steel Corporation, which was the first billion-dollar corporation.

J. Pierpont Morgan and Company An investment bank under the leadership of J. Pierpont Morgan that bought or merged unrelated American companies, often using capital acquired from European investors.

Mormons Members of the Church of Jesus Christ of Latter-day Saints, which dismissed other Christian denominations, emphasizing universal salvation and a modest lifestyle; Mormons were often persecuted for their secrecy and clannishness.

Morrill Land Grant Act (1862) Federal statute that allowed for the creation of land-grant colleges and universities, which were founded to provide technical education in agriculture, mining, and industry.

Samuel F. B. Morse (1791–1872) In 1832, he invented the telegraph and revolutionized the speed of communication.

mountain men Inspired by the fur trade, these men left civilization to work as trappers and reverted to a primitive existence in the wilderness. They were the first white people to find routes through the Rocky Mountains, and they pioneered trails that settlers later used to reach the Oregon country and California in the 1840s.

muckrakers Writers who exposed corruption and abuses in politics, business, consumer safety, working conditions, and more, spurring public interest in progressive reforms.

Mugwumps Reformers who bolted the Republican party in 1884 to support Democratic Grover Cleveland for president over Republican James G. Blaine, whose secret dealings on behalf of railroad companies had brought charges of corruption.

mulattoes Mixed-race people who constituted most of the South's free black population.

Benito Mussolini, or "*Il Duce*" (1883–1945) The Italian founder of the Fascist party who came to power in Italy in 1922 and allied himself with Adolf Hitler and the Axis powers during the Second World War.

National Association for the Advancement of Colored People (NAACP) Organization founded in 1910 by black activists and white progressives that promoted education as a means of combating social problems and focused on legal action to secure the civil rights supposedly guaranteed by the Fourteenth and Fifteenth Amendments.

National Industrial Recovery Act (1933) Passed on the last of the Hundred Days, it created public-works jobs through the Federal Emergency Relief Administration and established a system of self-regulation for industry through the National Recovery Administration, which was ruled unconstitutional in 1935.

National Labor Union (NLU) A federation of labor and reform leaders established in 1866 to advocate for new state and local laws to improve working conditions.

National Recovery Administration (NRA) (1933) Controversial federal agency that brought together business and labor leaders to create "codes of fair competition" and "fair labor" policies, including a national minimum wage.

National Security Act Congressional legislation passed in 1947 that created the Department of Defense, the National Security Council, and the Central Intelligence Agency.

National Socialist German Workers' Party (Nazi) Founded in the 1920s, this party gained control over Germany under the leadership of Adolf Hitler in 1933 and continued in power until Germany's defeat at the end of the Second World War. It advocated a violent anti-Semitic, anti-Marxist, pan-German ideology. The Nazi party perpetrated the Holocaust.

National Trades' Union Formed in 1834 to organize all local trade unions into a stronger national association, only to be dissolved amid the economic depression during the late 1830s.

nativists Members of a reactionary conservative movement characterized by heightened nationalism, anti-immigrant sentiment, and the enactment of laws setting stricter regulations on immigration.

natural rights An individual's basic rights that should not be violated by any government or community.

Navigation Acts Restrictions passed by the British Parliament between 1650 and 1775 to control colonial trade and bolster the mercantile system.

Negro nationalism A cultural and political movement in the 1920s spearheaded by Marcus Garvey which exalted blackness, black cultural expression, and black exclusiveness.

Negrophobia A violent new wave of racism that spread in the late nineteenth century largely spurred by white resentment for African-American financial success and growing political influence.

"neutrality laws" Series of laws passed by Congress aimed at avoiding entering a Second World War; these included the Neutrality Act of 1935, which banned loans to warring nations.

"New Democrats" Centrist ("moderate") Democrats led by President Bill Clinton that emerged in the late 1980s and early 1990s to challenge the "liberal" direction of the party.

"new economy" Period of sustained economic prosperity during the nineties marked by budget surpluses, the explosion of dot.com industries, low inflation, and low unemployment.

New France The name used for the area of North America that was colonized by the French. Unlike Spanish or English colonies, New France had a small number of colonists, which forced them to initially seek good relations with the indigenous people they encountered.

New Freedom Program championed in 1912 by the Woodrow Wilson campaign that aimed to restore competition in the economy by eliminating all trusts rather than simply regulating them.

New Frontier Proposed domestic program championed by the incoming Kennedy administration in 1961 that aimed to jump-start the economy and trigger social progress.

"new immigrants" Wave of newcomers from southern and eastern Europe, including many Jews, who became a majority among immigrants to America after 1890.

New Jersey Plan The delegations to the Constitutional Convention were divided between two plans on how to structure the government: New Jersey wanted one legislative body with equal representation for each state.

New Left Term coined by the Students for a Democratic Society to distinguish their efforts at grassroots democracy from those of the 1930s Old Left, which had embraced orthodox Marxism.

New Mexico A U.S. territory and later a state in the American Southwest, originally established by the Spanish, who settled there in the sixteenth century, founded Catholic missions, and exploited the region's indigenous peoples.

New Nationalism Platform of the Progressive party and slogan of former President Theodore Roosevelt in the presidential campaign of 1912; stressed government activism, including regulation of trusts, conservation, and recall of state court decisions that had nullified progressive programs.

"New Negro" In the 1920s, a slow and steady growth of black political influence occurred in northern cities where African Americans were freer to speak and act. This political activity created a spirit of protest that expressed itself culturally in the Harlem Renaissance and politically in "new Negro" nationalism.

New Netherland Dutch colony conquered by the English in 1667 and out of which four new colonies were created: New York, New Jersey, Pennsylvania, and Delaware.

New Orleans, Battle of (1815) Final major battle in the War of 1812, in which the Americans under General Andrew Jackson unexpectedly and decisively countered the British attempt to seize the port of New Orleans, Louisiana.

New South *Atlanta Constitution* editor Henry W. Grady's 1886 term for the prosperous post–Civil War South: democratic, industrial, urban, and free of nostalgia for the defeated plantation South.

William Randolph Hearst's *New York Journal* In the late 1890s, the *New York Journal* and its rival, the *New York World*, printed sensationalism on the Cuban revolution as part of their heated competition for readership. The *New York Journal* printed a negative letter from the Spanish ambassador about President McKinley and inflammatory coverage of the sinking of the *Maine* in Havana Harbor. These two events roused the American public's outcry against Spain.

Joseph Pulitzer's *New York World* In the late 1890s, the *New York World* and its rival, *New York Journal*, printed sensationalism on the Cuban revolution as part of their heated competition for readership.

Admiral Chester Nimitz (1885–1966) During the Second World War, he was the commander of central Pacific. Along with General Douglas MacArthur, he dislodged the Japanese military from the Pacific Islands they had occupied.

Nineteenth Amendment Constitutional amendment that granted women the right to vote in 1920.

Richard M. Nixon (1913–1994) He first came to national prominence as a congressman involved in the investigation of Alger Hiss, and later served as vice president during the Eisenhower administration. After being elected president in 1968, he slowed the federal enforcement of civil rights and appointed pro-Southern justices to the Supreme Court. He began a program of Vietnamization of the war. In 1973, America, North and South Vietnam, and the Viet Cong agreed to end the war and the United States withdrew. However, the cease-fire was broken, and South Vietnam fell to North Vietnam. In 1970, Nixon declared that the America was no longer the world's policemen and he would seek some partnerships with Communist countries, historically travelling to China and the Soviet Union. In 1972, he was reelected, but the Watergate scandal erupted shortly after his victory. He resigned the presidency under threat of impeachment.

nonviolent civil disobedience Tactic of defying unjust laws through peaceful actions championed by Dr. Martin Luther King Jr.

Lord North (1732–1792) The first minister of King George III's cabinet whose efforts to subdue the colonies only brought them closer to revolution. He helped bring about the Tea Act of 1773, which led to the Boston Tea Party. In an effort to discipline Boston, he wrote, and Parliament passed, four acts that galvanized colonial resistance.

North American Free Trade Agreement (NAFTA) Agreement eliminating trade barriers that was signed in 1994 by the United States, Canada, and Mexico, making North America the largest free-trade zone in the world.

North Atlantic Treaty Organization (NATO) Defensive political and military alliance formed in 1949 by the United States, Canada, and ten Western European nations to deter Soviet expansion in Europe.

Northwest Ordinance (1787) Land policy for new western territories in the Ohio valley that established the terms and conditions for self-government and statehood while also banning slavery from the region.

NSC-68 (1950) Top-secret policy paper approved by President Truman that outlined a militaristic approach to combating the spread of global communism.

nullification The right claimed by some states to veto a federal law deemed unconstitutional.

Barack Obama (1961–) In the 2008 presidential election, Senator Barack Obama mounted an innovative Internet-based and grassroots-oriented campaign. As the nation's economy nosedived in the fall of 2008, Obama linked the Republican economic philosophy with the country's dismal financial state and promoted a message of "change" and "politics of hope," which resonated with voters. He decisively won the presidency and became America's first person of color to be elected president.

Occupy Wall Street A grassroots movement protesting a capitalist system that fostered social and economic inequality. Begun in Zuccotti Park, New York City, during 2011, the movement spread rapidly across the nation, triggering a national conversation about income inequality and protests of the government's "bailouts" of the banks and corporations allegedly responsible for the Great Recession.

Sandra Day O'Connor (1930–) She was the first woman to serve on the Supreme Court of the United States and was appointed by President Reagan. Reagan's critics charged that her appointment was a token gesture and not a sign of any real commitment to gender equality.

Ohio gang In order to escape the pressures of the White House, President Harding met with a group of people, called the "Ohio gang," in a house on K Street in Washington, D.C. Members of this gang were given low-level positions in the American government and they used their White House connection to "line their pockets" by granting government contracts without bidding, which led to a series of scandals, most notably the Teapot Dome Scandal.

Old Southwest Region covering western Georgia, Alabama, Mississippi, Louisiana, Arkansas, and Texas, where low land prices and fertile soil attracted hundreds of thousands of settlers after the American Revolution.

Open Door policy Official U.S. insistence that Chinese trade would be open to all nations; Secretary of State John Hay unilaterally announced the policy in 1899 in hopes of protecting the Chinese market for U.S. exports.

open shop Business policy of not requiring union membership as a condition of employment; such a policy, where legal, has the effect of weakening unions and diminishing workers' rights.

open range Informal system of governing property on the frontier in which small ranchers could graze their cattle anywhere on unfenced lands; brought to an end by the introduction of barbed wire, a low-cost way to fence off one's land.

Operation Desert Shield After Saddam Hussein invaded Kuwait in 1990, President George H. W. Bush sent American military forces to Saudi Arabia on a strictly defensive mission. They were soon joined by a multinational coalition. When the coalition's mission changed to the retaking of Kuwait, the operation was renamed Desert Storm.

Operation Desert Storm (1991) Assault by American-led multinational forces that quickly defeated Iraqi forces under Saddam Hussein in the First Gulf War, ending the Iraqi occupation of Kuwait.

Operation Overlord The Allies' assault on Hitler's "Atlantic Wall," a seemingly impregnable series of fortifications and minefields along the French coastline that German forces had created using captive Europeans for laborers.

J. Robert Oppenheimer (1904–1967) He led the group of physicists at the laboratory in Los Alamos, New Mexico, who constructed the first atomic bomb.

Oregon Country The Convention of 1818 between Britain and the United States established the Oregon Country as being west of the crest of the Rocky Mountains and the two countries were to jointly occupy it. In 1824, the United States and Russia signed a treaty that established the line of 54°40′ as the southern boundary of Russia's territorial claim in North America. A similar agreement between Britain and Russia finally gave the Oregon Country clearly defined borders, but it remained under joint British and American control.

Oregon fever The lure of fertile land and economic opportunities in the Oregon Country that drew thousands of settlers westward, beginning in the late 1830s.

Osceola (1804?–1838) He was the leader of the Seminole nation who resisted the federal Indian removal policy through a protracted guerilla war. In 1837, he was treacherously seized under a flag of truce and imprisoned at Fort Moultrie, where he was left to die.

Overland Trails Trail routes followed by wagon trains bearing settlers and trade goods from Missouri to the Oregon Country, California, and New Mexico, beginning in the 1840s.

A. Mitchell Palmer (1872–1936) As the attorney general, he played an active role in the government's response to the Red Scare. After several bombings across America, including one at Palmer's home, he and other Americans became convinced that there was a well-organized Communist terror campaign at work. The federal government launched a campaign of raids and deportations and collected files on radical individuals.

Panic of 1819 A financial panic that began a three-year-long economic crisis triggered by a reduced demand of American imports, declining land values, and reckless practices by local and state banks.

Panic of 1837 A financial calamity in the United States brought on by a dramatic slowdown in the British economy and exacerbated by falling cotton prices, failed crops, high inflation, and reckless state banks.

Panic of 1873 A major economic collapse caused by President Grant's efforts to remove greenbacks from circulation; the resultant depression, in which thousands of businesses closed and millions lost their jobs, was then the worst in the nation's history.

Panic of 1893 A major collapse in the national economy after several major railroad companies declared bankruptcy, leading to a severe depression and several violent clashes between workers and management.

panning A method of mining that used a large metal pan to sift gold dust and nuggets from riverbeds during the California gold rush of 1849.

Rosa Parks (1913–2005) In 1955, she refused to give up her seat to a white man on a city bus in Montgomery, Alabama, which a local ordinance required of blacks. She was arrested for disobeying the ordinance. In response, black community leaders organized the Montgomery bus boycott.

Parliament Legislature of Great Britain, composed of the House of Commons, whose members are elected, and the House of Lords, whose members are either hereditary or appointed.

party bosses Powerful political leaders who controlled a "machine" of associates and operatives to promote both individual and party interests, often using informal tactics such as intimidation or the patronage system.

paternalism A moral position developed during the first half of the nineteenth century which claimed that slaves were deprived of liberty for their own "good." Such a rationalization was adopted by some slave owners to justify slavery.

Patriots Colonists who rebelled against British authority before and during the Revolutionary War.

patronage An informal system (sometimes called the "spoils system") used by politicians to reward their supporters with government appointments or contracts.

Alice Paul (1885–1977) She was a leader of the women's suffrage movement and head of the Congressional Committee of National Women Suffrage Association. She instructed female suffrage activists to use more militant tactics, such as picketing state legislatures, chaining themselves to public buildings, inciting police to arrest them, and undertaking hunger strikes.

Norman Vincent Peale (1898–1993) He was a champion of the upbeat and feel-good theology that was popular in the 1950s religious revival. He advocated getting rid of any depressing or negative thoughts and replacing them with "faith, enthusiasm and joy," which would make an individual popular and well liked.

Pearl Harbor Surprise Japanese attack on the U.S. fleet at Pearl Harbor on December 7, 1941, which prompted the immediate American entry into the war.

"peculiar institution" A phrase used by whites in the antebellum South to refer to slavery without using the word slavery.

Pennsylvania English colony founded by William Penn in 1681 as a Quaker commonwealth, though it welcomed people of all religions.

Pentagon Papers Informal name for the Defense Department's secret history of the Vietnam conflict; leaked to the press by former official Daniel Ellsberg and published in the *New York Times* in 1971.

People's party (Populists) Political party largely made up of farmers from the South and West that struggled to gain political influence from the East. Populists advocated a variety of reforms, including free coinage of silver, a progressive income tax, postal savings banks, regulation of railroads, and direct election of U.S. senators.

Pequot War Massacre in 1637 and subsequent dissolution of the Pequot Nation by Puritan settlers, who seized the Indians' lands.

perestroika Russian term for "economic restructuring"; applied to Mikhail Gorbachev's series of political and economic reforms that included shifting a centrally planned Commmunist economy to a mixed economy allowing for capitalism.

Commodore Matthew Perry (1794–1858) In 1854, he negotiated the Treaty of Kanagawa, which was the first step in starting a political and commercial relationship between the United States and Japan.

John J. Pershing U.S. general sent by President Wilson to put down attacks on the Mexican border led by Francisco "Pancho" Villa.

Personal Responsibility and Work Opportunity Act of 1996 (PRWOA) Comprehensive welfare-reform measure, passed by a Republican Congress and signed by President Clinton, that aimed to decrease the size of the "welfare state" by limiting the amount of government aid provided to the unemployed so as to encourage recipients to find jobs.

"pet banks" During President Andrew Jackson's fight with the national bank, Jackson resolved to remove all federal deposits from it. To comply with Jackson's demands, Secretary of Treasury Taney continued to draw on government's accounts in the national bank, but deposit all new federal receipts in state banks. The state banks that received these deposits were called "pet banks."

Pilgrims Puritan Separatists who broke completely with the Church of England and sailed to the New World aboard the *Mayflower*, founding Plymouth Colony on Cape Cod in 1620.

Gifford Pinchot (1865–1946) As the head of the Division of Forestry, he implemented a conservation policy that entailed the scientific management of natural resources to serve the public interest. His work helped start the conservation movement.

Elizabeth Lucas Pinckney (1722?–1793) One of the most enterprising horticulturists in colonial America, she began managing her family's three plantations in South Carolina at the age of sixteen. She had tremendous success growing indigo, which led to many other plantations growing the crop as well.

Pinckney's Treaty Treaty with Spain negotiated by Thomas Pinckney in 1795; established United States boundaries at the Mississippi River and the 31st parallel and allowed open transportation on the Mississippi.

Francisco Pizarro (1478?–1541) In 1531, he led his Spanish soldiers to Peru and conquered the Inca Empire.

"plain white folk" Yeoman farmers who lived and worked on their own small farms, growing food and cash crops to trade for necessities.

plantation mistress Matriarch of a planter's household, responsible for supervising the domestic aspects of the estate.

planter Owner of a large farm in the South that was worked by twenty or more slaves and supervised by overseers.

political "machine" A network of political activists and elected officials, usually controlled by a powerful "boss," that attempts to manipulate local politics.

James Knox Polk, or **"Young Hickory" (1795–1849)** As president, his chief concern was the expansion of the United States. Shortly after taking office, Mexico broke off relations with the United States over the annexation of Texas. Polk declared war on Mexico and sought to subvert Mexican authority in California. The United States defeated Mexico, and the two nations signed the Treaty of Guadalupe Hidalgo, in which Mexico gave up any claims on Texas north of the Rio Grande River and ceded New Mexico and California to the United States.

Pontiac's Rebellion An Indian attack on British forts and settlements after France ceded to the British its territory east of the Mississippi River, as part of the Treaty of Paris in 1763, without consulting France's Indian allies.

popular sovereignty Legal concept by which the white male settlers in a new U.S. territory would vote to decide whether or not to permit slavery.

Pottawatomie Massacre In retaliation for the "sack of Lawrence," John Brown and his abolitionist cohorts hacked five men to death in the pro-slavery settlement of Pottawatomie, Kansas, on May 24, 1856, triggering a guerrilla war in the Kansas Territory that cost 200 settlers' lives.

Powhatan Confederacy An alliance of several powerful Algonquian tribes under the leadership of Chief Powhatan, organized into thirty chiefdoms along much of the Atlantic coast in the late sixteenth and early seventeenth centuries.

Chief Powhatan Wahunsonacock He was called Powhatan by the English after the name of his tribe, and was the powerful, charismatic chief of numerous Algonquian-speaking towns in eastern Virginia representing over 10,000 Indians.

professions Occupations requiring specialized knowledge of some field; the Industrial Revolution and its new organization of labor created an array of professions in the nineteenth century.

Progressive party In the 1912 election, Theodore Roosevelt was unable to secure the Republican nomination for president. He left the Republican party and formed his own party of progressive Republicans, called the "Bull Moose" party (later Progressive Party). Roosevelt and Taft split the Republican vote, which allowed Democrat Woodrow Wilson to win.

Prohibition National ban on the manufacture and sale of alcohol that lasted from 1920 to 1933, though the law was widely violated and proved too difficult to enforce effectively.

proprietary colonies A colony owned by an individual, rather than a joint-stock company.

Protestant Reformation Sixteenth-century religious movement initiated by Martin Luther, a German monk whose public criticism of corruption in the Roman Catholic Church, and whose teaching that Christians can communicate directly with God, gained a wide following and led to the Protestant Reformation.

public schools Elementary and secondary schools funded by the state and free of tuition.

pueblos The Spanish term for the adobe cliff dwellings of the indigenous people of the southwestern United States.

Pullman strike (1894) A national strike by the American Railway Union, whose members shut down major railways in sympathy with striking workers in Pullman, Illinois; ended with intervention of federal troops.

Puritans English religious dissenters who sought to "purify" the Church of England of its Catholic practices.

Quakers George Fox founded the Quaker religion in 1647. They rejected the use of formal sacraments and ministry, refused to take oaths, and embraced pacifism. Fleeing persecution, they settled and established the colony of Pennsylvania.

race-based slavery Institution that uses racial characteristics and myths to justify enslaving a people.

Radical Republicans Senators and congressmen who, strictly identifying the Civil War with the abolitionist cause, sought swift emancipation of the slaves, punishment of the rebels, and tight controls over the former Confederate states after the war.

railroads Steam-powered vehicles that improved passenger transportation, quickened western settlement, and enabled commercial agriculture in the nineteenth century.

Raleigh's Roanoke Island Colony English expedition of 117 settlers, including Virginia Dare, the first English child born in the New World; colony disappeared from Roanoke Island in the Outer Banks sometime between 1587 and 1590.

A. Philip Randolph (1889–1979) He was the head of the Brotherhood of Sleeping Car Porters who planned a march on Washington, D.C., to demand an end to racial discrimination in the defense industries. To stop the march, the Roosevelt administration negotiated an agreement with the Randolph group. The demonstration would be called off and an executive order would be issued that forbade discrimination in defense work and training programs and set up the Fair Employment Practices Committee.

range wars In the late 1800s, conflicting claims over land and water rights triggered violent disputes between farmers and ranchers in parts of the western United States.

Ronald Reagan (1911–2004) In 1980, the former actor and governor of California was elected president. In office, he reduced social spending, cut taxes, and increased defense spending. During his presidency, the federal debt tripled, the federal deficit rose, programs such as housing and school lunches were cut, and the HIV/AIDS crisis grew to prominence in the United States. He signed an arms-control treaty with the Soviet Union in 1987 and authorized covert CIA operations in Central America. In 1986 the Iran-Contra scandal was revealed.

Reaganomics President Reagan's "supply-side" economic philosophy combining tax cuts with the goals of decreased government spending reduced regulation of business, and a balanced budget.

Reconstruction Finance Corporation (RFC) (1932) Federal program established under President Hoover to loan money to banks and other corporations to help them avoid bankruptcy.

Red Power Activism by militant Native American groups to protest living conditions on Indian reservations through demonstrations, legal action, and, at times, violence.

Redeemers Post–Civil War Democratic leaders who supposedly saved the South from Yankee domination and preserved the primarily rural economy.

Dr. Walter Reed (1851–1902) His work on yellow fever in Cuba led to the discovery that the fever was carried by mosquitoes. This understanding helped develop more effective controls of the worldwide disease.

reform Darwinism A social philosophy developed by Lester Frank War that challenged the ruthlessness of social Darwinism by asserting that humans were not passive pawns of evolutionary forces. Instead, people could actively shape the process of evolutionary social development through cooperation, innovation, and planning.

Reformation European religious movement that challenged the Catholic Church and resulted in the beginnings of Protestant Christianity. During this period, Catholics and Protestants persecuted, imprisoned, tortured, and killed each other in large numbers.

religious right Christian conservatives with a faith-based political agenda that includes prohibition of abortion and allowing prayer in public schools.

reparations As a part of the Treaty of Versailles, Germany was required to confess its responsibility for the First World War and make payments to the victors for the entire expense of the war. These two requirements created a deep bitterness among Germans.

Alexander Hamilton's Report on Manufactures First secretary of the Treasury Alexander Hamilton's 1791 analysis that accurately foretold the future of American industry and proposed tariffs and subsidies to promote it.

Republican ideology Political belief in representative democracy in which citizens govern themselves by electing representatives, or legislators, to make key decisions on the citizens' behalf.

republican simplicity Deliberate attitude of humility and frugality, as opposed to monarchial pomp and ceremony, adopted by Thomas Jefferson in his presidency

Republicans First used during the early nineteenth century to describe supporters of a strict interpretation of the Constitution, which they believed would safeguard individual freedoms and states' rights from the threats posed by a strong central government. The idealist Republican vision of sustaining an agrarian-oriented union was developed largely by Thomas Jefferson.

"return to normalcy" Campaign promise of Republican presidential candidate Warren G. Harding in 1920, meant to contrast with Woodrow Wilson's progressivism and internationalism.

Paul Revere (1735–1818) On the night of April 18, 1775, British soldiers marched toward Concord to arrest American Revolutionary leaders and seize their depot of supplies. Paul Revere famously rode through the night and raised the alarm about the approaching British troops.

Roaring Twenties The 1920s, an era of social and intellectual revolution in which young people experimented with new forms of recreation and sexuality. The Eastern, urban cultural shift clashed with conservative and insular Midwestern America, which increased the tensions between the two regions.

Jackie Robinson (1919–1972) In 1947, he became the first African American to play major league baseball. He won over fans and players and stimulated the integration of other professional sports.

rock-and-roll music Alan Freed, a disc jockey, noticed white teenagers were buying rhythm and blues records that had been only purchased by African Americans and Hispanic Americans. Freed began playing these records, but called them rock-and-roll records as a way to overcome the racial barrier. As the popularity of the music genre increased, it helped bridge the gap between "white" and "black" music.

John D. Rockefeller (1839–1937) In 1870, he founded the Standard Oil Company of Ohio, which was his first step in creating his vast oil empire. He perfected the idea of a holding company.

Roe v. Wade **(1973)** Landmark Supreme Court decision striking down state laws that banned abortions during the first trimester of pregnancy.

Roman Catholicism The Christian faith and religious practices of the Roman Catholic Church, which exerted great political, economic, and social influence on much of Western Europe and, through the Spanish and Portuguese Empires, on the Americas.

Romanticism Philosophical, literary, and artistic movement of the nineteenth century that was largely a reaction to the rationalism of the previous century; Romantics valued emotion, mysticism, and individualism.

Eleanor Roosevelt (1884–1962) She redefined the role of the presidential spouse and was the first woman to address a national political convention, write a nationally syndicated column, and hold regular press conferences. She travelled throughout the nation to promote the New Deal, women's causes, and organized labor, and to meet with African American leaders.

Franklin Delano Roosevelt (1882–1945) Elected during the Great Depression, Roosevelt sought to help struggling Americans through his New Deal programs that created employment and social programs, such as Social Security. After the bombing of Pearl Harbor, he declared war on Japan and Germany and led the country through most of the Second World War before dying of a cerebral hemorrhage.

Theodore Roosevelt (1858–1919) As the assistant secretary of the navy, he supported expansionism, American imperialism, and war with Spain. He led the Rough Riders, in Cuba during the War of 1898 and used the notoriety of this military campaign for political gain. As President McKinley's vice president, he succeeded McKinley after his assassination. His forceful foreign policy became known as "big stick diplomacy." Domestically, his policies on natural resources helped start the conservation movement. Unable to win the Republican nomination for president in 1912, he formed his own party of progressive Republicans: the "Bull Moose" party.

Roosevelt Corollary President Theodore Roosevelt's 1904 revision of the Monroe Doctrine (1823) in which he argued that the United States could use military force in Central and South American nations to prevent European nations from intervening in the Western Hemisphere.

Rough Riders The First U.S. Volunteer Cavalry, led in the War of 1898 by Theodore Roosevelt; they were victorious in their only engagement, the Battle of San Juan Hill near Santiago, Cuba, and Roosevelt was celebrated as a national hero, bolstering his political career.

Royal Proclamation of 1763 Statement issued by King George III in the wake of the Treaty of Paris which prohibited British colonists from settling any lands beyond the Appalachian mountains.

Nicola Sacco (1891–1927) In 1920, he and Bartolomeo Vanzetti were Italian immigrants who were arrested for stealing $16,000 and killing a paymaster and his guard. Their trial took place during a time of numerous bombings by anarchists and their judge was openly prejudicial; many liberals and radicals believe that their conviction was based on their political ideas and ethnic origin rather than the evidence against them.

Sacco and Vanzetti case The 1921 trial of two Italian immigrants that occurred at the height of Italian immigration and against the backdrop of numerous terror attacks by anarchists; despite a lack of clear evidence, the two defendants, both self-professed anarchists, were convicted of murder and were executed in 1927.

saloons Bars or taverns where mostly men would gather to drink, eat, relax, play games, and, often, to discuss politics.

salutary neglect Informal British policy during the first half of the eighteenth century that allowed the American colonies considerable freedom to pursue their economic and political interests in exchange for colonial obedience.

same-sex marriage The legal right for gay and lesbian couples to marry; it became the most divisive issue in the culture wars of the early 2010s as more and more court rulings affirmed this right in states and municipalities across the United States. In a landmark 2015 decision, the Supreme Court ruled in favor of legalizing same-sex marriage nationwide.

Sand Creek Massacre (1864) A brutal slaughter of unarmed Indian men, women, and children who had been promised protection by the territorial governor of Colorado; the massacre ignited warfare between Americans and Indians across the central plains for the next three years.

Sandinista Cuban-sponsored government that came to power in Nicaragua after toppling a corrupt dictator. The State Department believed that the Sandinistas were supplying the leftist Salvadoran rebels with Cuban and Soviet arms. In response, the Reagan administration ordered the CIA to train and supply guerrilla bands of anti-Communist Nicaraguans called Contras. A cease-fire agreement between the Contras and Sandinistas was signed in 1988.

Sandlot Incident Violence occurring during the Great Railroad Strike of 1877, when mobs of frustrated working-class whites in San Francisco attacked Chinese immigrants, blaming them for economic hardship.

General Antonio López de Santa Anna (1794–1876) In 1834, he seized political power in Mexico and became a dictator. In 1835, Texans rebelled against him and he led his army to Texas to crush their rebellion. He captured the missionary called the Alamo and killed all of its defenders, which inspired Texans to continue to resistance and Americans to volunteer to fight for Texas. The Texans captured Santa Anna during a surprise attack and he bought his freedom by signing a treaty recognizing Texas's independence.

Saratoga, Battles of Decisive defeat of 5,000 British troops under General John Burgoyne in several battles near Saratoga, New York, in October 1777; the American victory helped convince France to enter the war on the side of the Patriots.

scalawags White southern Republicans—some former Unionists—who served in Reconstruction governments.

Phyllis Schlafly (1924–) A right-wing Republican activist who spearheaded the anti-feminism movement. She believed feminists were "anti-family, anti-children, and pro-abortion." She worked against the equal rights amendment for women and civil rights protection for gays.

Scopes Trial Highly publicized 1925 trial of a high school teacher in Tennessee for violating a state law that prohibited the teaching of evolution; the trial was seen as the climax of the fundamentalist war on Darwinism.

Winfield Scott (1786–1866) During the Mexican War, he was the American general who captured Mexico City, which ended the war. Using his popularity from his military success, he ran as a Whig party candidate for President.

Sears, Roebuck and Company By the end of the nineteenth century, this company dominated the mail-order industry and helped create a truly national market. Its mail-order catalog and low prices allowed people living in rural areas and small towns to buy products that were previously too expensive or available only to city dwellers.

secession Shortly after President Abraham Lincoln was elected, southern states began dissolving their ties with the United States because they believed Lincoln and the Republican party were a threat to slavery.

Second Bank of the United States (B.U.S.) Established in 1816 after the first national bank's charter expired; it stabilized the economy by creating a sound national currency, by making loans to farmers, small manufacturers, and entrepreneurs, and by regulating the ability of state banks to issue their own paper currency.

Second Great Awakening Religious revival movement that arose in reaction to the growth of secularism and rationalist religion and spurred the growth of the Baptist and Methodist churches.

Second Industrial Revolution Beginning in the late nineteenth century, a wave of technological innovations, especially in iron and steel production, steam and electrical power, and telegraphic communications, all of which spurred industrial development and urban growth.

Second New Deal (1935–1938) Expansive cluster of legislation proposed by President Roosevelt that established new regulatory agencies, strengthened the rights of workers to organize unions, and laid the foundation of a federal social welfare system through the creation of Social Security.

second two-party system Domination of national politics by two major political parties, such as the Whigs and Democrats during the 1830s and 1840s.

Securities and Exchange Commission (1934) Federal agency established to regulate the issuance and trading of stocks and bonds in an effort to avoid financial panics and stock market "crashes."

Seneca Falls Convention (1848) Convention organized by feminists Lucretia Mott and Elizabeth Cady Stanton to promote women's rights and issue the pathbreaking Declaration of Sentiments.

"separate but equal" Principle underlying legal racial segregation, which was upheld in *Plessy v. Ferguson* (1896) and struck down in *Brown v. Board of Education* (1954).

separation of powers Strict division of the powers of government among three separate branches (executive, legislative, and judicial) which, in turn, check and balance each other.

September 11 On September 11, 2001, Islamic terrorists, who were members of the al Qaeda terrorist organization, hijacked four commercial airliners. Two were flown into the World Trade Center, a third into the Pentagon, and a fourth plane was brought down in Pennsylvania. In response, President George W. Bush launched his "war on terrorism." His administration assembled an international coalition to fight terrorism, which invaded Afghanistan after the country's government would not turn over Osama bin Laden. Bush and Congress passed the USA Patriot Act, which allowed government agencies to try suspected terrorists in secret military courts and eavesdrop on confidential conversations.

settlement houses Product of the late nineteenth-century movement to offer a broad array of social services in urban immigrant neighborhoods; Chicago's Hull House was one of hundreds of settlement houses that operated by the early twentieth century.

Seventeenth Amendment (1913) Constitutional amendment that provided for the direct election of senators rather than the traditional practice allowing state legislatures to name them.

Shakers Founded by Mother Ann Lee Stanley in England, the United Society of Believers in Christ's Second Appearing settled in Watervliet, New York, in 1774 and subsequently established eighteen additional communes in the Northeast, Indiana, and Kentucky.

share tenants Poor farmers who rented land to farm in exchange for a substantial share of the crop, though they would often have their own horse or mule, tools, and line of credit with a nearby store.

sharecroppers Poor, mostly black farmers who would work an owner's land in return for shelter, seed, fertilizer, mules, supplies, and food, as well as a substantial share of the crop produced.

Share-the-Wealth program Huey Long offered this program as an alternative to the New Deal. The program proposed to confiscate large personal fortunes, which would be used to guarantee every poor family a cash grant of $5,000 and every worker an annual income of $2,500. This program promised to provide pensions, reduce working hours, pay veterans' bonuses, and ensures a college education to every qualified student.

Shays's Rebellion Storming of the Massachusetts federal arsenal in 1787 by Daniel Shays and 1,200 armed farmers seeking debt relief from the state legislature through issuance of paper currency and lower taxes.

silent majority Term popularized by President Richard Nixon to describe the great majority of American voters who did not express their political opinions publicly—"the non-demonstrators."

Sixteenth Amendment (1913) Constitutional amendment that authorized the federal income tax.

slave codes Ordinances passed by a colony or state to regulate the behavior of slaves, often including brutal punishments for infractions.

Alfred E. Smith (1873–1944) In the 1928 presidential election, he won the Democratic nomination, but failed to win the presidency. Rural voters distrusted him for being Catholic and the son of Irish immigrants as well as for his anti-Prohibition stance.

Captain John Smith (1580–1631) A swashbuckling soldier of fortune with rare powers of leadership and self-promotion, he was appointed to the resident council to manage Jamestown.

Joseph Smith (1805–1844) In 1823, he claimed that the Angel Moroni showed him the location of several gold tablets on which the Book of Mormon was written. Using the Book of Mormon as his gospel, he founded the Church of Jesus Christ of Latter-day Saints, or Mormons. In 1839, they settled in Commerce, Illinois, to avoid persecution. In 1844, Joseph and his brother were arrested and jailed for ordering the destruction of a newspaper that opposed them. While in jail, an anti-Mormon mob stormed the jail and killed both of them.

social Darwinism The application of Charles Darwin's theory of evolutionary natural selection to human society; social Darwinists used the concept of "survival of the fittest" to justify class distinctions, explain poverty, and oppose government intervention in the economy.

social gospel Protestant movement that stressed the Christian obligation to address the mounting social problems caused by urbanization and industrialization.

social justice An important part of the Progressive's agenda, social justice sought to solve social problems through reform and regulation. Methods used to bring about social justice ranged from the founding of charities to the legislation of a ban on child labor.

Social Security Act (1935) Legislation enacted to provide federal assistance to retired workers through tax-funded pension payments and benefit payments to the unemployed and disabled.

Sons of Liberty First organized by Samuel Adams in the 1770s, groups of colonists dedicated to militant resistance against British control of the colonies.

Hernando de Soto (1500?–1542) A conquistador who explored the west coast of Florida, western North Carolina, and along the Arkansas river from 1539 till his death in 1542.

Southern Christian Leadership Conference (SCLC) Civil rights organization formed by Dr. Martin Luther King Jr. that championed nonviolent direct action as a means of ending segregation.

"southern strategy" This strategy was a major reason for Richard Nixon's victory in the 1968 presidential election. To gain support in the South, Nixon assured southern conservatives that he would slow the federal enforcement of civil rights laws and appoint pro-southern justices to the Supreme Court. As president, Nixon fulfilled these promises.

Spanish Armada A massive Spanish fleet of 130 warships that was defeated at Plymouth in 1588 by the English navy during the reign of Queen Elizabeth I.

Spanish flu Unprecedentedly lethal influenza epidemic of 1918 that killed more than 22 million people worldwide.

Herbert Spencer (1820–1903) As the first major proponent of social Darwinism, he argued that human society and institutions are subject to the process of natural selection and that society naturally evolves for the better. He was against any form of government interference with the evolution of society, like business regulations, because it would help the "unfit" to survive.

spirituals Songs with religious messages sung by slaves to help ease the strain of field labor and to voice their suffering at the hands of their masters and overseers.

spoils system The term—meaning the filling of federal government jobs with persons loyal to the party of the president—originated in Andrew Jackson's first term; the system was replaced in the Progressive Era by civil service.

Square Deal Roosevelt's progressive agenda of the "Three C's": control of corporations, conservation of natural resources, and consumer protection.

stagflation Term coined by economists during the Nixon presidency to describe the unprecedented situation of stagnant economic growth and consumer price inflation occurring at the same time.

Joseph Stalin (1879–1953) The Bolshevik leader who succeeded Lenin as the leader of the Soviet Union in 1924 and ruled the country until his death. During his totalitarian rule of the Soviet Union, he used purges and a system of forced labor camps to maintain control over the country, and claimed vast areas of Eastern Europe for Soviet domination.

Stalwarts Conservative Republican party faction during the presidency of Rutherford B. Hayes, 1877–1881; led by Senator Roscoe B. Conkling of New York, Stalwarts opposed civil service reform and favored a third term for President Ulysses S. Grant.

Stamp Act Act of Parliament requiring that all printed materials (e.g., newspapers, bonds, and even playing cards) in the American colonies use paper with an official tax stamp in order to pay for British military protection of the colonies.

Stamp Act Congress Twenty-seven delegates from nine of the colonies met from October 7–25, 1765 and wrote a Declaration of the Rights and Grievances of the Colonies, a petition to the King, and a petition to Parliament for the repeal of the Stamp Act.

Standard Oil Company Corporation under the leadership of John D. Rockefeller that attempted to dominate the entire oil industry through horizontal and vertical integration.

Elizabeth Cady Stanton (1815–1902) She was a prominent reformer and advocate for the rights of women, and she helped organize the Seneca Falls Convention to discuss women's rights. The convention was the first of its kind and produced the Declaration of Sentiments, which proclaimed the equality of men and women.

staple crops Profitable market crops, such as cotton, tobacco, or rice, that predominate in a given region.

state constitutions Charters that define the relationship between the state government and local governments and individuals, also protecting their rights from violation by the national government.

steamboats Ships and boats powered by wood-fired steam engines. First used in the early nineteenth century, they made two-way traffic possible in eastern river systems, creating a transcontinental market and an agricultural empire.

Thaddeus Stevens (1792–1868) As one of the leaders of the Radical Republicans, he argued that the former Confederate states should be viewed as conquered provinces, which were subject to the demands of the conquerors. He believed that all of Southern society needed to be changed, and he supported the abolition of slavery and racial equality.

Adlai E. Stevenson (1900–1965) In the 1952 and 1956 presidential elections, he was the Democratic nominee who lost to Dwight Eisenhower. He was also the U.S. Ambassador to the United Nations and is remembered for his famous speech in 1962 before the UN Security Council that unequivocally demonstrated that the Soviet Union had built nuclear missile bases in Cuba.

Stonewall Riots Violent clashes between police and gay patrons of New York City's Stonewall Inn in 1969; seen as the starting point of the modern gay rights movement.

Stono Rebellion A 1739 slave uprising in South Carolina that was brutally quashed, leading to executions as well as a severe tightening of the slave code.

Strategic Arms Limitation Treaty (SALT I) Agreement signed in 1972 by President Nixon and Secretary Brezhnev prohibiting the development of missile defense systems in the United States and Soviet Union and limiting the quantity of nuclear warheads for both.

Strategic Defense Initiative (SDI) (1983) Ronald Reagan's proposed space-based anti-missile defense system, dubbed "Star Wars" by the media, that aroused great controversy and escalated the arms race between the United States and the Soviet Union.

Levi Strauss (1829–1902) A Jewish tailor who followed miners to California during the gold rush and began making durable work pants that were later dubbed blue jeans or Levi's.

Student Nonviolent Coordinating Committee (SNCC) Interracial organization formed in 1960 with the goal of intensifying the effort to end racial segregation.

Students for a Democratic Society (SDS) Major organization of the New Left, founded at the University of Michigan in 1960 by Tom Hayden and Al Haber.

suburbia Communities formed from mass migration of middle-class whites from urban centers.

Suez crisis British, French, and Israeli attack on Egypt in 1956 after Nasser's seizure of the Suez Canal; President Eisenhower interceded to demand the withdrawal of the British, French, and Israeli forces from the Sinai peninsula and canal.

Sunbelt The label for an arc that stretched from the Carolinas to California. During the postwar era, much of the urban population growth occurred in this area.

the "surge" In early 2007, President Bush decided he would send a "surge" of new troops to Iraq and implement a new strategy. U.S. forces would shift their focus from offensive operations to the protection of Iraqi civilians from attacks by terrorist insurgents and sectarian militias. While the "surge" reduced the violence in Iraq, Iraqi leaders were still unable to develop a self-sustaining democracy.

Taft-Hartley Labor Act (1947) Congressional legislation that banned "unfair labor practices" by labor unions, required union leaders to sign anti-Communist "loyalty oaths," and prohibited federal employees from going on strike.

Taliban A coalition of ultraconservative Islamists who rose to power in Afghanistan after the Soviets withdrew. The Taliban leaders gave Osama bin Laden a safe haven in their country in exchange for aid in fighting the Northern Alliance, who were rebels opposed to the Taliban. After they refused to turn bin Laden over to the United States, America invaded Afghanistan.

Tammany Hall The "city machine" used by "Boss" Tweed to dominate politics in New York City until his arrest in 1871.

tariffs Taxes on goods imported from other nations, typically used to protect home industries from foreign competitors and to generate revenue for the federal government.

Tariff of 1816 A cluster of taxes on imports passed by Congress to protect America's emerging iron and textile industries from British competition.

Tariff of 1832 This tariff act reduced the duties on many items, but the tariffs on cloth and iron remained high. South Carolina nullified it along with the tariff of 1828. President Andrew Jackson sent federal troops to the state and asked Congress to grant him the authority to enforce the tariffs. Henry Clay presented a plan of gradually reducing the tariffs until 1842, which Congress passed and thereby ended the crisis.

Tariff of Abominations (1828) Tax on imported goods, including British cloth and clothing, that strengthened New England textile companies but hurt southern consumers, who experienced a decrease in British demand for raw cotton grown in the South.

tariff reform Effort led by the Democratic party to reduce taxes on imported goods, which Republicans argued were needed to protect American industries from foreign competition.

Zachary Taylor (1784–1850) During the Mexican War, he scored two quick victories against Mexico, which made him very popular in America. He used his popularity from his military victories to be elected the president as a member of the Whig party, but died before he could complete his term.

Taylorism Labor system based on detailed study of work tasks, championed by Frederick Winslow Taylor, intended to maximize efficiency and profits for employers.

Tea Party Right-wing populist movement, largely made up of middle-class, white male conservatives, that emerged as a response to the expansion of the federal government under the Obama administration.

Teapot Dome Affair Harding administration scandal in which Secretary of the Interior Albert B. Fall profited from secret leasing of government oil reserves in Wyoming to private oil companies.

Tecumseh (1768–1813) He was a leader of the Shawnee tribe who tried to unite all Indians into a confederation that could defend their hunting grounds. He believed that no land cessions could be made without the consent of all the tribes because they held the land in common. His beliefs and leadership made him seem dangerous to the American government and they waged war on him and his tribe. He was killed at the Battle of the Thames.

Tecumseh's Indian Confederacy A group of Native Americans under leadership of Shawnee leader Tecumseh and his prophet brother Tenskwatawa; its mission of fighting off American expansion was thwarted in the Battle of Tippecanoe (1811), when the confederacy fell apart.

Tejanos Texas settlers of Spanish or Mexican descent.

telegraph system System of electronic communication invented by Samuel F. B. Morse that could be transmitted instantaneously across great distances (first used in the 1840s).

Teller Amendment Addition to the congressional war resolution of April 20, 1898, which marked the U.S. entry into the war with Spain; the amendment declared that the United States' goal in entering the war was to ensure Cuba's independence, not to annex Cuba as a territory.

temperance A widespread reform movement, led by militant Christians, focused on reducing the use of alcoholic beverages.

tenements Shabby, low-cost inner-city apartment buildings that housed the urban poor in cramped, poorly ventilated apartments.

Tenochtitlán The capital city of the Aztec Empire. The city was built on marshy islands on the western side of Lake Tetzcoco, which is the site of present-day Mexico City.

Tet offensive Surprise attack by Viet Cong guerrillas and the North Vietnamese army on U.S. and South Vietnamese forces in 1968 that shocked the American public and led to widespread sentiment against the war.

Texas Revolution (1835–1836) Conflict between Texas colonists and the Mexican government that resulted in the creation of the separate Republic of Texas in 1836.

textile industry Commercial production of thread, fabric, and clothing from raw cotton in mills in New England during the first half of the nineteenth century, and later in the South in the late nineteenth century.

Thirteenth Amendment (1865) Amendment to the U. S. Constitution that freed all slaves in the United States.

Battle of Tippecanoe (1811) Battle in northern Indiana between U.S. troops and Native American warriors led by Tenskwatawa, the brother of Tecumseh, who had organized an anti-American Indian confederacy to fight American efforts to settle on Indian lands.

tobacco A cash crop grown in the Caribbean as well as the Virginia and Maryland colonies, made increasingly profitable by the rapidly growing popularity of smoking in Europe after the voyages of Columbus.

Gulf of Tonkin incident On August 2 and 4 of 1964, North Vietnamese vessels attacked two American destroyers in Gulf of Tonkin off the coast of North Vietnam. President Johnson described the attacks as unprovoked. In reality, the U.S. ships were monitoring South Vietnamese attacks on North Vietnamese islands that American advisers had planned. The incident spurred the Tonkin Gulf resolution.

Tonkin Gulf Resolution Congressional action that granted the president unlimited authority to defend U.S. forces abroad, passed in August 1964 after an allegedly unprovoked attack on American warships off the coast of North Vietnam.

Tories Term used by Patriots to refer to Loyalists, or colonists who supported the Crown after the Declaration of Independence.

Townshend Acts Parliamentary measures to extract more revenue from the colonies; the Revenue Act of 1767, which taxed tea, paper, and other colonial imports, was one of the most notorious of these policies.

Trail of Tears The Cherokees' eight-hundred mile journey (1838–1839) from the southern Appalachians to Indian Territory (in present-day Oklahoma); four thousand people died along the way.

transcendentalism Philosophy of a small group of New England writers and thinkers who advocated personal spirituality, self-reliance, social reform, and harmony with nature.

Transcontinental railroad First line across the continent from Omaha, Nebraska, to Sacramento, California, established in 1869 with the linkage of the Union Pacific and Central Pacific railroads at Promontory, Utah.

Transcontinental Treaty (Adams-Onís Treaty)(1819) Treaty between Spain and the United States that clarified the boundaries of the Louisiana Purchase and arranged the transfer of Florida to the United States in exchange for cash.

Treaty of Ghent (1814) Agreement between Great Britain and the United States that ended the War of 1812, signed on December 24, 1814.

Treaty of Guadalupe Hidalgo (1848) Treaty between United States and Mexico that ended the Mexican-American War.

Treaty of Paris Settlement between Great Britain and France that ended the French and Indian War.

Treaty of Versailles (1919) Peace treaty that ended the First World War, forcing Germany to dismantle its military, pay immense war reparations, and give up its colonies around the world.

trench warfare A form of prolonged combat between the entrenched positions of opposing armies, often with little tactical movement.

Trenton, Battle of A surprising and pivotal victory for General Washington and American forces in December 1776 that resulted in major British and Hessian losses.

triangular trade A network of trade in which exports from one region were sold to another region, which sent its exports to a third region, which exported its own goods back to the first country or colony.

Troubled Asset Relief Program (TARP) In 2008, President George W. Bush signed into law the bank bailout fund called Troubled Asset Relief Program (TARP), which required the Treasury Department to spend $700 billion to keep banks and other financial institutions from collapsing.

Harry S. Truman (1884–1972) As President Roosevelt's vice president, he succeeded him after his death near the end of the Second World War. After the war, Truman wrestled with the inflation of both prices and wages, worked with Congress to pass the National Security Act, and banned racial discrimination in the hiring of federal employees and ended racial segregation in the armed forces. In foreign affairs, he established the Truman Doctrine to contain communism, developed the Marshall Plan to rebuild Europe, and sent the U.S. military to defend South Korea after North Korea invaded.

Truman Doctrine (1947) President Truman's program of "containing" communism in Eastern Europe and providing economic and military aid to any nations at risk of Communist takeover.

trust A business arrangement that gives a person or corporation (the "trustee") the legal power to manage another person's money or another company without owning those entities outright.

Sojourner Truth (1797?–1883) She was born into slavery, but New York State freed her in 1827. She spent the 1840s and 1850s travelling across the country and speaking to audiences about her experiences as slave and asking them to support abolition and women's rights.

Harriet Tubman (1820–1913) She was born a slave, but escaped to the North. Then she returned to the South nineteen times and guided 300 slaves to freedom.

Frederick Jackson Turner An influential historian who authored the "Frontier Thesis" in 1893, arguing that the existence of an alluring frontier and the experience of persistent westward expansion informed the nation's democratic politics, unfettered economy, and rugged individualism.

Nat Turner (1800–1831) He was the leader of the only slave revolt to get past the planning stages. In August 1831, the revolt began with the slaves killing the members of Turner's master's household. Then they attacked other neighboring farmhouses and recruited more slaves until the militia crushed the revolt. At least fifty-five whites were killed during the uprising and seventeen slaves were hanged afterward.

Nat Turner's Rebellion (1831) Insurrection in rural Virginia led by black overseer Nat Turner, who killed slave owners and their families; in turn, federal troops indiscriminately killed hundreds of slaves in the process of putting down Turner and his rebels.

Tuskegee Airmen U.S. Army Air Corps unit of African American pilots whose combat success spurred military and civilian leaders to desegregate the armed forces after the war.

Mark Twain (1835–1910) Born Samuel Langhorne Clemens in Missouri, he became a popular humorous writer and lecturer and established himself as one of the great American satirists and authors. His two greatest books, *The Adventures of Tom Sawyer* and *The Adventures of Huckleberry Finn*, drew heavily on his childhood in Missouri.

William "Boss" Tweed (1823–1878) An infamous political boss in New York City, Tweed used his "city machine," the Tammany Hall ring, to rule, plunder, and sometimes improve the city's government. His political domination of New York City ended with his arrest in 1871 and conviction in 1873.

Twenty-first Amendment (1933) Repealed prohibition on the manufacture, sale, and transportation of alcoholic beverages, effectively nullifying the Eighteenth Amendment.

U-boats German military submarines (*Unterseeboot*) used during the First World War to attack enemy naval vessels as well as merchant ships of enemy and neutral nations.

Underground Railroad A secret system of routes and safe houses through which runaway slaves were led to freedom in the North.

Unitarians Members of the liberal New England Congregationalist offshoot, often well-educated and wealthy, who profess the oneness of God and the goodness of rational man.

United Farm Workers (UFW) Organization formed in 1962 to represent the interests of Mexican American migrant workers.

United Nations Security Council A major agency within the United Nations which remains in permanent session and has the responsibility of maintaining international peace and security. Originally, it consisted of five permanent members, (United States, Soviet Union, Britain, France, and the Republic of China), and six members elected to two-year terms. After 1965, the number of rotating members was increased to ten. In 1971, the Republic of China was replaced with the People's Republic of China, and the Soviet Union was replaced by the Russian Federation in 1991.

Universalists Members of a New England religious movement, often from the working class, who believed in a merciful God and universal salvation.

USA Patriot Act (2001) Wide-reaching Congressional legislation, triggered by the war on terror, which gave government agencies the right to eavesdrop on confidential conversations between prison inmates and their lawyers and permitted suspected terrorists to be tried in secret military courts.

U.S. battleship *Maine* American warship that exploded in the Cuban port of Havana on January 25, 1898; though later discovered to be the result of an accident, the destruction of the *Maine* was attributed by war-hungry Americans to Spain, contributing to the onset of the War of 1812.

utopian communities Ideal communities that offered innovative social and economic relationships to those who were interested in achieving salvation.

Valley Forge American military encampment near Philadelphia, where more than 3,500 soldiers deserted or died from cold and hunger in the winter of 1777–1778.

Cornelius Vanderbilt (1794–1877) In the 1860s, he consolidated several separate railroad companies into one vast entity, New York Central Railroad.

Bartolomeo Vanzetti (1888–1927) In 1920, he and Nicola Sacco were Italian immigrants who were arrested for stealing $16,000 and killing a paymaster and his guard. Their trial took place during a time of numerous bombings by anarchists and their judge was openly prejudicial. Many liberals and radicals believe that their conviction was based on their political ideas and ethnic origin rather than the evidence against them.

vertical integration The process by which a corporation gains control of all aspects of the resources and processes needed to produce and sell a product.

Amerigo Vespucci (1455–1512) Italian explorer who reached the New World in 1499 and was the first to suggest that South America was a new continent. Afterward, European mapmakers used a variant of his first name, America, to label the New World.

Vicksburg, Battle of (1863) A protracted battle in northern Mississippi in which Union forces under Ulysses Grant besieged the last major Confederate fortress on the Mississippi River, forcing the inhabitants into starvation and then submission.

Viet Cong Communist guerrillas in Vietnam who launched attacks on the Diem government.

Vietnamization Nixon-era policy of equipping and training South Vietnamese forces to take over the burden of combat from U.S. troops.

Francisco Pancho Villa (1877–1923) While the leader of one of the competing factions in the Mexican civil war, he provoked the United States into intervening. He hoped attacking the United States would help him build a reputation as an opponent of the United States, which would increase his popularity and discredit Mexican president Carranza.

Virginia Company A joint-stock enterprise that King James I chartered in 1606. The company was to spread Christianity in the New World as well as find ways to make a profit in it.

Virginia Plan The delegations to the Constitutional Convention were divided between two plans on how to structure the government: Virginia called for a strong central government and a two-house legislature apportioned by population.

Virginia Statute of Religious Freedom A Virginia law, drafted by Thomas Jefferson in 1777 and enacted in 1786, that guarantees freedom of, and from, religion.

virtual representation The idea that the American colonies, although they had no actual representative in Parliament, were "virtually" represented by all members of Parliament.

Voting Rights Act of 1965 Legislation ensuring that all Americans were able to vote; the law ended literacy tests and other means of restricting voting rights.

Wagner Act (1935) Legislation that guaranteed workers the right to organize unions, granted them direct bargaining power, and barred employers from interfering with union activities.

George Wallace (1919–1998) An outspoken defender of segregation. As the governor of Alabama, he once attempted to block African American students from enrolling at the University of Alabama. He ran as the presidential candidate for the American Independent party in 1968, appealing to voters who were concerned about rioting anti-war protesters, the welfare system, and the growth of the federal government.

war hawks In 1811, congressional members from the southern and western districts who clamored for a war to seize Canada and Florida were dubbed "war hawks."

War of 1812 Conflict fought in North America and at sea between Great Britain and the United States, 1812–1815, over American shipping rights and British efforts to spur Indian attacks on American settlements. Canadians and Native Americans also fought in the war.

war on terror Global crusade to root out anti-American, anti-Western Islamist terrorist cells launched by President George W. Bush as a response to the 9/11 attacks.

War Powers Act (1973) Legislation requiring the president to inform Congress within 48 hours of the deployment of U.S. troops abroad and to withdraw them after 60 days unless Congress approves their continued deployment.

War Production Board Federal agency created by President Roosevelt in 1942 that converted America's industrial output to war production.

"war relocation camps" Detention camps housing thousands of Japanese Americans from the West Coast who were forcibly interned from 1942 until the end of the Second World War.

Warren Court The U.S. Supreme Court under Chief Justice Earl Warren, 1953–1969, decided such landmark cases as *Brown v. Board of Education* (school desegregation), *Baker v. Carr* (legislative redistricting), and *Gideon v. Wainwright* and *Miranda v. Arizona* (rights of criminal defendants).

Booker T. Washington (1856–1915) He founded a leading college for African Americans in Tuskegee, Alabama, and become the foremost black educator in America by the 1890s. He believed that the African American community should establish an economic base for its advancement before striving for social equality. His critics charged that his philosophy sacrificed educational and civil rights for dubious social acceptance and economic opportunities.

George Washington (1732–1799) In 1775, the Continental Congress named him the commander in chief of the Continental Army which defeated the British in the American Revolution. He had previously served as an officer in the French and Indian War. In 1787, he was the presiding officer over the Constitutional Convention, but participated little in the debates. In 1789, the Electoral College chose Washington to be the nation's first president. Washington faced the nation's first foreign and domestic crises, maintaining the United States' neutrality in foreign affairs. After two terms in office, Washington chose to step down, and the power of the presidency was peacefully passed to John Adams.

Watergate (1972–1974) Scandal that exposed the criminality and corruption of the Nixon administration and ultimately led to President Nixon's resignation in 1974.

weapons of mass destruction (WMDs) According to the Bush Doctrine, these were in the hands of terrorist groups and rogue nations which required the United States to use preemptive military action in order to disable the threat.

Daniel Webster (1782–1852) As a representative from New Hampshire, he led the New Federalists in opposition to the moving of the second national bank from Boston to Philadelphia. Later, he served as representative and a senator for Massachusetts and emerged as a champion of a stronger national government. He also switched from opposing to supporting tariffs because New England had built up its manufactures with the understanding tariffs would protect them from foreign competitors.

Webster-Ashburton Treaty Settlement in 1842 of U.S.–Canadian border disputes in Maine, New York, Vermont, and in the Wisconsin Territory (now northern Minnesota).

Webster-Hayne debate U.S. Senate debate of January 1830 between Daniel Webster of Massachusetts and Robert Hayne of South Carolina over nullification and states' rights.

Western Front The contested frontier between the Central and Allied Powers that ran along northern France and across Belgium.

Whig party Political party founded in 1834 in opposition to the Jacksonian Democrats; Whigs supported federal funding for internal improvements, a national bank, and high tariffs on imported goods.

Whigs Another name for revolutionary Patriots.

Whiskey Rebellion (1794) Violent protest by western Pennsylvania farmers against the federal excise tax on corn whiskey, put down by a federal army.

Eli Whitney (1765–1825) He invented the cotton gin, which separated cotton from its seeds. One machine operator could separate fifty times more cotton than a worker could by hand, which led to an increase in cotton production and prices. These increases gave planters a new profitable use for slavery and a lucrative slave trade emerged from the coastal South to the Southwest.

Wilderness Road Originally an Indian path through the Cumberland Gap, it was used by over 300,000 settlers who migrated westward to Kentucky in the last quarter of the eighteenth century.

Roger Williams (1603–1683) Puritan who believed that the purity of the church required a complete separation between church and state and freedom from coercion in matters of faith. In 1636, he established the town of Providence, the first permanent settlement in Rhode Island and the first to allow religious freedom in America.

Wendell L. Willkie (1892–1944) In the 1940 presidential election, he was the Republican nominee who ran against President Roosevelt. He supported aid to the Allies and criticized the New Deal programs. Voters looked at the increasingly dangerous world situation and chose to keep President Roosevelt in office for a third term.

Wilmot Proviso (1846) Proposal by Congressman David Wilmot, a Pennsylvania Democrat, to prohibit slavery in any land acquired in the Mexican-American War.

Woodrow Wilson (1856–1924) In the 1912 presidential election, Woodrow Wilson ran under the slogan of New Freedom, which promised to improve of the banking system, lower tariffs, and break up monopolies. At the beginning of the First World War, Wilson kept America neutral, but provided the Allies with credit for purchases of supplies; however, the sinking of U.S. merchant ships and the Zimmermann telegram caused him to ask Congress to declare war on Germany. Wilson supported the entry of America into the League of Nations and the ratification of the Treaty of Versailles, but Congress would not approve the entry or ratification.

John Winthrop Puritan leader and Governor of the Massachusetts Bay Colony who resolved to use the colony as a refuge for persecuted Puritans and as an instrument of building a "wilderness Zion" in America.

woman suffrage Movement to give women the right to vote through a constitutional amendment, spearheaded by Susan B. Anthony and Elizabeth Cady Stanton's National Woman Suffrage Association.

Women Accepted for Voluntary Emergency Services (WAVES) During the Second World War, the increased demand for labor shook up old prejudices about gender roles in workplace and in the military. Nearly 200,000 women served in the Women's Army Corps or its naval equivalent, Women Accepted for Volunteer Emergency Service (WAVES).

Women's Army Corps (WAC) Women's branch of the United States Army; by the end of the Second World War nearly 150,000 women had served in the WAC.

women's movement Wave of activism sparked by Betty Friedan's *The Feminine Mystique* (1963); it argued for equal rights for women and fought against the cult of domesticity of the 1950s that limited women's roles to the home as wife, mother, and housewife.

women's work The traditional term referring to routine tasks in the house, garden, and fields performed by women. The sphere of women's occupations expanded in the colonies to include medicine, shopkeeping, upholstering, and the operation of inns and taverns.

Woodstock In 1969, roughly half a million young people converged on a farm near Bethel, New York, for a three-day music festival that was an expression of the flower children's free spirit.

Works Progress Administration (WPA) (1935) Government agency established to manage several federal job programs created under the New Deal; it became the largest employer in the nation.

Wounded Knee, Battle of Last incident of the Indians Wars took place in 1890 in the Dakota Territory, where the U.S. Cavalry killed over 200 Sioux men, women, and children who were in the process of surrender.

XYZ affair French foreign minister Tallyrand's three anonymous agents demanded payments to stop French plundering of American ships in 1797; refusal to pay the bribe led to two years of sea war with France (1798–1800).

Yalta Conference (1945) Meeting of the "Big Three" Allied leaders, Franklin D. Roosevelt, Winston Churchill, and Joseph Stalin, to discuss how to divide control of postwar Germany and eastern Europe

yellow journalism A type of news reporting, epitomized in the 1890s by the newspaper empires of William Randolph Hearst and Joseph Pulitzer, that intentionally manipulates public opinion through sensational headlines, illustrations, and articles about both real and invented events.

yeomen Small landowners (the majority of white families in the South) who farmed their own land and usually did not own slaves.

Yorktown, Battle of Last major battle of the Revolutionary War; General Cornwallis along with over 7,000 British troops surrendered to George Washington at Yorktown, Virginia, on October 17, 1781.

surrender at Yorktown Last battle of the Revolutionary War; General Lord Charles Cornwallis, along with over 7,000 British troops, surrendered at Yorktown, Virginia, on October 17, 1781.

Brigham Young (1801–1877) Following Joseph Smith's death, he became the leader of the Mormons and promised Illinois officials that the Mormons would leave the state. In 1846, he led the Mormons to Utah and settled near the Salt Lake. After the United States gained Utah as part of the Treaty of Guadalupe Hidalgo, he became the governor of the territory and kept the Mormons virtually independent of federal authority.

youth culture The youth of the 1950s had more money and free time than any previous generation and this allowed a distinct youth culture to emerge. A market emerged for products and activities that were specifically for young people such as transistor radios, rock records, *Seventeen* magazine, and Pat Boone movies.

Zimmermann telegram Message sent by a German official to the Mexican government in 1917 urging an invasion of the United States; the telegram was intercepted by British intelligence agents and angered Americans, many of whom called for war against Germany.

APPENDIX

THE DECLARATION OF INDEPENDENCE (1776)

When in the Course of human events, it becomes necessary for one people to dissolve the political bands which have connected them with another, and to assume among the powers of the earth, the separate and equal station to which the Laws of Nature and of Nature's God entitle them, a decent respect to the opinions of mankind requires that they should declare the causes which impel them to the separation.

We hold these truths to be self-evident, that all men are created equal, that they are endowed by their Creator with certain unalienable Rights, that among these are Life, Liberty and the pursuit of Happiness.—That to secure these rights, Governments are instituted among Men, deriving their just powers from the consent of the governed, —That whenever any Form of Government becomes destructive of these ends, it is the Right of the People to alter or to abolish it, and to institute new Government, laying its foundation on such principles and organizing its powers in such form, as to them shall seem most likely to effect their Safety and Happiness. Prudence, indeed, will dictate that Governments long established should not be changed for light and transient causes; and accordingly all experience hath shewn, that mankind are more disposed to suffer, while evils are sufferable, than to right themselves by abolishing the forms to which they are accustomed. But when a long train of abuses and usurpations, pursuing invariably the same Object evinces a design to reduce them under absolute Despotism, it is their right, it is their duty, to throw off such Government, and to provide new Guards for their future security.—Such has been the patient sufferance of these Colonies; and such is now the necessity which constrains them to alter their former

Systems of Government. The history of the present King of Great Britain is a history of repeated injuries and usurpations, all having in direct object the establishment of an absolute Tyranny over these States. To prove this, let Facts be submitted to a candid world.

He has refused his Assent to Laws, the most wholesome and necessary for the public good.

He has forbidden his Governors to pass Laws of immediate and pressing importance, unless suspended in their operation till his Assent should be obtained; and when so suspended, he has utterly neglected to attend to them.

He has refused to pass other Laws for the accommodation of large districts of people, unless those people would relinquish the right of Representation in the Legislature, a right inestimable to them and formidable to tyrants only.

He has called together legislative bodies at places unusual, uncomfortable, and distant from the depository of their public Records, for the sole purpose of fatiguing them into compliance with his measures.

He has dissolved Representative Houses repeatedly, for opposing with manly firmness his invasions on the rights of the people.

He has refused for a long time, after such dissolutions, to cause others to be elected; whereby the Legislative powers, incapable of Annihilation, have returned to the People at large for their exercise; the State remaining in the mean time exposed to all the dangers of invasion from without, and convulsions within.

He has endeavoured to prevent the population of these States; for that purpose obstructing the Laws for Naturalization of Foreigners; refusing to pass others to encourage their migrations hither, and raising the conditions of new Appropriations of Lands.

He has obstructed the Administration of Justice, by refusing his Assent to Laws for establishing Judiciary powers.

He has made Judges dependent on his Will alone, for the tenure of their offices, and the amount and payment of their salaries.

He has erected a multitude of New Offices, and sent hither swarms of Officers to harrass our people, and eat out their substance.

He has kept among us, in times of peace, Standing Armies without the Consent of our legislatures.

He has affected to render the Military independent of and superior to the Civil power.

He has combined with others to subject us to a jurisdiction foreign to our constitution, and unacknowledged by our laws; giving his Assent to their Acts of pretended Legislation:

For Quartering large bodies of armed troops among us:

For protecting them, by a mock Trial, from punishment for any Murders which they should commit on the Inhabitants of these States:

For cutting off our Trade with all parts of the world:

For imposing Taxes on us without our Consent:

For depriving us in many cases, of the benefits of Trial by Jury:

For transporting us beyond Seas to be tried for pretended offences

For abolishing the free System of English Laws in a neighbouring Province, establishing therein an Arbitrary government, and enlarging its Boundaries so as to render it at once an example and fit instrument for introducing the same absolute rule into these Colonies:

For taking away our Charters, abolishing our most valuable Laws, and altering fundamentally the Forms of our Governments:

For suspending our own Legislatures, and declaring themselves invested with power to legislate for us in all cases whatsoever.

He has abdicated Government here, by declaring us out of his Protection and waging War against us.

He has plundered our seas, ravaged our Coasts, burnt our towns, and destroyed the lives of our people.

He is at this time transporting large Armies of foreign Mercenaries to compleat the works of death, desolation and tyranny, already begun with circumstances of Cruelty & perfidy scarcely paralleled in the most barbarous ages, and totally unworthy the Head of a civilized nation.

He has constrained our fellow Citizens taken Captive on the high Seas to bear Arms against their Country, to become the executioners of their friends and Brethren, or to fall themselves by their Hands.

He has excited domestic insurrections amongst us, and has endeavoured to bring on the inhabitants of our frontiers, the merciless Indian Savages, whose known rule of warfare, is an undistinguished destruction of all ages, sexes and conditions.

In every stage of these Oppressions We have Petitioned for Redress in the most humble terms: Our repeated Petitions have been answered only by repeated injury. A Prince whose character is thus marked by every act which may define a Tyrant, is unfit to be the ruler of a free people.

Nor have We been wanting in attentions to our Brittish brethren. We have warned them from time to time of attempts by their legislature to extend an unwarrantable jurisdiction over us. We have reminded them of the circumstances of our emigration and settlement here. We have appealed to their native justice and magnanimity, and we have conjured them by the ties of our common kindred to disavow these usurpations, which, would inevitably interrupt our connections and correspondence. They too have been deaf to the voice of justice and of consanguinity. We must, therefore, acquiesce in the necessity, which denounces our Separation, and hold them, as we hold the rest of mankind, Enemies in War, in Peace Friends.

We, therefore, the Representatives of the united States of America, in General Congress, Assembled, appealing to the Supreme Judge of the world for the rectitude of our intentions, do, in the Name, and by Authority of the good People of these Colonies, solemnly publish and declare, That these United Colonies are, and of Right ought to be Free and Independent States; that they are Absolved from all Allegiance to the British Crown, and that all political connection between them and the State of Great Britain, is and ought to be totally dissolved; and that as Free and Independent States, they have full Power to levy War, conclude Peace, contract Alliances, establish Commerce, and to do all other Acts and Things which Independent States may of right do. And for the support of this Declaration, with a firm reliance on the protection of divine Providence, we mutually pledge to each other our Lives, our Fortunes and our sacred Honor.

Georgia
Button Gwinnett
Lyman Hall
George Walton

North Carolina
William Hooper
Joseph Hewes
John Penn

South Carolina
Edward Rutledge
Thomas Heyward, Jr.
Thomas Lynch, Jr.
Arthur Middleton

Massachusetts
John Hancock

Maryland
Samuel Chase
William Paca
Thomas Stone
Charles Carroll of
    Carrollton

Virginia
George Wythe
Richard Henry Lee
Thomas Jefferson
Benjamin Harrison
Thomas Nelson, Jr.
Francis Lightfoot Lee
Carter Braxton

Pennsylvania
Robert Morris
Benjamin Rush
Benjamin Franklin
John Morton
George Clymer
James Smith
George Taylor
James Wilson
George Ross

Delaware
Caesar Rodney
George Read
Thomas McKean

New York
William Floyd
Philip Livingston
Francis Lewis
Lewis Morris

New Jersey
Richard Stockton
John Witherspoon
Francis Hopkinson
John Hart
Abraham Clark

New Hampshire
Josiah Bartlett
William Whipple

Massachusetts
Samuel Adams
John Adams
Robert Treat Paine
Elbridge Gerry

Rhode Island
Stephen Hopkins
William Ellery

Connecticut
Roger Sherman
Samuel Huntington
William Williams
Oliver Wolcott

New Hampshire
Matthew Thornton

ARTICLES OF CONFEDERATION (1787)

TO ALL TO WHOM these Presents shall come, we the undersigned Delegates of the States affixed to our Names send greeting.

Whereas the Delegates of the United States of America in Congress assembled did on the fifteenth day of November in the Year of our Lord One Thousand Seven Hundred and Seventy-seven, and in the Second Year of the Independence of America agree to certain articles of Confederation and perpetual Union between the States of Newhampshire, Massachusetts-bay, Rhodeisland and Providence Plantations, Connecticut, New York, New Jersey, Pennsylvania, Delaware, Maryland, Virginia, North-Carolina, South-Carolina and Georgia in the Words following, viz.

Articles of Confederation and perpetual Union between the States of Newhampshire, Massachusetts-bay, Rhodeisland and Providence Plantations, Connecticut, New-York, New-Jersey, Pennsylvania, Delaware, Maryland, Virginia, North-Carolina, South-Carolina and Georgia.

ARTICLE I. The stile of this confederacy shall be "The United States of America."

ARTICLE II. Each State retains its sovereignty, freedom and independence, and every power, jurisdiction and right, which is not by this confederation expressly delegated to the United States, in Congress assembled.

ARTICLE III. The said States hereby severally enter into a firm league of friendship with each other, for their common defence, the security of their liberties, and their mutual and general welfare, binding themselves to assist each other, against all force offered to, or attacks made upon them, or any of them, on account of religion, sovereignty, trade or any other pretence whatever.

ARTICLE IV. The better to secure and perpetuate mutual friendship and intercourse among the people of the different States in this Union, the free inhabitants of each of these States, paupers, vagabonds and fugitives from justice excepted, shall be entitled to all privileges and immunities of free citizens in the several States; and the people of each State shall have free ingress and regress to and from any other State, and shall enjoy therein all the privileges of trade and commerce, subject to the same duties, impositions and restrictions as the inhabitants thereof respectively, provided that such restrictions shall not extend so far as to prevent the removal of property imported into any State, to any other State of which the owner is an inhabitant; provided also that no imposition, duties or restriction shall be laid by any State, on the property of the United States, or either of them.

If any person guilty of, or charged with treason, felony, or other high misdemeanor in any State, shall flee from justice, and be found in any of the United States, he shall upon demand of the Governor or Executive power, of the State from which he fled, be delivered up and removed to the State having jurisdiction of his offence.

Full faith and credit shall be given in each of these States to the records, acts and judicial proceedings of the courts and magistrates of every other State.

ARTICLE V. For the more convenient management of the general interests of the United States, delegates shall be annually appointed in such manner as the legislature of each State shall direct, to meet in Congress on the first Monday in November, in every year, with a power reserved to each State, to recall its delegates, or any of them, at any time within the year, and to send others in their stead, for the remainder of the year.

No State shall be represented in Congress by less than two, nor by more than seven members; and no person shall be capable of being a delegate for more than three years in any term of six years; nor shall any person, being a delegate, be capable of holding any office under the United States, for which he, or another for his benefit receives any salary, fees or emolument of any kind.

Each State shall maintain its own delegates in a meeting of the States, and while they act as members of the committee of the States.

In determining questions in the United States, in Congress assembled, each State shall have one vote.

Freedom of speech and debate in Congress shall not be impeached or questioned in any court, or place out of Congress, and the members of Congress shall be protected in their persons from arrests and imprisonments, during the time of their going to and from, and attendance on Congress, except for treason, felony, or breach of the peace.

ARTICLE VI. No State without the consent of the United States in Congress assembled, shall send any embassy to, or receive any embassy from, or enter into any conference, agreement, alliance or treaty with any king, prince or state; nor shall any person holding any office of profit or trust under the United States, or any of them, accept of any present, emolument, office or title of any kind whatever from any king, prince or foreign state; nor shall the United States in Congress assembled, or any of them, grant any title of nobility.

No two or more States shall enter into any treaty, confederation or alliance whatever between them, without the consent of the United States in Congress assembled, specifying accurately the purposes for which the same is to be entered into, and how long it shall continue.

No State shall lay any imposts or duties, which may interfere with any stipulations in treaties, entered into by the United States in Congress assembled, with any king, prince or state, in pursuance of any treaties already proposed by Congress, to the courts of France and Spain.

No vessels of war shall be kept up in time of peace by any State, except such number only, as shall be deemed necessary by the United States in Congress assembled, for the defence of such State, or its trade; nor shall any body of forces be kept up by any State, in time of peace, except such number only, as in the judgment of the United States, in Congress assembled, shall be deemed requisite to garrison the forts necessary for the defence of such State; but every State shall always keep up a well regulated and disciplined militia, sufficiently armed and accoutred, and shall provide and constantly have ready for use, in public stores, a due number of field pieces and tents, and a proper quantity of arms, ammunition and camp equipage.

No State shall engage in any war without the consent of the United States in Congress assembled, unless such State be actually invaded by enemies, or shall have received certain advice of a resolution being formed by some nation of Indians to invade such State, and the danger is so imminent as not to admit of a delay, till the United States in Congress assembled can be consulted: nor shall any State grant commissions to any ships or vessels of war, nor letters of marque or reprisal, except it be after a declaration of war by the United States in Congress assembled, and then only against the kingdom or state and the subjects thereof, against which war has been so declared, and under such regulations as shall be established by the United States in Congress assembled, unless such State be infested by pirates, in which case vessels of war may be fitted out for that occasion, and kept so long as the danger shall continue, or until the United States in Congress assembled shall determine otherwise.

ARTICLE VII. When land-forces are raised by any State of the common defence, all officers of or under the rank of colonel, shall be appointed by the Legislature of each State respectively by whom such forces shall be raised, or in such manner as such State shall direct, and all vacancies shall be filled up by the State which first made the appointment.

ARTICLE VIII. All charges of war, and all other expenses that shall be incurred for the common defence or general welfare, and allowed by the United States in Congress assembled, shall be defrayed out of a common treasury, which shall be supplied by the several States, in proportion to the value of all land within each State, granted to or surveyed for any person, as such land and the buildings and improvements thereon shall be estimated according to such mode as the United States in Congress assembled, shall from time to time direct and appoint.

The taxes for paying that proportion shall be laid and levied by the authority and direction of the Legislatures of the several States within the time agreed upon by the United States in Congress assembled.

ARTICLE IX. The United States in Congress assembled, shall have the sole and exclusive right and power of determining on peace and war, except in the cases mentioned in the sixth article—of sending and receiving ambassadors—entering into treaties and alliances, provided that no treaty of commerce shall be made whereby the legislative power of the respective States shall be restrained from imposing such imposts and duties on foreigners, as their own people are subjected to, or from prohibiting the exportation or importation of and species of goods or commodities whatsoever—of establishing rules for deciding in all cases, what captures on land or water shall be legal, and in what manner prizes taken by land or naval forces in the service of the United States shall be divided or appropriated—of granting letters of marque and reprisal in times of peace—appointing courts for the trial of piracies and felonies committed on the high seas and establishing courts for receiving and determining finally appeals in all cases of captures, provided that no member of Congress shall be appointed a judge of any of the said courts.

The United States in Congress assembled shall also be the last resort on appeal in all disputes and differences now subsisting or that hereafter may arise between two or more States concerning boundary, jurisdiction or any other cause whatever; which authority shall always be exercised in the manner following. Whenever the legislative or executive authority or lawful agent of any State in controversy with another shall present a petition to Congress, stating the matter in question and praying for a hearing, notice thereof shall be given by order of Congress to the legislative or executive authority of the other State in controversy, and a day assigned for the appearance of the parties by their lawful agents, who shall then be directed to appoint by joint consent, commissioners or judges to constitute a court for hearing and determining the matter in question: but if they cannot agree, Congress shall name three persons out of each of the United States, and from the list of such persons each party shall alternately strike out one, the petitioners beginning, until the number shall be reduced to thirteen; and from that number not less than seven, nor more than nine names as Congress shall direct, shall in the presence of Congress be drawn out by lot, and the persons whose names shall be so drawn or any five of them, shall be commissioners or judges, to hear and finally determine the controversy, so always as a major part of the judges who shall hear the cause shall agree in the determination: and if either party shall neglect to attend at the day appointed, without reasons, which Congress shall judge sufficient, or being present shall refuse to strike, the Congress shall proceed to nominate three persons out of each State, and the Secretary of Congress shall strike in behalf of such party absent or refusing; and the judgment and sentence of the court to be appointed, in the manner before prescribed, shall be final and conclusive; and if any of the parties shall refuse to submit to the authority of such court, or to appear or defend their claim or cause, the court shall nevertheless proceed to pronounce sentence, or judgment, which shall in like manner be final and decisive, the judgment or sentence and other proceedings being in either case transmitted to Congress, and lodged among the acts of Congress for the security of the parties concerned: provided that every commissioner, before he sits in judgment, shall take an oath to be administered by one of the judges of the supreme or superior court of the State where the case shall be tried, "well and truly to hear and determine the matter in question, according to the best of his judgment, without favour, affection or hope of reward:" provided also that no State shall be deprived of territory for the benefit of the United States.

All controversies concerning the private right of soil claimed under different grants of two or more States, whose jurisdiction as they may respect such lands, and the states which passed such grants are adjusted, the said grants or either of them being at the same time claimed to have originated antecedent to such settlement of jurisdiction, shall on the petition of either party to the Congress of the United States, be finally determined as near as may be in the same manner as is before prescribed for deciding disputes respecting territorial jurisdiction between different States.

The United States in Congress assembled shall also have the sole and exclusive right and power of regulating the alloy and value of coin struck by their own authority, or by that of the respective States—fixing the standard of weights and measures throughout the United States—regulating the trade and managing all affairs with the Indians, not members of any of the States, provided that the legislative right of any State within its own limits be not infringed or violated—establishing and regulating post-offices from one State to another, throughout all of the United States, and exacting such postage on the papers passing thro' the same as may be requisite to defray the expenses of the said office—appointing all officers of the land forces, in the service of the United States, excepting regimental officers—appointing all the officers of the naval forces, and commissioning all officers whatever in the service of the United States—making rules for the government and regulation of the said land and naval forces, and directing their operations.

The United States in Congress assembled shall have authority to appoint a committee, to sit in the recess of Congress, to be denominated "a Committee of the States," and to consist of one delegate from each State; and to appoint such other committees and civil officers as may be necessary for managing the general affairs of the United States under their direction—to appoint one of their number to preside, provided that no person be allowed to serve in the office of president more than one year in any term of three years; to ascertain the necessary sums of money to be raised for the service of the United States, and to appropriate and apply the same for defraying the public expenses—to borrow money, or emit bills on the credit of the United States, transmitting every half year to the respective States an account of the sums of money so borrowed or emitted,—to build and equip a navy—to agree upon the number of land forces, and to make requisitions from each State for its quota, in proportion to the number of white inhabitants in such State; which requisition shall be binding, and thereupon the Legislature of each State shall appoint the regimental officers, raise the men and cloath, arm and equip them in a soldier like manner, at the expense of the United States; and the officers and men so cloathed, armed and equipped shall march to the place appointed, and within the time agreed on by the United States in Congress assembled: but if the United States in Congress assembled shall, on consideration of circumstances judge proper that any State should not raise men, or should raise a smaller number of men than the quota thereof, such extra number shall be raised, officered, cloathed, armed and equipped in the same manner as the quota of such State, unless the legislature of such State shall judge that such extra number cannot be safely spared out of the same, in which case they shall raise officer, cloath, arm and equip as many of such extra number as they judge can be safely spared. And the officers and men so cloathed, armed and equipped, shall march to the place appointed, and within the time agreed on by the United States in Congress assembled.

The United States in Congress assembled shall never engage in a war, nor grant letters of marque and reprisal in time of peace, nor enter into any treaties or alliances, nor coin money, nor regulate the value thereof, nor ascertain the sums and expenses necessary for the defence and welfare of the United States, or any of them, nor emit bills, nor borrow money on the credit of the

United States, nor appropriate money, nor agree upon the number of vessels to be built or purchased, or the number of land or sea forces to be raised, nor appoint a commander in chief of the army or navy, unless nine States assent to the same: nor shall a question on any other point, except for adjourning from day to day be determined, unless by the votes of a majority of the United States in Congress assembled.

The Congress of the United States shall have power to adjourn to any time within the year, and to any place within the United States, so that no period of adjournment be for a longer duration than the space of six months, and shall publish the journal of their proceedings monthly, except such parts thereof relating to treaties, alliances or military operations, as in their judgment require secresy; and the yeas and nays of the delegates of each State on any question shall be entered on the Journal, when it is desired by any delegate; and the delegates of a State, or any of them, at his or their request shall be furnished with a transcript of the said journal, except such parts as are above excepted, to lay before the Legislatures of the several States.

ARTICLE X. The committee of the States, or any nine of them, shall be authorized to execute, in the recess of Congress, such of the powers of Congress as the United States in Congress assembled, by the consent of nine States, shall from time to time think expedient to vest them with; provided that no power be delegated to the said committee, for the exercise of which, by the articles of confederation, the voice of nine States in the Congress of the United States assembled is requisite.

ARTICLE XI. Canada acceding to this confederation, and joining in the measures of the United States, shall be admitted into, and entitled to all the advantages of this Union: but no other colony shall be admitted into the same, unless such admission be agreed to by nine States.

ARTICLE XII. All bills of credit emitted, monies borrowed and debts contracted by, or under the authority of Congress, before the assembling of the United States, in pursuance of the present confederation, shall be deemed and considered as a charge against the United States, for payment and satisfaction whereof the said United States, and the public faith are hereby solemnly pledged.

ARTICLE XIII. Every State shall abide by the determinations of the United States in Congress assembled, on all questions which by this confederation are submitted to them. And the articles of this confederation shall be inviolably observed by every State, and the Union shall be perpetual; nor shall any alteration at any time hereafter be made in any of them; unless such alteration be agreed to in a Congress of the United States, and be afterwards confirmed by the Legislatures of every State.

And whereas it has pleased the Great Governor of the world to incline the hearts of the Legislatures we respectively represent in Congress, to approve of, and to authorize us to ratify the said articles of confederation and perpetual union. Know ye that we the undersigned delegates, by virtue of the power and authority to us given for that purpose, do by these presents, in the name and in behalf of our respective constituents, fully and entirely ratify and confirm each and every of the said articles of confederation and perpetual union, and all and singular the matters and things therein contained: and we do further solemnly plight and engage the faith of our respective constituents, that they shall abide by the determinations of the United States in Congress assembled, on all questions, which by the said confederation are submitted to them. And that the articles thereof shall be inviolably observed by the States we respectively represent, and that the Union shall be perpetual.

In witness thereof we have hereunto set our hands in Congress. Done at Philadelphia in the State of Pennsylvania the ninth day of July in the year of our Lord one thousand seven hundred and seventy-eight, and in the third year of the independence of America.

The Constitution of the United States (1787)

We the People of the United States, in Order to form a more perfect Union, establish Justice, insure domestic Tranquility, provide for the common defence, promote the general Welfare, and secure the Blessings of Liberty to ourselves and our Posterity, do ordain and establish this Constitution for the United States of America.

Article. I.

SECTION. 1. All legislative Powers herein granted shall be vested in a Congress of the United States, which shall consist of a Senate and House of Representatives.

SECTION. 2. The House of Representatives shall be composed of Members chosen every second Year by the People of the several States, and the Electors in each State shall have the Qualifications requisite for Electors of the most numerous Branch of the State Legislature.

No Person shall be a Representative who shall not have attained to the Age of twenty five Years, and been seven Years a Citizen of the United States, and who shall not, when elected, be an Inhabitant of that State in which he shall be chosen.

Representatives and direct Taxes shall be apportioned among the several States which may be included within this Union, according to their respective Numbers, which shall be determined by adding to the whole Number of free Persons, including those bound to Service for a Term of Years, and excluding Indians not taxed, three fifths of all other Persons. The actual Enumeration shall be made within three Years after the first Meeting of the Congress of the United States, and within every subsequent Term of ten Years, in such Manner as they shall by Law direct. The Number of Representatives shall not exceed one for every thirty Thousand, but each State shall have at Least one Representative; and until such enumeration shall be made, the State of New Hampshire shall be entitled to chuse three, Massachusetts eight, Rhode-Island and Providence Plantations one, Connecticut five, New-York six, New Jersey four, Pennsylvania eight, Delaware one, Maryland six, Virginia ten, North Carolina five, South Carolina five, and Georgia three.

When vacancies happen in the Representation from any State, the Executive Authority thereof shall issue Writs of Election to fill such Vacancies.

The House of Representatives shall chuse their Speaker and other Officers; and shall have the sole Power of Impeachment.

SECTION. 3. The Senate of the United States shall be composed of two Senators from each State, chosen by the Legislature thereof for six Years; and each Senator shall have one Vote.

Immediately after they shall be assembled in Consequence of the first Election, they shall be divided as equally as may be into three Classes. The Seats of the Senators of the first Class shall be vacated at the Expiration of the second Year, of the second Class at the Expiration of the fourth Year, and of the third Class at the Expiration of the sixth Year, so that one third may be chosen every second Year; and if Vacancies happen by Resignation, or otherwise, during the Recess of the Legislature of any State, the Executive thereof may make temporary Appointments until the next Meeting of the Legislature, which shall then fill such Vacancies.

No Person shall be a Senator who shall not have attained to the Age of thirty Years, and been nine Years a Citizen of the United States, and who shall not, when elected, be an Inhabitant of that State for which he shall be chosen.

The Vice President of the United States shall be President of the Senate, but shall have no Vote, unless they be equally divided.

The Senate shall chuse their other Officers, and also a President pro tempore, in the Absence of the Vice President, or when he shall exercise the Office of President of the United States.

The Senate shall have the sole Power to try all Impeachments. When sitting for that Purpose, they shall be on Oath or Affirmation. When the President of the United States is tried, the Chief Justice shall preside: And no Person shall be convicted without the Concurrence of two thirds of the Members present.

Judgment in Cases of Impeachment shall not extend further than to removal from Office, and disqualification to hold and enjoy any Office of honor, Trust or Profit under the United States: but the Party convicted shall nevertheless be liable and subject to Indictment, Trial, Judgment and Punishment, according to Law.

SECTION. 4. The Times, Places and Manner of holding Elections for Senators and Representatives, shall be prescribed in each State by the Legislature thereof; but the Congress may at any time by Law make or alter such Regulations, except as to the Places of chusing Senators.

The Congress shall assemble at least once in every Year, and such Meeting shall be on the first Monday in December, unless they shall by Law appoint a different Day.

SECTION. 5. Each House shall be the Judge of the Elections, Returns and Qualifications of its own Members, and a Majority of each shall constitute a Quorum to do Business; but a smaller Number may adjourn from day to day, and may be authorized to compel the Attendance of absent Members, in such Manner, and under such Penalties as each House may provide.

Each House may determine the Rules of its Proceedings, punish its Members for disorderly Behaviour, and, with the Concurrence of two thirds, expel a Member.

Each House shall keep a Journal of its Proceedings, and from time to time publish the same, excepting such Parts as may in their Judgment require Secrecy; and the Yeas and Nays of the Members of either House on any question shall, at the Desire of one fifth of those Present, be entered on the Journal.

Neither House, during the Session of Congress, shall, without the Consent of the other, adjourn for more than three days, nor to any other Place than that in which the two Houses shall be sitting.

SECTION. 6. The Senators and Representatives shall receive a Compensation for their Services, to be ascertained by Law, and paid out of the Treasury of the United States. They shall in all Cases, except Treason, Felony and Breach of the Peace, be privileged from Arrest during their Attendance at the Session of their respective Houses, and in going to and returning from the same; and for any Speech or Debate in either House, they shall not be questioned in any other Place.

No Senator or Representative shall, during the Time for which he was elected, be appointed to any civil Office under the Authority of the United States, which shall have been created, or the Emoluments whereof shall have been increased during such time; and no Person holding any Office under the United States, shall be a Member of either House during his Continuance in Office.

SECTION. 7. All Bills for raising Revenue shall originate in the House of Representatives; but the Senate may propose or concur with Amendments as on other Bills.

Every Bill which shall have passed the House of Representatives and the Senate, shall, before it become a Law, be presented to the President of the United States: If he approve he shall sign it, but if not he shall return it, with his Objections to that House in which it shall have originated, who shall enter the Objections at large on their Journal, and proceed to reconsider it. If after such Reconsideration two thirds of that House shall agree to pass the Bill, it shall be sent, together with the Objections, to the other House, by which it shall likewise be reconsidered, and if approved by two thirds of that House, it shall become a Law. But in all such Cases the Votes of both Houses shall be determined by yeas and Nays, and the Names of the Persons voting for and against the Bill shall be entered on the Journal of each House respectively. If any Bill shall not be returned by the President within ten Days (Sundays excepted) after it shall have been presented to him, the Same shall be a Law, in like Manner as if he had signed it, unless the Congress by their Adjournment prevent its Return, in which Case it shall not be a Law.

Every Order, Resolution, or Vote to which the Concurrence of the Senate and House of Representatives may be necessary (except on a question of Adjournment) shall be presented to the President of the United States; and before the Same shall take Effect, shall be approved by him, or being disapproved by him, shall be repassed by two thirds of the Senate and House of Representatives, according to the Rules and Limitations prescribed in the Case of a Bill.

SECTION. 8. The Congress shall have Power To lay and collect Taxes, Duties, Imposts and Excises, to pay the Debts and provide for the common Defence and general Welfare of the United States; but all Duties, Imposts and Excises shall be uniform throughout the United States;

To borrow Money on the credit of the United States;

To regulate Commerce with foreign Nations, and among the several States, and with the Indian Tribes;

To establish an uniform Rule of Naturalization, and uniform Laws on the subject of Bankruptcies throughout the United States;

To coin Money, regulate the Value thereof, and of foreign Coin, and fix the Standard of Weights and Measures;

To provide for the Punishment of counterfeiting the Securities and current Coin of the United States;

To establish Post Offices and post Roads;

To promote the Progress of Science and useful Arts, by securing for limited Times to Authors and Inventors the exclusive Right to their respective Writings and Discoveries;

To constitute Tribunals inferior to the supreme Court;

To define and punish Piracies and Felonies committed on the high Seas, and Offences against the Law of Nations;

To declare War, grant Letters of Marque and Reprisal, and make Rules concerning Captures on Land and Water;

To raise and support Armies, but no Appropriation of Money to that Use shall be for a longer Term than two Years;

To provide and maintain a Navy;

To make Rules for the Government and Regulation of the land and naval Forces;

To provide for calling forth the Militia to execute the Laws of the Union, suppress Insurrections and repel Invasions;

To provide for organizing, arming, and disciplining, the Militia, and for governing such Part of them as may be employed in the Service of the United States, reserving to the States respectively, the Appointment of the Officers, and the Authority of training the Militia according to the discipline prescribed by Congress;

To exercise exclusive Legislation in all Cases whatsoever, over such District (not exceeding ten Miles square) as may, by Cession of particular States, and the Acceptance of Congress, become the Seat of the Government of the United States, and to exercise like Authority over all Places purchased by the Consent of the Legislature of the State in which the Same shall be, for the Erection of Forts, Magazines, Arsenals, dock-Yards, and other needful Buildings;—And

To make all Laws which shall be necessary and proper for carrying into Execution the foregoing Powers, and all other Powers vested by this Constitution in the Government of the United States, or in any Department or Officer thereof.

SECTION. 9. The Migration or Importation of such Persons as any of the States now existing shall think proper to admit, shall not be prohibited by the Congress prior to the Year one thousand eight hundred and eight, but a Tax or duty may be imposed on such Importation, not exceeding ten dollars for each Person.

The Privilege of the Writ of Habeas Corpus shall not be suspended, unless when in Cases of Rebellion or Invasion the public Safety may require it.

No Bill of Attainder or ex post facto Law shall be passed.

No Capitation, or other direct, Tax shall be laid, unless in Proportion to the Census or enumeration herein before directed to be taken.

No Tax or Duty shall be laid on Articles exported from any State.

No Preference shall be given by any Regulation of Commerce or Revenue to the Ports of one State over those of another; nor shall Vessels bound to, or from, one State, be obliged to enter, clear, or pay Duties in another.

No Money shall be drawn from the Treasury, but in Consequence of Appropriations made by Law; and a regular Statement and Account of the Receipts and Expenditures of all public Money shall be published from time to time.

No Title of Nobility shall be granted by the United States: And no Person holding any Office of Profit or Trust under them, shall, without the Consent of the Congress, accept of any present, Emolument, Office, or Title, of any kind whatever, from any King, Prince, or foreign State.

SECTION. 10. No State shall enter into any Treaty, Alliance, or Confederation; grant Letters of Marque and Reprisal; coin Money; emit Bills of Credit; make any Thing but gold and silver Coin a Tender in Payment of Debts; pass any Bill of Attainder, ex post facto Law, or Law impairing the Obligation of Contracts, or grant any Title of Nobility.

No State shall, without the Consent of the Congress, lay any Imposts or Duties on Imports or Exports, except what may be absolutely necessary for executing it's inspection Laws: and the net Produce of all Duties and Imposts, laid by any State on Imports or Exports, shall be for the Use of the Treasury of the United States; and all such Laws shall be subject to the Revision and Controul of the Congress.

No State shall, without the Consent of Congress, lay any Duty of Tonnage, keep Troops, or Ships of War in time of Peace, enter into any Agreement or Compact with another State, or with a foreign Power, or engage in War, unless actually invaded, or in such imminent Danger as will not admit of delay.

ARTICLE. II.

SECTION. 1. The executive Power shall be vested in a President of the United States of America. He shall hold his Office during the Term of four Years, and, together with the Vice President, chosen for the same Term, be elected, as follows:

Each State shall appoint, in such Manner as the Legislature thereof may direct, a Number of Electors, equal to the whole Number of Senators and Representatives to which the State may be entitled in the Congress: but no Senator or Representative, or Person holding an Office of Trust or Profit under the United States, shall be appointed an Elector.

The Electors shall meet in their respective States, and vote by Ballot for two Persons, of whom one at least shall not be an Inhabitant of the same State with themselves. And they shall make a List of all the Persons voted for, and of the Number of Votes for each; which List they shall sign and certify, and transmit sealed to the Seat of the Government of the United States, directed to the President of the Senate. The President of the Senate shall, in the Presence of the Senate and House of Representatives, open all the Certificates, and the Votes shall then be counted. The Person having the greatest Number of Votes shall be the President, if such Number be a Majority of the whole Number of Electors appointed; and if there be more than one who have such Majority, and have an equal Number of Votes, then the House of Representatives shall immediately chuse by Ballot one of them for President; and if no Person have a Majority, then from the five highest on the List the said House shall in like Manner chuse the President. But in chusing the President, the Votes shall be taken by States, the Representation from each State having one Vote; A quorum for this purpose shall consist of a Member or Members from two thirds of the States, and a Majority of all the States shall be necessary to a Choice. In every Case, after the Choice of the President, the Person having the greatest Number of Votes of the Electors shall be the Vice President. But if there should remain two or more who have equal Votes, the Senate shall chuse from them by Ballot the Vice President.

The Congress may determine the Time of chusing the Electors, and the Day on which they shall give their Votes; which Day shall be the same throughout the United States.

No Person except a natural born Citizen, or a Citizen of the United States, at the time of the Adoption of this Constitution, shall be eligible to the Office of President; neither shall any Person be eligible to that Office who shall not have attained to the Age of thirty five Years, and been fourteen Years a Resident within the United States.

In Case of the Removal of the President from Office, or of his Death, Resignation, or Inability to discharge the Powers and Duties of the said Office, the Same shall devolve on the Vice President, and the Congress may by Law provide for the Case of Removal, Death, Resignation or Inability, both of the President and Vice President, declaring what Officer shall then act as President, and such Officer shall act accordingly, until the Disability be removed, or a President shall be elected.

The President shall, at stated Times, receive for his Services, a Compensation, which shall neither be increased nor diminished during the Period for which he shall have been elected, and he shall not receive within that Period any other Emolument from the United States, or any of them.

Before he enter on the Execution of his Office, he shall take the following Oath or Affirmation:—"I do solemnly swear (or affirm) that I will faithfully execute the Office of President of the United States, and will to the best of my Ability, preserve, protect and defend the Constitution of the United States."

SECTION. 2. The President shall be Commander in Chief of the Army and Navy of the United States, and of the Militia of the several States, when called into the actual Service of the United States; he may require the Opinion, in writing, of the principal Officer in each of the executive Departments, upon any Subject relating to the Duties of their respective Offices, and he shall have Power to grant Reprieves and Pardons for Offences against the United States, except in Cases of Impeachment.

He shall have Power, by and with the Advice and Consent of the Senate, to make Treaties, provided two thirds of the Senators present concur; and he shall nominate, and by and with the Advice and Consent of the Senate, shall appoint Ambassadors, other public Ministers and Consuls, Judges of the supreme Court, and all other Officers of the United States, whose Appointments are not herein otherwise provided for, and which shall be established by Law: but the Congress may by Law vest the Appointment of such inferior Officers, as they think proper, in the President alone, in the Courts of Law, or in the Heads of Departments.

The President shall have Power to fill up all Vacancies that may happen during the Recess of the Senate, by granting Commissions which shall expire at the End of their next Session.

SECTION. 3. He shall from time to time give to the Congress Information of the State of the Union, and recommend to their Consideration such Measures as he shall judge necessary and expedient; he may, on extraordinary Occasions, convene both Houses, or either of them, and in Case of Disagreement between them, with Respect to the Time of Adjournment, he may adjourn them to such Time as he shall think proper; he shall receive Ambassadors and other public Ministers; he shall take Care that the Laws be faithfully executed, and shall Commission all the Officers of the United States.

SECTION. 4. The President, Vice President and all civil Officers of the United States, shall be removed from Office on Impeachment for, and Conviction of, Treason, Bribery, or other high Crimes and Misdemeanors.

ARTICLE III.

SECTION. 1. The judicial Power of the United States shall be vested in one supreme Court, and in such inferior Courts as the Congress may from time to time ordain and establish. The Judges, both of the supreme and inferior Courts, shall hold their Offices during good Behaviour, and shall, at stated Times, receive for their Services a Compensation, which shall not be diminished during their Continuance in Office.

SECTION. 2. The judicial Power shall extend to all Cases, in Law and Equity, arising under this Constitution, the Laws of the United States, and Treaties made, or which shall be made, under their Authority;—to all Cases affecting Ambassadors, other public Ministers and Consuls;—to all Cases of admiralty and maritime Jurisdiction;—to Controversies to which the United States shall be a Party;—to Controversies between two or more States;— between a State and Citizens of another State,—between Citizens of different States,—between Citizens of the same State claiming Lands under Grants of different States, and between a State, or the Citizens thereof, and foreign States, Citizens or Subjects.

In all Cases affecting Ambassadors, other public Ministers and Consuls, and those in which a State shall be Party, the supreme Court shall have original Jurisdiction. In all the other Cases before mentioned, the supreme Court shall have appellate Jurisdiction, both as to Law and Fact, with such Exceptions, and under such Regulations as the Congress shall make.

The Trial of all Crimes, except in Cases of Impeachment, shall be by Jury; and such Trial shall be held in the State where the said Crimes shall have been committed; but when not committed within any State, the Trial shall be at such Place or Places as the Congress may by Law have directed.

SECTION. 3. Treason against the United States, shall consist only in levying War against them, or in adhering to their Enemies, giving them Aid and Comfort. No Person shall be convicted of Treason unless on the Testimony of two Witnesses to the same overt Act, or on Confession in open Court.

The Congress shall have Power to declare the Punishment of Treason, but no Attainder of Treason shall work Corruption of Blood, or Forfeiture except during the Life of the Person attainted.

ARTICLE. IV.

SECTION. 1. Full Faith and Credit shall be given in each State to the public Acts, Records, and judicial Proceedings of every other State. And the Congress may by general Laws prescribe the Manner in which such Acts, Records and Proceedings shall be proved, and the Effect thereof.

SECTION. 2. The Citizens of each State shall be entitled to all Privileges and Immunities of Citizens in the several States.

A Person charged in any State with Treason, Felony, or other Crime, who shall flee from Justice, and be found in another State, shall on Demand of the executive Authority of the State from which he fled, be delivered up, to be removed to the State having Jurisdiction of the Crime.

No Person held to Service or Labour in one State, under the Laws thereof, escaping into another, shall, in Consequence of any Law or Regulation therein, be discharged from such Service or Labour, but shall be delivered up on Claim of the Party to whom such Service or Labour may be due.

SECTION. 3. New States may be admitted by the Congress into this Union; but no new State shall be formed or erected within the Jurisdiction of any other State; nor any State be formed by the Junction of two or more States, or Parts of States, without the Consent of the Legislatures of the States concerned as well as of the Congress.

The Congress shall have Power to dispose of and make all needful Rules and Regulations respecting the Territory or other Property belonging to the United States; and nothing in this Constitution shall be so construed as to Prejudice any Claims of the United States, or of any particular State.

SECTION. 4. The United States shall guarantee to every State in this Union a Republican Form of Government, and shall protect each of them against Invasion; and on Application of the Legislature, or of the Executive (when the Legislature cannot be convened), against domestic Violence.

ARTICLE. V.

The Congress, whenever two thirds of both Houses shall deem it necessary, shall propose Amendments to this Constitution, or, on the Application of the Legislatures of two thirds of the several States, shall call a Convention for proposing Amendments, which, in either Case, shall be valid to all Intents and Purposes, as Part of this Constitution, when ratified by the Legislatures of three fourths of the several States, or by Conventions in three fourths thereof, as the one or the other Mode of Ratification may be proposed by the Congress; Provided that no Amendment which may be made prior to the Year One thousand eight hundred and eight shall in any Manner affect the first and fourth Clauses in the Ninth Section of the first Article; and that no State, without its Consent, shall be deprived of its equal Suffrage in the Senate.

ARTICLE. VI.

All Debts contracted and Engagements entered into, before the Adoption of this Constitution, shall be as valid against the United States under this Constitution, as under the Confederation.

This Constitution, and the Laws of the United States which shall be made in Pursuance thereof; and all Treaties made, or which shall be made, under the Authority of the United States, shall be the supreme Law of the Land; and the Judges in every State shall be bound thereby, any Thing in the Constitution or Laws of any State to the Contrary notwithstanding.

The Senators and Representatives before mentioned, and the Members of the several State Legislatures, and all executive and judicial Officers, both of the United States and of the several States, shall be bound by Oath or Affirmation, to support this Constitution; but no religious Test shall ever be required as a Qualification to any Office or public Trust under the United States.

ARTICLE. VII.

The Ratification of the Conventions of nine States, shall be sufficient for the Establishment of this Constitution between the States so ratifying the Same.

The Word, "the," being interlined between the seventh and eighth Lines of the first Page, the Word "Thirty" being partly written on an Erazure in the fifteenth Line of the first Page, The Words "is tried" being interlined between the thirty second and thirty third Lines of the first Page and the Word "the" being interlined between the forty third and forty fourth Lines of the second Page.

Attest William Jackson Secretary done in Convention by the Unanimous Consent of the States present the Seventeenth Day of September in the Year of our Lord one thousand seven hundred and Eighty seven and of the Independance of the United States of America the Twelfth In witness whereof We have hereunto subscribed our Names,

G°. Washington
Presidt and deputy from Virginia

Delaware	Geo: Read Gunning Bedford jun John Dickinson Richard Bassett Jaco: Broom	Massachusetts	Nathaniel Gorham Rufus King

Connecticut — Wm. Saml. Johnson / Roger Sherman

Maryland
: James McHenry
: Dan of St Thos. Jenifer
: Danl. Carroll

New York — Alexander Hamilton

Virginia
: John Blair
: James Madison Jr.

New Jersey
: Wil: Livingston
: David Brearley
: Wm. Paterson
: Jona: Dayton

North Carolina
: Wm. Blount
: Richd. Dobbs Spaight
: Hu Williamson

South Carolina
: J. Rutledge
: Charles Cotesworth Pinckney
: Charles Pinckney
: Pierce Butler

Pennsylvania
: B Franklin
: Thomas Mifflin
: Robt. Morris
: Geo. Clymer
: Thos. FitzSimons
: Jared Ingersoll
: James Wilson
: Gouv Morris

Georgia
: William Few
: Abr Baldwin

New Hampshire
: John Langdon
: Nicholas Gilman

Amendments to the Constitution

The Bill of Rights: A Transcription

THE PREAMBLE TO THE BILL OF RIGHTS Congress of the United States begun and held at the City of New-York, on Wednesday the fourth of March, one thousand seven hundred and eighty nine.

THE Conventions of a number of the States, having at the time of their adopting the Constitution, expressed a desire, in order to prevent misconstruction or abuse of its powers, that further declaratory and restrictive clauses should be added: And as extending the ground of public confidence in the Government, will best ensure the beneficent ends of its institution.

RESOLVED by the Senate and House of Representatives of the United States of America, in Congress assembled, two thirds of both Houses concurring, that the following Articles be proposed to the Legislatures of the several States, as amendments to the Constitution of the United States, all, or any of which Articles, when ratified by three fourths of the said Legislatures, to be valid to all intents and purposes, as part of the said Constitution; viz.

ARTICLES in addition to, and Amendment of the Constitution of the United States of America, proposed by Congress, and ratified by the Legislatures of the several States, pursuant to the fifth Article of the original Constitution.

Note: The following text is a transcription of the first ten amendments to the Constitution in their original form. These amendments were ratified December 15, 1791, and form what is known as the "Bill of Rights."

Amendment I

Congress shall make no law respecting an establishment of religion, or prohibiting the free exercise thereof; or abridging the freedom of speech, or of the press; or the right of the people peaceably to assemble, and to petition the Government for a redress of grievances.

Amendment II

A well regulated Militia, being necessary to the security of a free State, the right of the people to keep and bear Arms, shall not be infringed.

AMENDMENT III

No Soldier shall, in time of peace be quartered in any house, without the consent of the Owner, nor in time of war, but in a manner to be prescribed by law.

AMENDMENT IV

The right of the people to be secure in their persons, houses, papers, and effects, against unreasonable searches and seizures, shall not be violated, and no Warrants shall issue, but upon probable cause, supported by Oath or affirmation, and particularly describing the place to be searched, and the persons or things to be seized.

AMENDMENT V

No person shall be held to answer for a capital, or otherwise infamous crime, unless on a presentment or indictment of a Grand Jury, except in cases arising in the land or naval forces, or in the Militia, when in actual service in time of War or public danger; nor shall any person be subject for the same offence to be twice put in jeopardy of life or limb; nor shall be compelled in any criminal case to be a witness against himself, nor be deprived of life, liberty, or property, without due process of law; nor shall private property be taken for public use, without just compensation.

AMENDMENT VI

In all criminal prosecutions, the accused shall enjoy the right to a speedy and public trial, by an impartial jury of the State and district wherein the crime shall have been committed, which district shall have been previously ascertained by law, and to be informed of the nature and cause of the accusation; to be confronted with the witnesses against him; to have compulsory process for obtaining witnesses in his favor, and to have the Assistance of Counsel for his defence.

AMENDMENT VII

In Suits at common law, where the value in controversy shall exceed twenty dollars, the right of trial by jury shall be preserved, and no fact tried by a jury, shall be otherwise re-examined in any Court of the United States, than according to the rules of the common law.

AMENDMENT VIII

Excessive bail shall not be required, nor excessive fines imposed, nor cruel and unusual punishments inflicted.

AMENDMENT IX

The enumeration in the Constitution, of certain rights, shall not be construed to deny or disparage others retained by the people.

AMENDMENT X

The powers not delegated to the United States by the Constitution, nor prohibited by it to the States, are reserved to the States respectively, or to the people.

AMENDMENT XI

Passed by Congress March 4, 1794. Ratified February 7, 1795.

Note: Article III, section 2, of the Constitution was modified by amendment 11.

The Judicial power of the United States shall not be construed to extend to any suit in law or equity, commenced or prosecuted against one of the United States by Citizens of another State, or by Citizens or Subjects of any Foreign State.

AMENDMENT XII

Passed by Congress December 9, 1803. Ratified June 15, 1804.

Note: A portion of Article II, section 1 of the Constitution was superseded by the 12th amendment.

The Electors shall meet in their respective states and vote by ballot for President and Vice-President, one of whom, at least, shall not be an inhabitant of the same state with themselves; they shall name in their ballots the person voted for as President, and in distinct ballots the person voted for as Vice-President, and they shall make distinct lists of all persons voted for as President, and of all persons voted for as Vice-President, and of the number of votes for each, which lists they shall sign and certify, and transmit sealed to the seat of the government of the United States, directed to the President of the Senate; — the President of the Senate shall, in the presence of the Senate and House of Representatives, open all the certificates and the votes shall then be counted; — The person having the greatest number of votes for President, shall be the President, if such number be a majority of the whole number of Electors appointed; and if no person have such majority, then from the persons having the highest numbers not exceeding three on the list of those voted for as President, the House of Representatives shall choose immediately, by ballot, the President. But in choosing the President, the votes shall be taken by states, the representation from each state having one vote; a quorum for this purpose shall consist of a member or members from two-thirds of the states, and a majority of all the states shall be necessary to a choice. [And if the House of Representatives shall not choose a President whenever the right of choice shall devolve upon them, before the fourth day of March next following, then the Vice-President shall act as President, as in case of the death or other constitutional disability of the President. —]* The person having the greatest number of votes as Vice-President, shall be the Vice-President, if such number be a majority of the whole number of Electors appointed, and if no person have a majority, then from the two highest numbers on the list, the Senate shall choose the Vice-President; a quorum for the purpose shall consist of two-thirds of the whole number of Senators, and a majority of the whole number shall be necessary to a choice. But no person constitutionally ineligible to the office of President shall be eligible to that of Vice-President of the United States.

AMENDMENT XIII

Passed by Congress January 31, 1865. Ratified December 6, 1865.

Note: A portion of Article IV, section 2, of the Constitution was superseded by the 13th amendment.

SECTION 1. Neither slavery nor involuntary servitude, except as a punishment for crime whereof the party shall have been duly convicted, shall exist within the United States, or any place subject to their jurisdiction.

SECTION 2. Congress shall have power to enforce this article by appropriate legislation.

Superseded by section 3 of the 20th amendment.

AMENDMENT XIV

Passed by Congress June 13, 1866. Ratified July 9, 1868.

Note: Article I, section 2, of the Constitution was modified by section 2 of the 14th amendment.

SECTION 1. All persons born or naturalized in the United States, and subject to the jurisdiction thereof, are citizens of the United States and of the State wherein they reside. No State shall make or enforce any law which shall abridge the privileges or immunities of citizens of the United States; nor shall any State deprive any person of life, liberty, or property, without due process of law; nor deny to any person within its jurisdiction the equal protection of the laws.

SECTION 2. Representatives shall be apportioned among the several States according to their respective numbers, counting the whole number of persons in each State, excluding Indians not taxed. But when the right to vote at any election for the choice of electors for President and Vice-President of the United States, Representatives in Congress, the Executive and Judicial officers of a State, or the members of the Legislature thereof, is denied to any of the male inhabitants of such State, being twenty-one years of age,* and citizens of the United States, or in any way abridged, except for participation in rebellion, or other crime, the basis of representation therein shall be reduced in the proportion which the number of such male citizens shall bear to the whole number of male citizens twenty-one years of age in such State.

SECTION 3. No person shall be a Senator or Representative in Congress, or elector of President and Vice-President, or hold any office, civil or military, under the United States, or under any State, who, having previously taken an oath, as a member of Congress, or as an officer of the United States, or as a member of any State legislature, or as an executive or judicial officer of any State, to support the Constitution of the United States, shall have engaged in insurrection or rebellion against the same, or given aid or comfort to the enemies thereof. But Congress may by a vote of two-thirds of each House, remove such disability.

SECTION 4. The validity of the public debt of the United States, authorized by law, including debts incurred for payment of pensions and bounties for services in suppressing insurrection or rebellion, shall not be

---

Changed by section 1 of the 26th amendment.

questioned. But neither the United States nor any State shall assume or pay any debt or obligation incurred in aid of insurrection or rebellion against the United States, or any claim for the loss or emancipation of any slave; but all such debts, obligations and claims shall be held illegal and void.

SECTION 5. The Congress shall have the power to enforce, by appropriate legislation, the provisions of this article.

AMENDMENT XV

Passed by Congress February 26, 1869. Ratified February 3, 1870.

SECTION 1. The right of citizens of the United States to vote shall not be denied or abridged by the United States or by any State on account of race, color, or previous condition of servitude—

SECTION 2. The Congress shall have the power to enforce this article by appropriate legislation.

AMENDMENT XVI

Passed by Congress July 2, 1909. Ratified February 3, 1913.

Note: Article I, section 9, of the Constitution was modified by amendment 16.

The Congress shall have power to lay and collect taxes on incomes, from whatever source derived, without apportionment among the several States, and without regard to any census or enumeration.

AMENDMENT XVII

Passed by Congress May 13, 1912. Ratified April 8, 1913.

Note: Article I, section 3, of the Constitution was modified by the 17th amendment.

The Senate of the United States shall be composed of two Senators from each State, elected by the people thereof, for six years; and each Senator shall have one vote. The electors in each State shall have the qualifications requisite for electors of the most numerous branch of the State legislatures.

When vacancies happen in the representation of any State in the Senate, the executive authority of such State shall issue writs of election to fill such vacancies: *Provided*, That the legislature of any State may empower the executive thereof to make temporary appointments until the people fill the vacancies by election as the legislature may direct.

This amendment shall not be so construed as to affect the election or term of any Senator chosen before it becomes valid as part of the Constitution.

AMENDMENT XVIII

Passed by Congress December 18, 1917. Ratified January 16, 1919. Repealed by amendment 21.

SECTION 1. After one year from the ratification of this article the manufacture, sale, or transportation of intoxicating liquors within, the importation thereof into, or the exportation thereof from the United States and all territory subject to the jurisdiction thereof for beverage purposes is hereby prohibited.

SECTION 2. The Congress and the several States shall have concurrent power to enforce this article by appropriate legislation.

SECTION 3. This article shall be inoperative unless it shall have been ratified as an amendment to the Constitution by the legislatures of the several States, as provided in the Constitution, within seven years from the date of the submission hereof to the States by the Congress.

AMENDMENT XIX

Passed by Congress June 4, 1919. Ratified August 18, 1920.

The right of citizens of the United States to vote shall not be denied or abridged by the United States or by any State on account of sex.

Congress shall have power to enforce this article by appropriate legislation.

AMENDMENT XX

Passed by Congress March 2, 1932. Ratified January 23, 1933.

Note: Article I, section 4, of the Constitution was modified by section 2 of this amendment. In addition, a portion of the 12th amendment was superseded by section 3.

SECTION 1. The terms of the President and the Vice President shall end at noon on the 20th day of January, and the terms of Senators and Representatives at noon on the 3rd day of January, of the years in which such terms would have ended if this article had not been ratified; and the terms of their successors shall then begin.

SECTION 2. The Congress shall assemble at least once in every year, and such meeting shall begin at noon on the 3d day of January, unless they shall by law appoint a different day.

SECTION 3. If, at the time fixed for the beginning of the term of the President, the President elect shall have died, the Vice President elect shall become President. If a President shall not have been chosen before the time fixed for the beginning of his term, or if the President elect shall have failed to qualify, then the Vice President elect shall act as President until a President shall have qualified; and the Congress may by law provide for the case wherein neither a President elect nor a Vice President shall have qualified, declaring who shall then act as President, or the manner in which one who is to act shall be selected, and such person shall act accordingly until a President or Vice President shall have qualified.

SECTION 4. The Congress may by law provide for the case of the death of any of the persons from whom the House of Representatives may choose a President whenever the right of choice shall have devolved upon them, and for the case of the death of any of the persons from whom the Senate may choose a Vice President whenever the right of choice shall have devolved upon them.

SECTION 5. Sections 1 and 2 shall take effect on the 15th day of October following the ratification of this article.

SECTION 6. This article shall be inoperative unless it shall have been ratified as an amendment to the Constitution by the legislatures of three-fourths of the several States within seven years from the date of its submission.

Amendment XXI

Passed by Congress February 20, 1933. Ratified December 5, 1933.

SECTION 1. The eighteenth article of amendment to the Constitution of the United States is hereby repealed.

SECTION 2. The transportation or importation into any State, Territory, or Possession of the United States for delivery or use therein of intoxicating liquors, in violation of the laws thereof, is hereby prohibited.

SECTION 3. This article shall be inoperative unless it shall have been ratified as an amendment to the Constitution by conventions in the several States, as provided in the Constitution, within seven years from the date of the submission hereof to the States by the Congress.

AMENDMENT XXII

Passed by Congress March 21, 1947. Ratified February 27, 1951.

SECTION 1. No person shall be elected to the office of the President more than twice, and no person who has held the office of President, or acted as President, for more than two years of a term to which some other person was elected President shall be elected to the office of President more than once. But this Article shall not apply to any person holding the office of President when this Article was proposed by Congress, and shall not prevent any person who may be holding the office of President, or acting as President, during the term within which this Article becomes operative from holding the office of President or acting as President during the remainder of such term.

SECTION 2. This article shall be inoperative unless it shall have been ratified as an amendment to the Constitution by the legislatures of three-fourths of the several States within seven years from the date of its submission to the States by the Congress.

AMENDMENT XXIII

Passed by Congress June 16, 1960. Ratified March 29, 1961.

SECTION 1. The District constituting the seat of Government of the United States shall appoint in such manner as Congress may direct:

A number of electors of President and Vice President equal to the whole number of Senators and Representatives in Congress to which the District would be entitled if it were a State, but in no event more than the least populous State; they shall be in addition to those appointed by the States, but they shall be considered, for the purposes of the election of President and Vice President, to be electors appointed by a State; and they shall meet in the District and perform such duties as provided by the twelfth article of amendment.

SECTION 2. The Congress shall have power to enforce this article by appropriate legislation.

AMENDMENT XXIV

Passed by Congress August 27, 1962. Ratified January 23, 1964.

SECTION 1. The right of citizens of the United States to vote in any primary or other election for President or Vice President, for electors for President or Vice President, or for Senator or Representative in Congress, shall not be denied or abridged by the United States or any State by reason of failure to pay poll tax or other tax.

SECTION 2. The Congress shall have power to enforce this article by appropriate legislation.

AMENDMENT XXV

Passed by Congress July 6, 1965. Ratified February 10, 1967.

Note: Article II, section 1, of the Constitution was affected by the 25th amendment.

SECTION 1. In case of the removal of the President from office or of his death or resignation, the Vice President shall become President.

SECTION 2. Whenever there is a vacancy in the office of the Vice President, the President shall nominate a Vice President who shall take office upon confirmation by a majority vote of both Houses of Congress.

SECTION 3. Whenever the President transmits to the President pro tempore of the Senate and the Speaker of the House of Representatives his written declaration that he is unable to discharge the powers and duties of his office, and until he transmits to them a written declaration to the contrary, such powers and duties shall be discharged by the Vice President as Acting President.

SECTION 4. Whenever the Vice President and a majority of either the principal officers of the executive departments or of such other body as Congress may by law provide, transmit to the President pro tempore of the Senate and the Speaker of the House of Representatives their written declaration that the President is unable to discharge the powers and duties of his office, the Vice President shall immediately assume the powers and duties of the office as Acting President.

Thereafter, when the President transmits to the President pro tempore of the Senate and the Speaker of the House of Representatives his written declaration that no inability exists, he shall resume the powers and duties of his office unless the Vice President and a majority of either the principal officers of the executive department or of such other body as Congress may by law provide, transmit within four days to the President pro tempore of the Senate and the Speaker of the House of Representatives their written declaration that the President is unable to discharge the powers and duties of his office. Thereupon Congress shall decide the issue, assembling within forty-eight hours for that purpose if not in session. If the Congress, within twenty-one days after receipt of the latter written declaration, or, if Congress is not in session, within twenty-one days after Congress is required to assemble, determines by two-thirds vote of both Houses that the President is unable to discharge the powers and duties of his office, the Vice President shall continue to discharge the same as Acting President; otherwise, the President shall resume the powers and duties of his office.

Amendment XXVI

Passed by Congress March 23, 1971. Ratified July 1, 1971.

Note: Amendment 14, section 2, of the Constitution was modified by section 1 of the 26th amendment.

SECTION 1. The right of citizens of the United States, who are eighteen years of age or older, to vote shall not be denied or abridged by the United States or by any State on account of age.

SECTION 2. The Congress shall have power to enforce this article by appropriate legislation.

AMENDMENT XXVII

Originally proposed Sept. 25, 1789. Ratified May 7, 1992.

No law, varying the compensation for the services of the Senators and Representatives, shall take effect, until an election of representatives shall have intervened.

PRESIDENTIAL ELECTIONS

Year	Number of States	Candidates	Parties	Popular Vote	% of Popular Vote	Electoral Vote	% Voter Participation
1789	11	**GEORGE WASHINGTON**	No party designations			69	
		John Adams				34	
		Other candidates				35	
1792	15	**GEORGE WASHINGTON**	No party designations			132	
		John Adams				77	
		George Clinton				50	
		Other candidates				5	
1796	16	**JOHN ADAMS**	Federalist			71	
		Thomas Jefferson	Democratic-Republican			68	
		Thomas Pinckney	Federalist			59	
		Aaron Burr	Democratic-Republican			30	
		Other candidates				48	
1800	16	**THOMAS JEFFERSON**	Democratic-Republican			73	
		Aaron Burr	Democratic-Republican			73	
		John Adams	Federalist			65	
		Charles C. Pinckney	Federalist			64	
		John Jay	Federalist			1	
1804	17	**THOMAS JEFFERSON**	Democratic-Republican			162	
		Charles C. Pinckney	Federalist			14	

Year	No.	Candidates	Parties	Electoral Vote	% Popular Vote	Popular Vote	% Voter Participation
1808	17	**JAMES MADISON**	Democratic-Republican	122			
		Charles C. Pinckney	Federalist	47			
		George Clinton	Democratic-Republican	6			
1812	18	**JAMES MADISON**	Democratic-Republican	128			
		DeWitt Clinton	Federalist	89			
1816	19	**JAMES MONROE**	Democratic-Republican	183			
		Rufus King	Federalist	34			
1820	24	**JAMES MONROE**	Democratic-Republican	231			
		John Quincy Adams	Independent	1			
1824	24	**JOHN QUINCY ADAMS**	Democratic-Republican	84	30.5	108,740	26.9
		Andrew Jackson	Democratic-Republican	99	43.1	153,544	
		Henry Clay	Democratic-Republican	37	13.2	47,136	
		William H. Crawford	Democratic-Republican	41	13.1	46,618	
1828	24	**ANDREW JACKSON**	Democratic	178	56.0	647,286	57.6
		John Quincy Adams	National-Republican	83	44.0	508,064	

Year	Number of States	Candidates	Parties	Popular Vote	% of Popular Vote	Electoral Vote	% Voter Participation
1832	24	**ANDREW JACKSON**	Democratic	688,242	54.5	219	55.4
		Henry Clay	National-Republican	473,462	37.5	49	
		William Wirt	Anti-Masonic }	101,051	8.0	7	
		John Floyd	Democratic }			11	
1836	26	**MARTIN VAN BUREN**	Democratic	765,483	50.9	170	57.8
		William H. Harrison	Whig }			73	
		Hugh L. White	Whig }	739,795	49.1	26	
		Daniel Webster	Whig }			14	
		W. P. Mangum	Whig }			11	
1840	26	**WILLIAM H. HARRISON**	Whig	1,274,624	53.1	234	80.2
		Martin Van Buren	Democratic	1,127,781	46.9	60	
1844	26	**JAMES K. POLK**	Democratic	1,338,464	49.6	170	78.9
		Henry Clay	Whig	1,300,097	48.1	105	
		James G. Birney	Liberty	62,300	2.3		
1848	30	**ZACHARY TAYLOR**	Whig	1,360,967	47.4	163	72.7
		Lewis Cass	Democratic	1,222,342	42.5	127	
		Martin Van Buren	Free Soil	291,263	10.1		
1852	31	**FRANKLIN PIERCE**	Democratic	1,601,117	50.9	254	69.6
		Winfield Scott	Whig	1,385,453	44.1	42	
		John P. Hale	Free Soil	155,825	5.0		
1856	31	**JAMES BUCHANAN**	Democratic	1,832,955	45.3	174	78.9
		John C. Frémont	Republican	1,339,932	33.1	114	
		Millard Fillmore	American	871,731	21.6	8	

Year	Number of States	Candidates	Parties	Popular Vote	% of Popular Vote	Electoral Vote	% Voter Participation
1860	33	**ABRAHAM LINCOLN**	Republican	1,865,593	39.8	180	81.2
		Stephen A. Douglas	Democratic	1,382,713	29.5	12	
		John C. Breckinridge	Democratic	848,356	18.1	72	
		John Bell	Constitutional Union	592,906	12.6	39	
1864	36	**ABRAHAM LINCOLN**	Republican	2,206,938	55.0	212	73.8
		George B. McClellan	Democratic	1,803,787	45.0	21	
1868	37	**ULYSSES S. GRANT**	Republican	3,013,421	52.7	214	78.1
		Horatio Seymour	Democratic	2,706,829	47.3	80	
1872	37	**ULYSSES S. GRANT**	Republican	3,596,745	55.6	286	71.3
		Horace Greeley	Democratic	2,843,446	43.9	66	
1876	38	Rutherford B. Hayes	Republican	4,036,572	48.0	185	81.8
		Samuel J. Tilden	Democratic	4,284,020	51.0	184	
1880	38	**JAMES A. GARFIELD**	Republican	4,453,295	48.5	214	79.4
		Winfield S. Hancock	Democratic	4,414,082	48.1	155	
		James B. Weaver	Greenback-Labor	308,578	3.4		
1884	38	**GROVER CLEVELAND**	Democratic	4,879,507	48.5	219	77.5
		James G. Blaine	Republican	4,850,293	48.2	182	
		Benjamin F. Butler	Greenback-Labor	175,370	1.8		
		John P. St. John	Prohibition	150,369	1.5		
1888	38	**BENJAMIN HARRISON**	Republican	5,477,129	47.9	233	79.3
		Grover Cleveland	Democratic	5,537,857	48.6	168	
		Clinton B. Fisk	Prohibition	249,506	2.2		
		Anson J. Streeter	Union Labor	146,935	1.3		

Year	Number of States	Candidates	Parties	Popular Vote	% of Popular Vote	Electoral Vote	% Voter Participation
1892	44	**GROVER CLEVELAND**	Democratic	5,555,426	46.1	277	74.7
		Benjamin Harrison	Republican	5,182,690	43.0	145	
		James B. Weaver	People's	1,029,846	8.5	22	
		John Bidwell	Prohibition	264,133	2.2		
1896	45	**WILLIAM MCKINLEY**	Republican	7,102,246	51.1	271	79.3
		William J. Bryan	Democratic	6,492,559	47.7	176	
1900	45	**WILLIAM MCKINLEY**	Republican	7,218,491	51.7	292	73.2
		William J. Bryan	Democratic; Populist	6,356,734	45.5	155	
		John C. Wooley	Prohibition	208,914	1.5		
1904	45	**THEODORE ROOSEVELT**	Republican	7,628,461	57.4	336	65.2
		Alton B. Parker	Democratic	5,084,223	37.6	140	
		Eugene V. Debs	Socialist	402,283	3.0		
		Silas C. Swallow	Prohibition	258,536	1.9		
1908	46	**WILLIAM H. TAFT**	Republican	7,675,320	51.6	321	65.4
		William J. Bryan	Democratic	6,412,294	43.1	162	
		Eugene V. Debs	Socialist	420,793	2.8		
		Eugene W. Chafin	Prohibition	253,840	1.7		
1912	48	**WOODROW WILSON**	Democratic	6,296,547	41.9	435	58.8
		Theodore Roosevelt	Progressive	4,118,571	27.4	88	
		William H. Taft	Republican	3,486,720	23.2	8	
		Eugene V. Debs	Socialist	900,672	6.0		
		Eugene W. Chafin	Prohibition	206,275	1.4		

Year		Candidates	Parties	Popular Vote	%	Electoral Vote	% Voter Participation
1916	48	**WOODROW WILSON**	Democratic	9,127,695	49.4	277	61.6
		Charles E. Hughes	Republican	8,533,507	46.2	254	
		A. L. Benson	Socialist	585,113	3.2		
		J. Frank Hanly	Prohibition	220,506	1.2		
1920	48	**WARREN G. HARDING**	Republican 16,143,407	60.4	404	49.2	
		James M. Cox	Democratic	9,130,328	34.2	127	
		Eugene V. Debs	Socialist	919,799	3.4		
		P. P. Christensen	Farmer-Labor	265,411	1.0		
1924	48	**CALVIN COOLIDGE**	Republican	15,718,211	54.0	382	48.9
		John W. Davis	Democratic	8,385,283	28.8	136	
		Robert M. La Follette	Progressive	4,831,289	16.6	13	
1928	48	**HERBERT C. HOOVER**	Republican	21,391,993	58.2	444	56.9
		Alfred E. Smith	Democratic	15,016,169	40.9	87	
1932	48	**FRANKLIN D. ROOSEVELT**	Democratic	22,809,638	57.4	472	56.9
		Herbert C. Hoover	Republican	15,758,901	39.7	59	
		Norman Thomas	Socialist	881,951	2.2		
1936	48	**FRANKLIN D. ROOSEVELT**	Democratic	27,752,869	60.8	523	61.0
		Alfred M. Landon	Republican	16,674,665	36.5	8	
		William Lemke	Union	882,479	1.9		
1940	48	**FRANKLIN D. ROOSEVELT**	Democratic	27,307,819	54.8	449	62.5
		Wendell L. Willkie	Republican	22,321,018	44.8	82	
1944	48	**FRANKLIN D. ROOSEVELT**	Democratic	25,606,585	53.5	432	55.9
		Thomas E. Dewey	Republican	22,014,745	46.0	99	

Year	Number of States	Candidates	Parties	Popular Vote	% of Popular Vote	Electoral Vote	% Voter Participation
1948	48	**HARRY S. TRUMAN**	Democratic	24,179,345	49.6	303	53.0
		Thomas E. Dewey	Republican	21,991,291	45.1	189	
		J. Strom Thurmond	States' Rights	1,176,125	2.4	39	
		Henry A. Wallace	Progressive	1,157,326	2.4		
1952	48	**DWIGHT D. EISENHOWER**	Republican	33,936,234	55.1	442	63.3
		Adlai E. Stevenson	Democratic	27,314,992	44.4	89	
1956	48	**DWIGHT D. EISENHOWER**	Republican	35,590,472	57.6	457	60.6
		Adlai E. Stevenson	Democratic	26,022,752	42.1	73	
1960	50	**JOHN F. KENNEDY**	Democratic	34,226,731	49.7	303	62.8
		Richard M. Nixon	Republican	34,108,157	49.5	219	
1964	50	**LYNDON B. JOHNSON**	Democratic	43,129,566	61.1	486	61.9
		Barry M. Goldwater	Republican	27,178,188	38.5	52	
1968	50	**RICHARD M. NIXON**	Republican	31,785,480	43.4	301	60.9
		Hubert H. Humphrey	Democratic	31,275,166	42.7	191	
		George C. Wallace	American Independent	9,906,473	13.5	46	
1972	50	**RICHARD M. NIXON**	Republican	47,169,911	60.7	520	55.2
		George S. McGovern	Democratic	29,170,383	37.5	17	
		John G. Schmitz	American	1,099,482	1.4		
1976	50	**JIMMY CARTER**	Democratic	40,830,763	50.1	297	53.5
		Gerald R. Ford	Republican	39,147,793	48.0	240	

Year	Number of States	Candidates	Party	Popular Vote	% of Popular Vote	Electoral Vote	% Voter Participation
1980	50	**RONALD REAGAN**	Republican	43,901,812	50.7	489	52.6
		Jimmy Carter	Democratic	35,483,820	41.0	49	
		John B. Anderson	Independent	5,719,437	6.6		
		Ed Clark	Libertarian	921,188	1.1		
1984	50	**RONALD REAGAN**	Republican	54,451,521	58.8	525	53.1
		Walter F. Mondale	Democratic	37,565,334	40.6	13	
1988	50	**GEORGE H. W. BUSH**	Republican	47,917,341	53.4	426	50.1
		Michael Dukakis	Democratic	41,013,030	45.6	111	
1992	50	**BILL CLINTON**	Democratic	44,908,254	43.0	370	55.0
		George H. W. Bush	Republican	39,102,343	37.4	168	
		H. Ross Perot	Independent	19,741,065	18.9		
1996	50	**BILL CLINTON**	Democratic	47,401,185	49.0	379	49.0
		Bob Dole	Republican	39,197,469	41.0	159	
		H. Ross Perot	Independent	8,085,295	8.0		
2000	50	**GEORGE W. BUSH**	Republican	50,455,156	47.9	271	50.4
		Al Gore	Democrat	50,997,335	48.4	266	
		Ralph Nader	Green	2,882,897	2.7		
2004	50	**GEORGE W. BUSH**	Republican	62,040,610	50.7	286	60.7
		John F. Kerry	Democrat	59,028,444	48.3	251	
2008	50	**BARACK OBAMA**	Democrat	69,456,897	52.92	365	63.0
		John McCain	Republican	59,934,814	45.66	173	
2012	50	**BARACK OBAMA**	Democrat	65,915,795	51.1	332	54.9
		Mitt Romney	Republican	60,933,504	47.2	206	

Candidates receiving less than 1 percent of the popular vote have been omitted. Thus the percentage of popular vote given for any election year may not total 100 percent.

Before the passage of the Twelfth Amendment in 1804, the electoral college voted for two presidential candidates; the runner-up became vice president.

ADMISSION OF STATES

Order of Admission	State	Date of Admission	Order of Admission	State	Date of Admission
1	Delaware	December 7, 1787	26	Michigan	January 26, 1837
2	Pennsylvania	December 12, 1787	27	Florida	March 3, 1845
3	New Jersey	December 18, 1787	28	Texas	December 29, 1845
4	Georgia	January 2, 1788	29	Iowa	December 28, 1846
5	Connecticut	January 9, 1788	30	Wisconsin	May 29, 1848
6	Massachusetts	February 7, 1788	31	California	September 9, 1850
7	Maryland	April 28, 1788	32	Minnesota	May 11, 1858
8	South Carolina	May 23, 1788	33	Oregon	February 14, 1859
9	New Hampshire	June 21, 1788	34	Kansas	January 29, 1861
10	Virginia	June 25, 1788	35	West Virginia	June 30, 1863
11	New York	July 26, 1788	36	Nevada	October 31, 1864
12	North Carolina	November 21, 1789	37	Nebraska	March 1, 1867
13	Rhode Island	May 29, 1790	38	Colorado	August 1, 1876
14	Vermont	March 4, 1791	39	North Dakota	November 2, 1889
15	Kentucky	June 1, 1792	40	South Dakota	November 2, 1889
16	Tennessee	June 1, 1796	41	Montana	November 8, 1889
17	Ohio	March 1, 1803	42	Washington	November 11, 1889
18	Louisiana	April 30, 1812	43	Idaho	July 3, 1890
19	Indiana	December 11, 1816	44	Wyoming	July 10, 1890
20	Mississippi	December 10, 1817	45	Utah	January 4, 1896
21	Illinois	December 3, 1818	46	Oklahoma	November 16, 1907
22	Alabama	December 14, 1819	47	New Mexico	January 6, 1912
23	Maine	March 15, 1820	48	Arizona	February 14, 1912
24	Missouri	August 10, 1821	49	Alaska	January 3, 1959
25	Arkansas	June 15, 1836	50	Hawaii	August 21, 1959

POPULATION OF THE UNITED STATES

Year	Number of States	Population	% Increase	Population per Square Mile
1790	13	3,929,214		4.5
1800	16	5,308,483	35.1	6.1
1810	17	7,239,881	36.4	4.3
1820	23	9,638,453	33.1	5.5
1830	24	12,866,020	33.5	7.4
1840	26	17,069,453	32.7	9.8
1850	31	23,191,876	35.9	7.9
1860	33	31,443,321	35.6	10.6
1870	37	39,818,449	26.6	13.4
1880	38	50,155,783	26.0	16.9
1890	44	62,947,714	25.5	21.1
1900	45	75,994,575	20.7	25.6
1910	46	91,972,266	21.0	31.0
1920	48	105,710,620	14.9	35.6
1930	48	122,775,046	16.1	41.2
1940	48	131,669,275	7.2	44.2
1950	48	150,697,361	14.5	50.7
1960	50	179,323,175	19.0	50.6
1970	50	203,235,298	13.3	57.5
1980	50	226,504,825	11.4	64.0
1985	50	237,839,000	5.0	67.2
1990	50	250,122,000	5.2	70.6
1995	50	263,411,707	5.3	74.4
2000	50	281,421,906	6.8	77.0
2005	50	296,410,404	5.3	77.9
2010	50	308,745,538	9.7	87.4

IMMIGRATION TO THE UNITED STATES, FISCAL YEARS 1820–2013

Year	Number	Year	Number	Year	Number	Year	Number
1820–1989	**55,457,531**	**1871–80**	**2,812,191**	**1921–30**	**4,107,209**	**1971–80**	**4,493,314**
1820	8,385	1871	321,350	1921	805,228	1971	370,478
1821–30	**143,439**	1872	404,806	1922	309,556	1972	384,685
1821	9,127	1873	459,803	1923	522,919	1973	400,063
1822	6,911	1874	313,339	1924	706,896	1974	394,861
1823	6,354	1875	227,498	1925	294,314	1975	386,914
1824	7,912	1876	169,986	1926	304,488	1976	398,613
1825	10,199	1877	141,857	1927	335,175		103,676
1826	10,837	1878	138,469	1928	307,255	1977	462,315
1827	18,875	1879	177,826	1929	279,678	1978	601,442
1828	27,382	1880	457,257	1930	241,700	1979	460,348
1829	22,520	**1881–90**	**5,246,613**	**1931–40**	**528,431**	1980	530,639
1830	23,322	1881	669,431	1931	97,139	**1981–90**	**7,338,062**
1831–40	**599,125**	1882	788,992	1932	35,576	1981	596,600
1831	22,633	1883	603,322	1933	23,068	1982	594,131
1832	60,482	1884	518,592	1934	29,470	1983	559,763
1833	58,640	1885	395,346	1935	34,956	1984	543,903
1834	65,365	1886	334,203	1936	36,329	1985	570,009
1835	45,374	1887	490,109	1937	50,244	1986	601,708
1836	76,242	1888	546,889	1938	67,895	1987	601,516
1837	79,340	1889	444,427	1939	82,998	1988	643,025
1838	38,914	1890	455,302	1940	70,756	1989	1,090,924
1839	68,069	**1891–1900**	**3,687,564**	**1941–50**	**1,035,039**	1990	1,536,483
1840	84,066	1891	560,319	1941	51,776	**1991–2000**	**9,090,857**
1841–50	**1,713,251**	1892	579,663	1942	28,781	1991	1,827,167
1841	80,289	1893	439,730	1943	23,725	1992	973,977
1842	104,565	1894	285,631	1944	28,551	1993	904,292
		1895	258,536	1945	38,119	1994	804,416
		1896	343,267	1946	108,721		

Year	Number	Year	Number	Year	Number	Year	Number
1843	52,496	1897	230,832	1947	147,292	1995	720,461
1844	78,615	1898	229,299	1948	170,570	1996	915,900
1845	114,371	1899	311,715	1949	188,317	1997	798,378
1846	154,416	1900	448,572	1950	249,187	1998	660,477
1847	234,968					1999	644,787
1848	226,527					2000	841,002
1849	297,024	**1901–10**	**8,795,386**	**1951–60**	**2,515,479**	**2001–13**	**10,501,053**
1850	369,980	1901	487,918	1951	205,717	2001	1,058,902
		1902	648,743	1952	265,520	2002	1,059,356
1851–60	**2,598,214**	1903	857,046	1953	170,434	2003	705,827
1851	379,466	1904	812,870	1954	208,177	2004	957,883
1852	371,603	1905	1,026,499	1955	237,790	2005	1,122,373
1853	368,645	1906	1,100,735	1956	321,625	2006	1,266,129
1854	427,833	1907	1,285,349	1957	326,867	2007	1,052,415
1855	200,877	1908	782,870	1958	253,265	2008	1,107,126
1856	200,436	1909	751,786	1959	260,686	2009	1,130,818
1857	251,306	1910	1,041,570	1960	265,398	2010	1,042,625
1858	123,126					2011	1,062,040
1859	121,282	**1911–20**	**5,735,811**	**1961–70**	**3,321,677**	2012	1,031,631
1860	153,640	1911	878,587	1961	271,344	2013	990,553
		1912	838,172	1962	283,763		
1861–70	**2,314,824**	1913	1,197,892	1963	306,260		
1861	91,918	1914	1,218,480	1964	292,248		
1862	91,985	1915	326,700	1965	296,697		
1863	176,282	1916	298,826	1966	323,040		
1864	193,418	1917	295,403	1967	361,972		
1865	248,120	1918	110,618	1968	454,448		
1866	318,568	1919	141,132	1969	358,579		
1867	315,722	1920	430,001	1970	373,326		
1868	138,840						
1869	352,768						
1870	387,203						

Source: U.S. Department of Homeland Security.

IMMIGRATION BY REGION AND SELECTED COUNTRY OF LAST RESIDENCE, FISCAL YEARS 1820–2013

Region and country of last residence	1820 to 1829	1830 to 1839	1840 to 1849	1850 to 1859	1860 to 1869	1870 to 1879	1880 to 1889	1890 to 1899
Total	128,502	538,381	1,427,337	2,814,554	2,081,261	2,742,137	5,248,568	3,694,294
Europe	99,272	422,771	1,369,259	2,619,680	1,877,726	2,251,878	4,638,677	3,576,411
Austria-Hungary	—	—	—	—	3,375	60,127	314,787	534,059
Austria	—	—	—	—	2,700	54,529	204,805	268,218
Hungary	—	—	—	—	483	5,598	109,982	203,350
Belgium	28	20	3,996	5,765	5,785	6,991	18,738	19,642
Bulgaria	—	—	—	—	—	—	—	52
Czechoslovakia	—	—	—	—	—	—	—	—
Denmark	173	927	671	3,227	13,553	29,278	85,342	56,671
Finland	—	—	—	—	—	—	—	—
France	7,694	39,330	75,300	81,778	35,938	71,901	48,193	35,616
Germany	5,753	124,726	385,434	976,072	723,734	751,769	1,445,181	579,072
Greece	17	49	17	32	51	209	1,807	12,732
Ireland	51,617	170,672	656,145	1,029,486	427,419	422,264	674,061	405,710
Italy	430	2,225	1,476	8,643	9,853	46,296	267,660	603,761
Netherlands	1,105	1,377	7,624	11,122	8,387	14,267	52,715	29,349
Norway-Sweden	91	1,149	12,389	22,202	82,937	178,823	586,441	334,058
Norway	—	—	—	—	16,068	88,644	185,111	96,810
Sweden	—	—	—	—	24,224	90,179	401,330	237,248
Poland	19	366	105	1,087	1,886	11,016	42,910	107,793
Portugal	177	820	196	1,299	2,083	13,971	15,186	25,874
Romania	—	—	—	—	—	—	5,842	6,808
Russia	86	280	520	423	1,670	35,177	182,698	450,101
Spain	2,595	2,010	1,916	8,795	6,966	5,540	3,995	9,189
Switzerland	3,148	4,430	4,819	24,423	21,124	25,212	81,151	37,020
United Kingdom	26,336	74,350	218,572	445,322	532,956	578,447	810,900	328,759
Yugoslavia	—	—	—	—	—	—	—	—
Other Europe	3	40	79	4	9	590	1,070	145

Region								
Asia	34	55	121	36,080	54,408	134,128	71,151	61,285
China	3	8	32	35,933	54,028	133,139	65,797	15,268
Hong Kong	—	—	—	—	50	166	247	102
India	9	38	33	42	—	—	—	102
Iran	—	—	—	—	—	—	—	—
Israel	—	—	—	—	—	—	—	—
Japan	—	—	—	—	138	193	1,583	13,998
Jordan	—	—	—	—	—	—	—	—
Korea	—	—	—	—	—	—	—	—
Philippines	—	—	—	—	—	—	—	—
Syria	—	—	—	—	—	—	—	—
Taiwan	—	—	—	—	—	—	—	—
Turkey	19	8	45	94	129	382	2,478	27,510
Vietnam	—	—	—	—	—	—	—	—
Other Asia	3	1	11	11	63	248	1,046	4,407
America	9,655	31,905	50,516	84,145	130,292	345,010	524,826	37,350
Canada and Newfoundland	2,297	11,875	34,285	64,171	117,978	324,310	492,865	3,098
Mexico	3,835	7,187	3,069	3,446	1,957	5,133	2,405	734
Caribbean	3,061	11,792	11,803	12,447	8,751	14,285	27,323	31,480
Cuba	—	—	—	—	—	—	—	—
Dominican Republic	—	—	—	—	—	—	—	—
Haiti	—	—	—	—	—	—	—	—
Jamaica	—	—	—	—	—	—	—	—
Other Caribbean	3,061	11,792	11,803	12,447	8,751	14,285	27,323	31,480
Central America	57	94	297	512	70	173	279	649
Belize	—	—	—	—	—	—	—	—
Costa Rica	—	—	—	—	—	—	—	—
El Salvador	—	—	—	—	—	—	—	—
Guatemala	—	—	—	—	—	—	—	—
Honduras	—	—	—	—	—	—	—	—
Nicaragua	—	—	—	—	—	—	—	—
Panama	—	—	—	—	—	—	—	—
Other Central America	57	94	297	512	70	173	279	649
South America	405	957	1,062	3,569	1,536	1,109	1,954	1,389
Argentina	—	—	—	—	—	—	—	—
Bolivia	—	—	—	—	—	—	—	—

Region and country of last residence	1820 to 1829	1830 to 1839	1840 to 1849	1850 to 1859	1860 to 1869	1870 to 1879	1880 to 1889	1890 to 1899
Brazil	—	—	—	—	—	—	—	—
Chile	—	—	—	—	—	—	—	—
Colombia	—	—	—	—	—	—	—	—
Ecuador	—	—	—	—	—	—	—	—
Guyana	—	—	—	—	—	—	—	—
Paraguay	—	—	—	—	—	—	—	—
Peru	—	—	—	—	—	—	—	—
Suriname	—	—	—	—	—	—	—	—
Uruguay	—	—	—	—	—	—	—	—
Venezuela	—	—	—	—	—	—	—	—
Other South America	405	957	1,062	3,569	1,536	1,109	1,954	1,389
Africa	15	50	61	84	407	371	763	432
Egypt	—	—	—	—	4	29	145	51
Ethiopia	—	—	—	—	—	—	—	—
Liberia	1	8	5	7	43	52	21	9
Morocco	—	—	—	—	—	—	—	—
South Africa	—	—	—	—	35	48	23	9
Other Africa	14	42	56	77	325	242	574	363
Oceania	3	7	14	166	187	9,996	12,361	4,704
Australia	2	1	2	15	—	8,930	7,250	3,098
New Zealand	—	—	—	—	—	39	21	12
Other Oceania	1	6	12	151	187	1,027	5,090	1,594
Not Specified	19,523	83,593	7,366	74,399	18,241	754	790	14,112

Total	8,202,388	6,347,380	4,295,510	699,375	856,608	2,499,268	3,213,749	6,244,379
Europe	7,572,569	4,985,411	2,560,340	444,399	472,524	1,404,973	1,133,443	668,866
Austria-Hungary	2,001,376	1,154,727	60,891	12,531	13,574	113,015	27,590	20,437
Austria	532,416	589,174	31,392	5,307	8,393	81,354	17,571	15,374
Hungary	685,567	565,553	29,499	7,224	5,181	31,661	10,019	5,063
Belgium	37,429	32,574	21,511	4,013	12,473	18,885	9,647	7,028
Bulgaria	34,651	27,180	2,824	1,062	449	97	598	1,124
Czechoslovakia	—	—	101,182	17,757	8,475	1,624	2,758	5,678
Denmark	61,227	45,830	34,406	3,470	4,549	10,918	9,797	4,847
Finland	—	—	16,922	2,438	2,230	4,923	4,310	2,569
France	67,735	60,335	54,842	13,761	36,954	50,113	46,975	32,066
Germany	328,722	174,227	386,634	119,107	119,506	576,905	209,616	85,752
Greece	145,402	198,108	60,774	10,599	8,605	45,153	74,173	37,729
Ireland	344,940	166,445	202,854	28,195	15,701	47,189	37,788	22,210
Italy	1,930,475	1,229,916	528,133	85,053	50,509	184,576	200,111	55,562
Netherlands	42,463	46,065	29,397	7,791	13,877	46,703	37,918	11,234
Norway-Sweden	426,981	192,445	170,329	13,452	17,326	44,224	36,150	13,941
Norway	182,542	79,488	70,327	6,901	8,326	22,806	17,371	3,835
Sweden	244,439	112,957	100,002	6,551	9,000	21,418	18,779	10,106
Poland	—	—	223,316	25,555	7,577	6,465	55,742	63,483
Portugal	65,154	82,489	44,829	3,518	6,765	13,928	70,568	42,685
Romania	57,322	13,566	67,810	5,264	1,254	914	2,339	24,753
Russia	1,501,301	1,106,998	61,604	2,463	605	453	2,329	33,311
Spain	24,818	53,262	47,109	3,669	2,774	6,880	40,793	22,783
Switzerland	32,541	22,839	31,772	5,990	9,904	17,577	19,193	8,316
United Kingdom	469,518	371,878	341,552	61,813	131,794	195,709	220,213	153,644
Yugoslavia	514	6,527	49,215	6,920	2,039	6,966	17,990	16,267
Other Europe	299,836	269,736	22,434	9,978	5,584	11,756	6,845	3,447
Asia	19,884	20,916	126,740	19,231	34,532	135,844	358,605	2,391,356
China	—	—	30,648	5,874	16,072	8,836	14,060	170,897
Hong Kong	3,026	3,478	—	—	—	13,781	67,047	112,132
India	—	—	2,076	554	1,692	1,850	18,638	231,649
Iran	—	—	208	198	1,144	3,195	9,059	98,141
Israel	—	—	—	—	98	21,376	30,911	43,669

Region and country of last residence	1820 to 1829	1830 to 1839	1840 to 1849	1850 to 1859	1860 to 1869	1870 to 1879	1880 to 1889	1890 to 1899
Japan	139,712	77,125	42,057	2,683	1,557	40,651	40,956	44,150
Jordan	—	—	—	—	—	4,899	9,230	28,928
Korea	—	—	—	—	83	4,845	27,048	322,708
Philippines	—	—	—	391	4,099	17,245	70,660	502,056
Syria	—	—	5,307	2,188	1,179	1,091	2,432	14,534
Taiwan	—	—	—	—	—	721	15,657	119,051
Turkey	127,999	160,717	40,450	1,327	754	2,980	9,464	19,208
Vietnam	—	—	—	—	—	290	2,949	200,632
Other Asia	9,215	7,500	5,994	6,016	7,854	14,084	40,494	483,601
America	277,809	1,070,539	1,591,278	230,319	328,435	921,610	1,674,172	2,695,329
Canada and Newfoundland	123,067	708,715	949,286	162,703	160,911	353,169	433,128	156,313
Mexico	31,188	185,334	498,945	32,709	56,158	273,847	441,824	1,009,586
Caribbean	100,960	120,860	83,482	18,052	46,194	115,661	427,235	790,109
Cuba	—	—	12,769	10,641	25,976	73,221	202,030	132,552
Dominican Republic	—	—	—	1,026	4,802	10,219	83,552	221,552
Haiti	—	—	—	156	823	3,787	28,992	121,406
Jamaica	—	—	—	—	—	7,397	62,218	193,874
Other Caribbean	100,960	120,860	70,713	6,229	14,593	21,037	50,443	120,725
Central America	7,341	15,692	16,511	6,840	20,135	40,201	98,560	339,376
Belize	77	40	285	193	433	1,133	4,185	14,964
Costa Rica	—	—	—	431	1,965	4,044	17,975	25,017
El Salvador	—	—	—	597	4,885	5,094	14,405	137,418
Guatemala	—	—	—	423	1,303	4,197	14,357	58,847
Honduras	—	—	—	679	1,874	5,320	15,078	39,071
Nicaragua	—	—	—	405	4,393	7,812	10,383	31,102
Panama	—	—	—	1,452	5,282	12,601	22,177	32,957
Other Central America	7,264	15,652	16,226	2,660	—	—	—	—

South America	15,253	39,938	43,025	9,990	19,662	78,418	250,754	399,862
Argentina	—	—	—	1,067	3,108	16,346	49,384	23,442
Bolivia	—	—	—	50	893	2,759	6,205	9,798
Brazil	—	—	4,627	1,468	3,653	11,547	29,238	22,944
Chile	—	—	—	347	1,320	4,669	12,384	19,749
Colombia	—	—	—	1,027	3,454	15,567	68,371	105,494
Ecuador	—	—	—	244	2,207	8,574	34,107	48,015
Guyana	—	—	—	131	596	1,131	4,546	85,886
Paraguay	—	—	—	33	85	576	1,249	3,518
Peru	—	—	—	321	1,273	5,980	19,783	49,958
Suriname	—	—	—	25	130	299	612	1,357
Uruguay	—	—	—	112	754	1,026	4,089	7,235
Venezuela	—	—	—	1,155	2,182	9,927	20,758	22,405
Other South America	15,253	39,938	38,398	4,010	7	17	28	61
Other America	6,326	—	29	25	25,375	60,314	22,671	83
Africa	—	8,867	6,362	2,120	6,720	13,016	23,780	141,990
Egypt	—	—	1,063	781	1,613	1,996	5,581	26,744
Ethiopia	—	—	—	10	28	302	804	12,927
Liberia	—	—	—	35	37	289	841	6,420
Morocco	—	—	—	73	879	2,703	2,880	3,471
South Africa	6,326	—	—	312	1,022	2,278	4,360	15,505
Other Africa	—	8,867	5,299	909	3,141	5,448	9,314	76,923
Oceania	12,355	12,339	9,860	3,306	14,262	11,353	23,630	41,432
Australia	11,191	11,280	8,404	2,260	11,201	8,275	14,986	16,901
New Zealand	—	—	935	790	2,351	1,799	3,775	6,129
Other Oceania	1,164	1,059	521	256	710	1,279	4,869	18,402
Not Specified	33,493	488	930	—	135	12,472	119	305,406

Region and country of last residence	1990 to 1999	2000 to 2009	2010	2011	2012	2013
Total	9,775,398	10,299,430	1,042,625	1,062,040	1,031,631	990,553
Europe	1,348,612	1,349,609	95,429	90,712	86,956	91,095
Austria-Hungary	27,529	33,929	4,325	4,703	3,208	2,061
Austria	18,234	21,151	3,319	3,654	2,199	1,053
Hungary	9,295	12,778	1,006	1,049	1,009	1,008
Belgium	7,077	8,157	732	700	698	803
Bulgaria	16,948	40,003	2,465	2,549	2,322	2,720
Czechoslovakia	8,970	18,691	1,510	1,374	1,316	1,258
Denmark	6,189	6,049	545	473	492	546
Finland	3,970	3,970	414	398	373	360
France	35,945	45,637	4,339	3,967	4,201	4,668
Germany	92,207	122,373	7,929	7,072	6,732	6,880
Greece	25,403	16,841	966	1,196	1,264	1,526
Ireland	65,384	15,642	1,610	1,533	1,694	1,765
Italy	75,992	28,329	2,956	2,670	2,946	3,233
Netherlands	13,345	17,351	1,520	1,258	1,294	1,376
Norway-Sweden	17,825	19,382	1,662	1,530	1,441	1,665
Norway	5,211	4,599	363	405	314	389
Sweden	12,614	14,783	1,299	1,125	1,127	1,276
Poland	172,249	117,921	7,391	6,634	6,024	6,073
Portugal	25,497	11,479	759	878	837	917
Romania	48,136	52,154	3,735	3,679	3,477	3,475
Russia	433,427	167,152	7,502	8,548	10,114	10,154
Spain	18,443	17,695	2,040	2,319	2,316	2,970
Switzerland	11,768	12,173	868	861	916	1,040
United Kingdom	156,182	171,979	14,781	13,443	13,938	15,321
Yugoslavia	57,039	131,831	4,772	4,611	4,488	4,445
Other Europe	29,087	290,871	22,608	20,316	16,865	17,839

Asia	2,859,899	3,470,835	410,209	438,580	416,488	389,301
China	342,058	591,711	67,634	83,603	78,184	68,410
Hong Kong	116,894	57,583	3,263	3,149	2,642	2,614
India	352,528	590,464	66,185	66,331	63,320	65,506
Iran	76,899	76,755	9,078	9,015	8,955	9,658
Israel	41,340	54,081	5,172	4,389	4,640	4,555
Japan	66,582	84,552	7,100	6,751	6,581	6,383
Jordan	42,755	53,550	9,327	8,211	7,014	5,949
Korea	179,770	209,758	22,022	22,748	20,802	22,937
Philippines	534,338	545,463	56,399	55,251	55,441	52,955
Syria	22,906	30,807	7,424	7,983	6,674	3,999
Taiwan	132,647	92,657	6,785	6,206	5,295	5,336
Turkey	38,687	48,394	7,435	9,040	7,362	7,189
Vietnam	275,379	289,616	30,065	33,486	27,578	26,578
Other Asia	637,116	745,444	112,320	122,417	122,000	107,232
America	5,137,743	4,441,529	426,981	423,277	409,664	399,380
Canada and Newfoundland	194,788	236,349	19,491	19,506	20,138	20,489
Mexico	2,757,418	1,704,166	138,717	142,823	145,326	134,198
Caribbean	1,004,687	1,053,357	139,389	133,012	126,615	121,349
Cuba	159,037	271,742	33,372	36,261	32,551	31,343
Dominican Republic	359,818	291,492	53,890	46,036	41,535	41,487
Haiti	177,446	203,827	22,336	21,802	22,446	20,083
Jamaica	177,143	172,523	19,439	19,298	20,300	19,052
Other Caribbean	181,243	113,773	10,352	9,615	9,783	9,384
Central America	610,189	591,130	43,597	43,249	39,837	44,056
Belize	12,600	9,682	997	933	875	969
Costa Rica	17,054	21,571	2,306	2,230	2,152	2,232
El Salvador	273,017	251,237	18,547	18,477	15,874	18,015
Guatemala	126,043	156,992	10,263	10,795	9,857	9,829
Honduras	72,880	63,513	6,381	6,053	6,773	8,795

Region and country of last residence	1990 to 1999	2000 to 2009	2010	2011	2012	2013
Nicaragua	80,446	70,015	3,476	3,314	2,943	2,940
Panama	28,149	18,120	1,627	1,447	1,363	1,276
Other Central America	—	—	-	-	-	-
South America	570,624	856,508	85,783	84,687	77,748	79,287
Argentina	30,065	47,955	4,312	4,335	4,218	4,227
Bolivia	18,111	21,921	2,211	2,113	1,920	2,005
Brazil	50,744	115,404	12,057	11,643	11,248	10,772
Chile	18,200	19,792	1,940	1,854	1,628	1,751
Colombia	137,985	236,570	21,861	22,130	20,272	20,611
Ecuador	81,358	107,977	11,463	11,068	9,284	10,553
Guyana	74,407	70,373	6,441	6,288	5,282	5,564
Paraguay	6,082	4,623	449	501	454	437
Peru	110,117	137,614	14,063	13,836	12,414	12,370
Suriname	2,285	2,363	202	167	216	170
Uruguay	6,062	9,827	1,286	1,521	1,348	1,314
Venezuela	35,180	82,087	9,497	9,229	9,464	9,512
Other South America	28	2	1	2	-	1
Other America	37	19	4	-	-	1
Africa	346,416	759,734	98,246	97,429	103,685	94,589
Egypt	44,604	81,564	9,822	9,096	10,172	10,719
Ethiopia	40,097	87,207	13,853	13,985	15,400	13,484
Liberia	13,587	23,316	2,924	3,117	3,451	3,036
Morocco	15,768	40,844	4,847	4,249	3,534	3,202
South Africa	21,964	32,221	2,705	2,754	2,960	2,693
Other Africa	210,396	494,582	64,095	64,228	68,168	61,455
Oceania	56,800	65,793	5,946	5,825	5,573	6,061
Australia	24,288	32,728	3,077	3,062	3,146	3,529
New Zealand	8,600	12,495	1,046	1,006	980	1,027
Other Oceania	23,912	20,570	1,823	1,757	1,447	1,505
Not Specified	25,928	211,930	5,814	6,217	9,265	10,127

—Represents zero or not available.

PRESIDENTS, VICE PRESIDENTS,
AND SECRETARIES OF STATE

	President	Vice President	Secretary of State
1.	George Washington, Federalist 1789	John Adams, Federalist 1789	Thomas Jefferson 1789 Edmund Randolph 1794 Timothy Pickering 1795
2.	John Adams, Federalist 1797	Thomas Jefferson, Dem.-Rep. 1797	Timothy Pickering 1797 John Marshall 1800
3.	Thomas Jefferson, Dem.-Rep. 1801	Aaron Burr, Dem.-Rep. 1801 George Clinton, Dem.-Rep. 1805	James Madison 1801
4.	James Madison, Dem.-Rep. 1809	George Clinton, Dem.-Rep. 1809 Elbridge Gerry, Dem.-Rep. 1813	Robert Smith 1809 James Monroe 1811
5.	James Monroe, Dem.-Rep. 1817	Daniel D. Tompkins, Dem.-Rep. 1817	John Q. Adams 1817
6.	John Quincy Adams, Dem.-Rep. 1825	John C. Calhoun, Dem.-Rep. 1825	Henry Clay 1825
7.	Andrew Jackson, Democratic 1829	John C. Calhoun, Democratic 1829 Martin Van Buren, Democratic 1833	Martin Van Buren 1829 Edward Livingston 1831 Louis McLane 1833 John Forsyth 1834
8.	Martin Van Buren, Democratic 1837	Richard M. Johnson, Democratic 1837	John Forsyth 1837
9.	William H. Harrison, Whig 1841	John Tyler, Whig 1841	Daniel Webster 1841

	President	Vice President	Secretary of State
10.	John Tyler, Whig and Democratic 1841	None	Daniel Webster 1841 Hugh S. Legaré 1843 Abel P. Upshur 1843 John C. Calhoun 1844
11.	James K. Polk, Democratic 1845	George M. Dallas, Democratic 1845	James Buchanan 1845
12.	Zachary Taylor, Whig 1849	Millard Fillmore, Whig 1848	John M. Clayton 1849
13.	Millard Fillmore, Whig 1850	None	Daniel Webster 1850 Edward Everett 1852
14.	Franklin Pierce, Democratic 1853	William R. King, Democratic 1853	William L. Marcy 1853
15.	James Buchanan, Democratic 1857	John C. Breckinridge, Democratic 1857	Lewis Cass 1857 Jeremiah S. Black 1860
16.	Abraham Lincoln, Republican 1861	Hannibal Hamlin, Republican 1861 Andrew Johnson, Unionist 1865	William H. Seward 1861
17.	Andrew Johnson, Unionist 1865	None	William H. Seward 1865
18.	Ulysses S. Grant, Republican 1869	Schuyler Colfax, Republican 1869 Henry Wilson, Republican 1873	Elihu B. Washburne 1869 Hamilton Fish 1869
19.	Rutherford B. Hayes, Republican 1877	William A. Wheeler, Republican 1877	William M. Evarts 1877

	President	Vice President	Secretary of State
20.	James A. Garfield, Republican 1881	Chester A. Arthur, Republican 1881	James G. Blaine 1881
21.	Chester A. Arthur, Republican 1881	None	Frederick T. Frelinghuysen 1881
22.	Grover Cleveland, Democratic 1885	Thomas A. Hendricks, Democratic 1885	Thomas F. Bayard 1885
23.	Benjamin Harrison, Republican 1889	Levi P. Morton, Republican 1889	James G. Blaine 1889 John W. Foster 1892
24.	Grover Cleveland, Democratic 1893	Adlai E. Stevenson, Democratic 1893	Walter Q. Gresham 1893 Richard Olney 1895
25.	William McKinley, Republican 1897	Garret A. Hobart, Republican 1897 Theodore Roosevelt, Republican 1901	John Sherman 1897 William R. Day 1898 John Hay 1898
26.	Theodore Roosevelt, Republican 1901	Charles Fairbanks, Republican 1905	John Hay 1901 Elihu Root 1905 Robert Bacon 1909
27.	William H. Taft, Republican 1909	James S. Sherman, Republican 1909	Philander C. Knox 1909
28.	Woodrow Wilson, Democratic 1913	Thomas R. Marshall, Democratic 1913	William J. Bryan 1913 Robert Lansing 1915 Bainbridge Colby 1920
29.	Warren G. Harding, Republican 1921	Calvin Coolidge, Republican 1921	Charles E. Hughes 1921
30.	Calvin Coolidge, Republican 1923	Charles G. Dawes, Republican 1925	Charles E. Hughes 1923 Frank B. Kellogg 1925

	President	Vice President	Secretary of State
31.	Herbert Hoover, Republican 1929	Charles Curtis, Republican 1929	Henry L. Stimson 1929
32.	Franklin D. Roosevelt, Democratic 1933	John Nance Garner, Democratic 1933 Henry A. Wallace, Democratic 1941 Harry S. Truman, Democratic 1945	Cordell Hull 1933 Edward R. Stettinius, Jr. 1944
33.	Harry S. Truman, Democratic 1945	Alben W. Barkley, Democratic 1949	Edward R. Stettinius, Jr. 1945 James F. Byrnes 1945 George C. Marshall 1947 Dean G. Acheson 1949
34.	Dwight D. Eisenhower, Republican 1953	Richard M. Nixon, Republican 1953	John F. Dulles 1953 Christian A. Herter 1959
35.	John F. Kennedy, Democratic 1961	Lyndon B. Johnson, Democratic 1961	Dean Rusk 1961
36.	Lyndon B. Johnson, Democratic 1963	Hubert H. Humphrey, Democratic 1965	Dean Rusk 1963
37.	Richard M. Nixon, Republican 1969	Spiro T. Agnew, Republican 1969 Gerald R. Ford, Republican 1973	William P. Rogers 1969 Henry Kissinger 1973
38.	Gerald R. Ford, Republican 1974	Nelson Rockefeller, Republican 1974	Henry Kissinger 1974
39.	Jimmy Carter, Democratic 1977	Walter Mondale, Democratic 1977	Cyrus Vance 1977 Edmund Muskie 1980

	President	Vice President	Secretary of State
40.	Ronald Reagan, Republican 1981	George H. W. Bush, Republican 1981	Alexander Haig 1981 George Schultz 1982
41.	George H. W. Bush, Republican 1989	J. Danforth Quayle, Republican 1989	James A. Baker 1989 Lawrence Eagleburger 1992
42.	William J. Clinton, Democratic 1993	Albert Gore, Jr., Democratic 1993	Warren Christopher 1993 Madeleine Albright 1997
43.	George W. Bush, Republican 2001	Richard B. Cheney, Republican 2001	Colin L. Powell 2001 Condoleezza Rice 2005
44.	Barack Obama, Democratic 2009	Joseph R. Biden, Democratic 2009	Hillary Rodham Clinton 2009 John Kerry 2013

FURTHER READINGS

CHAPTER 16

The most comprehensive treatment of Reconstruction is Eric Foner's *Reconstruction: America's Unfinished Revolution, 1863–1877* (1988). On Andrew Johnson, see Hans L. Trefousse's *Andrew Johnson: A Biography* (1989) and David D. Stewart's *Impeached: The Trial of Andrew Johnson and the Fight for Lincoln's Legacy* (2009). An excellent brief biography of Grant is Josiah Bunting III's *Ulysses S. Grant* (2004).

Scholars have been sympathetic to the aims and motives of the Radical Republicans. See, for instance, Herman Belz's *Reconstructing the Union: Theory and Policy during the Civil War* (1969) and Richard Nelson Current's *Those Terrible Carpetbaggers: A Reinterpretation* (1988). The ideology of the Radicals is explored in Michael Les Benedict's *A Compromise of Principle: Congressional Republicans and Reconstruction, 1863–1869* (1974). On the black political leaders, see Phillip Dray's *Capitol Men: The Epic Story of Reconstruction through the Lives of the First Black Congressmen* (2008).

The intransigence of southern white attitudes is examined in Michael Perman's *Reunion without Compromise: The South and Reconstruction, 1865–1868* (1973) and Dan T. Carter's *When the War Was Over: The Failure of Self-Reconstruction in the South, 1865–1867* (1985). Allen W. Trelease's *White Terror: The Ku Klux Klan Conspiracy and Southern Reconstruction* (1971) covers the various organizations that practiced vigilante tactics. On the massacre of African Americans, see Charles Lane's *The Day Freedom Died: The Colfax Massacre, the Supreme Court, and the Betrayal of Reconstruction* (2008).

The difficulties former slaves had in adjusting to the new labor system are documented in James L. Roark's *Masters without Slaves: Southern Planters in the Civil War and Reconstruction* (1977). Books on southern politics during Reconstruction include Michael Perman's *The Road to Redemption: Southern*

Politics, 1869–1879 (1984), Terry L. Seip's *The South Returns to Congress: Men, Economic Measures, and Intersectional Relationships, 1868–1879* (1983), and Mark W. Summers's *Railroads, Reconstruction, and the Gospel of Prosperity: Aid under the Radical Republicans, 1865–1877* (1984).

Numerous works study the freed blacks' experience in the South. Start with Leon F. Litwack's *Been in the Storm So Long: The Aftermath of Slavery* (1979). The Freedmen's Bureau is explored in William S. McFeely's *Yankee Stepfather: General O. O. Howard and the Freedmen* (1968). The situation of freed slave women is discussed in Jacqueline Jones's *Labor of Love, Labor of Sorrow: Black Women, Work and the Family, from Slavery to the Present* (1985).

The politics of corruption outside the South is depicted in William S. McFeely's *Grant: A Biography* (1981). The political maneuvers of the election of 1876 and the resultant crisis and compromise are explained in Michael Holt's *By One Vote: The Disputed Presidential Election of 1876* (2008).

CHAPTER 17

For masterly syntheses of post–Civil War industrial development, see Walter Licht's *Industrializing America: The Nineteenth Century* (1995) and Maury Klein's *The Genesis of Industrial America, 1870–1920* (2007). On the growth of railroads, see Richard White's *Railroaded: The Transcontinentals and the Making of Modern America* (2011) and Albro Martin's *Railroad Triumphant: The Growth, Rejection, and Rebirth of a Vital American Force* (1992).

On entrepreneurship in the iron and steel sector, and Thomas J. Misa's *A Nation of Steel: The Making of Modern America, 1865–1925* (1995). The best biographies of the leading business tycoons are Ron Chernow's *Titan: The Life of John D. Rockefeller, Sr.* (1998), David Nasaw's *Andrew Carnegie* (2006), and Jean Strouse's *Morgan: American Financier* (1999). Nathan Rosenberg's *Technology and American Economic Growth* (1972) documents the growth of invention during the period.

For an overview of the struggle of workers to organize unions, see Philip Bray's *There Is Power in a Union: The Epic Story of Labor in America* (2010). On the 1877 railroad strike, see David O. Stowell's *Streets, Railroad, and the Great Strike of 1877* (1999). For the role of women in the changing workplace, see Alice Kessler-Harris's *Out to Work: A History of Wage-Earning Women in the United States* (1982) and Susan E. Kennedy's *If All We Did Was to Weep at Home: A History of White Working-Class Women in American* (1979). On

Mother Jones, see Elliott J. Gorn's *Mother Jones: The Most Dangerous Woman in America* (2001). To trace the rise of socialism among organized workers, see Nick Salvatore's *Eugene V. Debs: Citizen and Socialist* (1982). The key strikes are discussed in Paul Arvich's *The Haymarket Tragedy* (1984) and Paul Krause's *The Battle for Homestead, 1880–1892: Politics, Culture, and Steel* (1992).

CHAPTER 18

The classic study of the emergence of the New South remains C. Vann Woodward's *Origins of the New South, 1877–1913* (1951). A more recent treatment of southern society after the end of Reconstruction is Edward L. Ayers's *Southern Crossing: A History of the American South, 1877–1906* (1995). A thorough survey of industrialization in the South is James C. Cobb's *Industrialization and Southern Society, 1877–1984* (1984).

On race relations, see Howard N. Rabinowitz's *Race Relations in the Urban South, 1865–1890* (1978). Leon F. Litwack's *Trouble in Mind: Black Southerners in the Age of Jim Crow* (1998) treats the rise of legal segregation, while Michael Perman's *Struggle for Mastery: Disfranchisement in the South, 1888–1908* (2001) surveys efforts to keep African Americans from voting. An award-winning study of white women and the race issue is Glenda Elizabeth Gilmore's *Gender and Jim Crow: Women and the Politics of White Supremacy in North Carolina, 1896–1920* (1996). On W. E. B. Du Bois, see David Levering Lewis's *W. E. B. Du Bois: Biography of a Race, 1868–1919* (1993). On Booker T. Washington, see Robert J. Norrell's *Up from History: The Life of Booker T. Washington* (2009).

For stimulating reinterpretations of the frontier and the development of the West, see William Cronon's *Nature's Metropolis: Chicago and the Great West* (1991), Patricia Nelson Limerick's *The Legacy of Conquest: The Unbroken Past of the American West* (1987), Richard White's *"It's Your Misfortune and None of My Own": A New History of the American West* (1991), and Walter Nugent's *Into the West: The Story of Its People* (1999). An excellent overview is James M. McPherson's *Into the West: From Reconstruction to the Final Days of the American Frontier* (2006).

The role of African Americans in western settlement is the focus of William Loren Katz's *The Black West: A Documentary and Pictorial History of the African American Role in the Westward Expansion of the United States*, rev. ed. (2005), and Nell Irvin Painter's *Exodusters: Black Migration to Kansas after Reconstruction* (1977).

The best account of the conflicts between Indians and whites is Robert M. Utley's *The Indian Frontier of the American West, 1846–1890* (1984). For the Sand Creek massacre, see Ari Kellman's *A Misplaced Massacre: Struggling over the Memory of Sand Creek* (2013). On the Battle of the Little Bighorn, see Nathaniel Philbrick's *The Last Stand: Custer, Sitting Bull, and the Battle of the Little Bighorn* (2010). On Crazy Horse, see Thomas Powers's *The Killing of Crazy Horse* (2010).

For a presentation of the Native American side of the story, see Peter Nabokov's *Native American Testimony: A Chronicle of Indian-White Relations from Prophecy to the Present, 1492–2000*, rev. ed. (1999). On the demise of the buffalo herds, see Andrew C. Isenberg's *The Destruction of the Bison: An Environmental History, 1750–1920* (2000).

CHAPTER 19

For a survey of urbanization, see David R. Goldfield's *Urban America: A History* (1989). Gunther Barth discusses the emergence of a new urban culture in *City People: The Rise of Modern City Culture in Nineteenth-Century America* (1980). John Bodnar offers a synthesis of the urban immigrant experience in *The Transplanted: A History of Immigrants in Urban America* (1985). See also Roger Daniels's *Guarding the Golden Door: American Immigration Policy and Immigrants since 1882* (2004). Walter Nugent's *Crossings: The Great Transatlantic Migrations, 1870–1914* (1992) provides a wealth of demographic information and insight. Efforts to stop Chinese immigration are described in Erika Lee's *At America's Gates: Chinese Immigration during the Exclusion Era* (2003).

On urban environments and sanitary reforms, see Martin V. Melosi's *The Sanitary City: Urban Infrastructure in America from Colonial Times to the Present* (2000), Joel A. Tarr's *The Search for the Ultimate Sink: Urban Pollution in Historical Perspective* (1996), and Suellen Hoy's *Chasing Dirt: The American Pursuit of Cleanliness* (1995).

For the growth of urban leisure and sports, see Roy Rosenzweig's *Eight Hours for What We Will: Workers and Leisure in an Industrial City, 1870–1920* (1983) and Steven A. Riess's *City Games: The Evolution of American Urban Society and the Rise of Sports* (1989). Saloon culture is examined in Madelon Powers's *Faces along the Bar: Lore and Order in the Workingman's Saloon, 1870–1920* (1998).

On the impact of Darwin's theory of evolution, see Barry Werth's *Banquet at Delmonico's: Great Minds, the Gilded Age, and the Triumph of Evolution in America* (2009). On the rise of realism in thought and the arts during the second half of the nineteenth century, see David E. Shi's *Facing Facts: Realism in American Thought and Culture, 1850–1920* (1995). The rise of pragmatism is the focus of Louis Menand's *The Metaphysical Club: A Story of Ideas in America* (2001).

Two good overviews of the Gilded Age are Sean Cashman's *America in the Gilded Age: From the Death of Lincoln to the Rise of Theodore Roosevelt* (1984) and Mark Summers's *The Gilded Age or, The Hazard of New Functions* (1996). Nell Irvin Painter's *Standing at Armageddon: The United States, 1877–1919* (1987) focuses on the experience of the working class.

For a stimulating overview of the political, social, and economic trends during the Gilded Age, see Jack Beatty's *Age of Betrayal: The Triumph of Money in America, 1865–1900* (2007). On the development of city rings and bosses, see Kenneth D. Ackerman's *Boss Tweed: The Rise and Fall of the Corrupt Pol Who Conceived the Soul of Modern New York* (2005). Excellent presidential biographies include Hans L. Trefousse's *Rutherford B. Hayes* (2002), Zachary Karabell's *Chester Alan Arthur* (2004), Henry F. Graff's *Grover Cleveland* (2002), and Kevin Phillips's *William McKinley* (2003). On the political culture of the Gilded Age, see Charles Calhoun's *Minority Victory: Gilded Age Politics and the Front Porch Campaign of 1888* (2008).

A balanced account of Populism is Charles Postel's *The Populist Vision* (2007). The election of 1896 is the focus of R. Hal Williams's *Realigning America: McKinley, Bryan, and the Remarkable Election of 1896* (2010). On the role of religion in the agrarian protest movements, see Joe Creech's *Righteous Indignation: Religion and the Populist Revolution* (2006). The best biography of Bryan is Michael Kazin's *A Godly Hero: The Life of William Jennings Bryan* (2006).

CHAPTER 20

An excellent survey of the diplomacy of the era is Charles S. Campbell's *The Transformation of American Foreign Relations, 1865–1900* (1976). For background on the events of the 1890s, see David Healy's *U.S. Expansionism: The Imperialist Urge in the 1890s* (1970). The dispute over American policy in Hawaii is covered in Thomas J. Osborne's *"Empire Can Wait": American Opposition to Hawaiian Annexation, 1893–1898* (1981).

Ivan Musicant's *Empire by Default: The Spanish-American War and the Dawn of the American Century* (1998) is the most comprehensive volume on the conflict. A colorful treatment of the powerful men promoting war is Evan Thomas's *The War Lovers: Roosevelt, Lodge, Mahan, and the Rush to Empire,*

1898 (2010). For the war's aftermath in the Philippines, see Stuart Creighton Miller's *"Benevolent Assimilation": The American Conquest of the Philippines, 1899–1903* (1982). On the Philippine-American War, see David J. Silbey's *A War of Frontier and Empire: The Philippine-American War, 1899–1902* (2007).

A good introduction to American interest in China is Michael H. Hunt's *The Making of a Special Relationship: The United States and China to 1914* (1983). John Taliaferro's *All the Great Prizes: The Life of John Hay* (2013) examines the role of this key secretary of state in forming policy.

For U.S. policy in the Caribbean and Central America, see Walter LaFeber's *Inevitable Revolutions: The United States in Central America,* 2nd ed. (1993). David McCullough's *The Path between the Seas: The Creation of the Panama Canal, 1870–1914* (1977) presents an admiring account of how the United States secured the Panama Canal. A more sober assessment is Julie Greene's *The Canal Builders: Making America's Empire at the Panama Canal* (2009). For a detailed treatment of Theodore Roosevelt's diplomacy as president, see James Bradley's *The Imperial Cruise: A Secret History of Empire and War* (2009).

CHAPTER 21

Splendid analyses of progressivism can be found in John Whiteclay Chambers II's *The Tyranny of Change: America in the Progressive Era, 1890–1920,* rev. ed. (2000), Steven J. Diner's *A Very Different Age: Americans of the Progressive Era* (1997), Maureen A. Flanagan's *America Reformed: Progressives and Progressivisms, 1890–1920* (2006), Michael McGerr's *A Fierce Discontent: The Rise and Fall of the Progressive Movement in America* (2003) and David Traxel's *Crusader Nation: The United States in Peace and the Great War, 1898–1920* (2006). On Ida Tarbell and the muckrakers, see Steve Weinberg's *Taking on the Trust: The Epic Battle of Ida Tarbell and John D. Rockefeller* (2008).

The evolution of government policy toward business is examined in Martin J. Sklar's *The Corporate Reconstruction of American Capitalism, 1890–1916: The Market, the Law, and Politics* (1988). Mina Carson's *Settlement Folk: Social Thought and the American Settlement Movement, 1885–1930* (1990) examines the social problems in the cities. Robert Kanigel's *The One Best Way: Frederick Winslow Taylor and the Enigma of Efficiency* (1997) highlights the role of efficiency and expertise in the Progressive Era.

An excellent study of the role of women in progressivism's emphasis on social justice is Kathryn Kish Sklar's *Florence Kelley and the Nation's Work: The Rise of Women's Political Culture, 1830–1900* (1995). On the tragic fire at the Triangle Shirtwaist Company, see David Von Drehle's *Triangle: The*

Fire That Changed America (2003). The best study of the settlement house movement is Jean Bethke Elshtain's *Jane Addams and the Dream of American Democracy: A Life* (2002).

On Theodore Roosevelt and the conservation movement, see Douglas Brinkley's *The Wilderness Warrior: Theodore Roosevelt and the Crusade for America* (2009) The pivotal election of 1912 is covered in James Chace's *1912: Wilson, Roosevelt, Taft, and Debs—The Election That Changed the Country* (2004) and Sidney M. Milkis's *TR, the Progressive Party, and the Transformation of Democracy* (2009). Excellent biographies include Kathleen Dalton's *Theodore Roosevelt: A Strenuous Life* (2002) and A. Scott Berg's *Wilson* (2013). The racial blind spot of Progressivism is assessed in David W. Southern's *The Progressive Era and Race: Reform and Reaction, 1900–1917* (2006).

CHAPTER 22

A lucid overview of international events in the early twentieth century is Robert H. Ferrell's *Woodrow Wilson and World War I, 1917–1921* (1985). For a vivid account of U.S. intervention in Mexico, see Frederick Katz's *The Life and Times of Pancho Villa* (1999). On Wilson's stance toward war, see Robert W. Tucker's *Woodrow Wilson and the Great War: Reconsidering America's Neutrality, 1914–1917* (2007). An excellent biography is John Milton Cooper Jr.'s *Woodrow Wilson: A Biography* (2010).

For the European experience in the Great War, see Adam Hochschild's *To End All Wars: A Story of Loyalty and Rebellion, 1914–1918* (2011), Margaret MacMillan's *The War That Ended Peace* (2013), and William Philpott's *Attrition: Fighting the First World War* (2015). Edward M. Coffman's *The War to End All Wars: The American Military Experience in World War I* (1968) is a detailed presentation of America's military involvement. See also Gary Mead's *The Doughboys: America and the First World War* (2000).

For a survey of the impact of the war on the home front, see Meirion Harries and Susie Harries's *The Last Days of Innocence: America at War, 1917–1918* (1997). Maurine Weiner Greenwald's *Women, War, and Work: The Impact of World War I on Women Workers in the United States* (1980) discusses the role of women in the war effort while Sara Hunter Graham's *Woman Suffrage and the New Democracy* (1996) traces the movement during the war to give women the vote. Ronald Schaffer's *America in the Great War: The Rise of the War Welfare State* (1991) shows the effect of war mobilization on business organization. Richard Polenberg's *Fighting Faiths: The*

Abrams Case, the Supreme Court, and Free Speech (1987) examines the prosecution of a case under the 1918 Sedition Act. See also Ernest Freeberg's *Democracy's Prisoner: Eugene V. Debs, the Great War, and the Right to Dissent* (2009).

How American diplomacy fared in the making of peace has received considerable attention. Thomas J. Knock connects domestic affairs and foreign relations in his explanation of Wilson's peacemaking in *To End All Wars: Woodrow Wilson and the Quest for a New World Order* (1992). See also John Milton Cooper Jr.'s *Breaking the Heart of the World: Woodrow Wilson and the Fight for the League of Nations* (2002), and Adam Tooze's *The Deluge: The Great War, America, and the Remaking of the Global Order* (2014).

The problems of the immediate postwar years are chronicled by a number of historians. The best overview is Ann Hagedorn's *Savage Peace: Hope and Fear in America, 1919* (2007). On the Spanish flu, see John M. Barry's *The Great Influenza: The Epic Story of the Deadliest Plague in History* (2004). Labor tensions are examined in David E. Brody's *Labor in Crisis: The Steel Strike of 1919* (1965) and Francis Russell's *A City in Terror: Calvin Coolidge and the 1919 Boston Police Strike* (1975). On racial strife, see Jan Voogd's *Race Riots and Resistance: The Red Summer of 1919* (2008). The fear of Communists is analyzed in Robert K. Murray's *Red Scare: A Study in National Hysteria, 1919–1920* (1955).

CHAPTER 23

For a lively survey of the social and cultural changes during the interwar period, start with William E. Leuchtenburg's *The Perils of Prosperity, 1914–32*, 2nd ed. (1993). Even more comprehensive is Michael E. Parrish's *Anxious Decades: America in Prosperity and Depression, 1920–1941* (1992). The best introduction to the culture of the 1920s remains Roderick Nash's *The Nervous Generation: American Thought, 1917–1930* (1990). See also Lynn Dumenil's *The Modern Temper: American Culture and Society in the 1920s* (1995).

The impact of woman suffrage is treated in Kristi Anderson's *After Suffrage: Women in Partisan and Electoral Politics before the New Deal* (1996). The best study of the birth-control movement is Ellen Chesler's *Woman of Valor: Margaret Sanger and the Birth Control Movement in America* (1992).

On the African American migration from the South, see James N. Gregory's *The Southern Diaspora: How the Great Migrations of Black and White Southerners Transformed America* (2005). See Charles Flint Kellogg's *NAACP: A History of the National Association for the Advancement of Colored People* (1967) for his analysis of the pioneering court cases against racial discrimination. Nathan Irvin Huggins's *Harlem Renaissance* (1971) assesses the cultural impact of the Great Migration on New York City. The emergence of jazz is ably documented in Burton W. Peretti's *The Creation of Jazz: Music, Race, and Culture in Urban America* (1992). Scientific breakthroughs are analyzed in Manjit Kumar's *Quantum: Einstein, Bohr, and the Great Debate about the Nature of Reality* (2010). See also Steven Gimbel's *Einstein: His Space and Times* (2015). The best overview of cultural modernism in Europe is Peter Gay's *Modernism: The Lure of Heresy from Baudelaire to Beckett and Beyond* (2009). On southern modernism, see Daniel Joseph Singal's *The War Within: From Victorian to Modernist Thought in the South, 1919–1945* (1982). Stanley Coben's *Rebellion against Victorianism: The Impetus for Cultural Change in 1920s America* (1991) surveys the appeal of modernism among writers, artists, and intellectuals. See also Charles J. Shindo's *1927 and the Rise of Modern America* (2010).

CHAPTER 24

On Harding, see Robert K. Murray's *The Harding Era: Warren G. Harding and His Administration* (1969). On Coolidge, see Amith Shlaes's *Coolidge* (2013). On Hoover, see Martin L. Fausold's *The Presidency of Herbert C. Hoover* (1985). The influential secretary of the Treasury during the 1920s is ably analyzed in David Cannadine's *Mellon: An American Life* (2006).

John Higham's *Strangers in the Land: Patterns of American Nativism, 1860–1925*, 2nd ed. (2002) details the story of immigration restriction. The controversial Sacco and Vanzetti case is the focus of Moshik Temkin's *The Sacco-Vanzetti Affair: America on Trial* (2009). For analysis of the revival of Klan activity, see Thomas R. Pegram's *One Hundred Percent American: The Rebirth and Decline of the Ku Klux Klan in the 1920s* (2011). The best analysis of the Scopes trial is Edward J. Larson's *Summer for the Gods: The Scopes Trial and America's Continuing Debate over Science and Religion* (1997). On Prohibition, see Daniel Okrent's *Last Call: The Rise and Fall of Prohibition* (2011). For the story of the invention of the airplane, see David McCullough's *The Wright Brothers* (2015).

On the stock market crash in 1929, see Maury Klein's *Rainbow's End: The Crash of 1929* (2000). Overviews of the depressed economy are found in Charles P. Kindleberger's *The World in Depression, 1929–1939*, rev. and enlarged ed. (1986) and Peter Fearon's *War, Prosperity, and Depression: The U.S. Economy, 1917–1945* (1987). On the removal of the Bonus Army, see Paul Dickson and Thomas B. Allen's *The Bonus Army: An American Epic* (2004).

CHAPTER 25

Two excellent overviews of the New Deal are Ira Katznelson's *Fear Itself: The New Deal and the Origins of Our Time* (2013) and David M. Kennedy's *Freedom from Fear: The American People in Depression and War, 1929–1945* (1999). A lively biography of Roosevelt is H. W. Brands's *Traitor to His Class: The Privileged Life and Radical Presidency of Franklin Delano Roosevelt* (2009). The Roosevelt marriage is well described in Hazel Rowley's *Franklin and Eleanor: An Extraordinary Marriage* (2011).

The busy first year of the New Deal is ably detailed in Anthony J. Badger's *FDR: The First Hundred Days* (2008). Perhaps the most successful of the early New Deal programs is the focus of Neil M. Maher's *Nature's New Deal: The Civilian Conservation Corps and the Roots of the American Environmental Movement* (2008). On the political opponents of the New Deal, see Alan Brinkley's *Voices of Protest: Huey Long, Father Coughlin, and the Great Depression* (1982). Roosevelt's battle with the Supreme Court is detailed in Jeff Shesol's *Supreme Power: Franklin Roosevelt vs. The Supreme Court* (2010). The actual effects of the New Deal on the economy are detailed in Elliot A. Rosen's *Roosevelt, the Great Depression, and the Economics of Recovery* (2005).

A critical assessment of Roosevelt and the New Deal is Amity Schlaes's *The Forgotten Man* (2007). James N. Gregory's *American Exodus: The Dust Bowl Migration and Okie Culture in California* (1989) describes the migratory movement. The dramatic Scottsboro court case is the focus of James Goodman's *Stories of Scottsboro* (1995). On the environmental and human causes of the dust bowl, see Donald Worster, *Dust Bowl: The Southern Plains in the 1930s* (1979). On cultural life during the 1930s, see Morris Dickstein's *Dancing in the Dark: A Cultural History of the Great Depression* (2009).

The best overview of diplomacy between the world wars remains Selig Adler's *The Uncertain Giant, 1921–1941: American Foreign Policy between the Wars* (1965). Robert Dallek's *Franklin D. Roosevelt and American Foreign Policy, 1932–1945* (1979) provides a judicious assessment of Roosevelt's foreign policy initiatives during the 1930s.

On Roosevelt's war of words with isolationists, see Lynne Olsen's *Those Angry Days: Roosevelt, Lindbergh, and America's Fight over World War II, 1939–1942* (2013), David Kaiser's *No End Save Victory: How FDR Led the Ntion into War* (2014), and Nicholas Wapshott's *The Sphinx: Franklin Roosevelt, the Isolationists, and the Road to World War II* (2015). See also David Reynolds's *From Munich to Pearl Harbor: Roosevelt's America and the Origins of the Second World War* (2001). For the Japanese perspective, see Eri Hotta's

Japan 1941: Countdown to Infamy (2014). On the surprise attack on Pearl Harbor, see Gordon W. Prange's *Pearl Harbor: The Verdict of History* (1986). Japan's perspective is described in Akira Iriye's *The Origins of the Second World War in Asia and the Pacific* (1987).

CHAPTER 26

For a sweeping survey of the Second World War, consult Anthony Roberts's *The Storm of War: A New History of the Second World War* (2011). The best detailed treatment of U.S. involvement is Rick Atkinson's multivolume Pulitzer prize–winning series, *An Army at Dawn* (2007), *The Day of Battle* (2008), and *The Guns at Last Light* (2013). Roosevelt's wartime leadership is analyzed in Eric Larrabee's *Commander in Chief: Franklin Delano Roosevelt, His Lieutenants, and Their War* (1987).

Books on specific European campaigns include Anthony Beevor's *D-Day: The Battle for Normandy* (2010) and Charles B. MacDonald's *A Time for Trumpets: The Untold Story of the Battle of the Bulge* (1985). On the Allied commander, see Carlo D'Este's *Eisenhower: A Soldier's Life* (2002). Richard Overy assesses the controversial role of air power in *The Bombing War: Europe, 1939–1945* (2013).

For the war in the Far East, see John Costello's *The Pacific War, 1941–1945* (1981), Ronald H. Spector's *Eagle against the Sun: The American War with Japan* (1985), John W. Dower's award-winning *War without Mercy: Race and Power in the Pacific War* (1986), and Dan van der Vat's *The Pacific Campaign: The U.S.-Japanese Naval War, 1941–1945* (1991).

An excellent overview of the war's effects on the home front is Michael C. C. Adams's *The Best War Ever: America and World War II* (1994). On the transformation to the wartime economy, see Arthur Herman's *Freedom's Forge: How American Business Produced Victory in World War II* (2012) and Maury Klein's *A Call to Arms* (2013). Susan M. Hartmann's *The Home Front and Beyond: American Women in the 1940s* (1982) treats the new working environment for women. Kenneth D. Rose tells the story of problems on the home front in *Myth and the Greatest Generation: A Social History of Americans in World War II* (2008). Neil A. Wynn looks at the participation of blacks in *The Afro-American and the Second World War* (1976). The story of the oppression of Japanese Americans is told in Greg Robinson's *A Tragedy for Democracy: Japanese Confinement in North America* (2009). On the development of the atomic bomb, see Jim Baggott's *The First War of Physics: The Secret History of the Atomic Bomb* (2010). The devastation caused by the atomic bomb is the focus of Susan Southard's *Nagasaki: Life after Nuclear War* (2015). For the controversy over America's policies towards the Holocaust, see Richard Breitman and Alan J. Lichtman's *FDR and the Jews* (2013).

A detailed introduction to U.S. diplomacy during the conflict can be found in Gaddis Smith's *American Diplomacy during the Second World War, 1941–1945* (1965). To understand the role that Roosevelt played in policy making, consult Warren F. Kimball's *The Juggler: Franklin Roosevelt as Wartime Statesman* (1991). The most important wartime summit meeting is assessed in S. M. Plokhy's *Yalta: The Price of Peace* (2010). The issues and events that led to the deployment of atomic weapons are addressed in Martin J. Sherwin's *A World Destroyed: The Atomic Bomb and the Grand Alliance* (1975).

CHAPTER 27

The cold war remains a hotly debated topic. The traditional interpretation is best reflected in John Lewis Gaddis's *The Cold War: A New History* (2005). Both superpowers, Gaddis argues, were responsible for causing the cold war, but the Soviet Union was more culpable. The revisionist perspective is represented by Gar Alperovitz's *Atomic Diplomacy: Hiroshima and Potsdam: The Use of the Atomic Bomb and the American Confrontation with Soviet Power*, 2nd ed. (1994). Also see H. W. Brands's *The Devil We Knew: Americans and the Cold War* (1993) and Melvyn P. Leffler's *For the Soul of Mankind: The United States, the Soviet Union, and the Cold War* (2007). On the architect of the containment strategy, see John L. Gaddis, *George F. Kennan: An American Life* (2011).

Frank Constigliola assesses Franklin Roosevelt's role in the start of the cold war in *Roosevelt's Lost Alliances: How Personal Politics Helped Start the Cold War* (2013). Arnold A. Offner indicts Truman for clumsy statesmanship in *Another Such Victory: President Truman and the Cold War, 1945–1953* (2002). For a positive assessment of Truman's leadership, see Alonzo L. Hamby's *Beyond the New Deal: Harry S. Truman and American Liberalism* (1973) and Robert Dallek's *The Lost Peace: Leadership in a Time of Horror and Hope, 1945–1953* (2010). The domestic policies of the Fair Deal are treated in William C. Berman's *The Politics of Civil Rights in the Truman Administration* (1970), Richard M. Dalfiume's *Desegregation of the U.S. Armed Forces: Fighting on Two Fronts, 1939–1953* (1969), and Maeva Marcus's *Truman and the Steel Seizure Case: The Limits of Presidential Power* (1977). The most comprehensive biography of Truman is David McCullough's *Truman* (1992).

For an introduction to the tensions in Asia, see Akira Iriye's *The Cold War in Asia: A Historical Introduction* (1974). For the Korean conflict, see Callum A. MacDonald's *Korea: The War before Vietnam* (1986) and Max Hasting's *The Korean War* (1987).

The anti-Communist crusade is surveyed in David Caute's *The Great Fear: The Anti-Communist Purge under Truman and Eisenhower* (1978). Arthur Herman's *Joseph McCarthy: Reexamining the Life and Legacy of America's Most Hated Senator* (2000) covers McCarthy himself. For a well-documented account of how the cold war was sustained by superpatriotism, intolerance, and suspicion, see Stephen J. Whitfield's *The Culture of the Cold War*, 2nd ed. (1996).

CHAPTER 28

Two excellent overviews of social and cultural trends in the postwar era are William H. Chafe's *The Unfinished Journey: America since World War II*, 6th ed. (2006), and William E. Leuchtenburg's *A Troubled Feast: America since 1945*, rev. ed. (1979). For insights into the cultural life of the 1950s, see Jeffrey Hart's *When the Going Was Good! American Life in the Fifties* (1982) and David Halberstam's *The Fifties* (1993).

The baby boom generation and its impact are vividly described in Paul C. Light's *Baby Boomers* (1988). The emergence of the television industry is discussed in Erik Barnouw's *Tube of Plenty: The Evolution of American Television*, 2nd rev. ed. (1990), and Ella Taylor's *Prime-Time Families: Television Culture in Postwar America* (1989).

On the process of suburban development, see Kenneth T. Jackson's *Crabgrass Frontier: The Suburbanization of the United States* (1985). Equally good is Tom Martinson's *American Dreamscape: The Pursuit of Happiness in Postwar Suburbia* (2000).

The middle-class ideal of family life in the 1950s is examined in Elaine Tyler May's *Homeward Bound: American Families in the Cold War Era*, rev. ed. (2008). Thorough accounts of women's issues are found in Wini Breines's *Young, White, and Miserable: Growing Up Female in the Fifties* (1992). For an overview of the resurgence of religion in the 1950s, see George M. Marsden's *Religion and American Culture*, 2nd ed. (2000).

The origins and growth of rock and roll are surveyed in Carl Belz's *The Story of Rock*, 2nd ed. (1972). The colorful Beats are brought to life in Steven Watson's *The Birth of the Beat Generation: Visionaries, Rebels, and Hipsters, 1944–1960* (1995).

Scholarship on the Eisenhower years is extensive. A balanced treatment is Jean Edward Smith's *Eisenhower in War and Peace* (2012). For the manner in which Eisenhower conducted foreign policy, see Evan Thomas's *Ike's Bluff: President Eisenhower's Secret Battle to Save the World* (2012).

The best overview of American foreign policy since 1945 is Stephen E. Ambrose and Douglas G. Brinkley's *Rise to Globalism: American Foreign Policy since 1938* 9th ed. (2011). For the buildup of U.S. involvement in Indochina, consult Fredrik Logevall's *Embers of War: The Fall of an Empire and the Making of America's Vietnam* (2012). The Cold War strategy of the Eisenhower administration is the focus of Chris Tudda's *The Truth Is Our Weapon: The Rhetorical Diplomacy of Dwight D. Eisenhower and John Foster Dulles* (2006). To learn about the CIA's secret activities in Iran, see Ervand Abrahamian's *The Coup: 1953, the CIA, and the Roots of Modern U.S.-Iranian Relations* (2013).

The impact of the Supreme Court during the 1950s is the focus of Archibald Cox's *The Warren Court: Constitutional Decision as an Instrument of Reform* (1968). A masterly study of the important Warren Court decision on school desegregation is James T. Patterson's *Brown v. Board of Education: A Civil Rights Milestone and Its Troubled Legacy* (2001).

For the story of the early years of the civil rights movement, see Taylor Branch's *Parting the Waters: America in the King Years, 1954–1963* (1988), Robert Weisbrot's *Freedom Bound: A History of America's Civil Rights Movement* (1990), and David A. Nicholas's *A Matter of Justice: Eisenhower and the Beginning of the Civil Rights Revolution* (2007). On Rosa Parks, see Jeanne Theoharis's *The Rebellious Life of Mrs. Rosa Parks* (2013). On the testy relationship of Eisenhower and his vice president, Richard Nixon, see Jeffrey Frank's *Ike and Dick: Portrait of a Strange Political Marriage* (2013).

Chapter 29

A superb analysis of John Kennedy's life is Thomas C. Reeves's *A Question of Character: A Life of John F. Kennedy* (1991). The 1960 campaign is detailed in Gary A. Donaldson's *The First Modern Campaign: Kennedy, Nixon, and the Election of 1960* (2007). The best study of the Kennedy administration's domestic policies is Irving Bernstein's *Promises Kept: John F. Kennedy's New Frontier* (1991). See also Robert Dallek's *Camelot's Court: Inside the Kennedy White House* (2013), Thurston Clarke's *JFK's Last Hundred Days* (2013), and Ira Stoll's *JFK, Conservative* (2013). For details on the still swirling conspiracy theories about the assassination, see David W. Belin's *Final Disclosure: The Full Truth about the Assassination of President Kennedy* (1988).

On LBJ, see the magisterial multivolume biography by Robert Caro's titled *The Years of Lyndon Johnson*. On the Johnson administration, see Vaughn Davis Bornet's *The Presidency of Lyndon B. Johnson* (1984). For an insider's perspective, see Joseph A. Califano's *The Triumph and Tragedy of Lyndon Johnson* (2015).

Among the works that interpret liberal social policy during the 1960s, John E. Schwarz's *America's Hidden Success: A Reassessment of Twenty Years of Public Policy* (1983) offers a glowing endorsement of Democratic programs. For a contrasting perspective, see Charles Murray's *Losing Ground: American Social Policy, 1950–1980* (1994). Also see Martha J. Bailey and Sheldon Danzinger's *Legacies of the War on Poverty* (2015).

On foreign policy, see *Kennedy's Quest for Victory: American Foreign Policy, 1961–1963* (1989), edited by Thomas G. Paterson, and Patrick J. Sloyan's *The Politics of Deception* (2015). To learn more about Kennedy's problems in Cuba, see Mark J. White's *Missiles in Cuba: Kennedy, Khrushchev, Castro and the 1962 Crisis* (1997). See also Aleksandr Fursenko and Timothy Naftali's *"One Hell of a Gamble": Khrushchev, Castro and Kennedy, 1958–1964* (1997).

American involvement in Vietnam has received voluminous treatment from all political perspectives. For an excellent overview, see Larry Berman's *Planning a Tragedy: The Americanization of the War in Vietnam* (1983) and *Lyndon Johnson's War: The Road to Stalemate in Vietnam* (1989), as well as Stanley Karnow's *Vietnam: A History*, 2nd rev. ed. (1997). An analysis of policy making concerning the Vietnam War is David M. Barrett's *Uncertain Warriors: Lyndon Johnson and His Vietnam Advisors* (1993). A fine account of the military involvement is Robert D. Schulzinger's *A Time for War: The United States and Vietnam, 1941–1975* (1997). On the legacy of the Vietnam War, see Arnold R. Isaacs's *Vietnam Shadows: The War, Its Ghosts, and Its Legacy* (1997).

Many scholars have dealt with various aspects of the civil rights movement and race relations in the 1960s. See especially Carl M. Brauer's *John F. Kennedy and the Second Reconstruction* (1977), David J. Garrow's *Bearing the Cross: Martin Luther King, Jr., and the Southern Christian Leadership Conference* (1986), and Adam Fairclough's *To Redeem the Soul of America: The Southern Christian Leadership Conference and Martin Luther King, Jr.* (1987). William H. Chafe's *Civilities and Civil Rights: Greensboro, North Carolina, and the Black Struggle for Freedom* (1980) details the original sit-ins. An award-winning study of racial and economic inequality in a representative American city is Thomas J. Sugrue's *The Origins of the Urban Crisis: Race and Inequality in Postwar Detroit* (1996).

CHAPTER 30

An engaging overview of the cultural trends of the 1960s is Maurice Isserman and Michael Kazin's *America Divided: The Civil War of the 1960s,* 3rd ed. (2007). The New Left is assessed in Irwin Unger's *The Movement: A History of the American New Left, 1959–1972* (1974). On the Students for a Democratic Society, see Kirkpatrick Sale's *SDS* (1973) and Allen J. Matusow's *The Unraveling of America: A History of Liberalism in the 1960s* (1984). Also useful are Todd Gitlin's *The Sixties: Years of Hope, Days of Rage,* rev. ed. (1993) and Bryan Burrough's *Days of Rage* (2015). For a focused study, see James T. Patterson's *The Eve of Destruction: How 1965 Transformed America* (2013). On the popularity of folk music and the role of Greenwich Village, see Stephen Petrus and Ronald D. Cohen's *Folk City* (2015).

For insights into the black power movement, see Peniel E. Joseph's *Stokely: A Life* (2014), and Joshua Bloom and Waldo E. Martin Jr.'s *Black against Empire: The History and Politics of the Black Panther Party* (2013).

Two influential assessments of the counterculture by sympathetic commentators are Theodore Roszak's *The Making of a Counter-Culture: Reflections on the Technocratic Society and Its Youthful Opposition* (1969) and Charles A. Reich's *The Greening of America: How the Youth Revolution Is Trying to Make America Livable* (1970). A good scholarly analysis that takes the hippies seriously is Timothy Miller's *The Hippies and American Values* (1991). A more recent assessment of the "culture wars" since the Sixties is Andrew Hartman's *A War for the Soul of America* (2015).

The best study of the women's liberation movement is Ruth Rosen's *The World Split Open: How the Modern Women's Movement Changed America,* rev. ed. (2006). The organizing efforts of Cesar Chavez are detailed in Ronald B. Taylor's *Chavez and the Farm Workers* (1975). See also Miriam Pawel's *The Crusades of Cesar Chavez: A Biography* (2014). The struggles of Native Americans for recognition and power are sympathetically described in Stan Steiner's *The New Indians* (1968).

The best overview of the 1970s and 1980s is James T. Patterson's *Restless Giant: The United States from Watergate to Bush v. Gore* (2005). On Nixon, see Melvin Small's thorough analysis in *The Presidency of Richard Nixon* (1999). A good slim biography is Elizabeth Drew's *Richard M. Nixon* (2007). A massive biography is Evan Thomas's *Being Nixon* (2015). An especially critical approach is Tim Weiner's *One Man Against the World: The Tragedy of Richard Nixon* (2015). For an overview of the Watergate scandal, see Stanley I. Kutler's *The Wars of Watergate: The Last Crisis of Richard Nixon* (1990). For the way the Republicans handled foreign affairs, consult Tad Szulc's *The Illu-*

sion of Peace: Foreign Policy in the Nixon Years* (1978). The Nixon White House tapes make for fascinating reading. See *The Nixon Tapes* (2014), ed. by Douglas Brinkley and Luke Nichter. Rick Perlstein traces the effects of Nixon's career on the Republican party and the conservative movement in two compelling books: *Nixonland: The Rise of a President and the Fracturing of America* (2007) and *The Invisible Bridge: The Fall of Nixon and the Rise of Reagan* (2014).

The Communist takeover of Vietnam and the end of American involvement there are traced in Larry Berman's *No Peace, No Honor: Nixon, Kissinger, and Betrayal in Vietnam* (2001). William Shawcross's *Sideshow: Kissinger, Nixon and the Destruction of Cambodia*, rev. ed. (2002), deals with the broadening of the war, while Larry Berman's *Planning a Tragedy: The Americanization of the War in Vietnam* (1982) assesses the final impact of U.S. involvement. The most comprehensive treatment of the anti-war movement is Tom Wells's *The War Within: America's Battle over Vietnam* (1994).

A comprehensive treatment of the Ford administration is contained in John Robert Greene's *The Presidency of Gerald R. Ford* (1995). The best overview of the Carter administration is Burton I. Kaufman's *The Presidency of James Earl Carter, Jr.*, 2nd rev. ed. (2006). A work more sympathetic to the Carter administration is John Dumbrell's *The Carter Presidency: A Re-evaluation*, 2nd ed. (1995). Gaddis Smith's *Morality, Reason, and Power: American Diplomacy in the Carter Years* (1986) provides an overview. Background on how the Middle East came to dominate much of American policy is found in William B. Quandt's *Decade of Decisions: American Policy toward the Arab-Israeli Conflict, 1967–1976* (1977). For a biography of Carter, see Randall Balmer, *Redeemer: The Life of Jimmy Carter* (2014).

CHAPTER 31

The rise of modern political conservatism is well told in Patrick Allitt's *The Conservatives: Ideas and Personalities throughout American History* (2009) and Michael Schaller's *Right Turn: American Life in the Reagan-Bush Era, 1980–1992* (2007).

On Reagan, see John Patrick Diggins's *Ronald Reagan: Fate, Freedom, and the Making of History* (2007), Richard Reeves's *President Reagan: The Triumph of Imagination* (2005), Sean Wilentz's *The Age of Reagan: A History, 1974–2008* (2008), and Thomas C. Reed's *The Reagan Enigma: 1964–1980* (2015). The best political analysis is Robert M. Collins's *Transforming America: Politics and Culture during the Reagan Years* (2007). For insights into the

1980 election, see Andrew E. Busch's *Reagan's Victory: The Presidential Election of 1980 and the Rise of the Right* (2005). On Reaganomics, see David A. Stockman's *The Triumph of Politics: Why the Reagan Revolution Failed* (1986).

For Reagan's foreign policy in Central America, see James Chace's *Endless War: How We Got Involved in Central America—and What Can Be Done* (1984) and Walter LaFeber's *Inevitable Revolutions: The United States in Central America*, 2nd ed. (1993). On Reagan's second term, see Jane Mayer and Doyle McManus's *Landslide: The Unmaking of the President, 1984–1988* (1988). For a masterly work on the Iran-Contra affair, see Theodore Draper's *A Very Thin Line: The Iran Contra Affairs* (1991). Several collections of essays include varying assessments of the Reagan years. Among these are *The Reagan Revolution?* (1988), edited by B. B. Kymlicka and Jean V. Matthews; *The Reagan Presidency: An Incomplete Revolution?* (1990), edited by Dilys M. Hill, Raymond A. Moore, and Phil Williams; and *Looking Back on the Reagan Presidency* (1990), edited by Larry Berman.

The 41st president is the focus of Timothy Naftali's *George H. W. Bush* (2007). On the 1988 campaign, see Sidney Blumenthal's *Pledging Allegiance: The Last Campaign of the Cold War* (1990). For a social history of the decade, see John Ehrman's *The Eighties: America in the Age of Reagan* (2005). On the Persian Gulf conflict, see Lester H. Brune's *America and the Iraqi Crisis, 1990–1992: Origins and Aftermath* (1993).

CHAPTER 32

Analysis of the Clinton years can be found in Joe Klein's *The Natural: The Misunderstood Presidency of Bill Clinton* (2002). Clinton's impeachment is assessed in Richard A. Posner's *An Affair of State: The Investigation, Impeachment, and Trial of President Clinton* (1999). The conflict between Clinton and Ginrich is explained in Elizabeth Drew's *The Struggle between Gingrich and the Clinton White House* (1996).

On changing demographic trends, see Sam Roberts's *Who We Are Now: The Changing Face of America in the Twenty-First Century* (2004). For a textured account of the exploding Latino culture, see Roberto Suro's *Strangers among Us: How Latino Immigration Is Transforming America* (1998). On social and cultural life in the 1990s, see Haynes Johnson's *The Best of Times: America in the Clinton Years* (2001). Economic and technological changes are assessed in Daniel T. Rogers's *Age of Fracture* (2011). The onset and growth of the AIDS epidemic are traced in *And the Band Played On: Politics, People, and the AIDS Epidemic,* 20th anniversary ed. (2007), by Randy Shilts.

On the religious right, see George M. Marsden's *Understanding Fundamentalism and Evangelicalism,* new ed. (2006) and Ralph E. Reed's *Politically Incorrect: The Emerging Faith Factor in American Politics* (1994).

On the invention of the computer and the Internet, see Paul E. Ceruzzi's *A History of Modern Computing,* 2nd ed. (2003), Janet Abbate's *Inventing the Internet* (1999), and Michael Lewis, *The New New Thing: A Silicon Valley Story* (1999). The booming economy of the 1990s is well analyzed in Joseph E. Stiglitz's *The Roaring Nineties: A New History of the World's Most Prosperous Decade* (2003).

For further treatment of the end of the cold war, see Michael R. Beschloss and Strobe Talbott's *At the Highest Levels: The Inside Story of the End of the Cold War* (1993) and Richard Crockatt's *The Fifty Years War: The United States and the Soviet Union in World Politics, 1941–1991* (1995).

On the transformation of American foreign policy, see James Mann's *Rise of the Vulcans: The History of Bush's War Cabinet* (2004), Claes G. Ryn's *America the Virtuous: The Crisis of Democracy and the Quest for Empire* (2003), and Stephen M. Walt's *Taming American Power: The Global Response to U.S. Primacy* (2005).

The disputed 2000 presidential election is the focus of Jeffrey Toobin's *Too Close to Call: The Thirty-Six-Day Battle to Decide the 2000 Election* (2001). On the Bush presidency, see *The Presidency of George W. Bush: A First Historical Assessment,* edited by Julian E. Zelizer (2010). See also Fred H. Israel and Jonathan Mann's *The Election of 2000 and the Administration of George W. Bush* (2003). Also see Dick Cheney's illuminating, if self-serving, account of his service as Bush's vice president in *In My Time: A Personal and Political Memoir* (2011).

On the attacks of September 11, 2001, and their aftermath, see *The Age of Terror: America and the World after September 11,* edited by Strobe Talbott and Nayan Chanda (2001). For a devastating account of the Bush administration by a White House insider, see Scott McClellan's *What Happened: Inside the Bush White House and Washington's Culture of Deception* (2008). On the historic 2008 election, see Michael Nelson's *The Elections of 2008* (2009). The best biography of Obama is David Maraniss's *Barack Obama: The Story* (2012). A conservative critique is provided in Edward Klein's *The Amateur: Barack Obama in the White House* (2012). For an insider's account of the Obama administration, see David Axelrod's *Believer: My Forty Years in Politics* (2015).

The Great Recession is explained in Alan S. Blinder's *After the Music Stopped: The Financial Crisis, the Response, and the Work Ahead* (2013). The Tea Party movement is assessed in Theda Skocpol and Vanessa Williamson's

The Tea Party and the Remaking of Republican Conservatism (2012) and Elizabeth Price Foley's *The Tea Party: Three Principles* (2012). The polarization of politics is the focus of Russell Muirhead's *The Promise of Party in a Polarized Age* (2015). The partisan gridlock in Congress is the focus of Thomas E. Mann and Norman J. Ornstein's *The Broken Branch: How Congress Is Failing America and How to Get it Back on Track* (2012). The tension between the conservative majority on the U.S. Supreme Court and the Obama administration is examined in Jeffrey Toobin's *The Oath: The Obama White House and the Supreme Court* (2012). On the growing economic inequality in America, see Joseph Stiglitz's *The Price of Inequality: How Today's Divided Society Endangers Our Future* (2013).

The emergence of Islamist radicalism is well analyzed in Michael Weiss and Hassan Hassan's *ISIS: Inside the Army of Terror* (2015) and Jesssica Stern and J. M. Berger's *ISIS: The State of Terror* (2015). The conflicts in the Middle East are the focus of Dominic Tierney's *The Right Way to Lose a War: America in an Age of Unwinnable Conflicts* (2015).

CREDITS

CHAPTER 16: p. 578: Smithsonian American Art Museum, Washington, DC/Art Resource; **p. 581:** Granger Collection; **p. 587:** Library of Congress; **p. 589:** Library of Congress; **p. 595:** Library of Congress; **p. 596:** Bettmann/Corbis; **p. 597:** Granger Collection; **p. 606:** Library of Congress; **p. 608:** Library of Congress.

PART 5: p. 615: Walter P. Reuther Library, Wayne State University; **p. 616:** David J. & Janice L. Frent Collection/Corbis.

CHAPTER 17: p. 618: Granger Collection; **p. 623:** Granger Collection; **p. 627:** National Archives **p. 633:** Wikimedia, pd; **p. 635:** Library of Congress; **p. 637:** Library of Congress; **p. 639:** Private Collection/Peter Newark American Pictures/Bridgeman Images; **p. 642:** Special Collections, Vassar College Libraries; **p. 648:** T.V. Powderly Photographic Collection, The American Catholic History Research Center University Archives, The Catholic University of America, Washington, D.C.; **p. 654:** PhotoQuest/Getty Images.

CHAPTER 18: p. 658: Granger Collection; **p. 663:** Library of Congress; **p. 669:** Corbis; **p. 670:** Special Collections, University of Chicago Library; **p. 671:** Library of Congress; **p. 672:** Library of Congress; **p. 678:** Kansas State Historical Society; **p. 682:** Corbis; **p. 684:** Keystone View Company/National Geographic Society/Corbis; **p. 690:** Stapleton Collection/Corbis.

CHAPTER 19: p. 698: © 2015 Delaware Art Museum/Artist Rights Society (ARS), New York *Wet Night on the Bowery*, 1911 (oil on canvas), Sloan, John (1871-1951)/Delaware Art Museum, Gift of the John Sloan Memorial Fund/Bridgeman Images; **p. 704:** William Williams Papers, Manuscripts and Archives Division, The New York Public Library, Astor, Lenox and Tilden Foundations, Art Resource, NY; **p. 706:** Library of Congress: **p. 707:** Granger Collection; **p. 708:** Bettmann/Corbis; **p. 710:** Bettmann/Corbis; **p. 713:** Stag at Sharkey's, 1909 (oil on canvas), Bellows, George Wesley (1882-1925)/Cleveland Museum of Art/Hinman B. Hurlbut Collection/Bridgeman Images; **p. 715:** Granger Collection; **p. 721:** Library of Congress; **p. 722:** Bettmann/Corbis; **p. 725:** Bettmann/Corbis; **p. 729:** Library of Congress; **p. 731:** Kansas State Historical Society; **p. 734:** Bettmann/Corbis; **p. 735 (top and bottom):** David J. & Janice L. Frent Collection/Corbis.

PART 6: p. 741: Bettmann/Corbis; **p. 743:** From the Collections of The Henry Ford Museum.

CHAPTER 20: p. 744: Frederic Remington Art Museum; **p. 749:** Granger Collection; **p. 753:** Bettmann/Corbis; **p. 758:** National Archives; **p. 761:** Granger Collection; **p. 768:** Granger Collection; **p. 770:** Corbis; **p. 772:** Granger Collection.

CHAPTER 21: p. 776: Granger Collection; **p. 780:** Granger Collection; **p. 783:** University of Illinois at Chicago Library; **p. 784:** Library of Congress; **p. 792:** Library of Congress; **p. 794:** Library of Congress; **p. 797:** NYPL/Art Resource, NY; **p. 799:** Culver Pictures/The Art Archive at Art Resource, NY; **p. 803:** Donald C. & Elizabeth M. Dickinson Research Center, National Cowboy & Western Heritage Museum; **p. 805:** Library of Congress; **p. 811 (top):** Corbis; **(bottom):** Granger Collection.

INDEX

Page numbers in *italics* refer to illustrations.